The Story of God Bible Commentary Series Endorsements

"Getting a story is about more than merely enjoying it. It means hearing it, understanding it, and above all, being impacted by it. This commentary series hopes that its readers not only hear and understand the story, but are impacted by it to live in as Christian a way as possible. The editors and contributors set that table very well and open up the biblical story in ways that move us to act with sensitivity and understanding. That makes hearing the story as these authors tell it well worth the time. Well done."

Darrell L. Bock
Dallas Theological Seminary

"The Story of God Bible Commentary series invites readers to probe how the message of the text relates to our situations today. Engagingly readable, it not only explores the biblical text but offers a range of applications and interesting illustrations."

Craig S. Keener
Asbury Theological Seminary

"I love The Story of God Bible Commentary series. It makes the text sing, and helps us hear the story afresh."

John Ortberg
Senior Pastor of Menlo Park Presbyterian Church

"In this promising new series of commentaries, believing biblical scholars bring not only their expertise but their own commitment to Jesus and insights into today's culture to the Scriptures. The result is a commentary series that is anchored in the text but lives and breathes in the world of today's church with its variegated pattern of socioeconomic, ethnic, and national diversity. Pastors, Bible study leaders, and Christians of all types who are looking for a substantive and practical guide through the Scriptures will find these volumes helpful."

Frank Thielman
Beeson Divinity School

"The Story of God Bible Commentary series is unique in its approach to exploring the Bible. Its easy-to-use format and practical guidance brings God's grand story to modern-day life so anyone can understand how it applies today."

Andy Stanley
North Point Ministries

"I'm a storyteller. Through writing and speaking I talk and teach about understanding the Story of God throughout Scripture and about letting God reveal more of His story as I live it out. Thus I am thrilled to have a commentary series based on the Story of God—a commentary that helps me to Listen to the Story, that Explains the Story, and then encourages me to probe how to Live the Story. A perfect tool for helping every follower of Jesus to walk in the story that God is writing for them."

Judy Douglass
Director of Women's Resources, Cru

"The Bible is the story of God and his dealings with humanity from creation to new creation. The Bible is made up more of stories than of any other literary genre. Even the psalms, proverbs, prophecies, letters, and the Apocalypse make complete sense only when set in the context of the grand narrative of the entire Bible. This commentary series breaks new ground by taking all these observations seriously. It asks commentators to listen to the text, to explain the text, and to live the text. Some of the material in these sections overlaps with introduction, detailed textual analysis and application, respectively, but only some. The most riveting and valuable part of the commentaries are the stories that can appear in any of these sections, from any part of the globe and any part of church history, illustrating the text in any of these areas. Ideal for preaching and teaching."

Craig L. Blomberg
Denver Seminary

"Pastors and lay people will welcome this new series, which seeks to make the message of the Scriptures clear and to guide readers in appropriating biblical texts for life today."

Daniel I. Block
Wheaton College and Graduate School

"An extremely valuable and long overdue series that includes comment on the cultural context of the text, careful exegesis, and guidance on reading the whole Bible as a unity that testifies to Christ as our Savior and Lord."

Graeme Goldsworthy
author of *According to Plan*

MARK

Editorial Board

of

The Story of God Bible Commentary

Old Testament general editor
Tremper Longman III

Old Testament associate editors
George Athas
Mark J. Boda
Myrto Theocharous

New Testament general editor
Scot McKnight

New Testament associate editors
Lynn H. Cohick
Michael F. Bird
Dennis R. Edwards

Zondervan editors

Senior acquisitions editor
Katya Covrett

Senior production editor, Old Testament
Nancy L. Erickson

Senior production editor, New Testament
Christopher A. Beetham

The Story of God
Bible Commentary

MARK |

Timothy G. Gombis
Tremper Longman III & Scot McKnight
General Editors

ZONDERVAN
ACADEMIC

ZONDERVAN ACADEMIC

Mark
Copyright © 2021 by Timothy G. Gombis

Requests for information should be addressed to:
Zondervan, *3900 Sparks Dr. SE, Grand Rapids, Michigan 49546*

Zondervan titles may be purchased in bulk for educational, business, fundraising, or sales promotional use. For information, please email SpecialMarkets@Zondervan.com.

ISBN 978-0-310-32715-8 (hardcover)

ISBN 978-0-310-12001-8 (ebook)

Cover design: Ron Huizinga
Cover image: iStockphoto ®
Interior composition: Kait Lamphere

21 22 23 24 25 26 27 28 29 30 31 32 /TRM/ 16 15 14 13 12 11 10 9 8 7 6 5 4 3 2 1

To Don and Becky, John and Linda

Old Testament series

1 ▪ Genesis—*Tremper Longman III*
2 ▪ Exodus—*Christopher J. H. Wright*
3 ▪ Leviticus—*Jerry E. Shepherd*
4 ▪ Numbers—*Jay A. Sklar*
5 ▪ Deuteronomy—*Myrto Theocharous*
6 ▪ Joshua—*Lissa M. Wray Beal*
7 ▪ Judges—*Athena E. Gorospe*
8 ▪ Ruth/Esther—*Marion Ann Taylor*
9 ▪ 1–2 Samuel—*Paul S. Evans*
10 ▪ 1–2 Kings—*David T. Lamb*
11 ▪ 1–2 Chronicles—*Carol M. Kaminski*
12 ▪ Ezra/Nehemiah—*Douglas J. Green*
13 ▪ Job—*Martin A. Shields*
14 ▪ Psalms—*Elizabeth R. Hayes*
15 ▪ Proverbs—*Ryan P. O'Dowd*
16 ▪ Ecclesiastes/Song of Songs—*George Athas*
17 ▪ Isaiah—*Mark J. Boda*
18 ▪ Jeremiah/Lamentations—*Andrew G. Shead*
19 ▪ Ezekiel—*D. Nathan Phinney*
20 ▪ Daniel—*Wendy L. Widder*
21 ▪ Minor Prophets I—*Beth M. Stovell*
22 ▪ Minor Prophets II—*Beth M. Stovell*

New Testament series

1 ▪ Matthew—*Rodney Reeves*
2 ▪ Mark—*Timothy G. Gombis*
3 ▪ Luke—*Kindalee Pfremmer DeLong*
4 ▪ John—*Nicholas Perrin*
5 ▪ Acts—*Dean Pinter*
6 ▪ Romans—*Michael F. Bird*
7 ▪ 1 Corinthians—*Justin K. Hardin*
8 ▪ 2 Corinthians—*Judith A. Diehl*
9 ▪ Galatians—*Nijay K. Gupta*
10 ▪ Ephesians—*Mark D. Roberts*
11 ▪ Philippians—*Lynn H. Cohick*
12 ▪ Colossians/Philemon—*Esau McCaulley*
13 ▪ 1, 2 Thessalonians—*John Byron*
14 ▪ 1, 2 Timothy, Titus—*Marius Nel*
15 ▪ Hebrews—*Radu Gheorghita*
16 ▪ James—*Mariam J. Kamell*
17 ▪ 1 Peter—*Dennis R. Edwards*
18 ▪ 2 Peter, Jude—*C. Rosalee Velloso Ewell*
19 ▪ 1, 2, & 3 John—*Constantine R. Campbell*
20 ▪ Revelation—*Jonathan A. Moo*
21 ▪ Sermon on the Mount—*Scot McKnight*

Contents

Author's Preface xi
The Story of God Bible Commentary Series xiii
Abbreviations xvii
Introduction 1
1. Mark 1:1–13 21
2. Mark 1:14–15 36
3. Mark 1:16–20 42
4. Mark 1:21–28 47
5. Mark 1:29–34 55
6. Mark 1:35–39 62
7. Mark 1:40–45 67
8. Mark 2:1–12 74
9. Mark 2:13–17 83
10. Mark 2:18–22 88
11. Mark 2:23–28 96
12. Mark 3:1–6 102
13. Mark 3:7–12 107
14. Mark 3:13–19 112
15. Mark 3:20–35 119
16. Mark 4:1–20 130
17. Mark 4:21–25 147
18. Mark 4:26–34 152
19. Mark 4:35–41 159
20. Mark 5:1–20 166
21. Mark 5:21–43 180
22. Mark 6:1–6a 192
23. Mark 6:6b–30 199
24. Mark 6:31–44 212
25. Mark 6:45–52 223
26. Mark 6:53–56 230
27. Mark 7:1–23 234
28. Mark 7:24–30 253
29. Mark 7:31–37 260

30. Mark 8:1–10 266
31. Mark 8:11–13 275
32. Mark 8:14–21 280
33. Mark 8:22–26 286
34. Mark 8:27–33 291
35. Mark 8:34–9:1 298
36. Mark 9:2–13 304
37. Mark 9:14–29 312
38. Mark 9:30–37 322
39. Mark 9:38–50 329
40. Mark 10:1–12 339
41. Mark 10:13–16 348
42. Mark 10:17–31 354
43. Mark 10:32–45 365
44. Mark 10:46–52 375
45. Mark 11:1–11 380
46. Mark 11:12–25 389
47. Mark 11:27–33 400
48. Mark 12:1–12 407
49. Mark 12:13–17 417
50. Mark 12:18–27 423
51. Mark 12:28–34 431
52. Mark 12:35–44 439
53. Mark 13:1–37 447
54. Mark 14:1–11 474
55. Mark 14:12–31 483
56. Mark 14:32–52 497
57. Mark 14:53–72 512
58. Mark 15:1–20 524
59. Mark 15:21–47 538
60. Mark 16:1–8 559
Appendix: Alternative Endings to Mark's Gospel 571
Scripture Index 575
Subject Index 599
Author Index 611

Author's Preface

I don't know whether Christians are supposed to have favorite parts of the Bible, but Mark is my favorite Gospel. Writing this commentary has been a thrilling process of discovery for me. For the invitation to contribute this volume, I am grateful to the series editors, Scot McKnight and Michael Bird, along with Katya Covrett at Zondervan. The editorial comments of Mike and Scot greatly improved my work, and I am happy with the final product.

I developed a special love for Mark's Gospel over the last few decades for a variety of reasons and have been helped in my understanding through extensive discussion with good friends. My interest in narrative readings of Mark was kindled by many conversations with Bruce Hansen during our PhD days at St. Andrews. Don Humphreys and I preached through Mark together and enjoyed many fruitful discussions about various features of the text and how the Gospel might be embodied in our community.

Elizabeth Davidhizar and Pastor Brenda DeVries are two good friends and ministry leaders, who have been partners of mine in this study. Each engaged aspects of the commentary as I wrote it and challenged me on several points, which sharpened my thinking. My sister, Leah Bare, and my mother, Kathryn Gombis, read every word and offered encouragement and editorial help.

I wrote some of the commentary during a restful and fruitful season while on a semester leave at Ridley Hall, Cambridge. I'm grateful to John VerBerkmoes, my dean at Grand Rapids Theological Seminary, for providing generous funding for my stay at Ridley and for his excellent and faithful leadership. I am able to experience fully the joy of my vocation and very little administrative frustration because of him. I'm delighted to thank Kurt Behrends of the Issachar Fund for providing generous support for travel on my sabbatical, as well.

Two couples have been dear friends to Sarah and me the last fifteen years, and our friendships have been forged in a variety of shared difficulties as well as in long, life-giving seasons. It would be impossible to imagine our lives without them. I'm so pleased to call Don and Becky Humphreys and John and Linda Mortensen friends, and I am happy to dedicate this volume to them.

The Story of God Bible Commentary Series

The word of God may not change, but culture does. Think of what we have seen in the last twenty years: we now communicate predominantly through the Internet and email; we read our news on iPads and computers; we can talk on the phone to our friends while we are driving, while we are playing golf, while we are taking long walks; and we can get in touch with others from the middle of nowhere. We carry in our hands small devices that connect us to the world and to a myriad of sources of information. Churches have changed; the "Nones" are rising in numbers and volume, and atheists are bold to assert their views in public forums. The days of home Bible studies are waning; there is a marked rise in activist missional groups in churches, and pastors are more and more preaching topical sermons, some of which are not directly connected to the Bible. Divorce rates are not going down, marriages are more stressed, rearing children is more demanding, and civil unions and same-sex marriages are knocking at the door of the church.

Progress can be found in many directions. While church-attendance numbers are waning in Europe and North America, churches are growing in the South and the East. More and more women are finding a voice in churches; the plea of the former generation of leaders that Christians be concerned not just with evangelism but with justice is being answered today in new and vigorous ways. Resources for studying the Bible are more available today than ever before, and preachers and pastors are meeting the challenge of speaking a sure word of God into shifting cultures.

Readers of the Bible change too. These cultural shifts, our own personal developments, the progress in intellectual questions, as well as growth in biblical studies and theology and discoveries of new texts and new paradigms for understanding the contexts of the Bible—each of these elements works on an interpreter so that the person who reads the Bible today asks different questions from different angles.

Culture shifts, but the word of God remains. That is why we as editors of The Story of God Bible Commentary series, a commentary based on the New International Version 2011 (NIV 2011), are excited to participate in this new series of commentaries on the Bible. This series is designed to address this generation with the same word of God. We are asking the authors to explain what the Bible says to the sorts of readers who pick up commentaries so they can understand not only what Scripture says but what it means for today. The Bible does not change, but relating it to our culture changes constantly and in differing ways in different contexts.

When we, the New Testament editors, sat down in prayer and discussion to choose authors for this series, we realized we had found fertile ground. Our list of potential authors was staggering in length and quality. We wanted the authors to be exceptional scholars, faithful Christians, committed evangelicals, and theologically diverse, and we wanted this series to represent the changing face of both American and world evangelicalism, with both ethnic and gender diversity. I believe this series has a wider diversity of authors than any commentary series in evangelical history.

The title of this series, emphasizing as it does the "Story" of the Bible, reveals the intent of the series. We want to explain each passage of the Bible in light of the Bible's grand Story. The Bible's grand Story, of course, connects this series to the classic expression *regula fidei*, the "rule of faith," which was the Bible's story coming to fulfillment in Jesus as the Messiah, Lord, and Savior of all. In brief, we see the narrative built around the following biblical themes: creation and fall, covenant and redemption, law and prophets, and especially God's charge to humans as his image-bearers to rule under God. The theme of God as King and God's kingdom guides us to see the importance of Israel's kings as they come to fulfillment in Jesus, Lord and King over all, and the direction of history toward the new heavens and new earth, where God will be all in all. With these guiding themes, each passage is examined from three angles.

Listen to the Story. We believe that if the Bible is God speaking, then the most important posture of the Christian before the Bible is to listen. So our first section cites the text of Scripture and lists a selection of important biblical and sometimes noncanonical parallels; then each author introduces that passage. The introductions to the passages sometimes open up discussion to the theme of the passage, while other times they tie this passage to its context in the specific book. But since the focus of this series is the Story of God in the Bible, the introduction leads the reader into reading this text in light of the Bible's Story.

Explain the Story. The authors follow up listening to the text by explaining each passage in light of the Bible's grand Story. This is not an academic series, so the footnotes are limited to the kinds of texts typical Bible readers and preachers readily will have on hand. Authors are given the freedom to explain the text as they read it, though you should not be surprised to find occasional listings of other options for reading the text. Authors explore biblical backgrounds, historical context, cultural codes, and theological interpretations. Authors engage in word studies and interpret unique phrases and clauses as they attempt to build a sound and living reading of the text in light of the Story of God in the Bible.

Authors will not shy away from problems in the texts. Whether one is examining the meaning of "perfect" in Matthew 5:48, the problems with Christology in the hymn of Philippians 2:6–11, the challenge of understanding Paul in light of the swirling debates about the old, new, and post-new perspectives, the endless debates about eschatology, or the vagaries of atonement theories, the authors will dive in, discuss evidence, and do their best to sort out a reasonable and living reading of those issues for the church today.

Live the Story. Reading the Bible is not just about discovering what it meant back then; the intent of The Story of God Bible Commentary series is to probe how this text might be lived out today as that story continues to march on in the life of the church. At times our authors will tell stories about what this looks like; at other times they may offer some suggestions for living it out; but always you will discover the struggle involved as we seek to live out the Bible's grand Story in our world.

We are not offering suggestions for "application" so much as digging deeper; we are concerned in this section with seeking out how this text, in light of the Story of God in the Bible, compels us to live in our world so that our own story lines up with the Bible's Story.

Scot McKnight, general editor New Testament
Lynn Cohick, Dennis Edwards, and Michael Bird, editors

AB	Anchor Bible
ABD	*Anchor Bible Dictionary*. Edited by David Noel Freedman. 6 vols. New York: Doubleday, 1992
ACCS	Ancient Christian Commentary on Scripture
Ant.	*Jewish Antiquities* (Josephus)
ANTC	Abingdon New Testament Commentaries
AYBC	Anchor Yale Bible Commentary
BDAG	Danker, Frederick W., Walter Bauer, William F. Arndt, and F. Wilbur Gingrich. *Greek-English Lexicon of the New Testament and Other Early Christian Literature*. 3rd ed. Chicago: University of Chicago Press, 2000
BECNT	Baker Exegetical Commentary on the New Testament
BibInt	Biblical Interpretation
BNTC	Black's New Testament Commentaries
BTNTS	Biblical Theology of the New Testament Series
CEB	Common English Bible
CSB	Christian Standard Bible
DJG	*Dictionary of Jesus and the Gospels*. Edited by Joel B. Green, Jeannine K. Brown, and Nicholas Perrin. 2nd ed. Downers Grove, IL: InterVarsity Press, 2013
DNTB	*Dictionary of New Testament Background*. Edited by Craig A. Evans and Stanley E. Porter. Downers Grove, IL: InterVarsity Press, 2000
DTIB	*Dictionary of Theological Interpretation of the Bible*. Edited by Kevin J. Vanhoozer, Craig G. Bartholomew, Daniel J. Treier, and N. T. Wright. Grand Rapids: Baker Academic, 2005
ESV	English Standard Version
Gk.	Greek
Heb.	Hebrew
J.W.	*Jewish War* (Josephus)
lit.	literally
LXX	Septuagint (Greek Old Testament)
NASB	New American Standard Bible
NET	New English Translation
NIBC	New International Biblical Commentary
NIVAC	New International Version Application Commentary

NRSV   New Revised Standard Version
NSBT   New Studies in Biblical Theology
NTGJC   New Testament Guides in Their Judaic Contexts
NTL   New Testament Library
OTP   *Old Testament Pseudepigrapha*. Edited by James H. Charlesworth. 2 vols. New York: Doubleday, 1983, 1985
PNTC   Pillar New Testament Commentary
WUNT   Wissenschaftliche Untersuchungen zum Neuen Testament
ZECNT   Zondervan Exegetical Commentary on the New Testament

The Gospel of Mark and the Story of God

The four Gospels that stand at the head of the New Testament are not the beginning of a story but are the continuation of a much longer narrative coming out of the Old Testament. They constitute the climax of the story of the God of Israel, as Jesus indicates at the opening of Mark: "'The time has come,' he said. 'The kingdom of God has come near'" (1:15). We must understand, therefore, what that story is about and where Mark is situated in that larger drama. Scripture reveals the account of God creating his world as a hospitable place for humanity, a wonderful and welcoming habitat for humanity's flourishing. All of creation was to be God's temple—his dwelling place—and humanity was the image of the creator God in that temple.[1] God called humanity to rule over creation on God's behalf, overseeing the spread of God's order of flourishing throughout the whole world, spreading God's glory worldwide.

And humanity was created by God with difference and diversity. Adam and Eve were "other" to one another, and the differences between them stood in for the many differences and distinctions that would develop among tribes, nations, and ethnicities. And all of this "otherness" was the richness of the created order, so that God's glory was a symphony and not just the sound of a single note. The differences between Adam and Eve were opportunities for conversation, exploration, learning about the other, and wondering at the multifaceted richness of the other. This pattern of relating was to be replayed and acted out by groups of people over time, so that tribes and nations would relate to one another fruitfully as partners in enjoying and spreading the reign of the one true creator God.

---

1. John Walton's works on Genesis 1–3, reading these chapters in their ancient context, are immensely useful for understanding the temple theology found there (John H. Walton, *The Lost World of Genesis One: Ancient Cosmology and the Origins Debate* [Downers Grove, IL: IVP Academic, 2009]; *The Lost World of Adam and Eve: Genesis 2–3 and the Human Origins Debate* [Downers Grove, IL: IVP Academic, 2015]). Cf. also G. K. Beale, *The Temple and the Church's Mission: A Biblical Theology of the Dwelling Place of God*, NSBT 17 (Downers Grove, IL: IVP Academic, 2004).

Tragically, humanity rebelled against God, and rather than overseeing the spread of God's order of flourishing they cast their lot with forces of disorder and chaos. They were banished from the garden of God's presence and began the long, terrible experience of living in a "Godless" world, inhabiting creation in a way that God did not intend. They were alienated from one another and from God, viewing one another with suspicion, fostering conflict and division, and seeking to assert power over the other.

Adding to the dilemma, cosmic enemies now fostered the oppression and degradation of humanity and creation. As Cain finds out in Genesis 4, the cosmic power of Sin had also entered the drama, fomenting murderous desires within Cain and fostering division, oppression, and exploitation (Gen 4:7). And just as rebellion had occurred in the human realm, there were also heavenly figures of spiritual authority who had rebelled against God's kingship and in mysterious ways were perverting and corrupting human experience in God's good but now hijacked world (Gen 6:1–4).

God, of course, was not at all content with this situation. He longed for his world to manifest his gracious reign, and so he called Abraham as the agent through whom he would reclaim the nations—all humanity—and bring them back into his blessing (Gen 12:1–3). Abraham's family grew into a nation while enslaved in Egypt, and God eventually liberated them in a powerful display of his supremacy over the gods of Egypt. Israel was God's elect people, chosen by God as a kingdom of priests who would be the national agent of God's reclamation of the nations. They were specially chosen to know God and then to help the nations of the world understand how they, too, might turn from idols to worship the one true God (Exod 19:6).

Israel was called to be a people of justice, taking active steps to cultivate national patterns of life and cultural practices whereby the poor were taken care of, along with the orphan and the widow, and to prevent people from falling into crushing debt or losing their land. They were to enjoy economic practices that spread blessing around and prevented vulnerable people from being exploited. They were not to mistreat any of the foreigners that lived in the land—those non-Israelites that worshiped other gods—for they had once been foreigners and aliens themselves before God brought them into his land of blessing (Exod 22:21; Lev 19:33–34). In all these ways and more, Israel's national life would be a return to living in God's good world according to God's gracious design. Their corporate practices and community dynamics would embody and manifest the kingship of the one true God.

In another sad turn in the story, Israel did not become this kind of people who were faithful to God by being obedient to his commission. They exploited the vulnerable—the poor, the orphan, and the widow. They mistreated foreigners, did not orient their national life and cultural practices according to God's justice, and did not become a people that embodied the reign of the creator God through compassion toward others. And they cut themselves off from the nations rather than cultivating relationships with them in order to discover together how to enjoy the reign of God. Some among them even longed for God to destroy the nations rather than to bless them. Jonah embodied this sort of bitterness toward the nations. When God commanded him to preach to Nineveh that God's destruction was imminent, Jonah refused to go. He knew that if God detected even a whiff of a hint of repentance, he would relent from his stated purpose and pour out restoring power, and that's precisely what Jonah wanted to avoid (Jonah 4:1–11).

Because Israel rejected the prophets who called them back to faithfulness, they were sent into exile. First, Israel, the northern kingdom, was sent into exile in 722 BC, taken captive to Assyria. Then, in 586 BC, Judah, the southern kingdom, was exiled to Babylon. Exile, however, was not to be the end of the story. God promised that he would one day return and bring his people back to himself. In a second-exodus event, he would once again redeem them, liberating them from captivity as he had once freed them from enslavement in Egypt. They would enjoy the reign of God in the land God had given to them and finally become the just people that would enjoy God's gracious and life-giving reign. And Israel would partner with the nations to march to Jerusalem and worship the God of Israel, who is also the Great King over all the nations, the God who rules heaven and earth.

Israel, then, is left in a posture of expectation, a time of waiting to see how God would fulfill his promises to save and restore his people. And as the centuries went by, the waiting only intensified. There was a brief flare-up of hope with the rise of the Hasmonean family in the early second century BC, an account of which is found in 1–2 Maccabees. In 167 BC, Judea was occupied by the ruling Seleucids, and the king, Antiochus Epiphanes, initiated a period of intense persecution, stamping out Jewish practices and killing thousands. A priest from a small town north of Jerusalem sparked a revolt against the king's forces and, together with his sons, rallied a fighting force that grew and eventually drove out the foreigners. One of the priest's sons, Judas Maccabeus (Judas the "Hammer"), led the rebellion until his death, after which his brothers took the lead.[2]

---

2. Joel Willitts, "The Maccabean Revolt and Hasmonean Statecraft," in *Behind the Scenes of the Old Testament: Cultural, Social, and Historical Contexts*, ed. Jonathan S. Greer, John W. Hilber, and John H. Walton (Grand Rapids: Baker Academic, 2018).

This rebellion led to the capturing of Jerusalem, the purification of the temple (remembered annually at the Jewish celebration of Hanukkah), and eventually an independent Judea in 146 BC. Was this the fulfillment of the promises of God to restore his kingdom among his people? It certainly would have seemed so in the early days of independent rule. Over time, however, the Hasmoneans turned out to be compromised by political intrigues and manipulation of the high priesthood.

The era of Judean independence came to an end in 63 BC, when Rome, the rising imperial power in the Mediterranean, began its long occupation with the arrival of Pompey the Great. The setting for Mark's narrative, then, within the context of the story of Scripture, is again one of intense longing on the part of God's people for salvation in the form of liberation from foreign occupation. The Maccabean heroes of recent generations past had shaped the popular Jewish imagination of what God's salvation would look like. They conceived of a heroic figure who would arise and lead a rebellion against their tormentors—someone who could rally a fighting force and march down to Jerusalem to drive out the Romans and purify the temple once again.

As we open the pages of Mark's Gospel, therefore, God's people are waiting for the fulfillment of God's promises.[3] They are desperate for salvation in far more pervasive and profound senses than modern readers can imagine. They are not merely longing for spiritual fulfilment, a general sense of purpose, or eternal life after death, but rather socio-political liberation and economic restoration.[4] They were longing for the kingdom of God and the return of God's kingship. Additionally, the Gospels reveal that God's people were spiritually captive, held in Satan's enslaving grip, which Mark depicts by the many exorcisms Jesus and his disciples perform. Judea had become the "strong man's house" (Mark 3:27), and God's people were desperate for release, renewal, and redemption.

---

3. Cf. Rikki E. Watts, *Isaiah's New Exodus and Mark*, WUNT 2/88 (Tübingen: Mohr Siebeck, 1997; repr., Grand Rapids: Baker Academic, 2000), for the manner in which the opening of Mark, along with a number of other narrative and structural features, recalls Isaiah's prophetic hope of a new exodus for God's people.

4. Herman C. Waetjen captures the class conflicts, political power plays, and other pressing social realities that were relevant for the characters that show up in Mark's Gospel and for Mark's first audiences. These involved class struggle, exploitation of the lower classes, "appalling hunger, unemployment, disease, and powerlessness" (*A Reordering of Power: A Sociopolitical Reading of Mark's Gospel* [Philadelphia: Fortress, 1989; repr., Eugene, OR: Wipf & Stock, 2014], 13). Alan Storkey also helpfully sets the Gospels within the larger political and economic situation of Judea in the first century (*Jesus and Politics: Confronting the Powers* [Grand Rapids: Baker Academic, 2005]).

Mark's Gospel, then, is a climactic chapter in the great story of Scripture. It continues the account of the God of Israel who redeemed his people from slavery in Egypt and set them in the land of promise, who appointed them as a light to the nations and sent them into exile for their unfaithfulness, and who made promises of restoration and salvation. His oppressed people are awaiting his return and longing for his salvation. As Mark's Gospel begins, the good news of God's salvation is announced to them.

Mark as the "UnGospel"

Mark is one of the four New Testament Gospels, and it rightly stands alongside its three canonical partners in portraying the life and ministry of Jesus. At the same time, Mark is a highly subversive and utterly unique Gospel. It begins abruptly and moves along at breakneck speed, with everything happening "immediately." Jesus is often confrontational, speaking to various characters in shocking, rude, and mystifying ways. Mark frequently describes Jesus as a teacher and portrays him as teaching, but rarely mentions any of the *content* of his teaching. Further, Jesus regularly and forcefully forbids anyone from speaking about him or talking about what he has done. Isn't this supposed to be "a Gospel," and aren't we supposed to want the good news to spread? So why all the commands to be silent?

Moreover, in Mark nothing seems to be going well. Jesus calls disciples who obey right away and follow him without question. Yet they soon begin to grow confused about Jesus and even try to talk him out of his mission. They repeatedly fail to listen to what he says, even though God shows up at one point and commands Jesus's followers to "listen to him!" (9:7). The disciples rebuke Jesus, betray him, deny him, and abandon him. The Gospel ends without any hint that the relationship between Jesus and the disciples has been repaired. And at the very close of Mark, some women followers of Jesus encounter a young man at the place where Jesus had been buried. He commands them to relay a message to Jesus's disciples and Peter, but they fail to do so out of fear. And that's the final line!

What kind of "Gospel" is this? As I said, if someone picks up Mark to read it and gives careful attention to it, she will come away with a very different impression of things than if she were reading Matthew, Luke, or John. *This is a very different Gospel.* The temptation might be to blend it with the other three Gospels and perhaps soften some of its edges, as some English translations often do.

Mark challenges its audiences since the disciples stand in for churches that hear it. It confronts us with our failures to listen to Jesus, to attend carefully to Jesus's teaching, to his constant upending of social norms, to the radically alternative character of the kingdom of God, and especially to the completely different sort of ruler Jesus is. Audiences that claim a Christian identity but have grown complacent and have accommodated to social patterns of their surrounding culture will be brought up short and confronted by Mark's portrayal, because it is anything but comforting.

Mark is a subversive Gospel because it overturns expectations and assumptions. His narrative addresses Christian audiences who know Jesus's teaching and who have made a Christian confession but who are failing to grasp the character of the gospel as thoroughly shaped by the cross of Christ. In this sense, they have not been listening to Jesus; they have not been perceiving what he is all about. And they are not moving toward understanding so that they identify with the shame and the power of the cross. Mark is not necessarily for unbelievers to learn about Jesus. It is for churches who have heard Jesus's teaching and have grown lax in giving attention to it, with the result that their social dynamics and community patterns have gradually been shaped by cultural values of power-seeking, prestige-questing, and social-credential accumulation. Mark aims to jolt such communities back to a faithfully kingdom-oriented reality.

Jesus and the Kingdom of God

Jesus is the focus of Mark's Gospel. But if we isolate Jesus from his mission, we will tragically misunderstand him. Jesus is God's appointed agent of kingdom rule, the one through whom God's kingdom comes into being. He is the king who rules on God's behalf, and the events that lead up to Jesus's crucifixion constitute his procession to coronation—his death on the cross. And the kingdom of God is a socio-political and economic reality that is a total way of life. The gospel Jesus proclaims is the announcement that God's reign has arrived, and he calls everyone to enter it through concrete social practices of service to the needy and hospitality to the marginalized. These two activities in Mark's Gospel are what it means to "follow" Jesus as communities that embody and enact his reign (9:37; 10:43–44).

It is important to stress the intimate relation and unbreakable bond between Jesus and his kingdom because many contemporary Christians assume that the gospel is about Jesus and his willingness to inhabit human hearts. This popular gospel is about changing someone on the inside, giving them a new perspective on life. It offers a sense of purpose, inner peace, and fulfillment in the present and an eternal destiny in the future. It portrays Christian discipleship in terms of reordering one's internal world of affections and emotions. For such audiences, Mark's Gospel will land like a thud. There just isn't any of that here. Jesus calls for complete lives, not just hearts. And he is forming communities of people that will receive the kingdom by undergoing a thorough transformation of community practices, habits, prejudices, ideological commitments, and social dynamics. Social rankings will be turned on their heads, and conceptions of leadership will be totally overthrown.

In Mark's Gospel, the status quo and life as we know it has resulted in Judea becoming the "strong man's house"—satanically enslaved space. The preaching of the gospel as a call to enter a radically alternative socio-political and economic reality is not a challenge for people to try harder or embrace the call to "a higher personal standard." It is an offer of relief to the oppressed, rest for the weary, hope for the beaten-down, and warm embrace for the rejected and outcast. It presents a sharp challenge to those benefiting from the status quo (Mark 10:17–23). Yet for anyone with eyes to see, the kingdom of God is the dynamic, life-giving reality of healing and restoration.

Jesus is central to the Gospel of Mark—of course he is! But he is central in that he is God's authorized agent of kingdom rule and the one through whom God initiates his kingdom. And "the gospel" in the Gospel of Mark is the proclamation of the arrival of God's kingdom and the call to enter it through the transformation of every aspect of life.

The Identity of Jesus in the Gospel of Mark

Jesus is a complex character in Mark. Not that he is complicated or hard to understand, but he occupies a central place in Scripture and brings together various narrative strands in the story of the Bible. He is a prophetic figure who confronts the powerful and exposes their exploitative and oppressive treatment of the weak and vulnerable. Mark consistently identifies Jesus with Elijah, the iconic prophet of Israel who often opposed the wicked Ahab and his wife, Jezebel. Mark also associates Jesus with John the Baptist, noting that Jesus reminds people of John and his radical mode of life and confrontational style.

Jesus is also an authoritative teacher in this Gospel. Characters routinely address Jesus as "teacher" or "rabbi." Mark often remarks that Jesus is teaching when he is performing an action, such as when he casts out a demon in 1:21–28. Mark piles up words for teaching in that episode and closes it with the crowd's amazement at Jesus's teaching, which comes with authority. *Yet none of Jesus's teaching appears here.* And this is not the only instance. In Mark,

Jesus is the authoritative teacher whose words have power and whose predictions always come to pass. As mentioned above, Mark's portrayal of Jesus in this way, while mentioning so little of his teaching, will strike audiences that are familiar with Jesus's teaching with the need to return to what Jesus has said and give renewed attention to it with the aim of living it.

The most common title that Jesus uses of himself in Mark is "Son of Man," which recalls a figure from Daniel 7 to whom God delegates authority to rule:

> In my vision at night I looked, and there before me was one like a son of man, coming with the clouds of heaven. He approached the Ancient of Days and was led into his presence. He was given authority, glory and sovereign power; all nations and peoples of every language worshiped him. His dominion is an everlasting dominion that will not pass away, and his kingdom is one that will never be destroyed. (Dan 7:13–14; cf. also vv. 26–27)

Beyond this, however, the title has prophetic notes, since this is how God consistently refers to Ezekiel throughout that prophet's ministry (e.g., Ezek 2:1). In Mark, Jesus as Son of Man is a figure of present humiliation who perseveres in faithfulness to God throughout his ministry of proclaiming the kingdom, healing the sick, casting out demons, and confronting injustice. He endures suffering, mistreatment, and death. God will vindicate him, however, by raising him from the dead and appointing him as his authorized agent of judgment and salvation. The Son of Man will return in power to bring in the fullness of God's kingdom in the end.

It is in this light that Jesus is the Messiah—the Christ—and Son of God. Jesus's identity as God's authorized agent of sovereign rule is obscured in Mark. That is, his glory is not fully on display as it was at the transfiguration (9:2–3). Audiences know that this is who Jesus is, for they hear of it right away in Mark's opening lines (1:1). But the other characters in Mark are unaware of Jesus's identity or are ignorant of its significance. Peter confesses Jesus to be the Christ/Messiah, but he dramatically misunderstands what that means. And no human figure in Mark identifies Jesus as the Son of God until the end where a Roman centurion does so (15:39). Apart from him, only God, demons, and Jesus know his true identity as the Son of God.

Mark focuses most on Jesus's identity as the suffering Son of Man, who is fully revealed as the Christ, the Son of God, *on the cross*, which is the means whereby God judges the present age and inaugurates the new-creation age of salvation.

The Cross in Mark

The cross is central to Mark's Gospel. Many readers will be familiar with the reality that it symbolizes the death of Jesus, which secures salvation for "many" (10:45). While the cross includes that in Mark, it is significant in much more far-reaching ways. The cross is a totalizing and relativizing reality that has cosmic, communal, social, political, economic, relational, and personal implications. It is "totalizing" in that it claims everything—every aspect of a community and the whole of a person. Nothing escapes its saving and judging power. And the cross is "relativizing," because it stands at the center of all reality, and everything else has its significance only in its light.

The cross shapes and orients Jesus's identity as ruler of God's kingdom, and it defines and determines the mode of life in that kingdom. Nearly the whole Gospel unfolds under the shadow of Jesus's death, since the plot to kill him is introduced very early in the narrative (3:6). Jesus's journey to Jerusalem is organized around three predictions of his suffering and death, along with teaching about discipleship characterized by followers taking up their crosses (8:31–32; 9:31; 10:33–34). Interestingly, because the cross is the means of God's victory in Jesus, Satan is portrayed as trying to prevent Jesus's crucifixion. Mark does not elaborate on Satan's temptation of Jesus in the wilderness at the Gospel's opening. He merely mentions that Jesus was thrust out into the desert to be tempted by Satan (1:12–13). The nature of the temptation is unstated.

The satanic temptation shows up, however, in 8:27–33. There, Peter confesses that Jesus is the Christ, and when Jesus predicts his suffering and death, Peter takes him aside and rebukes him. Peter's objection represents the disciples' desire for Jesus to enact the reign of God through power, with a spectacular military victory over their Roman oppressors. Jesus's counter-rebuke to Peter is crucial, and it informs how audiences perceive Satan's temptation upon subsequent readings from the beginning. Jesus calls Peter "Satan" because he has previously heard the satanic temptation to be a Messiah-in-power without going through the cross, and that temptation has come from Satan himself in the wilderness.

Jesus is only known faithfully when he is seen from the perspective of the cross. He is a cross-oriented king who calls disciples to take up their crosses and enter a cross-shaped kingdom. This is one of the main reasons Jesus constantly commands silence throughout Mark. To know Jesus simply from the perspective of bringing relief to so many who were longing for salvation is to know Jesus partially. He aims to inform and transform that partial, fractured vision of who he is and what his agenda is all about. The full revelation comes as Jesus hangs on the cross and dies, and we hear the dramatic confession of the centurion who "saw how he died," declaring that "surely this man was the Son of God" (15:39).

In Mark, the cross indicates a servant-oriented Messiah who gives himself as a ransom for many (10:45). And this entails cross-shaped leadership, where the greatest is the one who serves (vv. 43–44). The cross determines the mode of inclusive community life, which welcomes "nobodies" as if they were dignitaries. The cross is the central image in Mark for understanding Jesus, discipleship, and the church. It claims everything, and it is the only way of life that brings kingdom citizens into the life of the world to come.

The Author of Mark's Gospel

The author of the second Gospel is not named, and he nowhere inserts himself into the narrative. He does not imagine that his audiences will know who he is and accept what he writes about Jesus based on his reputation. The attribution of this Gospel to Mark comes from Papias, a bishop in Hierapolis in the first half of the second century AD. He had learned that Mark was Peter's "interpreter," with Mark recording what Peter had said on various occasions about Jesus's ministry.[5] If this is the same Mark as we find in the New Testament, and if all the references to Mark refer to the same person, then we may say a few things about him. He appears to be from Jerusalem, since his mother had a house in the city and hosted meetings of the early church (Acts 12:12). He would likely have known a number of key disciples.

Mark was Barnabas's cousin (Col 4:10) and traveled with him and Paul from Antioch on their first mission (Acts 13:13). He left midway through, however, and returned to Jerusalem (13:13; 15:37). For this reason, Paul did not want to take Mark along on a subsequent journey, which ended the partnership of Paul and Barnabas (15:39). Interestingly, Mark was with Paul while Paul wrote to Philemon from prison (Phlm 24), and during a later imprisonment Paul asks Timothy to bring Mark along with him (2 Tim 4:11). He is also with Peter in Rome ("Babylon") when the apostle writes his first letter (1 Pet 5:13). Mark, then, is quite ubiquitous in the pages of the New Testament, traveling with some of the major leaders of the early Christian movement. Perhaps most remarkably, he forms a bridge between the Jewish and non-Jewish wings of the early church, being a companion of both Peter and Paul.

---

5. Eusebius, *Hist. eccl.* 3.39.12–16.

Mark's identity and association with Peter is significant for the reception of this Gospel by the church as Scripture, but his identity is not important for understanding the second Gospel. The relationship between the author and Mark's Gospel is quite unlike that between Paul and his letters. If we were studying Romans, for example, it is useful to know as much as we can about Paul's life in order to interpret that letter, since he makes himself such a major factor in what he writes. The situation is very different when it comes to Mark. The character of the actual Mark does not bear in any way on our understanding of the narrative, since he does not insert himself into the drama or refer to his life in any way. Because it has been known in church tradition since the second century as "the Gospel according to Mark," and there is no reason to dispute this, I will refer throughout the commentary to Mark as the author.

The Intended Audience(s) of Mark's Gospel

For the last several centuries, scholars have sought to identify the historical community to which Mark belonged and for which he wrote. The search, however, has been inconclusive, for there is little internal or external evidence for any one location or intended destination, whether that is Galilee, Syria, or Rome.[6] Rather than directing his Gospel to any singular community, it is more likely that Mark intended his Gospel to have as wide a readership as possible.[7] In the same way that the author does not make himself a significant factor for understanding his narrative, the location from which he wrote likewise has no bearing on interpretation. The narrative, however, offers some clues about the sorts of audiences Mark had in mind.

It does not appear that Mark wrote with the same purposes as John, who states explicitly that he wrote his Gospel to awaken faith in hearers and readers, and to confirm the faith of those who read and heard it:

Jesus performed many other signs in the presence of his disciples, which are not recorded in this book. But these are written that you may believe that Jesus is the Messiah, the Son of God, and that by believing you may have life in his name. (John 20:30–31)

---

6. Dwight H. Peterson, *The Origins of Mark: The Markan Community in Current Debate*, BibInt 48 (Leiden: Brill, 2000).

7. Richard Bauckham, "For Whom Were the Gospels Written?," in *The Gospels for all Christians: Rethinking the Gospel Audiences*, ed. Richard Bauckham (Grand Rapids: Eerdmans, 1998).

John, then, is written to inform audiences about who Jesus is and what he taught, to persuade them to believe in him and to ground them in their faith.

Nils Dahl offers some reasons for regarding Mark as having a different purpose: Mark's Gospel addresses audiences that are already familiar with the gospel about Jesus, including his life and teaching. Mark ends without any resurrection appearances and with the failure of the women to relay the message of Jesus's resurrection to the disciples (16:8), which implies that Mark's intended audiences were already informed.[8] Further, the "messianic secret," which refers to Jesus's constant exhortations to keep quiet about him, is not a device whereby Mark keeps something hidden from his readers until the end. Audiences and readers know who Jesus is, not only because Mark identified Jesus in his opening statement but because they have heard God's declaration to Jesus at his baptism (1:11) and his announcement to the disciples at his transfiguration (9:7) that *Jesus is God's beloved Son.* Jesus's identity is hidden from characters in the narrative, but audiences know who he is. "Mark is not presenting the solution to something which has been an unanswered riddle; he is emphasizing the mysterious character of something with which his readers are familiar."[9]

In the long discourse about the coming destruction of the temple and the troubles of this age in Mark 13, Jesus twice does something remarkable. While privately speaking to a small group of disciples within the narrative, he turns to audiences and directly addresses them. First, referring to the "abomination that causes desolation," he exhorts readers of Mark directly, saying, "Let the reader understand" (v. 14). And at the end of his long address during which he has repeatedly urged his disciples to be watchful, to be on guard, to stay alert, and to be awake, he concludes by addressing all readers and audiences: "What I say to you, I say to everyone: 'Watch!'" (v. 37). This is a message that has direct reference to Christian readers and church audiences.

In contrast to the other Gospels, Mark is not written to lay out the basics of Jesus's identity and the content of his teaching. After all, not much of his teaching is relayed in Mark, and the instruction that is found here has to do with the word bearing fruit (4:1–20) and with attending carefully to what has been heard (13:1–37). Mark's purpose is not so much to proclaim the gospel as to *remind Christians of the true character of the gospel,* calling readers and audiences back to the reality of the gospel they had received.[10] Mark's intended

---

8. Nils A. Dahl, "The Purpose of Mark's Gospel," in *Jesus in the Memory of the Early Church* (Minneapolis: Augsburg, 1976), 55.

9. Dahl, "Purpose of Mark's Gospel," 56.

10. Dahl, "Purpose of Mark's Gospel," 58.

audiences, therefore, are churches that have received the gospel and envision themselves as participants in the kingdom of God, but they have grown complacent and are failing to embody and inhabit the kingdom of God according to its radically cross-shaped character.

The Approach of This Commentary

This commentary takes a narrative approach to Mark's Gospel, recognizing that Mark tells the story in a certain way in order to shape the imaginations of his audiences and readers and to effect transformation among them. I have attempted to discern, therefore, how the narrative does this and note the way it moves audiences to envision the kingdom of God, the identity of Jesus, and the path of discipleship to which they are called. I do not reflect on how the text sheds light on "the historical Jesus" or seek to discern other "behind the text" questions. While history is important, I focus on how historical matters inform what is happening *within the text*. My aim is to understand the narrative—informed by historical background and the biblical storyline—in order to grasp and articulate what Mark wants to impress upon audiences and readers.

And I mention "audiences" at times, rather than merely "readers," because most people who would have encountered Mark in the first few centuries would have done so as gathered groups hearing Mark read to them. The vast majority of people in the ancient world were illiterate, so they would not have encountered Mark's Gospel as a text to be read. Mark wrote it as a narrative to be read aloud to audiences. This is helpful to keep in mind as modern readers of texts collected in Bibles, since some of these episodes would have generated an unsettled reaction among audiences that might have responded with gasps or even verbal objections, such as when they heard Jesus speak harshly to the Syrian-Phoenician woman (7:27). And this is to say nothing of how an audience would react to Jesus's response to her quick reply.

For reasons stated above, I also focus on Mark's presentation to Christian audiences. I assume that many people reading this commentary are Christians, and I believe that Mark intends to challenge Christian readers to take a closer look at whether they really understand Jesus and the character of the kingdom. I want to represent this thrust of Mark, so in my comments I will note that Mark is confronting us—Christians! My study of this Gospel has unsettled me in countless ways and reconfigured how I envision being Christian, how I view God, and how I see the mission of the church. This has been a wonderful, though uncomfortable, experience. But since I think that this is what Mark has set out to do, I want to represent that in my comments. In some of my reflections in the "Live the Story" sections, I confront uncomfortable realities about the church in North America—my cultural setting—but I do not do so because I have an axe to grind. I want to faithfully represent Mark's searching and unsettling message for the contemporary church.

I also do not comment on Mark's relation to the other three Gospels. There are excellent commentaries that do this in order to highlight Mark's unique contribution. Such an approach has great value, but since there are other works that have done this, I have focused solely on Mark's narrative, attending to the details of his presentation and its intended effects on audiences and readers.

Literary and Theological Features of Mark's Gospel

The Disciples

Mark presents Jesus's disciples in quite a negative light. They begin well in dropping everything and following Jesus right away and without question. And when he sends them out on mission, they do what he told them to and experienced the power of the kingdom (6:12–13, 30). Apart from these bright moments, however, they routinely fail to understand Jesus, ignore what he says, respond to him sarcastically, grow more confused as the narrative progresses, and finally betray, deny, and abandon him. Why does Mark do this? In my view, Mark intends for Christian audiences to identify with the disciples. They, too, have committed themselves to Jesus and imagine that they are kingdom-of-God communities, but they need greater clarification about the cross-orientation of the gospel. Perhaps they, like Peter, are committed to their idea of who they want Jesus to be. While Mark is a tremendous challenge to Christian audiences, Jesus remains fully and faithfully committed to them throughout. He calls them "my disciples" when they are about to betray, deny, and abandon him, and when he is raised, his messenger wants word sent to "*his* disciples and Peter" (16:7).

Discipleship in Mark

Mark portrays discipleship as taking up one's cross and "following" Jesus as he goes to the cross. But what do these expressions mean in terms of actual practices? Discipleship is characterized in two ways: service and offering hospitality to the marginalized. After James and John had requested places of prominence in the kingdom, Jesus says that whoever wants to become great among you must be your servant, and whoever wants to be first must be slave of all. For even the Son of Man did not come to be served, but to serve, and to give his life as a ransom for many. (10:43–45)

Since the one who rules God's kingdom is a servant, all who inhabit it must also become servants and slaves of everyone else.

Not long before this, the disciples were arguing about who was the greatest. In response, Jesus states that service is what greatness in the kingdom is all about. He then goes on to speak about offering hospitality to the marginalized, welcoming as dignitaries those who are nobodies in terms of corrupted social values:

Sitting down, Jesus called the Twelve and said, "Anyone who wants to be first must be the very last, and the servant of all."

He took a little child whom he placed among them. Taking the child in his arms, he said to them, "Whoever welcomes one of these little children in my name welcomes me; and whoever welcomes me does not welcome me but the one who sent me. (9:35–37)

Insiders and Outsiders

The parable of the sower and the soils in 4:1–20 is foundational for understanding the rest of Mark's Gospel. Between the parable itself and the interpretation, Jesus says something shocking:

The secret of the kingdom of God has been given to you. But to those on the outside everything is said in parables so that,

"they may be ever seeing but never perceiving,
    and ever hearing but never understanding;
otherwise they might turn and be forgiven!" (4:11–12)

Jesus is not trying to eliminate the possibility of people coming to faith, and neither is he advocating for teaching and preaching that confuses rather than clarifies. This parable sets up much of what happens in Mark 4–8 and beyond, where "insiders" will demonstrate perception (seeing and hearing), while "outsiders" will manifest confusion at Jesus and his words.

In one of Mark's most brilliant ironies, as the narrative progresses the disciples grow in confusion at Jesus's words, while "outsider" characters routinely "see" and "hear" Jesus and respond faithfully to him. In chapter 5, three characters see and hear Jesus and fall down at his feet. They stand in contrast to the disciples, who grow more confused so that they do not even understand Jesus's plain statements, let alone his parables. The climax of this theme in chapters 4–8 is the Syrian-Phoenician woman, the ultimate outsider character, who demonstrates keen insight as to Jesus's identity and words and whom Jesus commends. The rest of Mark continues this narrative strategy of the upending of insiders and outsiders, culminating with the Roman centurion confessing that Jesus was the Son of God (15:39).

This theme reveals Mark's strategy of unsettling audiences by raising the question of whether they belong to God's kingdom. Do they really grasp the character of Jesus and the nature of the kingdom? Do they presume they are insiders when they manifest community dynamics and modes of life that run counter to the kingdom of God?

"Immediately"

Mark is a dramatic Gospel, filled with fast-paced action and moving from this episode to that incident before audiences have time to digest what just happened. The Greek term *euthys*, which means "immediately," occurs over forty times in Mark, which is unusual since it appears only about twelve times in the rest of the New Testament. In some episodes Mark uses this term with such repetition that it seems he is trying to overwhelm his audiences and readers. The NIV smooths out the narrative at some points, translating *euthys* with various synonyms like "just as" and "right away" rather than only using "immediately." This results in a more pleasing translation, but it obscures the fact that Mark intends to jar his audiences with the pace of his Gospel. Jesus is on the move, and his kingdom agenda just might leave you in the dust if you are comfortable and complacent. To get a sense of how Mark can at times pile up this word to jar his readers, consider Mark 1:21–31 in a more "woodenly literal" English translation, like the NASB.

Literary Sandwiches

Another device whereby Mark propels his narrative forward at breakneck speed is the use of *intercalation*, which simply has to do with inserting one episode inside another. It's easier to think of "literary sandwiches," which leaves readers with the impression that the action is cascading—so much is happening that Mark must break into episodes to report what has just happened! As just one example, amid narrating Jairus's plea to Jesus regarding his daughter, Mark tells the story of a woman who had been hemorrhaging for twelve years. The narrative then returns to conclude the raising of Jairus's daughter (5:21–43).

As we note in the commentary on this passage, the two incidents share several details so that they are mutually interpreting. But the effect of sandwiching one episode inside the other is to make audiences feel the frenetic pace of the drama, with people crowding Jesus, desperate for healing and restoration.

Secrecy Motif

Throughout the first half of Mark, Jesus continually commands various characters—his disciples, demons that he drives out, and people that he heals—to keep quiet about his identity. In one of the opening scenes, Jesus "drove out many demons, but he would not let the demons speak because they knew who he was" (1:34). After healing a leper, "Jesus sent him away at once with a strong warning: 'See that you don't tell this to anyone'" (1:43–44). When he raised up Jairus's daughter, "He gave strict orders not to let anyone know about this, and told them to give her something to eat" (5:43). And there are many more instances of this. These stern warnings from Jesus to keep quiet about him are quite mystifying, especially for Christian readers who have heard countless sermons on seizing every opportunity to talk about Jesus.

As I have already indicated, Mark is directed to Christian audiences and readers, challenging them with the reality that Jesus and the kingdom of God are more mysterious and wonderful than they know. Further, this Gospel causes churches to consider whether their social dynamics and corporate practices have drifted from embodying the radical character of the cross. Mark's Gospel is a call to return and give fresh consideration to the cruciform (i.e., cross-shaped) character of Jesus and the kingdom of God. Perhaps Christians and church communities ought to consider silence and careful reflection rather than feel the urgency to speak. After all, they may misrepresent Jesus and his reign, resulting in a grasp of the kingdom that Jesus calls satanic (4:15; 8:33). One of the most threatening things about this whole dynamic in Mark is that the huge crowds that gather to Jesus are indicators that the true nature of the gospel is being obscured. When a sentimentally hopeful gospel is preached that offers satisfaction of wants and needs, huge crowds will gather. But those crowds prove to be obstacles to Jesus throughout Mark, as we will see. When the cross is preached, and when Jesus ascends his throne in the shape of the cross, he dies utterly alone. In the age of megachurches and a focus on "ministry success," this is a powerful challenge.

Perception

As I indicated above, the parable of the sower and the soils in 4:1–20 is foundational to much that takes place in the remainder of the narrative. There,

Jesus speaks of some who will see but not perceive, and who will hear and not understand (v. 12). The disciples turn out to be such people as Mark unfolds. Jesus asks them in 8:17–18, "Do you still not see or understand? Are your hearts hardened? Do you have eyes but fail to see, and ears but fail to hear?" Meanwhile, a number of unexpected characters "hear" and "see" Jesus and respond to him in ways that the disciples do not. In Mark 5, the demon-possessed man, Jairus, and the woman all "see" and "hear" Jesus and run to him and fall down before him. The Syrian-Phoenician woman "heard" about Jesus (7:25). Jesus heals two blind men as parabolic actions that point to the need of the disciples (8:22–26; 10:46–52), and Bartimaeus "heard" Jesus coming through town and pleaded with him for healing (10:47). When Jesus asked him what he wanted, he replied that he wanted to see, the very thing for which the disciples should be pleading with Jesus.

Mark's Ending

Even though Mark's subversive storytelling characterizes the entire Gospel, the end still comes as a shock.[11] Rather than recounting resurrection appearances or programmatic commands to preach the gospel worldwide, Mark ends with failure. The women come to Jesus's burial place and find a young man sitting to the side of where Jesus was laid, and he announces that God has raised him and that the women should relay a message to the disciples and Peter. But the women remain silent because they were afraid. And that's how it ends—with failure.

The more one ponders how Mark concludes his Gospel, the more bizarre and profound it grows. It is a massive challenge to church audiences that want to belong to something successful. We want to be shaped by a narrative that ends well, that fires hope for the future. But Mark is a brilliant storyteller, and he knows that satisfying endings are far less effective than unsatisfying ones in provoking people to return to the beginning and give renewed consideration to just what this whole thing is all about.

A Map of Mark's Gospel

Mark 1:1–45

Mark introduces his Gospel, along with the main characters, John and Jesus, who is the Christ, the Son of God. Mark also provides a summary of the kinds of activities Jesus was involved in throughout his ministry. Without being exhaustive,

---

11. I assume, with most scholars, that Mark intended to end his Gospel at 16:8 and that the longer endings are inauthentic. See the appendix for a discussion of the ending and alternative endings.

he gives a sense of Jesus's ministry of *proclaiming the gospel of the kingdom* and *embodying the power of the kingdom through healing and driving out demons.*

Mark 2:1–3:6

This section is comprised of a series of conflict stories in Galilee between Jesus and the scribes and Pharisees. The action moves from suspicion about Jesus to outright hostility, so that by the end, the Pharisees depart to plot with the Herodians to kill Jesus.

Mark 3:7–35

In light of the threat from the scribes and Pharisees, Jesus "withdraws" with his disciples. He appoints the Twelve "to be with him" and "to be sent" to proclaim the gospel and to embody the gospel by driving out demons. Jesus also indicates the character of his new family: they are those who do the will of God.

Mark 4:1–34

Jesus teaches in parables. The sower and the seed (4:1–20) is the main parable to which Mark repeatedly refers.

Mark 5:1–8:21

This section elaborates on the prophetic quotation in 4:11–12 about seeing but not perceiving and hearing but not understanding. It closes with Jesus asking the disciples if this has happened to them (8:17–18). The "insider"/"outsider" dynamic that Jesus articulates in 4:11–12 works out in this narrative portion in ironically inverted ways, so that the disciples become increasingly confused, and outsiders routinely perceive ("see" and "hear") Jesus and come to him.

Mark 8:22–10:52

This section is framed by two healings of blind men. Jesus predicts his betrayal, suffering, death, and resurrection three times, and each time the disciples dramatically misunderstand or object to what he says, after which Jesus teaches them about discipleship. The expression "on the way" is repeated through-out this section, as Jesus and the disciples are "on the way" from Galilee to Jerusalem, where he will suffer and die.

Mark 11:1–12:44

Jesus and the disciples enter Jerusalem and go into the temple, where Jesus declares God's judgment on the temple and shuts it down. The temple author-ities react and enter into a series of confrontations with Jesus.

Mark 13:1–37

Jesus predicts the destruction of Jerusalem and its temple and gives counsel to the disciples regarding living in this age when all supposedly stable and predictable structures and institutions are being destroyed. He also refers to the return of the Son of Man, a distinct event from the series of destructions that characterize this age. He warns against looking for signs of his return and also against words of supposed safety—that God will save the temple and that he'll keep institutions from being destroyed during this age.

Mark 14:1–15:47

This section includes the betrayal, suffering, and death of Jesus at the hands of the Jerusalem authorities. Throughout this section, everyone abandons Jesus, and he dies alone. Further, while Jesus has determined the action throughout the Gospel, here he becomes passive and is acted upon by others. Yet everything is unfolding just as he predicted. Mark portrays Jesus's being led to the cross as his royal coronation: the cross-shaped king enters his cross-oriented reign.

Mark 16:1–8

This section is Mark's mystifying ending. Jesus is not in the grave. The young man says that he has been raised. The women are told to tell the rest of the disciples, but they flee and remain silent because of fear.

📖 LISTEN to the Story

¹The beginning of the good news about Jesus the Messiah, the Son of God, ²as it is written in Isaiah the prophet:

> "I will send my messenger ahead of you,
>   who will prepare your way"—
> ³"a voice of one calling in the wilderness,
> 'Prepare the way for the Lord,
>   make straight paths for him.'"

⁴And so John the Baptist appeared in the wilderness, preaching a baptism of repentance for the forgiveness of sins. ⁵The whole Judean countryside and all the people of Jerusalem went out to him. Confessing their sins, they were baptized by him in the Jordan River. ⁶John wore clothing made of camel's hair, with a leather belt around his waist, and he ate locusts and wild honey. ⁷And this was his message: "After me comes the one more powerful than I, the straps of whose sandals I am not worthy to stoop down and untie. ⁸I baptize you with water, but he will baptize you with the Holy Spirit." ⁹At that time Jesus came from Nazareth in Galilee and was baptized by John in the Jordan. ¹⁰Just as Jesus was coming up out of the water, he saw heaven being torn open and the Spirit descending on him like a dove. ¹¹And a voice came from heaven: "You are my Son, whom I love; with you I am well pleased." ¹²At once the Spirit sent him out into the wilderness, ¹³and he was in the wilderness forty days, being tempted by Satan. He was with the wild animals, and angels attended him.

Listening to the Text in the Story: Genesis 1:1; 22:2; Exodus 23:20; 2 Kings 1:8; Psalm 110; Malachi 3:1; 4:5–6; Isaiah 40:3, 9; 52:7–10; Romans 1:1–7; 1 Corinthians 15:1–8.

Beginnings are crucial. Some novelists manage to create unforgettable opening lines: "Call me Ishmael."[1] Or, "It was the best of times, it was the worst of times."[2] Those familiar with the Bible will recognize the first lines of the book of Genesis ("In the beginning God created . . .") and the prologue of the Gospel of John (1:1–18), "In the beginning was the Word." The openings of biblical narratives, like in other literature, often capture the entire drama in one brief statement or in a few paragraphs. The beginning of Mark's Gospel functions in precisely this way, summing up the whole of his narrative about Jesus Christ, the Son of God, who confronts and defeats Satan and inaugurates God's kingdom, beginning the work of restoring God's creation.

Mark opens with John the Baptist and his ministry of the preparation of God's people for the arrival of God's Messiah, readying them for Jesus's call to receive the kingdom by taking up their crosses. Many in Jesus's audiences were eager for the kingdom's arrival, but only those with prepared hearts would receive the teaching that challenged their commitments, cultural assumptions, and deeply held prejudices.

Sending John to prepare the way for Jesus is consistent with God's way of working throughout the biblical story. The quotation in Mark 1:2–3 is a blending of texts that come from pivotal moments in the story of God and his people. The first two lines come from Exodus 23:20 and Malachi 3:1, while v. 3 is a quotation of Isaiah 40:3. In Exodus 23:20, God tells Israel that he is sending his angel ahead of them to bring them safely into the land of promise. Malachi 3:1 is a prophecy that God's dramatic appearance at the great day of judgment and salvation will be preceded by a messenger who will prepare the way before the Lord. Exodus 23:20 comes from the early days of Israel's sojourn, and Malachi 3:1 comes from much later, after Israel had been sent into exile. Both texts—one from the Law and one from the Prophets—call God's people to get ready for the radical disruption that comes with God's arrival.

Mark blends these passages with Isaiah 40:3, a text from the beginning of the section of Isaiah that focuses on God's future restoration of Israel (Isa 40–55). The blended "quotation" therefore calls to mind previous, crucial turning points in God's relationship with his people and highlights how God's preparation for the sending of Jesus has precedents in the story of the Bible. And Mark wants his readers to see these instances through the lens of Isaiah, Israel's prophet who most significantly shaped messianic expectation.[3]

---

1. Herman Melville, *Moby-Dick: Or, The Whale* (New York: Random House, 1950), 1.

2. Charles Dickens, *A Tale of Two Cities* (New York: Bantam, 2003), 3.

3. Isaiah had a massive influence on how the New Testament writers conceived of Jesus's identity and mission. Isaiah is the only Old Testament figure Mark mentions by name, here and at 7:6, leading

Mark sets the stage for his narrative in terms of these significant scenes from the biblical narrative.

Mark also reveals Jesus's identity to his readers here. In v. 1, he calls Jesus "the Son of God," and at Jesus's baptism by John, God declares to Jesus, "You are my Son, whom I love; with you I am well pleased" (v. 11). Jesus's identity as God's Son recalls several biblical texts. In Genesis 22:1–2, God calls Abraham to take Isaac, "your son, your only son, whom you love," and sacrifice him as a burnt offering. Psalm 2 is a royal enthronement psalm that depicts Israel's king becoming God's son, the one appointed as priest, ruler, and judge on God's behalf. God's words to Jesus in Mark come directly from this psalm:

> He said to me, "You are my son;
>   today I have become your father." (v. 7)

And in Isaiah 42:1–4, especially v. 1, God speaks to his servant in words that echo in Mark 1:11:

> Here is my servant, whom I uphold,
>   **my chosen one in whom I delight;**
> **I will put my Spirit on him,**
>   and he will bring justice to the nations.
> He will not shout or cry out,
>   or raise his voice in the streets.
> A bruised reed he will not break,
>   and a smoldering wick he will not snuff out.
> In faithfulness he will bring forth justice;
>   he will not falter or be discouraged
> till he establishes justice on earth.
>   In his teaching the islands will put their hope.

A rich biblical tradition, therefore, informs how Mark speaks of Jesus as God's Son. He is God's appointed servant who will carry out God's will on earth. Mark's readers know who Jesus is, but one of the striking features of his Gospel is that many of the characters fail to grasp who Jesus is. This is a

---

some to call Mark's work "the Gospel according to Isaiah" (Joel Marcus, *Mark 1–8*, AB 27 [New York: Doubleday, 2000], 139–40, 147; Eugene M. Boring, *Mark: A Commentary*, NTL [Louisville: Westminster John Knox, 2006], 404–8). According to some commentators, Mark is mistaken when he cites a number of texts rather than simply Isaiah. It is more likely that Mark brings together several biblical references and wants his readers to think of them in terms of Isaiah's prophecies.

significant device whereby Mark both reveals Jesus's identity to his readers yet stresses the need to pay careful attention to the way in which Jesus embodies that identity.

EXPLAIN the Story

Mark sets his account of Jesus within the story of Scripture with his opening line: "The beginning of the good news about Jesus the Messiah" (v. 1), with "the beginning" possibly echoing Genesis 1:1.[4] Rather than telling a new story, this is a *continuation* of the unfinished story of the God of Israel that is awaiting its climax. "Gospel" (*euangelion*, "good news") situates Mark's work in terms of the hopes of Israel as expressed in the prophets. The Hebrew term (*basar*) for "good news" appears in several pivotal passages in Isaiah that anticipated God's future rescue of Israel:

> You who bring **good news** to Zion,
> go up on a high mountain.
> You who bring **good news** to Jerusalem,
> lift up your voice with a shout,
> lift it up, do not be afraid;
> say to the towns of Judah,
> "Here is your God!" (Isa 40:9)

In Isaiah 52:7, the prophet looked forward to being able to announce the inauguration of the life-giving and gracious reign of the God of Israel:

> How beautiful on the mountains
> are the feet of those who bring **good news**,
> who proclaim peace,
> who bring **good tidings**,
> who proclaim salvation,
> who say to Zion,
> "Your God reigns!"

---

4. Augustine, Irenaeus, and Origen saw in this allusion a unifying element between the gospel of Jesus Christ and the story of Israel's Scriptures. This was held in direct contrast to Marcion, an early figure who set the Old and New Testaments in opposition to each other, attributing them to different gods (Thomas C. Oden and Christopher A. Hall, eds., *Mark*, ACCS [Downers Grove, IL: InterVarsity Press, 1998], 2).

Israel had been scattered among the nations because of unfaithfulness, and they longed for God to gather his exiled people and reestablish his righteous rule. Many prophetic texts were filled with hope for the "good news" of God's triumph.

Early audiences of Mark in Greco-Roman settings would have been familiar with *euangelion* ("good news") from another context, too—its appearance in Roman imperial propaganda. Mark's reference to "the beginning of the good news about Jesus Christ" is similar to wording that appears on an inscription that dates from 9 BC, marking the birthday of Augustus:

> The providence which has ordered the whole of our life, showing concern and zeal, has ordained the most perfect consummation for human life by giving to it Augustus, by filling him with virtue for doing the work of a benefactor among men, and by sending in him, as it were, a savior for us and those who come after us, to make war to cease, to create order everywhere . . . ; the birthday of the god [Augustus] was *the beginning for the world of the good news* [*euangelion*] that has come to men through him.[5]

It is tempting to see here an indication that Mark's Gospel is deliberately anti-imperial, set in opposition to the notion that Caesar is divine, the embodiment of the gods. After all, Caesar received worship in the well-established emperor cult and was seen as the one who guaranteed the peace and order of the Rome Empire—the *Pax Romana*. Is Mark deliberately confronting Caesar's claims with his proclamation of Jesus as the Son of God?[6]

Jesus is certainly creating an alternative community that is utterly unique. He calls for radically new practices that will confront many well-established patterns of life in any culture, both Jewish and non-Jewish. Yet Jesus is focused more on establishing God's kingdom than on confronting Rome. In fact, if Mark's Gospel were a direct affront to Rome, we might wonder whether Jesus ceases to be relevant when Rome was no longer a dominant empire. Further, direct opposition of Rome and Caesar would easily play into violent strategies.

---

5. A. D. Nock, *Early Gentile Christianity and Its Hellenistic Background* (New York: Harper & Row, 1964), 37.

6. "Undeniably the first century Greco-Roman reader would have recognized the presence of Roman imperial language in Mark's incipit. To such a reader it would have appeared that Mark intentionally replaced Caesar with Jesus and thus attributed to Jesus the honor that was regularly reserved for the emperor alone" (Adam Winn, *Reading Mark's Christology under Caesar: Jesus the Messiah and Roman Imperial Ideology* [Downers Grove, IL: IVP Academic, 2018], 72). "We can hardly, then, read Mark's opening lines without recognizing that the Gospel's central character is on a collision course with Caesar" (Richard B. Hays, *Echoes of Scripture in the Gospels* [Waco, TX: Baylor University Press, 2016], 92).

Hopes for a military leader who would rally the Jews and take on the Romans were rampant in first-century Jewish culture. Throughout the Gospels, and especially Mark, Jesus constantly overturns this sort of expectation. Rather than facing down Rome with threats of superior violence, Jesus accomplished God's purposes by being the *victim* of Rome's violence. At the heart of Mark's Gospel is the paradoxical logic that God triumphs not through force of arms but through the cross.

In the end, the early Christian proclamation of "good news" about Jesus the Son of God would certainly have gotten Rome's attention (and it did), along with any earthly rulers who saw themselves as ultimate. Rulers who succumb to the illusion of ultimacy find themselves being reminded that only God is ultimate and that all earthly rulers are ordained by God and are accountable to him (Dan 4:34–37). To read Mark as setting forth an explicitly anti-imperial gospel, then, is to overstate his intentions. He proclaims the news about the reign of God in Jesus Christ without necessarily drawing the explicit corollary that God's reign opposes Rome's.[7]

Mark's use of *euangelion* frames his narrative in terms of the hopes of Israel for the long-awaited salvation of God. It also situates the kingdom of God as a unique entity that stands apart from and over against all other causes, nations, tribes, and earthly empires.

Jesus's Identity

Mark introduces Jesus as "the Messiah, the Son of God" (v. 1). "Messiah" (Heb. *mashiakh*), or "Christ" (Gk. *Christos*), signifies one appointed to carry out a certain task. In Isaiah 45:1, the pagan king Cyrus is God's "messiah," whom God appoints to dominate the international scene and ultimately bring about the rescue of Israel (Isa 45:1–7). "Messiah" is used as a title for Jesus at various points in Mark (8:29; 12:35; 13:21; 14:61; 15:32), and in 9:41 it is used as a proper name.[8] Jesus, then, is God's appointed agent of salvation for God's people.

Jesus is also called the "Son of God," a notion rich with biblical resonances. The nation of Israel was God's unique son (Exod 4:22–23; Hos 11:1), and Israel's king was called "God's son," indicating a special relationship to God.

---

7. For a helpful introduction to whether and to what extent the New Testament contains anti-imperial rhetoric, see Scot McKnight and Joseph B. Modica, eds., *Jesus Is Lord, Caesar Is Not: Evaluating Empire in New Testament Studies* (Downers Grove, IL: IVP Academic, 2013).

8. C. Clifton Black, *Mark*, ANTC (Nashville: Abingdon, 2011), 47. Craig Evans notes that three main scriptural passages shaped Jewish messianic expectation: Gen 49:10; Num 24:17; and Isa 11:1–6. See his article for how these texts shaped the development of messianic expectation in Judaism ("Messianism," *DNTB* 698–707).

The king was to reign in such a way as to enact God's own rule (2 Sam 7:13–14; Ps 2:7).[9] In Mark's presentation, Jesus is God's appointed king, representing God himself. But the identification of Jesus with the God of Israel is more intense than mere representation. In the ancient world the designation "son of" indicated that a person possessed the very same character as his father. Jesus is God's utterly unique Son in that he not only *represents* God *but is God himself.* Jesus shares in the identity of the God of Israel, the creator of all things.[10]

Mark uses these titles to develop his notion of Jesus's oft-misunderstood identity. While the disciples acknowledge that Jesus is indeed "the Christ," they continue to have a wrong conception of what this means. Peter confessed Jesus as "the Christ" in Mark 8:29, but then rebuked Jesus when he told his disciples that he was going to die and rise again (8:31–32). The disciples' imaginations were shaped by their culture's desires for a messiah who would come as a military conqueror. Mark wants his readers to question whether their conception of Jesus as the Christ is shaped by culture or by Scripture.

Mark uses the title "Son of God" in a similar way. In nearly every instance a character from the spiritual realm uses it of Jesus, whether God or demons. Humans, however, don't recognize Jesus as "Son of God" until the very end of the Gospel, when a Roman centurion confesses that Jesus is God's Son (Mark 15:39). This narrative device fits Mark's larger intention perfectly. God's people were supposed to "get" Jesus, but they fail to recognize his true identity. Mark forces his audience to confront the question: "Do you really recognize Jesus for who he is, and do you really understand what he requires of you?"

John Prepares the Way

Mark refers to John's ministry by citing the prophet Isaiah, but he then quotes three separate passages, as discussed above. The line from Malachi 3:1 comes from the prophet's prediction that God will send a figure to prepare his way when he returns to his people to judge and to save. This one is Elijah, the prophet who did not die but was taken up to heaven miraculously (2 Kgs 2:11–12): "See, I will send the prophet Elijah to you before that great and dreadful day of the LORD comes" (Mal 4:5).

Throughout Scripture, when God returns to his people, he warns his people to be ready and to be on the alert. God's angel went with Israel, which meant

---

9. Black, *Mark*, 48.

10. See Richard Bauckham, *Jesus and the God of Israel: God Crucified and Other Studies on the New Testament's Christology of Divine Identity* (Grand Rapids: Eerdmans, 2008), for the language of Jesus participating in the identity of the God of Israel. See also Michael F. Bird, *Jesus the Eternal Son: Answering Adoptionist Christology* (Grand Rapids: Eerdmans, 2017), 84–106.

that they were divinely protected, but he also warned of their need to watch their conduct carefully, since he would be ready to judge rebellion among God's people (Exod 23:21). And the prospect of God's return in Malachi was good news, except that it would involve an intense examination of the character of God's people and their patterns of life (Mal 3:5). The world-altering return of the God of Israel was called the "great and dreadful day of the LORD" (Mal 4:5).

In the same way, readers of Mark must prepare themselves. The restoration of God's reign is good news, but it involves a dramatic upsetting of "the normal way of doing things." As Mark proceeds, we'll see that the emergence of the kingdom and its king is of an entirely different order altogether. Be ready!

The description of John sets the tone for how readers are to encounter Mark's Gospel. First, John is in the wilderness (Mark 1:4), a place of great significance in Scripture and the history of Judaism. There Israel learned about dependence on God and being faithful to him before entering the land of promise. It is the place of new beginnings, "the place where Israel stood before crucial decisions (Deut 30:19), where they entered into the covenant and became God's people (Deut 29:12), where Israel is called to make a fresh start (Jer 2:2; Hos 2:14; 9:10), the route to a new Exodus (Isa 40–55)."[11] The mere mention of this location calls to mind a decisive new beginning.[12]

John's call to the wilderness also indicates a critique of the Jerusalem temple. The temple was the center of Jewish life, the place where heaven and earth met, where Jews encountered the God of Israel and found forgiveness. If there was to be any sort of renewal, surely it would begin at the temple, the place where God lives! John's call *away from the temple* was an implicit judgment on this central Jewish institution. As Mark progresses, we will see how Jesus is the new temple that replaces the old. Mark's point here, however, is that God is not found in the temple, but may be encountered in the desert.[13] This is an early sign that Jesus's agenda is going to involve a serious challenge to the status quo.

Second, John is "preaching a baptism of repentance for the forgiveness of sins" (Mark 1:4). Many Christians are familiar with the call to individual salvation, which involves repentance for the forgiveness of sins and results in a person having a right relationship with God. While closely related to this,

---

11. Boring, *Mark*, 39.

12. Because the wilderness was so critical in Israel's story, Jewish renewal movements often launched their efforts from the desert. The community at Qumran went to the desert to separate themselves from the unrighteous in Israel. Messianic pretenders led their followers into the desert in order to build their doomed movements (Acts 21:38; cf. Acts 5:36).

13. For a comparison of John's movement to contemporary Jewish renewal movements that involved a critique of the Jerusalem temple, see Nicholas Perrin, *Jesus the Temple* (Grand Rapids: Baker Academic, 2010), 17–45.

John's call is operating on the national level. This baptism was more likely a
ritual by which Jews joined John's renewal movement as a corporate body of
people rightly related to God and who were readying themselves for Israel's
messiah. "Forgiveness of sins" recalls the prophetic language of God restoring
the nation of Israel. In 2 Chronicles 7, God speaks to Solomon after the dedication of the temple and speaks of the relationship God has with the nation:

> I have heard your prayer and have chosen this place for myself as a temple
> for sacrifices.
>
> When I shut up the heavens so that there is no rain, or command locusts
> to devour the land or send a plague among my people, **if my people, who
> are called by my name, will humble themselves and pray and seek my
> face and turn from their wicked ways, then I will hear from heaven,
> and I will forgive their sin and will heal their land.** (2 Chr 7:12–14)

The Old Testament speaks clearly about how individuals relate to God, how
they are forgiven, and how they can walk in his ways. But Scripture also speaks
of national Israel's relation to God, how its sin can separate it from God, and
how repentance can secure forgiveness and restoration to a right relationship.

This national reality can also be seen in Jeremiah, where God speaks to
Jerusalem:

> I will hide my face from this city because of all its wickedness.
>
> Nevertheless, I will bring health and healing to it; I will heal my people
> and will let them enjoy abundant peace and security. I will bring Judah and
> Israel back from captivity and will rebuild them as they were before. **I will
> cleanse them from all the sin they have committed against me and will
> forgive all their sins of rebellion against me.** Then this city will bring me
> renown, joy, praise and honor before all nations on earth that hear of all
> the good things I do for it; and they will be in awe and will tremble at the
> abundant prosperity and peace I provide for it. (Jer 33:5–9)

John was calling out to Jews to form a body of people that would stand
in as the Israel that was rightly related to God, prepared for God to return to
his people. In this sense, John's baptism was a unique moment in the story of
God and his relation to his people. The baptism that we are familiar with and
which appears later in the New Testament—baptism "in the name of the Lord
Jesus" (cf. Acts 19:5)—has to do with individuals turning from sin to God,
having their sins forgiven, and being baptized to demonstrate their new life of

discipleship to Jesus. But John's baptism was a call to join a corporate movement of Jews to be the Israel that is rightly related to God. In fact, those responding to John's baptism could have been sinners needing to repent, but they also could have been righteous people who loved God and whose hearts were pure, people who wanted to separate themselves from the sinful nation and join a group intent on preparing themselves for the next step in God's saving program. While John's baptism was preparatory, the one coming after him was going to baptize them with the Spirit (Mark 1:8), referring to the fulfillment of God's promise to return by his Spirit and give life to his people (Isa 11:1–2; Joel 2:28–32).

Third, Mark indicates that John's movement was very popular and generated great excitement: "The whole Judean countryside and all the people of Jerusalem went out to him" (v. 5). In Mark's Gospel Jesus consistently encounters huge crowds, and John finds this same response. Mark portrays a nation desperate for God's salvation.

Fourth, Mark portrays John in terms of Israel's prophets, especially Elijah, who is described similarly in 2 Kings 1:8.[14] King Ahaziah's servants describe the man they encountered: "He had a garment of hair and had a leather belt around his waist." The king responds, "That was Elijah the Tishbite." Mark describes John in the same way: "John wore clothing made of camel's hair, with a leather belt around his waist," with the added detail that "he ate locusts and wild honey" (Mark 1:6). John is much like the radical prophet Elijah, calling out the sin of Israel's leaders (Mark 6:18), just as Elijah did. The confrontational prophetic mode is prominent in Mark's Gospel. He mentions John at a number of pivotal points (1:4; 6:14–29; 8:28), and his association of John (and Elijah) with Jesus casts Jesus as more of a confrontational figure than in the other three Gospels.

Jesus Initiates His Ministry

John's baptism as a rite of initiation into a renewal movement of preparation explains why Jesus is baptized. If we think about his baptism in terms of the public declaration after someone has come to faith, his baptism becomes theologically troubling. Jesus is not a sinner in need of salvation. Rather, Jesus, not yet anointed by the Spirit for ministry, seeks to do the will of God, and this leads him to join John's movement of people preparing themselves for the Lord's return.

Mark dramatically narrates the events that initiate Jesus's ministry. First, Jesus hardly gets out of the water before he sees heaven being ripped open and the Spirit descending on him (1:10).[15] This is the Spirit's anointing of Jesus for

---

14. Marcus, *Mark 1–8*, 156.

15. The verb for "torn open" (*schizō*) appears again in 15:38 with reference to the tearing of the veil when the Roman centurion recognizes that Jesus is the Son of God, forming an *inclusio*, a literary

the unique ministry to which God has called him. Second, Jesus hears God's declaration that "you are my Son, whom I love; with you I am well pleased" (v. 11). Mark implies that only Jesus hears this heavenly declaration of God's approval. This is an instance of how Mark develops the identity of Jesus for his readers. God knows who Jesus is, as does Jesus, and the readers are let in on this. But the human characters in Mark's story do not understand his identity.[16]

Third, Jesus barely has time to take in the heavenly declaration, because the Spirit immediately drives him into the wilderness for a climactic encounter with Satan (v. 12). Jesus's first task is to reverse the tragic failure of the initial human rebellion. Even though Adam and Eve failed in the garden, Jesus encounters Satan in the wilderness—a far less advantageous setting for such an encounter. Mark gives few details about Jesus's satanic encounter, but it must have involved the temptation to carry out his messianic role through some other route than the cross. When Jesus later hears a similar suggestion, he identifies it as satanic (Mark 8:31–35). The presence of the angels indicates some sort of divine aid. Humanity's original sin led to hostility with creation (Gen 3:14–21), and one of Judaism's hopes was a return to living in harmony with creation (Isa 11:6–9).[17] Jesus begins to restore humanity to its proper relation to creation by communing with the "wild animals" (v. 13).

LIVE the Story

Preparation

Mark begins his story of Jesus with the dominant note of preparation. When God acts dramatically on behalf of his people, he calls them to get ready. John the Baptist is sent to prepare God's people for the arrival of God's messiah. If they aren't rightly prepared, they will miss it. Tragically, they did miss it!

---

framing device, around Mark's Gospel. Further, the temple veil—likely the outer veil—was blue with a "whole vista of the heavens" embroidered on it, according to Josephus (*J. W.* 5.212). In Mark, then, there is a double tearing of the heavens at the opening and closing of Jesus's earthly ministry (David Ulansey, "The Heavenly Veil Torn: Mark's Cosmic *Inclusio*," *JBL* 110 [1991]: 123–25).

16. Hippolytus (170–235 AD), in beautiful poetic form similar to Paul in 2 Cor 4, comments on God's words to Jesus: "Listen to the Father's voice: 'This is my beloved Son, in whom I am well pleased.' This is he who is named the son of Joseph, who according to the divine essence is my only begotten. 'This is my beloved Son,' yes, none other than the One who himself becomes hungry, yet feeds countless numbers. He is my Son who himself becomes weary, yet gives rest to the weary. He has no place to lay his head, yet bears up all things in his hand. He suffers, yet heals sufferings. He is beaten, yet confers liberty upon the world. He is pierced in his side, yet repairs the side of Adam" (Oden and Hall, *Mark*, 15).

17. Francis J. Moloney, *The Gospel of Mark: A Commentary* (Grand Rapids: Baker Academic, 2002), 39.

When God himself showed up, they didn't recognize him. They took a three-year long look at Jesus and concluded that he was *not* God's messiah. We can't judge that generation for their blindness, because we would do the same thing. They missed it because they had fallen victim to the same blindness that afflicts us. We are often far more committed to our agendas, our preconceptions of what Jesus *must be like*, that we fail to see him for who he really is.

Those who follow the Christian calendar know that there are times throughout the year marked out for preparation. The Advent season—the four weeks leading up to Christmas—is just such a time. Advent shapes Christian hope and orients it according to the arrival of the Son of God. It's a time for the church to reflect on whether and to what extent they are prepared to welcome the Son of God into the world. This is one of the prayers from the Book of Common Prayer for the Advent season:

> Merciful God, who sent your messengers the prophets to preach repentance and prepare the way for our salvation: Give us grace to heed their warnings and forsake our sins, that we may greet with joy the coming of Jesus Christ our Redeemer; who lives and reigns with you and the Holy Spirit, one God, now and for ever. Amen.[18]

Seasons of intentional reflection and preparation are important because they are times we can subject our mindsets to purification, asking ourselves whether we've been taken captive to prejudices or other attitudes that corrupt our imaginations regarding being Christian. God's ways are different from our own, and we have the tendency to envision God's agenda in terms of our own thoughts.

Another way we may prepare for God to work on us is purposefully making the most out of times of fellowship with God's people, those times when we hear God's word. Here's a prayer of preparation for worship from Arthur Nelson's *A Book of Prayers*:

> Holy God, full of grace and just in all your ways, come to church with us this day with the urgency of your call to faith and the wonder of your large and magnificent promises.
>
> For so many in our times there are long stretches when the good news is stale news.

---

18. The Lectionary Page, www.lectionarypage.net/YearB/Advent/BAdv2.html.

For some there are times when they are unable to vouch for the gospel with the joy it deserves, caught in the abundance of life's chores. Spare us when so much distracts us. Spare us the corrosion of our enthusiasms, the impurity of our purposes and the deterioration of our courage. For if you do not enter our lives day after day, we may miss our charge to reach out to that segment of humanity that continues to stumble for unrighteousness's sake.

Say something today, God, by peace or persuasion, assurance or confirmation, as we anticipate by singing, listening, praying you're meeting us here with differing hopes and wounds.[19]

Baptism

Baptism is a Christian practice that symbolizes a break with the old and an initiation into something radically new. The early Christians baptized converts immediately after they confessed faith in Christ. In some settings, churches prefer to put an extended period of time between a person's confession of faith and their baptism. They may be motivated by a desire to see that a young Christian's faith is sincere and that they know what they've committed to. While this may be commendable, the first Christian generation baptized professing Christians right away, knowing that this was the first step of a lifelong growth process of coming to grips with the faith and the character of required commitment. While we may want to see to it that people really understand what they are doing, we might consider giving young believers an opportunity to concretely act out their faith. Such public acts flood our hearts with assurance by the Spirit, generate excitement in the community, and become the first steps of a lifelong journey in God's grace. We should seize opportunities like that to infuse fresh life and excitement into our church communities.

When I was in seminary, I had a conversation with a friend about whether baptism had lost its significance in a very "Christianized" America. If America is a place where one can be a professing Christian without being arrested or regarded as a radical, then is baptism really that big of a deal? Can we dispense with it?

A few weeks after this conversation, something happened that changed my perspective on baptism. A college student who had recently become a Christian was told by his parents that he could come to our church, attend

---

19. Arthur A. R. Nelson, *A Book of Prayers: A Guide to Public and Personal Intercession* (Downers Grove, IL: InterVarsity Press, 2012), 68–69.

Bible studies, and spend time with his new Christian friends as much as he wanted, *so long as he didn't get baptized.* He was from a Muslim family that understood clearly the significance of baptism—it meant turning his back on the faith he inherited. They feared losing their son and losing face with their community.

On the Sunday evening of his baptism, the church was unusually quiet and tense. Hysterical shouting and screaming could be heard coming through doors that led to the hallway near the baptismal pool. His mother and sister had come to confront him and were angrily cursing him for what he was doing to his family and to his inherited religion. It was a dramatic moment, but one that indicated the powerful symbolism of baptism.

The New Testament directly connects baptism with coming to faith. In Acts 2:38, Peter commands his audience, "Repent and be baptized, every one of you, in the name of Jesus Christ for the forgiveness of your sins." And in 1 Peter 3:21, he writes that "this water symbolizes baptism that now saves you also." But this is not to say that forgiveness from God is contingent on one's baptism, as if one is not finally reconciled to God until being dunked into and emerging out of actual water. In fact, Peter goes on to say that by baptism, he means "not the removal of dirt from the body but the pledge of a clear conscience toward God" (1 Pet 3:21).

Because the early church baptized converts directly after their confession of faith, those two acts were fused together to speak of one moment. It is that singular moment of turning to God that saves us. Because of the close association of baptism with conversion, the early church could talk about "those who were baptized" and "those who weren't baptized" as expressions synonymous to "the saved" and "the unsaved." Our theological problems with the language of the New Testament arise from our common practice of delaying for too long a person's baptism once they have professed faith. We will be helped by truly coming to grips with what the biblical language means, but we may also consider changing our practices so that they line up with those of the early church.

Repentance

John appeared, calling God's people to repent, to break radically from the norm, and to orient their lives differently, so that when Jesus appeared they would be ready to receive him. Repentance can be understood in several different senses. At conversion, people turn away from previous modes of life to a life of obedience to Jesus. Yet repentance is also one of the ongoing practices in the lives of God's people. The first of Martin Luther's ninety-five theses—the document that traditionally marks the beginning of the Reformation—regards repentance in this way: "When our Lord and Master Jesus Christ said, 'Repent' (Matt 4:17), he willed the entire life of believers to be one of repentance."[20]

Again, the Christian calendar provides special seasons for repentance, especially the season of Lent, which runs from Ash Wednesday in February to the Saturday before Easter Sunday. *Lent* comes from an old Germanic word for "springtime," and we can think of it as a spiritual "spring cleaning," a time for self-examination, quiet reflection before God, and special attention to where we need to make changes.

It is noteworthy that John called people out to the wilderness for this repentance. There is a sense in which the daily busyness of life can keep us from considering how we need to change. There is just too much noise and too many distractions for us to devote special attention to exposing our blind spots and discovering some of the undetected destructive practices that plague us. We may need to devote special seasons to this, or somehow take a break from the everyday so that we might devote ourselves to prayer and thoughtful reflection.

Several years ago, a friend of mine was granted a month-long sabbatical from his church and spent the month of June in Oxford, England. I was able to visit him for about eight days, intending to "get lots of writing done." That time was particularly stressful for our family and for me personally, and I found it difficult to slow down and collect my thoughts. In order to focus, I took long walks throughout Oxford, spending hours wandering alone in Christ Church meadows. I began to prayerfully reflect on the state of our family's life and the condition of my soul. I must confess that I did no writing at all, but that was one of the most fruitful weeks of my life. I was away from the noise of my everyday life long enough to give attention to some destructive patterns of thought and behavior. I filled my journal with reflections and made some basic decisions about relational patterns that needed to change.

When my wife and I reconnected, we had several long talks about some of these things, and that began a long stretch of seriously joyful flourishing in our family. I hadn't intended that time to be a season of repentance, but because I was able to get away and give sustained thought to dynamics in my life, I was able to identify some destructive habits to eliminate and strategize about cultivating alternative practices that would generate life-giving dynamics.

---

20. Martin Luther, "95 Theses," Internet Medieval Sourcebook, Dec 31, 1992, www.fordham .edu/halsall/source/luther95.txt.

CHAPTER 2

Mark 1:14–15

📖 LISTEN to the Story

¹⁴After John was put in prison, Jesus went into Galilee, proclaiming the good news of God. ¹⁵"The time has come," he said. "The kingdom of God has come near. Repent and believe the good news!"

Listening to the Text in the Story: Genesis 39:20; 1 Kings 18:15–18; 22:1–40; Psalm 95:3; 145:11–13; Jeremiah 37–39; Daniel 7:21–22; Acts 5:17–42; Colossians 1:13–14; 2 Timothy 3:10–12.

Mark 1:14–15 forms a bridge from the introduction (vv. 1–13) to the rest of the Gospel, and this brief passage foregrounds Jesus's preaching about the arrival of God's reign. The central thrust of the biblical story is God establishing his kingship over all creation through humanity. God's very identity is that he is the king of all creation, as many Psalms celebrate: "The LORD is the great God, the great King above all gods" (Ps 95:3; see also Pss 47:1–9; 103:19). But the visible reality of God's sovereignty in the world is something he has chosen to work out as a process. In Genesis 1–2 God commissions humanity to oversee the worldwide spread of God's rule through creation's flourishing. After humanity rebelled, God sought to establish his reign in Israel from which he would extend his gracious rule over all the nations. Tragically, Israel failed to submit to God's kingship, so the establishment of God's sovereignty became a future hope (Isa 45:23; Zech 14:9).

The longing for God's kingdom dominated Jewish culture in the centuries leading up to Jesus's arrival, so that when he came proclaiming the presence of the kingdom, everyone knew what this meant. And God's people were more than ready for this news. They were being oppressed by Rome, and many of their own leaders were corrupt and exploitative. The arrival of God's kingdom was "good news" for the oppressed, but it aroused suspicion among those in power. At various levels, many of the leaders among God's people had built their own "kingdoms" and were exploiting the system surrounding the temple for their own gain (Mark 11:17; 12:7, 38–40). Just as the Old Testament contrasted God's kingship to all earthly kingdoms and powers, those who have other agendas view God's kingdom as a threat (cf. Ps 2).[1] This is why Mark begins his narrative with the ominous note that Jesus's ministry begins just after John is thrown into prison. John's imprisonment sets the tone for Jesus's journey to a confrontation in Jerusalem that ends on a cross.

EXPLAIN the Story

Jesus's early ministry takes place in Galilee (v. 14), and Mark portrays him as both in continuity with John and distinct from him. Jesus comes "after John" in that his ministry is conducted *in the same manner*. They both exercised a prophetic ministry in that they both preached repentance and judgment. At several points, Mark associates Elijah with both John and Jesus (8:28; 9:2–13). Elijah is that confrontational figure who would not tolerate injustice, especially from King Ahab and his wife, Jezebel. In 1 Kings 18, Ahab sees Elijah coming and cries out, "Is that you, you troubler of Israel?" Elijah fires right back at him, reversing the accusation (1 Kgs 18:15–18). From the perspective of the religious leaders in Mark, John and Jesus are the "troublers of Israel," because they both disrupt a corrupted status quo.

But Jesus's ministry is also distinct from John's. John preached a baptism of repentance in *preparation* for the arrival of the messiah, whereas Jesus comes preaching that God's kingdom *has arrived*. Jesus indicates this already arrived reality with two expressions: "The time *has come*," and "the kingdom of God *has come near*" (Mark 1:15).

This was indeed good news. God's people were held in captivity under a reign of darkness and demonic oppression. Mark portrays Judea as spiritually enslaved under the satanic rule of the "strong man" (Mark 3:27). In fact, Judea had become the "strong man's house." With the arrival of Jesus, God was asserting his rule, and his reign was breaking out in formerly enslaved communities and overtaking previously enslaved people. God's restored order of life and flourishing is seen throughout Mark where demons are being cast out, the sick are being healed, the dead are being raised, and oppressors are being rebuked. The arrival of God's reign is an invasion, with the light breaking in

---

1. R. T. France, "Kingdom of God," *DTIB* 420–22.

on the darkness, signaling that the old age is on its deathbed—the old order
of darkness, demonic oppression, and injustice.[2]

The announcement of the kingdom came with a call to "repent and believe
the good news" (v. 15). Jesus demanded that his audiences reorder their lives
in terms of the new reality of God's reign as king. To repent (*metanoeð*) is to
change one's mind, to embrace new thought patterns, to expand the horizons
of current thought and behavior, and to imagine the new attitudes, redeemed
social practices, and life-giving patterns of behavior that are consistent with
inhabiting God's kingdom. To "believe the good news" is not merely an intellectual task but involves changing the way we conceive of living so that we
order our relationships and plan our days as if the reign of God is a reality
and not a pious fantasy. Jesus called for his people to see reality as God sees it,
to consider their lives as reconfigured by God's world-altering and radically
new reign.

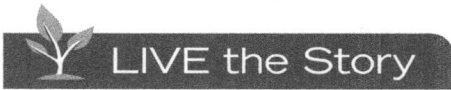

LIVE the Story

The Gospel of the Kingdom

I went to a Christian college for my undergraduate education and took a
required course on evangelism. While I am sure that we discussed various
biblical texts to discern what Scripture taught about salvation, all I remember
is that the class was focused mainly on technique. We discussed various evangelistic scenarios and strategized about turning conversations toward sharing
Christ with unbelievers, both friends and complete strangers. Our professor
assigned us to summarize our gospel presentation into something that could
be communicated in under three minutes. It was to include our testimony—a
brief narrative of how we received Christ—and an account of how someone
else could become a Christian. I must admit that I dreaded the sort of encounters the professor spoke of, as they seemed so scripted and formulaic. I did not
like the idea of engaging in conversation in a way that was manipulative, even
if I could tell myself that I was well-motivated.

Like many Christians, the teaching I had always received about evangelism
led me to regard "the gospel" as a presentation that a Christian may give a
non-Christian person in hopes that they would convert to being Christian.
On this scenario, "the gospel" is information about a personal transaction
whereby an individual can be reconciled to God. It usually starts out with the

---

2. Marcus, *Mark 1–8*, 175.

news that a person is a sinner and is headed for judgment after death. God, however, has made provision for forgiveness in the death of Jesus, and each sinner who receives Jesus is reconciled to God.

This understanding of the gospel may be familiar to many because it boils the Bible down to a succinct transaction and is easily understood. Further, it is the dominant way many Christians have described the gospel over the last few centuries in the West. Yet this is not how "the gospel" is used in the New Testament and especially in the four Gospels. *The gospel is the news about the arrival of the kingdom of God in Jesus.* And in Acts and Paul's letters, the gospel is about God's exaltation of Jesus as cosmic ruler and the establishment of kingdom communities around the world called churches (Rom 14:17; Col 1:13). "The gospel" is a much larger reality that stretches back to God's intentions from the beginning of the biblical story. It takes into account the narrative trajectory of creation, the rebellion of humanity, and God's call of Abraham and Israel, and it describes how God has initiated his universal reign in Jesus and is enacting that rule among his people gathered by God's Spirit as the church.

"The gospel"—the "good news"—is therefore *the set of language* that describes the multifaceted reality of God's creation of a people who embody the gracious reign of God in Christ through practices of joyful self-sacrifice, service, justice, love, compassion, care for the poor and for creation, confession of sin, and forgiveness. We can understand "the gospel," then, as *the announcement and related speech about* God's creation of a people who embody God's passionate pursuit of the whole of creation. In the New Testament, "the gospel" is the good news that God is currently doing this in Jesus and among Jesus's followers—the church.

We can draw several implications from this. First, "the gospel" is speech about God's establishment of his reign in Jesus. We are doing gospel work when we study in order to understand the precise character of Jesus Christ, God's appointed ruler, and the manner in which God brought the kingdom of God into existence through his death, resurrection, ascension, and current reign. And we are speaking about the gospel when we talk with others about Jesus as Lord over God's people.

Second, the gospel is speech about God's embodiment of his reign among the church—God's people brought together and united by God's Spirit. While it is daunting, I believe Christians should give serious consideration to the reality that the existence of a healthy church or churches—the social embodiment of God's reign—should determine the extent to which Christians talk about the gospel to unbelievers. I say this because it makes little sense to joyfully tell others about the arrival of God's reign into the world if we cannot point to healthy communities that depict this reality by the power of the Spirit.

On the positive side, however, because "the gospel" has to do with God's reign among his people, we are talking about "the gospel" when we describe the mode of life to which God calls us. When we speak about the wonders of reconciliation, about confession of sin and forgiveness, about the leveling of social status in the church and the joyful postures of service we are invited to inhabit—all of that is "gospel" talk because it has everything to do with behavior and conduct in the life-giving reign of King Jesus.

We can even be assured that we are engaging in "gospel" conversations with unbelievers when they point to the ways that churches fall short of God's intentions. We don't have to feel the pressure to deny such failures and shortcomings, as if we are salespeople trying to make the gospel look good. The "good news" is that God pours out forgiveness on people who engage in gospel practices, such as confession of sin and repentance. Reconciliation with others is the gospel mode of life to which God calls all people, so the practices of truth-speaking and frank admission of sins are crucial.

Third, the announcement of the gospel is attended with a call for repentance and faith. The gospel itself is not this call for a response, but rather the gospel *entails* a call. Repentance has to do with holistic change—a change of conception about my way of thinking and being in relation to the kingdom, and a change of direction regarding my holistic mode of life. Such a response comes along with "faith," which has been tragically misunderstood to mean merely "belief" or cognitive assent to objective truths about what God has done in Christ. Matthew Bates has shown, however, that "faith" in the first century had everything to do with *allegiance, loyalty,* and *fidelity.*[3] Jesus is God's appointed ruler over the people of God in the kingdom of God. Because this is the character of the reality to which people are called, the appropriate human response is *allegiance* expressed through a life-long pattern of repentance empowered by God's Spirit.

Now, all this information need not go into every evangelistic presentation. My point is that if our grasp of the gospel is not the news about the kingdom of God and about life within that kingdom, then our understanding is inadequate. The gospel is news about the arrival of the kingdom of God and speech about the dynamics and features of that kingdom, not information about a personal transaction that moves one from *sinner* to *one who is forgiven.* And it

---

3. Matthew W. Bates, *Salvation by Allegiance Alone: Rethinking Faith, Works, and the Gospel of Jesus the King* (Grand Rapids: Baker Academic, 2017); idem, *Gospel Allegiance: What Faith in Jesus Misses for Salvation in Christ* (Grand Rapids: Brazos, 2019).

does not start with personal sin and alienation from God but with God's intentions for creation and humanity. Further, it is not a one-size-fits-all message. As Jesus encounters a range of people in the Gospels, he speaks a kingdom word "on target" that is appropriate for each situation. He thinks from this larger narrative in a way that is appropriate to the need of the moment.

In communicating the gospel to outsiders (and in seeking to understand it ourselves), we should discern how the larger story would engage the life of this person or that community. That means we need to get to know people and communities, but it also means we need to pursue a thorough understanding of the larger scriptural story. We are seeking the sort of wisdom that can determine where confrontation is needed, or a word of tender comfort, or the offer of hope to a crushed soul, or the start of a long-term conversation with someone who needs greater understanding.

To faithfully communicate the gospel of the kingdom, Christians need to be patient and diligent students of Scripture, becoming conversant over time with the Christian story, so that they have the discernment to speak a life-giving word that meets the moment. This may be a challenge for those with a sense of urgency, but there is no virtue in meeting the moment with inadequate gospel comprehension.[4]

---

4. For a thorough discussion of the gospel of the kingdom and its distinction from a conversion-oriented message, see Scot McKnight, *The King Jesus Gospel: Revisiting the Original Good News* (Grand Rapids: Zondervan, 2011).

CHAPTER 3

Mark 1:16–20

📖 LISTEN to the Story

¹⁶As Jesus walked beside the Sea of Galilee, he saw Simon and his brother Andrew casting a net into the lake, for they were fishermen. ¹⁷"Come, follow me," Jesus said, "and I will send you out to fish for people." ¹⁸At once they left their nets and followed him.

¹⁹When he had gone a little farther, he saw James son of Zebedee and his brother John in a boat, preparing their nets. ²⁰Without delay he called them, and they left their father Zebedee in the boat with the hired men and followed him.

Listening to the Text in the Story: Genesis 35:10; Exodus 3:1–14; Deuteronomy 6:20–23; 1 Kings 19:19–21; Jeremiah 16:16–17; Galatians 6:14; 1 Peter 2:19.

God's call of his people is a consistently struck note throughout the biblical story. It stresses God's initiative, since it is only by God's grace that God's people belong to him. In Exodus 3, God calls Moses despite his lack of fitness for the task. God later calls Israel despite their being a slave nation under the thumb of the most powerful empire of the day (Deut 6:20–23). The common identity marker of God's people is that they are "called." God seeks us out, sets his love upon us, calls us by his grace, enters our realities, and saves us by his great power. This makes us "*his* people, the sheep of *his* pasture" (Ps 100:3). We play our part by entering the kingdom and celebrating our new identities as those called by God out of darkness into his marvelous light.

The account of Jesus calling his disciples relates directly to Mark's thematic statement in 1:14–15. Jesus's preaching of the kingdom includes his calling people to leave their well-established patterns of life to give him complete allegiance. His authoritative call demands an immediate response. Both sets of brothers in this passage respond *right away* by dropping what they're doing and leaving to follow Jesus. Just as he preaches the kingdom, they will too.

And just as he advances the kingdom into enemy territory, clearing away darkness by healing and casting out demons, so will they.

EXPLAIN the Story

Jesus's Authoritative Call

The call of the two sets of brothers follows the pattern of Elijah's call of Elisha (1 Kgs 19:19–21):

> So Elijah went from there and found Elisha son of Shaphat. He was plowing with twelve yoke of oxen, and he himself was driving the twelfth pair. Elijah went up to him and threw his cloak around him. Elisha then left his oxen and ran after Elijah. "Let me kiss my father and mother goodbye," he said, "and then I will come with you."
>
> "Go back," Elijah replied. "What have I done to you?"
>
> So Elisha left him and went back. He took his yoke of oxen and slaughtered them. He burned the plowing equipment to cook the meat and gave it to the people, and they ate. Then he set out to follow Elijah and became his servant.

Three elements of this call narrative shape Jesus's call of his disciples. First, Elijah took the initiative in the encounter. As he came across Elisha, he "went up to him." Second, without any introduction Elijah "threw his cloak around him," effectively calling Elisha and signaling that he should join him in the prophetic ministry. Third, Elisha responds by following Elijah: he "*left* his oxen and *ran after* Elijah. . . . *He set out to follow* Elijah and *became his servant.*"[1]

In the same way, Mark stresses Jesus's initiative. As Jesus is on his way he "sees" both pairs of brothers (vv. 16, 19), indicating Jesus's identification of who he wants to be his disciples. He then calls them to follow. Rather than announcing that he is taking applications for people to learn from him, he issues a commanding call for them to participate in kingdom work. Further, they will not be passive learners. They were to "follow," which in Mark indicates that Jesus's pattern of life and ministry was going to shape their lives comprehensively from now on. Just as Jesus came "after John," so that their ministries had continuity, Jesus's ministry would now shape the lives of the disciples.[2]

---

1. Marcus, *Mark 1–8*, 183.
2. Throughout Mark, "to follow" is synonymous with being a disciple (2:14, 15; 6:1; 8:34; 10:21, 28, 32, 52; 15:41; see Black, *Mark*, 70).

The new vocation to which Jesus calls these men is to "fish for people" (v. 17). Their task will include proclaiming the kingdom, but this image has surprising resonances in the Old Testament in texts that speak of judgment. It refers to the human instruments God uses to root out evildoers and punish them:

> "But now I will send for many fishermen," declares the LORD, "and they will catch them. After that I will send for many hunters, and they will hunt them down on every mountain and hill and from the crevices of the rocks. My eyes are on all their ways; they are not hidden from me, nor is their sin concealed from my eyes." (Jer 16:16–17)[3]

We noted in the previous section that Mark associates the ministries of John and Jesus with the confrontational prophet Elijah. Like these figures, the disciples in their proclamation of the kingdom will be confronting God's people with the need for radical repentance in order to participate in the kingdom of God.[4] It is striking—and a bit unsettling—that while

> Christian preachers have usually understood this passage as a call to evangelism: the disciples are to 'catch' outsiders and bring them into the church. . . . Jesus's call of Simon and Andrew should be understood as a call to participate—like John the Baptist—in declaring the imminence of judgment.[5]

The Disciples' Response

Simon and Andrew respond to Jesus's call "at once" (*euthys*, lit. "immediately," v. 18). Being a fisherman in the first century was not merely a job but an all-encompassing identity, determining everything about a person's life. To leave and follow Jesus meant a complete transformation of identity with a massive cost. The sons of Zebedee, too, left their father "with the hired men," indicating that their family may have been part of the area's managerial class (vv. 19–20).[6] While they did not leave their family destitute, they were turning their backs on a promising future and the potential of prominent social status.

Basil (ca. 329–79), the fourth-century bishop of Caesarea, turned his back on worldly ambitions in order to serve the church and later wrote about repentance:

---

3. See also Ezek 19:4–5; Amos 4:2.
4. Moloney, *Gospel of Mark*, 52.
5. Hays, *Echoes of Scripture in the Gospels*, 24–25.
6. Black, *Mark*, 70.

A beginning is made by detaching oneself from all external goods: property, self-importance, social class and useless desire, following the holy example of the Lord's disciples. James and John left their father Zebedee and the very boat upon which their whole livelihood depended. Matthew left his counting house and followed the Lord, not merely leaving behind the profits of his occupation, but also paying no heed to the dangers which were sure to befall both himself and his family at the hands of the magistrates because he had left the tax accounts unfinished. Paul speaks of the whole world being crucified to him, and he to the world. Thus, those who are strongly seized with the desire of following Christ can no longer be concerned with anything pertaining to this life, not even with the love of their parents or other relatives insofar as this runs counter to the calling of the Lord.[7]

LIVE the Story

Celebrating God's Call

Throughout Scripture, God's people consistently celebrate their identity as those called by God. According to the psalmist, "It is he who made us, and we are his" (Ps 100:3). In a letter that Paul intended to be used in the church's gathered worship, he begins with "praise be to the God and Father of our Lord Jesus Christ . . . [f]or he chose us in him before the creation of the world" (Eph 1:3–4). Using scriptural language to speak of Israel's call, Peter writes to scattered Christians these poetic words that shape their identity:

> But you are a chosen people, a royal priesthood, a holy nation, God's special possession, that you may declare the praises of him who called you out of darkness into his wonderful light. Once you were not a people, but now you are the people of God; once you had not received mercy, but now you have received mercy. (1 Pet 2:9–10)

When we gather as the church and hear Mark 1:16–20, we are reminded that we have been brought together by God's powerful call. Just like these two sets of brothers, our lives were interrupted and totally transformed by God's powerful summons to inhabit the kingdom of God.

We can faithfully live out the thrust of this text by keeping in mind that

---

7. Oden and Hall, *Mark*, 20.

when we gather for worship, we exist as God's people only through God's call—by God's grace alone. We are invited into God's presence, and we enjoy that when we maintain a posture of *reception*. All the good things in our lives, including our existence together as a community, are gifts from a gracious God. This is important because if we ever shift from this posture, we run the risk of imagining that our belonging to God's kingdom has come about by our own efforts or our own creativity or insight. This leads to arrogance and judgmentalism, as if we are somehow better than others. It also leads to anxiety, as though we need to maintain our status by performance.

This passage also reflects one vital component to God's call: mission. The biblical story consistently presents a missional God—the creator who has committed himself to pursuing his creation in love and triumphing over evil so that his creation might once again flourish. That means that those whom God calls are brought into his love *in order that they might participate with him in this mission.* Jesus calls disciples to extend and expand the call to participate in the kingdom of God. He does not call them to experience his love *at the expense of* others or *instead of* others. As I gather with my community, then, I am reminded that I am part of a people gathered to experience God's blessing and to strategize to embody God's desire to bless those beyond the walls of our church.

Too often God's call of us has become a theological topic of speculation that causes confusion. Some delight in emphasizing the election of believers and take a kind of comfort in a vision of God's sovereignty as one who chooses some to believe and others to perish. This causes other Christians to recoil at a conception of God in which he seems unconcerned about the mass of humanity that will perish. This also causes us to wonder why God has chosen us and not those we love—friends or family members.

Such a conception of election and of God's call falls short of how these are portrayed in Scripture. Through the Old and New Testaments, God's choosing and calling of a people has at least two components. First, God's love for his people and his rock-solid commitment to them. They have been on his heart and mind from eternity past, and this is something to celebrate. Second, God's call is his commissioning of his people as agents of his love to the nations, inviting others to participate in God's gracious rule. God's call of his people, therefore, has everything to do with God's love. God is on mission to pursue his creation and sweep them up into his love, and he calls a people into being to join him in this for the good of the world and for his glory.

CHAPTER 4

Mark 1:21-28

📖 LISTEN to the Story

²¹They went to Capernaum, and when the Sabbath came, Jesus went into the synagogue and began to teach. ²²The people were amazed at his teaching, because he taught them as one who had authority, not as the teachers of the law. ²³Just then a man in their synagogue who was possessed by an impure spirit cried out, ²⁴"What do you want with us, Jesus of Nazareth? Have you come to destroy us? I know who you are—the Holy One of God!"

²⁵"Be quiet!" said Jesus sternly. "Come out of him!" ²⁶The impure spirit shook the man violently and came out of him with a shriek.

²⁷The people were all so amazed that they asked each other, "What is this? A new teaching—and with authority! He even gives orders to impure spirits and they obey him." ²⁸News about him spread quickly over the whole region of Galilee.

Listening to the Text in the Story: Genesis 1; Judges 5:4–5; 1 Kings 18; Psalm 18:8–16; 29:1–11; Zechariah 13:1–2; Hebrews 4:12; James 3:14–17; 1 John 5:18–19

Exorcisms, and exorcists, were not uncommon in the ancient world. Josephus wrote about a Jewish man named Eleazar who released people from demonic possession. His method involved putting a ring that had a certain root on it near the afflicted person's nose, causing the demon to leave through that person's nostrils (*Ant.* 8.45–49). In a few places in the New Testament there are exorcists operating outside the circle of those whom Jesus's disciples knew. In Mark 9:38, John reports to Jesus that they had seen someone who did not belong to their group casting out demons in Jesus's name and had told him to stop. In Acts 19:13–19, Luke recounts that seven sons of a chief priest named Sceva were among some others who were casting demons out in the name of

Jesus. In the latter instance, things went very badly when a demon-possessed person gave all of them an awful beating, driving them from a house, naked and bleeding.[1]

Jesus is distinctive when he drives out demons. He does not use any items or a common stock of incantations. While he drove away sickness from many people and forcefully rebuked a storm (Mark 4:39), he only used exorcistic language when it came to addressing demons. Perhaps most importantly here, while the power at work to drive out demons is the Holy Spirit (cf. Mark 3:23–29), Jesus does not cast out demons by invoking God or the Holy Spirit. He has the authority himself to expel unclean spirits. Finally, Jesus's exorcising work is the manifestation of the advance of God's kingdom as it overtakes the satanic darkness that has overwhelmed and overcome God's people.[2]

Wherever Jesus goes, kingdom power is present, and it inevitably clashes with the kingdom of darkness. Mark opens and closes this brief episode by mentioning Jesus's authoritative teaching (vv. 21–22, 27) and includes the exorcism in the middle. It is interesting that teaching plays such a prominent role in this passage that does not include any of the content of Jesus's teaching. Mark seems to be more interested in portraying the authoritative and powerful word of Jesus rather than what exactly he is teaching. Other characters in Mark will question Jesus's authority to forgive sins (2:6–12) and to shut down the temple operations (11:27–28). But Mark's readers know from the beginning that Jesus comes with God's own authority and speaks a divinely authoritative word.

EXPLAIN the Story

This episode takes place in Capernaum, which is on the northern shore of the Sea of Galilee, just west of where the Jordan River flows into it. There is a synagogue in Capernaum today that dates from the fourth century AD, but it likely sits atop one that goes back to Jesus's day. Synagogues functioned as the centers of Jewish social life in the first century, including the study and discussion of Scripture. It's a small detail, but Mark notes that "*they* went to Capernaum," indicating that Jesus and his followers are on mission together, united in purpose. It is also significant that this takes place on a Sabbath day

---

1. For further instances of exorcism in the ancient world, see Graham H. Twelftree, *In the Name of Jesus: Exorcism among Early Christians* (Grand Rapids: Baker Academic, 2007).

2. Twelftree, *In the Name of Jesus*, 48–49.

in a synagogue. As Mark's Gospel progresses, Jesus's activities on the Sabbath provoke the judgment and disapproval of the Pharisees and scribes.

Jesus, the Authoritative Teacher

Mark stresses Jesus's teaching by repeating "teach" or "teaching" five times and by opening and closing the episode by mentioning Jesus's authoritative teaching.[3] By associating the dramatic exorcism with Jesus's teaching, Mark focuses our attention on Jesus's authority. This is also what impresses the crowd. His teaching is both "new" and authoritative (v. 27), and they recognize that it is completely different than how the scribes teach (v. 22). Scribes had a noble history in first-century Jewish culture, going back to Ezra, who studied and taught Scripture (Ezra 7:1–11).[4] Their interpretations of the law were regarded as authoritative, and they occupied places of public honor. A scribe "combined the offices of Torah professor, teacher and moralist, and civil lawyer, in that order."[5]

Jesus, however, is someone completely different. He is not merely weighing in on this or that interpretive issue in Scripture but speaking with an authority that stands outside the human realm. The association with the exorcism indicates that Jesus speaks a liberating word, one that gives life and brings renewal and redemption. While the scribes—and other religious leaders—may indeed be experts in interpretation, they have been able to do little to bring relief to those who are suffering and in the grip of the oppressive rule of darkness. The demon-possessed person remained in his enslaved condition, even with the scribes present.

The Demonic Confrontation

The presence and power of Jesus draws the demon out into the open and into this confrontation. The demon-possessed man says two things that indicate a challenge. First, he cries out, "What do you want with us?" This expression (lit. "What is there between us and you?") sets two sides against each other before a violent confrontation (Judg 11:12; 1 Kgs 17:18). The demon-possessed man effectively shouted, "You're my enemy, Jesus, and you and I are going to do battle!"

Second, the demon identifies Jesus. This strikes modern ears as very odd. Modern moviegoers might expect Jesus to have responded, "That's right!

---

3. David E. Garland, *A Theology of Mark's Gospel: Good News about Jesus the Messiah, the Son of God*, BTNTS (Grand Rapids: Zondervan, 2015), 266.

4. G. Thellman, "Scribes," *DJG* 841.

5. James R. Edwards, *The Gospel according to Mark*, PNTC (Grand Rapids: Eerdmans, 2002), 54.

Did everyone catch that? I'm Jesus of Nazareth and I'm the Holy One of God, so after I cast out this demon, you all must listen to me!" But that is not what is happening here. The act of naming is a power move. This is an attempt to dominate Jesus, to get the upper hand in the confrontation.[6] We might imagine fighters insulting one another before a big fight. They feel that if they can get the upper hand verbally, they can eventually defeat their opponent.

But Jesus comes with kingdom power, and he will have none of this. He turns back the initial move by summarily rebuking the demon: "Be quiet!" "Come out of him!" The impure spirit comes out, and everyone witnesses the power and authority of Jesus.[7] Jesus does the same thing to the raging storm in Mark 4:39, and it recalls the creator God's activity in bringing order to chaos (Gen 1). In the same way, Jesus speaks forcefully to liberate God's creation from the grip of oppressive forces. The kingdom of God brings *shalom* (God's order of universal flourishing), and God's reign is incompatible with demonic oppression. As these two realms of power clash, the light overtakes the darkness, with Jesus standing at the forefront of God's liberating kingdom. This also recalls God's promise to remove "the spirit of impurity" in the day of his return to Jerusalem (Zech 13:1–2).

The Crowd's Response

The crowd's reaction of amazement at Jesus's authoritative teaching opens and closes this episode (vv. 22, 27), and the news about what Jesus had done "spread quickly over the whole region of Galilee" (v. 28). It is easy to read this as an obviously positive development, but there are a few reasons for a more sober assessment. First, as Mark progresses, Jesus is not at all interested in getting the word out about his ministry. In fact, precisely the opposite! Jesus continually warns people not to tell anyone about what he has done for them (e.g., 1:44; 3:12; 5:43; 7:36). He knows that big crowds will obscure his ability to teach about the cross-shaped nature of the kingdom. Second, in several places the crowds hinder Jesus from carrying out his ministry (e.g., 1:45; 5:21–43). Lastly, the crowds that acclaim Jesus as he enters Jerusalem (11:9–10) are the same people whom the Jerusalem leaders manipulate into demanding Jesus's death (15:11–15).

---

6. Marcus, *Mark 1–8*, 192.

7. Athanasius captures well the notion that even though the demon rightly identifies Jesus, there is something twisted about truth coming from a wicked source: "He put a bridle in the mouths of the demons that cried after him from the tombs. For although what they said was true, and they did not lie when they said, 'You are the Son of God' and 'the Holy One of God,' yet he did not wish that the truth should proceed from an unclean mouth, and especially from such as those who under pretense of truth might mingle with it their own malicious devices" (Oden and Hall, *Mark*, 23).

Jesus knows that human hearts are fickle, and immediately positive responses are not always lasting (cf. John 2:24–25). In fact, in just a few chapters we will encounter Jesus telling a parable about how a good number of those who hear the news about the kingdom may have an immediately positive response but will not end up bearing lasting fruit (Mark 4:16–19).

LIVE the Story

The Kingdom Confronts the Darkness

The most dramatic aspect of this episode is certainly Jesus's exorcism of the demon inhabiting the man in the synagogue. This raises all sorts of questions regarding the demonic, especially whether Christians today will encounter demonically possessed people and the extent to which Christians have authority over demons. The challenge when it comes to this topic is that there is very little instruction for Christian churches about it in the New Testament. The disciples are given authority over demons when they are sent on a mission from Jesus (Matt 10:1; Mark 6:7; Luke 9:1–2), but no New Testament text authorizes the church to do this. And much of what we think we know about how demons operate and how we can interact with them comes from anecdotes and stories, perhaps from missionary accounts in other cultural contexts or from fictionalized accounts of spiritual warfare. These are very unreliable bases from which to reflect theologically. But what can we say from Scripture in reflecting on the demonic realm?

First, because we have been conditioned to look for the demonic in spectacular encounters, we may miss the fact that in Scripture people make themselves vulnerable to the demonic in some apparently mundane and unremarkable ways. These include harboring bitterness, anger, and jealousy, resulting in divisiveness and the refusal to forgive. Consider Genesis 4:2–8:

> Now Abel kept flocks, and Cain worked the soil. In the course of time Cain brought some of the fruits of the soil as an offering to the LORD. And Abel also brought an offering—fat portions from some of the firstborn of his flock. The LORD looked with favor on Abel and his offering, but on Cain and his offering he did not look with favor. So Cain was very angry, and his face was downcast. Then the LORD said to Cain, "Why are you angry? Why is your face downcast? If you do what is right, will you not be accepted? But if you do not do what is right, sin is crouching at your door; it desires to have you, but you must rule over it." Now Cain said to

his brother Abel, "Let's go out to the field." While they were in the field, Cain attacked his brother Abel and killed him.

The text does not indicate why God preferred Abel's sacrifice over that of Cain, but it may be that this is consistent with God's pattern of God subverting human expectations by preferring the younger over the older. Whatever the reason, this is an occasion for Cain to become angry and despondent. It is a dangerous situation because his growing jealousy and the fact that he is nurturing his anger makes him vulnerable to the spiritual power of Sin. The cosmic power of Sin—an active agent of destruction—is seeking to overtake Cain. He can resist it, but spiritual evil has a way of finding its way into a person through unchecked anger, growing jealousy, and the cultivation of resentment.

God speaks to Cain and offers him encouragement and a warning. The way of goodness is to recognize God's preference of Abel as the agent of blessing to all and to go on enjoying being blessed by God through Abel. If he goes down this road, he will faithfully inhabit God's *shalom*. The result, tragically, is the first murder.

It is easy to think that anger and resentment are so common that demonic involvement seems outlandish. Yet consider how irrationally we behave when we cultivate resentment. We can hardly think straight, and our desires for revenge become overpowering. We become violent and abusive. The devastating, long-lasting, and far-reaching effects of unchecked anger and jealousy are awful. Churches have been split, families have been divided, communities have been destroyed, and reputations have been ruined. There is good reason for Paul to urge his communities to pursue peace and reconciliation and to deal with anger before it transforms into settled bitterness: "Do not let the sun go down while you are still angry, and do not give the devil a foothold" (Eph 4:26–27).

Another fascinating text that makes this connection is the narrative of the rise of David and the downfall of Saul, beginning in 1 Samuel 18.

It happened as they were coming, when David returned from killing the Philistine, that the women came out of all the cities of Israel, singing and dancing, to meet King Saul, with tambourines, with joy and with musical instruments. The women sang as they played, and said,

"Saul has slain his thousands,
and David his ten thousands."

Then Saul became very angry, for this saying displeased him; and he said, "They have ascribed to David ten thousands, but to me they have

ascribed thousands. Now what more can he have but the kingdom?" Saul
looked at David with suspicion from that day on. (1 Sam 18:6–9 NASB)

Hearing David praised after defeating Goliath, "Saul became very angry,"
the same expression used of Cain in response to God's preference for Abel
(Gen 4:5). It points to an intense jealousy driven by a feeling of having been
slighted. Saul now sees David as a threat and regards him with suspicion. His
inflamed jealousy and his impulses for self-preservation drive him to suspect
David of plotting to supplant him as king.

What follows is striking. In some mysterious way, Saul's deep anger and
jealousy opens him up to spiritual evil.

Now it came about on the next day that an evil spirit from God came
mightily upon Saul, and he raved in the midst of the house, while David
was playing the harp with his hand, as usual; and a spear was in Saul's
hand. Saul hurled the spear for he thought, "I will pin David to the
wall." But David escaped from his presence twice. Now Saul was afraid of
David, for the LORD was with him but had departed from Saul. (1 Sam
18:10–12 NASB)

Saul's paranoia has driven him to murderous plotting and the first of a series
of attempted murders. As the story plays out, Saul gradually loses his mind.
His paranoia and obsession with eliminating David drive him to turn on his
own son, Jonathan, and to plot and scheme endlessly (1 Sam 20:30–33). Saul's
festering jealousy, his growing anger, his commitment to self-preservation at
all costs, and his suspicion that grew into self-destructive paranoia rendered
him vulnerable to influence from spiritual evil.

Consider how many church conflicts begin with one person being jealous
of the attention given to another. How often do church staffs fracture because
the drive for self-preservation and self-promotion becomes contagious? Turf
battles in churches, power-struggles in work environments, and so many other
social dynamics provoke reactions of jealousy, the cultivation of resentment,
and wounded pride. When anger isn't dealt with, it settles in the heart and
produces all sorts of socially destructive dynamics—manipulation, character
assassination, destructive competition, evil scheming, and gossip.

We might say, "Well, that's just normal stuff. That's not anything that
involves spiritual forces of evil or the demonic." Scripture portrays such situations otherwise. In addition to Paul's exhortation in Ephesians 4:26–27, James
connects social conflicts to a kind of "wisdom" that is "earthly, unspiritual,

demonic" (Jas 3:14–17). And Jesus connects his opponents' murderous desires to their kinship with Satan (John 8:37–44).

Many Western Christians imagine that "the demonic" is only at work in faraway places like Africa or in South American jungle tribes. Whatever the manifestation of the demonic in those places, we may be encountering the demonic when we meet people who are so captive to their anger that they cannot forgive others. This is why regular practices of restoration, including forgiveness of others and confessing sin to those we harm, are powerful measures against the power of darkness. This is likely why Paul's discussion in Ephesians 5:21–6:9 regarding how the new community should conduct itself in love and subjection to one another is followed by the rhetorically powerful section on divine warfare (6:10–18). In Paul's mind, the practices of love, peacemaking, and care for others are how the church wages spiritual warfare. These behaviors create a community by the Spirit that the powers of darkness cannot touch.

We must make a second point about the demonic realm from the New Testament. In a number of passages, we see that demons can oppress people who do not seem to have done anything. While many Christians today assume that psychological problems are a modern equivalent to ancient demonic possession, it seems better to assume that the demonic is real and that we very well may encounter demonically possessed people. In such situations, we should not imagine that we have authority to "cast them out." In Scripture, only Jesus's authorized apostles have this authority; it is not given to the church in general. Further, in the one episode in Acts where someone other than an apostle tries this, it goes very badly (Acts 19:13–17). Beyond this, there are warnings about speaking to entities in the spiritual realm that we don't fully comprehend (Jude 8–10). We should not presume that we can contact personal beings in the spiritual realm or that our well-intentioned words will have any effect.

What is powerful against the demonic realm is a spirit that submits to the lordship of Christ and a community that embodies the love of God in Christ for others (1 John 5:18–19). As we participate in practices of love, reconciliation, and forgiveness, we invite the life-giving and cleansing Spirit of God to overpower us, and we inhabit God's presence, the kingdom of God. These dynamics are powerful to liberate and cleanse from demonic oppression.[8]

---

8. For a helpful discussion of various views of spiritual warfare, see James K. Beilby and Paul Rhodes Eddy, eds., *Understanding Spiritual Warfare: Four Views* (Grand Rapids: Baker Academic, 2012).

Mark 1:29-34

📖 LISTEN to the Story

²⁹As soon as they left the synagogue, they went with James and John to the home of Simon and Andrew. ³⁰Simon's mother-in-law was in bed with a fever, and they immediately told Jesus about her. ³¹So he went to her, took her hand and helped her up. The fever left her and she began to wait on them. ³²That evening after sunset the people brought to Jesus all the sick and demon-possessed. ³³The whole town gathered at the door, ³⁴and Jesus healed many who had various diseases. He also drove out many demons, but he would not let the demons speak because they knew who he was.

Listening to the Text in the Story: 1 Samuel 1:1–2:11; 2 Kings 4:1–37; Psalm 138:6; 147:6; Luke 1:46–56; Romans 2:11; 1 Peter 1:17.

Women play a prominent role in Mark, as do other socially marginalized characters. Jesus's special attention to women resonates with God's grace to women throughout the biblical story. The narrative of Samuel, a significant biblical figure who leads Israel for a time and eventually anoints David as king, begins with a focus on his mother Hannah, the mistreated second wife of Elkanah. She was barren, while "her rival" had children and "kept provoking her in order to irritate her" (1 Sam 1:6). During one of their yearly visits to the Lord's house at Shiloh, Hannah was deeply discouraged and prayed for a child, promising to dedicate him to the service of the Lord if she were to conceive. The Lord heard her prayer, and she conceived and gave birth to a son. Her beautiful prayer of praise at Samuel's dedication is recorded in 1 Samuel 2:1–10:

> My heart rejoices in the LORD;
>   in the LORD my horn is lifted high.

> My mouth boasts over my enemies,
>> for I delight in your deliverance. (v. 1)

> The Lord sends poverty and wealth;
>> he humbles and he exalts.
> He raises the poor from the dust
>> and lifts the needy from the ash heap;
> he seats them with princes
>> and has them inherit a throne of honor. (vv. 7–8)

Hannah's poetic exultation became the basis for Mary's song of praise in Luke 1:46–55, another response of praise at the announcement of God's special favor to a woman.[1]

Hannah's prayer is an example of the prominent theme in Scripture of God's special attention to the poor, the outcast, and the marginalized. This note is sounded throughout the Bible's wisdom literature and celebrated in the Psalms. Even though "the Lord is exalted, he looks kindly on the lowly" (Ps 138:6). Psalm 147 celebrates the God of Israel as the one who "builds up Jerusalem; he gathers the exiles of Israel" (v. 2). "The Lord sustains the humble but casts the wicked to the ground" (v. 6). God gives special attention to the poor and lowly because he is not impressed with human achievement, impressive power, or the markers of high social standing (Rom 2:11; 1 Pet 1:17). The psalmist says it well:

> His pleasure is not in the strength of the horse,
>> nor his delight in the legs of the warrior;
> the Lord delights in those who fear him,
>> who put their hope in his unfailing love. (Ps 147:10–11)

This passage demonstrates Jesus's embodiment of this aspect of God's grace. In the first part, Jesus gives special attention to Simon's mother-in-law (Mark 1:29–31), and in the second, which is a summary statement of the many whom Jesus healed, he attends to the sick, demon-possessed, and those with various diseases (vv. 32–34).

---

1. Mary's song of praise is traditionally called Mary's "Magnificat" because this is the initial word in the first line of the Latin translation (Magnificat anima mea Dominum ["My soul magnifies the Lord"]).

EXPLAIN the Story

Jesus Heals Peter's Mother-in-Law

Mark captures the frenzied pace of the early days of Jesus's ministry with a pileup of uses of the Greek term *euthys* ("immediately"). Following the dramatic exorcism in the synagogue, word "immediately" spread (NIV "quickly"), and "immediately" after they left the synagogue (v. 29; NIV "as soon as"), the disciples "immediately told Jesus about her" (v. 30).

Mark emphasizes Jesus's care for Simon Peter's mother-in-law. As soon as he heard about her fever, he went to her and "took her hand" (v. 31). Francis Moloney states that it is unusual for a teacher to take the hand of a woman, as there is no recorded instance of a rabbi doing so.[2] This assertion argues from silence, but it is worth noting that in Mark Jesus touches all the "wrong" people—lepers, the unclean, and the dead. Here he touches a sick woman. Biblical purity codes had been misused to label all sorts of people and to either devalue or exclude them from the larger community. Here, as throughout Mark, Jesus steps across boundaries that have been erected to marginalize people, and in this instance a woman. The presence of the kingdom has a sanctifying effect, and Jesus, as the agent of the kingdom, radiates purity and healing.

After taking her hand, Jesus "helped her up." By using the Greek verb *egeirō* ("to raise up"), Mark subtly connects this healing with Jesus's resurrection. The same language is used when Jesus speaks of his coming resurrection (14:28) and when the young man reports that Jesus "has risen" (16:6). Mark also uses the verb to refer to healings (5:41; 9:27) so that readers get the impression that each healing and exorcism is an instance of resurrection life breaking out.[3] While the miracles that Jesus performs in Mark reveal his identity as the Son of God, they are also instances of the holistic work of the kingdom of God breaking in to destroy the kingdom of darkness. The ultimate expression of the kingdom is, of course, Jesus's death and resurrection.

Another indication of the dynamic character of the kingdom of God is that Mark does not merely write, "and she was well." Just as Jesus drove out the demons with an authoritative word (vv. 25–26), Mark describes her restoration in active terms: "The fever left her" (v. 31). "Both shrieking demons and bodily afflictions are distortions of the divine will that flee at the advent of Jesus."[4]

---

2. Moloney, *Gospel of Mark*, 55.
3. Black, *Mark*, 75.
4. Marcus, *Mark 1–8*, 199.

As a sign of her restoration, Simon's mother-in-law "began to wait on them." Jesus is not reinforcing a subservient role for women here. "Service" (*diakoneō*) and ministry in Mark is something that the angels do for Jesus in 1:13, and Jesus teaches that service is the indicator of true greatness (9:35; 10:43).[5] In fact, this is what Jesus himself came for, to serve rather than to be served (10:45). If anything, Peter's mother-in-law is an example of genuine discipleship.

Summary of Jesus's Busy Ministry

Verses 32–34 function as a summary statement of the dramatic effect of Jesus's ministry in Capernaum. In Jewish culture, the Sabbath was not over at midnight but rather at sunset, just as it began at sunset the previous day. At sunset the Sabbath regulations came to an end, and there was no longer a need to stay indoors. The spreading excitement had generated intense interest and great enthusiasm for seeing Jesus and being around him. With the close of the Sabbath, the floodgates opened, and people came rushing out of their homes and gathered to Simon Peter's house.

The dramatic language of movement gives the sense that Israel has been suffering under the oppression of demonic spirits and sickness for far too long. The opportunity for liberation generates loads of energy toward Jesus. As he is driving out demons (v. 34), Jesus once again demonstrates his authority over them by not permitting them to speak. He does this "because they knew who he was," the Son of God, the long-awaited Messiah bringing God's salvation. The revelation of how Jesus embodies this role, however, must wait until the end of the Gospel.

LIVE the Story

An Invasion of Purity with the Kingdom

In Mark's Gospel, Jesus is constantly touching people, mainly those he is not supposed to be touching according to the purity codes of his culture. In the episode after this one, Jesus heals a leper by speaking, but Mark emphasizes that *Jesus also touches him*. In the double episode of 5:21–43, Jesus is touched by a bleeding woman, and he touches a dead body. According to Leviticus 15, both make a person unclean. Mark intensifies things in 7:31–37, with Jesus doing all sorts of touching—he puts his fingers in a man's ears and seems to

---

5. Black, *Mark*, 75–76.

exchange spittle with him! This is not only disgusting to modern readers but extremely offensive in Jesus's ancient context.

In Mark, Jesus hangs out with the all the wrong people (Mark 2:15–17), and he touches everyone he isn't supposed to touch. For Mark, the kingdom of God is an invasion of purity because the kingdom is sanctifying space. Wherever Jesus is, that's where the presence of God's kingdom is located, and it has the power to reverse old patterns and dynamics. When Jesus touches unclean people, they are healed and made clean. In the kingdom of God, purity—rather than impurity—is contagious. This is one way for Mark to emphasize that all are warmly welcomed into God's kingdom.

This is a radical reversal of the sort of attitudes that pervaded first-century Jewish culture. Craig Blomberg surveys a range of Jewish texts to demonstrate the general concern to maintain one's purity through separation from the unclean and from sinners.[6] Such separation was crucial because contact with sinners made one impure. Further, if those considered "bad" were present, they might receive the message that they were okay, as if their behavior or status before God was being endorsed. Meals were not seen as opportunities for what we might call "outreach"; rather, they were mainly viewed as occasions "for insiders to have fellowship with one another."[7] Jesus's behavior, however, is a challenge to God's people to embody Jesus's glad invitation to marginalized groups to participate fully in the kingdom of God.

Corrupt cultural patterns are replicated in our day where we gather only with people who are like us—those that our established groups consider "approved." We have ways of signaling that certain people are "clean" and that others are "unclean." Our social practices assign greater and lesser value to people. Social worth is determined by gender, ethnicity, wealth, or any of a number of culturally generated measures of value. These ways of seeing people inevitably affect how the church evaluates people. And there are countless other corrupted lenses through which Christian cultures can view one another. These are particular measuring sticks whereby we assign greater or lesser value to people—marital status, parenting style, those touched by mental illness or other physical maladies. Passages like this one in Mark are supposed to shape churches' imaginations so that they envision everyone as welcome in the kingdom. Because God confers on everyone in the kingdom infinite worth, the church must find ways in its social practices of living in concert with God's way of thinking.

---

6. Craig L. Blomberg, *Contagious Holiness: Jesus's Meals with Sinners*, NSBT 19 (Downers Grove, IL: InterVarsity Press, 2005), 65–86.

7. Blomberg, *Contagious Holiness*, 86.

Blomberg writes about the need for Christians to develop habits of fellowshipping with varieties of people at every social location—those like us and those very much unlike us. Because many of our churches consist of people of the same ethnicity and social class, this will indeed be a challenge. Yet it is one we should embrace so that we don't end up falling into the community patterns that Jesus is challenging in Mark's Gospel.[8]

I spoke with a woman recently who had been divorced and who sought to return to the church to put her life back together. She timidly walked into a fellowship group on a Sunday morning in an effort to find community support. Finding an empty chair around a large table, she sat down next to a man, only to have his wife pull his chair closer to hers. This was a clear signal that the space she had entered was not kingdom space. She was a threat, "unclean." She realized she was unwelcome and never returned to that church. How different might things have been if she had been engaged in conversation? If that couple had the confidence that God's reign comes with an invasion of purity, an inviting space to which all are welcome?

My family was part of a church for several years that engaged this challenge. We joined a church plant in a very poor section of Springfield, Ohio, one filled with all the effects of urban poverty—homelessness, prostitution, drug addiction, and violence. We found ourselves sitting in church alongside people I was raised to view as dangerous and threatening—people like Ray, the crack addict, and Lisa, the prostitute. Our church services were followed by a common meal to which we invited people from the surrounding neighborhood. We also operated a food pantry from the church building and so developed relationships with people in the neighborhood over several years.

I will never forget a conversation I had with a woman who came to our food pantry for a supply that would feed her and her family for the week. As we sat together, she shared her story about how a recent difficulty had put her in a very tough financial situation. As she stood up to leave, she remarked to someone sitting next to her about how refreshing it was to be treated like a human being, as someone with dignity.

Because my full-time job was teaching the New Testament, I was struck by this very dynamic in the Gospels—that the kingdom brought with it an invasion of purity, freeing us to fellowship with people that our cultural values tell us are dangerous—"unclean." Because Jesus was constantly touching people with whom he was not supposed to have contact according to his cultural values, these were the very people I was supposed to get to know. And I began

8. Blomberg, *Contagious Holiness*, 172–73.

to see things in a different light: getting to know these people who were very different from me was a wonderful opportunity for me to experience the power and presence of God's kingdom. It was not something I was *supposed* to do but something I was *privileged* to do.

This realization came home to me in two small ways. First, one day I was walking through the neighborhood with my friend John. We were talking about how our conception of our ministry had changed over the course of a few years. Rather than seeing ourselves as the salvation of the people to whom we felt we were ministering, God had brought us to that neighborhood to save us, to bless us with his presence.

Second, I found that our family devotional time was transformed. For years we had routinely read Scripture in the mornings with our children before breakfast. Over time, as we read through the Gospels, I had regular opportunities to refer to the character of our church participation. We could draw direct lines from episodes of Jesus touching those considered "unclean" to our cultivation of friendships with the sort of people we encountered in the neighborhood.

Because churches are outposts of the kingdom of God on earth, they would do well to consider how they may be unintentionally making certain people feel unwelcome or like second-class Christians. Do certain ethnicities feel out of place in our churches? How about divorced people? Do single mothers feel that they don't belong in our communities? Mark invites us to consider how we can transform our imaginations and community dynamics, so that all are welcome and no one feels "unclean."

CHAPTER 6

Mark 1:35-39

📖 LISTEN to the Story

³⁵Very early in the morning, while it was still dark, Jesus got up, left the house and went off to a solitary place, where he prayed. ³⁶Simon and his companions went to look for him, ³⁷and when they found him, they exclaimed: "Everyone is looking for you!"

³⁸Jesus replied, "Let us go somewhere else—to the nearby villages —so I can preach there also. That is why I have come." ³⁹So he traveled throughout Galilee, preaching in their synagogues and driving out demons.

Listening to the Text in the Story: Exodus 33–34; Psalm 142; Daniel 6; James 5:17–18.

Ministers know the crucial character of prayer. Fears from within and without, pressures, anxieties, and the monumental task of ministry demand meditation on Scripture and time alone in prayer. Moses (Exod 32:9–14), David (Ps 142), Elijah (Jas 5:17–18), and Daniel (Dan 6) are all examples of leaders of Israel whose lives of prayer demonstrated dependence on God. Exodus 33–34 tells the story of Moses feeling the weight of leading God's people. His communication with God sustained him. He prayed for assurances from God that he would not abandon his people but that he would remain with them, and in a remarkable passage Moses asked to see God's glory (Exod 33:18). Exodus 33:19–34:8 relays the dramatic encounter between God and Moses in which God's glory passes him by, allowing Moses to get a glimpse of it. Moses's relationship of honest interchange with the God who was redeeming Israel carried him through the enormous pressure he faced in leading Israel out of Egypt and into the land of promise. Jesus's attempt to be alone to pray indicates his need for this same kind of sustaining relationship with God.

EXPLAIN the Story

Jesus Praying

The previous evening had been hectic with ministry activity, and it likely had been that way for quite some time. Mark has portrayed Galilee as desperate for the liberation and healing Jesus is bringing, and people have been crowding him and nearly piling all over him. Amid all this, Jesus wants to spend time in quiet prayer. Mark dramatically shifts the pace of the narrative by slowing things down, giving the sense of a quiet, deliberate early morning. He introduces the scene with repetitive and ponderous phrases: "Very early in the morning" repeats "while it was still dark," and after Jesus got up, he "left the house," which Mark repeats when he says that Jesus "went off."

Jesus went to a "solitary place," which is the same Greek term (*erēmos*) used earlier when John appears "in the wilderness" (1:4) and when Jesus was sent into "the wilderness" by the Spirit (1:12). As indicated earlier, the desert is a place of dramatic encounter with God throughout the biblical narrative, so this is more than an incidental detail. Jewish revolutionaries called people out to the desert in order to build a movement seeking to establish God's reign through military conquest.[1] While Jesus's agenda is to establish God's kingdom rule, his method is dramatically different. The Son of God ushers in God's reign through suffering and death, and his ministry will fly in the face of cultural expectations. This difficult mission is why Jesus is in the desert to pray.

The Disciples Disturb Jesus's Solitude

When the disciples awoke to find Jesus gone, they may have grown alarmed. They had left everything behind to follow him, so where was he? A few details indicate that Mark does not approve of their going out to look for Jesus. Their curiosity and impatience are preventing Jesus from the refreshment that solitude with God might bring. First, Mark uses a verb to refer to their searching in v. 36 that has negative overtones—they "hunt him down" (*katadiōkō*), and it is paired with *zēteō* in v. 37 ("everyone is looking for you" [*pantes zētousin se*]). Elsewhere in Mark, *zēteō* is used of searching for Jesus with misguided or malicious intent (3:32; 8:11–12; 11:18; 12:12; 14:1, 11, 55).[2] Second, while this is the first mention of Jesus praying, each subsequent mention of Jesus doing so in Mark includes some kind of failure by the disciples. In 6:46–50

---

1. Acts 21:38; Josephus, *J.W.* 2.13.4; 7.11.1. See Morna D. Hooker, *The Gospel According to Saint Mark*, BNTC (Peabody, MA: Hendrickson, 1993), 36.

2. Black, *Mark*, 79.

they are terrified by the storm. In 9:14–29, they fail to pray for an exorcism, and in 14:32–42 they fall asleep while Jesus is praying.[3] Jesus has called them to "follow," which means increasingly adjusting their thoughts and intentions to match Jesus's kingdom agenda. They are not yet on the same page as Jesus.

When they find him, they exclaim urgently, "Everyone is looking for you!" The whole town is wondering where Jesus is, and the sun has hardly been up. Jesus's emergence onto the public scene has aroused deep longings among the people for release from demonic oppression and sickness. Everyone is desperate for renewal and for the arrival of God's kingdom.

Jesus's Mission

Jesus responds in a way that does not address the disciples' message to him about the crowds. He simply restates his mission. He is on God's timetable, and what he does will be oriented not by the desires of the masses but by the kingdom of God. They must keep going to other towns so that he can continue to announce the arrival of God's kingdom. In his concluding statement, Mark associates Jesus's preaching with driving out demons (v. 39), indicating that kingdom proclamation and demonic expulsion are vitally connected. God's long-awaited kingdom reign has come, and Jesus announces it with healing power that drives out the darkness.[4]

Jesus will return to Capernaum as he travels through Galilee (2:1), but he also expects that the people to whom he has preached will begin to inhabit God's reign, enacting it in their renewed relationships and redeemed communal behaviors. The kingdom's arrival is a realized reality—it is here! The repentance and belief (v. 15) that Jesus calls for entails that his audience respond by living into the fullness of faith rather than chasing Jesus down for more impressive miracles.

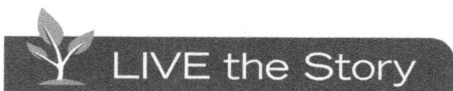

LIVE the Story

The Ambivalence of Popular Hunger for Jesus

Modern readers of Mark are likely to read the overwhelming response to Jesus on the part of the crowds as a positive development. The crowds are hungry for Jesus! They're coming to him in droves! Surely his ministry is a success at this point, right? We tend to measure the "success" or "effectiveness" of a ministry

---

3. Moloney, *Gospel of Mark*, 57.
4. Jesus's statement ("that is why I have come") is one of a handful in Mark's Gospel that captures the purpose of Jesus's ministry (1:24, 38; 2:17; 10:45); see Marcus, *Mark 1–8*, 203–4.

or a church based on the number of people it attracts. The more popular it is the more God must be pouring out his blessing. We evaluate churches based on how compelling the worship is or how much we like the preaching. In a consumeristic culture in which we are trained to evaluate everything based on our likes and dislikes, we cannot help but conceive of churches and ministries in this way. And this is precisely why Mark portrays the desperate hunger for Jesus on the part of the crowds ambivalently. That is, it is not entirely positive.

The hunger of the crowds demonstrates the desperation felt by many in Galilee and Judea for God's salvation. But like many in our culture, the desires of the crowds need to be redeemed. They want salvation, but they want it according to a distorted conception of God's messiah—one who will come as a triumphant hero. This is why Jesus keeps telling everyone in Mark to keep quiet about him. The great excitement gets in the way of his teaching about the cross-shaped kingdom and his identity as a cross-oriented Messiah. Mark presents a challenge for those of us in an entertainment-oriented and celebrity-obsessed culture to avoid being swept up by the excitement of crowds or popular approval. What matters is not popularity but the faithfulness of a ministry to the message that Jesus calls his people to be shaped by the cross. What matters is a church's corporate obedience to this call by enacting increasing faithfulness in loving, serving, and welcoming others.

In his day, Ezekiel encountered the same phenomenon. Amid God's order to proclaim judgment, God informed the prophet that the Israelites in exile actually loved to come and hear him preach:

> As for you, son of man, your people are talking together about you by the walls and at the doors of the houses, saying to each other, "Come and hear the message that has come from the LORD." My people come to you, as they usually do, and sit before you to hear your words, but they do not put them into practice. Their mouths speak of love, but their hearts are greedy for unjust gain. Indeed, to them you are nothing more than one who sings love songs with a beautiful voice and plays an instrument well, for they hear your words but do not put them into practice. When all this comes true—and it surely will—then they will know that a prophet has been among them. (Ezek 33:30–33)

What counts before God is hearing God's word and doing it (Mark 3:35). Immediate excitement and popularity usually fade (4:17–19). A ministry built on popularity is constructed on sand.

This is why Paul carefully cultivated a ministry presence that portrayed the cross and its scandal when he was with the Corinthians. He avoided putting on a dazzling display of rhetorical skill and impressing them with a powerful personal presence.

> And so it was with me, brothers and sisters. When I came to you, I did not come with eloquence or human wisdom as I proclaimed to you the testimony about God. For I resolved to know nothing while I was with you except Jesus Christ and him crucified. I came to you in weakness with great fear and trembling. My message and my preaching were not with wise and persuasive words, but with a demonstration of the Spirit's power, so that your faith might not rest on human wisdom, but on God's power. (1 Cor 2:1–5)

I grew up in a vibrant church setting with a thriving youth group and a bunch of friends with whom I attended summer camps and Christian concerts. I remember well the yearly conclusion of summer camp, when we would reaffirm our commitment to live as faithful disciples throughout the coming school year, as well as the "high" we would experience after concerts. We thought that these routine jolts of enthusiasm would carry us forward in our Christian lives. In those moments we could hardly conceive that we would ever depart from Christ or leave the life of the church. Sadly, however, those friends with whom I shared those moments have no connection at all to Christ. The strong emotional responses we experienced were not enough to drive a lifelong commitment to the sort of discipleship to which Jesus calls us.

I have a friend who has learned this lesson well. He is now the pastor of a small church in a rural part of the country. He had been in the military special forces and has a whole range of wild stories and outrageous experiences. For a time he would speak to men's groups and talk about his military service, during which he would relay his Christian testimony. Over the course of years, however, he was struck with the haunting question of whether this was bearing any fruit of developing in others a lifelong discipleship. Were his presentations of amazing accounts of military heroism merely entertaining? Was he doing anything to cultivate in others a trust in the power of God? Because he could not have confidence that this mode of ministry was bearing genuine gospel fruit, he increasingly turned down opportunities to speak and focused instead on ministering to his local community.

We would do well to consider Mark's ambivalent portrayal of the crowds throughout his Gospel, especially if we have unwittingly adopted the cultural value that what is popular must be good. What matters is a community's faithfulness in becoming increasingly conformed to the cross by sacrificially loving and serving others and one another in the name of Jesus.

CHAPTER 7

Mark 1:40-45

📖 LISTEN to the Story

⁴⁰A man with leprosy came to him and begged him on his knees, "If you are willing, you can make me clean."

⁴¹Jesus was indignant. He reached out his hand and touched the man. "I am willing," he said. "Be clean!" ⁴²Immediately the leprosy left him and he was cleansed. ⁴³Jesus sent him away at once with a strong warning: ⁴⁴"See that you don't tell this to anyone. But go, show yourself to the priest and offer the sacrifices that Moses commanded for your cleansing, as a testimony to them." ⁴⁵Instead he went out and began to talk freely, spreading the news. As a result, Jesus could no longer enter a town openly but stayed outside in lonely places. Yet the people still came to him from everywhere.

Listening to the Text in the Story: Leviticus 13–14; 2 Kings 5:1–14; Psalm 113; John 9; Philemon 1–25.

We noted previously that God takes special delight in blessing the marginalized—the poor, the orphan, and the widow. Those who are socially excluded are dear to his heart. We see this throughout the Old Testament, as God calls his people to care for the poor (Deut 14:28–29; Isa 3:14–15; Ezek 16:49). Psalm 113 celebrates both God's transcendence and his care for the least:

> The LORD is exalted over all the nations,
> > his glory above the heavens.
> Who is like the LORD our God,
> > the One who sits enthroned on high,
> who stoops down to look
> > on the heavens and the earth?
> He raises the poor from the dust
> > and lifts the needy from the ash heap;

> he seats them with princes,
>> with the princes of his people.
> He settles the childless woman in her home
>> as a happy mother of children.
> Praise the LORD. (vv. 4–9)

God reigns without any rival as the creator and supreme cosmic ruler, but he takes special care to bless the poor, the needy, and the barren woman. A childless woman in the ancient world bore tremendous social shame, since childbearing was so important. God's blessing of a woman was typically thought to be determined by how many children she had, so ancient cultures considered one who was childless to be the object of divine disapproval.

These sorts of assumptions were pervasive in Jesus's day, so that people with physical maladies (barrenness, blindness, leprosy) were cut off from their communities. This assumption is evident in John 9:1–2, where Jesus and his disciples come across a blind man. They ask him, "Rabbi, who sinned, this man or his parents, that he was born blind?" Lepers were treated in the same way. They were cut off from their communities, considered unclean, and likely reduced to begging for survival.

EXPLAIN the Story

The Leper's Request

The term *leprosy* covers a range of skin diseases in the ancient world, so this may not have been leprosy as we know it. Some skin diseases could be cured, and in such cases steps were provided for becoming "clean" (Lev 13–14).[1] The story of Naaman is an instance of someone with an incurable condition who was miraculously healed (2 Kgs 5:1–14). In certain instances, a skin disease could be caused by sin (Num 12:1–16; 2 Kgs 5:19–27; 2 Chr 26:19–21), though according to the regulations in Leviticus this was not always the case.[2] Over time, however, anyone with a skin disease was stigmatized as sinful and excluded from their communities.

This leper, like many of the people throughout Galilee, was desperate. He was labeled "unclean" and therefore in need of being restored to his community. He approached Jesus in abject humiliation, beseeching (*parakalōn*) him and falling

---

1. D. P. Wright and R. N. Jones, "Leprosy," *ABD* 4:277–82.
2. T. Omiya, "Leprosy," *DJG* 517–18.

on his knees (*gonypetōn*) (v. 40). Like other figures in Mark, he approaches Jesus in a submissive posture, indicating worship (Mark 5:6, 22, 33). His plea includes a statement of his faith in Jesus's ability to heal him: "You can make me clean."

Jesus's Response

Jesus's response to the leper is mysterious and challenging. First, "Jesus was indignant" (v. 41). As the marginal note in the NIV indicates, a number of manuscripts have the verb *splanchnizomai*, meaning that Jesus was "moved with compassion" rather than "indignant" (*orgizomai*). Among other criteria for judging which reading is more likely the original, textual critics prefer the more difficult one. This is because it makes more sense that when scribes were copying the text they changed the far more challenging verb to one that is less offensive, thinking that perhaps the scribe working before them had made a mistake. The reading in the NIV is the more difficult of the two and is likely the original.

But why does Jesus react this way? Two other episodes in Mark provide some help. In Mark 3:5 Jesus heals a man with a withered hand, a person who has been marginalized among the community and apparently is not being cared for by the Pharisees. Jesus is grieved at the Pharisees' hardness of heart and reacts with anger (*orgē*, the noun form of *orgizomai*). In Mark 10:13–14 Jesus's disciples prevent children from coming to him and Jesus, seeing this, is again indignant (*aganakteō*). In these two episodes Jesus reacts to the corrupted social codes and practices that marginalize those who need care. Here, too, Jesus reacts with anger at the broken community dynamics that ostracize one who needs healing and restoration. The man is degraded, humiliated, outcast, and not experiencing *shalom* according to God's intentions. Jesus is not indignant at this man but is moved with anger at the situation where community deterioration is at work. These are precisely the sorts of situations that the kingdom of God transforms. The Mosaic law had called for Israel to be a nation of justice and care for the marginalized. While Israel had failed, Jesus and his kingdom would embody this reality.

Mark emphasizes Jesus touching the leper, doubling up the verbs: "He reached out his hand and touched the man." As he did with Simon's mother-in-law and will continue to do throughout Mark's narrative, Jesus indicates that in the kingdom of God purity is contagious rather than impurity. According to John Chrysostom:

> He did not simply say, "I will, be cleansed," but he also "extended his hand, and touched him"—an act we do well to analyze. If he cleansed him merely by willing it and by speaking it, why did he also add the touch of his hand?

For no other reason, it seems to me, than that he might signify by this that he is not under the hand of the law, but the law is in his hands. Hence to the pure in heart, from now on, nothing is impure.[3]

At the commanding word of Jesus, "the leprosy left [*aperchomai*] him" (1:42). This expression parallels that of the demon being driven out in the previous episode (*exerchomai*, 1:26), thus associating the healing with exorcism. Not that the leprosy is because of demonic possession, but there is a similarity in that the presence of the kingdom of God invades the darkness and forcefully drives out demons and sickness.

To show his fidelity to the Mosaic law and to give the leper the opportunity to be restored to his community, Jesus exhorts the man to offer a sacrifice and to show himself to the priests. Jesus also strongly warns him to tell no one else what had happened. Jesus knows the intense desperation among God's people for God's deliverance and for the glory of God's kingdom. He is aware that hysteria can easily be whipped up so that it becomes increasingly difficult to communicate the cross-shaped reality of God's kingdom. He wants to avoid fostering and fueling triumphalist notions of the kingdom.

The Leper's Response

Rather than obeying what Jesus told him to do, the leper spread the news of what Jesus did for him. It would be easy to read this as a normal response. Mark does not say how long the man had leprosy nor how long he had been cut off from his community. And we can easily imagine his great joy at being physically and socially restored. Yet Jesus had strongly warned him to go directly to the priests, but the man disobeys, bringing negative consequences for Jesus's ministry: "As a result, Jesus could no longer enter a town openly but stayed outside in lonely places" (v. 45). Further, the man is prevented from being fully restored to his community, which would have taken place if he had been declared "clean" by the authorities.

LIVE the Story

Loving and Blessing without Calculation

This episode is a striking example of the logic at work in Jesus's ministry of healing and blessing. He is the agent of God's kingdom order of restoration

---

3. Oden and Hall, *Mark*, 26.

among his people, and so he is bringing freedom from demonic oppression and sickness. *And this is happening without any reference to whether the recipients are deserving or not.* In fact, the leper in this episode ends up ignoring Jesus's strong warning to tell no one what had happened and to show himself to the priest. But the man is healed because Jesus is infinitely generous and gracious, a reflection of the overwhelming generosity and grace of God.

Elsewhere, Jesus calls upon God's character as scandalously generous and ties it to the identity and conduct of the church:

> You have heard that it was said, "Love your neighbor and hate your enemy."
> But I tell you, love your enemies and pray for those who persecute you, that
> you may be children of your Father in heaven. He causes his sun to rise on
> the evil and the good, and sends rain on the righteous and the unrighteous.
> If you love those who love you, what reward will you get? Are not even the
> tax collectors doing that? And if you greet only your own people, what are
> you doing more than others? Do not even pagans do that? (Matt 5:43–47)

Jesus's disciples do not love people based on their fitness to be loved or their qualifications for receiving love. Followers of Jesus love others *because that is their identity.* They love their friends, and they love their enemies, because this manner of life reflects the character of the God who is loving and generous to his friends and enemies alike.

On the one hand, this should go without saying. Scripture is filled with indications that the fundamental identity marker of the church is that we are people who love one another as God loves us (Lev 19:18; John 13:35; 1 John 4:16–21). On the other hand, it is important to note the precise logic at work in the manner in which God loves, because there is a kind of language that I have heard in a variety of Christian contexts that represents a rationale that is different from the logic of God's love. Rather than a logic of overwhelming and scandalous generosity, we often fall captive to a logic of stinginess, one of parsimony.

I am referring to the language of "investment." Because the language of the marketplace is so pervasive in our wider culture, it is easy to adopt this language in Christian contexts. For example, a pastor or church leader might spot a younger person that she would like to cultivate for a potential leadership position, and she might say something like, "I am going to invest myself in this person to develop her for a leadership role."

I have heard others use this language, and I know I have used it too. In fact, after a long discussion with a colleague about this a few years ago,

I later referred to "investing in students" in a meeting, at which point he made a dramatic show of objecting to my language. Not only did this bring some comic relief to a department meeting, it highlighted the ubiquity of the language of capitalism and how it can subtly invade and orient relationships in other settings.

The framework from which the language of "investment" emerges is often used to speak of other ministry opportunities. A church board may evaluate certain outreach or service efforts based on whether the expenditures of time and energy are "worth it," given the expected "payoffs" or "benefits."

I think that something more profound is at work here than a simple choice of language. This subtle transformation of speech reflects a distortion of Christian identity. Rather than focusing attention on the identity of the church as generous givers and lovers without expectations, there is a turn to evaluating the fitness of the person I am "investing" in. Instead of envisioning an opportunity for the church to bless others with God's gifts to us, we now are evaluating "investment opportunities" based on expected outcomes.

This language changes the way I see myself and others. The difference between these alternative logics came home to me several years ago. One evening in a small group meeting, someone mentioned that they were looking for a mentor for a junior high school boy who had no adult role models in his life. Another person responded that perhaps there was a college student who could meet this need, which seemed to make good sense to the rest of us. Over the next few weeks, I could not get this boy out of my mind, and I was struck by the fact that I had the time and space in my life to cultivate a relationship with him. As I reflected on my thought processes, I realized that my imagination had been shaped by this logic of "investment." I knew that if a gifted young adult had asked me to mentor him that I would have found the time to do so. I would have seen such an opportunity as "worth my effort," a "worthy investment."

To make a long story short, I talked to the woman who brought this young boy to our attention, and we made plans for me to meet him and his family. Over the next several years, he became a significant part of our family life, and we also got to know him and his family, which led to great mutual benefit and blessing.

That experience taught me a few things about the biblical configuration of relationships. First, the New Testament consistently portrays relationships in the church in terms of siblingship.[4] We are "brothers and sisters" in the new

---

4. Joseph H. Hellerman, *When the Church Was a Family: Recapturing Jesus's Vision for Authentic Christian Community* (Nashville: B&H Academic, 2009).

family that God creates in Christ and by the Spirit. Some of us may be older siblings and others of us younger siblings, but the dominant note being struck here is *mutuality*. We are *together* in God's family, and no one is *above* anyone else. Our mentoring relationships are ones that God uses to bless *all* partners in the relationship, and so we should think in terms of mutual blessing. We engage one another in ways that invite God to bless both of us and each of us through one another and alongside one another. Second, I realized that because God does not love based on calculated results, I embody God's love faithfully when I do not calculate what I will get out of the situation. I cannot be on the lookout for someone who is *worthy of my love*, since that is not how God loves.

Today, when I consider ministry opportunities, I do not use the language of "investing" in others. Rather, I think about whether this or that opportunity will be one in which I can enjoy God's order of flourishing, into which people are invited without reference to their fitness or qualifications. This is valuable to keep in mind in a culture that regards people with disabilities or those in poorer communities as less valuable than those who have a higher social status or greater cultural honor. It is tempting to regard people who can contribute more effectively to the life of our church communities in terms of money or social prestige as worthy of "investment," but the church would do well to consider that this is a temptation to operate with a logic that does not represent the way God loves.

CHAPTER 8

Mark 2:1–12

📖 LISTEN to the Story

¹A few days later, when Jesus again entered Capernaum, the people heard that he had come home. ²They gathered in such large numbers that there was no room left, not even outside the door, and he preached the word to them. ³Some men came, bringing to him a paralyzed man, carried by four of them. ⁴Since they could not get him to Jesus because of the crowd, they made an opening in the roof above Jesus by digging through it and then lowered the mat the man was lying on. ⁵When Jesus saw their faith, he said to the paralyzed man, "Son, your sins are forgiven."

⁶Now some teachers of the law were sitting there, thinking to themselves, ⁷"Why does this fellow talk like that? He's blaspheming! Who can forgive sins but God alone?"

⁸Immediately Jesus knew in his spirit that this was what they were thinking in their hearts, and he said to them, "Why are you thinking these things? ⁹Which is easier: to say to this paralyzed man, 'Your sins are forgiven,' or to say, 'Get up, take your mat and walk'? ¹⁰But I want you to know that the Son of Man has authority on earth to forgive sins." So he said to the man, ¹¹"I tell you, get up, take your mat and go home." ¹²He got up, took his mat and walked out in full view of them all. This amazed everyone and they praised God, saying, "We have never seen anything like this!"

Listening to the Text in the Story: Exodus 34:4–7; Leviticus 4; Isaiah 43:25; 44:21–22; 55; Psalm 139:23; Luke 15; John 9.

This episode marks a transition in the narrative. To this point, Mark has established Jesus's authoritative identity as the one who brings in the kingdom of God. This episode is the first of five conflict stories that appear in 2:1–3:6, and as they progress the resistance to Jesus's authority intensifies.[1] This section opens (2:1–12) and closes (3:1–6) with two healing stories, framing three episodes that involve eating.[2]

> Mark 2:1–12—Jesus heals; scribes suspect blasphemy
>> Mark 2:13–17—Jesus eats with sinners, and Pharisees ask why
>> Mark 2:18–22—Jesus's disciples do not fast, and "some people" ask why
>> Mark 2:23–28—Jesus and disciples eat grain on the Sabbath,
>> and Pharisees ask why
> Mark 3:1–6—Jesus heals; Pharisees plot to kill Jesus

The two episodes that provide the "frame" for this section (2:1–12 and 3:1–6) have several similarities. First, Jesus "enters" into the midst of a large gathering—the crowded house and the synagogue. Second, Jesus heals and also uses the healing to provoke a response from those potentially opposing him. Third, Jesus discerns the thoughts of those who are opposed to what he is doing. Fourth, each healing confirms his opponents' suspicions despite the good that is done. Finally, both episodes end with someone leaving, though here there is a contrast. In the opening encounter, the healed man leaves, and everyone praises God (2:12). In the closing confrontation, the Pharisees leave and begin to plot to kill Jesus (3:6). The conclusions to these episodes demonstrate the growing opposition to Jesus, as his opponents progress from suspicion of blasphemy to murderous scheming.

In this passage we see Jesus displaying one of the key characteristics of God—forgiveness. Throughout Scripture, when God talks about himself, he stresses that he forgives sins. In the key biblical text where the God of Israel reveals his glory to Moses, God passes before Moses and proclaims his name:

> "The LORD, the LORD, the compassionate and gracious God, slow to anger, abounding in love and faithfulness, maintaining love to thousands, and forgiving wickedness, rebellion and sin. Yet he does not leave the guilty unpunished; he punishes the children and their children for the sin of the parents to the third and fourth generation." (Exod 34:6–7)

And in passages where God pleads with Israel to turn from sin, he bases his exhortations on his forgiving character. This well-known text from Isaiah appears in a context of forgiveness:

---

1. Black, *Mark*, 85.
2. Moloney, *Gospel of Mark*, 60.

"For my thoughts are not your thoughts,
    neither are your ways my ways,"
        declares the LORD.
"As the heavens are higher than the earth,
    so are my ways higher than your ways
    and my thoughts than your thoughts." (Isa 55:8–9)

This statement begins with "for," indicating that it is an argument giving reasons for what Israel should do, mentioned in the previous few statements:

Seek the LORD while he may be found;
    call on him while he is near.
Let the wicked forsake their ways
    and the unrighteous their thoughts.
Let them turn to the LORD, and he will have mercy on them,
    and to our God, for he will freely pardon. (Isa 55:6–7)

God is unlike any other god and unlike anyone and everyone else. He is not vindictive, and he does not castigate or scold those who call on him (Jas 1:5). Others may act this way, but God forgives those who call on him and delights to restore and renew and pour out his blessing. Forgiveness is a core characteristic of God, and the biblical narrative displays it consistently. In this passage in Mark, Jesus behaves just as the God of Israel does.

EXPLAIN the Story

This episode opens and closes with a focus on the paralytic, while in the middle, Mark reports the controversy that the pronouncement of forgiveness provokes among the scribes (vv. 6–10). There is a tragic irony here. The teachers of the law—those best positioned to respond well to Jesus—are offended by him in the midst of his mission to bring in the life-giving and healing reign of God.

The Crowded House (vv. 1–5)

This scene opens with Jesus having returned to Capernaum. While the NIV translates that he "had come home," the expression in Greek is less specific and may mean that he was at Peter's house.[3] Once again, word spreads of Jesus's

---

3. Marcus, *Mark 1–8*, 215. Jesus may have been using Peter's house as a base of operations while in Capernaum. In this case the phrase would be translated "at the house."

presence, and so a crowd gathers to such an extent that "there was no room left," and it spills over into the street. As he does in 1:21–27, Mark mentions Jesus's preaching without indicating the content of what he says (v. 2). But he portrays Jesus as an authoritative preacher by linking his preaching with his authoritative actions.

Mark narrates what happens next in such a matter-of-fact style that readers may fail to notice how outrageous it is. The friends of a paralyzed man climb to the roof of Peter's house and tear it apart to lower him, so that he might be healed by Jesus. Mark does not record Peter's reaction, but he could not have been pleased!

This also must have created a major disturbance for everyone gathered beneath. With dust and dirt and chunks falling on everyone and all around the people jammed into the overstuffed house, one wonders whether Jesus was able to continue teaching amid the disruption. Did he need to pause while the paralytic was lowered by his friends? And Mark doesn't say how they lowered the mat.

Mark leaves much unsaid, allowing our imaginations to fill in the details. Interestingly, he focuses solely on the action of the paralytic's friends, while the man himself is completely passive. In vv. 3–5 Mark notes that the men "came" to the house, "bringing" the man, who was "carried" by them. Trying to get him to Jesus, they "could not get him" there, so they "made an opening" in the roof, "digging" through it. They then "lowered" the man to Jesus. The friends are the subject of all the verbs. The only active description Mark gives of the paralytic is that he is "lying on" his mat (v. 4).

Jesus's response also involves the man's friends. He spoke to the paralytic when he saw "*their* faith" (v. 5). Jesus's perception of "their" faith may include the paralytic, but the group's over-the-top effort to get their friend to Jesus exhibits the faith that impresses Jesus.

What happens next is completely unexpected. Jesus says to the paralytic, "Son, your sins are forgiven" (v. 5). After the healings being reported thus far in Mark, readers expect to hear of the paralytic being healed. Certainly the paralyzed man, along with his friends and those gathered in the house expect the same. Jesus, however, announces that the man's sins are forgiven, which is a surprise. As the episode unfolds, it appears that Jesus uses this opportunity to confront his audience, and especially the scribes who are present, with the reality of his unique identity. If Jesus had simply healed the man, the scribes would have been able to remain passive observers, gathering information and considering how they might respond to him. But Jesus forces the issue.

The Controversy (vv. 6–10)

In this central section of the episode, Mark notes the presence of some scribes in the crowded house.[4] Their agitation comes in response to Jesus's declaration that the man's sins are forgiven. They consider this "blasphemy" since no human can claim to forgive sins. God alone does this (Exod 34:6–7), and Scripture is clear about how Israelites can obtain forgiveness (e.g., Lev 4). They take offense because Jesus claims to be playing the part of the God of Israel and is bypassing the Scripture-endorsed route for obtaining forgiveness. Though they are not reasoning aloud, they are thinking rightly in terms of Scripture. If Jesus is not God, then he is indeed blaspheming.

Mark often puts statements of Jesus's identity in the mouths (or here, in the minds) of other characters, leading his readers to draw conclusions about who Jesus is. Since Jesus is doing what only God can do, it must be that Jesus is identical with the God of Israel.

Jesus, in another indication of his divine identity, is aware of their thinking. Only God can discern the thoughts of humans (1 Sam 16:7; Ps 139:23; Prov 24:12), and Jesus knew "what they were thinking in their hearts."[5] He challenges them to reconsider their line of thinking (v. 8). Even though Jesus is confrontational toward his opponents in Mark, he is here inviting them to reconsider their approach. It is still possible for them to participate in the good that Jesus intends to do.

He then asks them a question that does not necessarily have a straightforward answer. "Which is easier: to say to this paralyzed man, 'Your sins are forgiven,' or to say, 'Get up, take your mat and walk'?" In one sense, it is easier to say that someone's sins are forgiven because this is not actually verifiable. Forgiveness takes place in the unseen realm, so anyone can easily say it. At the same time, it is not easy at all to say this since it will get you killed! No one went around casually blaspheming in Jesus's day. From this perspective, neither of the two statements are easy to say, but Jesus, of course, says them both. And he does so in order for his audience to know that he "has authority on earth to forgive sins" (v. 10).

Jesus is playing on the notion that it is easier to say that the man's sins are forgiven. The more difficult thing to say is that the man should get up

---

4. The NIV has "teachers of the law" for the Greek *tōn grammateōn* ("scribes"). Scribes played a range of roles in first-century Jewish culture, though "they shared in common a role as the keepers, interpreters and teachers of Israel's Scriptures and traditions that often led to their prominent roles in society and politics" (Thellman, "Scribes," *DJG* 844). They appear in Mark consistently in opposition to Jesus, apart from the scribe he encounters in Mark 12:28–34.

5. Marcus, *Mark 1–8*, 222.

and walk. That requires miraculous power and authority over sickness. The implication is that because Jesus can do the visible thing, he also has the authority to do what is invisible.[6]

Jesus's healing of this man becomes the occasion for a revelation of his divine identity. Joel Marcus points to the similarity of the language throughout the events of the exodus and Jesus's statement in v. 10. When Moses confronts Pharaoh, he announces that the God of Israel is going to act "so you may know that there is no one like me in all the earth" (Exod 9:14).[7] Jesus's language here is similar: "But I want you to know that the Son of Man has authority on earth to forgive sins" (v. 10).

The Conclusion (vv. 11–12)

Jesus's statement to the scribes in v. 10 functions as a point of transition to the conclusion of the episode. While the paralytic is the occasion of this confrontation, he's played a minor role to this point. Jesus, the man's friends, and the scribes have received most of the attention. Jesus now speaks directly to the man: "I tell you, get up, take your mat and go home" (v. 11). Emphasizing his immediate and unquestioning obedience, Mark succinctly reports that the man does precisely what Jesus told him to do. "He got up, took his mat and walked out in full view of them all" (v. 12).

That the entire crowd witnessed the event was necessary to furnish proof of Jesus's identity to them all, and the positive result is that God is praised (v. 12). This is Jesus's aim in bringing about this healing—to turn Israel's attention back to the God of Israel and to elicit thankfulness and worship to him for the goodness they enjoy.

LIVE the Story

Knowing God

When I teach how to read biblical narratives, I remind students to draw conclusions about the characters in the narrative based on how the narrative presents those characters. I will often point out that it is critical, yet difficult,

---

6. Chrysostom, writing in the fourth century about Jesus's authority to forgive sins, says this: "Whenever there was need to punish or to honor, to forgive sins or to make laws, Christ was fully authorized to do it. Whenever Christ had to do any of these much greater things, you will not characteristically find him praying or calling on his Father for assistance. All these things, as you discover in the text, he did on his own authority" (Oden and Hall, *Mark*, 27).

7. See also Exod 7:17; 8:10, 22; 9:14; 10:2 (Marcus, *Mark 1–8*, 218).

to try to set aside or forget what you know about God when you read biblical narratives. The reason I say this is that I want to stress the importance of allowing the biblical text to inform our thinking about God rather than holding tightly to our assumptions about who God is without letting the Bible reshape and reform them. As an exercise to demonstrate this, I will ask students to tell me about God. What is he like? What sort of things should we say about him? The answers usually include the three "omni-" terms. That is, the first things many of us say about God are that he is omniscient, omnipotent, and omnipresent. Other descriptions may be included, but it is interesting that we usually think about God in terms of attributes like these—terms that are not found in the Bible. The Bible does describe God's knowledge, power, and presence in ways that could be summed up with the three "omni-" terms, but there is also a good bit of complexity with each of these.

I raise this issue because biblical narratives have particular ways of constructing the character of God, portraying him as, among many other things, creator, king, judge, and wounded lover. To understand God, we should avoid generalizing attributes and instead pay close attention to the roles God plays in narratives and how he relates to others, the sorts of things he does, and what others say to and about him. Further, to grasp the character of God, it is crucial to reckon with how gospel narratives portray Jesus. After all, Jesus is the truest and most faithful representation of the unseen God (John 1:18; Heb 1:1–3).

Based on this text in Mark 2 and its biblical-theological context, one of the first things we ought to say about God is that he forgives. It is striking that as soon as Jesus sees the men lowering their friend down through the roof, he declares the man's sins forgiven. He could have, of course, done something else. He could have demonstrated his power by miraculously repairing the roof. He could have healed the man right away without raising the issue of forgiveness. Yet rather than doing these things, Jesus declares the man's sins forgiven. Forgiveness is Jesus's default setting. When he is in a crowded house and someone causes a huge commotion by tearing apart the roof and lowering a man down through it, Jesus forgives. Certainly Jesus's response is an intentional part of the narrative, designed to generate engagement with the scribes and to show that his authority had been delegated from God. Granting this, however, Jesus's authority is not generalized but has to do specifically with forgiveness of sins.

Jesus's behavior is consistent with the character of God revealed in Scripture. As cited above, when God has the opportunity to speak about himself, he speaks in terms of forgiveness. In Exodus 33 Moses tells God that he wants to know him:

Moses said to the LORD, "You have been telling me, 'Lead these people,' but you have not let me know whom you will send with me. You have said, 'I know you by name and you have found favor with me.' If you are pleased with me, teach me your ways so I may know you and continue to find favor with you. Remember that this nation is your people." (Exod 33:12–13)

In response, God would reveal to Moses his glory, which he does in a dramatic scene:

So Moses chiseled out two stone tablets like the first ones and went up Mount Sinai early in the morning, as the LORD had commanded him; and he carried the two stone tablets in his hands. Then the LORD came down in the cloud and stood there with him and proclaimed his name, the LORD. And he passed in front of Moses, proclaiming, "The LORD, the LORD, the compassionate and gracious God, slow to anger, abounding in love and faithfulness, maintaining love to thousands, and forgiving wickedness, rebellion and sin. Yet he does not leave the guilty unpunished; he punishes the children and their children for the sin of the parents to the third and fourth generation." (Exod 34:4–7)

The core identity of the God of Israel is his slowness to anger, his abundance of love and faithfulness, his steadfast love to thousands, and his proclivity to forgive. And his desire to forgive and restore is what sets him apart from anyone and everyone else, as he says in Isaiah 55:6–9.

What we think of God affects how we live and approach life. Unfortunately, we often assume that God's forgiveness is like ours—half-hearted, reluctant, incomplete. When we forgive, we often struggle not to hold on to anger and bitterness at others who have hurt us. And when we have an opportunity to forgive, it is tempting to articulate frustrations at someone, saying "I told you so," or otherwise verbally exacting some vengeance. But this is not how God forgives. The psalmist says this:

Then I acknowledged my sin to you
    and did not cover up my iniquity.
I said, "I will confess
    my transgressions to the LORD."
And you forgave
    the guilt of my sin. (Ps 32:5)

There is no intermediate step between our confession of sin and God's forgiveness. It is immediate. God stands ready to forgive, even eager to forgive. It is his inclination, his eager desire. There are two things we can draw from this. First, when we sin, we ought to be quick to confess our sins to God in prayer. He is not like us and will not chide us and scold us for failing or for deliberate folly. He is eager to forgive and restore us to life-giving pathways. Because of his delight in forgiving, we can have assurance to speak boldly and plainly before God about our sin. Second, we can walk through life with joy, being assured of God's delight in us and his pleasure in us. We are forgiven, and God is for us. That gives us confidence to face each day as inhabitants of the kingdom of God, a realm saturated with an atmosphere of forgiveness.

Mark 2:13-17

📖 LISTEN to the Story

¹³Once again Jesus went out beside the lake. A large crowd came to him, and he began to teach them. ¹⁴As he walked along, he saw Levi son of Alphaeus sitting at the tax collector's booth. "Follow me," Jesus told him, and Levi got up and followed him.

¹⁵While Jesus was having dinner at Levi's house, many tax collectors and sinners were eating with him and his disciples, for there were many who followed him. ¹⁶When the teachers of the law who were Pharisees saw him eating with the sinners and tax collectors, they asked his disciples: "Why does he eat with tax collectors and sinners?"

¹⁷On hearing this, Jesus said to them, "It is not the healthy who need a doctor, but the sick. I have not come to call the righteous, but sinners."

Listening to the Text in the Story: Isaiah 55:1–56:8; Matthew 11:28–30; Galatians 2:15–21; Romans 5:6–8.

This account of the call of Levi is the first of three controversies with religious leaders sandwiched between the framing episodes of 2:1–12 and 3:1–6. In each encounter, the scribes and Pharisees object in some way to Jesus's eating practices. Here, the scribes associated with the Pharisees object to Jesus eating with tax collectors and sinners. Jesus's eating habits are fully consistent with the character and behavior of the God of Israel throughout the biblical story. From the very beginning, God upsets human expectations. He chooses the younger Jacob over the older Esau. He calls a nation of slaves through whom he will redeem the nations of the world. In the same way, Jesus spends time with the outcasts in Israel to draw them to himself and calls the despised Levi as one of his followers.

God calls sinful Israel to himself in Isaiah 55–56, noting his character as the one who is eager to forgive and restore. One persistent struggle in the early church—seen in Acts 15 and Paul's letters to the Galatians and Romans—involved how and to what extent the Jewish believers in Jesus could embrace non-Jews as full participants in God's people. Arguing with his fellow Jewish Christians, Paul notes that even though they are "Jews by birth and not *sinful Gentiles*," they join non-Jewish believers in Jesus in being justified by faith (Gal 2:15–16). And Jesus didn't die for the "righteous" or for the "good" but for the "ungodly" (Rom 5:6–8). God's historic people had grown used to thinking of themselves as "righteous" and of gentiles as "sinners" and "ungodly." But they needed to consider themselves in these latter terms in order to become part of the group for whom Jesus died.

EXPLAIN the Story

This episode takes place in Capernaum beside the Sea of Galilee. Like each episode in this section, it opens with movement (2:1, 13, 18, 23; 3:1), continuing the portrayal of Jesus in Mark as being constantly in motion. Here, Jesus "went out beside the lake." In keeping with what has happened previously, Jesus draws a crowd and teaches them. Mark portrays Jesus as a teacher here, but doesn't mention what he teaches, just as in 1:21–27.

Jesus Calls Sinners (vv. 13–15)

As he was walking along, Jesus "saw" Levi. His taking notice of Levi stands in contrast to the scribes, who "saw" Jesus eating with sinners and tax collectors (v. 16). There is a difference here in vision. Jesus sees Levi, and presumably saw other individuals among the crowd in terms of hopes for redemption and transformation. The scribes can only see these individuals in their status as notorious sinners.[1]

Levi sits at the tax collector's booth. Tax collectors were considered traitors to the Jewish people and were therefore despised. They are lumped together with "sinners," not merely because they and other "sinners" happen to be imperfect people. These are well-known for their apparent disregard of God's law. They are notorious sinners—"professional sinners"—since by doing their job they are serving Rome and fostering the presence of impurity and uncleanness in Israel (i.e., the pagan Romans).[2] And they themselves were unclean because of their constant contact with the Romans. The foreign occupation of Israel was a persistent reminder that God's people were not enjoying the long-promised and desperately awaited salvation of God. It was widely assumed that

---

1. In Matt 9:9–13, Levi is referred to as "Matthew." In Mark's list of the Twelve in 3:16–19, Mark doesn't mention "Levi the son of Alphaeus," but only "James the son of Alphaeus" and "Matthew." It is likely that Mark has already begun to refer to "Levi" as "Matthew" in 3:18.

2. Black, *Mark*, 92.

God had not returned to redeem his people, partly because of the presence of such sinners among the people of God.

Surprisingly, when Jesus calls him, Levi responds immediately. "'Follow me,' Jesus told him, and Levi got up and followed him" (v. 14). The scribes and Pharisees throughout 2:1–3:6 are skeptical of Jesus, agitated at his claims and behavior. But when Jesus calls a notorious sinner, he responds without question. Not only this, but "many" tax collectors and sinners were eating with Jesus at Levi's house, "for there were many who followed him" (v. 15). The religious authorities object to Jesus, but the despised who respond to him enjoy his company and his blessing.

The Scribes' Objection (v. 16)

The teachers of the law who were Pharisees "see" Jesus eating with these notorious sinners and inquire about this to Jesus's disciples (v. 16). The Pharisees ate only with one another to ensure that they were ceremonially clean and ritually pure. They separated from sinners not only to maintain their purity but also to encourage these notorious sinners to repent, change their ways, and join them in careful and conscientious obedience to the God of Israel. In a sense, then, the scribes and Pharisees had a similar aim for tax collectors and sinners. Everyone wanted sinners to repent, but the Pharisaic strategy of *exclusion* differed dramatically from Jesus's ministry mode of *embrace*.

Jesus's Mission (v. 17)

This confrontation concludes with Jesus stating his mission in proverbial form. Jesus's answer functions in at least two ways. It answers the Pharisees' question of why he is eating with notorious sinners. Because of his identity as the one bringing God's restorative kingdom, he must go to those who need to be redeemed. He is the physician, so he must go to the sick. His answer is also an ironic rebuke of the teachers of the law, who already consider themselves righteous. They would never self-identify as "sinners." Because of this, they are in just as precarious a position as the notorious sinners they condemn through their exclusion. If they deny that they are "sinners," they have no place in God's kingdom.

LIVE the Story

Confronting Exclusive Churches

Throughout Mark 2:1–3:6, the scribes and Pharisees object to Jesus in various ways. In Mark 2:13–17, we see that they direct their question to Jesus's disciples and not to Jesus himself. This is unusual, but it is perhaps a sign of the complexity of Mark's aims in writing this Gospel. While Mark is recounting an episode in Jesus's ministry, he is also confronting his audience with Jesus's mode of life. This text confronts complacent churches of today and speaks to them. "Hey, complacent church, why is Jesus—the One you claim to represent, the One you call on for salvation, the One you claim to be the embodiment of the creator God on earth—why is he eating with all the wrong people, the notorious sinners, the ones on whom we were all convinced God was about to pour out his judgment? Why is he eating with them, running the risk of being seen to endorse them, *when you order your community habits to ensure you never run into them?*"

The question the Pharisees ask Jesus's disciples is a question put to the church. Mark would grant that all people desire to see sinners repent and begin new lives of joyful obedience. But such a desire is also found among those characters in Mark who oppose Jesus. Jesus, however, doesn't stop at merely desiring for sinners to repent. He goes to them, walks among them, calls them, sits and eats with them. If God's people are not among sinners, the question must be faced: Why does Jesus eat with sinners and tax collectors, but his disciples want nothing to do with them?

The routine patterns of church life may make spending time with sinners difficult for many of us. That is, we may consider that anyone is welcome to show up on a Sunday morning to attend one of our services. Because we are not intentionally excluding them, are we really to blame for them not showing up? Are there other creative ways to be spending time *as church communities* with outsiders so that we do not become exclusive communities?

My friend Charles came up with a creative idea. He began meeting on a weeknight at a local pub with a handful of people from his church. He asked others to invite interested friends who would not otherwise go to church but who wanted to engage in discussions related to the faith or what is in the Bible, or anything at all. This led to some interesting encounters, especially since it was unscripted and casual. Endeavors like this push us beyond what we might consider comfortable.

Saints and Sinners

Martin Luther famously wrestled with the question of whether Christians are "saints" or "sinners." Which is it? Are we wretched or renewed now that we're set right with God? There's a sense in which it is the better part of wisdom to hold on to both of these identities. Throughout Scripture, God attributes identity markers of great privilege and high honor to his people. We are "specially chosen," "uniquely loved," "blessed with every spiritual blessing in Christ." The purpose of identity markers given to us as God's people has to do with the blessing of driving home to our hearts that we are dearly loved by God.

While we celebrate these overwhelming blessings, we must be vigilant that we don't become arrogant or judgmental of others. We are only "holy" because of what God has done among us, to us, and on our behalf, for we are no better than anyone else.

Texts such as Mark 2:13–17 remind us that we must find ourselves alongside notorious sinners. The identity marker of "sinner" reminds us that we must always inhabit the place where we're receiving God's goodness without becoming arrogant. As the psalmist says, "Know that the LORD is God. It is he who made us, and we are his; we are his people, the sheep of his pasture" (Ps 100:3). In other words, God has brought us into his kingdom to enjoy his love. This didn't come about by our brilliance! And Paul reminds his readers that their salvation has come about by God's grace through his own faithfulness, not from them. It "is the gift of God—not by works, so that no one can boast" (Eph 2:8–9).

Mark 2:18–22

📖 LISTEN to the Story

¹⁸Now John's disciples and the Pharisees were fasting. Some people came and asked Jesus, "How is it that John's disciples and the disciples of the Pharisees are fasting, but yours are not?"

¹⁹Jesus answered, "How can the guests of the bridegroom fast while he is with them? They cannot, so long as they have him with them. ²⁰But the time will come when the bridegroom will be taken from them, and on that day they will fast.

²¹"No one sews a patch of unshrunk cloth on an old garment. Otherwise, the new piece will pull away from the old, making the tear worse. ²²And no one pours new wine into old wineskins. Otherwise, the wine will burst the skins, and both the wine and the wineskins will be ruined. No, they pour new wine into new wineskins."

Listening to the Text in the Story: Isaiah 54:4–8; John 16:7; Ephesians 4:7–13.

This is the central unit of Mark 2:1–3:6, a stretch of text that introduces the conflict between Jesus and the Pharisees, escalating to a climax in 3:6. The present episode explains why Jesus is a threat to the status quo. He is introducing something radically new, a way of life for God's people that is incompatible with their familiar ways of doing things. God had called Israel to manifest his kingdom through an economy of generosity, a politics of love, hospitality, and kindness, and a social program of caring for the poor and needy. Tragically, throughout the biblical story God's people regularly strayed from this life-giving, national calling and fell into patterns of exploitation, oppression, social conflict, and neglect of the needy among them.

As time passed, they grew comfortable with small compromises, injustices, and idolatries, so that when prophets like Jeremiah called them to repent and cultivate renewed ways of life, they didn't listen. Because of this, the brokenhearted prophet predicted God's judgment in the form of destruction and exile (e.g., Jer 4:5–6). But Jeremiah also looked ahead to the day when God would restore his people and transform their lived reality from oppression and despair to blessing, joy, and flourishing at the great restoration (31:23–40). That day had arrived in Jesus, and God was calling his people once again to a renewed way of life that demanded a departure from what was familiar—from the oppressed and oppressive reality that had sadly become the norm.

EXPLAIN the Story

This episode begins like the others in this section. "Some people" ask Jesus about the eating habits of his disciples (v. 18). In the previous episode, the scribes of the Pharisees had asked the disciples about Jesus's dining companions. Here, "some people" ask Jesus why his disciples do not fast like the disciples of John and the Pharisees (v. 18). This unspecified group is the scribes who belong to the Pharisees and who have been asking questions about the behavior of Jesus and his disciples throughout this section. Jesus gives a twofold answer. First, he speaks about his presence and absence, using the image of a bridegroom. Second, he relays two parables from everyday experience that speak of the new in relation to the old.

The Scribes' Question (v. 18)
The scribes' question has to do with the kind of fasting carried out by these two pious groups in an effort to hasten the day of salvation. John's disciples had repented and were preparing for the arrival of the God of Israel. The Pharisees were likewise intensely concerned with the honor of Israel's God and longed for God to return and save. The fasting by the disciples of John and of the Pharisees had to do with calling out to God to bring about the kingdom of God—the fulfillment of God's saving promises. Yet the scribes do not see Jesus's disciples fasting. Don't they also care about the salvation of Israel? Don't they want God to remember his promises, to show himself faithful to the covenant, and to vindicate his people?

Jesus's Presence and Absence (vv. 19–20)
Jesus answers the scribes using imagery drawn from prophetic passages that speak of the return of God to Israel, such as Isaiah 54:4–7:

"Do not be afraid; you will not be put to shame.
Do not fear disgrace; you will not be humiliated.
You will forget the shame of your youth
and remember no more the reproach of your widowhood.
For your Maker is your husband—
the LORD Almighty is his name—
the Holy One of Israel is your Redeemer;
he is called the God of all the earth.
The LORD will call you back
as if you were a wife deserted and distressed in spirit—
a wife who married young,
only to be rejected," says your God.
"For a brief moment I abandoned you,
but with deep compassion I will bring you back."

Jesus is indicating that *God has returned; their salvation is already here* (v. 19). It makes no sense for them to be urging God to act by fasting. God has acted, and the time has come—the kingdom of God has come in Jesus. Groups such as the disciples of John and the Pharisees should no longer be fasting but celebrating! In fact, fasting is inappropriate now that the bridegroom—God himself—has come.

Jesus continues, however, and his response takes a sober turn (v. 20). While the present is a time of celebration because of his presence among them, there will soon be an absence.[1] Jesus, the bridegroom, will be taken from them. This is quite shocking. According to biblically informed Jewish expectation, the bridegroom was supposed to bring full and final salvation. He was supposed to arrive and stay! But Jesus points to a day when he would be taken from them, referring to his impending death.

Jesus's answer involves both his presence and his absence. His disciples do not fast like other groups who long for God's kingdom because it has already come in Jesus. Yet when Jesus is "taken from them," that will again initiate a time of fasting because his disciples will be anticipating Jesus's return— his second coming—to bring in the kingdom fully. This is the situation for Christian disciples today. It is again a time of longing for God to restore all things. God has sent salvation "already," but we still live in the "not yet" as we await his coming in glory.

---

1. This is the first prediction of Jesus's death. Jesus later explicitly predicts his suffering and death three times in 8:31–33, 9:30–31, and 10:33–34.

Two Parables of Newness (vv. 21–22)

Jesus continues with two parables from everyday life. Though he is now present, he is going to be taken. But his absence is not a reversion to a previous moment in the story of God's work in the world. Even though Jesus is currently absent, the story has moved ahead. In the wisdom of God, Jesus's absence enables his presence. Only if Jesus ascends to the Father can he send the Spirit, who is the presence of Jesus himself among the church (John 16:7; Rom 8:9). Jesus is now paradoxically *both absent and present*, with his Spirit animating and empowering the radically new stage in the experience of God's people. This new reality—the church—is going to challenge old and established ways of doing things. While it is consistent with God's ways and while God operates "according to the Scriptures," this new move cannot be contained within the old structures of how God's people had been living. The church will be a community that waits, but not in the old way. God has come in Jesus, and though he is no longer on earth, his presence is among his people by the Spirit. So the new waiting is a step beyond the old mode of anticipation. It is a waiting that does not involve absence. God's presence is among us as we await his fully manifest presence.

This is the thrust of Jesus's two parables. The kingdom is a new reality that cannot fit within the confines of old realities, which is why the practice of Jesus's disciples will be different from that of John's and the Pharisees' disciples.[2] A new patch sewed onto an old garment ruins them both. And new wine poured into old wineskins bursts through and destroys the shriveled container and ruins the wine. In the same way, God's people must prepare for something new. Though related to the old, Jesus is establishing a new reality that he signals with an emphatic declaration: "New wine into new wineskins."[3]

LIVE the Story

Living the Paradox

The current era of God's work in the world involves paradox. A paradox is not a contradiction but involves holding together things that *appear* to be in contradiction but ultimately are not. The paradox in this passage involves the presence of Jesus, who was with his disciples during his earthly ministry

---

2. Hooker, *Mark*, 100.
3. Marcus, *Mark 1–8*, 238.

but soon was going to be absent, ascending to his heavenly throne after his death and resurrection. His absence, however, was going to bring about his presence in a new way, since at his ascension he sent the Spirit—the Spirit of Jesus himself—to dwell among his church. The contemporary life of the church, therefore, involves some complexity. Jesus is both absent and present, so we celebrate his presence with us by his Spirit, but we still await his coming in glory.

This makes the task of the church complex. In one sense we live in the world as God intended from the beginning—among a humanity restored to God and enjoying God's presence in his beautiful creation. In that sense we are the already saved and restored people of God (Eph 2:8). Because of this reality, we celebrate when we gather together as the church and give praise and thanks to God for his triumph over evil and the blessing of being fully restored to fellowship with him.

But in another sense, we are *not yet* saved and *not yet* fully restored. We are not living in the world as God intended, because we were supposed to enjoy this world as a place filled with God's presence and oriented by God's rule. Yet God is not present like he is supposed to be and not yet fully reigning over his creation as he one day will be. In the current moment, Jesus is the one who is on his way to his world to take up his rule (Rev 22:7). He has begun his reign in heaven but has not yet completed subduing all his enemies (1 Cor 15:25–28). And Paul says that "our salvation is nearer now than when we first believed," indicating that while we are already saved, we await the fullness of our salvation in the future (Rom 13:11). For now, "we eagerly await a Savior from [heaven], the Lord Jesus Christ" (Phil 3:20).

Because of this, our current experience involves pain and suffering and other hardships. It is tempting for many Christians to explain these aspects of reality away, to deny them or to emphasize only the triumphant aspects of Christian existence. But this is an inappropriate posture toward the world. Because God's world is not fully set right, we must mourn and lament when we face tragedy, pain, and suffering. It does not glorify God to give in to sentimentality by looking for the silver lining in bad situations. When we suffer, we must grieve. Not only is that a healthy response, it is an honest and a truthful one that resonates with what God knows about his world. But we can also have hope that when the Lord Jesus completes his triumph over evil, our hearts will be fully satisfied, and we will be able to participate in the celebration of evil's final destruction. And not only this, but even amid suffering God is working by his Spirit to do good to his people, triumphing in small ways over evil by turning pain into fuel for perseverance on the part of the people of God (Jas 1:2–4, 12).

The task of the church, therefore, is to live fully and truthfully into the reality of this world as it is. It is beautiful but broken; God has triumphed, but we await his final victory; we have been saved and restored, but we still experience pain, loss, and death. We cannot deny any aspect of our reality— neither the negative nor the positive. When we experience loss, we must grieve fully. When we feel pain, we must not give in to sentimentality and try to look on the bright side. In the face of brokenness we lament, grieve, and mourn. Yet we also celebrate because we are God's people. And celebration is an act of defiant faith. In the face of all that is still ugly in this world and the seemingly unbroken march of evil, we joyfully celebrate God's future victory, anticipating the day when he comes to vanquish evil for all time and fully restore creation for our complete and joyful satisfaction and for his great glory.

It is difficult to hold on to this paradox and to fully lean into this twin reality. I've discovered that this happens mainly when Christians suffer painful loss, such as the death of a loved one. A youth minister once relayed to me the story of a young person who had died in a car accident. He talked about the many high school students that attended the funeral who heard the gospel presented, wondering if perhaps their exposure to the gospel was the reason for this young man's death. I have heard many versions of this same sort of reasoning—the desire to make some kind of sense of human tragedy, to make everything fit.

The underlying assumption here is that the world in its current condition is just how God wants it to be. This leaves us in a place where we have to somehow justify our suffering, to make sense of the tragedies we endure. We try to piece it all together and look for good outcomes to painful events. This prevents us, however, from fully grieving the deep pains we suffer, and it flows from a misunderstanding of where we are in the story of God making all things new. Further, it robs our praying of the fuel that drives our longing for God to fulfill his promises of restoring creation.

It is not our task to demonstrate that tragedies are not all that tragic. We can both fully grieve and lament when we suffer, because awful things happen in this broken world that grieve the heart of God. And we can look forward in hope to the full restoration of all things in the future, when God makes all things new and brings a day when we will never again suffer loss. We grieve and feel the depths of our profound wounds. But we do not grieve as those without hope (1 Thess 4:13). We can pray that God will bring that day soon.

Praying the Paradox

About once a month our former church gathered to pray together. Below are a few excerpted sections of one of our prayer services, in which we expressed both lament and grief over the condition of our city, as well as hope for God's restoration in the future.

A Prayer for Springfield

Lord, we pray for the flourishing of Springfield.

From you, O Lord.

We pray for the lasting peace of this city.

From you, O Lord.

We pray for wisdom and compassion for the leaders in this city.

From you, O Lord.

We pray for comfort for families separated or grieving.

From you, O Lord.

For release of those trapped in cycles of violence.

From you, O Lord.

For safety and security for women and children.

From you, O Lord.

For refreshment for the weary and healing for the sick.

From you, O Lord.

For continuing faithfulness of the churches of this city.

From you, O Lord.

For tenacity of spirit for small Christian groups.

From you, O Lord.

For the mutual enrichment and support of those of different
    Christian traditions.

From you, O Lord.

You, Lord of all, we confess;

You, Lord Jesus, we glorify;

For you are the life of our bodies,

And you are the Savior of our souls.

A Prayer of Confession and Hope

Father, we confess to you our brokenness and despair.

Lord, have mercy.

We confess to you our wrongly directed hopes and ambitions.

Lord, have mercy.

We confess to you our selfish desires and our selfish habits.

Lord, have mercy.

We confess to you our foolish addictions and our enslaving and destructive practices.

Lord, have mercy.

Father, look upon our woundedness and our disappointments.

Lord, have mercy.

Father, look upon our crushed hopes and dreams.

Lord, have mercy.

Father, heal our hearts.

Lord, have mercy.

Father, stir up within us hope for goodness.

Create in us clean hearts.

Father, stir up within us hope for our true enjoyment of others.

Create in us true hearts.

Father, stir up within us a longing to enjoy your love.

Create in us hearts of love.

CHAPTER 11

Mark 2:23-28

📖 LISTEN to the Story

> [23]One Sabbath Jesus was going through the grainfields, and as his disciples walked along, they began to pick some heads of grain. [24]The Pharisees said to him, "Look, why are they doing what is unlawful on the Sabbath?"
>
> [25]He answered, "Have you never read what David did when he and his companions were hungry and in need? [26]In the days of Abiathar the high priest, he entered the house of God and ate the consecrated bread, which is lawful only for priests to eat. And he also gave some to his companions."
>
> [27]Then he said to them, "The Sabbath was made for man, not man for the Sabbath. [28]So the Son of Man is Lord even of the Sabbath."

Listening to the Text in the Story: Genesis 2:2–3; Exodus 20:8–11; Deuteronomy 23:25; 1 Samuel 21:1–6; Romans 14:5–9; Colossians 2:16.

This is the fourth of five episodes in Mark 2:1–3:6, the middle three of which revolve around food. To this point the Pharisees have been emerging as a presence in Mark, and in this episode they question Jesus directly. The scribes first questioned Jesus in 2:6, and after that it was the scribes of the Pharisees (v. 16). It is likely the same group in v. 18 who question Jesus about his disciples not fasting. Here, however, the Pharisees themselves question Jesus about his disciples' behavior on the Sabbath (v. 24). Mark uses this gradual emergence of the Pharisees over these five episodes to depict the growing opposition between them and Jesus.[1]

God set apart the Sabbath day because on that day he entered into his reign. After the six days of creation, he "rested." Not that he was worn out, but after constructing creation as his cosmic temple, he took his seat as king over

---

1. Moloney, *Gospel of Mark*, 68.

all he had made.[2] The Sabbath rhythm is part of creation and part of God's gracious instruction to Israel (Exod 20:8–11). They were to work six days and "rest" on the Sabbath, so that they might have lives attuned to the rhythm of creation. God's original intention was for his people to enjoy six days of work to sustain themselves and their families, and to set aside one day for rest and creative enjoyment. That is, rather than activities that led to sustenance, they were to fill that day with all sorts of activities they simply found enjoyable. Hiking, walking, visiting with friends and family, exploring, making up games to play—any and every sort of recreation Israel could imagine was to fill that one day of the week. In Exodus 16 God promised to provide for them enough food for the day, so that even if they did not work, they would be sustained.

To enjoy the Sabbath truly, therefore, required a huge amount of faith. To take a day off for nothing but frivolous activity would feel irresponsible! Yet their obedience in this matter was crucial, for God wanted them to depict in their national way of life the character of God, who loves humanity and delights when they enjoy his world. And he wants humanity to be refreshed by the cycle of work and rest, and in all of this God is glorified as the kind of God who longs to pour out lavish blessings on those who enjoy his gracious reign.

While God intended this to be an open-ended and life-giving command, by Jesus's day it had been turned into a restrictive ordinance, focused on all the sorts of things people should *not* do on that day. Sadly, rather than depicting through their national life a God who delighted in the joy of his people, their practice embodied the worship of a small-hearted, narrow-minded deity who would punish anyone having a good time. Rather than a delight, the Sabbath became a burden. The Pharisees' confrontation of Jesus in this passage manifests these contradictory conceptions of the Sabbath.

EXPLAIN the Story

The Pharisees' Objection (vv. 23–24)

This episode opens like the others in this sequence, with Jesus and his disciples on the move. As they were walking along, the disciples were picking "heads of grain" (v. 23). The Pharisees objected and complained to Jesus about what his disciples were doing, noting that it is "unlawful on the Sabbath" (v. 24).

---

2. John H. Walton's excellent work, *The Lost World of Genesis One: Ancient Cosmology and the Origins Debate* (Downers Grove, IL: IVP Academic, 2009), helpfully unfolds how Gen 1, read against the backdrop of the culture of the ancient world, describes the construction of creation as God's cosmic temple.

They apparently held to a strict conception of what it meant "to reap" grain and saw the disciples' actions as violating this standard. The Pharisees' concern for what was appropriate on the Sabbath likely had to do with their effort to move God to initiate the kingdom. This drove them to influence the people toward what they viewed as a careful and conscientious observance of the law.

The Biblical Analogy (vv. 25–26)

Jesus answers their question with his own question, one that reveals that they have missed the heart of God in their strict appropriation of God's word. They have come to observe the law in such a way as to make it an oppressive lord over humanity, whereas God gave the Torah ("instruction") for the flourishing of his people, as Jesus indicates in v. 27.[3] He sets up his interlocutors with a question from the Scriptures that puts them back on their heels. He says, in effect, "Your strict reading of the law sets up the observance of statutes and ordinances as an absolute, allowing no exceptions. Tell me, then, what you make of David going into the house of God and eating the consecrated bread? Would you be willing to say that this is an instance of an absolute being violated? Or, would you say that God's will was done in that situation? Isn't it the case that human need—of great concern to God—is perhaps also the point of the statutes and ordinances God gave to Israel?"

In the story, drawn from 1 Samuel 21:1–6, this is precisely what David did. He and his men were on the run from Saul and were in need. They were famished to the point of weariness, and so they went into the tabernacle and ate the consecrated bread.[4] These are the twelve loaves that represent the tribes of Israel and are placed on the tabernacle table every Sabbath to be eaten by the priests (Exod 40:23; Lev 24:5–9).[5]

---

3. Modern Bible readers unfortunately have a skewed view of the Mosaic law because the Hebrew *torah* is often translated as "law." In fact, the translation of the Bible in various languages and through several worldviews has distorted how we should understand God's gracious instruction to Israel. God gave his people the gift of Torah, giving them wisdom in how to walk in his love. "Torah" becomes *nomos* ("law") in Greek and then *lex* ("law") in Latin and now "law" in English. Each culture understands this term through how they view their own laws and their enforcement. Unfortunately, the original situation in which God chose his people and saved them and then gave them his instruction for how to enjoy his love has become a situation in which we imagine God primarily as a "lawgiver" who makes "demands" and punishes those who step out of line.

4. Abiathar is mentioned in v. 26 rather than Ahimelech, who appears in the episode in 1 Samuel 21:1–6. It may be that Mark is pointing to a larger unit of scriptural text in which Abiathar appears, since there were no chapters and verses in scriptural texts in the first century. Or, it may be that Mark is referring to a general period of time in David's life, and since Abiathar was high priest during David's reign he is especially associated with him (see the discussions in Edwards, *Mark*, 94–95; David E. Garland, *Mark*, NIVAC [Grand Rapids: Zondervan, 1996], 106; Robert H. Stein, *Mark*, BECNT [Grand Rapids: Baker Academic, 2008], 146–47).

5. Edwards, *Mark*, 94.

Jesus refers to this story as an instance where desperate human need trumped the meticulous observance of Mosaic instruction, and it points to the difference between how Jesus and the Pharisees view the law. For Jesus, God gave the law in order to provide for Israel's flourishing, to give them wisdom in how to walk in the love of God and of neighbor. It is filled with examples and suggestions for the kinds of practices that embody their care for one another that constituted the worship of God—and those two are intimately related to one another. The Mosaic law is saturated thoroughly by God's grace.

The Pharisees, on the other hand, have come to observe the law in order to present to God a purified people zealous for righteousness and holiness. The law had become the means to establishing a national identity of purity and rectitude in an effort to move God to bring the day of salvation nearer. Because of this, observance of the law became a burden and drew the Pharisees into a mode of relating to others whereby they became coercive and manipulative, condescending toward others in judgment. God's gracious instruction now became a restrictive and heavy burden, transformed into principles that had become more important than people.

Humanity and the Sabbath (vv. 27–28)
The Sabbath was God's good gift to humanity, for refreshment and joy. But it had been turned into something that felt far less than a gift, as if people were serving it rather than being refreshed by this special day. Jesus goes a step further to assert his lordship over the Sabbath. As Son of Man, Jesus is God's appointed agent of rule in the kingdom of God, and he has the authority to determine God's approved way of fulfilling the Sabbath. Jesus does not set himself against God's law. God's gracious instruction was always intended to direct Israel into the ways of life, so that they might fully enjoy God's blessing. Sabbath observance is one way their national life had gotten off track, and Jesus, far from overthrowing the law or nullifying it, is redirecting them toward God's original intentions.

LIVE the Story

Contemporary Sabbath Keeping
When it comes to thinking about the relation of Sabbath regulations to contemporary Christian discipleship, some Christians may want to point out that we are no longer under the Mosaic law. We are not obligated to submit to such regulations, as Paul indicates in a few passages (Col 2:16–17; Rom 14:5).

This is true to an extent, though this way of putting it perpetuates the mis-understanding Jesus intended to overturn. We must keep in mind that God's commands are not burdensome, but a joy and delight (1 John 5:3). God's word to his people gives life and brings liberation, and God gave the Torah to help his people understand how to inhabit God's love and blessing.

If we think of the Sabbath in terms of a heavy obligation, we are as mis-guided as many in Jesus's day. The Sabbath was not intended as a day to be heavily regulated, focused on all the things Israel was *prevented* from doing. God called Israel to embody the rhythms of life that he wove into the fabric of his good creation, with six days of work and one day of refreshment. They were to refrain from *work* and pursue any and all activities *that were not laborious*. This command was meant to be liberating, not constraining. Israel's national way of life was designed to depict the way that humanity would properly enjoy the gracious reign of the creator God.

Contemporary Christians inhabit the kingdom of God, which is God's restored order of flourishing under the lordship of Jesus Christ. Just as Jesus is Lord of the Sabbath, he is Lord over our lives, having claimed our bodies. We are not our own, but have been bought with a price (1 Cor 6:20; 7:23). And our lives within the kingdom of God are not oriented by constraint and limitation but by liberation and freedom for the recovery of our true humanity. And just as Israel's observance of the Sabbath would depict God's rule as joyfully liberating, we ought to imagine all the ways that our lives can portray the lordship of Jesus Christ as a gracious and refreshing reign.

My family had the opportunity to discover the joys of what a Sabbath rhythm meant for us. For about five years, our church met on Saturday nights, which freed up our Sundays. We developed the routine of sleeping in and enjoying a relaxing morning. I would put on music and make chocolate-chip waffles for breakfast, and we spent the rest of the morning without turning on the television or any of our other devices. Instead, we gathered in the living room and read books, the Sunday paper, or whatever else we wanted. About noon, we would head out for a long hike in the woods or do some other activity as a family. By the time we returned in the mid-afternoon, we were all relaxed and ready for quiet time, and some of us took an afternoon nap. In the evening, we regularly gathered with family friends for the conclusion of a wonderful day of refreshment.

Our Sundays became such a prized time that we took steps to protect them from incursion. I would make sure to have my Monday classes prepared by the previous Friday afternoon. And nobody thought to plan something on a Sunday without checking with the rest of the family. None of us thought that this was a heavy burden. Our Sundays were a delight! While our family has a different shape to it now—our children are all grown and out of the house—I still maintain this rhythm. I take a morning walk before church and make sure to keep my afternoon free to read something pleasurable or to take a nap. And in the evening, my wife and I conclude our week with dinner at the local Italian restaurant. My weeks are filled with busyness and obligations, and I have learned that living in concert with God's Sabbath rhythm is not a lifeless duty but a life-giving delight.

We might think of God's Sabbath rhythm as an alternative economy to the demanding economy that orients our contemporary world. We are encouraged to burn ourselves out in pursuit of career goals, achievement, and upward mobility. We are trained to maximize our time as we quest after promotions. All of this takes a heavy toll on our bodies and spirits, along with our relationships.

I remember a conversation I had with a friend at church who was recounting to me that he was by far the oldest person in his working group at his company. He said that he had been passed over for promotions and would probably retire at a much lower rank than others of his age. Yet he was content with that, because he deliberately made choices to spend time with his family and be involved in various efforts at the church rather than wear himself out in search of executive glory. That is someone whose life is oriented by a Sabbath economy rather than one that offers such apparent promise but is ultimately enslaving.

As Paul notes in Romans 14:5 and Colossians 2:16–17, non-Jewish Christians are free to choose the day they will experience refreshment and rest. Our weekly calendars may not line up according to one that is Jewish. But we would be wise to discern the rhythm of work and rest according to which God created the world and live in concert with it. God's good gift of the Sabbath is not a heavy burden. Its deep logic is not one of constraint or limitation. The Lord Jesus Christ has redeemed us—liberated us—into the freedom of the kingdom of God, so that we might experience in our bodies, minds, and souls the richness of God's good world as he intended.

CHAPTER 12

Mark 3:1-6

📖 LISTEN to the Story

¹Another time Jesus went into the synagogue, and a man with a shriveled hand was there. ²Some of them were looking for a reason to accuse Jesus, so they watched him closely to see if he would heal him on the Sabbath. ³Jesus said to the man with the shriveled hand, "Stand up in front of everyone."

⁴Then Jesus asked them, "Which is lawful on the Sabbath: to do good or to do evil, to save life or to kill?" But they remained silent.

⁵He looked around at them in anger and, deeply distressed at their stubborn hearts, said to the man, "Stretch out your hand." He stretched it out, and his hand was completely restored. ⁶Then the Pharisees went out and began to plot with the Herodians how they might kill Jesus.

Listening to the Text in the Story: Exodus 7–14; Ezekiel 34; Galatians 6:10.

This confrontation in the synagogue with the Pharisees concludes the section that stretches from 2:1–3:6. Over the course of these five episodes, the opposition between Jesus and the scribes and Pharisees intensifies. Initially they had come to check him out, but here they are resolutely against him. The opening episode (2:1–12) ends with everyone praising God, while this one closes with the Pharisees and Herodians plotting to kill the one they both perceive as a threat.[1]

Two dimensions of this passage reflect earlier movements in Scripture. First, the Pharisees' "stubborn hearts" recall Pharaoh's hardened heart in the events of the exodus (Exodus 7–14). In that foundational biblical story, Pharaoh became a character who was opposed to God's saving purposes. Through Moses, God had called Pharaoh to let his people go, but Pharaoh stubbornly refused.

---

1. Moloney, *Gospel of Mark*, 70–71.

If Pharaoh had done what God had commanded, he could have participated in the blessing of God through Israel. God intended to deliver Israel from slavery, bless them with their own land, and make them a blessing to the nations, including Egypt. But because he refused and hardened his heart, God confirmed him in that hardening, and he became an example of the fearsome love of God. God is so committed to redeeming the nations that he will harden people in unbelief if they choose to become obstacles to his saving mission. Like Pharaoh, the Pharisees had the opportunity to participate in the kingdom of God, but their stubbornness drove them to oppose Jesus and his mission.

Second, this passage recalls God's judgment on those shepherds of his people who have proven unfaithful. Despite the presence of many different religious authorities in Jesus's day, Mark portrays the immense and oppressive suffering of God's people. One of the main reasons for this was the unfaithful shepherds of God's people. The prophet Ezekiel called judgment down on them many years before:

> The word of the LORD came to me: "Son of man, prophesy against the shepherds of Israel; prophesy and say to them: 'This is what the Sovereign LORD says: Woe to you shepherds of Israel who only take care of yourselves! Should not shepherds take care of the flock? You eat the curds, clothe yourselves with the wool and slaughter the choice animals, but you do not take care of the flock. You have not strengthened the weak or healed the sick or bound up the injured. You have not brought back the strays or searched for the lost. You have ruled them harshly and brutally. So they were scattered because there was no shepherd, and when they were scattered they became food for all the wild animals. (Ezek 34:1–5)

The Pharisees in this episode do not seem concerned for the man with the withered hand. He appears marginalized, pushed aside or perhaps seated in the back. Rather than taking responsibility for him or even celebrating his healing, they are provoked to plot Jesus's murder after this event.

This episode captures in one incident the conflict between Jesus and the authorities in Mark. Jesus has come to inaugurate God's kingdom, which is good news for those who are marginalized and in need of care and healing. But this good news is a threat to the Pharisees, who initiate a plot to destroy the one inaugurating God's reign. Like Pharaoh they have become an obstacle to God's saving mission.

EXPLAIN the Story

Jesus had previously driven out an evil spirit in the synagogue in Capernaum on a Sabbath (1:21–28), and now he heals a man on a Sabbath in a synagogue. The man with the withered hand in this episode plays an incidental role, just like the paralytic in 2:1–12. His condition likely prevents him from making a living, leaving him in poverty.[2] He is also in the role of many others in Mark who suffer social ostracism possibly tinged with a note of moral judgment. The thinking is subtle, but those who suffered would have felt it keenly: "If there is something wrong with you, it is probably God's judgment and you are morally suspect."

The Pharisees who are present have a sinister motivation, hoping to gather information to use against Jesus (v. 2). They are not open to what he may do, and they are not looking for good to be done. They believed that if someone's life was in danger they could receive medical attention, but because there was no immediate threat in this case, they concluded that Jesus's healing of him violated God's law.[3] Their orientation is completely out of keeping with God's intentions, as they take a negative posture by noting what *cannot* be done on the Sabbath. The kingdom of God runs by a different logic and is oriented toward intentional goodness. There is a generosity of spirit that maintains that it is always appropriate to restore, to give life, and to heal.

Jesus seizes the initiative and sets the man front and center. Just as with the paralytic in 2:1–12, Jesus's goodness is a provocation to the Pharisees and their hard hearts. They are opposed to Jesus and his mission out of envy at his popularity and his challenge to their status and teaching (15:10). Jesus's question in v. 4 is an absolute softball, but it also reveals how Jesus interprets the law. To fail to do good on the Sabbath is to do evil, and for Jesus to refuse to heal the man when he has the power to do so is to kill rather than to save. Because of their commitment to opposing Jesus, however, they cannot answer his basic question. The fear of the Lord is the beginning of wisdom, but their stubborn opposition has turned them into silent fools.

Jesus's response of anger (*orgē*) and deep distress (*syllypeō*) is caused by their opposition to God's saving purposes. Leaders among God's people are called to care for people like the man with the withered hand, but as Athanasius notes,

---

2. Boring, *Mark*, 93.

3. Rabbinic texts contain discussions of Sabbath exceptions in cases of life-threatening conditions, childbirth, and circumcision (Mark L. Strauss, *Mark*, ZECNT [Grand Rapids: Zondervan, 2014], 147).

the Pharisees are there to discredit Jesus. "They had little interest in seeing the sufferer made whole."[4]

The man's response stands in sharp contrast. When Jesus gave the order, he immediately obeyed and "was completely restored" (v. 5). The tragic irony here is that the Pharisees actually do answer Jesus's question, though not verbally. They object to good being done on the Sabbath, but they apparently imagine that it is lawful to plot to kill. Their opposition to Jesus must have been nearly obsessive, since it drove them to scheme with the Herodians against him. "The Herodians" were not an organized party but were the supporters, servants, and officials associated with the pro-Roman Herodian dynasty.[5] The two groups were not natural allies at all and may have been bitterly opposed. After all, the Pharisees longed for God's restoration of Israel, which would have included the removal of the pagan Romans from the land.

LIVE the Story

Creatively Doing Good

Jesus's view of obedience to the law is neither passive nor negative. Rather than the approach of these Pharisees[6] of *avoiding* perceived violation of the law by doing good on the Sabbath, Jesus is *proactive* and *creative* about doing good to others and giving life. The Pharisees' approach was one of avoiding impurity rather than carrying out strategically planned and purposeful acts of goodness. This is precisely the opposite of how Jesus enacts the kingdom of God. He visits towns around Galilee, preaching the kingdom, healing, and casting out demons. The kingdom of God is neither a static reality nor a realm of purity that must be carefully maintained. Because it is animated by the life-giving power of God, it is dynamic and alive with God's own life, bringing about healing and restoration. It is a place of superabundant resources and where purity, rather than impurity, is contagious. This is why the postures of people who inhabit the kingdom do not have to be fearful, negative, or guided by avoidance.

Some years ago, when I was teaching Christian undergraduates, we had a discussion in class about the scriptural portrayal of obedience as a creative

---

4. Oden and Hall, *Mark*, 35.

5. H. Bond, "Herodian Dynasty," *DJG* 382; Strauss, *Mark*, 148.

6. The Pharisees are not uniformly negative characters in the New Testament. Many were part of the early church, and Paul never stopped being one, even after he became a Jesus follower (Acts 15:5; 23:6; Phil 3:5).

activity—how our imaginations are to be sparked and kicked into gear to come up with new ways of having solidarity with those who are suffering while spreading God's order of flourishing. A student asked me what this might look like in the small Midwestern town in which we all lived. I mentioned that they could visit with the pastors of a few local churches to find out if there were any elderly shut-ins who would like someone to visit with them or bring them a meal. Another idea would be to do some work to find out which young people in our town have no adult mentors in their lives. Perhaps these college students could get together and start a mentoring program to ensure that there are no kids in town who are marginalized or neglected. Our class session ended, and I didn't really think much more about that discussion.

I was surprised to find out later that some young women had taken up one of these suggestions. They had discovered that there were a number of junior high and high school girls who came from single-parent homes and weren't part of any local church. They formed a group for mutual support and began developing relationships with these younger girls, meeting with them regularly. One of these college students went on to become a full-time youth worker, developing mentoring programs in a major city. This group—and especially this one young woman—caught the biblical vision of obedience as a creative and proactive endeavor.

I have found that when I bring up the topic of obedience in Christian settings, it's as if everyone sits upright and immediately feels uptight. I think that this is because we naturally have a notion of obedience that represents the Pharisees' outlook in this episode: it is constrictive, limiting, and has to do with what we are supposed to avoid. Certainly there are prohibitions in Scripture, but many commands in the Bible are positive, pointing to the sorts of things we ought to be doing. And even these *positive* commands do not *limit* the range of what is possible. They are illustrative of the kinds of behaviors and community patterns we can enact so that we can more faithfully manifest God's reign in Jesus and enjoy his life-giving presence by the Spirit. When we focus on the possibilities for enjoying more of God's presence among us, drawing more effectively on his sustaining power and experiencing even more of his joy, our conception of obedience changes from a dark vision of what we must avoid to a hopeful, creative, and exciting one.

CHAPTER 13

Mark 3:7-12

📖 LISTEN to the Story

⁷Jesus withdrew with his disciples to the lake, and a large crowd from Galilee followed. ⁸When they heard about all he was doing, many people came to him from Judea, Jerusalem, Idumea, and the regions across the Jordan and around Tyre and Sidon. ⁹Because of the crowd he told his disciples to have a small boat ready for him, to keep the people from crowding him. ¹⁰For he had healed many, so that those with diseases were pushing forward to touch him. ¹¹Whenever the impure spirits saw him, they fell down before him and cried out, "You are the Son of God." ¹²But he gave them strict orders not to tell others about him.

Listening to the Text in the Story: 1 Samuel 5:1–5; Isaiah 49:6; Zechariah 8:20–23; 1 Maccabees 5:3–16; Philippians 2:9–11.

This passage is a summary of Jesus's ministry that marks a transition to a section of Mark that ends in 8:21, the episodes of which take place on and around the Sea of Galilee. Despite the opposition on the part of the Pharisees and Jesus's attempts to keep his popularity from spreading, his ministry is greatly expanding. People are pouring into Galilee, not only from Jerusalem and Judea but from areas beyond the borders of Israel (v. 8). This expansion is significant in light of God's promises concerning Israel's restoration while the nation was still in exile. When he restored Israel and brought them back to the land, he was going to reactivate their identity as a light to the nations. As the agent spreading God's salvation, Israel would draw the nations to worship the God of Israel (Isa 49:6). Zechariah articulates this vision found throughout the prophets:

This is what the LORD Almighty says: "Many peoples and the inhabitants of many cities will yet come, and the inhabitants of one city will go to another and say, 'Let us go at once to entreat the LORD and seek the LORD

Almighty. I myself am going.' And many peoples and powerful nations will come to Jerusalem to seek the Lord Almighty and to entreat him."

This is what the Lord Almighty says: "In those days ten people from all languages and nations will take firm hold of one Jew by the hem of his robe and say, 'Let us go with you, because we have heard that God is with you.'" (Zech 8:20–23)

Jesus's magnetic effect in drawing people from these lands indicates that the restoration of God's people is happening in fulfillment of God's promises.

This episode also recalls the portrayal of the God of Israel as exalted above all other gods (Pss 95:3; 96:4; Phil 2:9–11) and any other spiritual entity. First Samuel 5 recounts this reality in narrative form, relaying what happened after the ark of the covenant had been captured by the Philistines:

After the Philistines had captured the ark of God, they took it from Ebenezer to Ashdod. Then they carried the ark into Dagon's temple and set it beside Dagon. When the people of Ashdod rose early the next day, there was Dagon, fallen on his face on the ground before the ark of the Lord! They took Dagon and put him back in his place. But the following morning when they rose, there was Dagon, fallen on his face on the ground before the ark of the Lord! His head and hands had been broken off and were lying on the threshold; only his body remained. (1 Sam 5:1–4)

Dagon's having "fallen on his face on the ground before the ark of the Lord" indicates a posture of worship, just as impure spirits are doing in Mark 3:11. After having been set back up, Dagon again falls down in submissive worship before the ark, though this time with his head and hands cut off, pointing to his defeat in battle. The rest of this story points to God's continuing triumph over Dagon. While Dagon's hands had been cut off, "the Lord's hand was heavy" upon the people of Ashdod and its vicinity, with an outbreak of tumors (1 Sam 5:6). Just as the God of Israel was manifesting his sovereignty over a supposed competitor, Mark's report of the ongoing activity of Jesus with reference to the demonic realm indicates that Jesus shares in God's sovereignty over impure spirits.

EXPLAIN the Story

Just after the Pharisees began their murderous plotting (3:6), Jesus "withdrew" with his disciples to the lake, probably pointing to some of the more deserted areas to the north where the Jordan River empties into the Sea of Galilee (v. 7).[1] It is not that Jesus is fearing for his life; he knows what awaits him in his eventual confrontation, suffering, and death in Jerusalem. But his ministry is just getting underway, and there remains much to do.

Jesus's ministry had a powerful effect in both the human (vv. 8–10) and demonic realms (vv. 11–12). The dramatic language in this passage captures the disruption caused by the arrival of the kingdom of God. The crowd is so enormous that Jesus is under threat of being crushed. Mark points to "a large crowd" (v. 7), "many people" (v. 8), and "the crowd" (v. 9), which forces Jesus to ask for a small boat to keep them from "crowding him" (Gk. *thlibō*, "to crush"). And while the NIV portrays them "pushing toward" Jesus, Mark's Greek describes the crowd as "falling over" (*epipiptō*) Jesus in an effort to touch him (v. 10).

People have come from all over to see Jesus, both from the heart of Israel—Judea and Jerusalem—and the surrounding regions. The geographical places Mark mentions are significant because they are places concerning which Jews would have had suspicions and animosities, regions where "outsiders" to the people of God lived, such as "the regions across the Jordan and around Tyre and Sidon." And 1 Maccabees 5:3–16 portrays the enemies of God's people coming from Idumea.[2] This summary passage, therefore, functions to look ahead as Jesus will increasingly minister to outsiders and others on the fringes of historic Israel.[3]

Much like the crowds who were "falling over" Jesus wherever he went, when the "impure spirits" saw him they "fell down" (*prospiptō*) before him. They recognize his identity as the "Son of God," and their bowing portrays Jesus as sharing in God's sovereignty over demonic spirits. In a sense, this is a dramatic preview of the eschatological day of Christ at which "every knee will bow . . . and every tongue confess that Jesus Christ is Lord" (Phil 2:9–11 NASB).[4] This summary passage concludes with Jesus's strict refusal to allow the impure spirits to reveal his identity. Once again, the unclean spirits grasp Jesus's identity, though this recognition has no redemptive power. Yet in the human realm, even among his disciples, the need remains to have Jesus's identity and mission clarified.

This dramatic summary passage portrays the confrontation between the kingdom of God and the forces of darkness. Mark here presents Jesus—the

---

1. Edwards, *Mark*, 103.
2. Bruce Chilton et al., eds., *A Comparative Handbook to the Gospel of Mark: Comparisons with Pseudepigrapha, the Qumran Scrolls, and Rabbinic Literature*, NTGJC 1 (Leiden: Brill, 2010), 138.
3. Black, *Mark*, 104; Moloney, *Gospel of Mark*, 75.
4. Marcus, *Mark 1–8*, 261.

agent of kingdom presence on earth and its redeeming power—as healer of afflictions and one with authority over demons. Jesus has come to inaugurate the restoring reality that frees God's world from the grip of darkness and disease.

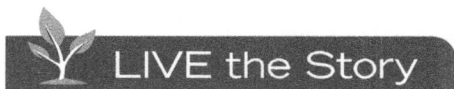

LIVE the Story

Bearing Contingency in Hope

Two interesting dynamics come together in this episode. First, note Mark's use of "touch" throughout his entire gospel narrative. Jesus is constantly touching people and being touched by them, and shockingly, the wrong kinds of people—typically those who would make him ceremonially unclean (1:41; 3:10; 5:27–31; 6:56; 7:33; 8:22). This is one way that Mark displays the power of the kingdom of God and how it comes with an invasion of purity. Rather than impurity, purity is contagious, as all kinds of people considered far from God are not only made acceptable but approved because of their faith (e.g., 5:25–34). Second, while Mark depicts overwhelming, large crowds streaming to Jesus, he does not describe them positively. They reveal an immense desperation for liberation from oppression among God's people, but they are also a hindrance to Jesus's ministry.

These two narrative devices coincide in this passage in a way that Augustine articulates well:

It is by faith that we touch Jesus. And far better to touch him by faith than to touch or handle him with the hands only and not by faith. It was no great thing to merely touch him manually. Even his oppressors doubtless touched him when they apprehended him, bound him, and crucified him, but by their ill-motivated touch they lost precisely what they were laying hold of. O worldwide church! It is by touching him faithfully that your "faith has made you whole!"[5]

The crowds in this passage are pressing in on Jesus and falling all over themselves to get to him. Just like the demons, they recognize him, but Mark reserves judgment about this being a saving recognition. This is not quite the "seeing" that indicates faith and leads to healing as in other episodes.

---

5. Oden and Hall, *Mark*, 38.

This is an excellent reminder to check our motives for seeking Jesus, especially when we encounter seasons when we are beset with sickness and disease. In *Reclaiming the Body: Christians and the Faithful Use of Modern Medicine*, Joel Shuman and Brian Volck provide a helpful guide for navigating the medical establishment as Christian bodies that are claimed by Christ and joined to the body of Christ.[6] They write about "bearing contingency in hope," which is their way of expressing our hopefulness in God's ultimate triumph over sickness, while not being able to guarantee that we will be healed in this life. They note that it is fully acceptable to pray for healing, as Paul did in 2 Corinthians 12:7–8. Paul writes that he was given a "thorn in the flesh" to keep him from exalting himself because of his incredible spiritual experiences. He prayed three times that it might be taken away, but received only the answer that God's grace was sufficient: "For power is perfected in weakness" (v. 9).

Before we are fully transformed into a radically new humanity in the new creation, clothed with a physical body from heaven (1 Cor 15:35–55), we can lay no claim on God to heal us from physical infirmities and sickness. And while some see the assurance of healing as great faith, it is simply not the case that we can guarantee an answer to our prayers for physical restoration. We can know with certainty, however, that amid pain and suffering God is at work to empower us to persevere, to unite us more closely with brothers and sisters in Christ, and to transform us into the image of his Son through the struggle and to ignite our hope *in* and fire our prayers *for* the coming restoration of all things. In these ways God's grace is sufficient, and God's power is made perfect in our weaknesses. After all, this current broken world order is not our final home. Those in Christ are headed for a world made new in the re-created new earth—our true home in which sorrow and pain will have no place.

This orientation toward physical illnesses is what Shuman and Volck mean by "bearing contingency in hope." We grieve our brokenness, and it is appropriate to pray for healing, but we hold the assurance of an answer lightly, knowing that we are caught up into God's greater purposes of healing his broken cosmos and confident that our greatest good is found in God's larger purposes. Our present health is *contingent*—we do not know whether we will be healed in this age—but we have *hope* in the restoration of all things, including our bodies. In this passage, Mark does not commend those who seek out Jesus for immediate relief. Such seeking honors God only when it leads to or is accompanied by persevering faith.

---

6. Joel Shuman and Brian Volck, *Reclaiming the Body: Christians and the Faithful Use of Modern Medicine* (Grand Rapids: Brazos, 2006), 39–40.

CHAPTER 14

Mark 3:13-19

📖 LISTEN to the Story

¹³Jesus went up on a mountainside and called to him those he wanted, and they came to him. ¹⁴He appointed twelve that they might be with him and that he might send them out to preach ¹⁵and to have authority to drive out demons. ¹⁶These are the twelve he appointed: Simon (to whom he gave the name Peter), ¹⁷James son of Zebedee and his brother John (to them he gave the name Boanerges, which means "sons of thunder"), ¹⁸Andrew, Philip, Bartholomew, Matthew, Thomas, James son of Alphaeus, Thaddaeus, Simon the Zealot ¹⁹and Judas Iscariot, who betrayed him.

Listening to the Text in the Story: Genesis 17:3–8; 35:9–10; Exodus 3; 19; Deuteronomy 5:1–27; 1 Kings 19:8–18; Matthew 5:1–7:29; John 12:23–26.

Coming just after a transition passage that summarizes Jesus's ministry, this is the first episode in a larger section that closes at 8:21. The previous section (1:14–3:6) also began with a call and commissioning narrative, similar to this one (1:16–20). Throughout 3:13–8:21 we find various reactions to Jesus and his preaching, drawing out what it means that insiders have the "secret of the kingdom of God" given to them, while outsiders get everything in mystifying statements (4:11–12). In this initial text Jesus calls and appoints twelve of his followers to "be with him" and to participate in his mission of proclaiming the kingdom and driving out demons.

The setting on a mountainside evokes many significant events that took place on or near mountains in the biblical story. Mountains are places of encounters with God, making this episode a solemn occasion.[1] Moses encountered God in the burning bush at "Horeb, the mountain of God" (Exod 3:1),

---

1. Black, *Mark*, 106; Moloney, *Gospel of Mark*, 76.

and later returned to the mountain to receive the law (19:1–25). Elijah, after his dramatic battle with the prophets of Baal, encounters God on the very same mountain (1 Kgs 19:1–18). Jesus's most well-known and longest recorded teaching, "the Sermon on the Mount," is set "on a mountainside" (Matt 5:1).

Jesus's selection and special appointment of twelve from among his followers involves renaming three of them, an action that often goes along with God's call and special appointment in the biblical story. In Genesis 17:3–8, at the beginning of his redemptive mission, God gives Abram the new name Abraham ("father of many") because he will be the father of many nations. Later, in Genesis 35:9–10 God gives Jacob, Abraham's grandson, the new name Israel ("contends with God"), which foreshadows his and the nation's contentious relationship with God. Jesus renames three of his disciples, perhaps because these three will have a special relationship with him, forming an inner circle with him in the rest of Mark (5:37; 9:2; 13:3; 14:33).[2]

Naming is significant because it indicates an identity, as when Naomi wants to be called Mara, which means "bitter" (Ruth 1:20–21). Her tragic losses had left her feeling that she had been treated bitterly by God, but that was not the end of the story, as the book of Ruth narrates a sweet redemption. In another biblical story, Nabal fully lives up to his name, as he behaves foolishly when he encounters David's men. After his quick-thinking wife, Abigail, rescues him, she says to David, "His name means Fool, and folly goes with him" (1 Sam 25:25).

An identity conferred by God, however, indicates a person drawn into the great drama of redemption and claimed by God for his saving purposes. It also points to God's intimate knowledge of a person. In this passage, Jesus changes the names of three of the disciples, an indication of their special intimacy with Jesus.

EXPLAIN the Story

This episode opens much like other calling passages in Mark, such as 1:16–20 and 2:13–14. Jesus is on the move and sees certain individuals and calls them, who then respond by coming to him. While the language is slightly different here, the pattern is the same. Jesus has certain ones that "he wanted" (v. 13), and he called them and they responded obediently by coming to him. The Twelve are a specially appointed group from among the many who are listening

---

2. Marcus, *Mark 1–8*, 268.

to and following Jesus. From that larger group, he appointed the Twelve for a unique task.

That Jesus calls twelve of his followers to be sent on his behalf points to their being a reconstituted Israel. It is not the case that they replace Israel or that what eventually becomes the church replaces Israel. Jesus is calling historic Israel to return to God in faithfulness, which means becoming a people of justice and a light to the nations. At the same time, Jesus is performing Israel's role in acting justly and, throughout this section and beyond, reaching out to the gentiles (e.g., 5:1–20; 7:24–30). The Twelve, called to be "with Jesus," are Israel *in nuce* ("in a nutshell"), a remnant intended to grow so that it absorbs many other Jews who join in faithfulness to the God of Israel.

Mark mentions four tasks in connection with his appointment of these disciples: they are to be with Jesus, they will be sent out by him, they will preach, and they will have authority over demons (vv. 14–15). We must note carefully how these are related to one another because they are not four simultaneous and equal activities. The first two (to be "with" Jesus and "sen[t] out") belong together and are primary, and the second two ("to preach and to have authority to drive out demons") are dependent on the first two. The fundamental appointment of the disciples is to be with Jesus, which involves being sent out.

At first glance it seems that being with Jesus and being sent out involves a paradox. How can they be with Jesus while being away from him? For Mark, however, being with Jesus does not merely indicate proximity to him. It means, rather, that their agendas must be ordered by his kingdom agenda. Being with Jesus in Mark means doing what Jesus says, following his lead, recognizing the manner in which he is the Messiah and the true nature of the kingdom, and letting that shape how they inhabit the kingdom of God. This is why "being with" is compatible with "being sent." They do not need to be near Jesus to be with Jesus in terms of doing the things he does and relating to others according to his example.[3] The expression also informs the disciples' negative behavior, such as when everyone flees from Jesus (14:50) or when Peter denies that he was "with that Nazarene, Jesus" (14:67).

The one main commission, therefore, to which Jesus appoints the disciples is that they would be "with him," and this involves for the Twelve the two tasks of proclaiming the kingdom of God and having authority over demons, which are also the two main facets of Jesus's ministry up to this point in Mark. Jesus has been preaching about the arrival of the kingdom of God, calling his

---

3. Marcus, *Mark 1–8*, 267.

hearers to repent and take on the mode of life that embodies the reign of God. And he has been driving out unclean and evil spirits, restoring God's peace and relieving the suffering and oppression of God's people. The disciples are to carry on this very same work.

When Mark names the disciples whom Jesus calls to himself (vv. 16–19), he notes that Jesus renames Peter, James, and John, pointing to a special intimacy these three have with Jesus, forming an inner circle among the specially selected Twelve.[4] To Simon, Jesus gives the name "Peter," which means "rock," which could indicate stability or persistence and courage. Instances come to mind where he displays leadership and strength, and we could conclude that because of the role he will play in the early church, Peter will need to be this sort of person. But it can also mean hardheadedness, stubbornness, and failure to learn. Again, one could find examples of Peter's failures and his slowness to rightly comprehend Jesus's identity and mission.[5]

Jesus names James and John the "sons of thunder," but like with Peter, Mark does not explain why Jesus does so or what it means. His renaming of these three, however, indicates the close relationship he enjoyed with them that he did not necessarily have with the others. Mark's comment that Judas Iscariot is the one "who betrayed him" further darkens the shadow cast over the narrative. Coupled with the indication that John had been put in prison (1:14) and that the Pharisees began to plot to kill Jesus (3:6), this adds to the threatening tone of Mark's Gospel. Jesus's ministry was directed toward an eventual confrontation in Jerusalem, and it was carried out almost entirely under the threat of dangerous opposition. Jesus persisted in the face of all of this.

LIVE the Story

Authority over Demons?

The first half of Mark's Gospel reports a number of exorcisms. Jesus enacts the invasion of God's kingdom into a satanically enslaved creation by healing and driving out demons, and in this passage he delegates his authority over demonic spirits to his twelve specially appointed disciples. We have already discussed the reality of demons earlier, but this passage raises the question of whether the authority to drive out demons that Jesus delegates to the Twelve extends to all of his followers, including the contemporary church. Do Christians today

---

4. Moloney, *Gospel of Mark*, 79.
5. Black, *Mark*, 107; Marcus, *Mark 1–8*, 268–69.

have the authority to cast out demons? In working toward a helpful way of thinking about this, we can make a number of points from Scripture.

First, the spiritual realm is real, and there seems to be an order to it. Satan is the chief agent of evil and God's cosmic archenemy, whose power does not rival God's and who is subject ultimately to God and will be destroyed in the end when God restores and reclaims his world. There are also archangelic spiritual figures of cosmic rule who operate at a macrolevel, orienting mindsets, ideologies, prejudices, and cultural imaginations, so that humanity walks in ways of disobedience and does not experience life in God's world as God intended.[6] And at a localized level, affecting individuals, there are demonic spirits, as we see portrayed in Mark.

At a broad, cosmic level, the church opposes Satan and the powers and authorities—the New Testament's terms for cosmic rulers opposed to God— not by direct engagement but by resisting the perverted and corrupted ways of life to which humanity is enslaved. The church's task is to identify these corruptions (pride, greed, sensuality, malice, and idolatry) and to resist being conformed to them, cultivating instead godly virtues such as humility, love for one another, commitment to God's people, service to the church, reconciliation, and forgiveness. After writing at length about becoming a community that cultivates such practices (Eph 5:21–6:9), Paul rhetorically sums up Ephesians by speaking about this sort of spiritual warfare. He calls on the church to put on God's virtues in order to stand firm against the cosmic forces of darkness (6:10–18). We should look to the exhortations throughout that letter, therefore, to figure out how to carry out practically this spiritual warfare. Paul speaks of behaviors such as dealing with anger in a godly way as a powerful tool against Satan's goal to divide the church (4:26–27). When the church becomes a community that manifests godly virtues, it serves notice to the evil cosmic powers regarding Christ's lordship over them (3:10). Rather than direct engagement with these forces, becoming faithful new-creation communities displays God's triumph in Christ and indicates that their day of eventual destruction is coming (1 Cor 15:25–28).

Regarding the church's engagement with localized demonic spirits, however, there is no clear direction in the New Testament indicating that Christians have authority to speak to demons or how they might do so. In light of this, I offer the following observations. First, apart from Jesus giving authority to the Twelve to drive out demons (and not to all his followers), we have no

---

6. For a description of these cosmic rulers and how they functioned in Paul's Jewish worldview, see Timothy G. Gombis, *The Drama of Ephesians: Participating in the Triumph of God* (Downers Grove, IL: IVP Academic, 2010), 35–58.

commands in the New Testament to do this. Second, the only instance of someone other than one of the Twelve (or Paul) attempting to drive out a demon is in Acts 19, and in this case it did not go well:

> Some Jews who went around driving out evil spirits tried to invoke the name of the Lord Jesus over those who were demon-possessed. They would say, "In the name of the Jesus whom Paul preaches, I command you to come out." Seven sons of Sceva, a Jewish chief priest, were doing this. One day the evil spirit answered them, "Jesus I know, and Paul I know about, but who are you?" Then the man who had the evil spirit jumped on them and overpowered them all. He gave them such a beating that they ran out of the house naked and bleeding. (Acts 19:13–16)

Third, there are warnings against speaking into the spiritual realm when we have little information about how this realm functions or about whether and how we should engage it. Jude and 2 Peter contain warnings against those who do not respect authority and the cosmic order that God has instituted:

> Bold and arrogant, they are not afraid to heap abuse on celestial beings; yet even angels, although they are stronger and more powerful, do not heap abuse on such beings when bringing judgment on them from the Lord. But these people blaspheme in matters they do not understand. They are like unreasoning animals, creatures of instinct, born only to be caught and destroyed, and like animals they too will perish. (2 Pet 2:10–12; cf. Jude 8–10)

Unfortunately, as Walter Wink and Michael Hardin note, many of the strategies for casting out demons or engaging spiritual entities are developed from personal anecdotes or stories about experiences that are subject to interpretation and embellishment.[7] There is much that we do not know about the demonic realm, and with no clear word from Scripture we ought to be very hesitant about assuming that we have authority over demonic spirits to engage them directly or perform exorcisms.

Fourth, what we do know is that from the context of James 4:1–10, 1 Peter 5:6–11, and Ephesians 5–6, the cultivation of communities of virtue is powerful against the darkness. When God's people pursue humility, Satan

---

7. "Response to C. Peter Wagner and Rebecca Greenwood," in *Understanding Spiritual Warfare: Four Views*, ed. James K. Beilby and Paul Rhodes Eddy (Grand Rapids: Baker Academic, 2012), 199.

(the personal name standing in for any and all forces of darkness) departs. It is best, then, to recognize the reality of personal agents of evil in the world, both at the cosmic and personal level. Yet since Scripture focuses not on these entities but on the positive pursuit of cultivating communities of love, justice, reconciliation, and self-giving love, this positive orientation ought to consume our attention. Because God dwells in power among this sort of community, we can be confident that when God is truly among us, we are protected from any and all spiritual forces of darkness (1 John 5:18). And if we encounter demon-possessed people, we should consider appealing to them to call on the Lord, who can cleanse and purify and make a person new. God is powerful over all spiritual entities. Since he has not clearly granted this authority to the church, we ought to be wary of assuming we have it.

Mark 3:20-35

📖 LISTEN to the Story

²⁰Then Jesus entered a house, and again a crowd gathered, so that he and his disciples were not even able to eat. ²¹When his family heard about this, they went to take charge of him, for they said, "He is out of his mind."

²²And the teachers of the law who came down from Jerusalem said, "He is possessed by Beelzebul! By the prince of demons he is driving out demons."

²³So Jesus called them over to him and began to speak to them in parables: "How can Satan drive out Satan? ²⁴If a kingdom is divided against itself, that kingdom cannot stand. ²⁵If a house is divided against itself, that house cannot stand. ²⁶And if Satan opposes himself and is divided, he cannot stand; his end has come. ²⁷In fact, no one can enter a strong man's house without first tying him up. Then he can plunder the strong man's house. ²⁸Truly I tell you, people can be forgiven all their sins and every slander they utter, ²⁹but whoever blasphemes against the Holy Spirit will never be forgiven; they are guilty of an eternal sin."

³⁰He said this because they were saying, "He has an impure spirit."

³¹Then Jesus' mother and brothers arrived. Standing outside, they sent someone in to call him. ³²A crowd was sitting around him, and they told him, "Your mother and brothers are outside looking for you."

³³"Who are my mother and my brothers?" he asked.

³⁴Then he looked at those seated in a circle around him and said, "Here are my mother and my brothers! ³⁵Whoever does God's will is my brother and sister and mother."

Listening to the Text in the Story: Psalm 68:18–20; Isaiah 49:24–25; Ezekiel 33:30–33; Hosea 1:9; Romans 9:6–33; 2 Corinthians 4:4; Ephesians 2:1–3; Hebrews 6:1–12; 1 John 5:16–17.

In this passage, Jesus clarifies who is his family—those who belong to him and are truly "with" him. In the previous episode, he had appointed a group of twelve disciples to be with him in a special way, sending them out on his behalf (3:13–19). In the passage after this one (4:1–20), Jesus will identify two groups of people: those who are insiders of the kingdom and those who are on the outside. In the present text, Jesus explains that his family is not determined by physical relations, but rather those who belong to him are those who recognize the reality of the kingdom of God and live into its fullness by doing what God says to do.

Jesus's physical family frames this passage, arriving at the house in vv. 20–21 and then calling for Jesus in vv. 31–35. This is an instance of a Markan "sandwich"—an account in which the opening and closing of an incident is wrapped around another situation. The encounter with the teachers of the law from Jerusalem is situated inside of this encounter with Jesus's family.

Jesus's family, part one (vv. 20–21)
  Jesus and the teachers of the law (vv. 22–29)
Jesus's family, part two (vv. 30–35)

This passage displays two inadequate responses to Jesus, one by his family and the other by the teachers of the law. After observing what has been going on with Jesus's ministry, his family concludes that he is out of his mind, and they just want to get him home and out of the public eye. The teachers of the law from Jerusalem have already judged Jesus negatively (2:1–3:6), but now they claim that Jesus is carrying out his ministry under the power of Satan. If disciples are identified in terms of being oriented by Jesus's agenda, then these two reactions are complete failures.

The clarification of those who truly are God's people is a common theme throughout the scriptural narrative. Membership in the people of God is not determined by birth or family connection, and those who are teachers of the law cannot assume that they are part of God's people. This is the awful message that the prophet Hosea delivers to Israel. Because of Israel's unfaithfulness to God, they are called "not my people" (Hos 1:9). Rather than being a just people who manifested the character of the God of Israel, they had turned to the worship of the gods of other nations. The fact that they were physical descendants from Abraham, Isaac, and Jacob did not prevent God from calling them "not my people."

Through the prophet Ezekiel, God warned that his people could take no comfort in their outward indicators of membership if they did not cultivate obedience. God speaks to Ezekiel in very similar terms to Mark 3:35:

As for you, son of man, your people are talking together about you by the walls and at the doors of the houses, saying to each other, "Come and hear the message that has come from the LORD." My people come to you, as they usually do, and sit before you to hear your words, but they do not put them into practice. Their mouths speak of love, but their hearts are greedy for unjust gain. Indeed, to them you are nothing more than one who sings love songs with a beautiful voice and plays an instrument well, for they hear your words but do not put them into practice. (Ezek 33:30–32)

Ezekiel's audience loved to hear him preach. If these people were around in our day, they would listen to online sermons and devour Christian books. They would thoroughly enjoy these resources and enthusiastically talk to their friends about them. But God tells Ezekiel that they're going to be destroyed because they hear God's words but are not interested in doing what God says to do (vv. 27–29).

A few other texts from Jesus's ministry run along similar lines. John the Baptist's preaching attracted the attention of some Pharisees and Sadducees, to whom John issues a warning against presumption of membership in God's family:

But when he saw many of the Pharisees and Sadducees coming to where he was baptizing, he said to them: "You brood of vipers! Who warned you to flee from the coming wrath? Produce fruit in keeping with repentance. And do not think you can say to yourselves, 'We have Abraham as our father.' I tell you that out of these stones God can raise up children for Abraham. The ax is already at the root of the trees, and every tree that does not produce good fruit will be cut down and thrown into the fire. (Matt 3:7–10)

Elsewhere, amid a tense confrontation, Jesus again identifies the family to which his opponents belong, disputing the claim that they have Abraham or God as their father:

Jesus said to them, "If God were your Father, you would love me, for I have come here from God. I have not come on my own; God sent me. Why is my language not clear to you? Because you are unable to hear what I say. You belong to your father, the devil, and you want to carry out your father's desires. He was a murderer from the beginning, not holding to the truth, for there is no truth in him." (John 8:42–44)

Membership in the family of Jesus does not depend on church affiliation, family lineage, or some other social indicator that may point to being part of God's people. Jesus's family is marked out by those who hear what Jesus says to do and respond by doing it. The opposite responses in this passage point to attributing the kingdom's power to Satan and actively preventing Jesus from carrying out his mission.

EXPLAIN the Story

Jesus's Family Seeks Jesus (vv. 20–21)

The opening and closing portions of this narrative—the two outer layers of the Markan "sandwich"—emphasize family and the domestic sphere. The episode takes place in "a house," where Jesus and his disciples have gathered to eat. Mark mentions Jesus's family in v. 21 and then repeats several times Jesus's family relations in vv. 31–35. The repetition of family and the setting in a house provide the context in which Jesus clarifies who truly belongs to him. A crowd has gathered and, as elsewhere in Mark, prevents Jesus from taking care of the basic needs of sustenance along with his disciples.

Jesus's physical family heard about what was going on with the massive crowds coming to Jesus, and their response places them alongside others who were threats to his ministry. They went "to take charge of him," which translates a verb (*krateō*) that elsewhere in Mark is used to refer to Herod's arrest of John the Baptist (6:17), the chief priests' desire to arrest Jesus (12:12), and Jesus's eventual arrest in Gethsemane (14:46). His family, like these other opponents of the kingdom of God, are seeking to prevent Jesus from carrying out his mission of bringing in the fullness of God's reign. And they are motivated by their conviction that Jesus is "out of his mind" (3:21). It is ironic that while Jesus is with "his family" (made up of those who have gathered to hear him), his physical family occupies positions as outsiders, obstacles to what God is doing in Jesus.

Conflict with the Teachers of the Law (vv. 22–30)

Just after Mark mentions the opinion of Jesus's family, he introduces the teachers of the law. They have come down from Jerusalem and render their verdict that Jesus is "possessed by Beelzebul! By the prince of demons he is driving out demons" (v. 22). Beelzebul is another name for Satan, who appears in Jewish literature as the ruler of demons.[1] The name used here may mean "lord of the house," which fits well with the domestic setting of this passage and the reference to "the strong man's house" in v. 27.[2]

Jesus ironically "calls" these scribes to himself (v. 23), much like he called his disciples previously in v. 13. This small detail, along with Jesus's warning to them in vv. 28–30, indicates Jesus's appeal to them. There is still an opportunity for them to change their opinion, to repent of their opposition, and participate in the power of the kingdom. He calls them aside and speaks to them in a series of "parables" (v. 23), sayings that invite them to seriously consider the truth of the situation, with the hope of greater understanding. Jesus's response to the teachers' claims about him unfolds in three stages.

First, in vv. 23b–26, Jesus questions their claim at the commonsense level: the claim is simply absurd in light of how power works and the self-interested character of rulers. "Does it really make sense for Satan to initiate an assault against himself? Is this really how things work? If Satan wants to continue his enslaving rule over humanity and at the same time begin an operation of freeing humanity from his enslaving power, wouldn't that result in the toppling of his reign? Does that make any sense? If this is really Satan doing this, then he's finished!" He wants them to critically scrutinize their reaction. Is it reasonable for them to have arrived at such a conclusion?

Second, in v. 27, Jesus utters the "riddle" of the binding of the strong man. "No one can enter a strong man's house without first tying him up. Then he can plunder the strong man's house." The "strong man" here is Satan, who is the "god of this age" (2 Cor 4:4) and the "ruler of the kingdom of the air" (Eph 2:2). God's cosmic archenemy has hijacked God's good world and holds humanity enslaved. In apocalyptic Jewish texts, Satan's main occupation is leading the nations astray into idolatry and the pursuit of pleasure and greed, keeping humanity from obeying God and thus walking in his blessing (e.g., Jub. 10.1–14). The tragedy in Mark is that even Israel has become "the strong man's house," overrun with demons and in desperate need of rescue from the domain of darkness.

Jesus, God's appointed agent of bringing in God's life-giving rule, is freeing people from demonic possession and bringing healing with the spread of God's kingdom presence. His point here is that they are drawing the wrong conclusion if they think he is in league with Satan. The obvious lesson they should learn is that the only way he can be driving out demons is if he has in

---

1. Cf. Jub. 10.8; 11.4–6; 2 En. 29.4–5; T. Dan 1.7–8.
2. Strauss, *Mark*, 168.

some sense already defeated Satan. That is, if he is plundering the strong man's house, then he must have already broken into his house and subdued him.[3] The "plunder" here is people: Jesus is snatching individuals from the enslaving grip of demonic possession, sickness, and even greed, in the case of Levi (Mark 2:13–17). The teachers of the law witness Jesus casting out demons, and they should draw the sensible conclusion that he is doing this because he has already triumphed over the strong man, Satan.

Jesus's third response is not spoken in the form of riddles, but comes as a straightforward warning (vv. 28–29). Beginning with the solemn "truly" (*amēn*; lit. "amen"), Jesus warns the teachers of the law that they are in danger of committing an eternally grievous error. For them to witness Jesus's actions, his healings and exorcisms, along with the relief and the restoration to flourishing he is bringing to many people, and then to attribute all of this to the work of Satan is to put oneself in danger of eternal judgment. They ought to be drawing the conclusion that Jesus is the agent of Israel's God who is inaugurating the long-awaited and life-giving kingdom. But they are witnessing the kingdom of God at work and labeling it the work of Satan. This is a fatal move.

To do this is to blaspheme "against the Holy Spirit." Blasphemy in Scripture is abusive speech that denigrates or defames other people (1 Tim 6:4), God (Rom 2:24), or angels (2 Pet 2:10–12). At his baptism the Spirit descended upon Jesus, and God ripped apart the heavens to enter the world and initiate his kingdom work through Jesus (Mark 1:10). To witness the effects of this divine invasion and say that Satan is at work is to defame the Holy Spirit.

In v. 29, Jesus indicates that if the teachers of the law continue in this conviction, their sin has eternal consequences. If they turn from their opinion and respond positively to Jesus at this point, they can find forgiveness. But to observe what is happening and conclude that Satan is at work rather than God is damnable. While people can find forgiveness for any other sin they commit, to maintain this opinion to the point of settled conviction makes them "guilty of an eternal sin."

Jesus Redefines His Family (vv. 31–35)

Returning to Jesus's family, Mark notes that whereas they had already set out to "seize" or "arrest" him (*krateō*, v. 21), they now arrive at the house (v. 31). Significantly, they are "standing outside," in a different relation to Jesus than those gathered around him inside. In the next passage, Jesus will talk about those who are "insiders" to the kingdom and those who are "outside" it

---

3. Hooker, *Mark*, 116.

(4:10–11), so the detail about his mother and brothers "standing outside" is important. They sent someone in "to call him," which is ironic because in Mark it is Jesus who calls. He has called disciples to follow him (1:16–20; 2:13–17), called the Twelve and appointed them to a special mission (3:13–19), and even called the teachers of the law earlier in this passage (v. 23). This calling from his family is the wrong sort of call, however, diverting him from his mission. It does not arise from God's redemptive mission for Jesus but from the conviction that Jesus is out of his mind (v. 21).[4]

We may wonder how Mary, Jesus's mother, could appear in any other way than as one who had a clear-eyed conception of Jesus's identity. How is she now portrayed as one who is calling Jesus away from his mission? We must keep in mind that while Mary knew that God had appointed her child as the agent of God's salvation, her conception of what that redemption would look like was shaped by her culture's expectations of dramatic victory over gentile enemies. Like everyone else, she had no idea about the sort of Messiah Jesus was going to be.[5] And now, Jesus is upsetting the status quo and challenging those in power. All of this was likely making his family uncomfortable, and now they are becoming an obstacle to his mission, much like the crowds have been thus far in Mark's narrative.

Someone reports to Jesus that his family is "outside looking for you," but Mark's terminology is slightly more ominous. The verb translated "looking" is *zēteō*, which appears when the disciples and the crowds seek out Jesus, getting in the way of his time of solitude and prayer (1:37). It indicates a wrong sort of seeking, especially when it is used of Jesus's opponents who search for opportunities to arrest him and put him to death (11:18; 12:12; 14:1, 11).[6]

When he hears of this, Jesus asks those sitting around him about the identity of his family. "Who are my mother and brothers?" Referring to those who have gathered to hear what he has to say, Jesus makes the stunning claim in v. 34 that these people are his true family. "Here are my mother and my brothers!"

The family of Jesus is made up of all those who do God's will (v. 35). Jesus's physical family is not currently doing God's will. They are calling Jesus away from

---

4. There are conceptual and auditory similarities between the family's opinion of Jesus and their standing outside the house. They believe he is *exestē* (lit. "standing outside" himself or "out of his mind," v. 21), and they are *exō zētousin* ("outside seeking," v. 32). These similarities link his family's opinion and their situation as "outsiders" to Jesus's true family. This is not the end of the story, of course, and surely more than one of his siblings became part of the family of faith after his resurrection, including James, a leader in the Jerusalem church (Acts 21:18).

5. Scot McKnight, *The Real Mary: Why Evangelical Christians Can Embrace the Mother of Jesus* (Brewster, MA: Paraclete, 2007), 73–86.

6. Black, *Mark*, 113.

carrying out God's mission. The teachers of the law from Jerusalem are not doing God's will, either. They are running directly contrary to what God wants by not only failing to recognize God at work but attributing what God is doing to Satan! Only those who are gathered around Jesus to hear about the kingdom of God are considered his family. Membership in the family of God is not determined by physical lineage, social credentials, educational training, or the approval of the self-appointed religious elite. Those who are eager to hear what God says so that they might carry out God's will are considered the family of God.

LIVE the Story

The Unpardonable Sin

Christians with sensitive consciences may read this passage and be overcome with anxiety, wondering, "Have I committed the unpardonable sin?" When I taught undergraduates, students would occasionally ask me—in the privacy of my office—whether what they had done could be considered the unpardonable sin. These were typically young people who had lived for some period of their lives in disobedience or in rebellion against their parents. They usually had some sexual relationship with a boyfriend or girlfriend and, after changing their ways and becoming once again obedient to the faith, wondered if they had done something unforgivable.

These conversations were great opportunities to talk about the God of Christian Scripture, who is far more gracious than we can imagine, far more loving and forgiving than we can grasp, and infinitely more eager to restore, cleanse, redeem, and bless sinners than we ever could be. These conversations also revealed the sort of guilt people carry around, built up over the years from hearing about a kind of God who, rather than being completely unlike us in his infinite heart of love, has a heart very much like ours—small, vindictive, and given to payback rather than joyful redemption.

It is important to understand how the Gospels speak about sin that is unpardonable, along with a few other passages in the New Testament that speak of something similar. First John 5:16–17 contains these words:

> If you see any brother or sister commit a sin that does not lead to death, you should pray and God will give them life. I refer to those whose sin does not lead to death. There is a sin that leads to death. I am not saying that you should pray about that. All wrongdoing is sin, and there is sin that does not lead to death.

This passage is somewhat similar to what we find in Mark 3. We find a further text along these lines in Hebrews 6:4–8:

> It is impossible for those who have once been enlightened, who have tasted the heavenly gift, who have shared in the Holy Spirit, who have tasted the goodness of the word of God and the powers of the coming age and who have fallen away, to be brought back to repentance. To their loss they are crucifying the Son of God all over again and subjecting him to public disgrace. Land that drinks in the rain often falling on it and that produces a crop useful to those for whom it is farmed receives the blessing of God. But land that produces thorns and thistles is worthless and is in danger of being cursed. In the end it will be burned.

This is one of the most difficult texts in the New Testament, and certainly for young believers or those with sensitive consciences about a past lived in sin, it can lead to sheer terror.

In bringing Mark 3:28–29 into biblical-theological conversation with these other passages of warning in the New Testament, there are a number of things we can say. First, regarding Mark 3:28–29, and the parallel passages in Matthew 12:32 and Luke 12:10, Jesus directs his words toward those who specifically attribute the power by which Jesus is ministering to Satan and not to the Spirit of God. The "unforgiveable sin," therefore, is something very specific and is not at all broadened to other "serious" sins, even those that burden the conscience. While Christians may be overwhelmed by guilt at times for sins previously committed, they should shape their minds and inform their consciences with the overwhelming goodness of God and his overpowering forgiveness.

Second, as mentioned above, Jesus speaks these terrifying words as a warning. The scribes who are hearing this are still in a position where they may repent of their sinful thinking. In fact, Jesus speaks these words to shock them into repentance, causing them to reconsider their ways and the eternal consequences of their current course.[7] By extension, even if a person today is running the risk of committing this specific sin—of reading the Gospels and attributing the power by which Jesus lived and ministered to Satan rather than to God—it is still possible for them to change their opinion. Such a person may still turn and affirm that Jesus is the Messiah, the appointed one of God,

---

7. Augustine says it well: "It is not that this was a blasphemy which under no circumstances could be forgiven, for even this shall be forgiven if right repentance follows it" (Oden and Hall, *Mark*, 45).

and that he lived and ministered and cast out demons by the power of God's Spirit. Sinners may still seek God while he may be found, and if a person is still alive, it is still an opportunity for her or him to turn to the Lord and be forgiven (Isa 55:6–7).

Third, 1 John 5:16–17 is intended to offer assurance that God restores and gives life to those who seek him. In the context of this letter, the "sin that does not lead to death" is some sort of visible sin, as John mentions at the beginning of v. 16 ("if you see . . ."). He is not referring to sins of motive or thought but to some kind of sinful, outward action that a believing member of the church community commits. John does not refer to the severity of the sin, but we may assume that he is referring to anything that perhaps in our day we might consider truly heinous, a behavior that shocks our sense of morality. The "sin that does not lead to death" is not specified because in the logic of the passage, a range of sins is in view, and John is emphasizing here the community's responsibility to engage the situation and pray for that person. He is likely also assuming that the community will take further steps too, such as graciously confronting the situation with encouragements to enter a process of restoration.

This discussion is set against the "sin that leads to death." John notes that his readers should not intercede for a person who is engaged in that sort of sin. What does John have in mind here? Just as with Mark 3, we must respect the context and let the whole of 1 John define what he means. John refers to the sin of those who are causing trouble in the church receiving this letter, those who are denying that Jesus came in the flesh and whose teaching and divisive behavior are causing trouble.[8] These are people who have set themselves deliberately against the truth of God and are attempting to destroy the work of God in the world. They are not church members who have fallen into sin, even shocking or heinous sin, through a failure to be vigilant against temptation. Such brothers and sisters are the very people for whom John exhorts the community to pray. But those who deny the truth about Jesus Christ and who actively propagate this error to the destruction of the church are the ones who commit the "sin that leads to death." In this sense, this passage resembles Mark 3.

Fourth, turning to Hebrews 6, this passage does indeed contain some strong words, but it is a warning to a community that has committed itself to following Jesus and is in some way being pressured to consider a departure from faithful discipleship (Heb 2:1–4; 3:12–14; 4:1–11; 10:19–39). The warning in Hebrews 6:4–8 is based on the reality that those who take in scriptural

---

8. Colin G. Kruse, *The Letters of John*, PNTC (Grand Rapids: Eerdmans, 2000), 192.

teaching and bear the fruit of disobedience can only expect judgment. And it does assume that it is possible for people to begin a pursuit of discipleship and then to depart. The writer is reminding his readers that it is necessary to remain faithful and to encourage one another to continue in steadfast discipleship until the end (10:24–25). He does, however, continue with words of grace:

> Even though we speak like this, dear friends, we are convinced of better things in your case—the things that have to do with salvation. God is not unjust; he will not forget your work and the love you have shown him as you have helped his people and continue to help them. We want each of you to show this same diligence to the very end, so that what you hope for may be fully realized. We do not want you to become lazy, but to imitate those who through faith and patience inherit what has been promised. (Heb 6:9–12)

The writer is encouraged that his readers are bearing the fruit of salvation because he has witnessed their past faithfulness. And God rewards such faithfulness with further empowerment to continue in lives of discipleship. But God's empowering grace must be matched by diligence in perseverance on their part. This passage does not ultimately have to do with the unpardonable sin but with the threat of apostasy—that is, the awful possibility that people who begin in the faith might depart from Christ.[9]

Ultimately, Jesus affirms the magnanimous forgiveness of God in Mark 3:28, noting that "people can be forgiven all their sins and every slander they utter." Taken on its own, this is a staggering statement of the grace and forgiveness that sinners may find with God. He is eager to forgive any and all sin. He cleanses thoroughly and never holds grudges. This is not, of course, permission to sin, nor an indicator that God takes sin lightly. Rather, it points to God's eagerness to embrace those who call to him. If Jesus holds out the possibility that even the teachers of the law who claim that God's work is powered by Satan, then the offer of forgiveness and restoration is held out to all until the day of judgment.

---

9. Apostasy has to do with the considered, voluntary, and conscious departure from faith in Christ on the part of a person who has been a disciple of Jesus Christ. It is a rare but real possibility. It should not be understood as "losing one's salvation," as if it is the result of a lapse into disobedience, however severe. Sustained disobedience may lead to apostasy, but this is not necessarily the case. Settled and permanent apostasy is in this sense an unforgivable sin. For a biblical and theological discussion of apostasy, see Scot McKnight, "Apostasy," *DTIB* 58–60.

CHAPTER 16

Mark 4:1–20

📖 LISTEN to the Story

¹Again Jesus began to teach by the lake. The crowd that gathered around him was so large that he got into a boat and sat in it out on the lake, while all the people were along the shore at the water's edge. ²He taught them many things by parables, and in his teaching said: ³"Listen! A farmer went out to sow his seed. ⁴As he was scattering the seed, some fell along the path, and the birds came and ate it up. ⁵Some fell on rocky places, where it did not have much soil. It sprang up quickly, because the soil was shallow. ⁶But when the sun came up, the plants were scorched, and they withered because they had no root. ⁷Other seed fell among thorns, which grew up and choked the plants, so that they did not bear grain. ⁸Still other seed fell on good soil. It came up, grew and produced a crop, some multiplying thirty, some sixty, some a hundred times." ⁹Then Jesus said, "Whoever has ears to hear, let them hear." ¹⁰When he was alone, the Twelve and the others around him asked him about the parables. ¹¹He told them, "The secret of the kingdom of God has been given to you. But to those on the outside everything is said in parables ¹²so that, "'they may be ever seeing but never perceiving, and ever hearing but never understanding; otherwise they might turn and be forgiven!'" ¹³Then Jesus said to them, "Don't you understand this parable? How then will you understand any parable? ¹⁴The farmer sows the word. ¹⁵Some people are like seed along the path, where the word is sown. As soon as they hear it, Satan comes and takes away the word that was sown in them. ¹⁶Others, like seed sown on rocky places, hear the word and at once receive it with joy. ¹⁷But since they have no root, they last only a short time. When trouble or persecution comes because of the word, they quickly fall away. ¹⁸Still others, like seed sown among thorns, hear the word; ¹⁹but the worries of this life, the deceitfulness of wealth and the desires for other things come in and choke the word, making it unfruitful. ²⁰Others, like seed sown on good soil, hear

the word, accept it, and produce a crop—some thirty, some sixty, some a hundred times what was sown."

Listening to the Text in the Story: Deuteronomy 6:4–9; Psalm 29; 111:10; Isaiah 6:9–10; Ezekiel 3:27; 12:1–3; James 1:19–25.

This passage plays a crucial role in Mark's Gospel, especially in the section that runs to 8:21. An *inclusio* frames this section, formed by the repetition of a prophetic citation having to do with failure to perceive. In 4:12 Jesus quotes Isaiah 6:9–10, and in 8:18 he cites Jeremiah 5:21. In 4:1–20 Jesus explains that his teaching is going to distinguish between those who are insiders to the kingdom and those who are outside of it. The insiders will grasp "the secret" of the kingdom, but those outside of it will hear Jesus's teaching as mystifying statements. As Mark 4–8 progresses, we will begin to see a few interesting dynamics develop. Characters who are assumed to be "outsiders" surprisingly demonstrate their "insider" status by responding to Jesus rightly, while those we suppose are obvious "insiders" grow increasingly dull in their understanding. Mark's brilliantly subversive narration through this section should cause readers to question their assumptions about who is inside and who is outside the kingdom.

Mark 4:1–20 contains an unusually long portion of Jesus's teaching. It consists of an introduction (vv. 1–2), a parable (vv. 3–9), an interlude in which Jesus speaks privately with his disciples (vv. 10–12), and the explanation of the parable (vv. 13–20). The passage makes two related points. First, Jesus teaches in parables in order to both obscure his teaching and make it plain. To those who are of the kingdom—those with ears to hear—Jesus's teaching will make sense. But outsiders to the kingdom will be confused by what Jesus says. Second, despite the prevalence of outsiders—those who do not bear the fruit of the kingdom— the kingdom will continue to grow, and the word will bear abundant fruit.

This passage evokes the scriptural theme of the disobedience of God's people expressed in terms of dulled senses. Jesus quotes Isaiah 6:9–10, a passage in which God commissions the prophet Isaiah to speak on God's behalf to his people, who have senses but no understanding or perception:

Then I heard the voice of the Lord saying, "Whom shall I send? And who will go for us?"
    And I said, "Here am I. Send me!"
    He said, "Go and tell this people:

'Be ever hearing, but never understanding;
  be ever seeing, but never perceiving.'
Make the heart of this people calloused;
  make their ears dull
  and close their eyes.
Otherwise they might see with their eyes,
  hear with their ears,
  understand with their hearts,
and turn and be healed." (Isa 6:8–10)

This passage from Isaiah follows a chapter that expresses God's relationship to Israel in agricultural terms, like the several parables in Mark 4. God had carefully cultivated a vineyard that produced only bad fruit (Isa 5:1–2), representing Judah, a people among whom God expected to find justice, but was filled with bloodshed instead (v. 7). Their judgment is expressed in terms of a failure of perception: "Therefore my people will go into exile for lack of understanding" (v. 13a).

God spoke to his people in similar language through the prophet Ezekiel, calling him to put on a dramatic representation of going off into exile:

The word of the LORD came to me: "Son of man, you are living among a rebellious people. They have eyes to see but do not see and ears to hear but do not hear, for they are a rebellious people.

"Therefore, son of man, pack your belongings for exile and in the daytime, as they watch, set out and go from where you are to another place. Perhaps they will understand, though they are a rebellious people." (Ezek 12:1–3)

In Mark 4:1–20, Jesus draws on this tradition to explain how it is that the proclamation of the kingdom will go out and be heard by many. Yet not all will perceive it; not everyone will grasp it with true understanding. Those who do understand demonstrate that they are kingdom inhabitants, but those who do not are outside the kingdom. As indicated above, genuine surprises await Mark's readers, as expectations of who is inside and who is outside the kingdom are subverted.

In the parable, three of the four types of soil fail to produce kingdom fruit, though the good soil of which Jesus speaks produces at an astounding rate. The kingdom of God, because its growth is powered by God, will not be prevented from growing and bearing fruit. God had promised his people that he would give them a new heart (Ezek 36:24–28). Though the proclamation of the kingdom faces the obstacle of people who fail to perceive aright, God's work will go on.

The unstoppable growth of the kingdom may be related to another image that is introduced in this section of Mark and that continues throughout chapters 4–8, and that is Jesus's sovereign kingship over the sea. Mark notes that the crowd was so large that Jesus "got into a boat and sat in it out on the lake" (v. 1). The Greek expression for what Jesus does is quite unusual. Jesus got "into a boat to sit on the sea" (*eis ploion embanta kathēsthai en tē thalassē*). Does he really mean for Jesus to be sitting "on the sea?" Who sits on the sea? Mark's first audiences would have immediately answered, "God!" This is a scriptural allusion that portrays Jesus in terms of the authoritative character of the creator God. Psalm 29 extols God's supreme power over a range of fearsomely awesome entities. In the ancient world, few were feared more than the sea, which was regarded as a chaotic and threatening deity. Psalm 29 portrays God as supreme over sea, thundering in triumph over "the waters" and "the flood" as a champion standing over a defeated foe:

> The voice of the LORD is over the waters;
>> the God of glory thunders,
>> the LORD thunders over the mighty waters. (v. 3)
> [. . .]
> The LORD sits enthroned over the flood;
>> the LORD is enthroned as King forever. (v. 10)

This psalm expresses a common image in Scripture, and Mark depicts Jesus as filling this role with reference to the sea that only the God of Israel plays. Jesus is doing what only the God of Israel, the creator God, can do. Jesus's stilling of the storm and waves (Mark 4:35–41) and his walking on the water (6:45–56) should also be understood in this light. Together with Mark's stress on Jesus as a teacher, this image puts emphasis on Jesus in his uniquely authoritative role. Jesus is not just any teacher. He is God himself, the one whose voice thunders over the sea. His word goes out, and despite the prevalence of hard hearts and dull senses, the fruit of the kingdom will be produced because of God's kingship.

EXPLAIN the Story

Introduction (vv. 1–2)

The introduction to this passage slows down the fast-paced narrative by extensively describing the scene. Most of the episodes to this point have been brief, spare in detail, and set in rapid-fire sequence. Mark slows down at this point to set this pivotal passage front and center. He opens the scene with Jesus beginning to teach by the Sea of Galilee.[1] He mentions this three times in vv. 1–2 ("teach," "taught" and "teaching"), which, combined with the allusion to Psalm 29, focuses our attention on Jesus as authoritative teacher. The crowd is so large that Jesus cannot stand on the shoreline to teach them. As his ministry has progressed, the gathered groups have grown in size so that this is his largest audience yet.

Jesus began to teach using parables, a term that can indicate a variety of stories, riddles, or fables. New Testament scholar C. H. Dodd offered this concise description: "At its simplest the parable is a metaphor or simile drawn from nature or common life, arresting the hearer by its vividness or strangeness, and leaving the mind in sufficient doubt about its precise application to tease it into active thought."[2] Parables appear throughout the Gospels in different forms, and Jesus uses them rather than straightforward lecture-style teaching, in order to provoke his hearers to ponder the realities associated with the kingdom. Jesus's use of parables in Mark, however, is more complex, as noted in vv. 10–12.

The Parable of the Sower (vv. 3–9)

The introduction (v. 3) and conclusion (v. 9) to the parable are designed to arrest attention, with Jesus repeating the exhortation to perceive with the senses. He urges his hearers, saying, "Listen!" The NIV represents the striking opening in v. 3 well with the exclamation point, but the Greek is even more emphatic. Mark includes appeals to the ears and eyes (*akouete. idou*, "Listen! Behold!"). It may be that the "behold" following Jesus's emphatic command to listen is merely a narrative device to begin a story, but in light of the importance of verbs of perception throughout the rest of Mark, it is better to read the opening of Jesus's parable with doubled-up commands to pay close attention: "Listen! Look! A farmer went out to sow . . ."[3] After he finishes speaking the parable, he repeats his exhortation to perceive it (v. 9).

---

1. When *hē thalassa* appears by itself, the NIV translates it as "the lake." When the same term appears in connection with its proper name, the NIV translates it as "Sea of Galilee." Other versions translate the term "the sea" whenever it appears. "Lake" is appropriate in that it represents the size of the Sea of Galilee, which is 65 square miles, roughly thirteen miles from north to south and about eight miles from east to west. For the sake of comparison, the smallest of the Great Lakes, Lake Ontario, is 7,320 square miles. While "lake" makes good sense for modern readers, it misses the allusion that ancient hearers would have caught. "The sea" was a threatening element and represented the anti-God forces of chaos that constantly threatened to undo creation. This characteristic of "the sea" is crucial in this passage, along with several others in Mark.

2. C. H. Dodd, *The Parables of the Kingdom* (New York: Scribner, 1961), 5.

3. Marcus, *Mark 1–8*, 292.

Jesus introduces a farmer who sows seed in a field by casting it abroad. Inevitably, the seed lands on different kinds of ground. Some of it lands along the trampled and hard-packed path, and because the seed does not fall into ruts prepared by the farmer, birds eat it up (v. 4). Other seeds fall on rocky places, where the soil is shallow (v. 5). Farmers would clear a field of rocks and boulders while tilling it, but some may have remained just under the surface. Because there's only a thin layer of soil in some places, the seed springs up quickly but dies, because it cannot put roots down deep (v. 6).

The third landing spot is "among thorns" (v. 7), which grow up around the plant and choke it out, preventing it from flourishing and producing grain. Finally, some seed finds good, rich soil that produces a wonderfully surprising amount, multiplying thirty, sixty, and a hundred times (v. 8). The uneven multiples (rather than thirty, sixty, ninety) may represent the abundant fruitfulness of the seed and rich soil that produces "explosive" growth.[4]

Agricultural metaphors are found throughout Scripture. When God speaks to his people through Isaiah about his expectations that they would be a fruitful people, he does so in the parable of the vineyard (Isa 5:1–7). Paul uses agricultural imagery when he speaks about his partnership with other early Christian ministers (1 Cor 3:5–9). One plants, says Paul, another waters, but it is God who makes things grow. The writer of Hebrews uses similar imagery to illustrate his point regarding those who enjoy rich spiritual blessings but do not bear fruits of obedience (Heb 6:7–8).

It only makes sense that agricultural metaphors appear so often. Many of the intended original audiences for biblical texts lived in agrarian cultures and were familiar with farming practices. Agrarian metaphors can also be especially helpful since they capture the complex realities involved with ministry and community life in the kingdom of God. Successful farming requires good soil, the right sort of planting technique, careful cultivation, and total dependence on the larger climatological forces that create good weather. And this is to say nothing of the mysteries involved in growth and life. Therefore, even though such images are common in Scripture, understanding these complex dynamics is perhaps something we have lost in our contemporary world that is the result of a powerful technological revolution. Unfortunately, our conception of Christian ministry is often shaped by our technologized, manipulated, and mechanized society.

Jesus concludes his parable with a strong exhortation to listen carefully and give close consideration (v. 9). In effect he is saying, "It is crucial that you

---

4. Black, *Mark*, 119.

get this! Your grasp of my ministry and the character of the kingdom rides on your understanding, so if you can hear what I am saying, then listen up!"

Jesus and the Disciples in Private (vv. 10–12)

At some point after his public teaching, the disciples ask Jesus about the parables, either about their meaning or why he is now using them in his teaching. Jesus responds with some shocking statements that raise serious theological questions. He tells them that "the secret of the kingdom" has been given to them, but he is speaking in parables in order to confuse those who are outside the kingdom to prevent them from repenting. For those outside the kingdom, "everything is said in parables" in the sense of confounding statements. Those who belong to the kingdom of God will increasingly perceive the identity of Jesus and the reality of the kingdom, but outsiders will be increasingly baffled, hearing only mystifying statements leading to confusion and remaining cut off from the secret of the kingdom.

Jesus reveals his intentions through the quotation from Isaiah 6:9–10 in v. 12. The "so that" preceding the quotation indicates the purpose of his use of parables. In their seeing, outsiders are going to be prevented from perceiving, and in their hearing they are going to be prevented from understanding: "Otherwise they might turn and be forgiven!" This strikes readers as completely counterintuitive to Jesus's mission. Does he not want people to repent and believe the gospel? Why else is he traveling around and preaching? Why does Jesus say this, and how can we deal with the difficult theological problem of Jesus intentionally confusing his hearers so that they will not have the opportunity to repent?

It certainly seems that Jesus is teaching a sort of "hard determinism" here, indicating that God has predestined certain people for damnation and that Jesus is intentionally teaching in a confusing way so that they will not repent and be saved. It appears that the choice to repent is not truly theirs, since God is purposefully keeping them from it. Yet within the larger context of Mark, Jesus's words here make good sense. As the narrative unfolds, it turns out that Jesus's words are a warning directed to insiders, those who are complacent about being "in" the kingdom. In fact, his real target is the disciples.

As Mark 4:1–8:21 progresses, those who assume they're "obviously in" are not the insiders they thought they were. The disciples, those who were told they were "in," begin to be confused by Jesus's words, while those who are "obviously out" demonstrate that they are insiders by rightly perceiving Jesus and responding to him faithfully. Unexpected characters grasp Jesus's difficult sayings, while the disciples grow increasingly baffled, even by Jesus's plain statements (e.g., 8:14–18).[5] In light of how this dynamic unfolds, therefore, Jesus's words in vv. 11–12 are meant as a warning to the complacent and presumptuous who assume that because of their status as insiders they do not need to pay close attention to Jesus to make sure they really "get" the true nature of the kingdom.

There is, therefore, no hard determinism here. Everyone's status with reference to the kingdom as insider or outsider is undetermined. Jesus's exhortations to "hear" and "listen" really do indicate that participation in the kingdom is open-ended and depends on hearers' response to Jesus and his teaching.[6]

The "secret of the kingdom" to which Jesus refers in v. 11 is not merely awareness of who Jesus is, since he has been drawing massive crowds wherever he goes. Mark's portrayal of the crowds as a threat to Jesus's ministry may point us in the right direction. The Greek term for "secret" (*mystērion*) refers to something that cannot be known unless God reveals it. Paul uses this term in several contexts with reference to the new work that God is doing in the church, uniting Jewish and non-Jewish Jesus-followers in one body (Rom 16:25; Eph 3:4–5; Col 1:26–27). This was unforeseen in the Scriptures but is a new move of God in anticipation of the fulfillment of prophetic expectations in the future age when Israel is restored along with the nations.

Interestingly, Paul uses the term in contexts in which he refers to his cross-shaped ministry, which subverts human assumptions about how things ought to be done (1 Cor 2:7; Eph 3:2–13). Rather than impressive displays of powerful rhetoric, Paul's ministry was one of weakness and suffering. And this was intentional, for he knew that his apostleship was most obviously authentic if it resembled the life of the one he represented. The cultural pressures to shape his ministry by self-assertion and self-promotion came from a sinister source. Paul conducted his ministry this way because this is the only way God works. If God triumphs through the cross, then his ministers must also be shaped by the cross, which is the wisdom of God (1 Cor 1:18–2:16). God's wisdom is his way of working, which subverts human assumptions about power and "the normal way of doing things."

The "secret of the kingdom" is closely related to this. *It has to do with the sort of Messiah that Jesus is and the kind of kingdom he is initiating.* The "secret" is the kingdom's countercultural character. God's kingdom does not

---

5. Beyond the discrete section of 4:1–8:21, this theme of outsiders "getting" Jesus and what he is about continues until the very end of the Gospel. The climactic confession of Jesus's identity in Mark is made by a Roman centurion, an obvious outsider to the people of God (15:39).

6. See also the helpful discussion of vv. 10–12 in Klyne Snodgrass, *Stories with Intent: A Comprehensive Guide to the Parables of Jesus*, 2nd ed. (Grand Rapids: Eerdmans, 2018), 157–64.

work in the way that the world works. It does not come by human power, military might, triumphant displays of self-importance, or violent overthrow of the Romans. And Jesus is not going to be that sort of Messiah, one who resembles a Maccabean hero, leading an uprising to finally rid the land of the hated Romans. Jesus is not going to play to cultural expectations. He is headed to the cross, his life is marked by the cross, his kingdom is the community shaped by the cross, and he calls others to to take up the cross and follow him in self-giving servanthood along with him.

The "secret" is that the kingdom starts in smallness and weakness and will come in power in the future age. The "secret" is that the kingdom includes many more people than everyone expected—especially from the sinners, outsiders, and gentiles. The reality that the kingdom has this character is one that many are going to miss, because they are absorbed with their own preconceived notions of what God *must* do, who Jesus *must* be, and how the kingdom *must* come. Popular expectations and assumptions, along with hatred of the Romans and desire for revenge and liberation, would cause many in Jesus's audience to overlook or reject the reality of Jesus's call to take up a cross and follow him in the way of the cross.

Jesus Interprets the Parable (vv. 13–20)
Jesus begins his interpretation of the parable with a tough word of challenge, indicating the importance of grasping his teaching (v. 13). He explains that the seed represents the word of the kingdom going out to the world, and it is cast abroad just like the seed is cast indiscriminately around the field, landing in spots that are variously prepared. Just as the parable contains four sorts of landing spots, there are four different kinds of reception of the word. As we consider the four soils, we need to keep in mind the "secret" of the kingdom. This will help us understand that Jesus is referring to "the word" in the specific sense of the message of a cross-shaped kingdom with a cross-oriented Messiah. We will also see that the responses to the word are more specific than is apparent on an immediate reading of this passage.

The seed that falls along the path and is eaten up by birds (v. 4) represents a situation in which Satan comes and takes away the word as soon as a person hears it (v. 15). This is not a general action on the part of Satan, one in which a person hears of salvation but then immediately forgets about it because the moment passes and it is removed from their memory. In the Gospel of Mark, Satan's opposition to Jesus is very specific, focused toward preventing Jesus from being the cross-directed Messiah who goes the way of weakness and self-giving love. Mark does not say much about Jesus's temptation by Satan in 1:12–13, and it seems that he wants his readers to regard the temptation in light of Jesus's rebuke to Peter in 8:33. Peter is enthusiastic about Jesus as Messiah but refuses to hear any talk of going to Jerusalem to be put to death. Satan's strategy in 1:12–13 most likely involves tempting Jesus to embody his role through some spectacular display, through grasping after power and prestige, leading a revolutionary movement to get rid of Rome and establish the kingdom of God. *Satan does not mind if Jesus is the Messiah, but he does not want him going to the cross.* He wants Jesus to be the Messiah shaped by the corruptions of this world—self-assertion, self-promotion, and grasping after power. The opposition of Satan to the cross should inform Satan's action of taking away the word in v. 15.

Keep in mind that all of Galilee was rife with kingdom fever, longing for the arrival of God's messiah. Jesus knows that this fervor is mixed with desires for a powerful, revolutionary messiah who would spark a military revolt through spectacular displays of heroism leading to an uprising. In this highly charged context, Jesus is preaching about an unexpected kingdom, an unanticipated Messiah, and a countercultural people of God. This is why he keeps tamping down expectations, telling people to keep quiet and not spread the word about him. If momentum grows, the expectations will get out of hand, and the message of the cross will be overshadowed.

All of this is to say that the way Satan "snatches away the word" is not by removing gospel preaching from a person's consciousness as we might conceive of it. Satan does so by obscuring its orientation by the cross, by taking away Jesus's message of a Messiah who goes to the cross, who refuses to grab for power, who gives his life for others, and who calls for kingdom participants to take up their crosses.

Satan takes away the word by clouding Jesus's message of the cross with mounting revolutionary fervor, so that people respond positively to Jesus because they think he is going to be the sort of messiah they want him to be. This is why Mark portrays the huge crowds as an obstacle to Jesus's ministry. They represent an indication that the message of the cross is being obscured. If they are responding out of a feeling that their desires are going to be met, the huge crowds, far from being a positive sign of the kingdom's health, represent what it looks like when Satan snatches away the word of the cross.

Ironically, modern readers of Mark usually regard popular and enthusiastic response to Jesus as a great thing. But we miss that in a culture of celebrity, self-promotion, and grasping after power, the gospel gets corrupted so that ministries are evaluated by their size, their "energy," and the celebrity magnetism of the pastor. Mark would not regard these realities kindly.

In vv. 16–17, Jesus interprets the seed that falls on the rocky places (v. 5). Like the seed that sprouts but withers quickly because of the shallow soil, these people hear the word and receive it immediately with joy. Perhaps Jesus is referring to the many who receive healing throughout Mark and others who are caught up in the hope and promise attached to the arrival of God's Messiah. But they "quickly fall away" because of the "trouble or persecution" that "comes because of the word." Jesus's call to a cross-shaped kingdom has nothing to do with sentimental notions of how great things will be after committing to follow Jesus. His call is to the hard road, to faithfulness to the point of the cross, and especially to crucifying foolish expectations that have their roots in culturally generated notions of how the kingdom ought to be. Trouble and persecution will alienate people who set out to follow Jesus because of sentimental hopefulness. When the true character of the kingdom is revealed, they are no longer interested.

In vv. 18–19, the third group of people are like the seed that lands among the thorns (v. 7). Just as the thorns grew up and choked the plants, the word is choked out and made unfruitful by "the worries of this life, the deceitfulness of wealth and the desires for other things." These things do not necessarily pull people away or cause them to depart, as in v. 17. Here, the word is rendered ineffective when other values and agendas enter in. It is choked from the inside.

Just as with Satan taking away the word by corrupting the message with a conception of the kingdom achieved through power, Jesus indicates that the worries of "this life" [lit. "this age," *tou aiōnos*], the deceitfulness of wealth, and the desires for other things are ways that the kingdom is corrupted. People initially respond to the word but then attach the kingdom agenda to some other earthly movement, such as loyalty to a political cause or party. Perhaps some people imagine that participation in the kingdom is a way to get rich, or that the kingdom can be advanced through financial resources. Both of these involve deception. The way humans imagine advancing a cause usually involves one or another kind of human strength—money, political power, or fame. Jesus does not refer to the "desires for other things" so that people will be tempted to depart the kingdom for them. He indicates the desires for other things that creep into the church's imagination that prevent God's people from faithfully embodying kingdom life.

These are all ways of choking the word, making it unfruitful. In these situations the word of the cross does not produce a cross-shaped community. Other desires have entered in, and another agenda is driving the community to be a different sort of people. It will always be the human temptation to shape the gospel into our own image, making Jesus the kind of Messiah we want him to be and transforming his kingdom after our own agendas.

Finally, in v. 20 Jesus interprets the seed that fell on good soil (v. 8), and by this time the meaning of this last response to the word is self-evident. These are the people who hear the word about the kind of Messiah that Jesus is and the true character of the kingdom, and they receive it. They recognize Jesus as the Son of God and perceive that his mission involves a march to the cross and that his kingdom calls for a radical commitment. And they embrace it. They see the way of discipleship along this difficult path as the true way of life, and they give themselves to it. These are the ones who become fruitful in an unexpectedly superabundant way. Against all expectations, the fruit multiplies at an exponential rate in accordance with Jesus's upside-down kingdom.

This passage is often read as an exhortation to avoid being one of the first three soils and to become cultivated soil in which the word can flourish. Insofar as audiences reflect on this text to discern the character of their reception of the cross-oriented preaching of the kingdom, they are reading the text faithfully. At the same time, the text is more of a description than an exhortation. Jesus is pointing ahead to the dynamics that are going to unfold in the rest of Mark's narrative. The word of the cross will be proclaimed, and it will find different responses. Big crowds will be so taken with news about the kingdom that they will fail to grasp its true character, and other agendas will overtake it so that it will not bear fruit. But cultivated soil will be found, as unexpected people rightly perceive what Jesus is about.

LIVE the Story

The "Secret" of the Kingdom

Jesus speaks of the secret of the kingdom given especially to his disciples. It is interesting that Jesus speaks of something secret, even while there is an overwhelming crowd attracted to Jesus. As I indicated above, the "secret" of the kingdom has to do with its cross-shaped character. Jesus is a cross-oriented Messiah who defies the expectations of his culture. He is not impressive by human standards. He is not a military hero who will play to the national longings for vengeance against the Romans. He will not confer social capital and prestige on those who follow him. And his kingdom is cross-shaped. It calls for repentance—a change of life-direction, a reorientation of relational patterns, and a transformation of ambition.

Because these are the realities of Jesus and his kingdom, many in Jesus's day missed it. It remained a "secret." Everyone was looking for the kingdom and God's messiah, but their expectations were shaped by their culture and driven by their longings for vindication. None of this is to pass judgment on the first-century Jewish culture from a standpoint of superiority. We need to hold this reality up to our own situations, in order to examine ourselves. In what ways do Jesus and his kingdom remain unknown to us? Is it a "secret" that we have not managed to find? Are our churches and Christian communities imitating the crowds in Mark? Is our enthusiasm about Jesus an indication of our passion for *our version* of Jesus and his kingdom?

Our culture of consumerism has oriented the way we think about doing ministry and going to church. We do demographic analyses and engage in market research, and there may be good reasons for doing so. We must take care, however, that our imaginations are not shaped by trying to please people or accommodating the gospel to what we think will make people happy. We may end up leaving the reality of Jesus and his kingdom far behind in our efforts to build impressive churches. Issuing this warning is infinitely far easier than heeding it, however.

During my seminary years, I was an intern in the college ministry of a large church. We told ourselves that while our ministry had big numbers and looked on the outside like a megachurch, we weren't a "church growth" church. We had been founded on the preaching of the word, and we told ourselves that our large numbers indicated faithfulness to God rather than shrewd market analysis. We were very attuned, however, to the reality of attendance week in and week out, and to the "energy" during our gatherings. I remember one particular Tuesday staff meeting, during which we spent hours vigorously discussing the timing of various segments during the service and the transitions between the opening, the music, and the message. Things had not gone smoothly the previous Sunday, and several of us were quite upset about the lack of "excellence" in our presentation. Our pastor in particular felt the pressure to continually produce a compelling Sunday morning experience because of the need to demonstrate healthy attendance numbers to the senior staff.

After that meeting, we went to lunch, and our pastor was visibly upset. He lamented that we had just spent four hours working through the superficial aspects of our presentation, as if all we did on a Sunday morning was put on a show. We talked about the difficulty of maintaining integrity within a large church that came with the pressure of performance reviews and the constant expectation of keeping up the "energy" in order to cultivate regular attendance.

Indeed, many pastors face this challenge. In a culture saturated with entertainment options, shaped to choose which offering from among many is the most pleasing, it is extremely difficult to build a ministry in which we preach a cross-shaped Messiah and call on people to join a cross-oriented kingdom. It is difficult to build and nurture communities that retain the shape of the cross. *A pastor's ambition to build a large church may be the first thing that should be nailed to the cross.* That may be the first step in fostering a community that finds and embodies the "secret" of the kingdom.

Satan: Enemy of God and of the People of God

This passage portrays Satan as taking away the word that is preached. It may be a frightening thought for some that we can hear the Scripture proclaimed and that Satan can take away what we have heard. Or perhaps it is discouraging that unbelievers can hear the gospel presented to them, and Satan blocks them from hearing it or removes it from their minds so that they do not remember anything they heard. But this passage, and others in the New Testament that portray Satan's activity, do not mean to communicate this.

Satan appears throughout Scripture as the archenemy of God and of God's people (Job 1–2; Zech 3:1–2). Throughout the New Testament, and very much in line with developments in contemporary Judaism, Satan is portrayed as the ruler of this present evil age who, in league with a range of other anti-God cosmic rulers, ensures the presence within human cultures of perverted ideologies, corrupted mindsets, selfish patterns of life oriented by greed, and various idolatries that enslave humanity. Paul calls him the "the god of this age" (2 Cor 4:4), and the "ruler of the kingdom of the air" (Eph 2:2), which indicates that he works mainly to pervert human experience at a very broad level, guaranteeing that this truly is "the present evil age" (Gal 1:4). In passages where Satan and his cosmic associates are mentioned, Paul notes his readers' former lives when they lived an accord with "the ways of this world," "gratifying the cravings of our flesh and following its desires and thoughts" (Eph 2:1–3).

For Paul, then, Satan works at a macrolevel to pervert human experience, so that humanity will be turned away from God by following their own desires in ways of life that are ultimately destructive. Satan does not work on each individual, and he is not omnipresent so that while one person is experiencing the temptation of Satan in one way, another person in some other part of the world is being attacked by Satan in another way. Some Christians imagine the activity of Satan in accord with fantastic novels or films that dramatize a kind of "spiritual warfare," so that the many episodes of our daily lives are arenas in which we encounter Satan in battle.

Satan's aim with regard to the church is to see it broken apart through division. In Ephesians 4:26, Paul exhorts his readers to avoid sinning through anger. They must see to it that anger in the church is dealt with properly so that it does not fester, become settled bitterness, and lead to division. Paul restates his exhortation in v. 27 by urging them to "not give the devil a foothold." He is not indicating that Satan is personally taking an interest in their community there in Asia Minor. Rather, Paul is noting that the enemy's method of destroying churches is through divisions that develop when people do not pursue reconciliation and the resolution of grievances. Engagement with Satan, then, is the metaphorical way of articulating concrete practices. That is, the manner in which the church battles Satan or participates in spiritual warfare is through pursuing practices of peacemaking in the church, graciously confronting conflicts, confessing sin, and forgiving one another in the same way that God has forgiven us in Christ (cf. vv. 31–32).

We find similar dynamics in James 4:1–10. Within this larger context, James is calling on his hearers to treat each other justly, to avoid fights in the church, and to put aside their selfish agendas in favor of experiencing joy together as a community. He rebukes them for their pride, which is the source of many of their conflicts. He will then go on to rebuke them for slandering and call on them to stop judging one another (vv. 11–12). In the middle of all of that, James tells them to submit to God and to resist the devil. If they do this, the devil will flee from them (v. 7). This is not an indication that they are somehow to confront Satan, God's cosmic archenemy who inhabits the spiritual realm. It is, rather, another way of talking about their resistance of temptations to give in to self-seeking, selfishness, and stubbornly pushing and praying for the advancement of their own agendas (v. 3). If they identify these sinful patterns and stop them, no longer judging and fostering conflicts, they will be resisting Satan, refusing to further his agenda of the destruction of their community. Cultivating humility in this way, seeking to foster the unity of the church, is their submission to God.

This is not to say that Satan is not real. He is, indeed. It is to properly identify his activity as perverting humanity by supplying an endless array of available patterns of destructive behavior that constitute disobedience to God, do tragic damage to communities and relationships, and are ultimately enslaving. When we give in to these enticing ways of life, we are "letting Satan fill our hearts" (cf. Acts 5:3) and are giving in to Satan's agenda. According to the New Testament, we properly resist Satan when we identify the many corruptions and distortions in our own lives and strenuously replace them by pursuing godly virtue.

We do not need to fear attacks from Satan himself, for in the spiritual realm we are in Christ, sealed by the Holy Spirit, protected from the evil one, and kept by the power of God (Eph 1:13; 1 John 5:18; Jude 1). As communities of faith, we recognize that Satan's strategies are for unsettled anger to lead to bitterness and to lead to outbursts of anger and slander against others, and for churches ultimately to divide. We resist Satan when we cultivate communities of humility, joy, self-sacrificial service, and mutual care. Perhaps this is why Paul does not only commend unity but commands his readers to "make every effort to keep the unity of the Spirit through the bond of peace" (Eph 4:3).

Becoming Fruitful Soil

As mentioned above, this parable is not necessarily a mini-sermon on how to avoid being a variety of bad soils and how to be good soil. The parable points ahead to the remainder of Mark's narrative, so that readers are attentive to the dynamics at work in the characters who do not bear fruit as well as those that do. As the Gospel progresses, Jesus does not expound on the aspects of how to grow in faith. There is more *showing* than *telling*. We see a range of characters respond to Jesus and either increase in confusion, on one hand, or grow in understanding and receive Jesus's commendation, on the other. So what can we learn from Mark's Gospel about growing in faith and becoming people in whom the word bears much fruit?

First, very simply, faithful disciples listen to what Jesus says and do it. When Jesus calls his disciples, they immediately drop everything and follow him (Mark 1:18). And Jesus says that his family is made up of all those who hear God's word and obey it (3:34–35). Growing in faith involves responding to the authoritative voice of God who spoke commandingly from heaven at Jesus's transfiguration: "This is my Son, whom I love. Listen to him!" (9:7). If we want to be people who bear much fruit, we will give careful attention to what Scripture says and consider the many ways God's word can move into our lives and transform us.

Second, three characters in Mark 5 demonstrate that a crucial aspect of fruitfulness is worship. The demon-possessed man, Jairus, and the bleeding woman all approach Jesus and fall at his feet in the posture of worship (vv. 6, 22, 33). In a day when so many are growing disenchanted with the church, we must remind ourselves of the necessity of gathering with God's people to give him praise and adoration. Scripture portrays Christian life *as worship* (cf. Rom 12:1–2), and when we come together we remind ourselves of what our entire lives and all reality is all about. In one sense, corporate worship is a distinct opportunity to praise God, but it is also a time of reorientation. We redirect our focus away from the many trivial pursuits that consume us and reframe our whole lives as taking place within God's kingdom. Not that we forget our mundane concerns, but we reconceive of them in terms of our fundamental identity as God's people, called into being for his glory and for our good.

Third, growing in faith entails a consideration of what it means for us to have our lives claimed by the cross. Jesus calls his disciples to take up their crosses and to follow him on the way to his cross (8:34). This call to discipleship is costly. The rich young man could not bear the thought of giving up all he owned to follow Jesus (10:17–22). On the other hand, the woman who anointed Jesus's head responded eagerly to this costly call, as she broke a vial of expensive nard, giving all she had to identify with Jesus's death (14:3–9). It is so tempting to look to these narratives for "principles of application" that are safe and that do not threaten our comforts. It is far more difficult to take an honest and sober look at our lives and discern whether there are leisurely pursuits that we can give up in order to become actively involved in meeting needs in our congregations and communities. Yet this is the sort of fruitfulness about which Jesus speaks.

Fourth, the father of the demon-possessed boy offers us the beautiful example of fruit bearing when he confesses his need of Jesus to help him overcome his unbelief (9:24). Growing in faith does not look like Christian superstardom where everything comes easily and we never suffer setbacks. A crucial component of being Christian is the routine practice of confession of sin and actively looking to God in Christ for help and empowerment by God's Spirit. God's people confess their inadequacy in the face of the pressures of life and the daunting prospects of ministry. To confess our need of God is not to admit failure but is itself an expression of faith in God, our only source of strength.

Finally, throughout Mark the soil that bears fruit is characterized by humility. Jesus says that in the kingdom of God there is a radical social reordering, where the first are last, and the last are first (10:31). This is the social vision that ought to shape our imaginations as we participate in the life of the people of God. Those who grow in faith embrace this reality through cultivating relationships with those on the margins of our communities, rather than only attending to those who share our same social status. Pursuing this radical social vision means that we may raise questions, just as Jesus's behavior did (2:16). The disciples provided a negative example in this regard when they saw the kingdom of God as an opportunity to attain power and prestige (10:37).

Much more could easily be said about becoming the sort of soil in which the word bears much fruit. These are simply a few of the examples in Mark that point to some of the ways that the Gospel portrays growth in faith.

LISTEN to the Story

²¹He said to them, "Do you bring in a lamp to put it under a bowl or a bed? Instead, don't you put it on its stand? ²²For whatever is hidden is meant to be disclosed, and whatever is concealed is meant to be brought out into the open. ²³If anyone has ears to hear, let them hear." ²⁴"Consider carefully what you hear," he continued. "With the measure you use, it will be measured to you—and even more. ²⁵Whoever has will be given more; whoever does not have, even what they have will be taken from them."

Listening to the Text in the Story: Proverbs 1:20–33; 2:1–22; Daniel 2:21; 2 Corinthians 4:3–6.

This passage extends Jesus's parabolic teaching in 4:1–20. The word that is proclaimed is that the kingdom takes the shape of the cross, but because of the audience's prejudices and expectations, the kingdom's true character is "hidden" from view. It must be revealed, however, and the revelation takes place not only in Jesus's preaching but in the responses of the disciples and eventually in the church that embodies the kingdom's reality. This movement from hiddenness to revelation demands attentiveness and careful discernment. Jesus is saying, "Pay close attention! If you do, you will receive greater understanding of this life-giving reality. If you fail to do so, even what little you grasp will be taken away."

Scripture is filled with similar exhortations, especially in the first chapter of Proverbs, which describes the call of wisdom:

> Let the wise listen and add to their learning,
>   and let the discerning get guidance—
> for understanding proverbs and parables,
>   the sayings and riddles of the wise.

The fear of the LORD is the beginning of knowledge,
    but fools despise wisdom and instruction. (Prov 1:5–7)

For the waywardness of the simple will kill them,
        and the complacency of fools will destroy them;
    but whoever listens to me will live in safety
        and be at ease, without fear of harm. (Prov 1:32–33)

God's wisdom is available to any who seek it, and he more than rewards those who long to know him. The same is true with Jesus's teaching about the kingdom of God and its cross-oriented character. Those who hold their own assumptions lightly and seek to grasp the kingdom's inner workings are rewarded with greater revelation.

EXPLAIN the Story

After interpreting the parable of the seed and the soils for his disciples, Jesus continues to speak to them in parables. He asks a question with an obvious answer about what to do with a lamp. No one puts it under a bed or a bowl, do they? That would either extinguish the light or ignite the bed. A lamp is for providing light, and one normally sets it in a place that allows maximum illumination. Jesus is referring to the dynamics associated with the secret of the kingdom. The true nature of the kingdom is largely hidden because so few people grasp its cross-shaped character. Yes, Jesus is drawing large crowds, but the fervor for liberation and their resentment at the occupying Romans are so strong that in their passion the crowds are not paying close enough attention to grasp what Jesus is all about. Even with this obstacle, however, the kingdom is not going to remain hidden. It is meant to be revealed, and Jesus is making it known in his preaching, in his ministry, and in the movement he is building. Just as a lamp illumines a dark room, revealing what was previously not visible, the kingdom's hiddenness is moving toward disclosure, revelation, and open demonstration.

Jesus then orders his disciples to pay close attention by repeating the exhortation from Mark 4:9 in v. 23: "If anyone has ears to hear, let them hear." Those who belong to the kingdom are responsible to lean in and give diligent attention to what is being said. Careful discernment is crucial, because other dynamics are always working to confuse and corrupt our understanding of Jesus and the nature of the kingdom. And to stress this, he repeats his previous call for a multisensory attentiveness from v. 3: "Listen! Look!" The Greek text in v. 24a is similar, and the NIV captures it well: "Consider carefully what you hear" (*blepete ti akouete*, lit. "see what you hear!"). Jesus had already noted that it is possible to hear but fail to listen, and to see but fail to perceive (v. 12). The possibility of their understanding the kingdom through their own hopes, dreams, fears, and prejudices is something they must guard against constantly. They can do so through persistent discernment and close attention to what Jesus is saying.

In vv. 24b–25, Jesus refers to the alternative responses of diligence and complacency. Those who pay close attention to what Jesus is saying will not only have understanding but will receive even more insight than they expected. On the other hand, those who are complacent, making little effort to grasp the character of the kingdom, will have even the little understanding that they do have taken away from them. The first half of this dynamic is promising. God is the one who gives light in this instance, and that is rightly the cause of praise. The second part, however, is a bit troubling. Will God really take away someone's understanding if they have only a small amount? How will beginners make progress in the faith if their small amount of understanding is taken away?

In the context of Mark, Jesus is not going after beginners in the faith. He is targeting the complacent and presumptuous, those who assume that they are insiders to the kingdom and presume that their special status means that they will be exalted rather than being servants. Jesus often chastises the disciples in Mark (4:40; 6:52; 8:17–18), and their presumption and failure to perceive is why. Mark wants the audiences that will hear his Gospel to be unsettled, to question themselves and examine whether complacency and presumption have taken hold.

LIVE the Story

Growing in Wisdom

Saint Anselm's famous saying "faith seeking understanding" described Christian pursuit of knowledge. Yet it also captures the character of how Jesus speaks of understanding the kingdom of God and the biblical nature of growing in wisdom. Those who give careful and obedient attention to what Jesus is saying will come to a greater understanding of it. The biblical dynamic of coming to understand God and his ways moves in an opposite direction from what we might expect. The modern project of growing in understanding follows René

Descartes (1596–1650) and his well-known procedure of doubting everything and establishing certain knowledge, starting from what the human mind could perceive and rationally establish. One only accepts what can be verified, and once one has firmly established knowledge, then one can begin to live in light of it. Understanding and knowledge, according to this way of thinking, *precede* commitment.

Scripture runs counter to this. The psalmist, reflecting the book of Proverbs, says, "The fear of the LORD is the beginning of wisdom; all who follow his precepts have good understanding" (Ps 111:10). The commitment to obey God is the first step toward rightly understanding oneself, others, God, the world, and how to navigate opportunities and challenges in life. Commitment *precedes* wisdom, and an obedient life *leads to* understanding. Jesus also teaches that discipleship precedes knowledge of the truth: "If you hold to my teaching, you are really my disciples. Then you will know the truth, and the truth will set you free" (John 8:31–32; cf. 7:17).

The skeptic does not have the freedom to critically examine Jesus's teaching and the character of the kingdom to determine if it satisfies rationally established criteria before repenting and entering into it. According to Jesus, there is no possibility of adopting a posture of critical distance so that one might coolly determine whether one will commit. Those who take this position will grow in confusion over the kingdom. It will not make any sense. Even the little grasp of it that one has will be taken away.

Jesus here reveals the "momentum" of two alternative postures toward Jesus's teaching. If someone wants to maintain their distance and critically assess what Jesus has to say, they cannot assume they are in a static position regarding kingdom realities. This posture toward the kingdom has momentum away from understanding the logic of Jesus's teaching and away from perceiving the power of the kingdom. This person will diminish in understanding and will increasingly lose sight of why the kingdom is worth one's complete commitment.

Alternatively, the one who lives into the reality of the kingdom will experience its life-giving power and the wonder of its counterintuitive logic. The more one serves and gives herself to loving others and meeting needs, the more she is flooded with God's own life and the more she inhabits—and is filled with—the power of God. Where one might think that genuine life is found in wealth and the accumulation of symbols of status, the upside-down nature of the kingdom means that life is found in self-expenditure and in providing hospitality to those with nothing to offer. *It is by practicing the wisdom of the cross that the wisdom of the cross appears truly wise and does so increasingly.*

And this happens to those with the eyes of faith who first give themselves to God and then grow in the set of habits whereby one's life is wedded to the kingdom of God.

Clement of Alexandria speaks of the sort of habitual practices that make up one's inhabiting of this new reality:

> A well, when pumped regularly, produces purer water. If neglected, and no one uses it, it changes into a source of pollution. Use keeps metal brighter, but disuse produces rust. For, in a word, exercise produces a healthy condition both in souls and bodies. So "No one lights a candle and puts it under a bowl, but upon a candlestick, that it may give light." For of what use is wisdom, if it fails to make those who hear it wise?[1]

---

1. Oden and Hall, *Mark*, 55.

Mark 4:26–34

📖 LISTEN to the Story

²⁶He also said, "This is what the kingdom of God is like. A man scatters seed on the ground. ²⁷Night and day, whether he sleeps or gets up, the seed sprouts and grows, though he does not know how. ²⁸All by itself the soil produces grain—first the stalk, then the head, then the full kernel in the head. ²⁹As soon as the grain is ripe, he puts the sickle to it, because the harvest has come." ³⁰Again he said, "What shall we say the kingdom of God is like, or what parable shall we use to describe it? ³¹It is like a mustard seed, which is the smallest of all seeds on earth. ³²Yet when planted, it grows and becomes the largest of all garden plants, with such big branches that the birds can perch in its shade." ³³With many similar parables Jesus spoke the word to them, as much as they could understand. ³⁴He did not say anything to them without using a parable. But when he was alone with his own disciples, he explained everything.

Listening to the Text in the Story: Ezekiel 31:6; Joel 3:13; 1 Corinthians 3:5–15; Revelation 14:14–20.

Earlier in Mark 4, Jesus had stressed the human obstacles to the growth of the kingdom. He drew a stark line between those who are "in" the kingdom and those who are "outside" of it and claimed that his teaching would hide the truth from some people while revealing it to others. Further, his discussion of the kingdom's reception has been somewhat negative, since there will be more who do not receive it than who do understand and bear its fruit. This passage (vv. 26–34), which concludes the parables section in Mark 4, opens up a different vista on the kingdom. Rather than focusing on human failure, Jesus emphasizes the certainty that God will build his kingdom.

These two parables have to do with the growth of the kingdom of God. The first parable (vv. 26–29) concerns the mysterious character of its growth, and the second (vv. 30–32) notes the astounding size and scope of its maturation. From an insignificant beginning, it becomes something staggeringly great. The parables section of chapter 4 closes in vv. 33–34 with a note of hope. Mark indicates that Jesus is speaking to the larger crowd at this point and not just the disciples, and he speaks to them in parables "as much as they could understand" (v. 33). He had said earlier that those who are kingdom insiders will gain understanding from the parables, while those outside the kingdom will be increasingly confused. Crucially, however, he has not identified who is in and who is out. That remains to be seen, and it depends on the response of those who hear Jesus's teaching. This closing note, then, balances the stark words of vv. 11–12 with the hope that Jesus is still looking for people with cultivated hearts to respond properly to the proclamation of the kingdom. As we noted earlier, as Mark unfolds, those who respond positively and those who grow confused will surprise readers of this Gospel.

The growth of the kingdom is due to God's power and not to any human genius, clever manipulations, calculated market research, or growth strategies. The contrast between God's working out his purposes in his own way and humans manipulating in order to bring about God's intentions is common in Scripture. Abraham received the amazing promise that even in his advanced age he was going to have an heir (Gen 15:4–6). The arrival of that child would be miraculous, but Abraham and Sarah reasoned that perhaps the promise would be brought about through the practice common to their culture of having a child through a slave girl (Gen 16:1–2). God had other plans, however, and intended to fulfill his promise through the completely unexpected pregnancy of Sarah at the age of ninety (Gen 18:9–15; Rom 4:18–21).

In Matthew 16:18 Jesus said, "I will build my church," and even the power of death would prove no obstacle. Jesus is building the kingdom of God, and he works through his people by his Spirit. The church does not just sit back and do nothing. But this is the important point: God's people need to discern how their efforts align with God's work in the world, so that we faithfully embody the corporate shape of Jesus himself in what we do. We all too easily try to accomplish God's purposes through our own wisdom, our own calculations and manipulations, and our own strategies, rather than simply embodying the reality of a cross-shaped kingdom with a cross-shaped king. When our efforts overshadow or become obstacles to the mysterious growth of the kingdom, we need to recalibrate our vision to be certain that we are pursuing God's agenda and not our own.

EXPLAIN the Story

The Mysterious Growth of the Kingdom (vv. 26–29)

To explain what the kingdom of God is like, Jesus uses a parable of a sower who scatters seed on the ground, like the one in vv. 3–8. After sowing the seed, the natural process of growth takes place without reference to human activity. The sower goes about his daily business, and to him the seed's persistent growth remains an utter mystery (v. 27). Apart from any human effort ("all by itself"), the seed sprouts and grows (v. 28). Jesus describes the persistent character of the growth in v. 28. It may be slow, but the growth is sure—"First the stalk, then the head, then the fuller kernel in the head."

Many of us are aware of how much maintenance a garden requires. For a few years, we lived in a rural area where we were able to plant a sizable garden. We had tomatoes, beans, potatoes, corn, and a few rows of sunflowers just for fun. My wife and I were acutely aware of the weather, watching out for the threat of frost in late spring and especially how much rain we were getting. We watched out for intrusive animals and weeded regularly. A garden does indeed require human maintenance and effort to provide the best conditions for plants to thrive. But Jesus focuses our attention not on human involvement but on the amazing process of growth that is beyond human control. I remember well plowing up the ground and preparing the area for planting. Looking at the barren patch of black dirt, I had no confidence that something I had my hand in would turn out to be something we could eat, and the process of growth always amazed me. We were soon eating delicious salsa that my wife had made completely from vegetables and herbs from our garden. And I would daily walk along my two rows of increasingly huge sunflowers, several of which reached a height of nine feet!

We may be able to water our gardens and enrich the soil in various ways, but the process of a small package of seeds turning into a flowering and richly productive garden is a mystery that is beyond human control. That mysterious growth is what the kingdom of God is like. It remains beyond human manipulation, and it cannot be engineered or forced (though many people still make the attempt). As Clifton Black notes, "The kingdom of God is pure gift."[1]

The Astounding Growth of the Kingdom (vv. 30–32)

In the second parable, Jesus again uses an agrarian metaphor and compares the kingdom to a tiny seed that eventually grows to become the largest of garden

---

1. Black, *Mark*, 127.

plants.[2] Certainly the growth of seeds into fruit-bearing plants is a mystery, but here the focus is on the astounding growth of the tiniest of seeds into the largest of plants. In fact, Jesus notes that this garden plant is so large that birds can find housing in its branches.

Just as with "the word" in the initial parable in 4:1–20, things begin small. The majority of people will not understand the word, and only a small minority will embrace it and bear fruit. The kingdom and the proclamation about its reality are hidden, unknown, and seemingly insignificant. Because God is the one building his kingdom, however, its growth is not only guaranteed, but its rate of growth will be astonishing. Just as a tiny mustard seed is completely out of proportion with the size of the fully grown plant, the kingdom's initial insignificance will be out of all proportion with its eventual size. Jesus likely is pointing, therefore, to the kingdom as an eventual worldwide empire that includes the nations within its rule.[3]

Conclusion to Jesus's Teaching in Parables (vv. 33–34)

While Mark notes that Jesus often taught in parables, this is the only section in his Gospel that records the content of Jesus's parabolic teaching (4:1–34). Mark's inclusion of these parables, then, is meant to be representative of the sort of parables Jesus used in his teaching. The summary of what Jesus taught "them" raises the question of what audience is in view here. Is this only the disciples, or does it include the whole crowd? Mark's reference to "them" and "they" in v. 33 and "them" in v. 34 refers to the larger crowd in view from v. 1. In v. 34 Mark contrasts what Jesus says to this larger group with what he taught "when he was alone with his own disciples." He is summarizing what Jesus taught to a larger audience that included his disciples and many more among the crowds who were following him. This is another indication that the line between who is in the kingdom and who is outside is ambiguous, so that the membership of the two groups is not fixed. Anyone can prove that they belong to the kingdom by their responsiveness to Jesus and his proclaimed word. And, alternatively, even those who consider themselves insiders need to be vigilant to remain attentive to Jesus's word, lest they demonstrate that they have hard hearts and are not of the kingdom as they presumed they were.

---

2. While we know today that the mustard seed is not the smallest of all seeds, it was common to speak of it in the ancient world in this way. Jesus was not giving a botany lesson but referring to what his hearers knew to help them understand the character of the kingdom (Strauss, *Mark*, 199; Boring, *Mark*, 139).

3. Several biblical texts depict empires as great trees and smaller nations as birds that find shade under its branches (Ezek 17; 31:1–14; Dan 4:10–12, 14). This image is likely pointing, therefore, to the kingdom of God as a worldwide empire in which the nations find refreshment and enjoy God's peace (Strauss, *Mark*, 200; Marcus, *Mark 1–8*, 331).

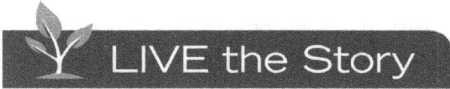 LIVE the Story

Ministry and the Mystery of the Kingdom

The mysterious character of the kingdom's growth provides a biblical framework to shape how ministers conceive of their task. Paul conceives of ministry in 1 Corinthians 3:5–15 through a similar organic metaphor, which contrasts Scripture's vision with an approach to ministry in a highly technologized culture. Certainly in my North American setting, if not also much of the Western world, the modern tools of demographic research, analysis of polling data, and studies on leadership and how to influence community dynamics have all shaped how we approach ministry. We may not say so explicitly in our churches, but in leadership meetings and strategic planning initiatives, we betray our fundamental conviction that we are capable of growing churches and predicting and executing development and expansion. This modern conception of ministry leaves us with the illusion that we can engineer, manufacture, or manipulate growth.

We can learn much from the organic metaphors in Scripture that describe the life of the church and the mysterious growth of the kingdom. In his book *Under the Unpredictable Plant*, Eugene Peterson reflects on the connections between farming and pastoral ministry. He stresses the importance of valuing a local setting: "Parish work is every bit as physical as farm work. It is *these* people, at *this* time, under *these* conditions."[4] Farmers who hold their particular location in high regard will not resent it but rather will seek to work with the land as it is. On the other hand, there is a dominant mode of modern agribusiness farming that is "impatient with the actual conditions of any farm." Such farmers bring in "big equipment to eliminate what is distinctively local so that machines can do their work unimpeded by local quirks and idiosyncrasies."[5] This approach to farming sees the land not as a rich resource to be cared for and nurtured and from which to draw sustenance but as something to be plundered and exploited for short-term gain.

These alternative approaches to farming have their parallels in ministry. Pastors face the temptation to take such an exploitative view of their churches. When they do, they "see the congregation as raw material to manufacture into an evangelism program, or a mission outreach, or a Christian Education learning center. Before I know it, I'm pushing and pulling, cajoling and

---

4. Eugene H. Peterson, *Under the Unpredictable Plant: An Exploration of Vocational Holiness* (Grand Rapids: Eerdmans, 1992), 131.

5. Peterson, *Unpredictable Plant*, 131.

seducing, persuading and selling."[6] Such an approach is taken by those who view ministry as a good career option rather than a calling.

Peterson points to the danger of *abstraction*—that is, relating to the church without regard to its particular location, its distinctive history, and the actual people who are its members. On one hand, our churches may be content to let ministers take such an approach. After all, people are used to being pushed around, manipulated, and shaken down by businesses, schools, and politicians. And the result may be applause and an increase in numbers. But, on the other hand,

> in the process I find myself dealing more and more in causes and gener-
> alities and abstractions, judging success by numbers, giving less and less
> attention to particular people, and experiencing a rapidly blurring memory
> of the complex interactions of crisscrossed histories that come partially into
> view each Sunday morning.[7]

Peterson presents an alternative to approaching pastoral ministry the way agribusiness farms the land. He reminds us that our "work is not to make a religious establishment succeed but to nurture the gospel of Jesus Christ into maturity." And this involves caring for a particular church and its particular people, which transforms the pastoral vision. "I never know how Christ is going to appear in another person, let alone in a congregation. I must be mindful of the conditions, treating as ever more particular and precious each of these parishioners." He goes on to say that "when I work in the particulars, I develop a reverence for what is actually there instead of a contempt for what is not, inadequacies that seduce me into a covetousness for someplace else."[8]

Peterson draws on Wendell Berry's work on farming to note that a farm is a "small-scale ecosystem," with "everything working with everything else in certain rhythms and proportions."[9] Wise farmers seek to understand each of these proportions and rhythms, seeking to foster their health and flourishing. He does not stubbornly "invade the place and decide that it is going to function on his rhythms and according to the size of his ego. If all a farmer is after is profit, he will not be reverential of what is actually there but only greedy for what he can get out of it."[10]

---

6. Peterson, *Unpredictable Plant*, 131.
7. Peterson, *Unpredictable Plant*, 132.
8. Peterson, *Unpredictable Plant*, 133.
9. Peterson, *Unpredictable Plant*, 133.
10. Peterson, *Unpredictable Plant*, 133.

In the same way, a wise pastor is sensitive to understand their congregation's rhythms and proportions, their unique history, and the interactions between various people. They view churches as being worked on and loved by the Spirit long before they came to town. "I must fit into what is going on. I have no idea yet what is taking place here; I must study the contours, understand the weather, know what kind of crops grow in this climate, be in awe of the complex intricacies between past and present, between the people in the parish and those outside."[11]

A focus on the particularity of community also shapes preaching. When pastors cultivate *affection for* and *loyalty to* their particular community, they maintain a posture of love and respect for those to whom they preach. They carry on a long-term dialogue over spiritual things, shaped by prayer and Scripture. Otherwise, Peterson states that proclamation can deteriorate into ranting, resentful bickering, or condescension.[12]

Peterson beautifully sums up this vision of ministry:

> Every parish is different, even more than each soul is different, for the parish is a compound of souls. What works in that place cannot be imposed on this place—this is unique, this place, this people. If I am dismissive of the uniqueness of this parish, or unwilling to acknowledge it, I will impose my routines on it for a few seasons, harvest a few souls, then move on to another parish to try my luck there, and in my belligerent folly I will miss the beauty and holiness and sheer divine life that was all the time there, unseen and unheard because of my rapacious religious ambitions.[13]

The agrarian metaphors in Scripture remind us that the focus of ministry is to be on faithfulness and careful cultivation of the life of the church over years. As Peterson says, such an approach to farming does not wear out the soil in a few decades. Rather, it takes the long view. It conceives of the land and its future into many generations. The same is true in a ministry context. Rather than focusing on results, pastors would do well to consider their work in terms of *cultivation*. This fosters humility by seeing their ministry as part of a much larger and longer process. And it puts them in a place where they are open to God's working in the church. Just as farmers are subject to larger weather forces and many other contingent dynamics, the work of ministry is to be done with open hands and with a posture of openness to God's blessing.

---

11. Peterson, *Unpredictable Plant*, 133.
12. Peterson, *Unpredictable Plant*, 135–36.
13. Peterson, *Unpredictable Plant*, 136.

CHAPTER 19

Mark 4:35-41

📖 LISTEN to the Story

> [35]That day when evening came, he said to his disciples, "Let us go over to the other side." [36]Leaving the crowd behind, they took him along, just as he was, in the boat. There were also other boats with him. [37]A furious squall came up, and the waves broke over the boat, so that it was nearly swamped. [38]Jesus was in the stern, sleeping on a cushion. The disciples woke him and said to him, "Teacher, don't you care if we drown?" [39]He got up, rebuked the wind and said to the waves, "Quiet! Be still!" Then the wind died down and it was completely calm. [40]He said to his disciples, "Why are you so afraid? Do you still have no faith?" [41]They were terrified and asked each other, "Who is this? Even the wind and the waves obey him!"

Listening to the Text in the Story: Job 38:11; Psalms 29:3–10; 107:23–32; Jonah 1–4.

This passage is the first of a series of episodes that portray Jesus's power over nature (4:35–41), demons (5:1–20), human illness (5:21–34), and death (5:35–43). This miracle story in which Jesus calms the storm is relayed in terms that recall the story of Jonah. Many of the same narrative elements are present: a journey in a boat, a great storm at sea, a sleeping main character, terribly frightened sailors, miraculous calming of the sea related to the main character, and a response of wonder by the sailors (Jonah 1:1–16).[1]

Mark's depiction of this episode in terms that allude to Jonah is not without

---

1. Strauss, *Mark*, 205–6. Several linguistic features intensify the allusion to Jonah. First, the disciples ask Jesus in v. 38, lit., "Don't you care that we're going to die [*apollymetha*]?" A related form of this Greek verb appears in Jonah 1:6 and 14 LXX. Second, in v. 39 Mark notes that the wind "died down" (*ekopasen*), the same Greek verb used in Jonah 1:11–12 LXX. Third, the response of the disciples in v. 41 is that they "feared a great fear" (*ephobēthēsan phobon*), the same expression used in Jonah 1:16 (Marcus, *Mark 1–8*, 333–37).

purpose. At the close of the previous passage, Jesus indicated that the astonishing growth of the kingdom and its eventual great size would allow for the birds to rest in its shade, a symbol of the kingdom's inclusion of the nations. Further, Jesus's exhortation that initiates this passage, "let us go over to the other side," is a call to head toward the region of the Decapolis, a large area that encompassed ten pagan cities. And a number of the episodes that follow take place in gentile territory (5:1–20; 7:24–36; 8:1–9). Mark portrays this episode in terms that recall Jonah because Jesus is undoing Jonah's reluctance to see the gentiles blessed by the God of Israel. And he is reversing the impulse present among his disciples that reflects the heart of Jonah to prefer that God judge the nations rather than save them.[2]

God commissioned the prophet Jonah to proclaim God's judgment against Ninevah (Jonah 1:1). He refused to go, however, because he had a very clear understanding of God's overpowering grace: "I knew that you are a gracious and compassionate God, slow to anger and abounding in love, a God who relents from sending calamity" (Jonah 4:2). Jonah so hated the Ninevites that he wanted to see them destroyed, and he knew that if God detected even a hint of repentance, he would relent from his intentions to destroy them. When God chose to relent from his intentions to destroy Ninevah, Jonah was so upset that he wanted to die (v. 3).

Far from reluctance, Jesus was eager to go to gentile territory and continue his mission of announcing the reign of God, driving out demons and healing the sick. While Israel was God's special possession, called to embody his kingdom of justice and peace, this role from the beginning was meant to draw the nations to the one true God and to extend his reign over all the whole earth. While many in Israel had developed an animosity toward the nations after the pattern of Jonah, Jesus displays God's heart for the flourishing of the nations.

EXPLAIN the Story

Jesus Calms the Storm (vv. 35–39)

Jesus had been in a boat teaching just offshore, and now his disciples join him "just as he was, in the boat" (v. 36), to go to the other side. It was already

---

2. There is a crucial biblical-theological connection between the appearance of "gentiles" in the New Testament and God's commissioning of Israel as "a light to the nations" (Isa 49:6 NRSV). The Greek term *ethnē* (often translated "gentiles" in English translations of the NT) is used in the LXX for "nations," so that "gentiles" are those non-Jewish nations to whom God originally sent Israel, in order to draw them to himself. Jesus's pattern of unhesitatingly going to the gentiles demonstrates his obedience to the God of Israel in reaching out to the nations with God's redeeming love.

evening (v. 35), so when the storm whipped up at night, the situation was especially terrifying.[3] Mark adds the tantalizing detail that "there were also other boats with him," continuing his depiction of a larger group of people receptive to Jesus's preaching. I referred previously to the relative size of the Sea of Galilee,[4] but furious winds could easily stir up waves large enough to threaten the sort of small boat in which they were traveling.

The contrast between Jesus and his disciples is striking. They are terrified, and he is asleep on a cushion in a covering under the stern. Modern readers who have sailed small boats in rough waters may understand how frightened the disciples might be while on tumultuous waters at night. Their terror, however, is magnified by the meaning of "the sea" in the ancient world. Across ancient cultures, the sea represented cosmic powers of chaos and was understood as a deity who threatened to undo the order of creation. This explains the fright of the disciples and Jesus's restful sleep. Just as the God of Israel dominates the sea and is exalted far above all symbols of earthly and cosmic power (Ps 29:3–10), Jesus is undisturbed by the roiling chaos of the sea.

The disciples rouse Jesus from his slumber, saying, "Teacher, don't you care if we drown?" (v. 38). It is easy to imagine that they are in quite a flustered state at this point. The question might strike Christian readers as impertinent, implying that perhaps Jesus does not care about his disciples. It may even seem at first glance that this is why Jesus rebukes them in v. 40. But the disciples' language is completely in line with the prayers of Scripture. Psalm 107:23–29 depicts scenes of sailors desperately crying out to God while in the midst of a storm. And Psalm 44:23–24 contains the language of intense and passionate wrestling with God:

> Awake, Lord! Why do you sleep?
> Rouse yourself! Do not reject us forever.
> Why do you hide your face
> and forget our misery and oppression?

The disciples' words to Jesus are not the reason for Jesus's rebuke, since they are consistent with the kind of language found in Scripture. Such blunt expressions may strike contemporary readers as impolite or irreverent, but this is likely the result of the difference between our cultural values and those of

---

3. Black, *Mark*, 133.
4. The Sea of Galilee is 65 square miles, roughly thirteen miles from north to south, and about eight miles from east to west. By comparison, the smallest of the Great Lakes, Lake Ontario, is 7,320 square miles.

ancient Israel. Contemporary Western Christians are heirs to a post-Victorian interpretation of the Christian faith that highlights politeness and exalts a placid disposition as a supreme virtue. For the ancient Israelites, however, pouring out one's extremely honest emotions before God was a manifestation of faith in God rather than the reverse.

Mark succinctly reports Jesus's action. He stood up and ordered the wind and waves, "Quiet! Be still!" (v. 39). Jesus rebuked the storm and spoke to the sea as if these were personal entities, displaying the same authority over the chaotic waters as that of God himself. Just as God spoke creation into existence and gave orders to the sea (Job 38:11), Jesus speaks to the sea, and it, along with the wind, immediately dies down and is completely calm.

> Jesus's mastery over the wind and waves demonstrates that he is the posses-
> sor of a power that the Old Testament consistently assigns to the Lord God
> alone. It is God who rebuked the waters and formed the dry land, God who
> parted the sea for Israel, God who made the storm be still.[5]

Jesus Rebukes His Disciples (vv. 40–41)

After Jesus rebukes the wind and the sea, he rebukes his disciples for their fear and their lack of faith. It is unclear, however, why Jesus rebukes them since they followed scriptural examples of calling out to God amid trouble (e.g., Ps 34:17). Why does that demonstrate a lack of faith? Moreover, it does not seem that Jesus is rebuking them merely for being afraid. In some way the disciples were afraid and did not believe. But what was Jesus expecting them to do?

Mark does not provide any clues as to what they should have done, but from the larger context we can surmise that Jesus was expecting them to calm the storm themselves. If this sounds outrageous, keep in mind that Jesus had been announcing the kingdom of God, declaring that the reign of God has invaded the realm dominated by Satan and demonic powers. And this reign was bringing with it the healing of creation and the restoration of humanity. God's original commission to humanity was to exercise rule and dominion over creation, overseeing its flourishing and managing its life-giving and humanity-sustaining capacities (Gen 1:28). Humanity had failed to rule creation for the glory of God, but this is precisely what Jesus has been doing in his ministry. Yes, he is God himself, but he is also the true human. Mark portrays him overseeing the spread of God's rule of *shalom* wherever he goes,

---

5. Hays, *Echoes of Scripture in the Gospels*, 69.

freeing people from demons and sickness and calling everyone to enter the life-giving kingdom of God. And he has called the disciples to be "with him" (Mark 3:14), to do what he does, and to partner with him in spreading God's rule and calling others to enter it.

There is a clear instance of God expecting his disciples to do the impossible in Mark 6. The miracle in which Jesus fed five thousand people with a few fish and loaves was supposed to be done by the disciples. Jesus challenged them in Mark 6:37 to feed the many thousands who have come to see him. And he can expect that his disciples could perform such a feat since they had just returned from a months-long mission, in which they had cast out many demons and healed many who were sick (vv. 12–13). Because they are "with Jesus," they have access to the miracle-working power of the kingdom of God. Their fear is a shrinking back from leaning into the fullness of being "with Jesus."

Because of this, their terror and wonderment in 4:41 is not a positive reaction of awe, but a negative reaction of confusion. Jesus had said that they were given the secret of the kingdom but that outsiders would grow increasingly confused (v. 11). Their failure at this point to participate with Jesus in kingdom power sets them on a trajectory through 8:17–18 and on to the end of Mark, in which their confusion only intensifies.

LIVE the Story

Living by Faith, Not Fear

Jesus puts the question to the disciples ("Why are you so afraid? Do you still have no faith?") in v. 40, introducing a theme that appears throughout Mark— the opposition of *faith* to *fear*. In the episodes that are sandwiched together in Mark 5, faith and fear are directly opposed, and fear appears throughout the Gospel as a clear indication that faith is absent.[6] Jesus preaches the gospel and calls for repentance and faith. And faith provides the conditions for the miraculous power of the kingdom to break out, bringing healing and restoration.

I grew up hearing stories of great faith that was rewarded in amazing ways. When I was young, we routinely had missionaries visiting our church and often hosted them in our home. I heard countless stories of rescue from dangerous situations and other life-threatening accounts. Over the years, such narratives that highlighted the spectacular left me wondering what great faith

---

6. Leroy A. Huizenga, *Loosing the Lion: Proclaiming the Gospel of Mark* (Steubenville, OH: Emmaus Road, 2017), 144.

would look like for me since so much of my life was pretty mundane and unremarkable. I suspect that many Christians feel the same way. In fact, when I was teaching undergraduates, a chapel speaker showed a video of his son and him scuba diving in a cage while feeding sharks. He used this as an example of doing great things for God and then went on to talk about how God wanted all of them to live exciting lives that involved taking big risks that demonstrated immense faith. I can understand that speakers like that man want to motivate Christian young people to engage with the faith in exciting ways, but I think that the implicit promises of wild experiences leave many people unprepared to deal with the manner in which faith works itself out in the daily routines of life. And they leave us with the illusion that unless we are doing things that are vividly remarkable, we are somehow falling short of the sort of faith to which God calls his people.

A far more hopeful and realistic approach is to consider how the dynamics of *faith* versus *fear* work in the sorts of situations we face consistently in the life of the church. I am thinking here of several conflict-resolution episodes in which I have been involved over the years. The kind of fear that Mark displays throughout his Gospel has to do with self-protection and self-preservation. Peter resists Jesus's words about going to the cross because that involves loss of life (8:31–33), and the rich young man rejects Jesus's exhortation to give up everything because that, very plainly, means giving up all that he has (10:17–31).

I have seen these same dynamics at work in the resolution of conflicts. When a conflict arises in the church, many people go into self-protect mode, adopting various postures that are ultimately destructive. They may shut down and nurse a grudge, gossiping about the other party in an effort to rally others to their side. Or they may lash out in an attempt to gain power over another person. Others may choose to ignore the conflict and simply leave a church rather than face the situation. Each of these responses demonstrate a lack of faith in the powerful resources that are available because of the presence of God among the church by the Spirit. Faith involves the confidence that kingdom dynamics are at work to bring about restoration if only they will give up postures of self-preservation and self-protection.

I was involved in a reconciliation of a conflict between several people in our church. We met together and spoke about the realities that God was present among us with his power to restore. We reminded ourselves that we needed to have the confidence that if we gave up trying to "win" and sought to truly hear and understand one another, we would be clearing room for the Spirit's dynamics of renewal to bring us together. I must admit that it was not easy and that for the first hour or so, we all displayed and witnessed a range of speech patterns oriented by fear. There were angry accusations and the recalling of past slights and attempts by the two parties to prove their case conclusively. For that first hour, I thought things were going to fall apart completely.

Then one of the participants adopted a humble posture of invitation. He stated that he could see that some of his behaviors were causing the others to feel bullied and not free to participate in a certain ministry with freedom. He said that he could see that because of how things were organized, the others were made to feel that their input was not valued. He then asked for clarification of how some of his relational patterns had caused pain and frustration in the past. This completely changed the tone of the whole conversation.

Each participant was then able to admit that their assumptions about the others and the manner in which they were relating were all contributing factors in the conflict. Every one of them admitted their faults, confessed their sins against the others, and forgave one another. They made a few concrete plans about how things would proceed from there. It was a beautiful experience that preserved our leadership team from fracture and deepened the relationships between everyone involved.

In this instance, faith involved the confidence that God's power was present in Christ and by the Spirit among us and that if we adopted self-giving postures shaped by the cross, God's restorative power would be unleashed. The fear that we all needed to overcome involved the impulses for self-preservation, the desire to be proven right, the suspicion that others were operating out of evil motives, and the temptation to manipulate the situation in order to come out on top.

In this episode in Mark, the disciples were afraid for their lives and did not have faith that the power of the kingdom was fully present and that they could participate in it fully. As we face the countless difficulties in our lives, we can pay close attention to how our fears drive us to adopt familiar patterns of self-protection and self-preservation. We can note these and refuse to give in to them. And we can begin to imagine what it might be like to enact faith—to take concrete steps to draw on the kingdom's power that is present among us.

CHAPTER 20

Mark 5:1-20

📖 LISTEN to the Story

¹They went across the lake to the region of the Gerasenes. ²When Jesus got out of the boat, a man with an impure spirit came from the tombs to meet him. ³This man lived in the tombs, and no one could bind him anymore, not even with a chain. ⁴For he had often been chained hand and foot, but he tore the chains apart and broke the irons on his feet. No one was strong enough to subdue him. ⁵Night and day among the tombs and in the hills he would cry out and cut himself with stones. ⁶When he saw Jesus from a distance, he ran and fell on his knees in front of him. ⁷He shouted at the top of his voice, "What do you want with me, Jesus, Son of the Most High God? In God's name don't torture me!" ⁸For Jesus had said to him, "Come out of this man, you impure spirit!" ⁹Then Jesus asked him, "What is your name?" "My name is Legion," he replied, "for we are many." ¹⁰And he begged Jesus again and again not to send them out of the area. ¹¹A large herd of pigs was feeding on the nearby hillside. ¹²The demons begged Jesus, "Send us among the pigs; allow us to go into them." ¹³He gave them permission, and the impure spirits came out and went into the pigs. The herd, about two thousand in number, rushed down the steep bank into the lake and were drowned. ¹⁴Those tending the pigs ran off and reported this in the town and countryside, and the people went out to see what had happened. ¹⁵When they came to Jesus, they saw the man who had been possessed by the legion of demons, sitting there, dressed and in his right mind; and they were afraid. ¹⁶Those who had seen it told the people what had happened to the demon-possessed man—and told about the pigs as well. ¹⁷Then the people began to plead with Jesus to leave their region. ¹⁸As Jesus was getting into the boat, the man who had been demon-possessed begged to go with him. ¹⁹Jesus did not let him, but said, "Go home to your own people and tell them how much the Lord has done for you, and how he has had mercy on you." ²⁰So the man went away

and began to tell in the Decapolis how much Jesus had done for him. And all the people were amazed.

Listening to the Text in the Story: Leviticus 11:1–8; Deuteronomy 14:8; 1 Samuel 5; 1 Kings 18; Romans 1:21–25.

In the previous passage, Jesus was traveling with his disciples into gentile territory on the other side of the Sea of Galilee. In terms of the dynamics of the biblical narrative, Jesus is fulfilling God's promise to Abraham to bless the nations. Jesus is the Messiah of Israel, the agent of the kingdom of God and the one calling God's historic people to repent and inhabit that kingdom. In addition to this, however, Jesus is also fulfilling God's purposes by reaching beyond Israel to extend the reach of God's gracious reign over the nations. He is doing among gentiles what he did in Israel—transforming uncleanness and advancing the kingdom of God by driving out demons and overthrowing the rule of Satan.

Mark emphasizes the authority and supremacy of Jesus as the Son of the Most High God in this passage. The legion of demons recognizes Jesus with this title in v. 7 and notes that he has authority over them by pleading with him (v. 10). Further stressing Jesus's supremacy, other characters in the passage plead with Jesus in a posture of submission. The demon-possessed man runs to Jesus and falls on his knees before him, representing a posture of subordination and worship (v. 6). The demons beg Jesus not to send them out of the region (v. 10). Later, they again beg Jesus to send them into the pigs (v. 12). The people plead with Jesus (v. 17), and finally the demon-possessed man begs Jesus to let him go with him (v. 18). Jesus occupies a position of authority in this passage, being fully in control and seizing the initiative, while the other characters are left to respond to him by making supplication to him.

The demons' recognition of Jesus's authority recalls the story in 1 Samuel 5 in which the ark of the covenant had been captured by the Philistines. Because of Israel's unfaithfulness, the nation had suffered a tremendous defeat by the Philistines and had seen the ark of the covenant captured by their enemies. To symbolize their triumph over Israel and their god's apparent defeat of the God of Israel, they put the ark in the temple of Dagon, their god (1 Sam 5:2). The next morning, however, they went into the temple and found Dagon "fallen on his face on the ground before the ark of the Lord"

(v. 3). The Philistines intended to symbolize the supremacy of Dagon to the God of Israel, but the prostration of Dagon before the ark indicated God's supremacy instead.

The Philistines "took Dagon and put him back in his place" (v. 3). The next morning, however, they again found Dagon fallen from his place in a posture of worship before the ark, except this time his head and hands were cut off (v. 4), indicating that the defeat of Israel by the Philistines was not the result of a heavenly defeat of the God of Israel by Dagon. The one true God, the God of Israel, had strategic purposes in allowing his people to be defeated, and it had nothing to do with being powerless against Dagon. Israel's God was powerful over any and all competitors and had cut off Dagon's head and hands, rendering him utterly powerless. The rest of the narrative portrays a victory tour around Philistia, for wherever the ark was taken God struck the Philistines with tumors, indicating that "the LORD's hand was heavy" upon the Philistines (v. 6). Whereas Dagon's hands had been cut off, Israel's God, without any human aid, had a strong hand against the Philistines as the ark was carried from town to town (vv. 7–12). Similarly, in Mark 5, the man possessed by the demons ran to Jesus and fell on his knees before him in a posture of worship. And the demons begged Jesus, recognizing his utter authority and supremacy over them.

In Mark 1:24, the first exorcism in this Gospel, the demon recognized the identity of Jesus as "the Holy One of God." Here in 5:7, however, the legion of demons identifies Jesus as the Son of "the Most High [God]"—a designation for God that indicates God's kingship over all the nations in addition to Israel (Deut 32:8; Dan 4:17).[1] It is used in biblical contexts in which gentiles recognize the ultimate authority of Israel's God (Gen 14:18–20; Num 24:16; Isa 14:14; Dan 3:26).[2] It also appears throughout the Psalms where other spiritual entities regarded as gods are in view. In such contexts, it means something like, "champion God," indicating that Israel's God is the one true creator God, who stands apart from and over all gods of the nations and all other spiritual entities. He is uniquely the king and sovereign lord over all (Pss 82:6; 83:18; 97:9). Jesus is the bearer of this very same authority, and as the ruler of creation he confronts the forces of evil and oppression where he finds them and liberates his creation from the grip of satanic darkness.

---

1. Marcus, *Mark 1–8*, 344.
2. Black, *Mark*, 136.

EXPLAIN the Story

The Demon-Possessed Man (vv. 1–5)

This episode is set in "the region of the Gerasenes" on the eastern shore of the Sea of Galilee (v. 1).[3] As soon as Jesus stepped out of the boat, he was immediately met by a man who was in a tragically oppressed condition (v. 2).[4] Descriptions of uncleanness dominate the passage, along with his mistreatment at the hands of others. The man is possessed by "an impure spirit" and lives among the tombs, which Mark mentions three times for emphasis (vv. 2, 3, 5). His contact with the dead makes him unclean according to Scripture (Num 5:2; 6:6; 9:6), so from a Jewish perspective he is not only a gentile, and therefore "unclean," but he is nearly radioactive in his uncleanness!

He is also tragically separated from human community, living among the tombs and behaving wildly. Mark stresses the attempts of others to control him in vv. 3–4, noting that "no one could bind him anymore" and that "no one was strong enough to subdue him." His terrifying behavior of crying out and gashing himself had led those who lived in the area to bind him with chains on his hands and feet, but with superhuman strength he had broken them and continued to harm himself. In a further note of tragedy, his breaking loose from bondage was not for the sake of freedom but for further self-harm. This man was clearly tortured by the impure spirit and in the grip of satanic self-destruction.

Mark's description of the man recalls the behavior of the prophets of Baal in 1 Kings 18. In their contest with Elijah, they called out to Baal to prove his supremacy, but to no avail (v. 26). They cried out louder and resorted to cutting and gashing themselves in an effort to bring about some kind of answer, but there was nothing (vv. 28–29). According to Scripture, worshipers of the one true God are free, enjoy human community, and flourish in God's good world as they enjoy the peaceful reign of God. Those who are idolatrous are dominated, oppressed, and end up in self-harm. As Paul charts the

---

3. This is likely a reference to the area on the eastern shore of the Sea of Galilee near the ancient city of Hippos. Gerasa is thirty-three miles southeast of the Sea of Galilee, though for a fisherman like Peter (Mark's source), who stayed largely in and around his hometown and seldom, if ever, ventured into this gentile area, anything in this direction could be regarded as "in the region of the Gerasenes." I owe this insight to Richard Bauckham, who spent considerable time with contemporary fishermen on the Sea of Galilee.

4. The NIV leaves out "immediately," which dramatically portrays the suddenness with which the man meets Jesus.

degradation of the gentile nations in Romans 1, he notes that the turn from the worship of the creator God (v. 23) results in degraded and dishonorable bodily behaviors (v. 24). The self-harm of the prophets in 1 Kings 18 points to the self-destructive character of idolatry and parallels the behavior of the man oppressed by the demon in Mark 5.

Jesus and the Demon-Possessed Man (vv. 6–10)

The demon-possessed man "saw Jesus from a distance" as soon as Jesus stepped out of the boat, and the man ran to him and fell on his knees before him (v. 6). The Greek verb *proskyneō* is often used to indicate a posture of worship (e.g., Matt 4:10; Luke 4:8; John 4:21; Heb 1:6; Rev 4:10). The two characters in the next episode, Jairus and the woman, behave similarly. In each of these instances a verb of perception (seeing Jesus or hearing about him; vv. 6, 22, 27, 33) is accompanied with falling down before him. These characters stand in contrast to the disciples, who are becoming confused as to Jesus's identity and mission. They are physically *with* him, but because of their lack of faith, they are failing to perceive who he is. The characters in Mark 5, however, see and hear Jesus in a way that leads to genuine perception, manifested by their response of worship and faith.

The account contains a confusing mixture of subjects, as Mark alternates between a singular spirit (vv. 2, 8, 9), many spirits (vv. 9, 12, 13), and the man himself (vv. 2–9, 10). It is difficult to determine who is speaking, a narrative device whereby Mark portrays the man as tragically confused and mentally tortured by the impure spirit(s). He cries out "at the top of his voice, 'What do you want with me, Jesus, Son of the Most High God?'"[5]

As indicated above, the title "Most High God" is used in biblical contexts where the gods of the nations are in view. According to Israel's biblical worldview, the God of Israel was the uniquely sovereign God who had no competitor and who alone was the creator of all things. His "divine council" reported to him and was filled with "gods" whom he had appointed to rule over the nations on his behalf. These figures had rebelled and were leading the nations astray into idolatry. Psalm 82 depicts the Most High God calling these gods to account and declaring their eventual judgment. This "legion" of demons recognizes Jesus's true identity, just as happens in 1:24, though because this episode takes place in gentile territory, Jesus is called "Son of the Most High God" rather than "Son of God."[6]

---

5. This expression ("What do you want with me?") is the same as that found in Jesus's first encounter with a demon-possessed man in Mark 1:24. It sets two sides against each other before a violent confrontation (Judg 11:12; 1 Kgs 17:18).

6. The title "Most High God" is used of God in the account of a demon-possessed slave girl who recognized Paul and Silas's motives for being in Philippi (Acts 16:16–24). In biblical texts that take

The demons recognize the authority of Jesus and his supremacy over them in this encounter. Their reaction to Jesus stands in contrast to that of the disciples in the previous episode, who are puzzled about his identity. Throughout Mark, characters in the supernatural realm rightly identify Jesus as the Son of God. Human characters, however, do not recognize his identity and mission, at least until a Roman centurion does so at the Gospel's climax (15:39).[7] Bizarrely, the legion of demons pleads with Jesus, appealing to God in v. 7: "In God's name don't torture me!" This may be an indication of the demonic intention with the man. The demons can only think of torturing this poor person, keeping him in this unspeakably tragic condition simply for the purposes of further torment. In a strange sort of projection of motives, they imagine that Jesus must want to do the same with them. Rather than torturing them, Jesus intends to free this man from their domination and eliminate them and their evil oppression from the region completely.

Mark indicates in v. 8 that the demon's dramatic plea came in response to Jesus's command to come out of the man. In demonic encounters, it is thought that the one who speaks first has the upper hand, along with the one who names the other, asserting dominance and taking control in the conflict. It might appear in v. 7 that the demon speaks first, but Jesus had already given the command and asked the demon its name. In this way, Mark narrates the desperate character of the man, but also of the demon in the face of Jesus and his supremacy. Mark does not explain the request to remain in the area (v. 10), but it may be that they want to hold out the possibility of torturing another person.[8]

Jesus Casts Out the Demons (vv. 11–13)

The demons again plead with Jesus (v. 12), this time to send them into a herd of pigs that "was feeding on the nearby hillside" (v. 11). From a Jewish perspective, the herd of pigs represents uncleanness that blankets this gentile territory. According to Deuteronomy 14:8, "The pig is also unclean; although it has a divided hoof, it does not chew the cud. You are not to eat their meat

---

place in gentile territories or whenever God and other gods are in view, biblical writers stress God's unique power to create (e.g., Ps 96:4–5; Acts 14:15; Eph 3:9) and his ultimate supremacy over all other supposed competitors.

7. According to Athanasius, the "spirits especially see through what is unseen by human eyes. They could tell if Christ was vulnerable and refuse him any obedience at all. As it is, what human disbelief doubts, the evil spirits see clearly: that he is God. For that reason they flee from him and fall at his feet, still crying out even as they once cried when he was in the body, 'We know who you are, the holy one of God,' and, 'Ah, what have I in common with you, Son of God? I implore you, do not torment me'" (Oden and Hall, *Mark*, 64).

8. Moloney, *Gospel of Mark*, 103.

or touch their carcasses" (cf. also Lev 11:7–8).[9] Jesus allowed them to go into the pigs, which resulted in their dramatic destruction. The pigs rushed down the steep bank into the Sea of Galilee and drowned.

While modern readers might be shocked at the senseless loss of animal life, from a first-century Jewish perspective Jesus was cleansing this gentile territory of its defilement and at the same time destroying the demons that were terrorizing this man. In the previous episode, Jesus had stilled the sea, representing his authority over the cosmic anti-God forces of chaos (4:35–41). Here, Jesus conquers this legion of demons and cleanses the region of these unclean animals. As the agent who brings in the rule of God, Jesus is overpowering and driving away the forces of evil, "rendering clean both people and place."[10]

A few things are striking about the pigs' destruction. First, the destruction of the animals appears to also be the destruction of the impure spirits. They are no longer around to harass and torment anyone else. They were destroyed along with the pigs, and the area is now purified. Second, they are destroyed in the sea, representing the waters of chaos. This calls to mind the celebration of Moses and Miriam after the Israelites passed through the Red Sea and the Egyptians were destroyed. The "Song of the Sea" in Exodus 15 celebrates Yahweh's use of the sea as a weapon with which to destroy Pharaoh's army.

> I will sing to the LORD,
>   for he is highly exalted.
> Both horse and driver
>   he has hurled into the sea. (v. 1)

> Pharaoh's chariots and his army
>   he has hurled into the sea. (v. 4)

> The deep waters have covered them;
>   they sank to the depths like a stone. (v. 5)

> But you blew with your breath,
>   and the sea covered them.
> They sank like lead
>   in the mighty waters. (v. 10)

---

9. A rabbinic text prohibits raising pigs: "None may rear swine anywhere" (m. Bava Qamma 7:7) (Moloney, *Gospel of Mark*, 104).

10. Moloney, *Gospel of Mark*, 104.

Just as God defeated Pharaoh's army in the sea, Jesus cleanses this gentile region and renews this man by destroying the impure spirits and impure animals in the sea.

The Townspeople Ask Jesus to Leave (vv. 14–17)

It is unclear if those who were "tending the pigs" were the owners of the herd or if they were looking after the herd on behalf of people in the town (v. 14). But these pig-herders go and report what has happened, and people from the town and countryside go out to witness what had taken place. What they find is astonishing, considering the outrageous measures they had previously taken to control this man. They now find him "sitting there, dressed and in his right mind" (v. 15). It is interesting that in the remainder of this narrative, the man is mentioned three more times. When he is sitting with Jesus, he is the one who *had been* possessed by the legion of demons (vv. 15, 18). But when those who had witnessed what had happened speak about the event, the man is referred to as "the demon-possessed man" (v. 16), as if the townspeople are not quite ready to conceive of a radical change in the man. They still see him as being harassed by the demon, whereas Jesus has already restored him and sees him for the new creation he has become.

Mark mentions twice that the townspeople "see" what has happened (vv. 14, 15). Though they "see," their seeing does not lead to genuine perception (cf. 4:12). On the contrary, when they took in what had happened, they were afraid (v. 15), just like the disciples in the previous episode (4:40–41). Throughout Mark, fear is often the opposite of faith, though not in every instance. In 5:33 Jesus commends the woman for her faith, even though she was also trembling with fear. Fear is a normal response to the mighty works of Jesus, but a decision confronts all those who respond this way. Will it be the cause of shrinking back and failing to live into the fullness of God's life-giving kingdom? Or will those who fear continue to press ahead to follow and obey Jesus, the agent of God's liberating and purifying rule? In this instance, their fear leaves them shaken. It grows into a rejection of Jesus, so that they plead with him to leave their region (v. 17).

The Man Reports Jesus's Triumph (vv. 18–20)

Just after the townspeople pleaded with Jesus to leave, the man begged to go "with him," indicating that he wanted to become one of Jesus's disciples (v. 18). Jesus had appointed the Twelve to be "with him" (3:14), and it appears that Jesus wants only the Twelve for that unique role.[11] While many are called to

---

11. Being "with" or "following" Jesus in Mark is one of the ways he indicates discipleship (1:16–20; 2:13–14; 3:13–19; 4:10). And this is something specific that his disciples do, while many more can inhabit the kingdom.

enter, inhabit, and enjoy God's life-giving kingdom, not all are called to play the unique role the Twelve play. But Jesus had another mission for this newly reclaimed and restored person. He sent him to his own people to report all that the Lord had done for him "and how he has had mercy on you" (v. 19). The man does this, relaying to people "in the Decapolis" what Jesus had done for him.[12] It is striking that Jesus tells the man to do this when we consider the other instances in Mark where Jesus prohibits people to speak concerning him. Yet this took place in gentile territory, where there was an absence of Jewish messianic fervor and thus less chance of misunderstanding Jesus's messianic identity and mission.

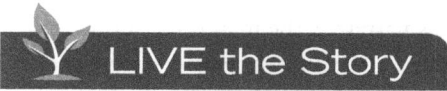

LIVE the Story

Unexpected Miracles

One of the interesting aspects of this episode is that the disciples are almost completely absent from it. They travel to the other side of the lake with Jesus, but after their brief mention in v. 1, they disappear entirely from this episode. Mark is not indicating anything negative about the disciples by leaving them out but rather focusing on Jesus and the events surrounding this exorcism and the man's miraculous transformation. One cannot help but wonder, however, about how the disciples were taking this in. They have traveled to gentile territory with Jesus, likely a location they have heard about but have never visited. They are immediately met by a terrifyingly wild madman possessed by a legion of demons, and an entire herd of unclean animals is roaming on the hillside. They are most definitely out of their comfort zone! They have the privilege, however, of witnessing God's redeeming power in the unexpected transformation of this person from madman to missionary.

For six years our family was involved in a church planted in the middle of a terribly impoverished urban neighborhood in Springfield, Ohio. We witnessed firsthand many of the problems associated with generational poverty and the devastating toll it takes on people. We also witnessed a few miraculous transformations.

For a few years, a woman with six children had been attending our church. She lived a chaotic and self-destructive life, and because her addictions put her children at risk, the state had taken them away at various times. Michelle

---

12. Jesus calls the man to tell others what "the Lord" had done for him, and the man goes and speaks about what "Jesus" has done. This is not an indication of the man's disobedience of Jesus but rather Mark's identification of Jesus as the God of Israel.

(not her real name) came fairly often to our services and to the meal we enjoyed together weekly, but mostly she sent her children. We were happy to look after them and to see that they had a good meal. Once in a while, when Michelle showed up, she would bring along a friend of hers, Sandra (also not her real name).

Sandra was a frightening person to speak with. Holding a conversation with her was quite an experience. She would seldom make much sense, speaking wildly about how much she hated her neighbor and wanted to get into a fistfight with her. She had violence in her eyes as she spoke incoherently about all the terrible things she knew her neighbor was planning against her. Talking with her reminded me, frankly, of the demon-possessed man in Mark 5. She seemed out of control and possessed by a deep anger that was frightening.

Because of the drama involved with Michelle's domestic life, much of our attention was given to her and the complications with state agencies that look after the safety of children. We spent hours talking with Michelle, visiting with her, and gave relatively little of our attention to Sandra. We saw her as just the person who came with Michelle and on whom we also kept a wary eye.

One Saturday evening—our church gathered for a service and a meal on Saturdays—Sandra approached a few of us and told us flatly that we needed to get her a Bible, "and one with big letters, because I don't see so good!" We were taken aback because this was the first we had heard of her interest in studying Scripture. She told us that after twenty-five years she was going to stop smoking pot, wanted to start reading the Bible, and wanted to be part of our community. What followed was a radical transformation that was shocking to witness. Within a few weeks, the intensity was gone from her eyes, and the anger had left her voice. Whereas previously she was unkempt and dirty, she was now looking after herself in both her cleanliness and diet. We helped her find a new apartment, and she began attending the midweek small group that met in our home. Sandra also began serving at our weekly meal, spending her Saturdays preparing food and staying after with us to clean up. And she began working at our monthly food bank, offering encouragement and a familiar face to the many people who showed up for assistance.

Sandra taught us much about ministry, especially about the need to cultivate postures of mutuality when ministering as upper-middle-class people to those in urban poverty. We discovered that it is very easy to slip into a paternalistic posture when ministering among underprivileged communities, a sure way to ensure that "helping" will perpetuate systemic problems. Yet Sandra also taught us about being alert to where God is at work. We were focused intensely on Michelle and her domestic issues, and rightly so. We were trying to be agents of help and relief. We wanted to be advocates to keep a family intact and to help Michelle move toward seeking her own good and her family's flourishing. But we were missing the transformative work going on in Sandra's life. Thankfully, she is a blunt and frank person, who arrested our attention and demanded that we play our roles as agents of God's grace in her life.

Considering the disciples in this narrative, it is understandable that they were likely uncomfortable and probably even paralyzed with fear. And considering how the narrative develops, they could not have been prepared for what they would find. When they hit land on the other side, the demon-possessed man appears out of nowhere! This episode is a great reminder for the church to be ready to be agents of God's goodness. We cannot predict who will have cultivated hearts ready to receive God's transforming grace. We can often be influenced to devote our energies and attention to what might look to us like "good opportunities." We need not apologize for using our good judgment, but we should also be ready to shift gears and nimbly adjust our agendas to be agents of God's love and life to those seeking relief, redemption, and renewal.

The Stigma of Mental Illness

The demon-possessed man in this episode experienced serious social stigmatization and exclusion because of his terrifying behavior, manifesting the reality that he was inhabited by demons. I am not at all suggesting that modern mental illness is a more appropriate way of conceiving of what the ancients thought of as demon possession, but I would like to draw an analogy to the dynamics of stigmatization and exclusion experienced by those afflicted with mental illness in our day. Sadly, many Christians fear exposure because they or a loved one suffers from a mental illness, and in some Christian communities there is great resistance to seeking the help of a counselor, psychologist, or medical professional. This is based on the assumption that somehow prayer and Christian practices should have the power to heal our spirits, and any nonphysical debilities are a sign of spiritual weakness or a lack of faith.

I have people I love in my family who have gone through seasons of darkness, and I know the confusion and loneliness that it can bring. I had the heartbreaking experience of talking with an undergraduate student some years ago who was suffering from a severe depression. He had been told by his Christian parents that it was simply a spiritual issue that could be sorted out through greater faith and more faithful prayer. Such counsel heaps guilt and frustration on top of a person who is already being crushed.

Heather Vacek notes that social stigma among churches is tragic because it "undermines core theological claims" regarding human identity and the calling of the church.[13]

> Both visible and invisible attributes that prompt stigma deepen suffering. Invisible or hidden mental illnesses bring distress because they force sufferers to limit awareness of their plight. A congregant who grieves alone following the death of her hospitalized brother because of her reluctance to share the details of his institutionalization demonstrates suffering generated from stigma-induced invisibility. In social situations, those who ail invisibly manage "undisclosed discrediting information" about themselves. Hiding a potentially stigmatizing attribute requires effort (and sometimes careful planning), but it is an effort that those who ail and their families deem worthwhile.[14]

Vacek commends an approach for the church toward those who suffer mental illness shaped by hospitality, which aligns so well with the dynamics of discipleship in Mark's Gospel. Purposefully giving our time and attention to those who suffer brings a measure of relief from the pains caused by stigmatization. Beyond that, churches can embody hospitality by engaging in long-term processes of drawing those who suffer into our communities, enveloping them with routines of hospitality and love that bring those who suffer from the margins of our community to the very center.[15]

Fear, Departure, and White Flight

A combination of fear and departure in vv. 14–17 of this episode provoke reflection on contemporary dynamics of fear and departure. Some commentators speculate regarding the possibility of an economic motive behind the townspeople's request of Jesus to leave. If that is the case, then Jesus is a threat to their profitability. It does not matter whether a man is restored; what matters is that we have lost these pigs as moneymakers! Whether an economic motive lies behind their request, there certainly is the presence of fear. The powerful outbreak of kingdom-of-God dynamics has restored this man, and it so rattles them that Jesus must depart the region.

While "white flight" is a complicated notion, it is quite a common phenomenon in the United States over the last seventy-five years or so and includes

---

13. Heather H. Vacek, *Madness: American Protestant Responses to Mental Illness* (Waco, TX: Baylor University Press, 2015), 163.

14. Vacek, *Madness*, 166.

15. Vacek, *Madness*, 169–80.

churches moving from urban centers to the suburbs.[16] Many white people in urban neighborhoods responded to the northern migration of African-Americans by moving to the suburbs. This is what is meant by "white flight," and it was motivated by fear of black people and the worry about economic loss in the form of potentially lower property value of their homes. The same dynamics of fear and departure at work in Mark 5 are at work in "white flight."

Historically, white congregations responded by selling their buildings in urban centers and rebuilding in the suburbs. Many changes followed in the wake of this move, including the manner in which churches played roles in communities. Church buildings in cities were on street corners, so that people walked past them often and regarded those churches as central to the life of the neighborhood. It was a meeting place to which they could walk. In the suburbs, however, churches were surrounded by large parking lots and set back from main thoroughfares, so that parishioners now become "commuters." Rather than being essential parts of a church community to which they "belonged," church membership now consists of "attending" a certain church, as if going to church is a show. Because owning a car is essential to being part of such suburban churches, the dynamics of discrimination and class division are woven into the fiber of this arrangement.

On one hand, we might think that the move of meeting places to the suburbs makes sense. After all, if that is where church members live, and it is inconvenient to drive back to the city, then why not meet where they actually live? I wonder, however, if such a move is driven by the individualistic character of American Christianity. Because so much of our ideology and practice of being Christian in America has to do with our own choice, churches inevitably respond to this, catering to the lowest common denominator of "what people want." For a church, then, to stay in a physical location that will cause a good number of people to leave the church is unthinkable. The corporate life of churches takes the shape of community desires, which are oriented by consumer preference. This is unfortunate, since the basic character and holistic mode of life for churches is supposed to be determined by service and oriented toward hospitality to the marginalized. For churches to participate in "white flight," leaving neighborhoods that suffer from relative neglect, is seriously problematic.

---

16. Mark Mulder notes that the responses on the part of white people to African-American northern migration and settlement in cities over the last century varies greatly. Many white people never moved and others moved but to different parts of the same city. Further, Mulder notes that the denominational history of churches is significant in understanding the decisions different communities made (see Mark T. Mulder, *Shades of White Flight: Evangelical Congregations and Urban Departure* [New Brunswick, NJ: Rutgers University Press, 2015], 5–6).

Mark Mulder offers churches—in all locations—a hopeful way to think about what they can do regarding neighborhoods in which they function as neighbors. His suggestions point the way also to how suburban churches can partner with urban churches to be involved in service and hospitality. Mulder notes that churches as sizable communities can advocate for housing availability. This is especially pertinent in my city (where Mulder also lives), Grand Rapids, Michigan, which is currently experiencing a building boom and gentrification, resulting in growing homelessness and the displacement of many from their communities. Churches can advocate for rezoning of neighborhoods for something other than single-family homes, so that affordable housing units can be built.

Churches can also take stock of the rich resources they have, such as well-outfitted industrial kitchens that can be put to use in service to their communities and to other neighborhoods. Our communities are also collections of people with leadership capacities, who can assist greatly in efforts to serve needy neighborhoods. Rather than giving in to fear resulting in departure, churches can begin to reimagine how they can respond in faith and creatively serve their neighborhoods.

CHAPTER 21

Mark 5:21-43

📖 LISTEN to the Story

²¹When Jesus had again crossed over by boat to the other side of the lake, a large crowd gathered around him while he was by the lake. ²²Then one of the synagogue leaders, named Jairus, came, and when he saw Jesus, he fell at his feet. ²³He pleaded earnestly with him, "My little daughter is dying. Please come and put your hands on her so that she will be healed and live." ²⁴So Jesus went with him.

A large crowd followed and pressed around him. ²⁵And a woman was there who had been subject to bleeding for twelve years. ²⁶She had suffered a great deal under the care of many doctors and had spent all she had, yet instead of getting better she grew worse. ²⁷When she heard about Jesus, she came up behind him in the crowd and touched his cloak, ²⁸because she thought, "If I just touch his clothes, I will be healed." ²⁹Immediately her bleeding stopped and she felt in her body that she was freed from her suffering.

³⁰At once Jesus realized that power had gone out from him. He turned around in the crowd and asked, "Who touched my clothes?"

³¹"You see the people crowding against you," his disciples answered, "and yet you can ask, 'Who touched me?'"

³²But Jesus kept looking around to see who had done it. ³³Then the woman, knowing what had happened to her, came and fell at his feet and, trembling with fear, told him the whole truth. ³⁴He said to her, "Daughter, your faith has healed you. Go in peace and be freed from your suffering."

³⁵While Jesus was still speaking, some people came from the house of Jairus, the synagogue leader. "Your daughter is dead," they said. "Why bother the teacher anymore?"

³⁶Overhearing what they said, Jesus told him, "Don't be afraid; just believe."

³⁷He did not let anyone follow him except Peter, James and John the brother of James. ³⁸When they came to the home of the synagogue leader,

Jesus saw a commotion, with people crying and wailing loudly. [39]He went in and said to them, "Why all this commotion and wailing? The child is not dead but asleep." [40]But they laughed at him.

After he put them all out, he took the child's father and mother and the disciples who were with him, and went in where the child was. [41]He took her by the hand and said to her, "*Talitha koum!*" (which means "Little girl, I say to you, get up!"). [42]Immediately the girl stood up and began to walk around (she was twelve years old). At this they were completely astonished. [43]He gave strict orders not to let anyone know about this, and told them to give her something to eat.

Listening to the Text in the Story: Leviticus 15:19–27; 1 Kings 17:17–24; 2 Kings 4:18–37; Psalm 113:5–9; James 1:9–11.

This long passage is another of Mark's "sandwiches"—an episode that has another episode wrapped within it. The incident of Jairus and his daughter opens in vv. 21–24a and concludes in vv. 35–43. In the middle of this account, Mark sets the episode of the woman with the affliction of bleeding (vv. 24b–34). This technique of narrating an episode within another one (called *intercalation*) increases the sense of drama and urgency in the Gospel narrative.

Several details relate these two episodes to one another. The two main characters, Jairus and the woman, are like the demon-possessed man in 5:6 in that they both perceive who Jesus is ("he saw," v. 22; "she heard," v. 27). This is especially significant in light of the disciples' confusion about Jesus in 4:41. Unlike the bewildered disciples, who are seeing but not perceiving, these two characters perceive Jesus and respond with faith and worship. They approach him and fall at his feet (vv. 22, 33), just like the demon-possessed man in the previous account (v. 6), knowing that Jesus is the one who can heal and save. Both accounts involve women who are unclean. The woman has perpetual menstrual bleeding, and Jairus's daughter is dead, and Jesus touches them both, a detail Mark emphasizes in both incidents. The number twelve links the episodes—the little girl is twelve years old (v. 42) and the woman's bleeding has continued for twelve years (v. 25). Both episodes involve "salvation," and both the woman and Jairus overcome their fear and exercise faith.[1] Finally, both

---

1. In vv. 23, 28, and 34 of the NIV, the Greek verb *sōzō* ("to save") is translated "healed." The term refers to rescue or preservation of life in some way and can indicate physical or spiritual salvation. Its appearances here are rightly translated "healed," but there is a sense in which the healings and

women are daughters—the little girl is obviously Jairus's daughter, and Jesus tenderly says to the woman, "Daughter, your faith has healed you" (v. 34).

This twofold account continues several narrative themes that Mark unfolds in his Gospel. The passage is loaded with verbs of perception (seeing, hearing, realizing, knowing), so that Mark is clearly extending his portrayal of how some will have eyes to see and ears to hear and will rightly grasp Jesus's identity and the nature of the kingdom. Yet some, on the other hand, will see but fail to perceive, and hear but fail to listen. It becomes clear, as Mark continues, that 4:1–20 is pivotal for his unfolding narrative. Further, these two incidents portray the purifying power of the kingdom of God with Jesus as its agent. With the invasion of the kingdom into this enslaved world comes an invasion of purity. Jesus has no need to fear becoming unclean by touching the woman and Jairus's daughter, since purity spreads wherever Jesus goes. The unfolding kingdom of God brings with it an outbreak of purifying and healing power.

The account of Jairus and his daughter exhibits a similar pattern to two healings performed by Elijah (1 Kgs 17:17–24) and Elisha (2 Kgs 4:18–37). In both of those accounts there is a desperate woman with a sick son. The two mothers in these scriptural stories speak strongly to the prophets, pleading with them to heal their sons. The incident with Elisha in 2 Kings 4 is especially intense, as the mother had originally been a childless, older woman (v. 14). She had served Elisha by offering to prepare him a room and hosting him as he traveled. Wanting to do something kind for the woman, Elisha told her that she was going to have a son (v. 16). The woman recoiled at the prophecy, indicating that she likely had hopes dashed in the past and did not want to have expectations excited only to be disappointed once again. Later, she had a child, but after several years the child had some sort of headache, which led to his sudden and unexpected death (vv. 18–21). She traveled to meet with Elisha and dramatically confronted him:

> When she reached the man of God at the mountain, she took hold of his feet. Gehazi came over to push her away, but the man of God said, "Leave her alone! She is in bitter distress, but the LORD has hidden it from me and has not told me why."
>
> "Did I ask you for a son, my lord?" she said. "Didn't I tell you, 'Don't raise my hopes'?" (vv. 27–28)

---

exorcisms in Mark are instances of God's wider work of salvation in the sense of delivering God's people from the oppression of sickness and demons.

Elisha traveled back with the woman and laid on top of the boy, who grew warm and eventually was restored to life.

In the same way, these two incidents in Mark portray two desperate situations—Jairus's daughter had died, and the woman had suffered for twelve years, defying the ability of doctors to cure her. And just as Jesus restored the demon-possessed man and enabled him to return to human community, in these two accounts Jesus again restores people and unites them to their loved ones and their communities. In doing so, Jesus is the faithful agent of the kingdom of the God of Israel, who

> raises the poor from the dust
>> and lifts the needy from the ash heap;
> he seats them with princes,
>> with the princes of his people.
> He settles the childless woman in her home
>> as a happy mother of children. (Ps 113:7–9)

EXPLAIN the Story

Jairus Pleads with Jesus (vv. 21–24a)

The episode begins with Jesus and his disciples returning from gentile territory by boat. As soon as they make it back to the other side, they are again mobbed by a crowd of people so large that they can hardly get out of the boat. When he had gone over to a gentile region, only the demon-possessed man came to him, but now that he's back in Jewish territory, eager crowds once again flock to him.[2]

Mark introduces Jairus, who was a synagogue leader, and who was among the crowd. While there are many similarities between these two episodes, Jairus's social location differs starkly from that of the woman with perpetual bleeding. He was a community leader and a central figure in the religious life of the community. While not a rabbi, he would have overseen the synagogue, may have led services, and probably had significant wealth.[3]

Jairus "saw Jesus," an expression of perception that highlights Jairus's awareness of Jesus's capacity to save his daughter. While he was a person of honor in the community, Jairus disregards his social status and humbles himself before

---

2. Moloney, *Gospel of Mark*, 106; Strauss, *Mark*, 228.
3. Marcus, *Mark 1–8*, 365; Black, *Mark*, 139.

Jesus in a posture of worship: he "fell at his feet" (v. 22) and "pleaded earnestly with him" (v. 23). His request to Jesus further demonstrates his faith in Jesus's power to save and restore: "Please come and put your hands on her so that she will be healed and live" (v. 23). Driving his urgency is the fact that Jairus knows his dearly loved daughter is near death (*eschatōs echei*, v. 23). He wants Jesus to put his hands on her in order to "save" her (*sōthē*, NIV: "she may be healed"). "Jesus went with him" (v. 24a), apparently to do just as Jairus had requested.

A Woman's Faith Miraculously Heals Her (vv. 24b–34)

The middle portion of the narrative, like the opening in v. 21, begins with a crowd mobbing Jesus (v. 24). And this increases the desperation of Jairus's situation—the crowd is blocking their progress to save his daughter. As in other places in Mark, the crowd is an obstacle to Jesus's ministry in general, and in this instance it proves fatal.

Amid the crowd is a woman "who had been subject to bleeding for twelve years" (v. 25), indicating perpetual menstruation. While modern readers rightly detect a serious medical need, the woman's plight is even more tragic because of her culture. Like the demon-possessed man in the previous episode, she is perpetually unclean and thus cut off from participation in the ritual worship of her people. Leviticus 15:19–27 details the ritual impurity of a woman during menstruation:

> When a woman has her regular flow of blood, the impurity of her monthly period will last seven days, and anyone who touches her will be unclean till evening.
> Anything she lies on during her period will be unclean, and anything she sits on will be unclean. Anyone who touches her bed will be unclean; they must wash their clothes and bathe with water, and they will be unclean till evening. Anyone who touches anything she sits on will be unclean; they must wash their clothes and bathe with water, and they will be unclean till evening. Whether it is the bed or anything she was sitting on, when anyone touches it, they will be unclean till evening (vv. 19–23).

This poor woman has been constantly unclean for over a decade and ostracized from her community, since, as the text above indicates, anyone who comes near her is defiled. She is also unable to have children and is now poor since she has spent everything on doctors in the attempt to be healed (v. 26). She occupies a very different social location than Jairus. She is an outcast, destitute, and cut off from worship.

Mark mentions her suffering three times (vv. 26, 29, 34), ironically indicating that she "had suffered a great deal under the care of many doctors" (v. 26). Rather than getting better from medical treatment, "she grew worse." Where doctors had exacerbated her condition, however, the woman knows that Jesus can help. Like Jairus, she perceives Jesus's ability to restore her. She "heard about Jesus" (v. 27), and this was genuine perception of him on her part. She demonstrates faith and adopts a posture of worship before him. Mark's comments about her thought process indicate her faith. She reasoned that if she just touched Jesus's clothing, she would be healed (v. 28). And she worships in v. 33 when she overcomes her fear and throws herself at Jesus's feet, confessing to him "the whole truth."

This healing account has some unique elements. Rather than making request to Jesus like Jairus did, the woman secretly touched Jesus's clothing and was healed instantly. Both she and Jesus felt the effect of healing power proceeding from Jesus. She felt instantly that her body was restored (v. 29), and Jesus knew that someone had received healing by touching him because "power had gone out from him" (v. 30).

Mark focuses on the detail of the woman touching Jesus in vv. 28–31. She plans to "just touch his clothes" and then does so, after which Jesus asks, "Who touched my clothes?" The disciples respond by demanding to know how he can ask, "Who touched me?" when there are loads of people crowding against him. This repetition emphasizes the reality that would have been on the minds of anyone who heard this narrative in the ancient world. Certainly her touch makes Jesus unclean, judging by Leviticus 15. Like in other episodes of Mark, however, kingdom dynamics unleash the purifying and healing power of God, so that purity is contagious rather than impurity.

When Jesus demands to know who had touched him, the disciples give voice to what an attentive reader might ask. In effect they say: "Jesus, there are crowds pressing in on you, so that you are hardly able to make your way to Jairus's house. People are jostling, pushing, and shoving in this chaotic rabble, and there are countless people who are touching your clothes and body. How can you possibly ask who touched you!?" What separates this woman from all the others who are touching Jesus in the jostling crowd is her faith. In her absolute desperation, she knew that Jesus could save her, and she acted on that knowledge.

The woman confessed everything to Jesus, even though she was "trembling with fear" (v. 33). While some characters in Mark give in to fear so that they don't exercise faith, the woman overcomes her fear, worships Jesus, and confesses everything to him. This nameless woman, even though she is utterly destitute, socially ostracized, and ritually impure, has ears to hear Jesus and eyes to see the truth about him. Because of that, Jesus tenderly speaks to her a word of sweet redemption. He calls her "daughter," indicating that she is no longer cut off from family and community. Jesus had described those who belong to his family in Mark 3:33–35:

> "Who are my mother and my brothers?" he asked. Then he looked at those seated in a circle around him and said, "Here are my mother and my brothers! Whoever does God's will is my brother and sister and mother."

The woman's response of faith makes her part of Jesus's family. While formerly she was cut off from ritual worship and the community of Israel, her faith puts her squarely within the kingdom of God. Because she now participates in God's restored order of *shalom*, Jesus bids her, "Go in peace and be freed from your suffering" (v. 34).

Jesus Heals Jairus's Daughter (vv. 35–43)

The press of the crowd and the healing of the woman have interrupted Jesus's progress to Jairus's daughter, who was said to be nearing death in the opening scene. As Jesus is concluding his conversation with the woman, some people from Jairus's house arrive to inform Jairus that his daughter has died. "Why bother the teacher anymore?" they ask (v. 35). This statement may be sarcastic, or perhaps it is a rebuke to Jesus.[4] If he had not delayed, he would have been able to save Jairus's precious daughter from death.[5] As Marcus notes, however, this passage points to the logic of the kingdom of God. It is not that one is saved only at the expense of another. The kingdom of God does not have a zero-sum calculus like the kingdoms of this world, where one only benefits by another losing. Where God rules as king, there is more than enough to go around.[6] Rather than an occasion for death to claim a victory, the delay becomes an opportunity for Jesus to triumph over the grave.

Jesus hears the message intended for Jairus and urges him to ignore it (v. 36). He exhorts Jairus to be like the woman who fought through her fears because of her faith. "Don't be afraid; just believe," Jesus tells him, and directs

---

4. Marcus, *Mark 1–8*, 370.

5. In a similar incident, Lazarus's sisters send the message to Jesus that "the one you love is sick" (John 11:3). Because of Jesus's delay, their brother dies, and when Jesus arrives in Bethany, Lazarus's sister Martha confronts him by saying, "If you had been here, my brother would not have died" (v. 21). Mary repeats this lament to Jesus (v. 32).

6. Marcus, *Mark 1–8*, 370.

him back to his house (v. 37). Jesus allows only Peter, James, and John to come with him, indicating for the first time in Mark that Jesus had a special relationship with these three, who were to become his inner circle.[7]

When they arrive at the house, Jesus finds a chaotic scene filled with commotion and the loud crying and wailing of mourners and relatives grieving the death of the little girl. Jesus confronts the mourners causing the commotion, claiming that the girl is not dead but merely asleep. While "sleep" also can indicate death, Jesus points to the girl's merely being naturally asleep and in need of being awakened (v. 39). The mourners mock him when he says this, but Jesus "put them all out" (*ekballō*, v. 40). The action this verb portrays is both more forceful than the NIV indicates and is quite suggestive. Mark uses *ekballō* to speak of Jesus "driving out" demons (1:34; 3:15, 23), so that Jesus driving out the mourners is somehow as characteristic of God's kingdom as his exorcisms.

Several details point toward Jesus's triumph over death in this incident. Mark repeats that Jesus "went in" (vv. 39-40), portraying his powerful entry to the abode of the dead to snatch this life from it. Two verbs also appear that are used with reference to Jesus being raised from the dead, so that Jesus's action points ahead to his own resurrection from the grave (vv. 41-42).[8] The NKJV captures Mark's strategic link of this miracle with God's conquest of death in raising Jesus: "'Little girl, I say to you, *arise*.' Immediately the girl *arose*." Finally, Jesus's touch of the girl is superfluous, since she is brought back to life by his powerful word. Yet it displays his fearlessness in the face of death and, once again, the purifying and life-giving power of the kingdom of God. Whereas touching a dead body would have made a person unclean (e.g., Lev 21:11; Num 19:11), God's kingdom operates in a new cosmic order that radiates cleansing power.

Seeing the girl rise and walk around causes everyone to be "completely astonished" and also draws Jesus's familiar and strict exhortation to keep quiet about what has happened (vv. 42-43a). His final command brings resolution to the desperation of Jairus to see his daughter saved from death. He orders that she be given something to eat (v.43b), giving her back into the care of her family and reuniting father and daughter in communal fellowship. Death destroys human lives and human community, and in conquering death Jesus restores life, family, and community.

---

7. These close associates are with Jesus at a few key points throughout Mark, including his transfiguration (9:2) and in Gethsemane (14:33) (Strauss, *Mark*, 233).

8. The Greek verbs *egeirō* ("to raise") and *anistēmi* ("to raise up") are used elsewhere in Mark with reference to Jesus's resurrection from the dead (8:31; 9:31; 10:34; 16:6; see Marcus, *Mark 1–8*, 372–73).

LIVE the Story

Faith and Healing

This passage connects faith and healing in a way that seems promising: Can we somehow guarantee healing from God if we have enough faith? This text, and others like it, seems to offer hope that perhaps there is a formula for divine healing. After all, if these characters are healed because of their faith, then perhaps a certain measure of faith on our part is sufficient to be healed from physical and mental afflictions. At the same time, many are aware of the anxiety and guilt that this discussion can generate. Many have prayed for years for healing and have felt guilty because they have assumed—or they are told by others—that their lack of faith is the reason for unanswered prayer. To reflect faithfully on the connection between faith and healing in this text and how it has significance for the contemporary world, we must understand the place of healing and faith in Mark's Gospel and then set this within a larger biblical-theological framework.

Jesus's statements in Mark that "your faith has healed you" are not as straightforward as they may seem. They should not be taken to endorse the assumption that if we have enough faith, healing is guaranteed. In Mark 5:34 Jesus tells the woman, "Daughter, your faith has healed you. Go in peace and be freed from your suffering." The Greek term here translated "healed" is a form of the verb *sōzō*, which means "to save" or "to rescue," and it points to her faith being effective to restore her in the sense that she has been drawn up into the redemptive power and presence of God's kingdom. In support of this, Jesus makes the further statement regarding her physical healing. So, he first commends her faith, which makes her a part of the kingdom of God, and follows this with the statement that she is also freed from her suffering.

A form of the same verb (*sōzō*) is used in Mark 10:52 when Jesus speaks to Bartimaeus after healing his blindness. Bartimaeus expresses his faith by rightly identifying Jesus as the Son of David and calling on him for mercy. Further, in response to Jesus's question ("What do you want me to do for you?"), Bartimaeus answers that he wants to see (v. 51). This is an important passage in the development of this section of Mark, one in which the disciples are desperately in need of vision and insight into Jesus and the kingdom. This is precisely the thing for which Bartimaeus asks, in contrast to James and John, who answer Jesus's same question in v. 36 with desires for prominence. At the end of this brief episode, Bartimaeus joins Jesus on the way to Jerusalem, indicating that he has become a true disciple—he has true perception—walking in the way of Jesus. All of this informs Jesus's statement to him that his faith has "saved" or "restored" (*sesōken*, from *sōzō*) him, drawing him into the power and presence of the kingdom so that he is renewed and restored to God. Jesus commends his spiritual perception, which is the very thing the disciples need to develop.

These two incidents do not employ the verb *therapeuō* ("to heal"), which is used in other contexts, pointing to a person being restored to health from some kind of sickness or physical illness. Mark uses this term in 1:34 to speak of the pattern of Jesus's ministry in Galilee. He also uses it in 6:5 to speak of what Jesus was able to do in a context where faith was lacking. His hometown largely rejected him, which left Jesus amazed at their lack of faith. Mark makes the intriguing statement that because of this, Jesus was unable to do any miracles except to heal (*therapeuō*) just a few sick people. Mark, then, portrays the kingdom of God as being attended by exorcisms and healings that point to its invading power, driving out the darkness of satanic oppression and sickness. He uses *therapeuō* to speak of this dynamic and does not comment on whether the healed person had faith. In fact, in Mark 6:5 Jesus is still able to heal (in the *therapeuō* sense) in a context where faith was lacking. But when Jesus commends people for their faith and notes that it is effective to draw them into the power of the kingdom, he uses the verb *sōzō*, pointing to God's saving power breaking out to overtake and renew a person.

Mark's narrative strategy, then, is to present healings and exorcisms as indications that the kingdom of God is invading this present evil age, depicted as an enslaved condition. Satan—the "god of this age" (2 Cor 4:4), "the strong man" (Mark 3:27)—holds the world in his enslaving and oppressive grip, and unclean spirits have overrun Israel. God's historic people are not only politically and economically oppressed by the Romans but are spiritually dominated by cosmic forces of darkness. Jesus's arrival on the scene comes with the liberating power of God's kingdom, freeing people from Satan's power and demonic enslavement and restoring many to wholeness through healing. Mark does not focus so much on individuals and their internal dispositions as good or bad candidates for healing, but rather on Jesus and his power to free people from sickness and death and the power of unclean spirits. That is, Mark's burden is to demonstrate the arrival of the kingdom and its restorative dynamics and life-giving power.

We ought to avoid moving too quickly, therefore, from isolated instances where faith and healing are connected to contemporary applications about the possibility of healing without understanding the character of Mark's larger portrait. After all, many are healed in Mark without any comment on their internal disposition of faith, and there are some instances of healing that are followed by disobedience. For example, in Mark 1:40–45 Jesus healed a leper and ordered him to keep quiet and follow proper procedure for restoration to his community. Instead, the man spread the news of what Jesus did, which inhibited Jesus's subsequent ministry. This does not invalidate or reverse his healing, but the incident fits Mark's overall depiction of the emergence of the kingdom of God. Healing and restoration are being spread around without any comment on whether certain individuals are deserving.

We must also keep in mind the "already-not yet" character of the kingdom of God in the rest of Scripture. God's kingdom has invaded the world in the death and resurrection of Jesus and the sending of the Spirit. God's life-giving Spirit has been poured out among us, so that our communities are outposts of kingdom life, experiencing its life-giving and restorative power. In this sense, the kingdom is *already here*. At the same time, the kingdom is *not yet here in its fullness*. We still await the future restoration of all things, when God's life-giving presence pervades all reality and he restores all things to himself. Only at this time will we experience complete wholeness as God intended. Only then will we be fully healed and restored, living in God's restored world in resurrected bodies forever.

Suffering, pain, and death are not God's will for creation, but they are inevitable aspects of this world in its broken condition. Because humanity cast its lot with anti-God forces in rebellion against God (Gen 3), we currently inhabit the world in a condition that resists God's rule and that is not operating according to God's will. In the end, God will heal and restore creation, including human bodies, and end suffering and death forever. That future day will consummate the new creation in which God's world fully and finally reflects God's will.

In the meantime, healing is indeed a blessing from God, in Mark and in the rest of Scripture, including the Elijah and Elisha healing narratives mentioned above. Sickness robs us of our health and can put enormous stress on families and communities. To be restored to health from an illness, disease, or injury may feel like a return to truly living. Following the example of Paul (2 Cor 12:8), it is surely right to pray to God, the one who "heals all your diseases" (Ps 103:3) for relief and wholeness. If we are restored, we ought to give thanks and celebrate the Lord's goodness. If we are not healed, we should not regard this as a lack of faith on our part, and we should resist the temptation to interpret this as some sort of message from God—either that we are being punished or in some way being tested for a specific reason.

It is wrong to assume that God is doing these things to us and that he has some hidden reason behind doing so. This is not how God works. He is not the author of evil (Jas 1:13), nor does he call us to try to get into his brain and figure out what hidden meaning there may be to our suffering. Our suffering and sickness are cruel realities in this broken creation. One day God will triumph over suffering and death in such a satisfying manner that the hearts of those who have been touched by pain will be fully at rest and filled with joy. And before that time comes, we can experience God's triumph in the midst of suffering, as God transforms it for his purposes. God is not the active agent behind our suffering, therefore, but he works in the midst of it for our good and his glory.

Suffering, pain, and death open opportunities for us to lament creation's broken condition along with God. God sees and feels the broken condition of his world and experiences it deeply. In Romans 8:18–27, Paul discusses the groaning of creation, of humanity, and of the Spirit of God, as believers await the transformation of their bodies. In that day, humanity will enjoy the restored world, and we will rule it faithfully on God's behalf so that it no longer suffers the awful effects of ruination and abuse. In the face of pain and suffering, many Christians feel the need to explain it away or look for a hidden divine logic behind it all. A better approach is to participate with God's Spirit in lamenting the broken condition of God's world. This approach brings a measure of relief as we speak truthfully about our pain and cry out to God to hasten the day when all things are made new.

One of the ways God triumphs over suffering and pain is that he works his purposes in the midst of it. When we suffer, God enters in and works for our good (Rom 8:28), empowering us when our faith is stressed and stretched so that we develop a persevering faith (Jas 1:2–4). The author of Hebrews calls on his audience to respond rightly amid trouble and stress, so that the suffering can be transformed into training from the Lord (Heb 12:7–11). Some Christians appeal to this passage to demonstrate that our suffering is God's "discipline" of his children, understood in terms of punishment. But the writer is not explaining the logic of suffering but exhorting his listeners to respond rightly amid suffering, so that it can be transformed into "training" from God, an opportunity for God to empower them for endurance, which will confirm to them that they are indeed God's children.

Much more could be said about suffering and pain, especially the opportunities these present for the church to engage and serve those who are suffering. To sum up, when it comes to sickness, it is right to pray for healing. Health, after all, is God's will! But we inhabit a world where God's will is not being done as it will be in the future when God restores all things and fully establishes his reign. If we are not healed and continue to experience sickness and suffering, we ought to be confident that even in this age, before God fully triumphs over all suffering and pain, we can still enjoy God's triumph over sickness, as God works by his Spirit to bring to bear a range of dynamics that make the kingdom among us truly effective and powerful.

CHAPTER 22

Mark 6:1–6a

📖 LISTEN to the Story

¹Jesus left there and went to his hometown, accompanied by his disciples. ²When the Sabbath came, he began to teach in the synagogue, and many who heard him were amazed.

"Where did this man get these things?" they asked. "What's this wisdom that has been given him? What are these remarkable miracles he is performing? ³Isn't this the carpenter? Isn't this Mary's son and the brother of James, Joseph, Judas and Simon? Aren't his sisters here with us?" And they took offense at him.

⁴Jesus said to them, "A prophet is not without honor except in his own town, among his relatives and in his own home." ⁵He could not do any miracles there, except lay his hands on a few sick people and heal them. ⁶He was amazed at their lack of faith.

Listening to the Text in the Story: Jeremiah 2:9–19; 20:1–6; Ezekiel 2:1–10; Luke 4:14–30; 13:33–34; Acts 7.

In the previous few episodes, Mark has narrated three positive reactions to Jesus, three instances of richly prepared soil. Each of the characters in Mark 5 —the demon-possessed man, Jairus, and the unnamed woman—see and hear of Jesus and rightly perceive who he is, and they approach him in postures of worship. Jesus now travels to his hometown and finds a very different reception. The townspeople also hear Jesus (v. 2), but their hearing is matched with a failure to perceive. Their familiarity with Jesus and the fact that they knew him as a common laborer prevent them from recognizing him as the Son of God, the agent who brings in the kingdom of God.

God's historic people have a long history of rejecting God's messengers. Acts 7 records the speech Stephen gave to the leaders of Jerusalem, in which he recounted Israel's consistent pattern of rejecting their God-provided redeemers.

God had appointed Joseph to be the agent of salvation for many around the ancient world, including his father Jacob, his brothers, and their families. Joseph's brothers rejected him, however, a move that God overturned, resulting in their rescue and blessing (Acts 7:9–16; cf. Gen 50:20). And the Israelites rejected Moses, whom God had called to deliver them from slavery in Egypt (Acts 7:17–29). Stephen concludes his speech with the provocative challenge, "Was there ever a prophet your ancestors did not persecute?" (v. 52). Jesus expresses the same sentiment sarcastically, which leads into his lament over Israel's capital:

> Surely no prophet can die outside Jerusalem! Jerusalem, Jerusalem, you who kill the prophets and stone those sent to you, how often I have longed to gather your children together, as a hen gathers her chicks under her wings, and you were not willing. (Luke 13:33–34)

The prophet Jeremiah was one of these persecuted, faithful proclaimers of God's truth to God's people. When God commissioned him to prophesy against Judah and its rulers, he told Jeremiah that he would face great opposition (Jer 1:19), and this proved to be the case. He was beaten and thrown into prison (20:1–6) and later put into a deep cistern (38:1–6), because his prophesying was resulting in discouragement (v. 4). The grief and frustration that God's prophets experience when God's people ignore or refuse to heed the prophetic word is shared by God himself. Jeremiah quotes God's lament over the defection of Judah:

> Cross over to the coasts of Cyprus and look,
>   send to Kedar and observe closely;
>   see if there has ever been anything like this:
> Has a nation ever changed its gods?
>   (Yet they are not gods at all.)
> But my people have exchanged their glorious God
>   for worthless idols. (Jer 2:10–11)

Mark's account of Jesus's rejection by his hometown continues this biblical theme of the rejection of God in his people's rejection of God's agents of salvation.

EXPLAIN the Story

After leaving Capernaum, where the previous episode took place, Jesus went with his disciples to his hometown of Nazareth. His teaching in the local synagogue on the Sabbath caused amazement (v. 2). This is an early indication that the "many who heard him" may end up responding positively to Jesus—hearing and truly perceiving. With the first few questions that they ask themselves, it appears that they are grasping for some explanation and may be open to receiving the truth of who Jesus is. Their questions run along precisely the right lines: they want to know what is behind what Jesus is doing and what is the wisdom or power by which he is doing what he is doing. They have yet to draw any conclusions.

Their initial amazement and subsequent inquisitiveness, however, take a dark turn. They are offended first because Jesus is a mere laborer. The term *tektōn* can indicate a "carpenter," but it is a slightly broader term pointing to a craftsman, artisan, or laborer. Jesus is not an authorized and recognized teacher, so they have trouble recognizing him as God's appointed spokesperson and the agent whereby God's kingdom comes in power. The book of Sirach, a Jewish text that dates from the early second-century BC, describes the value of the laborer in contrast to that of the scribe:

> All these [the plowman, the smith, the potter] rely on their hands,
>   and all are skillful in their own work.
> Without them no city can be inhabited,
>   and wherever they live, they will not go hungry.
> Yet they are not sought out for the council of the people,
>   nor do they attain eminence in the public assembly.
> They do not sit in the judge's seat,
>   nor do they understand the decisions of the courts;
> they cannot expound discipline or judgment,
>   and they are not found among the rulers. (Sir 38:31–33 NRSV)

The author then turns to ponder the task of the scribe:

> How different the one who devotes himself
>   to the study of the law of the Most High!
> He seeks out the wisdom of all the ancients,
>   and is concerned with prophecies;
> he preserves the sayings of the famous
>   and penetrates the subtleties of parables;
> he seeks out the hidden meanings of proverbs
>   and is at home with the obscurities of parables.
> He serves among the great
>   and appears before rulers;

he travels in foreign lands
>   and learns what is good and evil in the human lot.
He sets his heart to rise early
>   to seek the Lord who made him,
>   and to petition the Most High;
he opens his mouth in prayer
>   and asks pardon for his sins. (38:34–39:5 NRSV)

The common assumption of the respective tasks of laborers and scribes affected how the townspeople conceived of Jesus. "Hey, that's the carpenter who fixed my mother's broken chair. Who does he think he is, a scribe, a respected teacher of Torah? Who is he kidding?"

They also stumble over their familiarity with him. There is something exotic about the unknown, about someone we have not seen before so that we are unaware of his faults and failings. But they know Jesus and know his family. Nazareth was not a big town; it was the sort of place where everyone knows everyone else and word gets around. They were familiar with Jesus's family, as they were able to name his mother and siblings.[1] These two factors—that he is a laborer and that they know him and his family—become the cause of their stumbling (v. 3). The Greek term *skandalizō* points to such a serious objection that one is unable to accept the truth of what is being said. Many in his hometown are scandalized to the extent that they reject the gospel proclamation.[2]

At their rejection, Jesus states to them that "a prophet is not without honor except in his own town, among his relatives and in his own home," pointing to the immediate circumstance but also including the previous behavior of his family (Mark 3:20–35). Just as God's people have rejected and persecuted God's prophets through the centuries, stretching back to Moses, the prophet Jesus, proclaiming God's message to God's people, faces the same reaction.

Mark includes the arresting statement in v. 5 that Jesus "could not do any miracles there" (*ouk edynato*, lit. "was not able"). In some way the power and presence of the kingdom is affected by human faith. We may think of the kingdom of God as spaces where God's power is present. It is present in great power where humans welcome it, lean fully into it, and seek to actualize it through communal practices of self-giving love driven by an orientation toward God

---

1. Placher claims that identifying Jesus as Mary's son is an insult to him, since the normal mode of identification is by one's father in the first century (William C. Placher, *Mark*, Belief: A Theological Commentary on the Bible [Louisville: Westminster John Knox, 2010], 88). However, this does not appear to hint at Jesus's illegitimacy, but simply is an informal description (Boring, *Mark*, 166).

2. Hooker, *Mark*, 153.

and his glory. Human resistance, however, snuffs out kingdom power and marginalizes the life-giving presence of God. While the possibility of humans being able to thwart the work of God may strike us as troubling, it is only so if we have a static or absolute conception of God's power and presence rather than one that comes from attending closely to how God works among his people throughout Scripture. The prophet Ezekiel saw the glory of God depart from the temple and then from Jerusalem because of the unfaithfulness of God's people (Ezek 10). And in the book of Revelation, the risen Lord Jesus warns the church at Ephesus that if they do not repent from their complacency, the Spirit of Jesus will depart from them (Rev 2:5). Scripture portrays a direct correlation between the presence and power of God and the receptive faith of God's people. Where there is glad reception and hearty embrace of God's commands, God dwells there in power. Where there is resistance and rejection, God's presence is marginalized and muted.

Corresponding to the amazement of the townspeople (v. 2), the account closes with Jesus's being amazed at their lack of faith (v. 6). Having encountered overpowering crowds to this point in his ministry, and in light of the great faith demonstrated by the demon-possessed man, Jairus, and the unnamed woman, Jesus is stunned to encounter rejection in his hometown to the point that he is able to heal only a few sick people (v. 5).

LIVE the Story

The Scandal of a Crucified Christ

In a conversation just the other day about evangelism, someone mentioned the need to keep in mind that unbelievers may be offended by the cross. Such a reminder is important, but what is striking to me is that often in Scripture *God's own people are the ones offended by God's upside-down way of working*—by the identity of Jesus as a common laborer who is a crucified Messiah. In this very passage, God's historic people are offended by Jesus's identity and teaching, people who know Jesus well and who are amazed by all that he is doing. Bringing this closer to home, it is easy for Christians to be tripped up by God's way of working. We can fall prey to a worldly way of thinking and have our imaginations shaped by triumphalism and a longing for a Jesus of power and spectacle. We run the risk of being "scandalized" in the same way that those in Jesus's hometown were.

This dynamic of God's own people being scandalized by the reality of a crucified Messiah appears in a number of places in the New Testament.

In John 6:35, Jesus begins to speak to those who are following him about his identity as the "bread of life." Further, he proclaims that they need to eat his flesh and drink his blood so they can truly be his disciples (vv. 54–57). When he discerns that his hearers are objecting to what he is saying ("This is a hard teaching. Who can accept it?" v. 60), he asks them, "Does this offend [*skandalizei*] you? Then what if you see the Son of Man ascend to where he was before!" (vv. 61–62). This is a very odd statement. No one will actually see Jesus ascending to his heavenly throne, but in John's Gospel, Jesus's ascension begins at the cross (3:14; 8:28). They will see the Son of Man being lifted up on the cross, but will they recognize it through the eyes of faith as Jesus's ascent to his throne? Or will they merely see it as a crucifixion, the tragic end of Jesus's claims to be Messiah?[3]

Knowing that his teaching challenges worldly ways of thinking among God's people, Jesus presses the objectionable elements in arresting language. His teaching will offend, but his disciples must get used to embracing the offense of his teaching, since the center of the faith is going to be the greatest possible scandal—the call to recognize the one who hangs on a cross as Lord and God.

The Corinthian church had fallen into triumphalism, which drove their self-seeking pursuit for glory. Paul reminded them of the logic of the cross, depicting the character of the gospel over against the world's way of doing things:

Where is the wise person? Where is the teacher of the law? Where is the philosopher of this age? Has not God made foolish the wisdom of the world? For since in the wisdom of God the world through its wisdom did not know him, God was pleased through the foolishness of what was preached to save those who believe. Jews demand signs and Greeks look for wisdom, but we preach Christ crucified: a stumbling block [*skandalon*] to Jews and foolishness to Gentiles, but to those whom God has called, both Jews and Greeks, Christ the power of God and the wisdom of God. For the foolishness of God is wiser than human wisdom, and the weakness of God is stronger than human strength. (1 Cor 1:20–25)

God is unleashing his saving power in a way that defies all expectations of "how the world works." To human reasoning, it is foolishness that God would accomplish his purposes through a crucified Messiah, and the proclamation

---

3. Robert H. Gundry, *Commentary on the New Testament: Verse-by-Verse Explanations with a Literal Translation* (Peabody, MA: Hendrickson, 2010), 387.

of this message is folly. But the apostolic preaching of Christ crucified accomplishes God's saving purposes. Richard Hays wonderfully captures the heart of Paul's discussion:

> All of this is understandably baffling to Paul's hearers in the ancient Mediterranean world. Jews, who have suffered long under the burden of foreign oppression, quite reasonably look for manifestations of God's *power*: signs like those done by Moses at the time of the exodus, perhaps portending at last God's powerful deliverance of his people again from bondage. The Messiah should be a man of power, manifesting supernatural proofs of God's favor. Greeks, with their proverbial love of learning, quite reasonably look for *wisdom*: reasonable accounts of the order of things presented in a logically compelling and aesthetically pleasing manner. The Christ should be a wise teacher of philosophical truths. But no! God has blown away all apparently reasonable criteria: the Christ is a crucified criminal.[4]

The manner in which God works—God's "wisdom"—defies human expectations and common-sense calculations of the best ways to get things done. And this becomes a "scandal" to churches when such mindsets begin to grow among the people of God. It is utterly unexpected for God to save his people, to free his creation from the grip of sin and death, and to unleash on his world his own resurrection life through a common laborer who was misunderstood by his own family—one who was rejected by his hometown, abandoned by his followers, and ultimately put to death as a criminal. In the eyes of the world, it is completely backward.

This upside-down, expectation-defying wisdom is that which orients the church as a human community that operates unlike any other. The challenge for us in the contemporary world is being conformed to this divine "wisdom" in our orientation rather than being conformed to the "wisdoms" of this world (Rom 12:1–2; Jas 3:13–18). A community of self-giving love and service that looks out for the broken and marginalized and that is uninterested in social prestige is one that makes little sense in our world. We might say that joining such a community and making it the center of one's life is *scandalous*. But this is the life to which the Son of God calls us.

---

4. Richard B. Hays, *First Corinthians*, Interpretation (Louisville: Westminster John Knox, 1997), 31.

LISTEN to the Story

Then Jesus went around teaching from village to village. ⁷Calling the Twelve to him, he began to send them out two by two and gave them authority over impure spirits.

⁸These were his instructions: "Take nothing for the journey except a staff—no bread, no bag, no money in your belts. ⁹Wear sandals but not an extra shirt. ¹⁰Whenever you enter a house, stay there until you leave that town. ¹¹And if any place will not welcome you or listen to you, leave that place and shake the dust off your feet as a testimony against them."

¹²They went out and preached that people should repent. ¹³They drove out many demons and anointed many sick people with oil and healed them.

¹⁴King Herod heard about this, for Jesus' name had become well known. Some were saying, "John the Baptist has been raised from the dead, and that is why miraculous powers are at work in him."

¹⁵Others said, "He is Elijah."

And still others claimed, "He is a prophet, like one of the prophets of long ago."

¹⁶But when Herod heard this, he said, "John, whom I beheaded, has been raised from the dead!"

¹⁷For Herod himself had given orders to have John arrested, and he had him bound and put in prison. He did this because of Herodias, his brother Philip's wife, whom he had married. ¹⁸For John had been saying to Herod, "It is not lawful for you to have your brother's wife." ¹⁹So Herodias nursed a grudge against John and wanted to kill him. But she was not able to, ²⁰because Herod feared John and protected him, knowing him to be a righteous and holy man. When Herod heard John, he was greatly puzzled; yet he liked to listen to him.

²¹Finally the opportune time came. On his birthday Herod gave a banquet for his high officials and military commanders and the leading

men of Galilee. [22]When the daughter of Herodias came in and danced, she pleased Herod and his dinner guests.

The king said to the girl, "Ask me for anything you want, and I'll give it to you." [23]And he promised her with an oath, "Whatever you ask I will give you, up to half my kingdom."

[24]She went out and said to her mother, "What shall I ask for?"

"The head of John the Baptist," she answered.

[25]At once the girl hurried in to the king with the request: "I want you to give me right now the head of John the Baptist on a platter."

[26]The king was greatly distressed, but because of his oaths and his dinner guests, he did not want to refuse her. [27]So he immediately sent an executioner with orders to bring John's head. The man went, beheaded John in the prison, [28]and brought back his head on a platter. He presented it to the girl, and she gave it to her mother. [29]On hearing of this, John's disciples came and took his body and laid it in a tomb.

[30]The apostles gathered around Jesus and reported to him all they had done and taught.

Listening to the Text in the Story: Exodus 16; Leviticus 18:13, 16; 20:21; Deuteronomy 8:4; 29:5; 1 Kings 16:29–19:3; 21; Esther 1; 5:1–8; Acts 7.

This passage is another instance of a Markan sandwich, also called an *intercalation*, with one episode wrapped within another. The sending of the disciples by Jesus in 6:6b–13 and their return in v. 30 frames the story of the arrest and execution of John the Baptist. By bringing these two accounts together, Mark indicates that disciples of Jesus are not guaranteed a soft and easy life. On the contrary, those who are faithful may encounter dangerously threatening circumstances, just like John the Baptist did, and—as readers of Mark know—just like Jesus did. As in other places in Mark (e.g., 1:14), the treatment of John at the hands of Herod foreshadows the treatment of Jesus at the hands of the Jerusalem authorities and Pilate. And just as with John and Jesus, disciples sent out by Jesus are subject to the whims of wicked leaders and to unfolding political dynamics that have nothing to do with them. While the disciples return from this mission unharmed, many of them will later die as martyrs, pointing ahead to the countless faithful disciples through the ages who have endured persecution and died at the hands of others.

Jesus sends his disciples out on mission to proclaim repentance. They are calling Israel back to faithfulness to God, the one who brought them up out of Egypt and commissioned them to be a light to the nations. And, as Marcus points out, there are similarities between the instructions to the disciples in vv. 8–11 and God's provision for the Israelites during the exodus. In the same way that God sent manna from heaven to feed the Israelites (Exod 16), Jesus instructs his disciples not to bring any food with them but to depend on God's provision through people who will supply it for them. And just as God saw to it that the garments and shoes of the Israelites did not wear out during their sojourn (Deut 8:4; 29:5–6), Jesus orders his disciples to take with them only one garment.[1]

These similarities point to the thrust of Jesus's ministry in Mark whereby God is reconstituting his people Israel in a new exodus event, creating in Jesus a new community of followers who will make up the kingdom of God that spreads to the gentiles (i.e., the nations). Mark's narrative bears this out as Jesus calls Jews to follow him and inhabit the kingdom and as he also goes to gentile territories to spread the kingdom, in keeping with God's original intentions to bless the nations through Israel (Gen 12:3; Exod 19:6).

This text also contains allusions to the confrontational prophetic ministry of Elijah. The disciples' missionary activities remind people of the ministry of John the Baptist and of other biblical prophets, including Elijah (vv. 14–15). Just as John the Baptist rebukes Herod Antipas for his relationship with Herodias, Elijah had a series of confrontations with that legendarily wicked royal couple, Ahab and Jezebel. After his contest with the prophets of Baal on Mount Carmel, in which the God of Israel demonstrated his supremacy over Baal (1 Kgs 18:16–46), Elijah called for the slaughter of these false prophets. In response, Jezebel issued a threat to kill Elijah: "May the gods deal with me, be it ever so severely, if by this time tomorrow I do not make your life like that of one of them" (19:2). Elijah later accosted Ahab and Jezebel for their murderous theft of Naboth's vineyard, prophesying the death of Jezebel and judgment on the house of Ahab (1 Kgs 21).

Mark makes some interesting associations in Mark 6:14–15. The traveling ministries of the disciples cause the name of Jesus to "become well known," reminding people of John the Baptist, Elijah, and "the prophets of long ago." Each Gospel writer portrays Jesus through the use of different, though related, biblical images. Matthew portrays Jesus in terms of Moses, Israel's teacher and lawgiver, and Luke portrays him as the Lord, the cosmic ruler.

---

1. Marcus, *Mark 1–8*, 389.

John portrays Jesus as the Son of God who is one with God the Father. Mark, however, portrays Jesus in terms of Elijah, the confrontational prophet proclaiming repentance and calling God's people back to faithfulness. The disciples extend this image, carrying out their mission of preaching repentance, forcefully driving out demons, and like Elijah, healing many sick people (vv. 12–13).

EXPLAIN the Story

Sending of the Disciples (vv. 6b–13)

This initial section, the initial and outer part of the Markan sandwich, begins with the summary statement of Jesus going around and teaching from village to village. Interestingly, Mark mentions Jesus teaching, but again does not include the content of his teaching, as he does in a few other places, most notably 1:20–28. Like that passage, Mark portrays Jesus acting authoritatively, calling the disciples to himself and sending them out on mission, somewhat like the God of Israel calling his people to himself through the dramatic events of the exodus, commissioning them as a light to the nations. This is another way in which Mark depicts Jesus as the authoritative teacher, the one who has the power to drive out demons and who delegates this authority to his disciples to extend his ministry.

Jesus sent them out "two by two," a reflection of the pattern in the early church of ministry partnerships (6:7). In Acts, Paul and Barnabas travel together on mission, as do Paul and Silas and Peter and John.[2] As Black notes, sending the disciples in pairs ensures safety and corroboration.[3] Jesus gives to each pair a set of instructions in vv. 8–11 regarding their provisions and mode of ministry. They are to take nothing but a staff, indicating that the mission will be dangerous. Walking from town to town subjected the disciples to the dangers of bandits and wild animals.[4] And they were to take no provisions for themselves—"no bread, no bag, no money in your belts. Wear sandals but not an extra shirt" (vv. 8–9). This would have made them dependent on others to provide food and shelter for them, an indication that they are completely dependent on God to look after them, just as God provided for Israel during their sojourn in the desert.

---

2. Moloney, *Gospel of Mark*, 121.
3. Black, *Mark*, 152.
4. Marcus, *Mark 1–8*, 383.

When staying in a town and being welcomed into a house, the disciples are to stay in that house until they leave (v. 10), which Boring interprets as a prohibition from looking around for some better place to stay.[5] Jesus also mentions that in some places they will not be welcomed. He is not thinking of a town politely declining an offer but rather rejection of and opposition to the gospel proclamation.[6] When this happens, the disciples are to perform a symbolic act that indicates that the people are bringing judgment on themselves by not receiving the word about the kingdom. "Shaking the dust off the feet" was something that Jewish travelers did when they returned from pagan lands, leaving the impurity outside of the holy land of Israel.[7] This was an indication that the blame for the godlessness of the towns that rejected God's word would be their own and that they were bringing inevitable judgment on themselves. Paul performed a similar symbolic act in Corinth:

> When Silas and Timothy came from Macedonia, Paul devoted himself exclusively to preaching, testifying to the Jews that Jesus was the Messiah. But when they opposed Paul and became abusive, he shook out his clothes in protest and said to them, "Your blood be on your own heads! I am innocent of it. From now on I will go to the Gentiles." (Acts 18:5–6)

This passage is an exception to Mark's typical portrayal of the disciples throughout his Gospel narrative. Whereas he mostly presents them in a negative light, demonstrating their failure to rightly grasp Jesus's identity and faithfully respond to his cross-oriented gospel, in this text they respond positively. Jesus commissions them with specific instructions, and they do what Jesus says to do, preaching repentance, driving out demons, and healing people.[8] In fact, this is an instance of the disciples properly being "with Jesus," recalling Mark 3:13–15 where Jesus "called" the Twelve to himself and appointed them to be "with him." This commission involved the two tasks of preaching the kingdom and having authority to drive out demons. Here, then, even though they are sent out and separated from Jesus, they are "with" him in that they are operating according to his agenda and doing the very things he has been doing throughout his ministry.

---

5. Boring, *Mark*, 176.
6. Boring, *Mark*, 176; Marcus, *Mark 1–8*, 390.
7. Hooker, *Mark*, 157; Moloney, *Gospel of Mark*, 123.
8. The anointing with oil was a common practice in Judaism for healing (Matt 6:17; Jas 5:14). Cf. also C. Whalen, "Healing," *DJG* 362–70.

Opinions about Jesus (vv. 14–16)

The effect of the disciples' ministry was great, but Mark does not attribute the stir being generated to the disciples themselves. Rather, their ministry had the result of Jesus's name becoming well-known. This is another indication that the disciples are carrying out Jesus's intentions and operating on his agenda. They are not pointing to themselves and advancing their own cause, but their proclamation of the kingdom and of repentance results in Jesus's name being spread.

Word of this reaches Herod Antipas. This Herod, called here "king," was not actually a king but a tetrarch, which means "ruler of a quarter." After the death of his father Herod the Great in 4 BC, Herod Antipas had inherited rule over Galilee and Perea, a region to the east of the Jordan River.[9] Mark may be referring to him as a king because this was more or less the custom among commoners in those regions. Marcus, however, claims that Mark is using the term ironically, mocking the notion of his rule. He notes that Herod Antipas is hardly kingly at all, unable to control the events that unfold here. He cannot do what he wants with John, unable to shut him up or to protect him from Herodias. He is subject to his own passions, driven to make this foolishly boastful oath to Salome, and then controlled by his fear of the guests into carrying out what has been requested. He is easily manipulable, slave to his own passions, lusts, and fears.[10] While Marcus's suggestion is intriguing—and clearly Herod Antipas is a pathetic character in this narrative—we cannot say with confidence that Mark uses the title ironically. He may be just representing the common assumption of people who were unaware of the fine distinctions between titles made in Rome.[11]

When word of what is going on in Galilee reaches Herod, he speculates that John the Baptist has been raised from the dead, and Mark mentions this terrified speculation twice (vv. 14, 16), as if John has returned to haunt Herod and torture his guilty conscience. In repeating Herod's worry that John has been raised from the dead, Mark notes that Herod is the one who had him beheaded (v. 16), and this becomes the occasion for the flashback to how John's murderous execution came about. Mark also mentions the speculation of others who try to account for the miraculous powers at work through the disciples. Many associate the wonders being done with Elijah or the prophets

---

9. Herod Antipas, the son of Herod the Great and the Samaritan Malthace, ruled over Galilee and Perea, two disconnected territories, from 4 BC to 39 AD, after which he and Herodias were banished to Gaul (H. Bond, "Herodian Dynasty," *DJG* 381–82).

10. Marcus, *Mark 1–8*, 398–99.

11. Placher, *Mark*, 93.

of old. This is yet another association of the ministry of Jesus with Elijah. It portrays Jesus through the lens of that prophet's ministry as one of confrontation and powerful reorientation of Israel away from idolatry and toward repentance and embodiment of the kingdom of God.

The Arrest of John the Baptist (vv. 17–20)

The mention of John provides the opportunity for this flashback to the arrest and execution of John in vv. 17–29. John had been acting in the mode of a prophet of Israel, calling out a leader among God's people for conducting an adulterous relationship. Herod Antipas had divorced his wife and married Herodias, the wife of his brother Herod Philip, while the latter was still alive. This was a plain violation of the Mosaic law, which is the reason John confronted him (Lev 18:16; 20:21). As mentioned above, John's confrontation of Herod Antipas and Herodias recalls Elijah's conflicts with Israel's wicked royal couple, Ahab and Jezebel (1 Kgs 16:29–19:3; 21).

Because of John's prophetic denunciations, Herodias hated John and sought to kill him (v. 19), but Herod Antipas protected him. He had John arrested, but he was also afraid of him because he knew John was a righteous and holy man (v. 20), and to put him to death would have been to strike out against an innocent person and a representative of God. Herod also liked to listen to John (v. 20), which is a tragically ironic example of a type of soil (Mark 4:15–20)—the sort that enjoys hearing the preached word but has no intention of bearing the fruit of that word.

Herod's Party and John's Death (vv. 21–29)

Mark then relates the death of John the Baptist, which came about because of a rash vow made during a drunken feast. The scene recalls the banquet in the book of Esther at which King Ahasuerus says to his queen, "Now what is your petition? It will be given you. And what is your request? Even up to half the kingdom, it will be granted" (Esth 5:6). Herod was holding a banquet for his officials and military leaders, at which the daughter of Herodias, Salome, danced in some provocative fashion that aroused the king and his dinner guests.[12] While Mark does not elaborate on the sort of pleasure Herod and his officials took (v. 22), the verb Mark uses (*areskō*, "to please") appears in the LXX in contexts having to do with sexual pleasure (Gen 19:8; Judg 14:1, 3, 7; Job 31:10). This verb is also used in the similar expression regarding the

---

12. Mark does not mention the name of Herodias's daughter, but Josephus names her as Salome (*Ant.* 18.136; see Bond, "Herodian Dynasty," *DJG* 382).

pleasure Ahasuerus took in Esther (Esth 2:9).[13] According to Marcus, "the all-male audience and the extraordinary promise to which Herod is driven are evidence for a similar sexual connotation."[14]

When Herod Antipas makes his boastful oath to grant Salome whatever she asks, she quickly goes out to ask her mother how she might respond (v. 24). Without delay, Herodias sees her opportunity for vengeance on John and tells her daughter to ask for John's head. It is a grisly request, but the daughter's relaying of the request is even more gruesome: she wants John's head *on a platter*, presumably for display or further humiliation, demonstrating Herodias's hatred for John. One can imagine that Herodias often had vented her wrath over John's rebukes to her daughter, so that Salome also has been filled with similar rage not only to kill but to humiliate John.

This greatly distresses Herod, of course, because of his regard for John as a righteous and holy man, but his desire to save face in front of his dinner guests prevents him from backing down. He gives the order, and the deed is done. The executioner brought back John's head on a platter, who presented it to the girl and she to her mother.

In a sense this murderous and revolting meal is the opposite of the meal that takes place in the next episode (vv. 31–44). At Herod's banquet the executioner passed John's head to Salome, and Salome to her mother, whereas at the gathering with Jesus, he breaks the bread and gives it to his disciples, who pass it on to the crowd. The first meal is murderous, where a righteous man is put to death for being a faithful prophet calling out unrighteousness. The second meal is life giving, in which a small amount is multiplied for the sustenance of a large crowd. Mark's account closes with the disciples of John the Baptist claiming his body and giving it a proper burial (v. 29).

The Return of the Disciples (v. 30)

In this outer portion of the Markan sandwich, and after the close of the account of John the Baptist's death, Mark narrates the return of the disciples. In the opening episode, the disciples had done what Jesus told them to do. They were "with Jesus" while going out from him. They were operating by his authority and in his name so that *his* name spread, not theirs. They conducted their ministries in the same manner as Jesus had, preaching, driving out demons, and healing the sick. There are a few clues, however, that when the disciples return, they once again fall into ways of thinking that indicate their failure.

---

13. Marcus, *Mark 1–8*, 396.
14. Marcus, *Mark 1–8*, 396.

Mark notes that they return and report to Jesus "all *they* had done and taught." At the opening of this passage, their activities pointed to the reality of Jesus's ministry, and their authority was clearly delegated to them by Jesus. It does not come from them on their own. Here, however, the disciples point to their own activity and teaching, reporting to Jesus what *they* have done. This is a contrast to reporting what has been accomplished by God *through them*.

Several passages from Acts highlight this distinction. When Paul and Barnabas travel from Antioch to Jerusalem for the consultation to settle the issue of the gentiles being included in the people of God, Luke records that their arrival was followed by a report of their ministry: "When they came to Jerusalem, they were welcomed by the church and the apostles and elders, to whom they reported everything God had done through them" (Acts 15:4). And some years later, when Paul arrives again in Jerusalem, Luke uses a similar expression:

> When we arrived at Jerusalem, the brothers and sisters received us warmly. The next day Paul and the rest of us went to see James, and all the elders were present. Paul greeted them and reported in detail what God had done among the Gentiles through his ministry.
> When they heard this, they praised God. (Acts 21:17–20)

The reports of Barnabas in Acts 15 and Paul in Acts 21 point to *the activity of God being carried out through human agents*. The disciples, however, having experienced the power of the kingdom of God operating through them, return and rehearse the accomplishments as their own.[15]

In support of this interpretation is the subsequent behavior of the disciples in the following episode and beyond. They continue to misunderstand and respond wrongly to Jesus. When Jesus exhorts them to feed the large crowd, the disciples speak sarcastically and take offense (v. 37). Their response is unjustified since they have just returned from a missionary journey in which they witnessed the power of God and saw it work through them. Here, however, they resist Jesus's word, being brought up short by his statement and questioning the reasonableness of his command. In the episodes that follow, their confusion will increase. They are running the risk of demonstrating that they are outsiders, those whose meager understanding may be taken away (Mark 4:25).

---

15. Moloney, *Gospel of Mark*, 128.

LIVE the Story

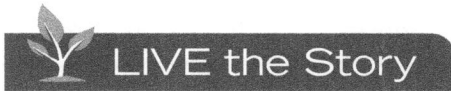

Suffering, Vindication, and Ministry Hardships

This passage indicates that Jesus's disciples, and especially those in gospel ministry, can expect suffering at the hands of evil people. This is a common theme throughout Scripture, though it is obscured or neglected by those who see the Christian life as the key to happiness and prosperity and view gospel ministry as a promising career path of worldly success. Just like John the Baptist, God's faithful people will endure suffering, and gospel ministers will face hardship. But in the same way that Jesus was exalted by God because of his faithfulness, God's servants will be vindicated if they persevere in the midst of suffering.

The early church leader Chrysostom (ca. 349–407) captures well the dynamics of suffering and vindication as it applies to John the Baptist:

> Note well the weakness of the tyrant compared to the power of the one in prison. Herod was not strong enough to silence his own tongue. Having opened it, he opened up countless other mouths in its place and with its help. As for John, he immediately inspired fear in Herod after his murder—for fear was disturbing Herod's conscience to such an extent that he believed John had been raised from the dead and was performing miracles! In our own day and through all future time, throughout all the world, John continues to refute Herod, both through himself and through others. For each person repeatedly reading this Gospel says: "It is not lawful for you to have the wife of Philip your brother." And even apart from reading the Gospel, in assemblies and meetings at home or in the market, in every place . . . even to the ends of the earth, you will hear this voice and see that righteous man even now still crying out, resounding loudly, reproving the evil of the tyrant. He will never be silenced nor the reproof at all weakened by the passing of time.[16]

It is important for pastors to keep this eschatological dimension in mind if and when they face the reality of persecution or trouble in ministry. This focus on future vindication by God for faithfulness will provide some measure of strength to persevere and relief from anxiety. And there are other things pastors can do to cope with suffering in ministry.

Pastors ought to consider building a personal support system and should

---

16. Oden and Hall, *Mark*, 82.

focus on doing this early in their ministry.[17] This may consist of select people within the church, a small group of people chosen carefully in whom the pastor can confide and from whom he can seek counsel. Of course, within this group the pastor will need to exercise caution and discernment regarding what she or he shares regarding others in the church. This support system should also include several other pastors, since, as Rediger notes, even pastors need a pastor—perhaps *especially* pastors, since pastoral ministry is such a unique vocation.[18] Pastors ought also to see a professional counselor, someone in whom they can confide and from whom they may gain counsel on handling various situations.

As I said, pastors would be wise to do this early in their ministry, because when an intense crisis hits, it's too late. Certain steps can be taken to seek help, of course, but looking for personal resources amid a community crisis is the worst time to do so. Well-established friendships with others in ministry, carefully cultivated friendships with certain people in the church, and a relationship with a professional who knows the pastor—each of these will provide great help to a minister who encounters ministry stresses that can often be profoundly destabilizing, both to a pastor and to his or her family.

There are also steps that those of us who are not in professional ministry can take. If we sit on a church leadership board, we can develop creative ways to support the pastor, especially during seasons of ministry stress. In such instances, boards can take steps to ensure that disgruntled parishioners or fellow board members cannot spread slander and gossip, by insisting that they answer for charges they bring.

Support of a pastor can take a variety of forms. In my case, I know how difficult it is to have a seminary professor in the congregation, someone with a doctorate in biblical studies. I know that there is the potential for my pastor to wonder what I am thinking about how he is treating a certain passage or the way he has packaged his sermon. Over the years I have labored to convey that I am not a threat to him. I routinely have offered words of support and encouragement after services, thanking him for his message and wishing him a good week. And I have noted that I am available to help out in any way I can and am glad to do so. Handling ministry stresses well is not the pastor's responsibility alone. The rest of us can creatively and graciously play our role in seeing to it that our pastors enjoy God's blessing of fruitful community life.

---

17. G. Lloyd Rediger, *Clergy Killers: Guidance for Pastors and Congregations under Attack* (Louisville: Westminster John Knox, 1997), 137.

18. Rediger, *Clergy Killers*, 137.

Glorifying God in Ministry, Not Ourselves

We had noted above that when the disciples returned to Jesus after proclaiming the kingdom, healing people, and casting out demons, they reported all that *they* had done rather than all that *God* had done *through them*. This highlights the challenge of seeing to it that in our participation in ministry we are glorifying God and not ourselves. How can we be careful to do this?

One way that this is typically done is by explicitly noting that God gets the glory for anything good that we do. I think that this is often well-motivated, but it can also function as a roundabout way of exalting ourselves. I have been around people who are happy to talk about all that they are doing for the Lord and are willing to more or less brag about it, so long as they punctuate each report with something like "but the Lord gets the glory," or "but, of course, it was all the Lord." This might leave us wondering just who exactly is getting the credit. And often such rhetoric has the value of making a person look both gifted and humble. They are doing great things, but at the same time they are just a lowly servant of God.

I reflected on this with a friend one time after I had preached a sermon some years ago. Afterward, my friend approached me and told me he really appreciated what I had to say. I responded by thanking him and told him that what he said meant a lot to me. He looked at me quizzically and said, "Aren't you supposed to say, 'The Lord gets the glory'?" I responded along these lines:

He just did get the glory! God was just glorified in our interchange, since God's glory is embodied through humans engaging with one another according to his design. When we delight together in all that he is doing among us, and when we satisfy each other's hearts by giving each other the gift of appreciation, we are *being the glory of God*. You want me to know that the work I put in to prepare this sermon had great value to you, and I genuinely receive that. That means so much to me, and I want you to know that you just blessed me. If I had simply said, "The Lord gets the glory," I fear that I run the risk of not taking you seriously, and that does not glorify God. But I want you to know that you just gave me the great gift of being assured that I spoke a good word from the Lord, so thank you. Further, if I simply say, "The Lord gets the glory," that may indicate that I *obviously* know that what I said came directly from God, and that feels to me like dangerous presumption. So, very simply, thank you for saying what you did.

I think there are other ways we can speak carefully so that God is glorified in our ministries. God is glorified in the church when everyone feels included and shares together in the joy of ministry and when no one person lifts himself or herself above others. I knew a pastor who was always careful to share credit for ideas and ministry efforts. He always talked about what "we" were doing and intentionally spoke of others when reporting on ministry-strategy sessions, highlighting their input. At one staff meeting, he reported that he and another pastor were talking about plans for a new initiative and proceeded to lay out the vision, mentioning the other person repeatedly. Later, I spoke to this other pastor, who noted that the idea wasn't really his and that he felt he was largely listening in that previous conversation. But the way the conversation was reported made him feel validated, and it made him feel that his contribution was highly valued. It gave him confidence to speak up more regularly from that point forward.

I have also been in ministry contexts where the opposite occurs. I have seen people take credit for the ideas and contributions of others, which creates bitterness and resentment. This results in a situation where God is not being glorified because of the discouragement that it breeds in the church.

I think it is noteworthy that Paul, the apostle we often envision as a solitary hero working alone, is always careful in his letters to indicate that he is someone who ministers on a team, as one servant of the Lord along with others. He opens and closes his letters by noting his associates, and he regularly puts the spotlight on their efforts. Such a careful rhetorical strategy dignifies the efforts of others, and because it brings delight and joy to the hearts of those who love and serve the Lord, it brings glory to God.

LISTEN to the Story

³¹Then, because so many people were coming and going that they did not even have a chance to eat, he said to them, "Come with me by yourselves to a quiet place and get some rest."

³²So they went away by themselves in a boat to a solitary place. ³³But many who saw them leaving recognized them and ran on foot from all the towns and got there ahead of them. ³⁴When Jesus landed and saw a large crowd, he had compassion on them, because they were like sheep without a shepherd. So he began teaching them many things.

³⁵By this time it was late in the day, so his disciples came to him. "This is a remote place," they said, "and it's already very late. ³⁶Send the people away so that they can go to the surrounding countryside and villages and buy themselves something to eat."

³⁷But he answered, "You give them something to eat."

They said to him, "That would take more than half a year's wages! Are we to go and spend that much on bread and give it to them to eat?"

³⁸"How many loaves do you have?" he asked. "Go and see."

When they found out, they said, "Five—and two fish."

³⁹Then Jesus directed them to have all the people sit down in groups on the green grass. ⁴⁰So they sat down in groups of hundreds and fifties. ⁴¹Taking the five loaves and the two fish and looking up to heaven, he gave thanks and broke the loaves. Then he gave them to his disciples to distribute to the people. He also divided the two fish among them all. ⁴²They all ate and were satisfied, ⁴³and the disciples picked up twelve basketfuls of broken pieces of bread and fish. ⁴⁴The number of the men who had eaten was five thousand.

Listening to the Text in the Story: Exodus 16; Numbers 11:1–25; 20:1–13; 27:15–23; 1 Kings 17:7–16; 2 Kings 4:42–44; Luke 24:13–35; 1 Corinthians 11:17–34.

The meal depicted in this passage stands in stark contrast to the previous one. Herod's dinner was filled with drunken partying, lascivious dancing, manipulative scheming, foolish boasting, and grisly death. The meal Jesus serves to this large crowd out in the open is miraculous and displays the power of the kingdom, while also signaling a return to some familiar dynamics in Mark after the interlude of the disciples' initial apostolic mission to Israel.[1] While they had been called to be "with Jesus," Mark portrays the disciples as regularly failing to be on Jesus's agenda. Mark 6:7–13 is a departure from this, however, as Jesus sends them out, and they, while being away from him, are "with Jesus" in that they carry out his agenda. They did what he told them to do and did the very things he was doing—proclaiming repentance, driving out demons, and healing the sick. Because of this, Jesus's name was spreading. This is all just as it should have been, with Jesus's disciples listening to *him*, extending *his* ministry, and making *his* name great.

We noted in the previous section, however, that upon their return they revert to their previous form. They announced to Jesus all that *they* had done, rather than all that had been accomplished *through* them. This dynamic intensifies in 6:31–44, as the disciples grow in their complacency, fail to grasp Jesus's agenda of caring for God's people, and resist Jesus when he exhorts them to be faithful shepherds.

In v. 34, Mark notes that Jesus looked on the crowds and "had compassion on them, because they were like sheep without a shepherd." This language comes from Numbers 27:17. Numbers 27 depicts the transition of leadership from Moses to Joshua. In 27:12–14 God lets Moses view the land that he is going to give to his people. Moses, however, will not lead them there because of his disobedience in the Desert of Zin. In this incident, recorded in Numbers 20:1–13, God had instructed Moses to speak to the rock in order to provide water for the people (v. 8). Moses had grown frustrated with the people, however, and struck the rock twice instead of speaking to it. Further, he vented his anger at the Israelites in such a way that he inappropriately identified himself with God over against the Israelites, saying, "Listen, you rebels, must we bring you water out of this rock?" (v. 10). This offended God's holiness—his utter uniqueness—and because of this, Moses was not allowed to lead God's people into the land (v. 12).

This is why Moses needed to hand over leadership of God's people to Joshua. As he was overlooking the land God would give his people, Moses said to the Lord:

---

1. Their mission is apostolic in that they are sent out, and they are called "apostles" in v. 30, indicating probably that they were sent to Israel on this initial mission. Yet these are also the ones later known as apostles, so it may point to that. Here I only mean their initial sending.

> May the LORD, the God who gives breath to all living things, appoint
> someone over this community to go out and come in before them, one
> who will lead them out and bring them in, so the LORD's people will not
> be like sheep without a shepherd. (Num 27:16–17)

The Lord directed Moses to appoint Joshua as leader over God's people,
which Moses did. Mark's reference to this passage is yet another one that
comes from the exodus sojourn of God's people in the desert. And it highlights
the necessity of faithful shepherds who will care for and lead God's people.
Mark 6:31–44 displays this need when Jesus calls on his disciples to care for
the people who have followed them and who are in need of being fed. The
Numbers passage also highlights the need for faithful shepherds who will
rightly recognize their place in relation to God and in relation to God's people.
Moses committed the grave error of identifying himself with God, the one who
supplies Israel's needs and who puts up with their complaining. The disciples
in Mark have yet to consistently grasp the role Jesus calls them to play in being
"with him" and ministering to God's people on God's behalf. This role does
not lift them up above others but rather makes them servants. They have yet
to get this quite right.

EXPLAIN the Story

A Crowd Follows Jesus and His Disciples (vv. 31–34)

This episode opens with Jesus and his disciples again being crowded by a
huge mob of people. The crush and constant rush of people, with their
coming and going, was so great that there was no time even to eat (v. 31).
Jesus therefore calls them and only them to come along with him to get
some rest. Mark emphasizes that Jesus intended for only his disciples to
join him, as he wanted time with them and to give them time to rest. Mark
does this by repeating the Greek phrase *kat' idian*, translated "by yourselves"
(v. 31) and "by themselves" (v. 32). The crowds, however, again hinder
Jesus and his aims with his disciples. While modern readers may regard the
reports of the huge crowds in Mark as a positive sign of Jesus's popularity,
Mark consistently portrays them as an obstacle to what Jesus is trying to do
(e.g., 1:35–37, 45; 4:1).

Mark uses the term *erēmos* three times in this passage (vv. 31, 32, 35). The
NIV translates it "a quiet place" in v. 31 and "a solitary place" in v. 32. It is
"a remote place" in v. 35. The term may indicate any of these, but it most

often points to the desert or wilderness, the place of dramatic and climactic encounters with God. This is the place to which John called people in Mark 1:4, and to which the Spirit thrust Jesus for his encounter with Satan (1:12). Jesus went there to pray before his disciples pursued him and interrupted his time alone with God (1:35). Mark's stress on "the desert" or "wilderness" as the location to which Jesus called his disciples indicates that this was intended to be an encounter with God and a time of rest and refreshment for the disciples. As happens throughout Mark, however, a divine appointment for rest and nourishment is interrupted. Mark's narrative style leaves both his audience and his characters breathless!

When the disciples left in response to Jesus's call (v. 32), the crowds saw it and "recognized them" (v. 33). Marcus suggests that this detail plays a part in the developing theme of the disciples' inflated sense of themselves due to their "success."[2] Things had been going well in vv. 12–14, where the disciples' activities resulted in the spread of Jesus's name. But here, the focus is now on *them*, which contributes to their sense of triumph, demonstrated by their "announcing" to Jesus all that they had done (v. 30). Just as Moses wrongly regarded his place and the character of his leadership in Numbers 20, the disciples are faltering here. Their vision of themselves in relation to Jesus and the tasks to which he calls them is becoming clouded, and this will play out in the rest of this episode as they respond wrongly to Jesus's exhortation to care for the people as faithful shepherds.

With all the mentions of "they" and "them" in vv. 32–33, referring to the disciples, the sudden focus on Jesus in v. 34 is striking. Mark zeroes in on his coming to shore, his seeing the large crowd, and his response of compassion. This will stand in contrast to the disciples' regard for the crowds in the remainder of the narrative. Jesus, however, looks on the crowds with compassion because they are God's people in need of care, nurture, and faithful leadership.[3] Interestingly, Jesus's compassion drives him to teach "them many things" (v. 34). This is another place in which Mark portrays Jesus as an authoritative and life-giving teacher but without mentioning the content of his teaching (cf. 1:21–28).

The Disciples Fail to Feed the Crowd (vv. 35–37)

While Jesus looks after the people as a shepherd, teaching them, much like God provided for Israel in the wilderness, the day grows late, and the disciples

---

2. Marcus, *Mark 1–8*, 417.

3. As Black notes, "like sheep without a shepherd" is scriptural language for "the mass of Israel needing sustenance by God's deputy, who provides help for the helpless" (1 Kgs 22:17; 2 Chr 18:16; Ps 95:7; Ezek 34; see Black, *Mark*, 158).

address Jesus with an emerging, dire situation. They are in the wilderness, a remote place, and the people will need to eat and look for provisions for nightfall. The disciples, however, do not care for the people as Jesus does. They ask him to "send the people away" to begin the search for something to eat, imagining that perhaps they can "buy themselves something to eat" (v. 36). Rather than caring for them as shepherds, the disciples want to leave the people to fend for themselves. They rightly recognize the need, but fail to regard it through the lens of kingdom power. Rather than thinking creatively about how to provide for the people, caring for them as Jesus did, they imagine a financial solution, throwing the people back on their own resources. In such a remote place, there certainly would be very little that they could have done for themselves. It is not as though they are modern travelers on a highway, where a rest stop could be expected, at which they could buy something to eat and drink.

Jesus's exhortation is tersely and strongly stated: "You give them something to eat" (v. 37). In effect he says, "You feed them! Faithful shepherds do not send away helpless sheep, leaving them to fend for themselves. Care for them. Love them and look after them as shepherds after my own heart." This may strike some readers as a shockingly unreasonable exhortation on Jesus's part. How on earth would they be able to feed these people? There was no food around. What were they supposed to do?

Keep in mind, however, that the disciples had just returned from a long season of ministry where they had seen the power of the kingdom firsthand (6:6b–13, 30). While being away from Jesus, having been sent out by him, they were "with him" in that they were doing the things he had been doing— driving out demons and healing people of their diseases and sicknesses. Having taken no bread, no bag, and no money, they had their needs met and had witnessed God providing for them. Having seen the miracle-working power of the kingdom, Jesus can rightly expect that the ones who had announced to him all that they had done would now be able to draw on kingdom power to meet the needs of the crowds. Sadly, the disciples' vision has become clouded. Because they have grown self-satisfied and complacent, they are no longer rightly reckoning with kingdom power and are failing to care for God's people as Jesus does. They can now only see the impossibility of the situation. They want to solve the problem by sending the people away to fend for themselves.

Intensifying the situation, they respond to Jesus with sarcasm. As Marcus notes, the amount of money they mention is outrageous.[4] They have grown

---

4. Marcus, *Mark 1–8*, 407.

impatient with Jesus, forgetting all that they have learned to this point and failing in their vision of the kingdom and its power. In a twist on the exodus allusions that pervade this passage, it is not the people who argue with God over the lack of food in the wilderness, but the disciples who argue with Jesus.[5] The ones called to shepherd God's people experience a failure of kingdom vision.

Jesus Feeds the Crowd through the Disciples (vv. 38–44)

Jesus, however, does not respond to them with harsh rebuke or by brushing them off and feeding the crowd by himself. This portion of the text proceeds with a very different tone and at a very different pace. It is slow and methodical, with Jesus setting things right. Rather than dismissing the disciples as failures, he makes them full participants in the miraculous provision. He first directs them to find out how much food is currently available. They do so and report back that there are five loaves and two fish (v. 38). Jesus then directs the disciples to instruct the people to sit in large groups "on the green grass" (v. 39) and ready themselves to receive a meal.[6] The allusion to the "green pastures" of Psalm 23:1 helps to fill out this scene as one in which God as a good shepherd looks after his people with great care, providing a lavish meal in the midst of "a remote place."[7] Further, that the people "ate and were satisfied" (Mark 6:42) hearkens back to the instruction in Deuteronomy 8:10 regarding the posture of the people when they enter the land: "When you have eaten and are satisfied, praise the LORD your God for the good land he has given you."[8] These scriptural references and the slowed and deliberate pace of vv. 38–44 contribute to the sense of a relaxed, refreshing, restful, and lavish feast. There was, after all, more than enough to go around![9]

This passage, then, depicts Jesus as the shepherd of God's people. In a remote place, God provides for basic needs. And according to the logic of the kingdom, there is more than anyone needs. Whereas the disciples looked at the needs of the moment and saw only that the people should be sent away to fend

---

5. Mary Ann Beavis, *Mark*, Paideia (Grand Rapids: Baker Academic, 2011), 106.

6. The language of "groups of hundreds and fifties" and Jesus's use of the disciples as agents who multiply his ability to distribute food to the crowd recall Exodus 18:1–25, in which Jethro instructs Moses to make use of deputies to resolve disputes, selecting capable men "as officials over thousands, hundreds, fifties and tens" (v. 21; see Moloney, *Gospel of Mark*, 131).

7. Beavis, *Mark*, 106.

8. Placher, *Mark*, 95.

9. It is tempting to discern meaning in the numbers in this passage. Do the twelve baskets signify Israel? And what might the five thousand mean? As Placher notes, the numbers point in all sorts of directions (Placher, *Mark*, 99). According to Black, it may be that the number five thousand merely indicates that Jesus fed a very large number of people (*Mark*, 160).

for themselves, Jesus's actions should reconfigure the disciples' imagination. They had witnessed the power of the kingdom while away on mission, but they needed to be reminded of the other-worldly dynamic of plenty that is at work where the kingdom of God is present. Finally, this passage displays the grace of God as embodied in the actions of Jesus toward the disciples. Rather than setting the disciples aside because of their failure to live into the fullness of the kingdom as they had been doing on their initial mission, Jesus makes them unwitting agents of blessing. He has them investigate regarding their current resources, direct the people to sit in groups, distribute the food as he makes it available, and gather what is left over.

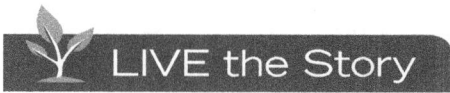

LIVE the Story

The Church as a Place of Nourishment and Service

This passage holds significant lessons for the life of the church. Jesus and the disciples see the crowd very differently, and they have opposing ideas about the resources available. Jesus looks with compassion on the crowd and directs his disciples to feed them. The disciples, however, want the crowd to fend for themselves and ask Jesus to send them away. All they can see is that they have no food and no way to feed all these people. But the loving care that Jesus demonstrates, and his feeding of the crowd, are an example for the disciples—and the church today—to follow. Just as Jesus sought to lovingly shepherd the crowd through the disciples, he aims to lovingly bless the needy in our world through the church.

There are a number of values and cultural patterns that are up and running in our world that press us into the mold of the disciples, working against the mission to which Jesus calls us. First, the ideology of individualism and its associated ways of life have shaped our world today. Stemming from the Enlightenment—which envisioned each person as becoming a citizen of the world, seeking education and social status through the accumulation of various luxury goods—individualism tends to set people against each other in competition.[10] We look out for ourselves and are tempted to devalue our commitments to family and to our local communities. In our social-media age, each person is building their own online brand, seeking the admiration of others through "likes" and "follows." The many cultural dynamics that flow

---

10. Pankaj Mishra explores how the Enlightenment spawned the individualism that spread Western ways of life across the world and feeds the current varieties of political unrest and violence in his stimulating book, *Age of Anger: A History of the Present* (New York: Picador, 2017).

from individualism have shaped us to envision those who are needy like the disciples in this episode: let them fend for themselves. You've got to look out for yourself.

This cultural value is displayed in the way that middle-class churches view those in poverty. We imagine that they are to blame for their difficult situation. We tend to think that if they had worked harder or made better decisions, they would be better off. Our individualistic culture shapes us to see those in need and ourselves as isolated individuals, who are responsible to build our own lives and provide for ourselves. We do not look at such people through the lens of the many biblical commands to actively take note of those without food and clothing, and to care for them (e.g., Matt 25:31–46; Jas 2:14–17; 1 John 3:16–18).

Another cultural pattern against which Christians and churches struggle is that of consumerism. Like businesses that want to grow by appealing to consumer desires, churches are tempted to grow and thrive by doing the same. Church leaders are certainly aware of the struggle to foster healthy biblical community life while also being extremely sensitive to the perceived need to keep people happy. After all, there are bills to pay and a budget with staff salaries and other necessities. They are all too cognizant of the reality that when people are unhappy, they leave and start attending the church across town. When fewer people attend, giving goes down, and that creates seemingly unbearable troubles. Churches are pressured, therefore, to offer programs and activities that will appeal to the widest number of people—programs for parents, for children, and for people at every age of life.

Pastors and church leaders rarely set out purposely to appeal to consumer desires. Yet the complexities of our modern world slowly and subtly creep in and end up shaping the vision of our communities in more pervasive ways than we can imagine. The problem here is that the church is not supposed to be the place where we have our desires and wishes fulfilled; rather, it is to be a base for mission and a site for service to those with real needs.

These cultural dynamics that subtly affect the vision of churches—individualism and consumerism—orient us to see things just as the disciples did. When people had the very real need for food, the disciples looked around and saw no way of responding to Jesus's command to provide for them. In the same way, when these worldly values shape the imagination of churches, we will tend to overlook the many resources we have for such needs. And this is tragic, especially when many of our churches will somehow find the money when it comes to new building projects or will even borrow money for such enterprises.

The power of this passage in Mark, however, is not merely that Jesus performs an impressive miracle to demonstrate his identity. Jesus is unleashing and participating in the dynamics of the kingdom of God, which has endless supplies for the church's mission to meet the needs of those within the church and to extend itself for the blessing of the needy in surrounding communities.

Embodying Jesus in the Church's Meals

Paul's discussion of the Lord's Supper in 1 Corinthians 11 is well-known to many Christians—at least a part of it. Many churches read it aloud when they take communion or when they celebrate the Eucharist.[11] Most readings of this passage begin with the familiar words of vv. 23–24: "For I received from the Lord what I also passed on to you: The Lord Jesus, on the night he was betrayed, took bread, and when he had given thanks, he broke it and said, 'This is my body, which is for you; do this in remembrance of me.'" And they end the reading at v. 27 or perhaps v. 32. Insofar as this passage is read in Christian gatherings, that is a good thing. But when we begin and end at these points, we miss that Paul's "instructions" here are really more of a harsh rebuke—perhaps even a rant!

The unit of text in which Paul stings the Corinthians begins at v. 17 and ends at v. 34, and it concerns the meal that the church eats together to symbolize and embody their unity as the people created by and oriented by the death of Jesus. Rather than being a ten-minute add-on to a church service, in which a thimbleful of juice and a small cracker are consumed, the meal was just that—a meal. The church was supposed to gather together for an entire meal, one to which the rich would bring more than they could eat so that they could share it and eat together with the poor. This would have symbolized and portrayed the new reality that God had created in the death and resurrection of Jesus—a unified group of people brought together only by the call of God in Christ, made into a new family with bonds stronger than natural relations. No one had status above anyone else, but all gathered at the same table to celebrate their unity.

Doing this in the first-century Greco-Roman context would have been socially subversive and revolutionary. Customary meals in Corinth would have symbolized and portrayed a thoroughly Corinthian reality: the rich would eat only with the rich, and the poor would be shut out. Different social classes did not mix, and the segregated meals upheld Corinthian values. Rich people

---

11. Various Christian traditions have different names for this celebration: "the Lord's Supper," "communion," "the Eucharist," depending on how they view this rite, whether as an ordinance or a sacrament. "Eucharist" comes from the Greek term *eucharistia*, which means "thanksgiving."

mattered more and did not associate with the lowly. After all, doing so was shameful. In fact, social climbers would strive to be invited to meals by wealthier people in hopes that their social status could be elevated. Eating with those lower on the social ladder would bring them shame, diminishing any social capital they had accumulated.

Paul confronts the Corinthians because they are eating the Lord's meal in the same way that they eat a normal Corinthian meal. They are symbolizing and portraying a reality that is at odds with the reality that God had brought about. They are upholding and reinforcing a worldly, corrupted Greco-Roman reality when they eat together. There are divisions among them (v. 18), and because of this Paul says in v. 17 that it is a bad thing that they even gather as the church! Paul wishes they would not even come to church, because they are corrupting the work of God with their perverted practice. They should not fool themselves into thinking that they are celebrating the Lord's meal, because it is most certainly not (v. 20). It is some other meal—a pagan meal, if anything! Rather than the rich bringing plenty and sharing with the poor, the rich members are bringing good bread, wine, and cheese and are eating it with their social peers while shutting out the poor. They are getting drunk on good wine and eating until they are full, while the poor are going hungry (vv. 21–22). Paul accuses them of despising the church of God—a serious charge. They are eating and drinking in an unworthy manner and are guilty of the body and blood of the Lord (v. 27), bringing judgment upon themselves, resulting in sickness and death (v. 30). Apparently, God is very concerned with how the church eats its meals together.

In some Christian traditions, this passage is read individualistically, and the Lord's Supper is taken as an opportunity to examine one's inner life to determine if there is any unconfessed sin. It is certainly good to examine oneself and confess sin, but Paul is focused on the corporate practice of guarding the unity of the church and preserving the work of God in uniting rich and poor, slave and free, Jew and non-Jew in Jesus's new family. Eating in an unworthy manner means participating in the division of the church into rich and poor, while supposedly celebrating the death of Christ, which brought about unity. Everyone in the church, then, must examine whether they are participating in division, fostering a situation in which some people feel marginalized and shut out. If they are doing so, they ought to repent and begin fostering dynamics of inclusion and participation in God's work of uniting his people. If the community judges itself and is transformed into a more inclusive body, then it will not face judgment—it will avoid being condemned along with the rest of the world (v. 32).

The conclusion to this passage is rarely noted, but it comes in vv. 33–34: "So then, my brothers and sisters, when you gather to eat, you should all eat together. Anyone who is hungry should eat something at home, so that when you meet together it may not result in judgment."

In the death of Jesus, God created a new people made up of individuals from every social class, tribe, and language. Rather than gathering only with those who look the same and sound the same, God's power is demonstrated in creating a new social reality in Christ and by the Spirit under the lordship of Jesus. When the church gathers and celebrates the meal rightly, it proclaims the Lord's death until he comes (v. 26). When the church gathers and eats a meal that excludes the poor or tolerates divisions, it proclaims that God does not have the power to create a new people and that Jesus died for no purpose (cf. Gal 2:21). This is serious, indeed, and indicates why Paul has such harsh words for the Corinthians and why God brought about such serious consequences in the life of the Corinthian community.

CHAPTER 25

Mark 6:45–52

📖 LISTEN to the Story

⁴⁵Immediately Jesus made his disciples get into the boat and go on ahead of him to Bethsaida, while he dismissed the crowd. ⁴⁶After leaving them, he went up on a mountainside to pray.

⁴⁷Later that night, the boat was in the middle of the lake, and he was alone on land. ⁴⁸He saw the disciples straining at the oars, because the wind was against them. Shortly before dawn he went out to them, walking on the lake. He was about to pass by them, ⁴⁹but when they saw him walking on the lake, they thought he was a ghost. They cried out, ⁵⁰because they all saw him and were terrified.

Immediately he spoke to them and said, "Take courage! It is I. Don't be afraid." ⁵¹Then he climbed into the boat with them, and the wind died down. They were completely amazed, ⁵²for they had not understood about the loaves; their hearts were hardened.

Listening to the Text in the Story: Exodus 9:33–35; 33:17–34:7; 1 Samuel 6:6; 1 Kings 19:11–12; Job 9:8–11; Psalm 77:16–20; Isaiah 43:16–17.

This episode has some similarities with the previous calming-of-the-sea incident that Mark recounts in 4:35–41. While the present passage has some unique features, its most puzzling detail occurs in v. 48, with Jesus intending to "pass by them." Why does he do this? It is easy to imagine that perhaps Jesus is upset with them and so is registering his displeasure. Or, maybe Jesus is testing them and wants to see how they will do during adverse circumstances. Is this what Mark is portraying?

This enigmatic episode makes good sense when we consult the rich tradition in Scripture of God revealing himself to humanity. In a number of these passages, God's self-revelation occurs in contexts that indicate God's "passing by" people in order to make himself known to them. In the foundational passage in this tradition, Exodus 33:17–34:7, Moses has been called to lead Israel out from Egypt and has asked that God reveal himself so that Moses will know him and his ways. After all, God has called him to this monumental task, and Moses wants to know more about the one he is serving. God acquiesces to Moses's request. He is going to reveal to Moses his glory—that is, he "will cause all my goodness to pass in front of you" (33:19). This expression occurs twice in v. 22 ("When my glory *passes by*, I will put you in a cleft in the rock and cover you with my hand until I have *passed by*"), and once more in 34:6, so that "passing by" becomes an expression for God's self-revelation.

This language occurs again in a similar scenario, this time with Elijah after his battle with the prophets of Baal on Mount Carmel. Elijah had fled to Horeb, the mountain of God (1 Kgs 19:8), where he had a fascinating divine encounter. God asks Elijah what he is doing there (vv. 9, 13), and Elijah informs God about what has just occurred and that he alone is left among those who are faithful to God. God responds by preparing Elijah for a *theophany*—a revelation of God to a human: "The LORD said, 'Go out and stand on the mountain in the presence of the LORD, *for the LORD is about to pass by*'" (v. 11).

In Job 9:8–11, Job wonders at God's unknowability, the incapacity of humans to fathom God's wisdom and the impossibility of finally capturing what God is like so as to figure out his ways. This poetic passage brings together two critical features of our episode:

> He alone stretches out the heavens
>> and treads on the waves of the sea.
> He is the Maker of the Bear and Orion,
>> the Pleiades and the constellations of the south.
> He performs wonders that cannot be fathomed,
>> miracles that cannot be counted.
> When he passes me, I cannot see him;
>> when he goes by, I cannot perceive him.

Job portrays God as the one who treads on the waves of the sea, a common theme in Scripture (Ps 77:16–20; Isa 43:16–17) and one that relates directly to what Jesus does in Mark 6. Job also uses the language for God's self-revelation ("when he passes me," "when he goes by") that occurs throughout Scripture.

So Mark uses language and imagery that brings together some biblical threads. Rather than being upset with his disciples, Jesus is revealing himself to them as the one in whom the God of Israel is acting to bring about his purposes. Just as the God of Israel makes a way through the waters, treading on the waves of the sea, Jesus does the same. This passage also resonates with other instances in Mark in which Jesus warns people not to talk about him or tell others what he has done for them. Mark wants his audiences to know that God is mysteriously at work in Jesus, but that there is also something unknowable about all of this. This should lead to a holy reticence: "Mark is teaching his readers to wonder and to listen more deeply before they start talking about things too wonderful for their understanding."[1]

EXPLAIN the Story

Jesus Gets Alone to Pray (vv. 45–46)

After the feeding of the five thousand in the previous episode, Mark uses a strong verb (*anankazō*, "to force" or "to compel") to demonstrate that Jesus took the initiative in sending his disciples "on ahead of him to Bethsaida." He "*made* his disciples get into the boat" (v. 45).[2] This situation of self-revelation was orchestrated by Jesus himself, as he sent the disciples ahead of him and also sent away the crowd.[3] Jesus is now alone so that he can pray. He had previously sought solitude for prayer but had been interrupted by the disciples, who were searching for him (1:35–37). Like the crowds who have become obstacles to Jesus's ministry, the disciples had hindered Jesus's ability to find quiet time and a secluded space for prayer. Here, he goes "up on a mountainside," a setting that is rich with resonances of an encounter with God.[4] The two theophanies to Moses and Elijah, in which the Lord had "passed them by" had taken place on mountains (Exod 34:2, 6; 1 Kgs 19:11). In this episode, we find Jesus on a mountainside in prayer as he prepares to pass by his disciples in an act of self-revelation.

Jesus Goes to His Disciples (vv. 47–50)

As the disciples make their way across the Sea of Galilee, Jesus is alone on the land, and he "sees" the disciples straining against the wind. This verb of

1. Richard B. Hays, *Reading Backwards: Figural Christology and the Fourfold Gospel Witness* (Waco, TX: Baylor University Press, 2014), 26.

2. Moloney, *Gospel of Mark*, 134.

3. Mark uses the same verb for Jesus's sending away the crowd (*apolyō*) in v. 45 that the disciples used in requesting that Jesus send the people away so that they might find something to eat in the previous episode (v. 36). Jesus eventually accedes to their request, but only after feeding and caring for the people.

4. Moloney, *Gospel of Mark*, 134.

discernment ("he saw") is important in Mark, as it occurs in situations where Jesus looks on people with compassion or when he spots a person he is about to call as a disciple (1:16, 19; 2:5, 14; 3:34; 8:33; 10:14). Marcus notes that this "seeing" likely involved supernatural insight, since they were far away and it was still night.[5] Far from playing games with the disciples, Jesus is driven by love, compassion, and care for them.

Just before dawn, Jesus went out to them, walking on the water. As indicated above, Scripture speaks of God treading upon the sea (Ps 77:16–20; Isa 43:16–17), pointing to God's sovereign power over hostile forces that threaten the stability and order of creation (cf. Ps 29:3–11). Mark uses the language of theophany to speak of Jesus passing by his disciples, so that this is some sort of self-revelation to them (v. 48). Jesus is not testing his disciples, nor is he intentionally ignoring them, as if he wanted to race ahead of them to Bethsaida without getting a ride from them in the boat. This is certainly a strange scenario, but because of the scriptural backdrop to this episode, it appears that Jesus was revealing to them his identity as the agent of God's salvation, the one who will go ahead of them and make a pathway through the sea.

The disciples, however, do not recognize him. They saw him and were terrified because they thought he was a ghost (vv. 49–50). Jesus reassures them: "Take courage! It is I. Don't be afraid."[6] Jesus's expression of his identity would have caught the attention of Mark's first Jewish audiences, since they are the same words Yahweh uses in Exodus 3:14 when he revealed himself to Moses (LXX: *egō eimi ho ōn*, "I am who I am"). The Greek expression translated here as "It is I" in the NIV is *egō eimi*.[7] This further reinforces the self-revelatory aspect of this episode.

The Disciples' Continuing Confusion (vv. 51–52)

As Jesus gets into the boat with the disciples, the disciples "were completely amazed," which Mark indicates is not a commendable response to what they have seen. The reason for their amazement is that "they had not understood about the loaves; their hearts were hardened" (v. 52). They had been with Jesus when he had calmed the storm after being asleep in the boat (4:35–41),

---

5. Marcus, *Mark 1–8*, 423.

6. Moloney notes that Jesus's words are similar to those spoken in theophanic situations in the Old Testament; cf. Exod 3:14; Judg 6:11–24 (*Gospel of Mark*, 134).

7. It may be that Jesus is merely indicating his identity ("Don't be afraid, it's me!"), but because of the strong scriptural tradition initiated by God's self-identification with these words, it is more likely that Jesus is indicating his identity as Yahweh, whose very name denotes "his active, upholding, uncircumscribed, everlasting presence, which allows no rival force to withstand it" (Marcus, *Mark 1–8*, 147; cf. also Boring, *Mark*, 190).

and they had just witnessed him feeding large crowds with a few scraps of food. But rather than gain insight as to Jesus's identity from what he had done, they are in the same bewilderment as when they had asked, "Who is this? Even the wind and the waves obey him!" (4:41).

That the disciples' hearts are hardened indicates that they are in danger of being revealed as outsiders who do not grasp the mystery of the kingdom (4:11), or perhaps even enemies who are opposed to it (3:5).[8] Mark's expression is passive—they do not "harden" their hearts; their hearts "are hardened." This may point to God as the agent of hardening, or it may be that their lack of careful attentiveness to Jesus has brought them inevitably to this place.

What is Mark doing in this episode? Again, he portrays the disciples in a negative light, and it is striking that Jesus seems to be expecting the impossible from them. We should keep in mind that Mark's portrayal is intended to have an effect on those who hear or read his Gospel. Mark wants to generate discussion, provoking audiences to ask one another, *What were the disciples supposed to learn from the loaves? Did Jesus expect them to learn from their experience of the power of the kingdom while they were on mission (6:6–13, 30), so that they would be able to extend his ministry by caring for others (6:37)?* Audiences who hear Mark's Gospel can remind one another that the realities of the kingdom are open to examination and that God gives greater light to those who strive to perceive what is going on (4:21–25). The "meaning" of this episode is found in Mark's portrayal for the purpose of unsettling audiences, leading them to ask whether they are being foolishly presumptuous in assuming they understand the unfathomable mysteries associated with God's work in Jesus. Is their current understanding of Jesus shaped by their own cultural expectations, prejudices, hopes, and fears? Or are they open to receiving a gift of insight as they strive to grasp the character of Jesus as he truly is?

LIVE the Story

Following King Jesus on Mission

Jesus is revealing himself to his disciples as the powerful agent of kingdom presence. He is inviting them to participate in kingdom realities by following him and doing as he does. They would gain greater insight if they would seek a clearer vision of Jesus's identity and lean into kingdom realities, but they end

---

8. Boring, *Mark*, 191; Black, *Mark*, 166. "Hardness of heart" is a theme with significant biblical roots, stretching back to Pharaoh's response of opposition to the God of Israel (Exod 9:33–35) and including Israel's leaders who disobey (e.g., 2 Chr 36:13) as well as Israel's rebellion (Ps 95:6–8).

up growing confused and obtuse as they fail to recognize Jesus for who he is. Following Jesus on his mission to spread the healing effects of his kingdom requires a cultivation of faith, for it will involve taking on modes of life and practices that run against the grain of how we are wired and what our culture says is desirable and acceptable.

Jesus says as much in John 12:25–26: "Anyone who loves their life will lose it, while anyone who hates their life in this world will keep it for eternal life. Whoever serves me must follow me; and where I am, my servant also will be. My Father will honor the one who serves me." So, the question is, Where is Jesus? Where can we expect to find him, so that we may be doing the sorts of things he is doing? Throughout Mark and the other three Gospels, Jesus is routinely going to marginalized people and spending time with them. If we truly see who Jesus is and if we understand his mission, we will follow him in doing the same.

I recently spent two afternoons with the chaplain staff and several volunteers at the local county jail. It is located just five miles from where I live, and I drive past it quite often, but it is not at all the sort of place where I feel comfortable. I sat with a chaplain as he taught a class, and watched as he interacted with the inmates. I also had the chance to talk with several of them myself. I felt in my body the very real discomfort and tension of being in a place that was utterly unfamiliar to me, and I tried my best to feel relaxed. After all, the chaplain had informed me that most of the inmates would be watching me to determine if I was judging them or looking down on them in some way.

I spoke with another chaplain who had given up a promising career as an executive at a local company in order to head up the chaplaincy program throughout the state. He had sat on the board of this ministry for a few years and grew so compelled by its vision that he took the position as the main chaplain. We talked about the forgotten men who are incarcerated and how visiting with them was an opportunity to encounter Jesus, since the county jail is precisely the sort of place Jesus would be.

One of the things that struck me about these two chaplains is that they were filled with such joy, and they seemed to know Jesus in powerful ways because they had given up much in worldly terms in order to follow Jesus on mission in this specific way. I expressed to one of them that I wanted to get involved with the program by teaching classes on the Bible, to which he responded by asking me about my motivation. Why did I want to do this? I told him that I had been thinking about Jesus's words to the sheep and the goats at the final judgment in Matthew 25. The sheep would inherit the kingdom because they had visited those in prison (v. 36), and the goats were headed for judgment because they did not (v. 43). Jesus identifies himself as being the one that the sheep had visited and the one that the goats had neglected. I told him that I wanted more encounters with Jesus, and because of that passage this seemed like a great opportunity for me. He informed me that I needed to be prepared to be changed by this ministry and that it would certainly be challenging.

Now, it may be the case that not everyone can immediately give up their careers, drop their commitments, and make such a dramatic change in their life by becoming a chaplain at the local jail. But if we think of our lives as enmeshed within the kingdom community of our church, there may be an opportunity to support others who do take such dramatic steps. One chaplain noted that his church plays a major supporting role in his ministry by taking special interest in him, knowing that his work can be stressful and draining. And they produce loads of baked goods that he brings with him to the jail each Friday.

These chaplains and their staff of volunteers demonstrate that they recognize Jesus as he has revealed himself in Mark's Gospel. He is God himself who comes with kingdom presence, bringing healing and restoration and inviting others to join him in going to the marginalized and the forgotten in order to fully experience the life-giving power of God. If we claim to recognize and know Jesus, we will manifest that reality by looking for creative ways to be where Jesus is and to do the sorts of things he is doing.

CHAPTER 26

Mark 6:53–56

📖 LISTEN to the Story

⁵³When they had crossed over, they landed at Gennesaret and anchored there. ⁵⁴As soon as they got out of the boat, people recognized Jesus. ⁵⁵They ran throughout that whole region and carried the sick on mats to wherever they heard he was. ⁵⁶And wherever he went—into villages, towns or countryside—they placed the sick in the marketplaces. They begged him to let them touch even the edge of his cloak, and all who touched it were healed.

Listening to the Text in the Story: Numbers 15:38–39; Deuteronomy 22:12; 33:26; Psalm 107; Acts 5:15–16.

This summary passage brings to a close a portion of Mark's Gospel marked by activity in and around the Sea of Galilee in boats, which opened in 4:35.[1] This larger section began with a series of episodes in which Jesus demonstrated his mastery over the sea, sickness, and unclean spirits. Several features are common in Mark's summary sections thus far (1:32–34; 3:7–12; 6:53–56), including:

- a brief description that sets the scene (1:32a; 3:7a; 6:53)
- a portrayal of people from everywhere being drawn to Jesus (1:33; 3:7b–8; 6:54–55)
- an emphasis on need for relief from suffering and sickness (1:32b; 3:10b; 6:55b–56a)
- Jesus's power to heal (1:34; 3:10a; 6:56b).[2]

---

1. Strauss, *Mark*, 290.
2. Black, *Mark*, 167.

Mark depicts the people of Galilee as desperate for relief from suffering and rushing to Jesus to be healed. Jesus has compassion on all whom he encounters, whether in towns, villages, or countryside, and he embodies the care of the God of Israel who loves to come to the aid of his people when they call to him (Deut 33:26; Pss 18; 34; 107).

EXPLAIN the Story

When Jesus and the disciples reached land, they were immediately swarmed with people. Mark draws a sharp contrast between the reactions to Jesus by people throughout the region and that of the disciples in the previous episode. The disciples saw Jesus and were terrified because they did not recognize him, thinking he was a ghost. Alternatively, these people recognize Jesus (v. 54) and respond by rushing to him because they see him as one who can heal and restore. This perception and subsequent reaction is similar to other characters who also contrast starkly with the disciples. The demon-possessed man in Mark 5 "saw Jesus from a distance" and immediately "ran and fell on his knees in front of him" (v. 6). Jairus, when he sees Jesus (v. 22), and the hemorrhaging woman, when she hears of Jesus (v. 27), each respond the same way (vv. 22, 33). Whereas the disciples seem to be fulfilling the prophetic words Jesus cites from Isaiah 6 about seeing but not perceiving, other characters are acting on Jesus's exhortation to pay close attention: "Whoever has ears to hear, let them hear" (4:9).

Especially striking is the behavior of people throughout the region: they are selflessly caring for one another. Like the friends who picked up the lame man and carried him to Jesus (2:1–12), the people are here portrayed as acting on behalf of the sick. Mark emphasizes through repetition their frantic efforts and extreme exertion on behalf of the afflicted. He depicts them running throughout the region and carrying the sick to Jesus, placing them in the marketplaces (vv. 55–56), so that they might have access to Jesus for healing. In several places, Mark portrays the crowds in his Gospel in a negative light. They impede Jesus's ability to carry out his ministry (3:9, 20; 5:24), and ultimately the Jewish leadership will turn the crowds against Jesus (15:11). Here, however, they are responding in a way that is commendable.

This care for others is yet another contrast with the disciples, along with the Pharisees. To this point the disciples have been either confused (4:35–41; 6:52), arrogant (6:35–37), or insolent (v. 37). Soon, they will behave very badly by responding to each of Jesus's predictions of his suffering and death

with utter selfishness, unconcerned with Jesus's impending passion and crucifixion (8:31–33; 9:30–35; 10:32–45). And the Pharisees have long since
decided that Jesus must die, as they initiated a plot to destroy him on the very
Sabbath that they had refused to endorse a good deed (3:1–6).

The relation of faith and the presence of healing power here is exactly the
opposite of that in Jesus's hometown. The inhabitants of Nazareth took offense
at Jesus, with the result that he "could not do any miracles there, except lay his
hands on a few sick people and heal them. He was amazed at their lack of faith"
(6:5–6). In this summary passage, however, the divine power is radiating from
Jesus so that if any sick person were to "touch even the edge of his cloak" they
would be healed (v. 56), indicating the presence of strong faith among these
crowds. A similar powerful outbreak of healing takes place in Mark's earlier
summary in 3:7–12 and with the hemorrhaging woman in 5:25–34. Mark
puts special emphasis here on the overwhelming force of divine power that is
flowing from Jesus. Rather than touching Jesus himself (3:10) or his garment
(5:30), if anyone even touched the *edge* of his cloak, they would be healed.

LIVE the Story

Divine Perception

We have seen the contrast developing in Mark between those who are seeing
but not perceiving (the disciples, the Pharisees), and those who see Jesus or
hear about him, and respond to him rightly. Here, the people in the towns
Jesus visits demonstrate true discipleship because they perceive Jesus and dash
around to find anyone and everyone who is in need to bring them to Jesus for
healing. Faithful perception of who Jesus is involves active discipleship in the
form of meeting concrete needs.

Our church is not large, but it includes an unusually large number of
people with seminary degrees and more than a few with doctorates in theology and biblical studies. We enjoy rich discussions with each other and are
grateful for the resources we have for ministries of teaching and instruction
in Scripture and doctrine. One of our members, Margaret, possesses neither a
theological degree nor much interest in discussing doctrine. She has taken the
lead, however, in forging a connection between our church and a local charity
that helps homeless families get into sustainable housing. She has coordinated
with other churches to raise funds to purchase an impressive number of mobile
homes and has arranged for work crews to refurbish them. This effort provides
the charity with affordable housing options in our city, where rising costs are

making affordable housing increasingly difficult to find. I have had the delight of working with Margaret over the last several years. I will always remember the time when she said at the end of a committee meeting during which we discussed service to the needy: "Well, this is what it's all about, isn't it?"

She was exactly right. Acquisition of biblical and theological knowledge is crucial for rightly articulating who we are in Christ and why we love and serve the way that we do. Indeed, doctrine and practice must always be kept together. In one sense, doctrine is the language we speak to make sense of our identity and the manner of life to which God calls us in Christ. I am grateful for Margaret, because the initiative she takes to do good is an example of true discipleship. Her perception of the heart of the faith has driven her to seek out ways to serve those in need and provide opportunities for our church, and related churches, to participate in that service.

Throughout Scripture, insight into the work of God is not only manifest in service, but is clearly a divine gift. And while it comes only from God, this gift does not eliminate our responsibility. We can put ourselves in position for God to act to open our eyes and increase our perception of kingdom realities. I often open a new semester of teaching with the following prayer from *The Book of Common Prayer*, asking God to do his work of transformation through our study:

Blessed Lord, who caused all holy Scriptures to be written for our learning: Grant us so to hear them, read, mark, learn, and inwardly digest them, that we may embrace and ever hold fast the blessed hope of everlasting life, which you have given us in our Savior Jesus Christ; who lives and reigns with you and the Holy Spirit, one God, for ever and ever. Amen.[3]

---

3. The Lectionary Page, www.lectionarypage.net/YearA/Pentecost/AProp28.html.

CHAPTER 27

Mark 7:1–23

📖 LISTEN to the Story

¹The Pharisees and some of the teachers of the law who had come from Jerusalem gathered around Jesus ²and saw some of his disciples eating food with hands that were defiled, that is, unwashed. ³(The Pharisees and all the Jews do not eat unless they give their hands a ceremonial washing, holding to the tradition of the elders. ⁴When they come from the marketplace they do not eat unless they wash. And they observe many other traditions, such as the washing of cups, pitchers and kettles.)

⁵So the Pharisees and teachers of the law asked Jesus, "Why don't your disciples live according to the tradition of the elders instead of eating their food with defiled hands?"

⁶He replied, "Isaiah was right when he prophesied about you hypocrites; as it is written:

'These people honor me with their lips,
    but their hearts are far from me.
⁷They worship me in vain;
    their teachings are merely human rules.'

⁸You have let go of the commands of God and are holding on to human traditions."

⁹And he continued, "You have a fine way of setting aside the commands of God in order to observe your own traditions! ¹⁰For Moses said, 'Honor your father and mother,' and, 'Anyone who curses their father or mother is to be put to death.' ¹¹But you say that if anyone declares that what might have been used to help their father or mother is Corban (that is, devoted to God)—¹²then you no longer let them do anything for their father or mother. ¹³Thus you nullify the word of God by your tradition that you have handed down. And you do many things like that."

¹⁴Again Jesus called the crowd to him and said, "Listen to me, everyone, and understand this. ¹⁵Nothing outside a person can defile them by going into them. Rather, it is what comes out of a person that defiles them." [¹⁶]

¹⁷After he had left the crowd and entered the house, his disciples asked him about this parable. ¹⁸"Are you so dull?" he asked. "Don't you see that nothing that enters a person from the outside can defile them? ¹⁹For it doesn't go into their heart but into their stomach, and then out of the body." (In saying this, Jesus declared all foods clean.)

²⁰He went on: "What comes out of a person is what defiles them. ²¹For it is from within, out of a person's heart, that evil thoughts come—sexual immorality, theft, murder, ²²adultery, greed, malice, deceit, lewdness, envy, slander, arrogance and folly. ²³All these evils come from inside and defile a person."

Listening to the Text in the Story: Numbers 18:8–13; Psalm 15; Isaiah 29:13; Jubilees 22.16; Acts 10:1–11:18; Romans 14:14–17; Ephesians 2:11–22.

Throughout Mark's Gospel, the inclusive character of the kingdom of God presents a challenge to many of Jesus's contemporaries. Here, Jesus clarifies the basis on which people are included in the kingdom and reveals that the Pharisees' standard for inclusion is deficient. He claims that what makes a person clean or unclean is not a set of rules determined by human tradition but a person's conformity to the character of the kingdom (v. 15).

The controversy in this passage involves what is "clean" and "unclean," along with what is "holy" and "common." In Scripture, these two sets of binaries are related but not the same. The people of Israel were "holy," set apart from the nations as God's special possession and for the purpose of being God's agent of mission to the other nations of the world. And within Israel, priests were "holy" unto the Lord, set apart from others for the special purpose of being near the Lord and performing the ritual sacrifices. The rest of the Israelites, on this scenario, were "common," and this distinction was not a moral one. The priests were no better or worse than others, but they were set apart for a special role on behalf of the rest of the nation.

The other distinction was between "clean" and "unclean," which involved ritual purity, defining who could approach the Lord (the "clean") and who could not participate in ritual worship at the temple (the "unclean"). This distinction *at times* involved a moral judgment, but not always. For example, a person with a skin rash was "unclean" until he recovered and was "cleansed," restoring his ability to participate in ritual worship (Lev 13:1–46). And a woman was "unclean" for a time after childbirth (Lev 12:1–8) and during her period of menstruation (Lev 15:19). There was no moral judgment on such people—far from it, as the birth of a child is something to celebrate! Often the circumstances that make a person unclean are "breaches of boundaries," such as torn skin and bodily discharges, or exceptions to what is considered normal, such as when animals "combined characteristics thought to be proper to different environments (e.g., lobsters, which live in the sea but walk on legs)."[1] On the other hand, "defilement" could also come from behaviors we consider "moral," such as deviant sexual practices (Lev 18:24).[2]

The social configuration oriented by these distinctions was based on Israel being God's dwelling place, the nation on earth among which God resided (Deut 4:20; 7:6). This was their holiness—they alone were God's special possession, and God's presence was a great blessing (Lev 26:3–12). It also meant, however, that the nation needed to take special care to behave in ways that did not defile the land and offend God (Lev 26:14–33).[3] If they were not circumspect in observing these instructions, God's presence might "break out" in judgment, which is what happened to Aaron's sons, Nadab and Abihu, when they offered an unauthorized sacrifice before the Lord:

> Aaron's sons Nadab and Abihu took their censers, put fire in them and added incense; and they offered unauthorized fire before the LORD, contrary to his command. So fire came out from the presence of the LORD and consumed them, and they died before the LORD. Moses then said to Aaron, "This is what the LORD spoke of when he said:
>
> 'Among those who approach me
>   I will be proved holy;
> in the sight of all the people
>   I will be honored.'" (Lev 10:1–3; cf. Exod 19:22)

Modern Christians may be tempted to regard the instructions in Scripture about "clean" and "unclean," "common" and "holy" as a primitive or legalistic set of rituals. These instructions, however, revolve around the notion of relating to the holiness of God and reflect a proper social ordering that guaranteed God's favor. This central purpose fueled debates in the first century among Jews about

---

1. D. deSilva, "Clean and Unclean," *DJG* 142.
2. deSilva, "Clean and Unclean," 145.
3. deSilva, "Clean and Unclean," 145.

what was "clean" and "unclean" that may seem archaic and pointless in our day. We would do well to consider, however, that many of our debates about how our churches should gather in worship, what sort of music we ought to sing, and what version of the Bible we should use are driven by this same impulse. We feel that there is an order to our gatherings that pleases God, while practices that make us uncomfortable or that are foreign to us are somehow offenses to God. Our "worship wars" today are every bit as intense as the debates within Judaism over the lines between "clean" and "unclean" in the first century.

Over the centuries, the conception of this system of social ordering among Jews was gradually distorted by prejudice, suspicion, fear, and judgment, so that it became a set of distinctions whereby some groups could exclude others. By the first century, Jews commonly assumed that they were supposed to avoid people from other nations, since non-Jews were "unclean." We can see this assumption at work in the middle to late second-century BC in Jubilees, a Jewish text:

> Separate yourselves from the gentiles, and do not eat with them, and do not perform deeds like theirs. And do not become associates of theirs. Because their deeds are defiled, and all of their ways are contaminated, and despicable, and abominable. (22.16)[4]

The same conviction is on display in the narrative about Peter and his interactions with Cornelius in Acts 10:28: "You are well aware that it is against our law for a Jew to associate with or visit a Gentile." The assumption here is that for a Jew to go into the house of a gentile and share a meal, the Jewish person would become unclean. Peter's vision on the roof in vv. 8–17 taught him that he was to regard no person as unclean or unacceptable to God based on cultural assumptions and prejudices: "But God has shown me that I should not call anyone impure or unclean" (v. 28).

Mark 7 portrays the Pharisees as having their own ideas about clean and unclean. They were not priests who ministered in the temple, but they practiced the purity rituals in accordance with the instructions given to priests. Only priests were required to ritually wash for the purposes of purification, along with washing the utensils used in the tabernacle (and later, the temple). The Pharisees, however, washed their hands, along with their bowls and cups, when they ate their meals. They envisioned contact with "common" people

---

4. *OTP* 2:98. The Letter of Aristeas, a Jewish text from sometime in the late second-century BC, also contains this sentiment: "To prevent our being perverted by contact with others or by mixing with bad influences, [Moses] hedged us in on all sides with strict observances connected with meat and drink and touch and hearing and sight, after the manner of the Law" (142) (*OTP* 2:22).

in the marketplace as potentially defiling, making them unclean. Therefore, they ritually washed before eating to maintain purity. Again, it is easy to sit in judgment over the Pharisees, but many Christians behave this way in our day, imagining that as we go out into "the world" we are contaminated with impurity and are in contact with "defilement." When we gather as a church, we assume that we are washed and purified.

It is notable that Mark situates this text (7:1–23) between two striking passages that subvert corrupted notions of clean and unclean that exclude or marginalize people. In 6:53–56, many who are sick touch Jesus and are healed. As we have seen in other contexts, rather than impurity spreading through touch, Jesus spreads purity and healing. The kingdom of God explodes with life-giving and restorative power, which is why Jesus encounters people fearlessly. The Pharisees, on the other hand, shun sinners, along with the sick, in order to maintain a self-constructed purity.

Mark follows 7:1–23 with Jesus going to Tyre, a gentile region, and entering a house. The Jewish texts cited above indicate that Jesus's Jewish culture would have regarded this as unlawful (cf. Acts 10:28; 11:2–3). There he encounters a gentile woman with a demon-possessed daughter, who falls at his feet and who becomes, as we will see in the next section, the singularly exemplary figure in a strategic section of Mark's narrative (7:24–30).

In Mark 7:1–23, therefore, Jesus clarifies the nature of the kingdom of God by indicating the sort of people who are welcome within it. He is not overturning or attacking the Mosaic law, but has as his target the Pharisaic tradition that had developed over time to exclude people, which was a distortion of how God sees people.[5] The kinds of people who are acceptable are those with an inner orientation toward God rather than those who have outward lives of conformity to tradition but who are inwardly corrupt. Jesus is not here overturning, attacking, or critiquing the Mosaic law.

⚒ EXPLAIN the Story

The Pharisees and Scribes Question Jesus (vv. 1–5)

The scene opens with the Pharisees and teachers of the law gathering around Jesus.[6] They are not there innocently, as they have already committed

---

5. Michael F. Bird, "Jesus as Law-Breaker," in *Who Do My Opponents Say I Am? An Investigation of the Accusations against Jesus*, ed. Scot McKnight and Joseph B. Modica (London: T&T Clark, 2008).

6. The NIV has "teachers of the law" for the Greek *grammateōn* ("scribes" in the NASB and ESV; "legal experts" in the CEB). Scribes played a range of roles in first-century Jewish culture, though

themselves to scheming with the Herodians to kill him (3:1–6). Further, they are "from Jerusalem," which is a detail easily passed over. In Mark, Jerusalem is not necessarily a neutral location; it is where Jesus is headed to be betrayed into the hands of those who will crucify him (10:32–34).[7]

The Pharisees and scribes "saw" Jesus's disciples eating with unwashed hands (v. 2), yet another significant verb of perception. Jesus has already noted that some people would see but not perceive (4:12). In the previous episode, the townspeople "recognized" Jesus and rushed to meet him wherever they "heard" he was going to be (6:53–56). Their perception of Jesus drove them to seek him out for healing. This is in contrast to the disciples who "saw" Jesus (v. 49), but failed to understand (v. 52). In the passage that follows this one, the Syrian-Phoenician woman "heard" about Jesus and immediately went to him and fell at his feet (7:25). Jairus and the woman with the incessant bleeding did the same (5:22, 33). Like the disciples, however, the Pharisees and scribes "saw" Jesus but failed to perceive, tragically fulfilling the prophecy from Isaiah 6:9–10 that Jesus quotes in Mark 4:12. Their seeing reveals the Pharisees' sinister motivation. They detect a difference in practice and perceive an opportunity to find fault. Rather than seeking Jesus commendably, they set themselves up as judges and expect Jesus and his disciples to explain themselves.

They raise the issue of Jesus's disciples not washing their hands. They assume that the disciples' hands are "defiled," because they likely had contact with people at some point throughout the day who may have been ritually unclean. The Pharisees had applied the holiness instructions from the temple to everyday life, which led them to "give their hands a ceremonial washing" (7:3) and wash their "cups, pitchers and kettles" in accordance with the "tradition of the elders" (vv. 3–4). The Mosaic law did not require these measures for everyone in everyday life, but only for the priests before eating in the temple rituals (Num 18:8–13) and before offering sacrifices (Exod 30:18–21; 40:31).[8] According to Marcus, the Pharisees were operating "on the theory that every Jew should live as a priest, and every Jewish home should become like the Temple."[9]

"they shared in common a role as the keepers, interpreters, and teachers of Israel's Scriptures and traditions that often led to their prominent roles in society and politics" (G. Thellman, "Scribes," *DJG* 844). They appear in Mark consistently in opposition to Jesus, apart from the scribe he encounters in Mark 12:28–34. I will use "teachers of the law" and "scribes" interchangeably in the discussion that follows.

7. Moloney, *Gospel of Mark*, 138.

8. Marcus, *Mark 1–8*, 442; Placher, *Mark*, 101.

9. Marcus, *Mark 1–8*, 442. Mark states that "all the Jews" have this practice, which sounds like an overstatement. But it is standard language for explaining certain practices to outsiders. The Letter of Aristeas tells the story of the translation of the Old Testament into Greek and notes that the translators washed their hands in the course of their prayers "as is the custom of all the Jews" (305) (Strauss, *Mark*, 299; Boring, *Mark*, 199).

Jesus Responds to the Pharisees and Scribes (vv. 6–13)

Jesus responds with a harsh rebuke, critiquing the Pharisees and scribes' hypocritical allegiance to human tradition that allows them to excuse—or even to justify—their disobedience to God's clear commands. In their view, the traditions of the elders were not developed in order to stand in the way of honoring God. Just the opposite! The Pharisees and scribes followed their tradition precisely because they were convinced that it was an extension of the Mosaic law, helping them to observe God's commands faithfully. In fact, they may not have seen any distinction between God's commands revealed to Moses on Sinai and the traditions of the fathers that elaborated upon it. In their view, their lives were characterized by worship, and their "holiness" was pleasing to the Lord. Jesus cites Isaiah 29:13, however, to rebuke their "worship" as pointless. They are standing in the same place as the targets of Isaiah's rebuke, since they are actually following human rules and teaching others to do the same. Though they would not have thought of themselves as doing this, Jesus says that they "have let go of the commands of God and are holding on to human traditions" (v. 8). The Pharisees and scribes were certainly aware of this passage in Isaiah, so to hear it used against them must have stung and strengthened their resolve to oppose and destroy Jesus.

Jesus now turns the heat up on his accusation. Beyond distinguishing between the traditions of the elders, on one hand, and the commands of God, on the other, in vv. 6–8, he now charges them with "setting aside the commands of God in order to observe your own traditions" (v. 9). They are more faithful to their community standards and social conventions than to God's clear commands. As an example of this, Jesus cites two Scripture passages in which God commands Israel to honor parents and authorizes severe punishment for all who curse them (v. 10; cf. Exod 20:12; 21:17; Lev 20:9; Deut 5:16). Rather than carefully following God's clear priority to care for one's mother and father, they exploit the allowance of declaring certain funds "an offering" to God in order to keep it from being used to support their parents.

Jesus is not implying here that all the Pharisees do this, but it is characteristic of how at least some of them are more loyal to their tradition than to God, which leads them to do "many things like that" (v. 13). Their fidelity to their own socially constructed code of holiness over the clear commands of Scripture has deluded them into conceiving of themselves as more faithful to God than everyone else. They presume they can pass judgment on others, marginalizing them, putting others down and lifting themselves up—all based on their traditions. If they were self-confessedly imperfect people who were striving to be faithful to God's commands while teaching others to do the same, they would not have been the target of Jesus's rebuke. But they are congratulating themselves on their standards of holiness, even while they are creating havens in their lives for sin in the form of greed and selfishness. Their misuse of the distinction between "clean" and "unclean" based on their tradition has caused them to fail to reckon faithfully with the realities of Jesus and life in the kingdom of God.

Jesus Clarifies the Nature of the Kingdom (vv. 14–23)

The discussion of distinctions between "clean" and "unclean" and the Pharisees' critique of the disciples has everything to do with the nature of the kingdom of God. The assumption behind such distinctions is that they set the limits of who are members of God's kingdom. The implicit question is, Who is acceptable to God? And the assumed answer of the Pharisees is that everyone who behaves the way they do is pleasing to God and inhabits God's kingdom. And they could claim to be building on Scripture in constructing the boundaries of the kingdom of God through certain social practices. Jesus, then, is not critiquing the Mosaic law when he dismantles their conception of who is truly pleasing to God. He is clarifying what Scripture itself teaches.

Jesus calls the crowd to himself and addresses them in vv. 14–15. He exhorts them to pay close attention with two Greek imperative verbs (*akousate*, "listen!"; *synete*, "understand!"). His arresting exclamation recalls his words in 4:3, 9 when he framed the parable of the sower in twin exhortations to pay close attention ("Listen! Look!" v. 3; "Whoever has ears to hear, let them hear," v. 9).

Jesus states that "nothing outside a person can defile them by going into them. Rather, it is what comes out of a person that defiles them" (v. 15). In the immediate situation, the disciples' handwashing practices have nothing to do with their acceptance before God. Whether or not they have washed after returning from the market, their eating does not make them acceptable or unacceptable to God. What matters with God is the core of a person—their desires, their private practices, the orientation of their heart. Some of the Pharisees would be indicted by Jesus's words here and would find themselves outside the kingdom ("defiled") because of their practice of setting aside God's commands in favor of fostering their greed and selfishness. Their manipulative loyalty to traditional practices that allowed them to set aside God's commands prevented them from having hearts shaped by love for God and love for others. They may indeed have washed hands so that they see themselves as "clean," but this self-evaluation was really self-deception. Before God, they were unacceptable.[10]

---

10. The NIV translation does not include v. 16 because it is very likely not original. Some manuscripts contain the words of 4:23, probably because a scribe perceived the two contexts as quite similar.

Jesus leaves the crowd and explains further what he means to his disciples (vv. 18–23), though this elaboration comes in the context of a rebuke. The disciples ask "about this parable," though it is not at all clear that Jesus has spoken in a parable. This is why Jesus rebukes them in v. 18: "Are you so dull?" He has spoken plainly and not in a parable or cryptic saying, and they have failed to reckon with what he has said.

This request and Jesus's rebuke partake of the developing dynamic in Mark whereby the disciples increase in misunderstanding. Beginning in 4:1–20, where Jesus indicates that those outside the kingdom will see and hear but not perceive or understand, the disciples have been gradually failing to recognize Jesus's identity and to grasp what he is saying. They responded to Jesus with sarcasm when he had exhorted them to feed the crowd (6:37), and in the previous episode their understanding has diminished, and their hearts have hardened (6:52). As we have noted previously, Mark develops this dynamic to confront his audiences with the question of whether they are faithfully paying close attention to Jesus so that they truly understand his identity and the nature of the kingdom. After all, the disciples' nearness to Jesus has not always resulted in good fruit. Without humility and cultivated hearts that are receptive to the truth of the cross-shaped kingdom and the cross-directed Jesus, audiences will manifest increasingly dull hearts and minds, and their understanding will diminish.

Jesus explains in vv. 18–19 that the food a person eats does not make them unacceptable to God since food enters the body and is later expelled. It does not touch "the heart"—a person's affections, orientation to God, commitment to love others, and relation to Jesus's teaching. God is not concerned about social status; God's kingdom is made up of people who in their holistic mode of being look to him in faith and love.

Mark adds the editorial statement in v. 19 that "In saying this, Jesus declared all foods clean," which raises a difficult interpretive question. Is Jesus overturning the food laws in Scripture that function as authoritative commands for Jews? If this were so, Jesus would be abrogating the clear teaching of Scripture.[11] This comment is better understood if we distinguish between Jesus's original context and Mark's intention that his Gospel reach an international audience. In Jesus's initial context, he is emphasizing to his audience that their behaviors that meet or fail to meet socially constructed expectations do not determine a person's status in the kingdom of God. They are not clean or unclean if they wash or do not wash before meals according to the traditions

---

11. Cf. the food laws of Lev 7:26–27; 11; 19:26; Deut 12:21–25 (Boring, *Mark*, 203).

of the elders. What matters is a person's disposition—their internal posture toward God and others that matches their lives of love for God and others. This was the thrust of Jesus's words in his initial context, and that initial audience included only Jews.

Mark's report of this narrative in his Gospel will reach audiences that comprise both Jews and non-Jews, so his editorial comment likely does not entail the notion that Jesus is overthrowing God's commands that determine the Jewish diet. He has in mind the people who make up gospel communities now that God's kingdom work has reached beyond the borders of Judea and Galilee and has brought in the gentiles. In declaring all foods clean, Mark has in mind here all the food that various people eat, including Jews and non-Jews. This does not mean that Jewish Christians are permitted to eat a nonkosher diet, since Jewish Christians would still be subject to the Mosaic law, their authoritative Scripture.[12] Since the Mosaic law never applied to non-Jews, the diet in Scripture does not apply to them.

Mark's comment is in line with Paul's in Romans 14:14 where he states to his Roman audiences that "I am convinced, being fully persuaded in the Lord Jesus, that nothing is unclean *in itself.*" Leviticus 11 and Deuteronomy 14 are two passages in the Mosaic law in which God gave commands to Israel about what foods they were to regard as unclean, noting that "*for you* it is unclean" (Deut 14:10). Therefore, it is not that these foods are unclean in themselves, but just that God had Israel maintain this unique diet in order to remain distinct from the surrounding nations. For the nations, however, these foods are not unclean, and so there is no reason why non-Jews in Mark's day should observe these dietary laws. And now that the gospel has gone to the nations, the boundary markers of God's people are broken down. God's singular, international family will eat together, but may have different menus.[13]

Jesus summarizes and expands upon his point in vv. 20–23. What makes a person unacceptable to God is not that they fail to meet the socially constructed standards of the leadership of God's people. Rather, the evil thoughts that proceed from within a person are what prevent them from being welcomed into God's presence. The vice list in vv. 21–22 indicates a heart populated by evil

---

12. Modern Western Christians might sense that Jesus's audience would have heard this as a word of liberation, as if they no longer needed to hold to a restrictive and limited diet but were set free to eat any and all foods without fear of harsh reprisals for failing to observe the law's strict requirements. But this would be to misunderstand the nature of the law and the character of the food laws, along with the possibility that they would be or could be abrogated. See the "Live the Story" discussion below.

13. For more on these dynamics as they relate to Acts 10, see Chris A. Miller, "Did Peter's Vision in Acts 10 Pertain to Men or the Menu?" *Bibliotheca Sacra* 159 (July–Sept 2002): 302–17. See the discussion of the Mosaic law in relation to Jewish Christians under "Live the Story" below.

inclinations and rebellious thoughts. It is not merely that a person is imperfect, but that these dynamics are welcomed and nurtured within a person's heart, being embodied by outward practices of sin and injustice. Those things put someone outside the people of God.

And this is nothing new. Scripture contains many statements that sum up what pleases God, indicating what kind of person is given a glad welcome into the presence of God. Psalm 15 is one of these:

> LORD, who may dwell in your sacred tent?
>> Who may live on your holy mountain?
> The one whose walk is blameless,
>> who does what is righteous,
>> who speaks the truth from their heart;
> whose tongue utters no slander,
>> who does no wrong to a neighbor,
>> and casts no slur on others;
> who despises a vile person
>> but honors those who fear the LORD;
> who keeps an oath even when it hurts,
>> and does not change their mind;
> who lends money to the poor without interest;
>> who does not accept a bribe against the innocent.
> Whoever does these things
>> will never be shaken.

God is not looking for perfect people. God's kingdom belongs to those with hearts oriented toward God that are matched by lives of goodness toward others, the pursuit of justice, and love for God and neighbor. Meeting social expectations constructed by Christian cultures is utterly irrelevant to membership in the kingdom of God.

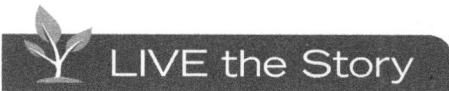

LIVE the Story

Constructing Social Standards of Holiness

It is easy to demonize the Pharisees as we encounter them on the pages of the Gospels, since they are so often the opponents of Jesus. The logic, however, that drove them is similar to the practical piety of many Christian traditions today. In seeking to please God by presenting to him a nation of people who were uniquely devoted, the Pharisees adopted in everyday life the holiness practices of the priests in the temple. Contemporary Christians may imagine that the radical lives of the apostles are uniquely pleasing to God—certainly more so than the piety of run-of-the-mill, everyday Christians—so that being "radically sold out" like Paul should become the goal for all Christians. I was part of a church for a time that taught that the qualifications for elders in 1 Timothy 3:1–7 and Titus 1:5–9 were the highest standard of godliness. Therefore, these attributes and characteristics are what all Christians should strive for.

Those who teach along these lines are not badly motivated in their desire for the church to take seriously its commitment to being the people of God in the world. They make two miscalculations, however, that have negative consequences. First, they take scriptural instructions that God intended for a very distinct form of service and apply those to all of God's people. The Pharisees took the temple instructions and applied them to all of life. They thought that this would have the benefit of sanctifying more spheres of life than just activities in the temple. However, trying to help God out, at least in this instance, had the negative consequences of drawing lines of clean and unclean where God never intended them to be drawn. In the church that I spent some time in, applying these lists that describe the sort of people who should lead the church to everyone as a standard for Christian discipleship had similar negative effects. New Christians were presented with tough goals for their lives of discipleship that did not allow time to let them take some baby steps in the faith and figure out, under the guidance of patient mentoring, how to reconfigure their lives to match the new commitment they made. This led to a lot of discouragement.

We also discovered that this misapplication of Scripture, along with the culturally shaped lenses through which these passages were understood, inadvertently set up scales of holiness measuring a Christian's love for and commitment to God. This resulted for us in community dynamics of judgment, with church members evaluating one another based on devotional practices and lifestyle choices. Our church became a community that fostered fear of exposure, where authenticity was threatening because no one wanted to be found out as someone who did not measure up.

These dynamics are replicated when we see Christians measuring themselves and one another by whether they have the "right" books on their shelves, whether they're listening to the "right" podcasts, reading the "most faithful" Bible translation, raising their children according to the agreed-upon "godly" parenting method, or voting for the approved political candidate from the "right" party.

Certain practices that become popular in Christian culture can inadvertently become such measuring sticks. Some years ago there was a fad where Christian girls were taking pledges and wearing purity rings to signify their commitment to avoiding sex before marriage. This immediately created a sort of caste system among young Christians based on experiences while dating. And even dating practices were drawn into this social dynamic, as the notion became widespread that only "courtship" was the "biblical" way to find a spouse.[14]

The second mistake that these well-intended people make is that they do not reckon with the diversity in calling among the people of God. God called *one tribe* among Israel's twelve tribes to play the priestly role. They were no better or worse than the other tribes; they were simply the one group called as priests among God's holy people. Their holiness was *functional*, and God was just as pleased with Israelites who were priests as he was with those who were farmers. And while God gave apostles, prophets, evangelists, and pastors and teachers to the church (Eph 4:11), they are no better or worse than members of Christ's body that are called to serve in relatively unremarkable or "ordinary" ways. God loves apostles and evangelists and is pleased when they are faithful. And God loves bricklayers and others who serve the community in unremarkable and unspectacular ways. God called Paul to be an apostle, but we forget that there were loads of people in the early church who were not called to be apostles. There was no doubt a certain mode of life that was necessitated by Paul's apostolic call, but this was unique to him. It is a grave mistake to set up Paul's life as the standard of devotion against which ordinary Christians should measure their lives.

The Pharisees may have been well-motivated in their desires to be a group that was dedicated to renewing Israel's faithfulness to God, but their application of temple purity to everyday life brought them to the point where they were passing judgment on others who, in their view, were unconcerned with holiness. In the same way, we must be on the lookout for the constant temptation to adopt standards of holiness that seem especially pleasing to God but that end up doing damage to God's people.

Our misapplication of God's call for Christian spirituality is revealed in how we talk about the Christian life. I recently asked one of my classes if they were okay with the following statement: "Christians are called to a higher

---

14. This way of understanding courtship became a fad in the 1990s with the publication of Josh Harris's book, *I Kissed Dating Goodbye* (Colorado Springs: Multnomah, 1997). Harris later disavowed the views he espoused in the book and called for the publisher to cease its publication (Sarah McCammon, "Evangelical Writer Kisses an Old Idea Goodbye," National Public Radio, December 17, 2018, www.npr.org/2018/12/17/671888011/evangelical-writer-kisses-an-old-idea-goodbye).

standard." Of course, by that point in the semester, they knew I had a habit of subjecting typical Christian sentiments to scrutiny, but most of them said that yes, Christians were called to a higher standard. I objected. I went on to explain that when we speak this way to ourselves and to one another, we conceive in our minds of a vertical scale with measurements. The lower regions of the scale are where ordinary life takes place, and the higher readings on the scale are what God calls Christians to. And we unconsciously fill the scale with lifestyle choices and habits that come from whatever church culture we were raised in.

Among a number of other problems, this way of talking does not take into account that "holiness" language in the Bible does not indicate "higher" or "better" but just "different." God had called Israel to be a radically *different* sort of people, with different social practices, an alternative set of politics, and a distinct network of economic exchanges. As I mentioned above, Israel was "holy" among the nations, though God loved all the nations; and the Levites were "holy" among Israel, though God loved all the tribes of the nation. When we conceive of "higher" standards, we construct a scale of what pleases God more and then have a humanly constructed measure with which we can pass judgment against one another, just like the Pharisees whom Jesus confronted. This highlights the necessity of discerning carefully how Scripture configures spirituality and holiness. We may consider ourselves well-motivated in constructing hierarchies of holiness, calling people to be truly committed to God, but if we are fostering community dynamics of judgment, we may need to revisit our reading of Scripture.

Human Tradition

The Pharisees whom Jesus confronted had come to hold fast to their traditions and were no longer following God's clear commands to love and honor their parents. Of course, the Pharisees would not have thought that their traditions stood in any tension at all with Scripture. *They might not even have thought that they had traditions*, but were simply people whose lives were oriented by Scripture. They probably would have said, just as many Christians do today, "We are people of the book! We do not follow tradition, we're biblical!" Jesus, however, was able to discern not only a difference between the traditions handed down to them from their elders and between Scripture, but a wide chasm.

Just as the Pharisees discovered, so Christians ought to recognize today and in every age and culture that *we do indeed have traditions*. They develop naturally and inevitably as we teach Scripture throughout the generations. We naturally summarize the content of Scripture and emphasize certain biblical texts rather than other ones, and we come up with systems to help us organize biblical content. What we must realize is that when we do this, *we do it from a place of privileging our own perception of what is important*. And this is shaped by our social and cultural location, our race and ethnicity, our family heritage, nationality, and denomination. We may tell ourselves that we are being biblical as we speak from Scripture about our way of life, but we inevitably choose certain passages in Scripture to talk about. It is no stretch to claim that Western Protestant churches spend far more time in Paul's letter to the Romans, speaking about the salvation of the individual, than in the Old Testament prophetic literature, calling out the injustices of economic inequality. I would also venture a guess that not many suburban Protestant churches that claim to be "biblical" hear sermons on the sin of home-improvement projects from Isaiah 5:8–9.

As church cultures hand down the faith to further generations, cultural prejudices and assumptions inevitably get mixed in and shape the way Christians conceive of the faith. Paul says that these cultural assumptions that distort the Christian faith are passed on through human tradition but originate in sinister, anti-God spiritual forces: "See to it that no one takes you captive through hollow and deceptive philosophy, which depends on human tradition and the elemental spiritual forces of this world rather than on Christ" (Col 2:8). He is not warning against the study of philosophy as an academic discipline, but rather against ideologies, mindsets, cultural patterns, and ways of thinking that develop in all cultures over time. He especially has in mind here those ideologies and patterns of life that are destructive and exploitative of others, such as the thought that one race of people is better than another, or that rich people are more important than the poor, or that people in power have the prerogative to mistreat those in weaker positions.

Matthew Avery Sutton narrates a tragic example of just this dynamic in his masterful work *American Apocalypse: A History of Modern Evangelicalism*. In chronicling the growth of evangelicalism in the 1920s and beyond, Sutton demonstrates that racist attitudes and segregationist policies strongly shaped the developing evangelical movement. Many white evangelicals rejected calls from black evangelical church leaders who wanted to join newly formed evangelical organizations. Further, many white Christian leaders opposed anti-lynching legislation, and no less an evangelical authority than *Moody Monthly* expressed its disagreement with granting African-Americans the right to vote.[15] Sutton notes that evangelicals thought that segregation and racism were plainly taught in their inerrant Bibles:

---

15. Sutton, *American Apocalypse: A History of Modern Evangelicalism* (Cambridge, MA: Belknap, 2017), 130–34.

Most fundamentalists not only practiced segregation on Sunday mornings; many also defended racial hierarchies in the broader society. Presbyterian minister and popular radio preacher Donald Grey Barnhouse appealed to nineteenth-century biblically inspired arguments to justify the inferior social position of African Americans. In a sermon on "the black man" preached over the Columbia Broadcasting System, he moved from emphasizing the unity of all people in Christ to the allegedly inferior nature of African Americans. He claimed that they still bore the "curse of Ham" and that God had destined "the colored peoples" to serve the "Semites" (Jews) and "Japhethites" (white Gentiles). "The streams of history," he explained, "have run in the channels that God marked out for them with His prophetic finger so long ago." By grounding racial differences in a supposedly inerrant Bible text, fundamentalists made it very difficult for opponents of segregation to mount an attack.[16]

A racially segregated church, however, runs directly counter to clear New Testament teaching. In Galatians 2, Paul argues that in the death of Jesus, God has united in one body the multiethnic people of God, and this unity must be embodied in social practices where visible fellowship depicts this transformative reality. Any segregation of God's people along ethnic or racial lines is an offense against the truth of the gospel (Gal 2:14). In Ephesians 2:11–14, Paul argues much the same, claiming that in his death, Christ has united people from all ethnicities and brought them together as one social entity to God the Father. God's people are one in Christ, and they are the communities on earth among whom God dwells by his Spirit. Based on this reality, Paul says there are grave consequences for anyone who breaks up God's people:

> Don't you know that you yourselves are God's temple and that God's Spirit dwells in your midst? If anyone destroys God's temple, God will destroy that person; for God's temple is sacred, and you together are that temple. (1 Cor 3:16–17)

Further, Paul calls down curses against anyone who teaches anything that opposes this reality:

> But even if we or an angel from heaven should preach a gospel other than the one we preached to you, let them be under God's curse! As we have

---

16. Sutton, *American Apocalypse*, 133.

already said, so now I say again: If anybody is preaching to you a gospel other than what you accepted, let them be under God's curse! (Gal 1:8–9)

So, how is it that a Christian culture that sees itself as "biblical" comes to do just what the Pharisees were doing? How did Bible teachers who militantly opposed mixing human tradition with the teaching of Scripture set aside the clear teaching of Scripture in preference for human traditions? How did they end up passing on culturally determined and corrupted biblical interpretations that plainly opposed God's purposes? It is not enough to claim to be biblical, nor to fire up our resolve to not let anything like this happen to our church. As I said, human traditions develop naturally, and we inevitably conceive of the Christian faith through the lenses of what our teachers handed on to us and how our culture shapes us.

We can perhaps find hope, however, in cultivating humility and listening to our culture's critiques of the church. People outside the church are often a wonderful resource for pointing out where the church has been hypocritical. We do not have to see criticism as a threat to us, for it can be a great gift. If we have faults pointed out to us, we can be set in the perfect position for repentance and the cultivation of life-giving patterns of community behavior. We can also develop relationships with Christian churches that are from other traditions. When we relate to others, we often see the differences more clearly, and perhaps these will reveal where we fall short of gospel practices. We do not have to compare ourselves to see who is better, but if relating to a church constituted by another ethnicity reveals prejudices, then we can discern where we need to repent and cultivate new attitudes and behaviors.

Favoring human tradition over God's commands is not a reality that ended with the Pharisees. It is human, and it is a habit that is still with us.

The Mosaic Law and Jewish Christians

Mark's comment that Jesus declared all foods clean may strike modern Bible readers as fairly unremarkable. This statement fits into a generally accepted scenario in which the Mosaic law is now obsolete or irrelevant now that Christ has come to earth, died, and been raised to new life. It is common for Western Christians to view the Mosaic law as an oppressive system of rules, and the food laws as "limiting" what Jews could eat. We may imagine that Jews for generations labored under this legalistic arrangement and longed to be free, eating what they would have wanted and living like their non-Jewish neighbors.

This generally assumed scenario has been called into question by the last generation of biblical scholarship, especially with a more accurate understanding of first-century Judaism. With a better informed vision of the historical situation among Jews in the first century, we can read the New Testament afresh to see more clearly how the biblical text presents the relationship between Jewish and non-Jewish Christians, and between Jewish Christians and the law of Moses. First, it is not right to say that Jews for generations were laboring under the legalistic and oppressive regime of the Mosaic law. Certainly, Jesus discerns that some Jewish teachers are laying huge burdens on their followers as they teach distortions of Scripture, driven by impure motives (Luke 11:46). But this is a rebuke of unfaithful teachers and not a faithful conception of the "good" law (Rom 7:12, 16), the "perfect law that gives freedom" (Jas 1:25). After all, Jesus makes this programmatic statement about his ministry:

> Do not think that I have come to abolish the Law or the Prophets; I have not come to abolish them but to fulfill them. For truly I tell you, until heaven and earth disappear, not the smallest letter, not the least stroke of a pen, will by any means disappear from the Law until everything is accomplished. (Matt 5:17–18)

Second, the Mosaic law was given through Moses to Israel as a good gift (Deut 4:8). It functioned as their holistic guide to life. God had delivered Israel out of bondage in Egypt and brought them into the good land to settle them there. He gave his instruction through Moses to teach Israel how to remain in his love. Again, the Mosaic law did not consist in "standards" that Israel needed to live up to. It contained instructions in how Israel could inhabit God's love now that God had graciously and powerfully brought them into it. The law functioned like Israel's national constitution, with instruction that governed all areas of life. And in teaching the nations to worship the one true God, Israel was not supposed to teach the nations to become part of Israel. Israel alone was Israel, and the nations were supposed to become acquainted with God through their contact with Israel. And they would not have followed the law of Moses like Israelites, but they would have become acquainted with the God of Israel through consultation with the law of Moses. All of this is to say that the Mosaic law functioned for Israel as their holistic guide to life. The nations were not to relate to the law of Moses the way that Israel did.

This is important for understanding what was going on in the New Testament era. When Jesus came, died, and was raised from the dead, that did not bring the Mosaic law to an end. Jewish followers of Jesus still related to God through their lives conducted within a Jewish identity, oriented by the law of Moses. They became obedient to Jesus *as Jews* and did not need to leave their Jewishness behind because of their Christian identities. We see this throughout the narrative of Acts, as the first generation of the church, certainly in Jerusalem, was entirely Jewish and gathered daily at the temple (Acts 5:12). Paul is the exception, as he was called to the gentile world to preach the gospel and establish churches among the nations beyond the borders of Judea. Yet he never ceased being a Jew and living out his Christian discipleship as a Jew. He maintained his identity as a Pharisee until the end of his life (Acts 23:6; 26:5–7) and was in a hurry during his third missionary journey to return to Jerusalem to be there for the Jewish festival of Pentecost (19:21; 20:16) and to worship at the Jerusalem temple (21:24–26).

In Galatians and Romans—and at the Jerusalem Council in Acts 15—Paul argued that gentiles were to remain gentiles and did not have to take on Jewish identity in order to enjoy salvation in Christ. The Western church has learned this lesson well, but we need to keep in mind that Jewish believers were also not to be subject to pressure to become non-Jewish. They, too, were welcome to the one God in Christ and by the Spirit, and were free from any pressure to change ethnicity to enjoy salvation.

This larger scenario helps to make sense of a text like Mark 7:19, where Mark states that Jesus declared all foods clean. It is not that Jews no longer needed to follow the law of Moses—the Scriptures that were given as a gift to their people and that continued as the word of God to define and orient their ethnic identity. In fact, Jews in the first century likely loved and enjoyed their diet and had no interest in eating the foods of other nations. At any rate, the force of Mark's words is that all people who eat any sorts of foods are all welcome to the one God who rules over and welcomes all nations, tribes, and tongues.

CHAPTER 28

Mark 7:24-30

²⁴Jesus left that place and went to the vicinity of Tyre. He entered a house and did not want anyone to know it; yet he could not keep his presence secret. ²⁵In fact, as soon as she heard about him, a woman whose little daughter was possessed by an impure spirit came and fell at his feet. ²⁶The woman was a Greek, born in Syrian Phoenicia. She begged Jesus to drive the demon out of her daughter.

²⁷"First let the children eat all they want," he told her, "for it is not right to take the children's bread and toss it to the dogs."

²⁸"Lord," she replied, "even the dogs under the table eat the children's crumbs."

²⁹Then he told her, "For such a reply, you may go; the demon has left your daughter."

³⁰She went home and found her child lying on the bed, and the demon gone.

Listening to the Text in the Story: 1 Kings 14:11; 21:19–24; Isaiah 23; Ezekiel 26:1–28:19; Philippians 3:2; Galatians 3:28.

This is one of the most challenging passages in Mark's Gospel. We have already noted that Jesus comes off as a confrontational character in Mark, which is why people throughout the Gospel associate him with Elijah (6:15; 8:28). But here he speaks with such apparent rudeness to this poor woman, insulting her and treating her in such degrading fashion, that interpreters are left befuddled. This simply does not seem like the gracious and compassionate Jesus, the one who is meek and mild, tender and kind. One explanation for Jesus's words is that he is stressing Israel's priority in salvation. The gospel will indeed go to the nations, but it is first good news for Israel.

While it is true that one of the narrative threads in the Gospel is Jesus calling Jews to return to being faithful to the God of Israel, Mark has more strategic purposes in this passage. He places this encounter just after Jesus's reorientation of the Pharisees' conception of who is inside the kingdom of God and who is on the outside (7:1–23). He had made the point that it is irrelevant whether one measures up to a social group's culturally constructed standard of holiness. What matters is a person's holistic orientation toward God. Rather than assessing the dressed-up, external appearance that meets the evaluation of others, God evaluates people based on who they truly are.

Jesus's conversation with the Syrian-Phoenician woman relates directly to the point he makes in vv. 1–23, and Mark sets up this situation to make Jesus's point in emphatic fashion. According to the Pharisees' standards of clean and unclean, this woman is obviously the furthest from the kingdom of God that one can get. She is radically unclean, being a woman, a gentile, ethnically Syrian-Phoenician, and having a demon-possessed daughter. Yet, in contrast to the disciples and the Pharisees, when she perceives Jesus, she not only rushes to him and prostrates herself in a posture of worship, she immediately grasps the toughest parabolic saying in the whole Gospel.

This passage also has a strong connection to Mark 4:1–20, especially Jesus's words in vv. 11–12:

> The secret of the kingdom of God has been given to you. But to those on the outside everything is said in parables so that, "they may be ever seeing but never perceiving, and ever hearing but never understanding; otherwise they might turn and be forgiven!"

Those who are outsiders to the kingdom are those who are mystified by Jesus's statements, while those who are insiders hear and understand; they see and rightly perceive. Mark presses his ironic narrative device most strongly here, where the disciples increasingly grow in confusion while people who culturally don't measure up continue to grasp what Jesus is saying. This episode is the climax of this dynamic, and the Syrian-Phoenician woman demonstrates that she is located at the very center of God's kingdom. Jesus delivers his most confrontational word, and she gives it right back to him, demonstrating a heart that is oriented toward God. She is the prime example of good soil that responds fruitfully (4:20).

EXPLAIN the Story

This episode takes place in Tyre, which is in Syria, to the north of Galilee. This detail would have raised eyebrows among the first audiences of Mark's

Gospel, since this was enemy territory. Israel's prophets railed against Tyre, proclaiming judgment (Isa 23; Ezek 26:1–28:19), and Jews and Tyrians in the first century detested each other.[1] That Jesus went into a house in Tyre increases the tension even more and would have at least raised the urgent question among Jewish audiences of Mark as to whether this house was that of a Jew or gentile. There were likely some Jews living in Tyre, but because Mark leaves the ethnic identity of the owner unstated, it may well have been a gentile's house.[2] Jesus's attempt to keep his presence and identity a secret was to no avail.

Mark introduces the woman in v. 25, noting that "as soon as she heard about" Jesus, she came and fell at his feet. Again, Mark uses a verb of perception ("she heard"), which is associated with many characters in his Gospel, though all do not respond faithfully. The disciples and Pharisees "see" or "hear" Jesus but fail to respond in a commendable manner. She responds, like a few others, by rushing to Jesus and falling before him in a posture of worship (cf. 5:6, 22, 33). Measured by the Pharisees' standard of acceptability, and even by common first-century Jewish assumptions, this woman is about as far away from the God of Israel as one can get. Think about the strikes she has against her: she is a woman, and not only is she a non-Jew, what's worse is that she is a Syrian-Phoenician living in enemy territory. And she lives with uncleanness all the time, since her daughter is "possessed by an impure spirit" (v. 25).

She continually pleaded with Jesus to "drive the demon out of her daughter," and Jesus continually responded to her in terms of his strong rebuff. The Greek verbs in vv. 26–27 are in the imperfect tense, indicating repeated action in the past. She "kept on begging" (*ērōta*) Jesus to do this, while he "kept on responding" (*elegen*) to her in this way. While Jesus speaks in more or less parabolic fashion in v. 27, there is no avoiding the reality that he is referring to her as a dog.[3] Even in our day, it's a harsh insult to call a woman "a dog," but in the ancient Near East, dogs were regarded as unclean scavengers and not as pets (1 Kgs 14:11; 21:19–24; Phil 3:2; Rev 22:15).[4] This amounted to an ethnic slur, which is shocking but strategic when the context and narrative purposes of Mark are taken into account. Jesus's dismissive insult would have resonated

1. Black, *Mark*, 177; Beavis, *Mark*, 123. Josephus, after referring to other nations, states that Tyrians held the strongest ill will against the Jews (*Against Apion* 1.70).

2. The situation may have been similar to that of Peter in Acts 10. Luke notes a few times that Peter welcomed gentiles into his house (10:23) and later went into a gentile's house (10:25; 11:12). And when Peter returns to Jerusalem, Jewish Christians confront him for going into a gentile's house (11:3).

3. Hooker, *Mark*, 183.

4. Beavis, *Mark*, 124; Strauss, *Mark*, 312.

strongly when it was first read to Jewish audiences. And other audiences who would have been familiar with Jewish culture would recognize that she is an obvious "outsider" and that Jesus's words represent strong Jewish sentiment.

This insult, however, only serves to set up the woman's clever response to Jesus. Mark casts the spotlight on her reply with his emphatic introduction of her statement: literally, "but she answered and says to him . . ." (v. 28).[5] She responds with a parable of her own, noting that "even the dogs under the table eat the children's crumbs." Mark gives no details indicating whether this woman is poor or wealthy, whether she has high or low status. Yet by her response she presents herself most humbly before Jesus. She has the most cultivated heart of any character in this larger section of Mark 4:1–8:21. She is not offended at Jesus's dismissive remark but rather adopts a posture of humility as one who is happy to receive a few table scraps. And she is the only person in Mark's Gospel who addresses him as "Lord."[6]

This humility stands in contrast to the disciples' sarcastic response to Jesus in 6:37, a humility that, along with her quick reply, manifests her cultivated heart. Whereas others have hearts that are uncultivated soil and thus take offense at Jesus's word or are confused by it, this woman receives the word and responds in a way that Jesus commends. Alert readers will recall the parable of the sower and the soils in 4:1–20 when they read Jesus's response to her: *dia touton ton logon* (lit. "because of this word"). Jesus's "word" has gone out, and even though it came to her in a tough and mystifying manner, she gave "a word" right back to Jesus.

Jesus sends her home to her daughter after telling her that the demon has left. The close of the episode is somewhat anticlimactic, since the woman and her interchange with Jesus stands at the center. This episode is not, then, an example of Jesus mistreating this poor woman. We would do well to keep in mind Mark's narrative moves. He draws a connection between this episode and the previous one, in which Jesus confronts the Pharisees for their corrupted conception of the kind of people whom God approves. This woman is the heroine of Mark 4:1–8:17. She is the model of a cultivated heart, the kind of person who sees Jesus clearly, adopts a posture of humility toward him, and responds faithfully to his word. She stands at the very center of the kingdom of

5. Marcus notes that Mark employs a historical present here (*legei*, "says," or "said"), a present-tense verb that may be translated as past action, which is the only appearance of a historical present in this episode, a feature that further highlights her response (*Mark 1–8*, 469). This emphatic introduction in the Greek text is translated by the NIV in an economy of words: "'Lord,' she replied . . ."

6. Boring, *Mark*, 214.

God, upsetting first-century cultural expectations and offending the Pharisees' conceptions of who belongs and who does not.

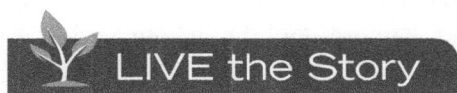

LIVE the Story

Creating Inclusive Church Cultures

In a paper for a spiritual formation class, a gifted student named Emily wrote the following, reflecting on her experience growing up in her church:

> One of the first things I was taught in church was that we read the Bible and obey it because it is the word of God. I remember wondering where this book came from; how do we know it wasn't written by a bunch of humans trying to trick us? However, I never asked questions like this, because there was a strong "unspoken" culture at my church. One of the unspoken rules was to never question the Bible. Another unspoken rule was that we weren't supposed to talk about difficult topics. I found creation to be a difficult topic, especially as a kid. My church used the creation story as an opportunity to teach us where men got their authority and women messed everything up. I often felt guilty as a girl and did not understand why I was made female if this was such a problem. Since I wasn't supposed to question where the Bible came from or why God hated women, I had to take what was given me and trust my pastors. I did not understand that Jesus is our well of truth, not the adults in my church. As a result, I believed God was a man who only made women so that men could have assistants. Since I was only second best, who was I to ask anything about God? I dealt with it, troubling as it was.[7]

While there is much to reflect on here, I want to especially focus on how all church communities are cultures that are shaped by countless forces and hidden assumptions, so that they become microcultures with "unspoken" rules. These rules are implicit and hidden from the people that participate in the community, but everyone feels them. They are "blind spots," but those who are marginalized or mistreated feel them especially strongly and feel the pressure to keep quiet about them, as if they will be punished or judged by the community as sinful if they point them out.

Certainly, Jewish communities in the first century would have felt that

---

7. Shared with permission.

Jesus's engagement with the Syrian-Phoenician woman was scandalous, just as Jesus's touching many unclean people throughout Mark's Gospel offended their prejudices. God's kingdom is a scandalously inclusive reality, constituted by all those who call upon the name of the Lord. And throughout Scripture, God consistently delights to offend typical human patterns of evaluating people. He chooses the younger over the older, which goes against cultural patterns (e.g., Gen 25:23; Rom 9:12). And he "looks at the heart" rather than making judgments as people do by evaluating the external appearance (1 Sam 16:7; Rom 2:11).

Many church cultures in America are prone to these dynamics in specific ways, especially with regard to race and gender. Michael Emerson and Christian Smith have demonstrated how the evangelical church is affected by American cultural patterns of racial division, so that the orientation of church life in America is strongly determined by racial practices and prejudices.[8] And evangelical biblical and historical scholars have helpfully exposed the cultural dynamics that shape contemporary church practice and traditional interpretations of the Bible, so that Christian women, like Emily, feel subjugated, repressed, and even oppressed within their churches.[9]

Ministry leaders who want to foster life-giving communities where no woman is marginalized but each person knows and feels they are essential would do well to consult helpful books like *Half the Church* by Carolyn Custis James.[10] She articulates the cultural assumptions that affect many Christians who read their Bibles to envision women as occupying a subservient place in the church. She offers a hopeful way forward for men and women to inhabit God's kingdom joyfully. And Brenda Salter McNeil has offered a rich resource to help communities embody God's reconciling work in the gospel that bridges racial divides.[11]

The desire to create inclusive church communities is not an impulse that

---

8. Michael O. Emerson and Christian Smith, *Divided by Faith: Evangelical Religion and the Problem of Race in America* (New York: Oxford University Press, 2001). See also Mary Beth Swetnam Mathews, *Doctrine and Race: African American Evangelicals and Fundamentalism between the Wars* (Tuscaloosa: University of Alabama Press, 2017).

9. On the historical and sociological factors that have shaped contemporary evangelical interpretations of Scripture regarding gender and the subjection of women in evangelical churches, see Margaret Lamberts Bendroth, *Fundamentalism and Gender, 1875 to the Present* (New Haven: Yale University Press, 1996); Betty A. DeBerg, *Ungodly Women: Gender and the First Wave of American Fundamentalism* (Macon, GA: Mercer University Press, 2000); Kathryn Joyce, *Quiverfull: Inside the Christian Patriarchy Movement* (Boston: Beacon, 2009).

10. Carolyn Custis James, *Half the Church: Recapturing God's Global Vision for Women* (Grand Rapids: Zondervan, 2010).

11. Brenda Salter McNeil, *Roadmap to Reconciliation: Moving Communities into Unity, Wholeness and Justice* (Downers Grove, IL: InterVarsity Press, 2016). See also the many publications of John

arises from cultural sensitivities that are "liberal" or driven by secular values that favor "diversity." The God whom Christians confess and worship is a diverse community—Father, Son, and Spirit. And he is also the Great King over all the earth, who is putting fractured humanity back together, building a multicultural community that will render to him praise in every language and from every culture. The God who made every human in his image loves his entire creation, and the church of Jesus Christ is radically inclusive to the extent that it will offend human prejudices. God's people are revealed as those who humbly recognize hatred in their own hearts and the divisions in their cultures and who participate with the Spirit to sustain communities that run against the grain of cultural animosities. If people feel marginalized or unwelcome in our churches because of their gender or race or ethnicity, we should examine ourselves to see if we are filled with some other spirit than the Spirit of Christ and stand in need of repentance.

Perkins and the ministry resources available from the Christian Community Development Association (https://ccda.org/).

CHAPTER 29

Mark 7:31-37

📖 LISTEN to the Story

³¹Then Jesus left the vicinity of Tyre and went through Sidon, down to the Sea of Galilee and into the region of the Decapolis. ³²There some people brought to him a man who was deaf and could hardly talk, and they begged Jesus to place his hand on him.

³³After he took him aside, away from the crowd, Jesus put his fingers into the man's ears. Then he spit and touched the man's tongue. ³⁴He looked up to heaven and with a deep sigh said to him, "*Ephphatha!*" (which means "Be opened!"). ³⁵At this, the man's ears were opened, his tongue was loosened and he began to speak plainly.

³⁶Jesus commanded them not to tell anyone. But the more he did so, the more they kept talking about it. ³⁷People were overwhelmed with amazement. "He has done everything well," they said. "He even makes the deaf hear and the mute speak."

Listening to the Text in the Story: Genesis 1:31; Exodus 4:10–12; Ecclesiastes 3:11; Isaiah 35:5–6; Romans 8:12–30.

Scripture tells the story of creation through to new creation. God created a good world in which humanity would flourish along with the rest of creation, enjoying God's presence and glorifying God in all things. Sin has ravaged that creation, but God is at work in Jesus to make all things new. Throughout Mark, Jesus enacts the kingdom of God on earth, a powerful and life-giving reality depicted by an invasion of purity, the driving out of demons, and acts of healing human brokenness and sickness. In this episode, Mark depicts Jesus restoring this man's hearing and speech in terms of God's acts of creation and new creation.

At the close of the episode, the people who brought the man to Jesus are overwhelmed with amazement and say, "He has done everything well." This declaration recalls Genesis 1:31: "God saw all that he had made, and it was very good."[1] Jesus's action here, then, recalls God's work of creation, his provision of a flourishing order marked by goodness. This notion is strengthened by the similarities to Ecclesiastes 3:11: "He has made everything beautiful in its time."

The crowd states further that "he even makes the deaf hear and the mute speak," drawing on Isaiah 35:5–6, which looks ahead to the restoration of all things when creation is made new:

> Then will the eyes of the blind be opened
>   and the ears of the deaf unstopped.
> Then will the lame leap like a deer,
>   and the mute tongue shout for joy.
> Water will gush forth in the wilderness
>   and streams in the desert.

Jesus's healing of this man is an instance of God's work of new creation—restoring what was broken and bringing life and flourishing where sickness and injury brought about enslavement and degradation.

Readers of this passage may also recall God's conversation with Moses in Exodus 4, in which Moses argued for his inadequacy for the task to which God had called him:

> Moses said to the LORD, "Pardon your servant, Lord. I have never been eloquent, neither in the past nor since you have spoken to your servant. I am slow of speech and tongue."
>
> The LORD said to him, "Who gave human beings their mouths? Who makes them deaf or mute? Who gives them sight or makes them blind? Is it not I, the LORD? Now go; I will help you speak and will teach you what to say." (Exod 4:10–12)

God is the one who creates and who renews creation from the devastation brought on by sin, sickness, and death. Just as God did with Moses, Jesus here loosens this man's tongue and opens his ears so that he might enjoy blessing and participate with his community in the flourishing of God's good creation.

---

1. Boring, *Mark*, 218.

EXPLAIN the Story

This event takes place in the Decapolis, a gentile region just southeast of the Sea of Galilee (7:31). Jesus had arrived there after having gone north through Sidon—deeper, that is, into a gentile region—before returning south and remaining outside of Jewish territory. Just as in Mark 2:1–12, a group of people bring to Jesus a man in need of healing. This man is "deaf and could hardly talk" (7:32). Like others who suffered from physical illness or injury, this man's condition went beyond physical limitation. Boring notes that in an oral and aural culture, rather than a visual or print culture like the modern West, inability to speak or hear cut a person off from their community.[2] The man's friends beg Jesus to touch and heal him, just as in the previous episode the woman with a demon-possessed daughter begged Jesus to drive out the demon.

Significantly, this man's ability to perceive is impaired. The parable of the sower and seed stands over this entire section of Mark from 4:1 to 8:17. Jesus had warned that there would be those who see and do not perceive and who hear but do not understand. Here, Jesus is not only bringing about new creation, restoring a person's ability to participate in God's good order of flourishing, but he is also granting perception and giving it especially to those who plead for it (cf. Prov 2:1–11). Over the last several chapters of Mark, the disciples have been seeing but not truly perceiving or understanding. And Peter is about to speak rightly (Mark 8:27–30), but then speak wrongly in a dramatic way (8:31–33). The disciples need—as do Mark's audiences and modern readers of Mark—the gift of perception, and they need God's touch so that they may speak coherently. To receive these from God, they need to look to God for insight and wisdom, so that they can become like the Syrian-Phoenician woman, this gentile crowd, and the many other people in Mark who see or hear about Jesus and rush to him in postures of worship.

Throughout Mark, Jesus has been touching people he is not supposed to touch, but here things get extreme. Not only does Jesus touch this man, but he puts his fingers into the man's ears, spits in his hands, and touches the man's tongue. Even modern readers may be disgusted, but in the ancient world spitting was a grave insult, and spittle was regarded as equivalent to excrement.[3] Far from being as concerned as the Pharisees about contracting

---

2. Boring, *Mark*, 216.
3. Placher, *Mark*, 107.

impurity unintentionally, Jesus is going out of his way to touch in culturally offensive ways! He is unaffected, however, by uncleanness and impurity.
Because he is the agent of the kingdom of God, he drives away uncleanness
and impurity wherever he goes. It is as if Mark presses this subversive dynamic
of the power of purity to the point of being obnoxious. God's renewing power
is so great that there is nothing to fear.

Jesus then raises his eyes to heaven, sighs deeply, and exclaims, "Be opened!"[4]
The Greek term Mark uses to refer to Jesus's "deep sigh" (*estenaxen*) is related
to the Spirit's deep groaning in Romans 8:26 (*stenagmois*). In that passage, Paul
depicts the deep groaning of creation (v. 22) and of God's redeemed people
(v. 23) for the coming new creation. Just as all creation groans as it longs for
the full realization of redemption, God's Spirit also groans along with the
prayers of God's people for the fullness of the new creation to come. Mark 7:34
depicts Jesus's own desire for creation to be healed and to experience renewal
in this specific instance of a man burdened by deafness and the inability to
speak. And we should not be surprised that Jesus's reaction to the brokenness
of creation is the same as that of the Spirit, since the Spirit is "the Spirit of
Jesus Christ" (Phil 1:19), and Paul notes that Jesus is also praying in concert
with the Spirit's groaning in Romans 8:27.

Jesus's prayer for this man's renewal—his experience of new creation—is
answered powerfully as his "ears were opened, his tongue was loosened and
he began to speak plainly" (Mark 7:35). This man is like others in Mark's
Gospel whom Jesus healed and who were now able to enjoy the richness of
full restoration to their communities. As in other places in Mark, Jesus commands everyone to remain silent about what they have witnessed (v. 36). Here,
however, this is somewhat surprising. If the man can now speak coherently,
why should he and others keep quiet? Isn't it worth spreading the good news
about Jesus doing God's work of restoration?

Jesus has been commanding silence throughout his ministry in Mark
because there remains much to ponder about the mystery of the kingdom.
The gospel being preached is indeed good news, but the great enthusiasm
over Jesus's work of freeing humanity from the grip of Satan, sin, and death
may prevent people from listening closely to Jesus's message about the cross-
shaped character of the kingdom of God. As we have already seen and will see
again in Mark 8, the disciples themselves still don't understand Jesus and this
fundamental aspect of the kingdom he brings.

---

4. The command for the man's ears to be opened is spoken in Aramaic ("*Ephphatha!*"), which
Mark translates for non-Jewish audiences.

LIVE the Story

Longing for New Creation

The North American Christian culture that I inhabit is a fairly comfortable one. Our church communities have not been touched with suffering and persecution in the way that many cultures have been throughout the history of the church. Indeed, today many Christians around the world face serious difficulties such as poverty and hunger, economic injustice, and even persecution. The comfort with which I am familiar can breed complacency when it comes to helping those who are less fortunate, and I have noticed that it has led to a serious lack of hope and longing for the new creation. After all, if life is good for us, why pray for God to come and make all things new? Why pray earnestly for the Lord to return and set creation right?

It seems to me that the more we know pain and suffering—either our own experience of it or our solidarity with those who suffer—the more we will think of the future day of Christ when God returns to make all things new. Such a focus sustains kingdom life in this age, and it also leads us to pray regularly for that day to come soon. After portraying the future restoration of heaven and earth, the closing passage of Revelation sums up the entire Bible by noting that the Spirit and the church are praying for the Lord's return: "The Spirit and the bride say, 'Come!' And let the one who hears say, 'Come!'" (Rev 22:17). Just as in Romans 8:18–23, John depicts the Spirit groaning along with creation, believers, and Jesus himself for the restoration of creation. Revelation indicates that this is to be the earnest and regular prayer of the church.

A friend of mine has a young child with a rare and severe condition, and he and his wife have been told that their son will almost certainly not live past his late teens. We have talked extensively about the pain of living with a child who will likely predecease his parents and siblings. This reality has generated in them a longing for the renewal of creation when children will not face the awful reality of death. They mention more than other people the hope of the resurrection and the blessed promises of the goodness of life in the future, restored creation. Their focus is so clearly on that day when God makes all things new. Christians who have experienced the untimely loss of a spouse or loved one can find comfort in the future hope of God's complete and glorious defeat of death and the resurrection of his people unto the fullness of eternal life.

My wife and I experienced the deep pain of loss after a number of late-term miscarriages. Some well-meaning Christian friends asked us if we were going to share the pain of loss with our other children. They were concerned that after praying for healthy deliveries, our children's faith might be affected by the deep disappointment and grief. We found that it was a good opportunity to share with our children the Christian reality of hope in the new creation, when children would not die and parents' hearts would not be crushed. The Christian faith is not a sentimental outlook where every dark cloud has a silver lining. We can fearlessly face the harsh realities of loss and the deep pain of death with the confidence that our hearts will one day be satisfied, because God will defeat death and banish suffering forever. Christians do indeed grieve, but not as the world does (1 Thess 4:13). We have hope. It is not that every difficulty will somehow have a good outcome, but our confidence is that God will triumph one day and that we will share in that victory along with those we have lost. That is the day for which we hope and pray.

CHAPTER 30

Mark 8:1–10

¹During those days another large crowd gathered. Since they had nothing to eat, Jesus called his disciples to him and said, ²"I have compassion for these people; they have already been with me three days and have nothing to eat. ³If I send them home hungry, they will collapse on the way, because some of them have come a long distance."

⁴His disciples answered, "But where in this remote place can anyone get enough bread to feed them?"

⁵"How many loaves do you have?" Jesus asked.

"Seven," they replied.

⁶He told the crowd to sit down on the ground. When he had taken the seven loaves and given thanks, he broke them and gave them to his disciples to distribute to the people, and they did so. ⁷They had a few small fish as well; he gave thanks for them also and told the disciples to distribute them. ⁸The people ate and were satisfied. Afterward the disciples picked up seven basketfuls of broken pieces that were left over. ⁹About four thousand were present. After he had sent them away, ¹⁰he got into the boat with his disciples and went to the region of Dalmanutha.

Listening to the Text in the Story: Exodus 16; Joshua 9:6, 9; Psalm 107:1–9; Acts 2:39; 22:21; 1 Corinthians 11:17–34; Galatians 2:12; Ephesians 2:12, 17.

This is the second feeding story in Mark's Gospel, and the narrative structure proceeds in similar fashion to the one in Mark 6:31–44:

Narrative element	Mark 6:31–45	Mark 8:1–10
The setting	"a quiet place" (v. 31); "a solitary place" (v. 32), both translations of *erēmon topon* (lit. "wilderness")	"this remote place" (v. 4), *erēmia* ("wilderness")
People in need	large crowd, "like sheep without a shepherd" and in need of food (vv. 34–36)	large crowd who have come from far away and are in need of food (vv. 1–3)
Jesus's response	"had compassion [*esplanch-nisthē*] on them" (v. 34)	"I have compassion [*splanchnizomai*] for them" (v. 2)
Jesus intends to feed the crowd	Jesus tells the disciples to feed the crowd when they raise the issue (vv. 35–37)	Jesus raises the issue (vv. 2–3)
The disciples' view	request Jesus to send the crowd away (vv. 35–36)	no way to feed the crowd in the remote location (v. 4)
Meager resources	five loaves, two fish (vv. 38, 41)	seven loaves, a few small fish (vv. 5, 7)
Jesus provides and hosts a feast	"Taking . . . , he gave thanks and broke . . ."; gives to disciples to distribute (v. 41)	"When he had taken . . . and given thanks, he broke . . ."; gives to disciples to distribute (v. 6)
Crowd's response	"all ate and were satisfied" (v. 42)	"the people ate and were satisfied" (v. 8)
Superabundant plenty	twelve baskets full of leftovers (v. 43)	seven baskets full of leftovers (v. 8)
Mark notes the size of the crowd	five thousand (v. 44)	four thousand (v. 9)
Conclusion	Jesus sends away the crowd and orders his disciples into a boat (v. 45)	Jesus sends away the crowd and gets into a boat with his disciples (v. 10)[1]

[1] This chart is an adaptation of Clifton Black's helpful layout (*Mark*, 182).

In addition to the many similarities between the two accounts, there are some notable differences. This feeding takes place in gentile territory, whereas the other occurred among Jews in Galilee. The similarities, in addition to the developing theme of the disciples' increasing dullness, serve to emphasize at least one significant feature of this second feeding. In the first episode, it is the narrator who notes that Jesus "had compassion on them, because they were like sheep without a shepherd" (6:34). In the present passage, however, it is Jesus who states at length that he has compassion for the people, that they have been with him for three days, and that they have nothing to eat. He dwells further on his concern for them by highlighting the peril of the situation: "If I send them home hungry, they will collapse on the way, because some of them have come a long distance" (v. 3). As we will discuss below, it is as if Jesus is giving the disciples a second opportunity, hinting that they should take the lead at this point in hopes that they have learned something from the last feeding. Mark notes in 6:52, however, that they had learned nothing from witnessing the feeding and that they are still not alert to the manner in which the dynamics of the kingdom of God can multiply meager resources to meet needs.

Like the previous feeding narrative, this one resonates with a number of scriptural threads. Psalm 107 speaks of the compassionate and gracious character of God, who rescues and meets the needs of the desperate in a variety of situations, including those who are hungry in the desert wastelands:

> Some wandered in desert wastelands,
>> finding no way to a city where they could settle.
> They were hungry and thirsty,
>> and their lives ebbed away.
> Then they cried out to the LORD in their trouble,
>> and he delivered them from their distress.
> He led them by a straight way
>> to a city where they could settle.
> Let them give thanks to the LORD for his unfailing love
>> and his wonderful deeds for mankind,
> for he satisfies the thirsty
>> and fills the hungry with good things. (Ps 107:4–9)

Beyond portraying the character of God in meeting the needs of the desperate, Jesus is also enacting God's desire to bless the nations—the gentiles. God had called Israel to be a blessing to the nations—to be the means by which God brought humanity back to himself and healed ethnic, national, and socioeconomic divisions. This work of God in the gospel is often portrayed in the New Testament through meals, which served as crucial social events that demonstrated solidarity among those who were invited and participated. In Galatians 2:12, Paul writes about an event that took place in Antioch, when Peter came from Jerusalem to visit that multiethnic church. Because the Antioch church was made up of Jews and non-Jews, their common meals depicted the international character of the church. When Peter visited, he experienced fellowship across ethnic boundary lines, which was likely very uncomfortable for Peter. After all, the Jerusalem church was monocultural, made up only of Jewish Christians, and Peter had formerly thought that it was unlawful to share a meal with gentiles (Acts 10:28). But when some others came from the Jerusalem church, men who did not agree that gentiles could be part of God's kingdom and remain gentiles, he was intimidated and withdrew from eating alongside non-Jews, inviting Paul's vigorous confrontation. The "truth of the gospel" (Gal 2:14) is that God's new people is made up of Jesus-followers from any and every ethnicity, since God longs to enjoy fellowship with all of humanity. The meal depicted here in Mark 8 resonates with some of these themes, as Jesus leads his disciples to enjoy fellowship with gentiles and to bless them in the name of the gracious and compassionate God of Israel, the God who is also the Great King over all nations.

EXPLAIN the Story

In the previous episode, Jesus had been somewhere in the Decapolis, to the southeast of the Sea of Galilee, in gentile territory (7:31). Mark situates this feeding account in the same region, linking the two passages with the introductory comment that it took place "during those days" (8:1). As in so many of the accounts in his Gospel, Mark notes that another large crowd had gathered, much like the first feeding that had taken place earlier (6:34).

They were in another "remote place" (*erēmia*, "wilderness," v. 4), where it was difficult to get food, and because they had none Jesus called his disciples to himself to share with them his concern over the critical need for the crowd to eat. In the previous feeding episode, the narrator sets the stage, noting for readers that Jesus looked with compassion on the crowd that stood in need of food. Here, however, Jesus speaks directly to the disciples regarding his compassionate concern. He notes that this multitude of gentiles has been "with me" for three days (v. 2), which is a striking detail, given that Jesus had called the disciples to be "with him" (3:14) in the sense of orienting their hearts, minds, and lives according to Jesus's agenda. This is yet another subtle reminder that while the disciples are in a process of unraveling in confusion, the gentile crowds are doing what the disciples are failing to do. They are tracking with Jesus, listening to what he says and remaining "with him" to the neglect of their own bodily needs.

Jesus plainly states his concern about the crowd in vv. 2–3, and Mark's quotation portrays Jesus lingering over his compassion, as if he is trying to get the disciples' attention. He is recalling for them the previous episode and giving them a second chance to step up, to be "with him" by sharing his concern for the gentile crowd. In the last feeding, the disciples had responded poorly to Jesus after he had challenged them to feed the crowd themselves (6:37). Here, he sets them up for success, describing his own concern at length, so that perhaps this time they will choose a better course. He wants to provide for the crowd because they have come from far away, and if they leave without eating, they will collapse as they return home.[1]

The disciples, however, do not get it. Mark had noted earlier that they did not understand about the loaves (6:52), and here they demonstrate that they still are not tracking with Jesus. They have seen Jesus previously work precisely this miracle, yet they ask, "Where in this remote place can anyone get enough bread to feed them?" (v. 4). Hearers of Mark would be exasperated at this point. "You just saw Jesus do this very thing! You saw him provide food in the wilderness, driven by compassion!"

Seemingly resigned, Jesus asks them how many loaves they have. They reply that they have seven, and so Jesus takes the loaves and multiplies them. He directs the crowd to sit on the ground and takes the bread, gives thanks, and gives them to the disciples to distribute to the people (v. 6). Just as in the previous feeding (6:41), the disciples become inadvertent servants as they distribute the food to the people. This is a note of grace and displays the goodness and kindness of God even to reluctant, dull, and uncomprehending disciples. The disciples' slowness of heart and mind does not prevent them from being the agents of God's blessing to the needy.

Mark notes that the people ate and were satisfied (v. 8). And just as before,

---

1. The expression "a long distance" is biblical language that indicates more than geographical distance. In the Old Testament, Israel was "near" to God (Ps 148:14 NASB), while the nations were "far away" (Deut 28:49; 29:22; see Marcus, *Mark 1–8*, 487). Essential to the gospel is God's work of bringing all humanity to himself, uniting Jews and gentiles in one new family in Christ. God sends Paul "far away to the Gentiles" (Acts 22:21) and brings near those who were "far off" (Eph 2:13, 17 NRSV; Moloney, *Gospel of Mark*, 153).

there was more food than was needed. Wherever Jesus is present, the power of the kingdom of God is at work, and it is a power that provides more than is necessary. God's life-giving presence animates the kingdom of God, so wherever there is kingdom presence there is an altered cosmic order of super-abundant flourishing. At Jesus's table there is always more than enough, always plenty for everyone to enjoy, a reality symbolized by the disciples picking up the "seven basketfuls of broken pieces that were left over" (v. 8).[2]

Now that they have been cared for, the crowd can be sent away. Jesus dismisses them, and the episode concludes with Jesus getting into a boat with his disciples and departing for Dalmanutha (vv. 9–10).[3]

☘ LIVE the Story

Cultivating an Imagination of Abundance

I have noticed in myself and among many Christians an attitude of arrogant judgment toward the experience of Israel in the Old Testament. Israel experienced the dramatic rescue of God from Egypt and God's gracious provision in the land of promise. They were regularly delivered by God, but they just as regularly fell into idolatry and disobedience. Contemporary Christians often question how on earth Israel could have constantly failed to "get it," assuming that if they were in Israel's place they would have behaved more faithfully. Jesus's disciples behaved just as Israel did. They witnessed Jesus's miraculous provision in the first feeding (6:31–45), but when they were faced with precisely the same situation, they were bewildered as to how to respond, asking where they were going to get provisions to feed all these people in such a remote location.

Mark challenges church audiences to consider whether they have imaginations that are in the same condition as the disciples, unable to recognize the overwhelming abundance of the kingdom that is able to meet the needs around them. These two feeding narratives in Mark (6:31–45; 8:1–10) are

---

2. Commentators speculate about the meaning of the numbers in this episode. Mark mentions the number seven three times (vv. 5, 6, 8) and puts this crowd at 4,000 (v. 9). Placher proposes a set of connections that highlight the gentile context of this event, claiming that for "first-century readers, fascinated by number symbolism, this passage would have cried out, 'This time Jesus is feeding *Gentiles*'" (*Mark*, 109). Marcus, however, doubts that there is any discernible significance. These numbers have a variety of associations in the Old Testament and Jewish literature, and no common feature stands out that makes any meaningful contribution to this text (*Mark 1–8*, 489–90). It may be best, then, to refrain from making any certain associations, especially since Mark does not.

3. The location of this place name is unknown, though it appears to be on the western shore of the Sea of Galilee, in Jewish territory.

not merely stories of something miraculous that Jesus did, proving that he has divine power. They are meant to shape the church's imagination about the superabundant power of the kingdom and the reality that God calls the church to live with open hands.

The Western church is set within a culture that has its values shaped largely by an economic vision of scarcity. The fundamental conviction of scarcity is that *we live in a world of limited goods.* We imagine that there is not enough to go around, so we must hoard our resources and be stingy with our money and time. This vision of the world, our place in it, and what we have has had a profound affect on churches and has fostered attitudes and practices that shape us into communities that do not resemble the kingdom of God. Like Israel, we have been blessed with amazing material resources, but we fail to live the lives of plenty to which Jesus calls the church.

God's economy operates with a different orientation. The kingdom of God, initiated by Jesus, is an economy of superabundant flourishing, not of scarcity. God's world is a world of plenty, where there is more than enough to go around. The church's imagination must be recaptured so that we can live into the fullness of a life of abundance embodied by community practices of sharing and hospitality. The task of having imaginations shaped by God's kingdom involves discerning the ways our churches have mindsets and practices oriented toward scarcity, and how we can have minds renewed so that we begin to cultivate mindsets and practices that embody abundance. Here are just a few examples of how we might do this.

We imagine that our church property is just that—*our* property. This building is our building, and this stuff is our stuff, to be used by us for our own purposes. We forget that everything we have belongs to God and that we only enjoy it as God's good gift to be used for our enjoyment and for purposes of God's mission in the world. Churches might consider creatively using their building and property to do as Jesus did in these two feeding passages. They can host meals for the larger community, providing the space and food and inviting others to enjoy God's plenty. There may be low-income families in the area that need a regular meal, or elderly shut-ins who cannot get out regularly to eat. Welcoming others to a meal is a great way to find out about people who have needs. And it is a great way to share the plenty with which God has blessed us.

And churches can do this without thinking of it as an evangelistic opportunity, or exploiting it to get people to join. Churches that take steps like this may be thinking of how they can "capitalize" (an economic term) on it, looking for a "return on investment." It is easy to think this way, but we may discern that such thinking simply points to how our imaginations have been captured by a worldly economic vision. Why else would a church undertake such an effort, if not to capitalize on it for some gain? Following the economic logic of Mark, the church does this to enjoy the rich blessings of participating in the kingdom of God. We do this so that we can have more of the life of God among us and feel the joy of being a people who live with open hands, sharing our plenty with others. We do this so that we can be a community that does the sorts of things Jesus did, sharing plenty without asking for anything in return.

Just think of the benefits to the church. People would need to plan, work together, and coordinate efforts to carry out something like this. It would foster communication and participation in the church, with the promise that our hearts will be filled with joy by the Spirit as we live the life of the exalted Jesus. People might need to make sacrifices of time and energy, missing out on other activities and opportunities. But they would be doing so for specifically Christian purposes, and they would enjoy the confirmation in their own hearts that they are truly partaking of the kingdom.

It would be *inconvenient*, but that might open up discussions of how *convenience* and *efficiency* have become dominant economic values in our culture. Because such values have shaped so many aspects of our lives, we have been robbed of rich community life and been cut off from our neighbors. But the kingdom of God is the rich reality that orients the life of the church, and such an effort might allow us to recover that community life for ourselves and share it with others who are hungering for it.

Churches might also consider finding out about single-parent families in the area and offering after-school activities in their building, along with tutoring. Again, this would require volunteers, training, and coordination. And this, too, can be something that churches undertake without an eye toward evangelism or recruitment. Rather than thinking about "return on investment," the church focuses on sharing resources with others in order to bring relief to stressed families and care for children. These are the very people Jesus is concerned about in Mark (cf. 10:13–16)—those with no social capital, who have fallen through the cracks of society, and who cannot add to the church's bottom line. They may not join the church, and even if they do they are not going to be big financial givers. But such an effort flows from the church's imagination reshaped by God's kingdom, where there is more than enough to go around. It focuses the church's imagination on those God is concerned about, and it shapes us into the kind of community that lives with an open hand. It is hard work from one perspective, but it is the kind of effort that invites God's rich blessings of joy and fellowship, tapping us ever more deeply into the power of the Spirit, who floods our hearts and relationships with God's life-giving presence.

There are so many more creative ways that churches can identify practices of plenty, as we live in a very needy world. We can care for the homeless, refugees, and the elderly. We can offer our spaces and resources to bring about dialogue with ethnic and religious minorities in our communities, finding out how we can be a resource for peacemaking in an increasingly fractured and conflicted culture. The church is the kingdom of God, the space where God is recovering an economy of plenty. We confess that God owns "the cattle on a thousand hills" (Ps 50:10), but does our community life profess that God actually owns very little? It is not just the world that needs to learn that all creation belongs to God. The church needs to learn this—for our own joy and the development of our shriveled imaginations.

LISTEN to the Story

¹¹The Pharisees came and began to question Jesus. To test him, they asked him for a sign from heaven. ¹²He sighed deeply and said, "Why does this generation ask for a sign? Truly I tell you, no sign will be given to it." ¹³Then he left them, got back into the boat and crossed to the other side.

Listening to the Text in the Story: Exodus 17:1–7; Judges 6; Luke 1:5–25; 1 Corinthians 1:18–25.

Two very different questions might be asked when faced with a prediction of a supernatural event. On the one hand, one might ask, "How can this be?" One might also ask, "How can I know that this will take place?" These don't seem like very different questions, but they are, in fact, worlds apart. They are divergent postures toward God and reveal hearts that are in quite different places.

In Luke 1:26–38 the angel Gabriel announced to Mary that she was going to have a son and that this would be a virginal conception—a miracle. Mary, quite astounded by this news, asks, "How will this be, since I am a virgin?" (v. 34). Gabriel explains to her that this will happen by God's Spirit. Mary's response to Gabriel is regarded as a response of faith, since she is commended by Gabriel and later by Elizabeth, the mother of John the Baptist (vv. 39–45). Her question had to do with trying to get her head around what she had heard, expressing that this was not the normal process for how children come into the world.

Zechariah, a priest who was also a relative of Mary, had previously received a visit from Gabriel. Gabriel had also revealed to him an astounding message— that he and his barren wife were going to have a son. Zechariah's response may not seem too dissimilar to Mary's. He responded by asking, "How can I be sure of this? I am an old man and my wife is well along in years" (Luke 1:18). Based on Gabriel's response, this was not an appropriate question. The two responses may not seem terribly different, but they are going in completely

275

opposite directions. Mary's question arises from a heart of faith. She believes what she's hearing, but wants help processing how it might come about. Zechariah, on the other hand, wants proof, some assurance that he can trust what he is hearing.

These represent two different postures toward God—one that receives his word and responds with obedience, and one that is skeptical and hesitant and wants more proof before going forward. Gideon's conversation with the angel of the Lord in Judges 6 proceeds much like Zechariah's in Luke 1. Gideon responds to the angel of the Lord with sarcasm and later asks for proof that what God is saying is truly going to happen—twice!

In their encounter with Jesus in this passage, the Pharisees demonstrate a less than commendable response to God. In fact, they behave worse than Zechariah and Gideon in their desire for a sign from God. There are times in Scripture when signs are given (e.g., Exod 4:8–9, 17, 28; 10:1–2; Deut 4:34),[1] typically to authenticate a divinely authorized spokesperson, but as we will see below, the Pharisees are standing in as props in the satanic attempt to transform Jesus into a different sort of Messiah.

EXPLAIN the Story

Jesus here returns to Jewish territory, and as soon as he does so some Pharisees seek him out to question him. They are not here with good motives, but to "test him" (*peirazontes*, v. 11). This is the same term used in Mark 1:13 when Satan "tested" or "tempted" Jesus in the wilderness. Mark is here aligning the Pharisees with Satan in their opposition to Jesus.[2] That seems like a dramatically harsh association, but there are several dynamics going on here. First, the Pharisees have already decided to plot with the Herodians to kill Jesus (3:6), and their associates, the scribes, have accused him of operating by the power of Satan (3:22).

Second, and to the heart of this passage, they are not necessarily "testing" Jesus to determine anything. They are *tempting* him, just as Satan did, to become a power-oriented Messiah, one that wins followers with impressive displays and overpowering feats. And it is not that they truly desire to believe or that they will follow Jesus if they see something impressive enough. That is not so much what Mark is aiming at here. Their intention is yet another

---

1. Strauss, *Mark*, 338.
2. Black, *Mark*, 185.

attempt to turn Jesus away from his mission, which is to go to the cross. Jesus is a cross-directed, cross-oriented Messiah who initiates a cross-shaped kingdom. And this is precisely what Satan is trying to prevent. This is why Jesus is always discouraging people from spreading the word about him and why he puts no faith in big crowds.

Jesus responds in v. 12 with a deep sigh, just as he did in 7:34 when he healed the deaf and mute man. There, Jesus was longing for God's restoration of all things, when brokenness will be transformed into wholeness. In this passage, Jesus is expressing grief over the Pharisees' hard-heartedness and enslavement to sinful blindness, embodying God's own response to the corruption of creation.

Jesus uses biblical language in referring to the Pharisees that recalls sinful and rebellious groups of people. "This generation" associates them with the sinful humanity that invited God's judgment at the flood (Gen 7:1) and the grumbling Israelites who wandered in the wilderness (Deut 1:35; 32:5, 20; Ps 95:10–11).[3] He refuses to give them a sign because he discerns the nature of their request.[4] They are not asking from a posture of faith that desires to understand more about the kingdom of God. Nor does their request merely come from wrong motives. They have seen his miraculous healings and exorcisms and have otherwise observed his ministry, and they are demanding that he turn from his mission and become a different sort of Messiah, one who does not represent the character of Israel's God. It is not that Jesus is harshly treating a group of people who are seeking after truth. He is refusing to be deterred from his mission. He embodies this refusal in the concluding scene, when "he left them," got into the boat with his disciples, and continued on with the work of the kingdom of God (v. 13).

LIVE the Story

Looking for Signs

The Pharisees in this passage demand a sign, and I pointed to a few other passages in Scripture in which characters do the same. They are rarely commended, nor are they commendable characters. We ought to draw the

---

3. Strauss, *Mark*, 339.

4. In John's Gospel, Jesus's miraculous deeds are "signs" of his identity and mission, but this is a narrative strategy particular to John. In Mark's Gospel, the powerful works of Jesus are not "signs" in this same sense. They are characteristic of his work of freeing Israel from oppression and demonic enslavement, spreading shalom and initiating the kingdom of God (Black, *Mark*, 185–86; Boring, *Mark*, 222).

conclusion that the biblical witness calls into question a common way of determining things in our day. That is, looking for a sign to judge ultimate realities is a bad idea, and looking for a sign to determine the "right" course of action is also not a wise course to take.

If we encounter people who are seeking the truth about ultimate things—the reality of God and of his claim on our lives in Christ Jesus—we can offer them the biblical witness to the revelation of God in Christ and seek to articulate a clear account of what God has done in Christ. We can point to the life of the church—that transformed and being-transformed people among whom God displays his new-creation power. If there is a wish or demand for something plainer, clearer, or *more urgently real*, then that is not a wish or demand that we can countenance. God reveals himself in the testimony of the Gospel writers and through the preaching of the church regarding Jesus. There are no overwhelming displays of divine power or pyrotechnics we can offer or conjure up. In this sense, *the desire for something more than what God offers us in Scripture* should be interpreted in light of the Pharisees' desire for a sign.

Humanity must respond to the portrait of God in Christ in Scripture, and if we are not compelled by that to commit ourselves to God, there is nothing further that would compel us. John Chrysostom, archbishop of Constantinople in the fourth and fifth centuries, expresses this well:

> But for what sign from heaven were they asking? Maybe that he should hold back the sun, or curb the moon, or bring down thunderbolts, or change the direction of the wind, or something like that? . . . In Pharaoh's time there was an enemy from whom deliverance was needed. But for one who comes among friends, there should be no need of such signs.[5]

Further, from the broader sweep of Scripture, it is unwise for us to seek to determine a course of life based on looking for "signs" of God's will. The notion that there is a specific divine plan for each individual person that we can find if we discern its signs in the midst of life is quite common in certain sectors of Christian culture, a notion that I think flows from the desire to see each person's life as significant, and significant to God. Beyond this, it comes from our desire to see God as intimately concerned about the details of our lives. Now, each person is indeed dear to God, and God is most definitely and utterly concerned about all that goes on in our lives. But the notion of a specific will that must be discovered by reading situations and the signs we

---

5. Oden and Hall, *Mark*, 101.

might find hidden in the episodes of our lives is one that is far more pagan that it is Christian.[6]

Rather than navigating life looking for signs of God's will, it is a far more fruitful approach to cultivate a heart and mind shaped by God's priorities for his people in an attempt to discern how our lives might fit into that. God's purposes are for our growth in wisdom, in our commitment to God's mission for his people in the world, and in our becoming more deeply connected in the body of Christ. When we are absorbed in these pursuits, we are already participating in God's will, and the other details of our lives can be sorted out in conversation with wise friends and older siblings in the faith. We make decisions based on our growing into the image of God as truly restored humans, not as pagans seeking to interpret random events or occurrences that may or may not have any explanation. God has spoken plainly in Christ, and we ought not seek for anything more. We find God's will for our lives revealed in Scripture. It is up to us, in conversation with our church families, to determine how God's purposes might be unfolded in the narratives of our lives.

---

6. Bruce K. Waltke, *Finding the Will of God: A Pagan Notion?*, 2nd ed. (Grand Rapids: Eerdmans, 2016).

CHAPTER 32

Mark 8:14–21

¹⁴The disciples had forgotten to bring bread, except for one loaf they had with them in the boat. ¹⁵"Be careful," Jesus warned them. "Watch out for the yeast of the Pharisees and that of Herod."

¹⁶They discussed this with one another and said, "It is because we have no bread."

¹⁷Aware of their discussion, Jesus asked them: "Why are you talking about having no bread? Do you still not see or understand? Are your hearts hardened? ¹⁸Do you have eyes but fail to see, and ears but fail to hear? And don't you remember? ¹⁹When I broke the five loaves for the five thousand, how many basketfuls of pieces did you pick up?"

"Twelve," they replied.

²⁰"And when I broke the seven loaves for the four thousand, how many basketfuls of pieces did you pick up?"

They answered, "Seven."

²¹He said to them, "Do you still not understand?"

Listening to the Text in the Story: Isaiah 6:9–10; Jeremiah 5:21; Ezekiel 12:2; Romans 8:5–17; 1 Corinthians 1:18–2:16.

This episode concludes a major section of Mark that began in 4:1–20. In that passage, Jesus told the parable of the seed and soils, which is the word of the kingdom that people respond to in various ways. In the middle of that passage, Jesus speaks to his disciples about what is happening when he teaches in parables:

He told them, "The secret of the kingdom of God has been given to you. But to those on the outside everything is said in parables so that, 'they may be ever seeing but never perceiving, and ever hearing but never understanding; otherwise they might turn and be forgiven!'" (vv. 11–12)

Since that point in the narrative, the disciples have grown increasingly dull and have been confused by what Jesus says. This stands in stark contrast with other characters who, despite their social locations as apparent outsiders, reveal that they rightly perceive who Jesus is and what he is saying. This dynamic reaches a climax here, as Jesus utters a prophetic formula in v. 18 that is strikingly similar to the citation of Isaiah 6:9–10 in Mark 4:11–12.

Mark's negative portrayal of the disciples' increasing confusion is not because he has something against them. He wants his audiences to reconsider their understanding of Jesus. They may call themselves disciples, but do they truly understand the gospel in the fullness of its cross-orientation? Are they succumbing to the temptation to shape the gospel in terms that reinforce their own values and in ways that make them comfortable?

Jesus's question in v. 18 comes from the language of Jeremiah 5:21 and Ezekiel 12:2, and it is reminiscent of Isaiah 6:9–10. In Jeremiah 5, God proclaims judgment against Jerusalem for their sin and their presumption that because they are Israelites, they can go on sinning without worrying that God will judge them. They speak in pious platitudes (v. 2), but their lives are full of sin, and they ignore the warnings of the prophets that judgment is coming (v. 13). They are much like some of the characters Jesus has encountered, such as the Pharisees and, at times, the disciples. Many in Jesus's day considered themselves loyal to the God of Israel, but the fact that they had other aims and intentions in mind demonstrates that their hearts were far from God. This is why Jesus raises the question using Jeremiah's words: "You foolish and senseless people, who have eyes but do not see, who have ears but do not hear" (Jer 5:21).

The disciples are indeed foolish and senseless. Mark intensifies his use of language having to do with sensory perception in this passage, piling up and repeating terms for sight, hearing, and understanding. He also situates it between two healings of perception (7:31–37 and 8:22–26), indicating that this is what the disciples need. It will take a miraculous work of God to open their minds and give them understanding.

EXPLAIN the Story

At the close of the previous episode, Jesus and the disciples had gotten into a boat to cross to the other side. This is the final in a series of boat journeys in Mark, one of the features that holds 4:1–8:21 together. The narrator notes that they had forgotten to take bread along with them, apparently from among the leftovers of the feeding. They did, however, have one loaf. Some commentators speculate that the singular loaf of bread is a reference to Jesus as the one who is the source of life and sustenance for the disciples and for the audiences of churches that will hear the Gospel read to them.[1] Regarding this as a reference to Jesus adds nothing to the passage, however, and Mark does not exploit this detail to shape Jesus's identity in the narrative. Further, this image is more at home in John's Gospel, which describes Jesus with a range of metaphors, including naming him "the bread of life" (John 6:35). Their having one loaf merely sets up the situation in which they could recognize that they may have brought along inadequate provisions.

Jesus issues a strong warning, using two imperative verbs in succession, both having to do with sensory perception: "Look! Watch out!" (v. 15).[2] He warns them to be on the lookout for the yeast of the Pharisees and of Herod. Yeast, or leaven, is a small bit of fermented dough that is inserted into a larger portion of dough and that will eventually pervade the whole in order to make it rise while baking. This metaphor appears often throughout Scripture to indicate a small element that is introduced and eventually pervades something larger. It could be used in a neutral sense (e.g., Matt 13:33), but it more often appears in a negative context, pointing to the effects of sin in a community (1 Cor 5:6; Gal 5:9).[3]

What might Jesus be referring to here? We should consider first what these characters are doing in Mark's Gospel before speculating about negative character traits in general. The manner in which the Pharisees and Herod operate in Mark is a complex of motivations, attitudes, aims, and behaviors that run counter to the dynamic of the kingdom of God, which is a cross-shaped and servant-oriented reality. Herod and the Pharisees, however, operate from self-preservation, self-protection, and self-advancement as they scratch and claw to hold on to power and their positions of authority. Because of this, Jesus is a threat, and so they find themselves plotting and scheming to do away with him. Or, if they cannot get rid of him, they seek to transform him into the sort of Messiah who will applaud them for their prestige and endorse their positions in the current system of power.

They see no value in doing good to others, in welcoming outcasts and sinners, or in celebrating the restoration of the demon-possessed and the healing of the sick. All that matters for them is holding on to their possessions

---

1. Boring, *Mark*, 226–27; Marcus, *Mark 1–8*, 509.

2. The Greek text situates the two imperative verbs (*horate, blepete*) next to each other: "Look! Watch out for . . ."

3. Black, *Mark*, 186; Strauss, *Mark*, 345.

and position, protecting their turf and preserving their social status. If Jesus were the sort of Messiah that endorsed the power games of Herod and the Pharisees, then he would have been applauded by crowds and approved by the religious authorities. The Pharisees would have been delighted if he had endorsed their agenda, and they certainly tried to move him into their camp (8:11–13). In Mark 10:42–45, Jesus contrasts worldly leaders with the sort of servants Jesus wants his disciples to be. Rather than lording authority over others and advancing their own agendas and flaunting their prestige, disciples of the cross-directed Son of Man will pursue servanthood if they are faithful.

Therefore, the small element that can eventually pervade a larger body is the self-orientation that seeks advancement, leadership that goes the way of self-promotion, and self-absorption that mistreats and exploits others. This sort of character resists the call to enter the self-sacrificing kingdom of God and ends up rejecting the gospel of the kingdom. It misses the secret of the kingdom because "the message of the cross is foolishness to those who are perishing" (1 Cor 1:18). The tragedy is that such people can influence churches so that this mindset spreads among others, with the likely result of a popular and apparently "thriving" ministry that is detached from the message of the cross.

The disciples discuss among themselves Jesus's words and demonstrate that they misunderstand him in two ways. They do not grasp that Jesus is speaking parabolically, referring to motivations, character traits, attitudes, and behaviors rather than to actual bread (v. 16). And they fail to recall what just happened when Jesus fed multitudes (vv. 19–20). They only have one loaf with them, but if Jesus can multiply five loaves to feed four thousand, it is nothing to multiply one loaf to feed a small group! Jesus calls the two feeding episodes to their attention and brings the last four chapters of Mark to a climax by asking a series of questions that exposes their lack of perception. Do they have hardened hearts? Are they the ones who are failing to perceive who Jesus is and the powerful kingdom dynamics of abundance that are at work among them? Jesus had stated in 4:10–12 that the secret of the kingdom had been given to the disciples and that everyone else would be confused by Jesus's parables and would not understand. Yet we have increasingly seen the disciples confused and failing to perceive, while apparent outsiders perceive and understand Jesus, responding to him rightly. Jesus here confronts the disciples with the peril of their situation: Are you demonstrating that you are outsiders to the kingdom of God? Does your confusion at my words indicate that you need to make your calling and election sure (cf. 2 Pet 1:10)?

LIVE the Story

Leadership Watchfulness

Ministry leaders face the constant pressure to perform their roles within the church in terms of worldly leadership approaches. This pressure is nothing new. In Acts 20, Paul exhorts the Ephesian church leaders to "keep watch over yourselves and all the flock of which the Holy Spirit has made you overseers. Be shepherds of the church of God, which he bought with his own blood" (v. 28). Because of the range of dynamics and temptations in having responsibility for the church, they must be vigilant over their own hearts and minds in addition to looking after the flock. And Paul uses shepherding terminology ("flock," "shepherds"), which situates ministry leadership in terms of humble service. Being a shepherd was a menial task in the ancient world, occupying a low social status. And shepherding involved looking after sheep, tending to them and their needs and ensuring they were led to places with food and water. Shepherds focused on the sheep and their needs, whereas ministry leaders often conceive of their career trajectories because of how many view contemporary ministry in terms of business leadership.

If one does a basic search for Christian leadership books online or walks into a Christian bookstore, they are likely to be overpowered by the available resources. One common feature I have discovered is that many Christian leadership books draw on secular leadership principles and sprinkle episodes from the Gospels into the discussion as examples of "Jesus's leadership style." Now, one can understand that there is indeed a wealth of wisdom in the world for Christians to consult on a range of topics. Jesus however, is at pains to note that other, worldly dynamics, both among God's people (the Pharisees) and out in the world (Herod), are always subtly creeping into the hearts and minds of Christian leaders, who are called to lead in radically different ways than leaders of the world. Whereas leaders in the world often play to popular opinion, cultivate a persona based on power and prestige, and draw attention to themselves, Christian leaders are called to shepherd the souls of those entrusted to their care. Further, the word of the cross—the call to give up everything—will never be popular, and ministry leaders need to be careful to avoid diminishing that word in favor of something more pleasing, interesting, and compelling—something that will help them build their "platform" or raise their public profile.

I have a colleague who does not like to hear talk about "leadership" at all when it comes to the church. I am starting to think he is onto something.

While Scripture does indeed present pastors and ministers as leaders and as leading, *the dominant frame of reference is responsible care for the church*. The focus of those who are responsible for the care of church communities ought to be on the health of each person and the flourishing of the community. Women and men who serve in these ways have everyone in the church on their minds and in their hearts, and they mention them all in their prayers. They visit with elderly shut-ins, sit with those who are sick, bring comfort to the grieving, and celebrate joyful seasons of life with others. Such faithful pastors see themselves as part of the community, called to serve. Yet they also stand in need of nurture and care themselves, which should lead them to cultivate relationships of mutuality and interdependence.

The danger I see of thinking about ministry from a "leadership" perspective is that my conceptions of what leadership looks like are all drawn from business, politics, and other areas of public life, such as education. The leaders that I recognize in these other arenas take bold action and are ambitious. They build their public stature by leaving the place they came from in order to achieve bigger, better, and more. If people connected to them are not part of the leader's ambitious plans, they are often seen as expendable. Other personal obstacles to success are likewise removed, no matter the relational messes left behind. While we might consider it "normal" to conceive of this kind of leadership in business or politics, this is precisely what Jesus is warning the disciples about. In effect he is saying, "Don't let this kind of leadership model shape how you think about the responsible care I am calling you to exercise among my people."

The ancient model of a shepherd looking after sheep is giving way in our day to pastors as CEOs and business leaders. This contemporary model shapes imaginations in profound and pervasive ways. Ministry practitioners would do well to heed Jesus's exhortation to be careful, to be watchful, and to critically assess their own motivations for the sorts of ministry postures and strategies they enact.

CHAPTER 33

Mark 8:22–26

📖 LISTEN to the Story

²²They came to Bethsaida, and some people brought a blind man and begged Jesus to touch him. ²³He took the blind man by the hand and led him outside the village. When he had spit on the man's eyes and put his hands on him, Jesus asked, "Do you see anything?"

²⁴He looked up and said, "I see people; they look like trees walking around."

²⁵Once more Jesus put his hands on the man's eyes. Then his eyes were opened, his sight was restored, and he saw everything clearly. ²⁶Jesus sent him home, saying, "Don't even go into the village."

Listening to the Text in the Story: 2 Kings 6:8–23; Isaiah 56:9–12; John 9; Ephesians 1:15–23.

This is a striking episode because of how unusual it is that Jesus's initial healing is not exactly successful. Is it that Jesus does not have the necessary power to heal this man, or perhaps just this one time he was unable to do the job? If we read this account in isolation, it is indeed mystifying. Yet this passage plays a critical and fascinating role in the narrative progression of Mark, functioning as a hinge. It closes the first half of the Gospel and opens the next major section. It looks backward to the disciples' need for sight and for understanding, and it looks ahead to what Mark is doing in the next major section.

This episode forms an *inclusio* (a literary device that brackets a section of text) with the healing of the blind man Bartimaeus in 10:46–52. These two healings of blind men frame a section in which Jesus predicts his suffering and death three times, and each time the disciples misunderstand him, ignore him, and display astonishing selfishness. After each of these predictions and misunderstandings, Jesus teaches them about discipleship:

Two-stage healing—8:22–26
  Prediction of Son of Man's suffering and death (3x: 8:31; 9:31; 10:33–34)
  Disciples' misunderstanding and selfishness (3x: 8:32–33; 9:32–34;
    10:35–41)
  Jesus teaches about discipleship (3x: 8:34–9:1; 9:35–37; 10:42–45)
  Healing of Bartimaeus—10:46–52

Within this section Jesus is no longer teaching large crowds but speaking directly to his disciples about discipleship. It is also marked by indications of being "on the way" or "on the road," expressions that point to Jesus's journey from Galilee to Jerusalem to go to the cross.[1]

Mark 8:22–10:52 reveals that the disciples have failed to watch out for the yeast of the Pharisees and of Herod. Rather than follow Jesus's instructions to conform their lives to the kingdom of God, they desire places of prominence. Yet they are still "with Jesus" in some sense as he makes his way to Jerusalem. If 4:1–8:21 raised the question of whether the disciples are in the kingdom or are blind and deaf, 8:22–26 and the larger unit of 8:22–10:52 indicate that their vision can indeed be restored. Jesus can heal their blindness, but it will take some time, and it may not be easy.[2]

Mark's placement of this two-stage healing episode also indicates that it is an enacted parable. Just after this episode, Mark narrates the conversation between Jesus and his disciples, in which Jesus asks what they think about his identity, after which Peter makes his climactic confession of Jesus as the Christ (8:27–30). This is a high point, but it is immediately followed by Jesus rebuking Peter after Peter rejects the reality of Jesus's cross-directed mission (vv. 31–33). Taking all of this into consideration, then, we are pursuing the wrong issue if we inquire as to why Jesus could not heal the man immediately. The two-stage healing of this blind man plays a crucial narrative role as an enacted parable of what is happening with Peter: he sees to some extent, but still needs greater clarity. And it points ahead to what is happening with the disciples leading up to 10:46–52. They are in need of Jesus to continue to heal their blindness and to restore their spiritual perception.

⚓ EXPLAIN the Story

Just like some other situations in Mark, the blind man has friends who bring him to Jesus for healing and beg Jesus to touch him so that he might be

---

1. Black, *Mark*, 189; Boring, *Mark*, 232.
2. Black, *Mark*, 190.

healed (cf. 2:3; 7:32). And like other healings in this Gospel, Mark stresses Jesus's touch, again emphasizing that the purifying and healing power of the kingdom radiates outward from Jesus and overwhelms impurity, uncleanness, and injury. And this dynamic of the kingdom drives fearless kingdom conduct. Rather than cutting off contact with the poor, blind, deaf, and unclean, kingdom citizens engage them, serve them, and offer hospitality. The yeast of the Pharisees is to shun sinners and the unclean and to ignore the injured (3:1–6), the sort of behavior Jesus warns against (8:15). Mark's emphasis on touch includes the group's request for Jesus to touch the man (v. 22), Jesus's taking him by the hand (v. 23), and then, stunningly, his spitting on the man's eyes and twice putting his hands on him (vv. 23, 25).

Jesus leads the man outside the city (v. 23) and afterward commands him to return home quietly without going into the village (v. 26). This reflects the theme in Mark of Jesus wanting to keep his messianic identity quiet out of concern that escalating popularity will overshadow the cross-orientation of his identity and message. Jesus then spits on the man's eyes, which is a shocking detail to modern readers, though it may have been a healing procedure of some ancient healers.[3]

After Jesus's first attempt, the man claims that he sees people looking like trees walking around. After Jesus's second attempt, Mark notes emphatically that the man was indeed restored and his vision was truly clarified. After Jesus's searching questions to the disciples about their blindness and lack of apprehension (vv. 17–21), the result of Jesus's touch resounds: "Then his eyes were opened, his sight was restored, and he saw everything clearly" (v. 25). What Jesus had done for this man, he will continue to be doing with his disciples. Audiences of Mark who are attuned to Mark's narrative strategy will adopt the place of the disciples and allow themselves to be questioned by Jesus about their vision and understanding. And they will seek to have their eyes continually opened, their sight increasingly restored, and their vision of the kingdom constantly expanded.

LIVE the Story

The Work of Imagination Transformation

In this section of Mark, Jesus is clarifying the vision of his disciples, transforming them from blind people into those that truly see the realities of the

---

3. Boring, *Mark*, 233; Adela Yarbro Collins, *Mark: A Commentary*, Hermeneia (Minneapolis: Fortress, 2007), 393.

kingdom as *reality itself.* The church inhabits the new age—the kingdom of God—and we do so by having eyes and ears constantly attuned to this new world so that we see it, hear and taste it, and get to know it better by living in it more fully. This is a massive challenge for us, since the media that we consume each day shapes our imaginations so that we live in *this world*—a world created and sustained by media companies that make money by attracting and holding our attention.

Paul recognizes that the audiences that hear his letters have minds thoroughly shaped by the ideologies and thought patterns of their surrounding cultures, and he knows that the task of reshaping their imaginations is a massive one. This is why in Ephesians he prays for his readers' enlightenment:

> I keep asking that the God of our Lord Jesus Christ, the glorious Father, may give you the Spirit of wisdom and revelation, so that you may know him better. I pray that the eyes of your heart may be enlightened in order that you may know the hope to which he has called you, the riches of his glorious inheritance in his holy people, and his incomparably great power for us who believe. (Eph 1:17–19)

We can participate in God's project of renovating our imaginations in several ways. First, we can learn to discern, or "see through," the messages that come at us constantly through various media, such as advertising. When my sons were young, they would often watch baseball or golf on television with me, and we would engage in this discernment process together. When a commercial would appear, we would express in an exaggerated and obnoxious manner the feeling or desire that the advertisement was attempting to create in us as its intended target. When a young, good-looking man was wearing a certain deodorant that *obviously* attracted the attention of a beautiful woman, we would shout, "I want to be popular, admired, and adored, so I'm going to buy that deodorant and have fulfilling relationships!"

We can take a similar approach to all the ways this world's messages come at us to shape our imaginations. How does our culture work on us to create in us dissatisfaction with what we currently have? In what ways am I made to feel discontent with my relationships and with my current station in life? What fills my mind and what shapes my desires so that I fail to see ministry and service opportunities, but only envision possibilities for career advancement or progression toward accumulating bigger, better, and more possessions?

Second, we can memorize Scripture passages that focus on having our imaginations—our minds and hearts—transformed, such as Romans 12:1–2:

Therefore, I urge you, brothers and sisters, in view of God's mercy, to offer your bodies as a living sacrifice, holy and pleasing to God—this is your true and proper worship. Do not conform to the pattern of this world, but be transformed by the renewing of your mind. Then you will be able to test and approve what God's will is—his good, pleasing and perfect will.

Another excellent text is Ephesians 4:22–24:

You were taught, with regard to your former way of life, to put off your old self, which is being corrupted by its deceitful desires; to be made new in the attitude of your minds; and to put on the new self, created to be like God in true righteousness and holiness.

We can turn these passages over and over in our minds throughout the day, thinking creatively about the ways our world shapes us to love, desire, imagine, fear, and hope according to its agendas. And we can develop the capacities to begin imagining what it might look like to do so according to God's intentions for us.

Finally, we can pray that God would open our eyes in the same way that Jesus was seeking to clarify the vision of his disciples. We can pray routinely and simply that God would do this, perhaps even by adapting Paul's prayer in Ephesians 1:

Father, in Christ and by your Spirit, we pray that you would open the eyes of our hearts that we may be enlightened and that we may know the hope to which you have called us, the riches of your glorious inheritance in your holy people, and your incomparably great power for us who believe. Amen.

CHAPTER 34

Mark 8:27–33

📖 LISTEN to the Story

²⁷Jesus and his disciples went on to the villages around Caesarea Philippi. On the way he asked them, "Who do people say I am?"

²⁸They replied, "Some say John the Baptist; others say Elijah; and still others, one of the prophets."

²⁹"But what about you?" he asked. "Who do you say I am?"

Peter answered, "You are the Messiah."

³⁰Jesus warned them not to tell anyone about him.

³¹He then began to teach them that the Son of Man must suffer many things and be rejected by the elders, the chief priests and the teachers of the law, and that he must be killed and after three days rise again. ³²He spoke plainly about this, and Peter took him aside and began to rebuke him.

³³But when Jesus turned and looked at his disciples, he rebuked Peter. "Get behind me, Satan!" he said. "You do not have in mind the concerns of God, but merely human concerns."

Listening to the Text in the Story: Daniel 7; Psalm 118; Isaiah 52:13–53:12; Romans 1:1–5; 1 Corinthians 2:1–8; 1 Timothy 3:16.

Mark places this conversation between Jesus and his disciples, especially Peter, just after the two-stage healing of the blind man (8:22–26). That healing sheds light on this episode and functions as an enacted parable of how Peter and the disciples partially understand who Jesus is, but their comprehension requires further clarification. This is also the first mention of Jesus speaking to his disciples "on the way" to Jerusalem (v. 27).[1] This conversation takes place in

---

1. The expression "on the way" is found throughout 8:22–10:52, pointing to Jesus's teaching about the path of discipleship as he and his disciples make their way to Jerusalem. The NIV sometimes translates *hodos* ("way," "path," "road") as "road[side]," and this term forms an *inclusio* around the final episode of this section (10:46, 52; see Black, *Mark*, 191; Boring, *Mark*, 237).

Caesarea Philippi, about twenty-four miles north of the Sea of Galilee. From here they will journey to Jerusalem, where Jesus faces a confrontation with the Jerusalem leadership and, as he predicts throughout 8:22–10:52, betrayal, rejection, suffering, and death.

This text includes the first of three passion predictions by Jesus. After each prediction (cf. 9:31–32; 10:32–34), the disciples either misunderstand him, ignore him, or display stunning selfishness. In this passage, after Jesus predicts his suffering and death, Peter rejects his statement and rebukes him for suggesting that this is his purpose in going to Jerusalem. Peter's rebuke is simply another escalation of the disciples' misunderstanding throughout Mark. He is not merely baffled by how God's purposes could be accomplished through suffering and death. He completely rejects how God is working out his purposes in and through Jesus.

Throughout Scripture, however, God always works in ways that subvert, upend, or baffle human calculations for accomplishing results. Because of the world's corruptions, people grasp for power and prestige to establish their identities and tend to manipulate a situation to bring about a desired end. When God promised Abraham an heir, though he and Sarah had no children, Abraham and Sarah reasoned that perhaps they could accomplish God's purposes through Hagar, Sarah's servant (Gen 16:1–3). But God later gave Abraham an heir when he was a hundred years old and Sarah was ninety. In that time, just as now, that runs against all human expectations.

Paul notes that the rulers of this age—the cosmic forces that determine worldly ways of thinking—do not understand God's wisdom or his mode of operating. God's logic and way of working run contrary to worldly wisdom. But the rulers of this age did not understand God's way of working, which is why they mysteriously orchestrated situations, events, and the motivations of human rulers so that Jesus would be put to death. But because God wins by losing, triumphs through defeat, and brings about the transformation of the cosmos through the death of Christ, the evil powers that rule this present age came to see that their triumph was their defeat (1 Cor 2:1–8).

The cross is the wisdom of God, even though it confounds human reasoning. Exaltation comes through humiliation; triumph comes through defeat. The Son of Man and the people loyal to him will suffer temporarily, but they will be vindicated by God and receive an eternal kingdom (Dan 7:13–14, 21–22, 27). And Isaiah prophesies about God's servant who will be oppressed and rejected, will suffer and die, but who ultimately will be vindicated by God (Isa 52:13–53:12). All of this is why Jesus says that this is the way the Son of Man "must" go (Mark 8:31). These things "must" happen, not merely because they are foreordained, but because this is God's mode of working, even though going the way of weakness, suffering, shame, rejection, and death is repugnant to human ways of thinking. Humans, even those who have committed themselves to Jesus, must constantly repent from worldly ways of thinking, having their minds and hearts constantly reoriented by how God works and away from ways of accomplishing God's purposes that are "convenient," "effective," "efficient," "successful," or "impressive."

EXPLAIN the Story

This episode takes place in Caesarea Philippi, far to the north. From here Jesus will begin his journey southward to Jerusalem. He initiates a discussion with his disciples about his identity, asking first what others are saying about him (v. 27). Again, as at other times in Mark, popular opinion associates Jesus with Elijah and John the Baptist, along with other unnamed prophets (v. 28; see 6:14–15; 9:4–5, 11–13; 15:35–36). In Mark's Gospel, Jesus is a confrontational and enigmatic character, and the mode of his ministry reminds people of biblical figures who came in a similar mode, speaking truth to power and calling out unrighteousness.

Jesus then asks the disciples about his identity (v. 29), and Peter answers, "You are the Messiah" (*ho christos*, "the Christ").[2] Peter answers rightly, as readers of Mark know well, since the narrator identifies Jesus as the Christ in the opening of the Gospel (1:1). Mark does not associate Jesus with any preexisting notions about who the Messiah was supposed to be and what he was supposed to do. Rather, Jesus's mission, ministry, and teaching define what it is to be the Messiah. This is especially significant, as this section of Mark (8:22–10:52) focuses on Jesus's journey to Jerusalem to give his life and during which he teaches about cross-oriented discipleship. He will dash all false hopes of a triumphalist messiah who will deliver a dramatic military victory over the Romans.

This is why Jesus follows Peter's identification with a warning in v. 30 "not to tell anyone about him." Throughout the rest of the narrative, the disciples are still captivated by hopes for liberation and places of prominence in God's kingdom (9:34; 10:35–37). Just as the enacted parable in the previous episode demonstrates, along with Peter's subsequent response in v. 32, the disciples may rightly identify Jesus as the Christ, but they are still in need of having their eyes opened regarding just what this means.

---

2. "Messiah" is the English translation of the Hebrew *mashiach*, and "Christ" is the English translation of the Greek *christos*, the Greek rendering of *mashiach*. On the diversity of Jewish messianic expectation, see M. F. Bird, "Christ," *DJG* 115–25.

Jesus begins this education process by teaching the disciples about what "must" take place. He taught them "that the Son of Man must suffer many things and be rejected by the elders, the chief priests and the teachers of the law, and that he must be killed and after three days rise again" (v. 31). The title "Son of Man" recalls a range of associations from Scripture. God addresses the prophet Ezekiel with this designation, and it appears in Daniel 7 in association with God's suffering people and a figure whom God vindicates (Dan 7:13–14, 21–22, 27).[3] These associations resonate strongly with Mark's portrayal of Jesus as a prophetic character whom God appoints to bring in God's kingdom and who will come in power in the future.[4]

Jesus says that the Son of Man "must" first suffer and die before being raised and vindicated by God, using a Greek verb (*dei*, "it is necessary, it must") that points to two realities: (1) Jesus is executing God's predetermined will of inaugurating God's kingdom and overthrowing the rule of Satan; and (2) the necessity of this taking place is according to God's character and the manner in which God works. God's thoughts and ways are not humanity's thoughts and ways. While the disciples hoped for a military triumph and places of prominence, God subverts human designs by working through the cross. In the wisdom of God, human power only reinforces the enslaving rule of Satan, while the cross liberates and transforms the cosmos.

Mark notes that Jesus "spoke plainly about this," indicating that he no longer is speaking allusively or in parables (Mark 8:32). The Greek expression here ties this statement back to the preaching of the word in 4:1–20: *kai parrēsia ton logon elalei* (lit. "and he spoke the word boldly"). In 4:1–20, Jesus speaks about the proclamation of "the word"—the message of a cross-directed Messiah calling disciples to inhabit a cross-oriented kingdom. Those who are of the kingdom will receive it and bear fruit, while those outside are confused by it. That Jesus spoke "the word" plainly to the disciples indicates that he is teaching them explicitly about the nature of his mission and ministry and the manner in which God is going to accomplish his purposes.

Peter responds by taking Jesus aside and rebuking him (v. 32). He is no longer confused by what Jesus is saying, since Jesus has been so direct. Peter outright rejects "the word." Rather than failing to comprehend how Jesus's suffering and death could accomplish God's purposes, Peter in effect says, "No,

---

3. "Jesus used the phrase not as a title, not because he was claiming to 'be' the messianic Son of man, but because he accepted for himself the role of obedient faith which the term evokes, and because he called others to share that calling with him" (Hooker, *Mark*, 93).

4. For a discussion of how the Old Testament informs Jesus's identity as the Son of Man, see Hays, *Echoes of Scripture in the Gospels*, 57–61.

that is not how this is going to go. You do not understand, Jesus. Going down to defeat is no way to overthrow the reign of Satan and establish the kingdom of God. You are reading from the wrong script!"

In response to Peter's rebuke, Jesus counter-rebukes Peter, addressing him as "Satan," doing so in a dramatic way by emphatically turning to him and ensuring that the rest of the disciples hear him (v. 33). We had noted in discussing Mark 4:15 that Satan snatches away the word when the cross-shaped character of the kingdom is diminished. Peter longs for the kingdom, but he wants the kingdom to come through triumph rather than through the cross. His rejection of Jesus's teaching is an instance of Satan snatching away the word, eliminating the cross from the kingdom. Jesus calling Peter "Satan" also indicates that Jesus is familiar with what he is hearing from Peter, having encountered this notion previously in the wilderness (1:13). Mark excludes many details in his account of Jesus's temptation in 1:12–13, but astute readers of Mark will remember that temptation when they read of Jesus associating Peter with Satan. Satan is not opposed to Jesus being the Christ, the Son of God. He is opposed to Jesus going to the cross, since that will ensure the overthrow of his enslaving rule. Satan tempts Jesus to be Messiah through power and spectacular display rather than through self-sacrificing love (cf. Matt 4:1–11; Luke 4:1–13).

Jesus exhorts Peter to "get behind me," which is a command to get back in line and follow Jesus and to return to Jesus's agenda and reject his own. Jesus wants Peter to listen, to learn, and to cultivate his heart so that he can receive the "word" of the cross-shaped kingdom and embrace it rather than rejecting it.[5] Peter has his mind set on worldly concerns, seeking to accomplish God's ends by human means—by power, military conquest, and violence. God's wisdom appears as foolishness in light of human reasoning. But human wisdom merely reinforces the enslaving grip of Satan's reign. God's liberating word of the cross confounds human wisdom and shatters the kingdom of Satan.

LIVE the Story

Jesus Refuses to be a Populist Messiah

Peter and the disciples had clear ideas about the sort of Messiah Jesus would be. After all, they had imaginations filled with what constituted a "successful" leader, especially the chosen agent of God's kingdom rule. They expected

---

5. Boring, *Mark*, 242.

someone compelling and winsome, a powerful speaker, someone who could draw big crowds and fire them up before leading them into action. Jesus, however, refuses to be pressed into the mold of these expectations. His identity and mission run in precisely the opposite direction. And it is important to keep in mind that the expectations that Jesus is going to reject *are those found among his followers.*

Jesus's refusal to reflect or endorse these expectations represents a powerful challenge to the contemporary church. Jesus's identity, mission, and message— along with the realities of the kingdom of God—confront worldly norms of how things ought to be done and what constitutes "success." And they aim to reconfigure the church's imagination to see God, themselves, culture, and community through the lens of the cross-shaped gospel as the people of a cross-directed Messiah. It is especially relevant for churches set within cultures that define success in terms of prestige, social status, political power, and numerical growth. Jesus tells Peter that he is going to Jerusalem to suffer, be rejected, and to die. This is the way that God works and the manner in which the kingdom of God comes in power. This runs directly counter to Peter's conception of how the victory of the kingdom of God should come about. Peter's imagination represents a worldly way of seeing that affects the imagination of many churches around the world and certainly in North America.

It is shocking to consider elements of Mark's narrative. Satan is a character who wants the gospel to be "successful," with a triumphant arrival in Jerusalem followed by a powerful victory over the Romans and the spectacular liberation of God's people. He wants to prevent Jesus from going to Jerusalem to suffer and die, since this is consistent with the way that God works out his program throughout Scripture. Peter articulates this vision, which is why Jesus identifies him as "Satan." This is not what we would expect.

Many in our day would see the great crowds that gathered around Jesus as evidence of Jesus's successful ministry. Certainly the increasingly large crowds are a good thing, are they not? But Mark does not present them this way. They are regularly obstacles to Jesus carrying out his ministry. And Jesus keeps telling everyone throughout the Gospel to keep quiet about him and what he has done. This is completely out of keeping with impulses we might have about spreading the word and initiating a marketing strategy to let as many as possible know about Jesus. What is going on here?

The reality that Jesus refuses to reflect populist desires for the sort of Messiah he should be has implications for contemporary churches. We should not seek to become the sort of communities that reflect worldly notions of "success," avoiding the marks of what our culture defines as "failure." The most important thing about the gospel in Mark is that the kingdom of God takes the shape of the cross, is ruled by a Christ who goes to the cross, and is constituted by a people whose corporate life is oriented by the cross. A community that claims to be an outpost of the kingdom of God is not a failure if they do not grow, increase in cultural power, or make their mark in society. Those are not appropriate measures for the church. While we may be tempted to evaluate a church as "successful" if it is growing numerically, adding building space and multiplying programs, such a view is evidence of having minds set on merely human concerns and not those of God.

A minister is a "failure" if she or he does not communicate faithfully that the gospel calls the church to turn away from grasping for cultural power or relevance. Ministers fail when they downplay the reality that the cross is at the center of the gospel and is the topic of the gospel from beginning to end. In the remainder of this section of Mark, Jesus calls disciples to take up their crosses and to cultivate a community life of hospitality to the vulnerable and of service to the marginalized. Communities of disciples serve the needy and keep watch over their imaginations so that they do not develop desires to play to crowds or cultivate the approval of those with wealth or social capital. In Mark, the cross-oriented identity of Jesus directly confronts a church mindset that is oriented by growth in numbers and cultural influence.

The attributes of a "successful" ministry reflect the true character and behavior of the Lord of the church—hospitality to those in need and service to those who do not have anything to offer the church in terms of prestige. The message of the cross in Mark calls churches to crucify their imaginations and desires, for only then will they enjoy the power of the resurrection in their communities. This is not an alternative strategy to accomplish goals of growth and power. It is the subversive and paradoxical way of life to which Jesus calls the church.

CHAPTER 35

Mark 8:34–9:1

📖 LISTEN to the Story

³⁴Then he called the crowd to him along with his disciples and said: "Whoever wants to be my disciple must deny themselves and take up their cross and follow me. ³⁵For whoever wants to save their life will lose it, but whoever loses their life for me and for the gospel will save it. ³⁶What good is it for someone to gain the whole world, yet forfeit their soul? ³⁷Or what can anyone give in exchange for their soul? ³⁸If anyone is ashamed of me and my words in this adulterous and sinful generation, the Son of Man will be ashamed of them when he comes in his Father's glory with the holy angels."

⁹:¹And he said to them, "Truly I tell you, some who are standing here will not taste death before they see that the kingdom of God has come with power."

Listening to the Text in the Story: Deuteronomy 1:19–46; Psalm 78; Galatians 1:6–10; Philippians 2:1–18; 3; Revelation 12:10–11.

This passage is a continuation of the conversation between Jesus and the disciples about his identity and mission as they begin the journey to Jerusalem. Just after Jesus counter-rebuked Peter (v. 33), he called on everyone around him, along with the disciples, to hear just what it means to have minds set on God's concerns rather than human concerns. After calling Peter "Satan," Jesus exhorted him to "get behind me," a call for Peter to take his position *behind* Jesus, listening to him and following his agenda as he takes the road to Jerusalem to be betrayed, rejected, and crucified. The connection between his words to Peter and his teaching in this passage is clear from the Greek text. Jesus tells Peter to "get behind [*opisō*] me," the same term that he uses to describe "whoever wishes to follow behind [*opisō*] me"

(v. 34, lit. translation).[1] Peter and the disciples have minds and hearts shaped by their culture so that they desire to see God's kingdom only come in glory and triumph. They want God's purposes fulfilled, but they do not understand that in God's wisdom, glory only comes through suffering and death. Beyond merely failing to grasp Jesus's mission, Peter actually rebukes Jesus for talking about it.

Jesus's teaching runs against the grain of the surrounding culture, which he calls "this adulterous and sinful generation" (v. 38). Scripture refers to Israel with similar expressions when they were unfaithful to God as he led them out of Egypt and into the land of promise. They were "a stubborn and rebellious generation, whose hearts were not loyal to God, whose spirits were not faithful to him" (Ps 78:8). Moses recounts how they came to "the hill country of the Amorites, which the LORD our God is giving us" (Deut 1:20). He exhorted them: "Go up and take possession of it as the LORD, the God of your ancestors, told you. Do not be afraid; do not be discouraged" (v. 21). They refused, however, and complained that God had evil intentions in bringing them out from Egypt "to deliver us into the hands of the Amorites to destroy us" (v. 27). After hearing of God's judgment on them for their disobedience, that "no one from *this evil generation* shall see the good land I swore to give your ancestors, except Caleb son of Jephunneh" (vv. 35-36), the Israelites attempted to take the land, even though God told them he would not be with them. This ended in disaster and defeat (v. 44).

Mark portrays the larger Jewish culture as similarly disobedient to God, for they want God's kingdom, but their imaginations were so limited that they could only conceive of human, worldly means of bringing it about. Jesus is calling the disciples to have minds and hearts shaped by his teaching and not by the prevailing cultural desire for a military triumph over the Romans.

EXPLAIN the Story

After the dramatic and intense exchange of rebukes with Peter in 8:32-33, Jesus addresses as wide an audience as possible, for what he is about to say is crucial. He "called the crowd to him along with his disciples" (v. 34). This is unusual, as Jesus typically begins by teaching to a general audience before

---

1. Boring, *Mark*, 243. The NIV translates this clause as "whoever wants to be my disciple," which captures well that Jesus is indeed giving instruction on discipleship.

calling his disciples aside to give them further instruction. Mark arrests his audience's attention by breaking this pattern.[2] The passage that follows this one stresses Jesus's words even more, with God putting an exclamation point on what Jesus says by thundering from the heavens, "This is my Son, whom I love. Listen to him!" (9:7).

Jesus announces to the gathered crowd that if anyone wishes "to follow behind me" (lit. translation; *opisō mou akolouthein*), they must "deny themselves" (v. 34). He is referring specifically to Peter's rejection of Jesus's mission to go to the cross and the fact that Peter has in mind "merely human concerns" rather than "the concerns of God" (v. 33). Disciples must recognize that their attempts to prevent Jesus from going to the cross have a satanic origin. They must deny their human reasoning that God's kingdom can be brought in by earthly political means or by military triumph, and they must turn from their desires for glory and honor. Disciples follow behind Jesus on his path to the cross, for this is the only way to glory in the end.

Jesus calls disciples to "take up their cross and follow me" (v. 34). Each follower must put to death their attempts to shape the kingdom according to human reasoning. While each person takes up their own cross, this is not generalized in the sense that "everyone has their own struggles." The cross in the first century was the symbol of imperial capital punishment and of the Roman Empire's domination over Judea. It was a shameful and humiliating symbol of defeat and loss. Followers must surrender any notion of defeating the Romans through violence, cultural triumphalism, or hopes for military victory and independence. In effect, Jesus is saying, "Identify yourselves as shamefully defeated ones with reference to your enemies, the Romans. Surrender and embrace the loss of the hope of establishing the kingdom through force. Follow me on the road to rejection, betrayal, and death—in the hope of resurrection." According to Mark's Gospel, the community of Jesus's followers is not marked by triumphalism but by surrender and loss, embodied through service and hospitality.

In vv. 35–38, Jesus provides the rationale and grounding logic for his radical call, indicated by the "for" (*gar*) in v. 35. In God's design, *now* is the time for rejection, suffering, and death for disciples, and exaltation comes *in the future*. Because the Son of Man will enter into his glory only by going to the cross, disciples will only share in his glory by following Jesus on this path. If anyone tries to preserve their life during the present age, "to save" it, they will lose it (v. 35). Seeking to establish the glorious kingdom now through any sort of political or military victory results in the loss of one's soul when the

---

2. Boring, *Mark*, 243.

kingdom comes in glory in the future. Such an attempt is a commitment to the kingdom of Satan, since it is fighting the perceived enemy (Rome) with the weapons supplied by the enslaving reign of God's cosmic enemy. Satan's oppressive grip over humanity is demonstrated by the excitement of revolutionary fervor, which will erupt in violence resulting in death and destruction. Even though fighting for political power and attempting to control the course of history makes good sense to human ways of thinking, this is not God's plan. On the other hand, anyone who follows the Son of Man who is raised only after being crucified, anyone who "loses their life for me and for the gospel," will in fact "save" their life (v. 35).

What good is it to gain control of the levers of political power in the present age *if you are destroyed with this age* (v. 36)? This is what Jesus means by gaining "the whole world," yet forfeiting one's soul. And one's "soul" is infinitely valuable, so disciples must be careful where they cast their lot (v. 37). Because the Son of Man is coming in power in the future, going the way of the cross now with Jesus is the wisest course, even though it runs counter to human impulses for self-preservation.

When Jesus speaks of the possibility of being "ashamed of me and my words" in v. 38, he recalls "the word" that was preached in 4:1–20 and "the word" that Jesus spoke plainly to his disciples in 8:32—the message of a cross-directed Messiah that calls disciples to inhabit a cross-shaped kingdom. If anyone is ashamed to participate in a community that does not grasp for power, that does not seek political influence, and that embraces loss and defeat with the confidence of resurrection in the future, then Jesus himself will not claim that person as a participant in his kingdom when he comes to establish it in power. This is not a general statement of being ashamed to identify as a Christian in the wider culture. It is a specific reference to claiming one's place in a community of surrender, even though others who identify as God's people think that God's will is accomplished through human means. Jesus is working out the will of "his Father," which calls him to the cross now before he inaugurates his Father's glorious kingdom in the future.

Jesus's statement in 9:1 is probably best read with the passage under discussion, since the introduction of a time indicator in 9:2 points to a new episode. His reference to the kingdom of God coming with power may point either to the transfiguration, which the disciples are about to witness in 9:2–13, or to his resurrection, which he has mentioned in v. 31.[3] In the narrative of Mark,

---

3. Black, *Mark*, 197; Moloney, *Gospel of Mark*, 176–77. See Strauss's discussion for the range of views of Jesus's statement (*Mark*, 375–76).

however, the disciples are not present at the empty tomb to witness that the resurrection has occurred. Only the women who arrive at Jesus's tomb find it empty (16:1–5). A young man announces to them, "He has risen! He is not here" (v. 6). While the women are not mentioned in 9:1, Mark later indicates that they are present at this point in the story: "In Galilee these women had followed him and cared for his needs. Many other women who had come up with him to Jerusalem were also there" (15:41).

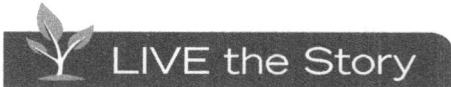

LIVE the Story

The Cross and the Culture Wars

Jesus's call for disciples to lose their lives in this present age so that they might gain them in the future presents a massive challenge to Christians caught up in culture wars. Frances FitzGerald, in her book *The Evangelicals*, narrates the history of evangelical Christianity in America as a struggle to gain political power in order to influence the moral culture of the nation.[4] This is an impulse that was present from the country's founding and has been on display over the last century, as conservative Christians have allied themselves with the Republican Party and its various leaders. Over the closing decades of the twentieth century and into the twenty-first, this alliance has solidified, so that many evangelicals conceive of an equivalence between voting Republican and being Christian. And they imagine that advancing the political fortunes of the party somehow also advance the kingdom of God.

FitzGerald details how Dwight Eisenhower exploited Billy Graham's popularity to spread the message of anti-communism and foster patriotism in the cause of guaranteeing national security. Graham portrayed America as uniquely Christian, and his preaching was filled with calls for America to repent and turn back to God in the hopes that God would preserve the nation from foreign threats.[5]

Over the last fifty years, the alliance between conservative Christians and the Republican Party has focused on retaking the Supreme Court in order to somehow roll back gay rights and overturn the legality of abortion. Because these efforts involve political agitation and demonization of political

---

4. Frances FitzGerald, *The Evangelicals: The Struggle to Shape America* (New York: Simon & Schuster, 2017). For another recent and extraordinarily insightful history of the political involvement of American evangelicals, see Matthew Avery Sutton, *American Apocalypse: A History of Modern Evangelicalism* (Cambridge, MA: Belknap, 2014).

5. FitzGerald, *Evangelicals*, 178.

opponents, Christian efforts have enflamed the culture war in America. Animosity and public rhetoric—on all sides—has become increasingly vitriolic and destructive. Sadly, despite the intentions of many conservative Christians, to be a "Christian" in America is now taken to mean one who is angry, judgmental, and bigoted.[6]

Christians in America have much to contemplate regarding their behavior and attitudes toward others. Mark's Gospel, however, identifies the root of the problem as the desire to gain control through political power in order to influence and determine the shape of American culture. Rather than seeking control through power, Jesus calls disciples to lose their lives in this world in order to gain them in the next. America is not the kingdom of God, and Christians seeking to "impact the culture" are fighting a losing battle.[7] Even if it were possible to "win" the culture war, it would require that we cast our lot with a kingdom of this world, forfeiting our place in the kingdom of God that is coming in the future. As Jesus asks, what good is it if we gain control of the levers of power to establish America as we want it, if we forfeit our souls?

It will require a radical change of mindset for many American Christians to see themselves most fundamentally as citizens of God's kingdom rather than as American citizens. Just as the disciples could hardly understand how Jesus's program could possibly work, many American Christians can hardly imagine that giving up the fight to control culture would be a good thing. Jesus's call is indeed radical. It confronts our worldly desires for cultural power and influence just as it did in the first century. But if we want to participate in the kingdom of God when it comes in power, we must answer Jesus's call to give up the effort to gain power and political influence.

---

6. David Kinnaman and Gabe Lyons, *unChristian: What a New Generation Really Thinks about Christianity . . . and Why It Matters* (Grand Rapids: Baker, 2012).

7. James Davison Hunter surveys Christian strategies to influence or change the culture and discusses why each of these ultimately fail (*To Change the World: The Irony, Tragedy, and Possibility of Christianity in the Late Modern World* [New York: Oxford University Press, 2010]).

CHAPTER 36

Mark 9:2-13

LISTEN to the Story

²After six days Jesus took Peter, James and John with him and led them up a high mountain, where they were all alone. There he was transfigured before them. ³His clothes became dazzling white, whiter than anyone in the world could bleach them. ⁴And there appeared before them Elijah and Moses, who were talking with Jesus.

⁵Peter said to Jesus, "Rabbi, it is good for us to be here. Let us put up three shelters—one for you, one for Moses and one for Elijah." ⁶(He did not know what to say, they were so frightened.)

⁷Then a cloud appeared and covered them, and a voice came from the cloud: "This is my Son, whom I love. Listen to him!"

⁸Suddenly, when they looked around, they no longer saw anyone with them except Jesus.

⁹As they were coming down the mountain, Jesus gave them orders not to tell anyone what they had seen until the Son of Man had risen from the dead. ¹⁰They kept the matter to themselves, discussing what "rising from the dead" meant.

¹¹And they asked him, "Why do the teachers of the law say that Elijah must come first?"

¹²Jesus replied, "To be sure, Elijah does come first, and restores all things. Why then is it written that the Son of Man must suffer much and be rejected? ¹³But I tell you, Elijah has come, and they have done to him everything they wished, just as it is written about him."

Listening to the Text in the Story: Exodus 19:3–25; 24:9–16; 34; Deuteronomy 18:15; 1 Kings 19:1–18; Psalm 118:22; Isaiah 53:3; Daniel 7:9; Malachi 4; Revelation 1:13–14.

The revelation of Jesus in his heavenly glory follows immediately after the previous passage, in which he speaks about disciples taking up their crosses to follow him on the road to Jerusalem to suffer and die. Those who lose their lives in the present age will participate with the Son of Man in his kingdom when he comes in glory in the future. Jesus leads Peter, James, and John up to a high mountain to gain a preview of this glorious and heavenly reality that is to come, and they hear God's emphatic proclamation that they are to listen to his Son. This is God's exclamation point that confirms what Jesus has said regarding disciples who lose their lives now to save them later. As Placher notes, God's voice from heaven identifying Jesus as God's beloved Son opens the first half of Mark's Gospel (1:11), just as God's voice "from the cloud" confirming his identity opens the second half (9:7).[1]

The setting on "a high mountain" recalls biblical scenes in which humans encounter God throughout Scripture. Moses encountered God on Mount Sinai at key points in the book of Exodus, including one passage with which Mark 9 strongly resonates:

> When Moses went up on the mountain, the cloud covered it, and the glory of the LORD settled on Mount Sinai. For six days the cloud covered the mountain, and on the seventh day the LORD called to Moses from within the cloud. To the Israelites the glory of the LORD looked like a consuming fire on top of the mountain. Then Moses entered the cloud as he went on up the mountain. And he stayed on the mountain forty days and forty nights. (Exod 24:15–18; cf. also 19:3–25; 34)

Elijah also encountered God on a mountain after his contest with the prophets of Baal (1 Kings 19). The appearance of Moses and Elijah in the present episode speaking with Jesus invites Mark's audiences to recall these previous divine encounters. Moses and Elijah may be taken to represent the revelation of God through the law and the prophets. Beyond this, however, and more to the point of the thrust of Mark's narrative, they are two characters who rejected the luxuries of royal courts and suffered the consequences of confronting defiant rulers.[2] Further, both were vindicated by God by ascending to glory. Elijah was transported to heaven (2 Kgs 2:9–12), and Moses's burial place remained a mystery (Deut 34:5–8), with subsequent tradition suggesting that he was exalted to heaven.[3] While Moses and Elijah spoke *on behalf of God*, Jesus is *the definitive revelation of God*, the authorized agent of the kingdom of God to whom the disciples must pay close attention. Moses spoke of the

---

1. Placher, *Mark*, 123.
2. Placher, *Mark*, 127.
3. Moloney, *Gospel of Mark*, 179.

prophet who was to come: "The LORD your God will raise up for you a prophet like me from among you, from your fellow Israelites. You must listen to him" (Deut 18:15).

EXPLAIN the Story

Mark sets this dramatic scene in terms of previous divine encounters. "After six days" recalls the six days the cloud covered the mountain in Exodus 24:15–16. Jesus brings along the three disciples who make up his inner circle, Peter, James, and John, and leads them up "a high mountain" (Mark 9:2). The description of the heavenly glory breaking out is quite sudden. The passive voice of the verb ("he was transfigured") indicates that God powerfully acted upon Jesus to break open the veil of earthly reality and to reveal Jesus in his heavenly splendor and power as the Son of Man. Mark's description of Jesus's clothes becoming "dazzling white, whiter than anyone in the world could bleach them" recalls Daniel's vision of God on his throne and John's vision of Jesus in Revelation:

> And the Ancient of Days took his seat.
> His clothing was as white as snow;
>   the hair of his head was white like wool.
> His throne was flaming with fire,
>   and its wheels were all ablaze. (Dan 7:9)

And when I turned I saw seven golden lampstands, and among the lampstands was someone like a son of man, dressed in a robe reaching down to his feet and with a golden sash around his chest. The hair on his head was white like wool, as white as snow, and his eyes were like blazing fire. (Rev 1:12–14)

Jesus had said that some of his disciples would not die before they saw the kingdom of God coming in power (9:1), and this display of Jesus in his heavenly glory is a foretaste of that future reality.

Peter, ever the impetuous disciple, speaks up, and Mark notes in an editorial comment that he did so from two motivations (v. 6). First, ignorance, as he "did not know what to say." Beyond this, however, Mark hints that what he had to say was not well-motivated, since "they were so frightened [*ekphoboi*]." When characters react with fear (*phobos*) in Mark, they are not acting from faith (4:40; 5:15, 36; 6:20, 50; 10:32; 11:18, 32; 12:12; 16:8). Being afraid is the opposite of a faithful response to the revelation of Jesus's identity (cf. 6:49–51). Peter's fearful response is not mere ignorance but demonstrates a lack of understanding of the revelation of Jesus in his glory.

This illuminates what Peter meant by his desire to "put up three shelters— one for you, one for Moses and one for Elijah" (v. 5). His suggestion is an attempt to sidestep or resist what Jesus had already made clear—that glory only comes after rejection, suffering, and death (8:31–32). Peter wants to make the glory permanent, to hold on to it, hoping that God's purposes can somehow be accomplished without suffering and death. The revelation of Jesus in his heavenly glory is but a foretaste of what is to come on the far side of suffering and death, meant to confirm that exaltation is indeed on its way. Peter, however, is still consumed by "merely human concerns" (8:33). He is still working from an inadequate understanding of Jesus's mission and God's wisdom.

God then dramatically enters the scene as a "cloud appeared and covered them" (v. 7). In divine encounters, the appearance of a cloud signals God's awesome presence (e.g., Exod 40:34–38; 1 Kgs 8:10–11).[4] Just as God announced Jesus's identity as his beloved Son at Mark's opening, so here he affirms the same, with the additional command, "Listen to him!" God's dramatic arrival resembles his appearance in Job 38:1, where he enters the debate between Job and his friends with an emphatic rebuke to the human wisdom that "obscures my plans with words without knowledge." Jesus has spoken the word of God, revealing the divine plan that the kingdom takes the shape of the cross and only comes through suffering and death. Any other way is the pathway of destruction. The disciples, flinching at the thought of having joined a movement destined for failure and wanting to somehow devise an alternative plan, must attend carefully to Jesus's call to join him on the way to the cross. They must listen!

Just as this awesome event began, overtaking the disciples by surprise, it suddenly concludes (v. 8). They looked around, and the glory was gone, as were Moses and Elijah. On the way down the mountain, Jesus reiterated his now familiar warning to keep quiet about what they had seen, though this time with a slight twist. They are to tell no one "until the Son of Man has risen from the dead" (v. 9). Indeed, it would do no good to have the disciples talking about what they had seen in their muddled state about how God works out his purposes. Their excitement over what they had witnessed would only

---

4. Placher, *Mark*, 129.

confuse and mislead others. They need to see the reality of what Jesus has been talking about before they can speak of it to others, and they will indeed eventually become the apostolic expositors of what God has brought about in Jesus's death and resurrection. For now, however, Jesus enjoins silence.

The disciples kept to themselves what they had seen, but as they descended the mountain, they were trying to work out how all of this could make sense. It is not that they were trying to figure out what "resurrection" meant, as this was a commonly understood notion among Jews.[5] They were struggling to get their heads around the reality that resurrection glory only comes about by suffering and death. How can this be? They may have also been asking themselves whether it was possible to somehow divert Jesus from this plan or perhaps see if he was willing to modify his intentions so that it would not have to go this way.

When they ask Jesus about the notion common among the teachers of the law that Elijah would come first (v. 11), it is as though they are going back to what they had been taught while growing up, revisiting points in the cultural story they inherited in order to figure out if things could possibly work out otherwise. In effect they are saying, "Wait a minute, Elijah is supposed to come first and restore all things, right? Well, since the Romans are still occupying the land, that hasn't happened yet. So, if we are still waiting for that to happen, perhaps Elijah will come soon and bring renewal, and you will not have to die but could enter directly into your glory!"

Jesus affirms that this is indeed the order—Elijah comes first to restore all things. "But," Jesus in effect asks in v. 12, "why is it written in Scripture that the Son of Man must first suffer and be rejected if that is *not* how God is going to work out his purposes?" Scripture speaks of God accomplishing his saving work through the suffering and eventual vindication of his appointed agent in passages like Isaiah 53:3–12 and Psalms 22:6 and 118:22.[6] Jesus then delivers to his disciples the news that may have made their hearts sink: Elijah *did* come first. He came in the person of John the Baptist, preaching repentance and calling everyone to prepare for the arrival of God's reign and for God's agent of the kingdom's inauguration. Yet, evil people treated him as they wished

---

5. While the origins and development of Jewish notions of resurrection are unclear, it was a well-established idea by the time of the first century. It involved "the concrete act of God raising the dead from their tombs. Its theological dimensions include restoring and exalting God's covenant people, ushering in God's kingdom of justice and peace (or eternal life), and inaugurating God's new creation. Within this context one may understand Jesus's miracles of raising the dead, his teaching concerning resurrection, as well as the significance of Jesus's own resurrection" (K. L. Anderson, "Resurrection," *DJG* 775).

6. Strauss, *Mark*, 389.

and ended up putting him to death. This is the way it must all unfold, even though it runs against the hopes and dreams generated by "human concerns." John the Baptist, coming in the role of Elijah, experienced the divine pattern of suffering and vindication, the same experience that awaits Jesus and all who are faithful to him.

LIVE the Story

Letting Go of This World for Life in the World to Come

Peter and the disciples have been given a vision of the glory of the kingdom that is to come. They are having trouble understanding the reality that this kingdom only comes about through suffering and death. This is counterintuitive to how humans accomplish things. We imagine that establishing God's kingdom on earth comes about through force or through an earthly political process whereby we assert our rights and control the levers of power. It is very difficult to let go of this way of seeing things. When Peter sees the vision of Jesus in his glory, he wants to hold on to it. "Why can't we have this here and now?" But God's rule over this world remains a future reality, and everyone who goes the way of the cross will fully enjoy it when it comes in its fullness.

Paul articulates the same dynamic in Galatians 2:20 when he says that he has "been crucified with Christ and I no longer live, but Christ lives in me." Further, in Galatians 6:14 he says that he has no other boast, no other claim to an identity or significance, except "the cross of our Lord Jesus Christ, through which the world has been crucified to me, and I to the world." Paul regards himself as dead to this world. His earthly identity formed through accomplishments and a well-cultivated claim to social significance are all on the cross; he is dead to that reality. He makes no claims to assert his privileges and prerogatives, since the cross has killed him with reference to this world and has made him a full participant in the kingdom of God that is to come in the future.

But that does not make him completely passive in this world. It is not that he has entirely let go of this world, so that he just gives up on everything and everyone. This leads him to living in this world in a completely new way. "The life I now live in the body, I live by faith in the Son of God, who loved me and gave himself for me" (2:20). His life is now wrapped up completely in the life of Jesus Christ, and he conducts the remainder of his time on earth as a living embodiment of the life of Jesus. The way this works out for Paul is by letting go of an assertion of his own rights, his quests for power, and his control over others. He has given up on his former conception of how God *must* do things, including his previous dreams for his people Israel. Rather than cultivating personal prestige and power, Paul now cultivates weakness. Rather than establishing his own significance, he serves others in the same way that Jesus came to serve and give his life for others (cf. Mark 10:45).

In the previous "Live the Story" section, I discussed how many American Christians have succumbed to the subtle equation over time of America with the kingdom of God. Because we imagine that it is possible to establish a righteous nation that truly pleases God, bringing security and blessing, we have fallen prey to associating the cause of Christ with earthly political agendas. And this has happened on both the political right and left. Other nations in the West have made similar errors, and this temptation is a constant threat for the church.

Jesus is pressing on his disciples the reality that the kingdom in its glory and power will not come in this age but in the one to come. Jesus calls the church to let go of our deeply embedded hopes for a glorious kingdom here and now. But this does not mean that the kingdom is not now already here. It was present with the arrival of Jesus Christ into the world. Paul speaks of the kingdom as already present when he says to the Colossians that God "has rescued us from the dominion of darkness and brought us into the kingdom of the Son he loves" (Col 1:13). In Romans 14:17, he states that the kingdom of God presently consists of "righteousness, peace and joy in the Holy Spirit."

Churches participate in the kingdom of God now through cultivating communities of peacemaking and joy, as they seek to live out *as communities* the very life of Jesus Christ on earth. Just as Jesus went the way of suffering and death in anticipation of entering into his glorious reign in the future, the church now gives up earthly pursuits of political power as it embraces the cross in the hope of fully enjoying the reign of God in the future. The church will always be tempted to be like Peter and hold on tightly to present visions of glory, in the hope of establishing God's kingdom of righteousness in this age. But this hope will lead us away from the cross toward the cultivation of political power. These hopes must be put to death, for Christians are dead to this world. We are fully alive to the kingdom of God when we let go of such earthly hopes. And this happens through active engagement here and now in cultivating communities of mutual service, love, hospitality, and peacemaking.

Christians claim their place in the kingdom that is to come by identifying the needy in their communities and serving them with joy. We advertise to others that we are destined to inherit all things in the future when we let go of questing after political power and instead cultivate practices of caring for the poor, the orphan, and the widow. Letting go of this world is an active community pursuit of reconciling broken relationships, learning the practice of forgiveness, and vigilantly resisting the temptation to see the "other" in our culture as the enemy. The resentment stirred up by our hotly contested political climate forces us to see hope in making alliances with political parties to gain social leverage. These are the attitudes we must put on the cross, so that we will share in the glory of Jesus Christ when he comes to fully establish his kingdom on earth.

CHAPTER 37

Mark 9:14–29

📖 LISTEN to the Story

¹⁴When they came to the other disciples, they saw a large crowd around them and the teachers of the law arguing with them. ¹⁵As soon as all the people saw Jesus, they were overwhelmed with wonder and ran to greet him.

¹⁶"What are you arguing with them about?" he asked.

¹⁷A man in the crowd answered, "Teacher, I brought you my son, who is possessed by a spirit that has robbed him of speech. ¹⁸Whenever it seizes him, it throws him to the ground. He foams at the mouth, gnashes his teeth and becomes rigid. I asked your disciples to drive out the spirit, but they could not."

¹⁹"You unbelieving generation," Jesus replied, "how long shall I stay with you? How long shall I put up with you? Bring the boy to me."

²⁰So they brought him. When the spirit saw Jesus, it immediately threw the boy into a convulsion. He fell to the ground and rolled around, foaming at the mouth.

²¹Jesus asked the boy's father, "How long has he been like this?"

"From childhood," he answered. ²²"It has often thrown him into fire or water to kill him. But if you can do anything, take pity on us and help us."

²³"'If you can'?" said Jesus. "Everything is possible for one who believes."

²⁴Immediately the boy's father exclaimed, "I do believe; help me overcome my unbelief!"

²⁵When Jesus saw that a crowd was running to the scene, he rebuked the impure spirit. "You deaf and mute spirit," he said, "I command you, come out of him and never enter him again."

²⁶The spirit shrieked, convulsed him violently and came out. The boy looked so much like a corpse that many said, "He's dead."

²⁷But Jesus took him by the hand and lifted him to his feet, and he stood up.

²⁸After Jesus had gone indoors, his disciples asked him privately, "Why couldn't we drive it out?"

²⁹He replied, "This kind can come out only by prayer."

Listening to the Text in the Story: Numbers 14:11; Deuteronomy 32:20; Psalm 86:11; Romans 4:18–24; 1 Timothy 6:11–12.

This episode concludes the first of three cycles in which Jesus's predictions of his suffering and death are followed by the disciples' misunderstanding and Jesus's teaching on discipleship. The following episode (9:30–32) begins the second cycle. Mark focuses in this passage on the failure of the disciples to minister to God's people from a posture of prayerful dependence on God. The disciples are Jesus's chosen agents of blessing to God's people, called to extend Jesus's kingdom ministry. Their unfaithfulness, however, prevents others from experiencing the liberation and healing power of God's kingdom.

God had called Israel to play this role, being a light to the nations and a kingdom of priests (Exod 19:6; Isa 42:6; 49:6). They were not chosen as God's favorite nation over against all the other nations. Rather, God called Israel to himself, and this nation became his special possession *because he loved the nations and wanted to call them back to himself*, extending to them his life-giving reign and his blessing. Israel, however, proved unfaithful to God and his designs for them to be a servant nation. Their constant disobedience frustrated God, who called them a faithless and unbelieving people. In his conversation with Moses, the God of Israel says, "How long will these people treat me with contempt? How long will they refuse to believe in me, in spite of all the signs I have performed among them?" (Num 14:11). Jesus's question in Mark 9:19 echoes this lament.

In Deuteronomy 32:20 God says, "I will hide my face from them, . . . and see what their end will be; for they are a perverse generation, children who are unfaithful." In the Old Testament, a heart of unbelief and unfaithful behavior are virtually the same. Israel had not merely failed to believe facts about God. They failed to become a people who embodied faith in God by responding faithfully to his commands and his commission.

The reality that God's servants must prove faithful is the issue in this text. The disciples have not heeded Jesus's warning about being wary of the "yeast of the Pharisees and that of Herod" (8:15), and so they have sunk to the level of the teachers of the law, being unable to drive out the demon from the boy.

EXPLAIN the Story

The wonder of the experience on the mountain for Jesus and his inner circle of Peter, James, and John is short-lived, for they return to encounter a situation filled with tension.[1] They discover that the rest of the disciples are arguing with the scribes (v. 14).[2] While Mark is silent regarding the subject of the intense discussion, it appears to be about why the disciples cannot cast out the demon from the man's son. The heated debate is taking place in the midst of "a large crowd."

Just as in many other places in Mark's Gospel, when "all the people saw Jesus" they immediately reacted in a way that contrasts starkly with the disciples and other negative characters such as the scribes and Pharisees. They were "overwhelmed with wonder and ran to greet him" (v. 15). Mark typically notes the "wonder" and "amazement" of various characters at the close of an episode, and this reaction is not always positive. In Mark 1:27, the people who witness Jesus's exorcism in the synagogue rightly perceive his power and the authority of Jesus's teaching. Yet, in 6:51–52 the disciples' amazement is coupled with their lack of understanding and the hardness of their hearts. Here, the people are amazed after they "see" Jesus, indicating that they have a true perception of him, and they respond positively by rushing to him to greet him. Their reaction stands in contrast to the disciples and the scribes, who do not respond to Jesus when he questions them (v. 16). Mark notes this amazement early in the episode in order to set up this contrast and also to focus on the faithlessness of the disciples. They have not prayerfully depended on God in carrying out their ministry, failing to do as Jesus did in 7:31–35, where Jesus "looked up to heaven and with a deep sigh" healed the deaf and mute man (v. 34).[3]

Jesus asks what their argument is about, a question that a man in the crowd answers rather than the disciples or scribes (v. 17). The man's response contains an interesting indication of the unity of the ministry of Jesus and the disciples. He says, "I brought *you* my son," but Jesus has been up on the mountain with his three disciples. The fact that he had brought the boy to the other disciples,

---

1. Moloney, *Gospel of Mark*, 183.
2. The NIV has "teachers of the law" for the Greek *grammateis* ("scribes"). Scribes played a range of roles in first-century Jewish culture, though "they shared in common a role as the keepers, interpreters and teachers of Israel's Scriptures and traditions that often led to their prominent roles in society and politics" (Thellman, "Scribes," *DJG* 844). They appear in Mark consistently in opposition to Jesus, apart from the scribe he encounters in Mark 12:28–34.
3. Boring, *Mark*, 273.

yet describes this as having brought him to Jesus, indicates that the disciples are authorized as agents of kingdom power just as Jesus is. He has called them to be "with him" (3:14), and their earlier ministry had resulted in the spread of Jesus's name, pointing again to the unity of the disciples and Jesus (6:12–14).

The father describes the awful plight of his son, who is terrorized by a demon that has robbed the boy of his ability to speak and often violently thrashes him around, putting him in fatal danger. He has brought him to Jesus (i.e., to the disciples) with the plea that the spirit be driven out, but the disciples have been unable to do so (v. 18). Like other instances of demonic harassment and sickness in Mark, this affliction has not merely affected the boy. It has obviously tormented the father, who must look on helplessly as his son is besieged. And the boy cannot enjoy the blessings of community life, since he cannot speak. God's designs for humanity to enjoy the life-giving arrangement of flourishing in community are being tragically hindered by this instance of satanic enslavement.

Jesus's rebuke in v. 19 is shocking: "You unbelieving generation, how long shall I stay with you? How long shall I put up with you?" It appears initially to be directed at this poor father, who is desperate to see his son freed from his demonic tormentor. After all, he is the one who is speaking with Jesus. Jesus's strong words, however, are directed to the disciples rather than to the man or the crowds. The man has simply come to Jesus for relief from suffering, and the crowd has acted commendably in recognizing Jesus, being amazed and rushing to greet him. Jesus is rebuking the disciples for their failure to prayerfully look to God in carrying out the ministry to which Jesus has called them. He had similarly addressed the Pharisees (8:12), whom he had called "this adulterous and sinful generation" (8:38). He had also warned the disciples to avoid becoming like the Pharisees (8:15), but they have not heeded his word. Jesus notes at the end of this episode that the disciples needed to pray in order to exorcise the demon, something they apparently did not do (9:29).

Jesus orders that the boy be brought to him, and when the spirit sees Jesus it throws the boy into convulsions (v. 20). His father tells Jesus that the demon has tortured him in terrifying ways since childhood, which increases the tragedy since the child is a precious life ruined and plundered by the enslaving grip of Satan's kingdom. The father asks Jesus, "If you can do anything, take pity on us and help us" (v. 22).

Jesus's response to the man is arresting. Throughout Mark, Jesus does not behave like the placid and gentle figure that many people expect, especially those who grew up with picture Bibles in which a peaceful and tender Jesus seems to glide through gospel episodes as if to a soundtrack of easy-listening music, setting everyone at ease.[4] In Mark's Gospel, Jesus is often associated with Elijah, the confrontational prophet, so some of his reactions are shocking and not easily explained. At first glance it appears that Jesus is affronted by the father's hedging, as if he is sarcastically rebuking him for his tepid request. But Jesus is not rebuking the father, a man whose suffering is exacerbated by the failure of the disciples to cast out the spirit. The man stands with other positive characters in Mark, just like the friends of the lame man (2:3–4), Jairus (5:22–23), and the Syrian-Phoenician woman in 7:25–26. Each of these, along with some others, sought Jesus's help on behalf of someone else. Like these others, he approached Jesus with a humble request and has done nothing to warrant Jesus's rebuke.

Jesus is more likely looking at the disciples when he says, "*If* you can?" He is grieved that their failure has cast a shadow of doubt in the man's heart, angry that the disciples have failed God's people. They were appointed to extend Jesus's mission of bringing relief from the oppression of enslavement to demonic oppression and sickness. They were to be agents of the life-giving kingdom of God. Still eyeing the disciples, Jesus proclaims that "everything is possible for one who believes," (*tō pisteuonti*, which could also be translated as "for one who is faithful"). The disciples are the unfaithful and unbelieving generation, failing to embody the same posture as Jesus of looking to God for enablement to direct kingdom power that heals and drives out demons. Their focus is misdirected, as they are caught up in arguing with the scribes.

Again, rather than the disciples responding to Jesus, the man speaks, with a beautiful confession of his faith in Jesus and a plea for Jesus to help him overcome his unbelief (v. 24). While his statement could be read as a confession that there is a pocket of unbelief that remains in his heart, this is really a reflection of commendable faith. He is an example for the disciples, the kind of plea *they* should be making to Jesus. The father stands alongside the Syrian-Phoenician woman as a hero in Mark's Gospel. He is completely honest before Jesus. He is a father who is at his wits' end having watched his son ceaselessly ravaged by an evil spirit. In hope, he came to Jesus, only to be disheartened at the disciples' inability to help him. His plea to Jesus is a way of putting himself completely in Jesus's hands, confessing his faith that Jesus can indeed drive away the evil spirit. He recognizes his limitations and his doubts, admits to internal contradictions and hesitation about whether he could ever see his son flourish, and puts himself completely before God for help.

---

4. Cf. Mark Galli, *Jesus Mean and Wild: The Unexpected Love of an Untamable God* (Grand Rapids: Baker, 2008).

As he does in other places, Mark dramatically sets the scene for Jesus's exorcism. Jesus looks around at the crowd that is rushing to the scene and then commands the demon to leave the child. The demon leaves, but not before thrashing the boy once more on his way out. The boy appears to be dead, but just as Jesus did with the young girl in 5:41, he "took him by the hand and lifted him to his feet, and he stood up" (v. 27). By doing this, Jesus embodies the resurrection dynamics that are at work in his ministry and that he will experience in his own death and resurrection. Jesus enacts the life-giving power of the kingdom.

The episode closes with a brief, private conversation between Jesus and his disciples. They ask why they were unable to cast out the demon, and Jesus responds that "this kind can come out only by prayer" (v. 29). Readers may wonder if there are *kinds* of demons and whether the disciples were unable to cast this one out because they merely used the wrong technique. The focus of Jesus's words, however, is on the fact that the disciples did not pray. Their inability stemmed from their lack of a prayerful posture that looks to God.

LIVE the Story

The Surprising Textures of Faith

The disciples are clearly a model of unfaithfulness, or unbelief, in this text in that they fail to inhabit the dependent posture of prayerfulness that will enable them to draw on the power of the kingdom. The father of the demon-possessed boy, however, is a model of the sort of faith that the disciples should have displayed. Now, that may be surprising, since we might expect that strong faith in Scripture looks like never doubting or having to struggle with the complexities of this world and the difficulties and mysteries of Christian discipleship. The father's plea to Jesus, however, provides us with an opportunity to clarify some of the dimensions and textures of biblical faith.

First, in thinking about what faith is *not*, we can say that faith is not the complete absence of intellectual doubt, nor does it entail always having an answer to any question that arises because of the hardships and troubles we see in this world. The posture of "faith seeking understanding" receives the biblical testimony about ourselves, the world, and God and works toward making sense of what is currently confusing. Matthew Bates also notes that faith is not the opposite of assessing evidence.[5] That is, faith does not entail

---

5. Matthew W. Bates, *Salvation by Allegiance Alone: Rethinking Faith, Works, and the Gospel of Jesus the King* (Grand Rapids: Baker Academic, 2017), 15.

the death of one's intellect, as if critical thinking were somehow opposed to biblical faith. Nor is faith a leap in the dark, and it is not the cultivation of some kind of optimistic sense that everything is going to work out.[6]

Faith involves the conviction that what Scripture says about the identity of Jesus and the reality of the kingdom of God is true, and this entails a complete reordering of one's life around this reality. Faith is an *intellectual* activity, because I conceive and know the realities of Jesus and the kingdom, and I see that these are all real. And faith has a *volitional* dimension—I inwardly own these realities and confess them publicly. Finally, faith is *active* in that I am loyal to King Jesus and reconfigure my life so that it is wrapped up into his kingdom purposes and projects.

But what about doubt? Does the expression of this man ("I do believe; help me overcome my unbelief!") and the recognition of latent doubt in my heart and mind play any part in faith? I believe that it does. The father in this narrative is honest about the condition that his messed up and terribly afflicted situation has left him in. His son has been ravaged for years, and Jesus's disciples are no help at all, but only a cruel disappointment. Faced with all this, he still confesses that he believes that Jesus can help him, and he is also completely honest about the condition of his heart. His situation has left him in the difficult place of living with God's promises while also inhabiting a world of suffering where things do not work out the way they are supposed to.

This sort of posture is displayed throughout the Bible. The prophets routinely argue with God, struggling to make sense of his plans as he reveals them. They agonize over the many dimensions of the terrible situation of being among God's rebellious people who are facing God's coming judgment. Enduring a brutally difficult ministry, Jeremiah complained to God with words that many of us would hardly dream of uttering in prayer:

> You deceived me, LORD, and I was deceived;
>   you overpowered me and prevailed.
> I am ridiculed all day long;
>   everyone mocks me.
> Whenever I speak, I cry out
>   proclaiming violence and destruction.
> So the word of the LORD has brought me
>   insult and reproach all day long. (Jer 20:7–8)

---

6. Bates, *Salvation by Allegiance Alone*, 18.

The prophet Habakkuk does the same when he receives the prophecy of God's destruction of his people by the Babylonians. He argues that there's no way God can use an evil people to bring about his purposes: "Your eyes are too pure to look on evil; you cannot tolerate wrongdoing. Why then do you tolerate the treacherous? Why are you silent while the wicked swallow up those more righteous than themselves?" (Hab 1:13). He reminds God of his character and argues that there's just no way God can possibly do this.

Jesus himself is an example of this, as we will see later in Mark. On the cross, at the culmination of unspeakable torture, he cries out in argumentative lament: "My God, my God, why have you forsaken me?" (Mark 15:34). And John sees the souls of the martyrs in heaven, crying out to God, "How long, Sovereign Lord, holy and true, until you judge the inhabitants of the earth and avenge our blood?" (Rev 6:10). All these instances are striking because across our Christian traditions, "niceness," "being upbeat and encouraging," and "cheerfulness" are highly prized dispositions and seen as manifestations of Christian virtue. But the examples above are all instances of faithful people wrestling with the realities of their world and how those can fit with a God who is a righteous king over all of it. These biblical figures manifest genuine faith, however, because they cry out *to God* with their questions, their angst, and their struggle. They do not try to damp down their doubts and questions or ignore them. *They expressed them to God.*

I believe it is difficult for many of us to grow comfortable with this reality that faith speaks its doubts frankly to God. Some years ago I began a class session with Christian undergraduates with a slide, on which I displayed the lyrics to the well-known hymn, "It Is Well with My Soul" in one column, and the lyrics to the U2 song "Wake Up, Dead Man" on the other. I realize that not many people know of this U2 song, since it is the final song on one of their less popular albums, "Pop." The song can be found easily, and its lyrics are located on the band's website.

I let students read through the lyrics to these alternative pieces of music and then asked which of the songs they thought was more "biblical"—either representing Scripture or being written based on Scripture. I got the responses I expected, as student after student stated that the classic hymn "It Is Well with My Soul" was drawn from the Bible. What they didn't realize is that the hymn expresses an approach to tragedy and suffering that is not represented in Scripture. While the words sound so noble, to face trauma and outrageous injustices and remain unruffled is not how participants in the biblical drama react to such things. This is far more representative of the Victorian virtue of placidity, an era in which many Christians felt that remaining calm amid stressful situations reflected godliness. This sentiment certainly remains with us today. The central issue many students had with the U2 song was that it expressed doubt and even anger at the state of things and seemed to blame God for why things were so messed up (the song contains a much stronger expression than "messed up"). Indeed, the song does this.

But what the students didn't realize is that the song was written based on Eugene Peterson's rendering of Psalm 44:23–26:

> Get up, GOD! Are you going to sleep all day?
>   Wake up! Don't you care what happens to us?
> Why do you bury your face in the pillow?
>   Why pretend things are just fine with us?
> And here we are—flat on our faces in the dirt,
>   held down with a boot on our necks.
> Get up and come to our rescue.
>   If you love us so much, *help us!*[7]

Bono, the lead singer of U2, said this about "Wake Up, Dead Man":

> Really, this is in the tradition of the Psalms of David, which offer an honest dialogue with God. I always wondered why was David so beloved of God? I think it was probably honesty. Because in a lot of the psalms he's really giving out: "Where are you when you're needed? Call yourself God? Look, I'm surrounded by my enemies. You got me into this, get me out of here!" It's so direct. I think it's very important that people feel able to address God from whatever state they're in, whether that's devotion or anger. Both are present here.[8]

In Scripture, faith includes the courage to be honest about doubts, about the struggle to imagine that God truly is good, and that he will redeem his people and his world in the end. We would do well to bring these doubts to God in prayer. The Northumbria Community prays this simple prayer during evening prayer. We adopted it at our church and added the line from Mark 9:24:

---

7. Eugene H. Peterson, *The Message: The New Testament, Psalms and Proverbs in Contemporary Language* (Colorado Springs, CO: NavPress, 1995), 611.
8. U2 and Neil McCormick, *U2 by U2* (New York: HarperCollins, 2006), 334.

Lord, you have always given
bread for the coming day;
and though I am poor,
today I believe.
Lord, you have always given
strength for the coming day;
and though I am weak,
today I believe.
Lord, you have always given
peace for the coming day;
and though of anxious heart,
today I believe.
Lord, you have always kept
me safe in trials;
and now, tried as I am,
today I believe.
Lord, you have always marked
the road for the coming day;
and though it may be hidden,
today I believe.
Lord, you have always lightened
this darkness of mine;
and though the night is here,
today I believe.
Lord, you have always spoken
when time was ripe;
and though you be silent now,
today I believe.[9]
We believe, Lord; help us overcome our unbelief.

---

9. Northumbria Community, "Evening Prayer," www.northumbriacommunity.org/offices
/evening-prayer/.

CHAPTER 38

Mark 9:30-37

📖 LISTEN to the Story

³⁰They left that place and passed through Galilee. Jesus did not want anyone to know where they were, ³¹because he was teaching his disciples. He said to them, "The Son of Man is going to be delivered into the hands of men. They will kill him, and after three days he will rise." ³²But they did not understand what he meant and were afraid to ask him about it.

³³They came to Capernaum. When he was in the house, he asked them, "What were you arguing about on the road?" ³⁴But they kept quiet because on the way they had argued about who was the greatest.

³⁵Sitting down, Jesus called the Twelve and said, "Anyone who wants to be first must be the very last, and the servant of all."

³⁶He took a little child whom he placed among them. Taking the child in his arms, he said to them, ³⁷"Whoever welcomes one of these little children in my name welcomes me; and whoever welcomes me does not welcome me but the one who sent me."

Listening to the Text in the Story: Genesis 18:1–5; Deuteronomy 17:14–20; Daniel 4:28–37; Philippians 2:5–11; Hebrews 13:2; Revelation 3:20.

This is the second in the cycle of three predictions of Jesus's death and resurrection, followed by the disciples' misunderstanding. The first cycle ran from 8:31–9:29; this one begins here and ends at 10:31. Jesus's prediction is plainly and frankly stated, and the contrast between what awaits him in Jerusalem and the disciples' selfish arguing is as stark as it is tragic. After his prediction, Jesus teaches about true greatness, which involves service to the least and offering hospitality to the socially marginalized.

In teaching about service, Jesus says that "anyone who wants to be first must be the very last, and the servant of all" (v. 35). Jesus models this servant orientation throughout his ministry and most explicitly in giving himself for the life of the world. This pattern is completely consistent with God's self-revelation and how he has called for leaders of his people to take the form of servants.

In his instruction to Israel about appointing a king, God's priorities are clearly demonstrated. The king is to be one of God's own choosing (Deut 17:15). Further, he must be one whose heart is for the Lord and not set on riches. And he must consider himself as one of the people rather than exalted above his fellow Israelites:

> The king, moreover, must not acquire great numbers of horses for himself or make the people return to Egypt to get more of them, for the LORD has told you, "You are not to go back that way again." He must not take many wives, or his heart will be led astray. He must not accumulate large amounts of silver and gold.
>
> When he takes the throne of his kingdom, he is to write for himself on a scroll a copy of this law, taken from that of the Levitical priests. It is to be with him, and he is to read it all the days of his life so that he may learn to revere the LORD his God and follow carefully all the words of this law and these decrees and not consider himself better than his fellow Israelites and turn from the law to the right or to the left. Then he and his descendants will reign a long time over his kingdom in Israel. (Deut 17:16–20)

The great king Nebuchadnezzar learned the lesson of what true kingship looks like under the sovereignty of the creator God. He prided himself on the greatness of what he had achieved, looking over the city of Babylon and musing: "Is not this the great Babylon I have built as the royal residence, by my mighty power and for the glory of my majesty?" (Dan 4:30). After he was turned into a beast for a time, however, he learned the reality that his position was delegated to him by God: "Now I, Nebuchadnezzar, praise and exalt and glorify the King of heaven, because everything he does is right and all his ways are just. And those who walk in pride he is able to humble" (v. 37).

The true path to exaltation is revealed in the pattern of Jesus's obedient self-giving, which Paul lays out in Philippians 2:5–11. Jesus reveals God in that while he enjoyed all the privileges and prerogatives of existing in the form of God, he poured himself out, took the form of a servant, and became obedient even to the point of death on the cross (Phil 2:6–8). Because he did that, "God exalted him to the highest place and gave him the name that is above every name" (v. 9). That is, God bestowed on Jesus the name Yahweh, declaring that Jesus had revealed the very heart and character of God by setting aside privileges and expending himself for the sake of others. God's exaltation of Jesus indicates for all time that servanthood is the pathway to glory. This is the very lesson that Jesus elaborates here for the disciples.

EXPLAIN the Story

This episode is set in Capernaum, which Mark notes is a stop "on the way" to Jerusalem. Readers and hearers of Mark know that "the way" leads to betrayal and crucifixion in Jerusalem, and Mark emphasizes this narrative momentum by mentioning "the way" twice (vv. 33–34).[1] Jesus purposefully found a place where they could be alone "because" (v. 31) he wanted to be able to speak explicitly and clearly with them about what was going to happen to him in Jerusalem. Mark's summary of what Jesus taught them is succinct: "The Son of Man is going to be delivered into the hands of men. They will kill him, and after three days he will rise."

Reflecting what happens to the servant in Isaiah 53, Jesus's passive expression that he "is going to be delivered into the hands of men" invites reflection on the varied actors involved in the drama. This is, of course, the action of God, as Jesus's death and resurrection is the means whereby God accomplishes salvation.[2] In his death, God puts to death the old age, breaking the enslaving satanic grip over creation and inaugurating the new creation.[3] But Jesus is also handed over by Judas, who betrays him to the Jewish authorities. Like the servant, however, Jesus will be vindicated by God, who will raise him from the dead after three days (cf. Isa 53:10–12). As Boring notes, the expression "handed over" (*paradidotai*) expresses what happens to disciples who faithfully follow Jesus. It happened to John the Baptist (1:14) and is going to happen to the disciples, who will be betrayed by their closest friends and family (13:9–12).[4]

Despite Jesus's plain statement of what is going to happen to him when his journey "on the way" leads him to Jerusalem, the disciples fail to understand what he says (v. 32). Further, they are "afraid to ask him" (*ephobounto auton eperōtēsai*) for clarification. As we have noted previously, when characters react

---

1. The Greek term *hodos* can be translated "the road," as in the NIV in v. 33, or "the way," as in the NIV in v. 34.

2. Moloney, *Gospel of Mark*, 187.

3. Michael J. Gorman, *The Death of the Messiah and the Birth of the New Covenant: A (Not So) New Model of the Atonement* (Eugene, OR: Cascade, 2014), 1–2.

4. Boring, *Mark*, 277.

with fear (*phobos*) in Mark, they are not acting in faith (4:40; 5:15, 36; 6:20, 50; 10:32; 11:18, 32; 12:12; 16:8). They have a perfect opportunity to be taught by Jesus, since they are "in the house" with him in Capernaum (v. 33). Like the man with the demon-possessed son in the previous episode, they could have confessed their lack of understanding and asked Jesus to clear up any confusion. But again, they are silent.

Their silence and failure to inquire further may be rooted in something more than simple incomprehension. Their minds are still stuck on human concerns rather than the concerns of God, as indicated by their conversation. Jesus asks what they were arguing about "on the road." The repetition of the expression "on the road/way" in vv. 33–34 highlights the shocking contrast between Jesus's mission of self-giving and the concerns of the disciples. They do not respond to Jesus's question out of shame, because "on the way" they were arguing "about who was the greatest" (v. 34).

Mark slows down the narrative flow when he introduces Jesus's teaching. They are already in his presence, but Mark dramatically describes Jesus's actions: "Sitting down, Jesus called the Twelve and said" (v. 35). The kingdom of God is counterintuitive to how the world works, a reign in which everything is turned on its head, following the character of the God who chooses the younger over the older, who triumphs through the cross, and who manifests his kingship by self-giving love. Because of that, true greatness follows the logic of this upside-down kingdom: "Anyone who wants to be first must be the very last, and the servant of all" (v. 35).

Again, Mark slows down and dramatically introduces Jesus's actions through repetition in v. 36: "He took a little child whom he placed among them. Taking the child in his arms, he said to them." Jesus "took" a child whom he placed among the disciples. The narrative is repetitive when Jesus then "takes" the child in his arms. The child does not represent innocence or trust but rather one who is socially marginalized and vulnerable. Children in the ancient world had the least social status and no legal rights.[5] They lacked social capital and could be regarded as those who "did not matter" in the eyes of the world. They stood in contrast to those with wealth or high social standing, precisely the opposite of those regarded as significant, and they were easily overlooked by those arguing over who is the greatest.

Jesus's revolutionary teaching is emphasized by the repetition of "welcome" here, which appears four times: "Whoever *welcomes* one of these little children in my name *welcomes* me; and whoever *welcomes* me does not *welcome* me but

---

5. Black, *Mark*, 215; Boring, *Mark*, 281.

the one who sent me" (v. 37). "Welcoming" a person indicates offering them hospitality, something strategically important in the ancient world, and also practiced in our day, especially in non-Western cultures. One gains in social status by opening one's home and going to great lengths to offer gracious hospitality to those with higher social status. We, like the ancients, would be very happy and eager to do this for people who are well-known or politically powerful, since doing so confers honor on us. But Jesus tells the disciples that they are to do this for those who have no social status, who cannot confer honor on them. They are to treat with great honor those who do not matter in the eyes of the world.

And they are not to do this simply out of the goodness of their hearts or out of obligation. It is their honor and privilege to do this, for when they welcome the socially insignificant and marginalized, they open their homes and offer hospitality to the greatest of all guests! When they welcome "nobodies," they welcome Jesus himself, and not only him, but God himself.

Jesus is revealing the dynamics of the kingdom of God while "on the way" to Jerusalem to give his life on the cross. This is true greatness, whereas the disciples are mired in worldly ways of thinking by arguing about who is first and who is the greatest. They have it precisely backward, for greatness in the kingdom of God is characterized by service and hospitality. Gregory of Nyssa's exhortation captures Jesus's teaching beautifully:

> Let vanity be unknown among us. Let simplicity and harmony and a guileless attitude weld the community together. Let each remind himself that he is not only subordinate to the brother at his side, but to all. If he knows this, he will truly be a disciple of Christ.[6]

LIVE the Story

Hospitality: Welcoming God

Hospitality—and specifically hospitality to the least—is supremely important to God, for it is rooted in God's very nature. Theologian Cornelius Plantinga speaks of the relationships among the Father, Son, and Holy Spirit in these terms.[7] Theologians often speak of these relationships in terms of *perichoresis*, which depicts the Trinity in terms of movement in and around. The three

---

6. Oden and Hall, *Mark*, 120.
7. Cornelius Plantinga Jr., *Engaging God's World: A Christian Vision of Faith, Learning, and Living* (Grand Rapids: Eerdmans, 2002), 20–21.

persons are not merely statically existing alongside each other but are eternally welcoming and entering one another, delighting in one another's excellencies, perfections, and wonders. The Father is always welcoming the Son and the Spirit into himself to be known, gloried in, and enjoyed, and the Son and the Spirit are always doing the same (John 1:1; 17:20–23; 1 Cor 2:10–11). This eternal community of mutual delight is always offering and enjoying hospitality.

God also delights to take up offers of hospitality from humanity. In Genesis 18:1–5, the Lord appeared to Abraham and accepted his invitation to stay with him and be refreshed. The writer of Hebrews looks back on this episode when he exhorts his audience to practice hospitality (Heb 13:2). After all, you never know whom you will be welcoming! Jesus manifests this characteristic of God when he meets two disciples on the road to Emmaus:

> As they approached the village to which they were going, Jesus continued on as if he were going farther. But they urged him strongly, "Stay with us, for it is nearly evening; the day is almost over." So he went in to stay with them. (Luke 24:28–29)

And when the exalted Jesus speaks to the church at Laodicea, he expresses his desire for their repentance and restoration in terms of hospitality: "Here I am! I stand at the door and knock. If anyone hears my voice and opens the door, I will come in and eat with that person, and they with me" (Rev 3:20).

When churches look for leaders, they seldom remember that one of the practices that ought to characterize pastors is hospitality (1 Tim 3:2). Considering how important this is for God and how it reflects his heart and his own existence, the necessity of this characteristic in leaders of God's people makes perfect sense.

As with all Christian practices, however, this is not something we merely *ought* to do. It is our privilege and high honor, for when we serve the least and roll out the welcome to the marginalized we are offering hospitality to Jesus and to God. This utterly promising prospect should change our conception of things and shape the way we speak of Christian service.

I have discovered that the reality that God dwells among his people sometimes *misshapes* Christian imagination. God does indeed inhabit the church as the new temple (1 Cor 3:16; Eph 2:21–22), and we celebrate this when we gather as his people. But it is wrong for Christians to think that we are the *possessors* or *containers* of God and that we have the prerogative to dispense his blessings to others as we see fit. From one perspective, God does indeed dwell among us. But this should not lead us to complacency. This passage in Mark's Gospel demonstrates that churches should see themselves from another perspective too. We are a people in need of God, and the way we enjoy God's presence among us is by serving those in need and welcoming the socially marginalized.

This reality has been helpful to me in setting before our church a hopeful and promising vision for participation in service. Along with other churches in our city, we participate in a program that helps homeless families get into sustainable housing. Four times each year, we welcome four to five families into our church building for a week, as they work with a local charity to find a job—if they need one—and a home. This undertaking requires the efforts of many volunteers. People stay overnight at the church, provide meals, and spend time with the families in the evening. In the weeks leading up to our hosting week, I regularly make announcements in our service, and I avoid manipulative or guilt-oriented motivational tactics. Rather than an approach that reflects the mentality of "God did this for us, so we should," or, "we have so much, so we ought to," I've taken an alternative approach shaped by Jesus's words in Mark 9. This is one of my announcements:

Good morning.

Beginning in two weeks from today, we'll be welcoming homeless families to stay in the church building for a week through the IHN program that is helping them get into sustainable housing. This is a wonderful opportunity for us to be doing the sorts of things Jesus talks about doing—the behaviors and activities that lie at the heart of the Christian faith—caring for the poor and serving the needy.

We are a church and not a government agency. So, we don't serve because we're *obligated*; this is not something we *should* do. *We get to do this.* We serve people who are in need because doing so *benefits us.* It sustains us in our Christian identity and connects us to the life of God. Jesus said: "Whoever welcomes people in need, people neglected by society, and does so in my name welcomes me; and whoever welcomes me does not welcome me but the one who sent me."

In providing hospitality for these families, then, we are experiencing the presence of God and of Jesus. There are many ways you can participate, so please see the sign-up sheets on the board out by the front desk.

CHAPTER 39

Mark 9:38-50

📖 LISTEN to the Story

³⁸"Teacher," said John, "we saw someone driving out demons in your name and we told him to stop, because he was not one of us."

³⁹"Do not stop him," Jesus said. "For no one who does a miracle in my name can in the next moment say anything bad about me, ⁴⁰for whoever is not against us is for us. ⁴¹Truly I tell you, anyone who gives you a cup of water in my name because you belong to the Messiah will certainly not lose their reward.

⁴²"If anyone causes one of these little ones—those who believe in me—to stumble, it would be better for them if a large millstone were hung around their neck and they were thrown into the sea. ⁴³If your hand causes you to stumble, cut it off. It is better for you to enter life maimed than with two hands to go into hell, where the fire never goes out. ⁴⁵And if your foot causes you to stumble, cut it off. It is better for you to enter life crippled than to have two feet and be thrown into hell. ⁴⁷And if your eye causes you to stumble, pluck it out. It is better for you to enter the kingdom of God with one eye than to have two eyes and be thrown into hell, ⁴⁸where

> "'the worms that eat them do not die,
>   and the fire is not quenched.'

⁴⁹Everyone will be salted with fire.
⁵⁰"Salt is good, but if it loses its saltiness, how can you make it salty again? Have salt among yourselves, and be at peace with each other."

Listening to the Text in the Story: Numbers 20:1–13; Joshua 7; Proverbs 6:16–19; Romans 2:11; 1 Corinthians 3:16–17.

The disciples are with Jesus in Capernaum, and he has been teaching them about service to the least and hospitality to the marginalized. Whereas Peter had objected to Jesus going to Jerusalem to suffer and die after his first prediction (8:31–33), here, after his second, John voices a misunderstanding of what it means to be a disciple, after which Jesus elaborates on how to relate to other disciples within the kingdom of God.

In v. 38 John articulates a common human error, one that Christians today may be prone to fall into, and one that occurs among God's people throughout Scripture. This is the assumption of exclusivity—the notion that *our group*, or perhaps one's denomination or theological tradition, is the one that is especially faithful to God, and the others must be brought into line. God loves us uniquely and is favorably disposed toward us—not the others—and it is our task to set others right. The apostle Paul encountered this assumption throughout his ministry, as Jewish Christians had difficulty accepting non-Jewish Christians into the family of God on equal footing. He countered this mindset with the conviction that "God does not show favoritism" (Rom 2:11). No one has an inside track with God. Since *all* have sinned—both Jews and gentiles—and *all* have been justified on the same basis, *all* people of any ethnicity or social class who are in Christ stand in God's grace, and there is no room for boasting in one's status over any other group (Rom 1:18–3:31).

Moses fell into a similar error, one that often befalls other ministers. That is the arrogant presumption, perhaps driven by ministry frustrations, that any human can stand with God over against God's people. Moses had been leading Israel and had grown frustrated with their complaining. They were in the Desert of Zin and had no water, which drove the Israelites again to complain and to quarrel with Moses (Num 20:1–5). He and Aaron sought God's counsel, and the Lord commanded them to speak to the rock so that it might pour forth water for the people and their livestock (vv. 6–8). Moses, however, made the mistake of speaking to the people out of exasperation, presumptuously identifying himself with God and chastising the people: "Listen, you rebels, must we bring you water out of this rock?" He then further disobeyed God by striking the rock rather than speaking to it, as God had commanded (vv. 10–11).

Moses paid dearly for this misjudgment. "But the LORD said to Moses and Aaron, 'Because you did not trust in me enough to honor me as holy in the sight of the Israelites, you will not bring this community into the land I give them'" (v. 12). Moses did not rightly reckon that the Lord alone is God, the one who provides for his people, reserving the right to judge or save as he sees fit. Moses's role in God's saving program was as an agent, the leader of God's people. That he set himself alongside God was an offense to God's holiness. This episode in Numbers closes by delivering the lesson: "These were the waters of Meribah, where the Israelites quarreled with the LORD and *where he was proved holy among them*" (v. 13).

John makes a similar misjudgment in this episode when he notes that the disciples have seen other people doing good in Jesus's name, and they told them to stop. After all, "he was not one of us" (Mark 9:38). Jesus delivers to the disciples a lesson about exclusivity that draws out what he had taught them in the previous episode about hospitality. The kingdom of God is bigger than they are, and they ought not to presume that they have an inside track with God or that they stand alongside God over against others who are doing good in Jesus's name.

EXPLAIN the Story

This is a continuation of the previous episode, with Jesus and the disciples in Capernaum. They are "on the way" to Jerusalem where Jesus will be delivered up to suffering and death, and he has for a second time predicted everything that will take place there. The disciples are fixed with a different mindset, however, being consumed with human concerns rather than God's priorities, and they have just been spending their time "on the way" arguing about who was the greatest among them (v. 34). After calling them to himself and placing a child among them, Jesus teaches them about what it means to be first in God's kingdom—true greatness is characterized by service and hospitality.

The Temptation to Exclusivity (v. 38)
John's statement to Jesus indicates that the disciples are still captivated by human concerns, finding it difficult to orient their hearts and minds according to the way of the Lord. He informs Jesus that they "saw someone driving out demons in your name," and that the disciples "told him to stop, because he was not one of us" (v. 38). Mark does not indicate just who these other disciples might be, and there is no way to determine their identity. It is useful, however, to focus on the effect of this episode on Mark's varied audiences. Just as the disciples must face how they relate to other groups of disciples, this account confronts communities of Jesus-followers with a warning about exclusivity and the issue of how they should relate to other churches.

In the previous episode, the disciples were consumed with being the greatest, and Jesus taught them the antidote to this, which is service and hospitality to those with no social capital. Here, a related temptation has overtaken them—the tendency to be loyal to a group rather than being open to others through service and hospitality. The irony of John's justification for telling this other person to stop is heightened in the Greek text: *hoti ouk ēkolouthei hēmin* (lit. "because he was not following us"). John, representing the sentiment of the rest of the disciples, makes the same mistake as Moses in Numbers 20, presuming that they are on Jesus's side over against another group of Jesus's followers. Further, the disciples are supposed to be *following Jesus—they are not called to have followers*. They are supposed to be following Jesus "on the way" to Jerusalem and to be "with him" (Mark 3:14), living and acting according to *his agenda*. Yet while they are physically with him, they are not listening to him and orienting their thinking according to his teaching on discipleship. They have not heeded Jesus's warning to watch out for the yeast of the Pharisees (8:15). They have fallen prey to being exclusive of others and concerned with group loyalty.

Jesus's Teaching about Intercommunity Relations (vv. 39–48)

Jesus responds to John's statement with three lessons about relating to other groups of Jesus-followers. First, in vv. 39–40, he tells them not to hinder others who are doing good in his name. John identifies the person they saw as one who was doing the very things Jesus was doing—"driving out demons" (v. 38). Jesus's mission, the same one to which he called the disciples (3:15), involved freeing God's people from satanic enslavement as the chief agent of God's renewing kingdom presence. Anyone who is doing good to God's people in the same manner as Jesus and in Jesus's name "is not against us." According to Jesus, such a one is "for us" and will not "say anything bad about me." This is clearly someone who has taken up his cross to follow Jesus, one who is not "ashamed of me and my words," and Jesus will not be ashamed of him when the Son of Man "comes in his Father's glory with the holy angels" (8:34–38). Because of this, the disciples are not to stop him but are to regard him as a partner. In the same way, Mark's audiences are to regard other communities of Jesus-followers as fellow members of God's family and fellow citizens of the kingdom of God rather than opponents or competitors.

Second, in v. 41 Jesus expands in an unexpected way on his previous teaching about hospitality. Rather than repeating his exhortation to his disciples to show hospitality to others who are doing good in his name, Jesus says that God rewards *others* who demonstrate service and hospitality *to the disciples*. Jesus had previously upended the scale of perceived social status when he had said that "anyone who wants to be first must be the very last, and the servant of all" (9:35). Here, Jesus puts the disciples in the place of outsiders who are served and welcomed with hospitality. This transforms their conception as those who have the inside track with Jesus but must confer honor on others. Intensifying the lesson that the kingdom of God levels the field of social worth, the disciples are to regard themselves as standing in need of being served and welcomed by others. God's kingdom is bigger than they are. They do not stand in the center, dispensing God's blessings as they see fit. It is their blessed privilege to serve and welcome others, and God also blesses with his presence others who serve the disciples. The lesson for Mark's audiences is to see themselves as blessed participants *along with others* in God's kingdom.

The third lesson involves taking sin seriously, and it is tempting in our contemporary context to read these words in an individualistic manner, as if Jesus is referring to personal and private sins (vv. 42–48).[1] This is not, however, his intent.[2] The severe measures in vv. 43–48 reinforce Jesus's warning in v. 42, which must be understood within the context of the temptation toward group loyalty and exclusivity. Jesus commands the disciples in vv. 36–37 to serve the least and offer hospitality to the socially marginalized. These are the precious "little ones" who are vulnerable to being wounded when groups of disciples square off in battle with one another out of group loyalty. The desire for great-ness often leads to the cultivation of a following, which must be maintained by calls for personal loyalty and group allegiance. If the disciples are caught up in this idolatrous mindset, the "little ones," like the child Jesus had set in their midst, end up being casualties.

Jesus defines "these little ones" as "those who believe in me," referring to those whom the disciples are responsible to care for through service and hospitality (v. 42). As Mark's Gospel is heard in church communities, it is a reference to any member of the body—all Christians, especially those who are vulnerable and on the margins of the community. The "stumbling" in view here refers to losing faith.[3] When powerful people build their followings and criticize other groups in order to shore up group loyalty, young Christians or those turned off by controversy and division may lose heart or grow disillu-sioned. They may turn away from the faith, losing interest in following Jesus.

---

1. Careful readers of the NIV will note that vv. 44 and 46 are omitted from the text. While they appear in the KJV, they were added later by a scribe, as they "do not appear in the earliest and best Greek manuscripts" (Strauss, *Mark*, 414).

2. These expressions for dealing seriously with sin appear in Matt 5:27–30 where Jesus warns against cultivating inward lust that leads to sexual sin. Here, however, these same expressions appear in a different context, appealing to the audience to deal seriously with sins that destroy community.

3. The Greek verb *skandalisē* ("stumble") also occurs in Mark 6:3 to refer to those in Jesus's home-town who took such offense that they rejected him and the truth he proclaimed. The related noun appears in this same sense in 1 Cor 1:23, referring to the preaching of Christ crucified, "a stumbling block [*skandalon*] to Jews." In these contexts, the stumbling in view refers to something that causes one to turn away from faith in Christ.

Jesus's warning is breathtaking. In effect he says, "If anyone causes one of these little ones to become a casualty in quests for personal glory that result in drawing boundaries to define group loyalty, it would be better for them to be killed in the most horrifying way possible than to face God's judgment." Jesus refers to a large millstone to which a donkey would be attached. As the donkey walked, the millstone would grind grain. It is a terrifying thought to die by having such a massive rock fitted around one's neck and being cast into the sea, preventing a proper burial.[4] Yet it is better to have this happen than to await the sort of judgment that will come on those who cause one of Jesus's disciples to lose faith.

As mentioned above, at first glance it appears that Jesus is warning individuals that severe measures must be taken to deal with private sin so that they avoid stumbling and "enter life" (v. 45) or "enter the kingdom of God" (v. 47). It makes better sense, however, to regard Jesus's words as directed toward communities to deal severely with elements within them that foster dynamics of sinful exclusivity and destructive group loyalty. Just like Paul's metaphor of the body of Christ that has many body parts (1 Cor 12:12–31), Jesus envisions communities as bodies that must confront those parts that cause stumbling— either causing "little ones" to lose faith or putting the community in danger of facing God's judgment.[5]

If a member of the church causes others to set themselves against other Jesus-following communities, the church must deal severely with that situation to avert judgment. That person must be confronted with the reality that they are putting "little ones" at risk and placing the community in danger. And they must be exhorted to repent and return to joyful participation in community dynamics of renewal in the form of service and hospitality. If they do not turn from their destructive path, the church must have the gospel-oriented courage to put that person out, so that the community as a whole may continue on its way toward entering the life of the kingdom of God. While it is a terribly grievous thing to expel a person from the community, it is better that they "cut off" this body part than for the community as a whole to face the judgment of God.[6]

---

4. Boring, *Mark*, 283.

5. Black, *Mark*, 218–19.

6. "Hell" (*geenna*, "Gehenna") here "refers to the place of punishment at the judgment. The term derives from the name of a valley located on the south slope of Jerusalem, the Valley of Hinnom (Josh 15:8; 18:16), where Ahaz and Manasseh followed the 'detestable practices of the nations' by burning sacrifices to Molech and even sacrificing their own sons in the fire (2 Chron 28:3; 33:6; 2 Kings 16:3). Associated with such practices as these, the Hinnom Valley came to be associated with the most horrific images of divine judgment (Jer 7:30–33; 19:1–13; 32:34–35; cf. Is 31:9; 66:24)" (J. G. Green, "Heaven and Hell," *DJG* 371).

Exhortation to Community Judgment (v. 49–50)

Jesus's final words in this section have to do with the necessity of communities to judge among themselves when it comes to intercommunity conflict. Before communities can enter the kingdom of God, they will be judged as to whether they were at peace with other Jesus-following communities. No one can escape this judgment. That is the force of the expression that "everyone will be salted with fire" (v. 49). Being communities of reconciliation and peacemaking is the fundamental character of the church, and if a community loses this orientation and its associated practices, it can no longer be called a church of Jesus Christ. This is what Jesus means by the proverbial saying in v. 50: "Salt is good, but if it loses its saltiness, how can you make it salty again?" Jesus calls his followers to the ongoing practice of community self-evaluation to determine whether they are cultivating exclusivity and group loyalty: "Have salt among yourselves." That is, look to your own community with discernment so that you are rooting out impulses and attitudes that make you posture yourselves against others. The final word to John and the disciples concerns the mindset of shutting others down who are doing Jesus's work in his name. It is the same word that he delivers to the church as they regard other Jesus-following communities: "Be at peace with each other."

LIVE the Story

Judgment and the People of God

Jesus has some pretty tough things to say about judgment in this passage, which may raise serious questions in the minds of some Christians. Are we not already justified by faith so that we have no fear of God's judgment? Paul says in Romans 8:1 that "there is now no condemnation for those who are in Christ Jesus." Then why these tough words of warning to the disciples and, by extension, to the church? Should Christians fear that if they do not deal sufficiently with sin they will be "thrown into hell?" These are serious questions that may shake the confidence of some. There is no cause for anxiety, however, though Christians ought to understand how God's judgment works in the present and the future.

For all those who are in Christ, the judgment that our sin deserves has been poured out on Jesus Christ in his death, so that we are at peace with God, forgiven, justified, and standing in the grace of God (Rom 5:1–2). When the day of Christ comes in the future—that great day of judgment and salvation—we can be confident that we will not face judgment but will be welcomed into the fullness of God's saving work (1 John 3:2; Jude 21, 24–25). We have been baptized into Christ, participating in his body, the church, the people gathered by God's Spirit and being empowered to persevere to the end. The only thing that awaits us is the full revelation of our identity as God's people and the transformation of our bodies. We will be vindicated and saved on that great day.

The present age, however, is a time of ongoing judgment, and this has relevance for God's people. The hardships and suffering that we face purify the church. This is God's refining work that prepares his people for the day of judgment. The pressures of life in their wide variety have a purifying effect in that those who are not truly God's children may depart (cf. 1 John 2:19). God uses these same struggles, however, to produce perseverance in his children. When they face trouble, they do not leave but cry out to God for mercy and grace (Rom 8:15). This is why New Testament writers exhort their audiences to respond to trouble and difficulty by being grateful for it (Jas 1:2) and by exploiting it as an opportunity to draw on God's grace that empowers us to endure (Heb 12:7; Jas 1:2–4).

It is crucial that believers respond to trouble not by retaliating against others who harm us but by pursuing reconciliation with others with whom we are in conflict or by seeking the help of the church to persevere through a painful season. The many forms of suffering we face arise naturally in the course of living in a fallen world. And we should envision these situations as God's refining judgment by which he purifies us for the day of Christ. When we respond well, God transforms trouble into fuel for perseverance. Referring to these dynamics, Peter says that the present age is the "time for judgment to begin with God's household" (1 Pet 4:17). Not that God is judging us when we suffer, but we can envision the hardships or troubles that we face as God's purifying work, whereby he works perseverance in us and prepares us for the day of Christ.

Bringing this broader discussion around to relate it to the judgment in Mark 9:38–50, the church participates in this purifying work by identifying dynamics and practices among them that are destructive of community life. That is, the church must grow in self-critical discernment to purify itself of behaviors that are divisive and dynamics that set the community in competition with other churches. When the church does so, it enjoys constant renewal by God's Spirit and prepares itself for the day of judgment and salvation. When it fails to do so, it puts itself in danger of judgment now and perhaps condemnation later. We can see this in Paul's exhortations to the Corinthians.

In 1 Corinthians 11:28–30, Paul tells the Corinthians that they are behaving in a way that is bringing God's judgment on them:

> Everyone ought to examine themselves before they eat of the bread and drink from the cup. For those who eat and drink without discerning the body of Christ eat and drink judgment on themselves. That is why many among you are weak and sick, and a number of you have fallen asleep.

The Corinthians were exploiting one another and breaking up into factions, doing damage to the body of Christ that the Spirit was working to unify (1 Cor 3:16–17). At the same time, they were eating the Lord's Supper, which was supposed to be a meal that depicted the unified church. This is why they were eating the meal "unworthily" and experiencing God's judgment. In response to this, Paul exhorted them to judge their community behaviors and seek to repent from divisive and destructive practices. They needed to "examine themselves" to identify the causes of division, in order to avoid judgment.

Paul wanted the Corinthians to understand that they were being disciplined by the Lord to bring about their repentance. And this was happening to avoid their being "finally condemned with the world" at the day of Christ (11:32).

To conclude, then, believers should not live in constant anxiety, wondering whether they will face judgment at the day of Christ. The way we keep ourselves in the love of God (Jude 21) is by serving and loving one another and cultivating practices as communities whereby we serve and love other church communities. The New Testament writers exhort the gathered church to cultivate discernment to be always on the lookout for dynamics of division within the body. When we spot these, we must have gospel courage to confront these dynamics in a way that leads toward repentance, reconciliation, and renewal. This is the ongoing "judgment" that is the work of the church, and when we participate in this we can grow in confidence that when we arrive together at the day of Christ, it will indeed be a day of great celebration.

Seeing Churches as Partners and Not Competitors

A few decades ago, I was part of a church that prided itself on careful analysis and study of Scripture and clear and compelling Bible teaching. We told ourselves that we were not like other churches that were not as faithful to Scripture, filling their preaching with anecdotes and stories rather than lengthy biblical exposition. This self-understanding as a community that was uniquely faithful to God and Scripture led us to have a critical and condescending posture toward other churches. Looking back on my time at that church,

I am grateful for many things I learned about Scripture and ministry, but I am also grieved that many of our attitudes were divisive, opposing what God was working to produce by his Spirit in his citywide and worldwide family.

Our church had a large college ministry and had groups that met at various Los Angeles colleges and universities. I was part of a campus ministry at one school, where once a year the various Christian campus ministries got together for a special celebration of our shared Christian identity. While our group was invited, we refused to participate because we envisioned those groups as failing to uphold sound doctrine and the ministry model that flowed clearly from Scripture. I now see that our attitude and behavior were the very ones that Jesus condemns in this passage.

The church that I currently am part of models the sort of partnership with other churches that Jesus speaks about. We partner with churches of other denominations in our city to serve and welcome homeless families as they seek to get into sustainable housing. We meet regularly with these churches in an effort that is coordinated by Family Promise/Inter-Faith Hospitality Network, a local charity, and we share ideas of how to serve effectively and faithfully.[7] This effort has had a wonderful effect on our church, strengthening bonds of friendship and partnership among ourselves as we work together. It has also developed in our church a posture of mutuality toward other fellowships. We have had to communicate and coordinate with them to solve problems and meet challenges together. This fosters an attitude of mutual respect and care. Rather than focusing on what divides us, we see ourselves as united in a common effort to discover God's grace together as we join in the very practices that Jesus talks about in Mark 9:30–50—service and hospitality.

---

7. Information about Family Promise can be found at their website: www.familypromisegr.org/home.

LISTEN to the Story

¹Jesus then left that place and went into the region of Judea and across the Jordan. Again crowds of people came to him, and as was his custom, he taught them.

²Some Pharisees came and tested him by asking, "Is it lawful for a man to divorce his wife?"

³"What did Moses command you?" he replied.

⁴They said, "Moses permitted a man to write a certificate of divorce and send her away."

⁵"It was because your hearts were hard that Moses wrote you this law," Jesus replied. ⁶"But at the beginning of creation God 'made them male and female.' ⁷'For this reason a man will leave his father and mother and be united to his wife, ⁸and the two will become one flesh.' So they are no longer two, but one flesh. ⁹Therefore what God has joined together, let no one separate."

¹⁰When they were in the house again, the disciples asked Jesus about this. ¹¹He answered, "Anyone who divorces his wife and marries another woman commits adultery against her. ¹²And if she divorces her husband and marries another man, she commits adultery."

Listening to the Text in the Story: Genesis 1:27; 2:24; Exodus 21:10–11; Deuteronomy 24:1–4; Malachi 2:13–17; 1 Corinthians 6:16; Ephesians 5:22–33; 1 Peter 3:7.

Jesus and his disciples have left Capernaum on their way to Jerusalem and have gone into the region of Judea and across the Jordan. This passage appears in the second of three prediction cycles, in which Jesus teaches about discipleship. This is important to keep in mind, because this larger context determines what Jesus says about marriage and divorce. He is not laying down generalized rules that can be applied easily to any situation. His purpose is more specific: he is teaching about how disciples orient their lives in the kingdom of God. They seek God's heart in Scripture and direct their lives toward service and care for others rather than living for themselves and satisfying their own desires.

God's intentions for marriage are clearly set out in the creation account, according to Jesus, who cites Genesis 1:27 and 2:24. In the former passage, the image of God is corporate and communal—together, male and female are the image of God. And in Genesis 2:24, the woman is created from the man, and they are made for each other. Jesus explains that this is why "a man will leave his father and mother and be united to his wife, and the two will become one flesh" (Mark 10:7–8). God's design of a union of two that are made one is for the propagation of humanity throughout the earth, but the union also serves the flourishing of community life and provides for the protection of the most vulnerable.

This is seen in several passages. In Exodus 21:10–11, God commands husbands to protect and provide for their wives, even if they marry a second wife.[1] In Malachi 2:13–17 God says he is coming in judgment because of the unfaithfulness of men toward their wives, whom they should be protecting (v. 16). In the ancient world, women were socially vulnerable, and men were in positions of power. Because God is on the side of the weak and vulnerable, husbands would imitate the character of God by protecting and caring for their wives as those who lived with a "weaker partner" (1 Pet 3:7). That phrase is not to diminish the capacities of women in any way, but simply reflects the first-century social arrangements in which men were dominant. In that social context, Paul's exhortations to husbands to love their wives as Christ loves the church are radical (Eph 5:22–33; Col 3:19).

Because of their position of social advantage and leverage, men could divorce their wives for any reason. According to David Instone-Brewer, in the first-century Jewish culture the specifics of Exodus 21:10–11 were debated, and while both men and women could theoretically get a divorce, women were at a disadvantage and had to ask a court to compel their husbands to divorce them. Based on Moses's teaching in Deuteronomy 24:1, the dominant Jewish understanding was that the grounds "for divorce in this passage could only be used by men."[2] This is the broader biblical and social setting within which Jesus's teaching on marriage and divorce appears.

---

1. Polygamy was common in the ancient world and found among many significant figures in the Old Testament, including Abraham, Jacob, and Moses. The Mosaic law did not forbid polygamy, but it called for husbands to treat each of their wives with equity and fairness.

2. D. Instone-Brewer, "Divorce," *DJG* 213.

The context for this passage, therefore, is one in which God's heart is for the vulnerable, and his intentions are for the protection of women and children. Participants in a marriage manifest God's character by faithfulness to one another. Many in the first century—exclusively men—who were engaged in debates about marriage and divorce were seeking to use Scripture to endorse their selfish desires. But this is not the way that disciples of Jesus inhabit the kingdom of God.

EXPLAIN the Story

Leaving Capernaum, Jesus and his disciples traveled through Judea and across the Jordan. Just as throughout Mark's Gospel, crowds thronged to Jesus, and "he taught them" (v. 1). As is typical in his narrative, Mark does not mention what Jesus taught them, as he is more interested in portraying Jesus as the authoritative teacher rather than describing the content of his teaching.[3] The Pharisees also came to Jesus, but their intention is more sinister—they are "testing" (*peirazō*) him in order to trap him by his answer (v. 2). It is significant that this episode takes place across the Jordan, the territory over which Herod Antipas ruled. The Pharisees may be trying to trap Jesus into a situation where he speaks out against Herod. This would put a target on his back and perhaps create a situation where he is killed, just as John the Baptist was arrested and later executed for calling out Herod's inappropriate relationship with his brother's wife (6:18).[4] The same verb (*peirazō*) is used in Mark 1:13 of Satan's testing of Jesus in the wilderness and of the Pharisees in 8:11. They have aligned themselves with Satan, opposed to Jesus's work. After all, they have already decided to plot with the Herodians to kill him (3:6).

Jesus responds by asking them what Moses has commanded them (v. 3). He is inviting them to think through Scripture and to reflect on the heart of God and God's intentions for marriage. The Pharisees could have recalled Exodus 21:10–11, in which God commanded men to provide protection for their first wife if they took a second one. They could also have drawn upon any passage that articulated how Scripture reflects God's intentions of caring for and providing for the socially vulnerable. Since Moses was regarded as having written the first five books of the Bible, any text in that corpus of Scripture that articulated a positive conception of marriage was available to them.

---

3. Boring, *Mark*, 286.
4. Strauss, *Mark*, 423.

They responded, however, by pointing to Deuteronomy 24:1–4, in which Moses refers to a man who divorces his wife, writing her a certificate of divorce and sending her away:

> If a man marries a woman who becomes displeasing to him because he finds something indecent about her, and he writes her a certificate of divorce, gives it to her and sends her from his house, and if after she leaves his house she becomes the wife of another man, and her second husband dislikes her and writes her a certificate of divorce, gives it to her and sends her from his house, or if he dies, then her first husband, who divorced her, is not allowed to marry her again after she has been defiled. That would be detestable in the eyes of the LORD. Do not bring sin upon the land the LORD your God is giving you as an inheritance.

In this text, Moses is not concerned with God's purpose in marriage, nor is he giving instructions about divorce. He is speaking about an exceptional situation in which two partners in an original marriage divorce and marry other people.[5] After that subsequent marriage, Moses forbids the two partners to remarry each other if they divorce again. Moses's prohibition in v. 4 is the focus of this passage, and the contingencies of an original breakup mentioned in vv. 1–3 are mentioned only by way of setting up the situation. That is, Moses's instruction about writing a certificate is not a command but rather a concession to the sort of sinful practices the Israelites had fallen into.

The Pharisees' choice of this specific biblical text therefore indicates their strategy of using Scripture against Scripture, just as Jesus accused them of doing in Mark 7:8–13.[6] They were setting aside Scripture's revelation of the heart of God in favor of a human tradition derived from a purposeful misreading of Scripture. They have isolated a detail in one passage and are giving that text greater weight than Scripture's clear voice regarding marriage. The result is their rejection of God's intention (Gen 2:24), based on their twisting of Scripture, so that it endorses their privilege of power over others and their selfish choices.[7] The motivation for their preferred way of reading Deuteronomy 24:1–4 is determined by their desires.

---

5. Hooker, *Mark*, 236.

6. Moloney, *Gospel of Mark*, 194–95.

7. In the first century, Pharisees debated the significance of Deut 24:1–4 for divorce. They generally agreed that this passage mandated the writing of a divorce certificate and that only men could justify a divorce based on this text. Further, "something indecent about her" (v. 1) was commonly understood to refer to adultery. The Pharisees also debated the meaning of the phrase translated in the NIV as "something indecent" (Heb. *erwat dabar*, "a cause of indecency," v. 1). The school of Hillel

Jesus responds by pointing to the proper thrust of Deuteronomy 24 and indicating the attitudes that disciples should have regarding God's intentions for marriage. Moses's instruction in Deuteronomy was not meant to be used as a lens through which God's people viewed marriage. Rather, writing a certificate was a concession given in the tragic case of divorce, and it was designed to protect a woman who would be in a disadvantaged and vulnerable position.[8] Jesus identifies the Pharisees with the rebellious Israelites in Moses's day when he says that "it was because your hearts were hard that Moses wrote you this law" (v. 5). The theme of hardness of heart in Mark, as in the rest of Scripture, has to do with stubborn unresponsiveness to God, a condition that indicates satanic enslavement.

God's intention from creation was for man and woman to image God together, representing the faithful and loving creator on earth by joining together to enjoy God's reign and to oversee the spread of God's order of flourishing (citing Gen 1:27 in Mark 10:6). In Genesis 2:24, God intended for a man and woman to come together to form a union: "So they are no longer two, but one flesh" (Mark 10:8). Jesus captures God's heart for marriage by concluding that "what God has joined together, let no one separate" (v. 9).[9]

After this public discussion, the disciples have a conversation with Jesus "in the house," a location in Mark's Gospel in which Jesus often gives private instruction to his disciples (7:17; 9:28, 33). This is an instance of the disciples behaving commendably. Previously, they were too afraid to ask Jesus either to clarify or expand on what he had said—an inappropriate response (9:33–34). Here, however, they "asked Jesus about this" (v. 10). Jesus states that if a man divorces his wife and marries another woman, he commits adultery against his original wife (v. 11). And a woman who divorces her husband and marries another man, she likewise commits adultery against her original husband (v. 12).

Jesus gives no conditions for divorce here, but simply states that divorce and remarriage lead to a condition in which the departing partner of an original

---

argued that the phrase contains two conditions for divorce. A man could divorce his wife (1) for adultery (*erwah*, "indecency"), and (2) for any other reason, understanding "a cause" (*dabar*) as "any cause." That is, the school of Hillel split the phrase (*erwat dabar*) in order to create a wide range of possibilities for men to divorce their wives. The school of Shammai, on the other hand, limited the cause of divorce to adultery alone, understanding the two terms together (*erwat dabar*) to refer to the singular condition, i.e., "a cause of indecency" refers to adultery (Instone-Brewer, "Divorce," *DJG* 213).

8. A woman with a certificate of divorce would be regarded as single and available for marriage.

9. The Greek expression *anthrōpos mē chōrizetō* may literally be translated as "let no man separate" and has specific force in the first-century Jewish culture, in which men had the social advantage and thus the prerogative of divorce. The NIV translation ("let no one separate") is appropriate, however, since in many contemporary contexts both women and men may pursue a divorce.

union commits adultery when they form a new one. It is important to keep in mind the larger context of Mark to understand what Scripture teaches about divorce and remarriage. Jesus is not laying down a singular rule that governs any and every situation. He is speaking, rather, to the orientation of the heart of those who are his disciples. Rather than using scriptural concessions to endorse selfish desires to get rid of a spouse and pursue a relationship with someone else, disciples reflect God's faithfulness by pursuing fidelity to their spouse. This is the way of life for members of God's kingdom. Jesus is here standing in the prophetic tradition of Malachi by identifying the corrupted motives of those who selfishly pursue divorce (Mal 2:13–17).[10]

Those who take up their cross and follow Jesus on the road to Jerusalem do not cultivate corrupted motives. They resist the appeal of walking away from a marriage in order to pursue other opportunities. Jesus does not address exceptional situations, such as when a spouse is abusive, neglectful, or abandons a marriage. Mark does not present Jesus as legislator but as the one who calls for disciples to pursue faithfulness rather than selfishness. This is the overall thrust of Moses's commands about marriage in Scripture.

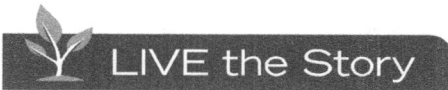

LIVE the Story

Discipleship, Marriage, and Divorce

Mark sets this discussion of marriage and divorce within a larger frame of discipleship. This is a properly Christian and fruitful lens through which to look at marriage, especially when we consider the many factors at work in our lives, including the wider culture and how it shapes us. On the one hand, we have to contend with our selfish orientation and the individualistic ideologies that foster an attitude of looking out for ourselves at the expense of others. On the other, our culture promotes many romantic notions that leave us with unrealistic conceptions of marriage. What wisdom can we gain from the wider witness of Scripture regarding the heart of God for marriage, and how might we think faithfully about the realities of divorce?

Disciples of Jesus Christ are those who are attentive to the heart of God. They view marriage as permanent and cultivate faithfulness to their partner in fulfillment of their wedding vows. They do not think about abandoning their partner or escaping their covenantal commitment. This is the priority that Jesus reflects in this passage in Mark. He is addressing the impulse among

---

10. Boring, *Mark*, 288.

men to look for a way out of their marriages at the expense of the physical, social, and emotional hardship of their vulnerable wives and children. Jesus states plainly that faithful disciples do not look for legal loopholes. Moreover, disciples must take account of an avenging God who takes up the cause of the vulnerable (Deut 10:18; Ps 82:3). Marriages shaped by fidelity reflect God's faithfulness and establish family units that bless others.

Inevitably, various external and internal forces put tremendous stress on marriages, driving wedges between marital partners. In those situations, disciples of Jesus Christ strive for fidelity and draw on God's grace to endure the crucible that marriage inevitably becomes. Disciples serve one another and sacrifice their own desires for the sake of the other person and for the flourishing of their covenantal relationship.

Christians conceive of marriage, along with everything else, through the lens of the cross, for they are shaped by the cross and seek to have their entire lives thoroughly oriented by the cross. According to Paul, "We always carry around in our body the death of Jesus, so that the life of Jesus may also be revealed in our body" (2 Cor 4:10). This points to the death-life paradox that lies at the heart of the gospel. Just as God poured out resurrection life on Jesus as he went to the cross, God pours out resurrection power wherever there are cross-shaped lives. When spouses adopt cross-shaped postures toward each other through service, sacrifice, and support, they enjoy together the life of God in their relationship. When they cultivate cruciform attitudes toward each other and speak cross-oriented words to each other, God floods their marriage with resurrection life.

When husbands pursue patterns of love and service, refusing to exploit social advantages for their own gain and holding lightly to their personal agendas (career, hobbies, friends) in order to foster the flourishing of their wives, they enjoy divine empowerment and participate in God's own joy. And when they keep watch over their sinful and selfish internal impulses, attitudes, and behavior and choose to envision ways that these must be nailed to the cross, they enjoy the empowering presence of God in ever greater ways. Disciples are those who follow Jesus on the way to the cross, having already taken up their crosses (Mark 8:34). Therefore, the fundamental impulse from which I operate must not be "what I want" or "what I deserve" or "I'm not going to put up with this." Disciples' lives are marked by the cross; my expectations, dreams, fantasies, romantic visions, and plans for what I want my marriage to be—these must be nailed to the cross in order for us to see what our lives and marriages can be when they unfold within God's life-giving kingdom.

Unfortunately, many churches in the modern West, especially North

America, have not helped couples think realistically and soberly about disciple-oriented marriage. We have fallen prey to post-Victorian romantic notions, along with conceptions of weddings and marriages shaped by the modern wedding industry. We tend to focus on helping people "find the right one" rather than on helping spouses navigate the crucible of marriage in a culture that fosters selfishness and unfaithfulness. Marriage is not the climax of a romantic story but rather the beginning of a journey of two individuals getting to know themselves and each other. As those who have been married for decades can attest, spouses know the least about each other on their wedding day. A marriage is the unfolding process of strangers exploring and discovering the one they married.

In God's design, the church is the safe haven within which this delicate and complex process of exploration can take place. Unfortunately, many churches have fallen prey to the idolatry of the nuclear family, focusing on families within the church rather than *the family that is the church*. In the New Testament, the church is not composed of families, but rather *is* a family. Disciples who are a nuclear family unit are part of the larger family of the church and should be able to draw on that family's nurture, love, support, and counsel. They should not feel pressure to be a perfect family in public, hiding any cracks, faults, or failings. They should be welcomed within a context of freedom to take the time and have the space to figure things out.

Unfortunately, marriages fall apart for a variety of reasons. Church leaders would do well to understand the heart and mind of God in Scripture for the protection of the socially vulnerable—almost always women—when this happens.[11] Churches can actualize their cross-shaped identities by setting aside other agendas and being safe havens for spouses who are trying to figure out their relationship. As a singular family (the theological reality) made up of nuclear family units (a modern invention), the church cannot put pressure on spouses and demand that they work things out, getting their act together before they can rejoin the fellowship. The church ought to be the safest and most fruitful place within which to work through relational confusion and difficulty.

If breakdown continues, churches should be alert to ways they can look after spouses who have been mistreated, neglected, or abandoned. Church leaders ought to be aware of the grave danger of offending a holy and righteous

---

11. Two great starting points are David Instone-Brewer, *Divorce and Remarriage in the Bible: The Social and Literary Context* (Grand Rapids: Eerdmans, 2002) and Richard B. Hays, *The Moral Vision of the New Testament: A Contemporary Introduction to New Testament Ethics* (New York: HarperCollins, 1996), 347–78.

God, whose wrath is stirred up when the vulnerable are mistreated among the people who call on one who judges impartially (1 Pet 1:17).

In situations of divorce, Scripture provides robust counsel for navigating redemptive pathways forward among God's people. Within the new-creation reality of God's kingdom, where God's life-giving Spirit dwells with resurrection power, there is always hope for renewal and joy. There are no dead ends for disciples. Those who have experienced divorce—both for those who have been wronged and those who have done wrong—can find hope and healing. No one is beyond the scope of God's renewing and redeeming work.

Mark 10:13-16

📖 LISTEN to the Story

¹³People were bringing little children to Jesus for him to place his hands on them, but the disciples rebuked them. ¹⁴When Jesus saw this, he was indignant. He said to them, "Let the little children come to me, and do not hinder them, for the kingdom of God belongs to such as these. ¹⁵Truly I tell you, anyone who will not receive the kingdom of God like a little child will never enter it." ¹⁶And he took the children in his arms, placed his hands on them and blessed them.

Listening to the Text in the Story: Exodus 22:21; Deuteronomy 10:12–22; John 3:1–21; Acts 10:1–11:18; Romans 3:21–24; Galatians 2:15–21; James 2:1–13; Revelation 7:9.

On the road to Jerusalem, Jesus is teaching his disciples about the character and identity—the orientation of life and self-understanding—of those who inhabit God's kingdom. According to Jesus, disciples welcome and provide hospitality to the socially marginalized and serve the needy (Mark 9:35–37). For in the kingdom of God, all markers of identity that have their origin in cultural systems of value are obliterated. God's people are servants of all, inhabiting God's reign in which the first are last and the last are first. All are loved by God, and all are welcomed gladly without any reference to gender, ethnicity, national origin, or social class. Jesus has also issued harsh warnings about exclusivity—that temptation to presume that any group has an inside track with God, having unique access to the exclusion of others (9:36–50).

These dynamics figure prominently throughout Scripture. God commanded Israel to treat foreigners who resided among them with justice and love, since they themselves were foreigners in Egypt (Exod 22:21; Deut 10:12–22). God had delivered Israel powerfully and had brought them into a land of plenty, where they were to live with generosity:

Circumcise your hearts, therefore, and do not be stiff-necked any longer. For the LORD your God is God of gods and Lord of lords, the great God, mighty and awesome, who shows no partiality and accepts no bribes. He defends the cause of the fatherless and the widow, and loves the foreigner residing among you, giving them food and clothing. And you are to love those who are foreigners, for you yourselves were foreigners in Egypt. Fear the LORD your God and serve him. Hold fast to him and take your oaths in his name. (Deut 10:16–20)

The generosity of God's people is founded on God's identity and the identity of Israel. God is impartial, so no one can escape his judgment if they treat foreigners with injustice or neglect the poor. God reigns over all creation, not merely Israel, so he loves everyone and wants all people to enjoy his gracious reign of goodness and plenty. And Israel's identity is a people who were once foreigners and who have been treated with great magnanimity. They were a slave people who were liberated and situated in a land of plenty, so they must now live generously.

The temptation to hoard God's blessing and to exclude others based on ethnicity or socioeconomic status is constant and remained a struggle in the early church. The first generation of Jesus's followers were all Jewish, and they struggled to understand how God's salvation could reach to non-Jews. Peter saw this clearly after God spoke to him in a vision and sent him to Caesarea:

Then Peter began to speak: "I now realize how true it is that God does not show favoritism but accepts from every nation the one who fears him and does what is right. You know the message God sent to the people of Israel, announcing the good news of peace through Jesus Christ, who is Lord of all." (Acts 10:34–36)

James also draws on God's identity and the identity of God's people in order to rebuke his audiences for ordering themselves according to corrupted social values. If they gather together and give rich people a prominent seat, while telling the poor to sit in the back, they have "become judges with evil thoughts" (Jas 2:4). Showing deference to the wealthy or to anyone with an exalted social status is an offence to God just as much as murder or adultery is an offence (vv. 8–11). God draws people into his kingdom without any reference to their worldly status. He has "chosen those who are poor in the eyes of the world to be rich in faith and to inherit the kingdom he promised those who love him" (v. 5). The paradoxically liberating identity of God's people, therefore, is as those who deserve nothing but who have been given everything. Owning this identity puts us in a place where we live with open hands, serving and welcoming anyone and everyone.

EXPLAIN the Story

While Jesus and the disciples were still in the house on the other side of the Jordan River, unnamed people were bringing little children to him "for him to place his hands on them" (v. 13). As is typical of Jesus in this Gospel, Mark emphasizes Jesus's touch (1:41; 6:56; 7:33). This brief episode opens and closes with Jesus placing his hands on these small children (vv. 13, 16). In fact, Mark portrays this emphatically by repeating his actions, with Jesus taking the children in his arms, placing his hands on them, and blessing them. Jesus pays great attention and gives affection to people that his disciples consider not worthy of his time.

The disciples respond by attempting to prevent these people from bringing their children to Jesus, showing again that they have not learned from him. Just previously, in 9:36–37, Jesus took a child in his arms and taught them to welcome little children. Further, he warned them harshly about being exclusive of others of his followers in 9:38–50. They are behaving like the Pharisees, who were passing judgment on Jesus for spending time with tax collectors and sinners (2:15–17).

At this, Jesus is indignant, a strong emotional response at this violation of kingdom dynamics (v. 14). His exhortation to the disciples is just as forceful, and he repeats it positively and negatively for emphasis. The NIV might be read in a passive and gentle manner: "Let the little children come to me." But his response contains two imperative verbs that amounts to a harsh rebuke: "Allow [*aphete*] the children to come to me, and stop preventing [*mē kōlyete*] them!"[1] Far from being unwelcome, children are precisely the sort of people who are central to the kingdom of God. Everyone has access to Jesus, since belonging to the kingdom does not depend on social status or any other culturally constructed evaluation.

Jesus presses even further, building on the common cultural assumption that children had no social status or leverage. Jesus says that in order to enter into the kingdom, one must receive it like one who has no leverage, no rank,

---

1. The negative (*mē*) with a present-tense imperative verb (*kōlyete*) may be translated as "stop preventing" rather than merely "do not prevent," since it is a present, ongoing action that Jesus is calling the disciples to cease.

and no social capital. One must own the reality that in the kingdom, socially constructed valuations of people are obliterated. This is, of course, offensive to people who associate their value with their socially constructed identity, their standing in the community, and what they have accomplished. This is not a call for self-abasement but for disciples to regard themselves as loved by God alongside others who are loved by God, the servant king who gives himself for the life of others. This position of "loved along with others loved by God" is depicted in v. 16, as Jesus gathers up the children in his arms and blesses them. Far from preventing children from coming to Jesus, the disciples should be celebrating Jesus's blessing of them, seeing the children as ones to emulate.

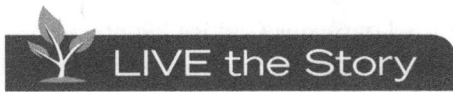

LIVE the Story

Hospitality and Care for the Least among Us

In his sober assessment, historian John Fea describes how American evangelicals are a subculture oriented by fear, nostalgia, and a search for political power.[2] This fear on the part of white evangelicals has historically been directed toward Native Americans, black people before and after the Civil War, and immigrants. By "nostalgia," Fea has in mind a yearning for an idealized past that never really existed. And the political power he describes is the quest for access to people of influence through the American political process. These social habits of heart and mind have produced an evangelical culture of resentment toward outsiders.

These attitudes and habits are a grave threat if we consider the hospitable practices Jesus commands his disciples to cultivate. Genuine hospitality does not have to do with welcoming those like us, but with providing a warm welcome to those who are unlike us—the social, ethnic, national, and racial other.[3] For white American evangelicals, this demands that we cultivate the habits of heart and mind that see fear, nostalgia, and quests for power as fatal, for they prevent us from being and becoming the sort of church Jesus calls us to be. If we are not communities that are advocates for and warmly welcome immigrants and the poor, we must confess that we are not interested in being the church as Jesus commanded us to be. We must consider whether we understand ourselves as "others" in relation to God, those who have been the recipients of outrageously gracious hospitality.

---

2. John Fea, *Believe Me: The Evangelical Road to Donald Trump* (Grand Rapids: Eerdmans, 2018).
3. Joshua W. Jipp, *Saved by Faith and Hospitality* (Grand Rapids: Eerdmans, 2017).

This is the very dynamic on display in Deuteronomy 10. In speaking to the church in Mark 10, Jesus represents the heart of God summarized in this passage:

> And now, Israel, what does the LORD your God ask of you but to fear the LORD your God, to walk in obedience to him, to love him, to serve the LORD your God with all your heart and with all your soul, and to observe the LORD's commands and decrees that I am giving you today for your own good?
>
> To the LORD your God belong the heavens, even the highest heavens, the earth and everything in it. Yet the LORD set his affection on your ancestors and loved them, and he chose you, their descendants, above all the nations—as it is today. Circumcise your hearts, therefore, and do not be stiff-necked any longer. For the LORD your God is God of gods and Lord of lords, the great God, mighty and awesome, who shows no partiality and accepts no bribes. He defends the cause of the fatherless and the widow, and loves the foreigner residing among you, giving them food and clothing. And you are to love those who are foreigners, for you yourselves were foreigners in Egypt. Fear the LORD your God and serve him. Hold fast to him and take your oaths in his name. He is the one you praise; he is your God, who performed for you those great and awesome wonders you saw with your own eyes. Your ancestors who went down into Egypt were seventy in all, and now the LORD your God has made you as numerous as the stars in the sky. (Deut 10:12–22)

I noted above that the cultivation of certain habits of heart and mind is a grave threat and fatal to being the church because God's words are so severe to Israel. The heart of God has not changed:

> Do not mistreat or oppress a foreigner, for you were foreigners in Egypt.
>
> Do not take advantage of the widow or the fatherless. If you do and they cry out to me, I will certainly hear their cry. My anger will be aroused, and I will kill you with the sword; your wives will become widows and your children fatherless. (Exod 22:21–24)

Caring for the vulnerable through hospitality and service are practices that lie near and dear to the heart of God. God sought out and redeemed a helpless and vulnerable people when he rescued Israel from Egypt. He delights to care for the vulnerable and those in desperate need. To be faithful to God involves cultivating the habits of heart and mind that make us hospitable communities for those in need.

There are many steps we can take to participate with God in shaping us into these kinds of communities. First, we can assess the ideologies that keep us from doing the things that Jesus talks about doing. I have noticed that when I talk about God's heart for immigrants, the homeless, the poor, and other marginalized populations, some middle-class white Christians routinely bring up more or less the same objections, and they draw on certain ideologies that do not come from Scripture. Notions of individual responsibility, the importance of national laws, and the need for border security seem to dominate our imaginations. When I hear sentiments driven by these values from Christians, I often wonder how such protestations will fly on the day of judgment when we have to answer for why we did not care for the marginalized as God has commanded his people to do.

White evangelical Christians believe it is possible to work to change national laws and public policy, especially when they feel that their interests are at stake. Some of us seem to forget this, however, when it comes to looking out for immigrants and refugees. Yet the prophets are filled with rebukes and condemnations of God's people for failing to look out for those in need. We will search in vain for passages excusing God's people for neglecting the poor because of the latter's bad choices and failure to keep a steady job. We ought to consider it a nonnegotiable that we care for marginalized populations among us.

Second, we can assess the sources of the fear, suspicion, and anxiety we feel when we think about marginalized populations, such as immigrants and refugees. Media outlets and cable news channels make their money by stoking the fears, anger, and in some cases, the resentment of their viewers. There is very little that is as addictive as fear, anger, and resentment, and cable channels posing as "news" sow this fear in their viewers to keep them glued to their sets, thus bringing in millions of dollars in advertising revenue. Christians must ask themselves if they are being duped by this money-making enterprise into being filled with resentment toward foreigners and others who are in need.

Third, many churches will feel helpless and overwhelmed at the possibilities and complications when it comes to serving marginalized people, such as immigrants and refugees. But there are many opportunities for local action and agencies that would welcome a group from a church to participate in efforts to relocate refugees and to help immigrants integrate into the life of the new communities to which they've arrived. In our town, Bethany Christian Services can link churches to people in need.[4] It takes little more than a few internet searches to find a few agencies that can facilitate such service, but it requires a vision of the genuine identity and mission of God's people to take the initiative and sustain the effort.

---

4. www.bethany.org.

CHAPTER 42

Mark 10:17–31

📖 LISTEN to the Story

17As Jesus started on his way, a man ran up to him and fell on his knees before him. "Good teacher," he asked, "what must I do to inherit eternal life?"

18"Why do you call me good?" Jesus answered. "No one is good— except God alone. 19You know the commandments: 'You shall not murder, you shall not commit adultery, you shall not steal, you shall not give false testimony, you shall not defraud, honor your father and mother.'"

20"Teacher," he declared, "all these I have kept since I was a boy."

21Jesus looked at him and loved him. "One thing you lack," he said. "Go, sell everything you have and give to the poor, and you will have treasure in heaven. Then come, follow me."

22At this the man's face fell. He went away sad, because he had great wealth.

23Jesus looked around and said to his disciples, "How hard it is for the rich to enter the kingdom of God!"

24The disciples were amazed at his words. But Jesus said again, "Children, how hard it is to enter the kingdom of God! 25It is easier for a camel to go through the eye of a needle than for someone who is rich to enter the kingdom of God."

26The disciples were even more amazed, and said to each other, "Who then can be saved?"

27Jesus looked at them and said, "With man this is impossible, but not with God; all things are possible with God."

28Then Peter spoke up, "We have left everything to follow you!"

29"Truly I tell you," Jesus replied, "no one who has left home or brothers or sisters or mother or father or children or fields for me and the gospel 30will fail to receive a hundred times as much in this present age: homes, brothers, sisters, mothers, children and fields—along with persecutions—and in the age to come eternal life. [31]But many who are first will be last, and the last first."

Listening to the Text in the Story: Deuteronomy 8:10–18; Psalm 49; Proverbs 8:18–21; 11:4, 25, 28; 19:17; 23:5; Jeremiah 9:23–24; Luke 16:19–31; 1 Timothy 6:6–10, 17–19; James 2:1–13; 5:1–6.

This conversation between Jesus and the man who ran up to him concludes the second of three cycles, in which Jesus predicts his death in Jerusalem, the disciples respond poorly, and Jesus teaches about discipleship. The final cycle begins with Jesus's third prediction in 10:32–34, and the entire section concludes with Jesus's giving sight to Bartimaeus in Jericho (10:46–52). Jesus had just rebuked the disciples for preventing little children coming to him so that he could bless them. The kingdom belongs "to such as these," said Jesus, indicating that those who inhabit the kingdom are those with no social status and little social leverage. He continued with the bold statement that "anyone who will not receive the kingdom of God like a little child will never enter it" (v. 15). The present passage relates directly to what precedes, for here we have a man with great wealth desiring to inherit eternal life.

Wealth is a complex reality throughout Scripture. It can be a sign of God's blessing. After all, in Deuteronomy 28:1–14 God promised abundant blessing for Israel if they kept the covenant and obeyed him. It then seems fairly straightforward to draw a line from the reality of one's material wealth to their godliness. Proverbs 10:22 seems to endorse this perspective: "The blessing of the LORD brings wealth, without painful toil for it." On the other hand, the book of Job is written to counteract this misapplication of the covenant blessings and curses to all of life. That is, it may seem like a kind of wisdom, in light of Deuteronomy 28, to identify a person with wealth as someone blessed by God and someone who is poor or who has various hardships as a person who is disobedient and in need of repentance. After counseling Job "biblically," Job's friends hear from God some pretty terrifying news about their supposedly wise counsel: "I am angry with you [Eliphaz] and your two friends, because you have not spoken the truth about me" (Job 42:7).

Further, Proverbs has much to say about the meaninglessness of wealth and how it can vanish in an instant (e.g., Prov 23:5). A person might be rich through unjust means and then use his status of social leverage to exploit and oppress the poor (22:16). A number of New Testament passages speak to these socially unjust arrangements, such as when the apostles harshly rebuke churches that have fallen into the practice of favoring the rich (1 Cor 11:17–34; Jas 2:1–13).

Scripture warns against the temptation to trust in riches to secure good outcomes rather than depending on God and looking to him for security. A closely related dynamic is the temptation for the rich to imagine that their wealth is their identity. Jeremiah issues this warning:

This is what the LORD says:

> "Let not the wise boast of their wisdom
>   or the strong boast of their strength
>   or the rich boast of their riches,
> but let the one who boasts boast about this:
>   that they have the understanding to know me,
> that I am the LORD, who exercises kindness,
>   justice and righteousness on earth,
>   for in these I delight,"
>   declares the LORD. (Jer 9:23–24)

"Boasting" involves a claim to significance and reveals how one sees their own identity and value. Riches and strength are realities of this world and are temporary and unreliable. The one who has her identity wrapped up in wealth will be devastated when it is gone. And none of these fading realities are of any relevance when it comes to their relationship to God and his kingdom.

EXPLAIN the Story

In the preceding episode, Jesus had explained that the kingdom of God belongs to children—that is, to those who have no social status—and that the kingdom must be received by people who hold on to nothing else than God for meaning and identity. The larger context for this passage is Jesus's teaching about discipleship, as he makes his way to Jerusalem for his climactic confrontation with the Jewish authorities. There he will be "delivered into the hands of men. They will kill him, and after three days he will rise" (9:31). After stopping in a house (10:10–16), Jesus is now again "on the way" (*hodos*, "way," "road") to Jerusalem (v. 17).

Jesus's Conversation with the Rich Man (vv. 17–22)

As Jesus makes his way, a man runs up to him and approaches him in much the same honorable way as did other positive characters in Mark: he "fell on his knees before him" (v. 17; cf. 5:1–6, 22, 33; 7:25). He addresses Jesus as "good teacher" before asking what he must do to inherit eternal life. Some might regard the man as being more interested in "doing" as opposed to "believing," but we should not imagine that he is caught up in a sort of legalistic mindset, wrongly focused on wanting to know how many good works are enough to get into heaven. Jesus had just spoken about the sort of posture disciples must adopt to receive the kingdom. This larger section of Mark in which Jesus teaches about discipleship (8:22–10:52) involves an intentionally cultivated posture toward God that involves both attitudes and practices. This conversation does not involve, then, a "law-gospel" contrast that sets doing in opposition to believing. The man's question is a valid one, as it involves the very topic about which Jesus has been speaking.

Jesus's response in v. 18 is somewhat provocative and a bit mystifying: "Why do you call me good? No one is good—except God alone." Jesus is not denying his own goodness and reserving goodness only for God. After all, he knows his identity as God's beloved Son. Twice he has heard God proclaim his approval of and love for him (1:11; 9:7). So this is not an abstract debate about the nature of goodness or an opportunity for Jesus to explain his relative goodness and God's absolute goodness. The man's address of Jesus as "good teacher" is an instance of the sort of flattery that a typical rich man would employ to wheel and deal in an effort to gain leverage in a negotiation. And while it may be subtly manipulative, he is not depicted here as an evil character, as manifested by his humble approach. This is simply how he has come to navigate his way through the world.

Jesus's response—"Why do you call me good?"—makes more sense in terms of his prophetic character throughout Mark, especially his refusal to be impressed by large crowds. Here, Jesus gently waves aside the man's flattery. Jesus is available to speak the truth to anyone who will listen. He does not need to be flattered, and he cannot be manipulated by someone seeking to gain an advantage. While such behavior comes naturally to this man, it is exactly the sort of posture toward others that runs counter to what Jesus meant by receiving the kingdom as a child. One who *receives* the kingdom does not seek to *gain* it through manipulative strategies that might have purchase with people. On this scenario, Jesus is kindly unmasking the man's motivation. It is as if Jesus is asking, "What is your agenda? Why do you feel it is necessary to approach me in this way?"

Jesus points the man to God's commandments, especially the second table of the Ten Commandments (Exod 20:12–17; Deut 5:16–21). These commands have to do with community life and relate to what Jesus has been teaching about the formation of a just community of disciples who serve and offer hospitality.[1] Again, Jesus is not setting him up for failure by mentioning the impossible standard of God, knowing he cannot genuinely keep God's commands. Jesus's answer here summarizes in brief what constitutes obedience to God, in the fashion of the Ten Commandments themselves and passages like Micah 6:8 and Psalm 15.

The man responds in v. 20 that he has kept these commands since the time of his childhood. This is not arrogance or foolish presumption. It is simple honesty that he has rendered to God sincere and faithful obedience throughout his life. At this point in the narrative, the man seems to be on the right track and seems so near to receiving the kingdom. And this sense of the narrative's positive trajectory continues with Jesus's dramatic and considered gaze, in addition to Mark's highly unusual comment that Jesus "loved him" (v. 21).

There is a hint, however, that perhaps this man will not ultimately meet Jesus's previously stated criterion for entering the kingdom: "Anyone who will not receive the kingdom of God like a little child will never enter it" (v. 15). The man certainly desires to enter the kingdom, as his desperate inquiry of Jesus indicates. He will balk, however, at entering it as a child. He notes that he has kept God's commands "from my youth" (*ek neotētos mou*, v. 20), which signals that he is no longer a child. He has grown up and has inherited or accumulated wealth and is now operating in the world of grown men and important people, unable to hold his possessions and possibilities loosely so that he might enter the kingdom in the only way Jesus indicates one can—as a child.

Jesus then issues his call for the man to become a disciple. This is the only time that Mark indicates that Jesus looked at someone "and loved him," but his calls for others to follow him are typically preceded by Jesus "seeing" them (1:16, 19; 2:14). Just as in those previous instances, this points to Jesus's penetrating knowledge of this man. He tells him that there is one further thing he must do, which is to sell all of his possessions, give to the poor, and reckon that his riches are in heaven. "Then come, follow me" (v. 21). Not everyone in Mark's Gospel receives a call to discipleship like this man did. When the demon-possessed man in Mark 5 wanted to follow Jesus, his request was refused, and Jesus told him to stay where he was and report what God had

---

1. Black, *Mark*, 225–26.

done for him. And other characters are not called as disciples, though Jesus blesses them, heals them, and exorcizes demons from them. The disciples, however, are called to follow Jesus, and though they are often obtuse, each of them had immediately left everything to take up Jesus's call.

Jesus has the prerogative to appoint any character to any role within the kingdom. In effect he says, "Follow me, along with my disciples who have left everything, on the road to Jerusalem where I will give everything—my life—for the life of the world." Jesus is not calling this man to do anything extraordinary, but is commanding him simply to do as he and his disciples are doing. He must face the cost of taking up his cross, giving himself and all his possessions completely to God.

Though the momentum in the narrative had been moving toward this man receiving the kingdom, he dejectedly turns away and departs. Mark notes that he is unable to take up Jesus's call because of his great wealth (v. 22). His accumulated status and his worldly means are too much to give up. The cost of discipleship is too high.

Jesus Teaches about the Rich and the Kingdom (vv. 23–27)

After the man departed, Jesus paused dramatically, looking around so that his statement had maximum effect on his disciples: "How hard it is for the rich to enter the kingdom of God!" (v. 23).[2] Jesus had just been teaching that to receive the kingdom one must embrace the reality of having no social status in the kingdom, no cultivated case for value apart from being loved and welcomed by God. Yet the wealthy—depicted by the man who departed— have significant investment and attachment to this world, and it is a massive challenge to let go of it, becoming as one who has nothing.

The disciples respond to Jesus's words with amazement (v. 24). Just as in our day, the wealthy get what they want and are usually the first in line for anything that is in high demand. They get "preferred" service and are regarded as "most valuable," so the disciples would expect this to be the same with the kingdom. They may also have been expecting Jesus to curry favor with this man as a way to advance his own agenda. Certainly this is how many leaders of Christian organizations operate toward the wealthy. Placher suggests that since many would have assumed that the wealthy were more pleasing to God, since riches were a sign of blessing, if they cannot enter the kingdom, where does that leave the disciples?[3]

---

2. Jesus pausing and looking around before speaking is a common feature of Mark (cf. 3:5, 34; 8:33).

3. Placher, *Mark*, 145.

Jesus then repeats what he had said, though with a few twists. First, a note of grace. Mark is a challenging Gospel, and he often portrays the disciples as failing and being rebuked by Jesus. His address to them here, however, is a moment of endearment. He calls them "children" (v. 24). This is not a note of condescension but of ownership. Jesus is claiming the disciples as his own, as members of the kingdom. After speaking about the necessity to receive the kingdom as children, for Jesus to call them "children" is to indicate that they belong. Despite their failings, hard-heartedness, slowness to listen, and misdirected motives, they are still "on the way" with Jesus, and they are still his.

He then generalizes his statement to refer to anyone in v. 24. It is difficult for anyone to enter the kingdom of God. It requires a transformation of the imagination and renovation of the heart for people to put to death their hopes and dreams for this world along with their previous conceptions of themselves and what gave them significance. To live in this world according to impulses of self-advancement and self-preservation and then to receive Jesus's call to take up a cross—the imperial instrument of capital punishment—is extremely difficult, if not impossible. He then reapplies what he has been saying to the wealthy. Referring to the biggest animal the disciples had ever seen and the smallest opening they knew about, Jesus says that it is every bit as possible for the rich to enter the kingdom as a camel to go through the eye of a sewing needle (v. 25).[4]

At this, the amazement of the disciples intensifies, becoming resignation and hopelessness (v. 26). Well, then, who can possibly be saved? If the rich—the preferred group above all others—cannot be saved, then how can anyone? Jesus responds by saying that with humans it is indeed impossible, but that all things are possible with God (v. 27). The typical human methods of getting things done and advancing a cause involve pleasing people, manipulating situations, granting favors, exercising strength, asserting power, using shrewdness and good business sense, and perhaps even employing shady means. But with God, none of this accomplishes anything. God cannot be pushed around, manipulated, paid off, impressed, or intimidated. Everything is upside-down with God, and human ways accomplish nothing in regard to his kingdom. It must be received apart from any human means and any cultural valuations of human worth. Jesus calls the fit and the unfit; he welcomes sinners and tax-collectors and touches the unclean. Assumed human conceptions of "how things get done" count for nothing and may even become obstacles for those who must learn to receive the kingdom as those with no social worth.[5]

---

4. Hooker, *Mark*, 242–43.
5. Moloney, *Gospel of Mark*, 203.

For anyone to enter the kingdom—especially the rich—it must be the work of God. Only God can transform a person.

Sacrifice and Reward (vv. 28–31)

Peter speaks up in v. 28 and notes that he and his fellow disciples have left everything, unlike the rich man to whom Jesus had been speaking. And he is right. When Jesus called them, they each immediately left their old lives behind—their possessions, their identity, their families—to follow him (1:17–20; 2:14).

Jesus acknowledges what they have done, but indicates that they will be rewarded both in the present age and in the age to come, when the kingdom will be fully realized. To become part of the kingdom of God is to join a new family oriented around obedience to Jesus rather than flesh and blood relations (cf. Mark 3:31–35). This is the ideal vision of the church: those who have left the way of the world are brought into a new "world" and attached to others by new relational ties. New prospects for genuine flourishing emerge. Yet further Jesus notes that during this age, all these good gifts one receives will include persecutions (v. 30). Community life in the time before the fullness of the kingdom will not be easy. Stresses within and pressures without are what disciples can expect. The age to come, however, will bring the relief, restoration, and joy of eternal and unending life with God.

Finally, in discussing the rich and everyone else, Jesus notes that this present and future reality is one that overturns expected estimations of personal worth. "Many who are first will be last, and the last first" (v. 31). There will likely be wealthy people in the kingdom, along with the poor, and people from every ethnicity. But the worldly constructions of personal value will be reversed and overturned. This new reality will be one that exalts the lowly and humbles the exalted.

LIVE the Story

The Obstacles to Discipleship That Money Creates

This passage in Mark obviously deals with the touchy subject of wealth and how earthly riches can be a threat to discipleship. Those with great wealth in this world have a difficult challenge when it comes to following Jesus because of their many attachments. The more a person possesses, the more difficult it becomes to hold things loosely and conceive of giving them up to follow Jesus. It would be easy at this point to reflect on this passage by taking a "how-to" approach, outlining steps or principles for stewarding material resources. In my view, however, this would not be faithful to the passage. Jesus is not suggesting principles for stewardship but directly addressing how wealth is an obstacle to discipleship.

It is important to identify just what it means to be wealthy. I was shocked recently to see just where my household ranked in comparison to worldwide incomes. This can be discovered quite easily. An online income calculator indicates that an annual income of $50,000 puts a person in the top .31 percent worldwide.[6] That is pretty surprising, especially because very few people making that much money feel very "wealthy." This may be because we measure ourselves against those who have much greater amounts of money or property, or because we see so many portrayals of wealthy people in various media. Further, we measure ourselves against people who have big houses and have the options in life that seem to come with financial abundance. Chances are, however, that if you have the money to purchase a book like this one, you are richer than you think!

It is worth considering, then, the threats that wealth presents to pursuing discipleship to Jesus and to participating faithfully in the body of Christ. First, those with financial means may be tempted to use their money to exploit others in the church. Paul addresses this issue with the Corinthians at several points in his first letter to them. It appears that those with means were seeking to resolve conflicts by taking others to court, where their superior wealth and social connections would give them leverage (1 Cor 6:1–11). Further, the rich were shutting out the poor when they came together to celebrate the Lord's Supper. The rich were bringing fine food and wine to the meal and eating their fill and drinking to the point of drunkenness. Only then were they allowing the poor to join them to eat the leftovers (11:17–34). Paul says that they were despising the church of God by humiliating the poor (v. 22), and that such behavior put them in danger of being condemned along with the world (v. 32).

Like the Corinthians, it is easy for church communities to divide along the same socioeconomic lines that separate our surrounding cultures. Those who live in better neighborhoods and enjoy leisure activities may fellowship only with others in the church that are like them. When we consider social activities as church communities, however, we ought to consider that God has created one new family out of people from every background. The ways that we socialize to develop closer connections must be oriented with an eye to the realities of what God is cultivating among us.

---

6. The *New York Times* has an income calculator that can be used to determine where one's income is ranked by city, county, state, and in the United States (www.nytimes.com/interactive/2012/01/15/business/one-percent-map.html).

Second, churches face the temptation to curry favor with the wealthy. James rebukes churches that are so delighted to see a rich person enter that they give him a place of honor, while treating the poor with contempt by seating them in the back or off to the side (Jas 2:1–4). James says that when churches adopt these behaviors, they have become "judges with evil thoughts" (v. 4). Such favoritism is a violation of Scripture (v. 9). James goes on to excoriate the wealthy who have engaged in exploitative practices against the poor. This is a terrifying passage when we consider that many contemporary Christians enjoy the benefits of economic systems and structures that deliver goods and services while making life hard for the poor:

> Now listen, you rich people, weep and wail because of the misery that is coming on you. Your wealth has rotted, and moths have eaten your clothes. Your gold and silver are corroded. Their corrosion will testify against you and eat your flesh like fire. You have hoarded wealth in the last days. Look! The wages you failed to pay the workers who mowed your fields are crying out against you. The cries of the harvesters have reached the ears of the Lord Almighty. You have lived on earth in luxury and self-indulgence. You have fattened yourselves in the day of slaughter. You have condemned and murdered the innocent one, who was not opposing you. (Jas 5:1–6)

A third threat to faithful discipleship is the temptation for churches with wealth to become complacent, associating their comfortable buildings, large staffs, and plentiful resources with God's approval. The exalted Lord Jesus confronts the church at Laodicea for falling into this error: "You say, 'I am rich; I have acquired wealth and do not need a thing'" (Rev 3:17). The Laodicean church likely did not articulate this attitude explicitly, but Jesus discerns their complacency and unwarranted self-sufficiency beneath a veneer of presumed godliness. He does not see them as they envision themselves. Rather, they need to open their spiritual eyes to see their true condition:

> But you do not realize that you are wretched, pitiful, poor, blind and naked. I counsel you to buy from me gold refined in the fire, so you can become rich; and white clothes to wear, so you can cover your shameful nakedness; and salve to put on your eyes, so you can see. (Rev 3:17–18)

A fourth threat is one that ministry practitioners face—the temptation to minister from a desire for financial gain. Paul warns Timothy about this in his first letter to him. He speaks of ministers who depart from apostolic teaching and have an unhealthy interest in "controversies and quarrels" and who generate constant conflict. Paul discerns in these people a corrupted ministry motivation, one driven by a desire for money (1 Tim 6:4–5). Paul continues:

> Godliness with contentment is great gain. For we brought nothing into the world, and we can take nothing out of it. But if we have food and clothing, we will be content with that. Those who want to get rich fall into temptation and a trap and into many foolish and harmful desires that plunge people into ruin and destruction. For the love of money is a root of all kinds of evil. Some people, eager for money, have wandered from the faith and pierced themselves with many griefs. (1 Tim 6:6–10)

Many churches in the West, and certainly many in North America, have resources that would astonish Christians in other parts of the world. But such prosperity has not always fed spiritual growth and vitality. Money creates rivalries and generates conflict among pastoral staff members and church leaders. And pastors can face the temptation to avoid confronting sin or fail to speak boldly out of fear of losing a well-paid position. I have a friend who was a bivocational pastor for nearly a decade. He taught junior high school and later kindergarten special education in order to serve a small church that could only pay him a meager salary. He was often worn out, but he told me that the freedom he felt was worth it and that he would never be a full-time minister. Money was never an issue between him and the church. He could care for his church without concern that his job was ever at stake. And when something difficult needed to be said, he was free to say it.

Most approaches to money and financial issues among Western Christians involve how to "manage" it or how to be faithful stewards. Without dismissing these notions, Jesus's words must also be considered carefully here. Indeed, Jesus does not call everyone to give up everything, but those who cling to this fact out of some desire for comfort are perhaps the very ones who need to weigh carefully what Jesus has to say about the manner in which riches can become obstacles to following Jesus.[7]

---

7. Craig L. Blomberg, *Christians in an Age of Wealth: A Biblical Theology of Stewardship* (Grand Rapids: Zondervan, 2013), 107.

CHAPTER 43

Mark 10:32-45

LISTEN to the Story

³²They were on their way up to Jerusalem, with Jesus leading the way, and the disciples were astonished, while those who followed were afraid. Again he took the Twelve aside and told them what was going to happen to him. ³³"We are going up to Jerusalem," he said, "and the Son of Man will be delivered over to the chief priests and the teachers of the law. They will condemn him to death and will hand him over to the Gentiles, ³⁴who will mock him and spit on him, flog him and kill him. Three days later he will rise."

³⁵Then James and John, the sons of Zebedee, came to him. "Teacher," they said, "we want you to do for us whatever we ask."

³⁶"What do you want me to do for you?" he asked.

³⁷They replied, "Let one of us sit at your right and the other at your left in your glory."

³⁸"You don't know what you are asking," Jesus said. "Can you drink the cup I drink or be baptized with the baptism I am baptized with?"

³⁹"We can," they answered.

Jesus said to them, "You will drink the cup I drink and be baptized with the baptism I am baptized with, ⁴⁰but to sit at my right or left is not for me to grant. These places belong to those for whom they have been prepared."

⁴¹When the ten heard about this, they became indignant with James and John. ⁴²Jesus called them together and said, "You know that those who are regarded as rulers of the Gentiles lord it over them, and their high officials exercise authority over them. ⁴³Not so with you. Instead, whoever wants to become great among you must be your servant, ⁴⁴and whoever wants to be first must be slave of all. ⁴⁵For even the Son of Man did not come to be served, but to serve, and to give his life as a ransom for many."

Listening to the Text in the Story: Deuteronomy 17:14–20; Proverbs 25:6–7; Isaiah 53:1–12; Luke 11:43; 14:7–11; 20:45–47; 1 Corinthians 3:5–9; 2 Corinthians 4:7–18; 8:9; 11:1–12:10; Ephesians 3:7–8.

As Jesus and the disciples make their way to Jerusalem, Jesus for the third time predicts his suffering and death. This is followed by the most preposterous response from the disciples. They ignore what he has said and approach Jesus to request seats of prominence when the kingdom comes in glory. Their request clearly demonstrates that they are not taking to heart Jesus's teaching on the nature of discipleship. Jesus is giving a performance of cross-directed and cross-oriented leadership in the most strategic way possible, and he goes on at the end of the passage to contrast worldly leadership with that which is "cruciform"—shaped by the cross.

Paul modeled this mode of leadership throughout his ministry, and he writes about it in his letters. The Corinthian church was situated in a culture that celebrated clever and creative rhetoric and powerful oratory. But Paul intentionally shaped his ministry among them in a "cruciform" manner:

> When I came to you, I did not come with eloquence or human wisdom as I proclaimed to you the testimony about God. For I resolved to know nothing while I was with you except Jesus Christ and him crucified. I came to you in weakness with great fear and trembling. My message and my preaching were not with wise and persuasive words, but with a demonstration of the Spirit's power, so that your faith might not rest on human wisdom, but on God's power. (1 Cor 2:1–5)

Much like our contemporary ministry contexts that exalt celebrity preachers, the Corinthians rallied around certain early church figures, breaking into groups around Apollos, Peter, and Paul (1 Cor 1:12). Paul was aghast at this, exhorting the church to be unified around Christ. After all, the early apostles and preachers are not to be exalted, but are only servants of Christ:

> What, after all, is Apollos? And what is Paul? Only servants, through whom you came to believe—as the Lord has assigned to each his task. I planted the seed, Apollos watered it, but God has been making it grow. So neither the one who plants nor the one who waters is anything, but only God, who makes things grow. The one who plants and the one who waters have one purpose, and they will each be rewarded according to their own labor. For we are co-workers in God's service; you are God's field, God's building. (1 Cor 3:5–9)

Paul struggled mightily with the Corinthian church, which he loved dearly, to convert them from a mindset that exalted celebrities to a vision of ministry that embraced humility. In 2 Corinthians 11:1–12:10, he contrasted his ministry against the "super-apostles" that had captivated the Corinthians with their impressive credentials and exciting style. These "false apostles" were boasting the way the world does (2 Cor 11:18), whereas Paul boasted about his sufferings and weakness (vv. 23–30). Paul's "boasting" in this passage is so countercultural that he presents the following as one of his most powerful claims to be a genuine apostle:

> The God and Father of the Lord Jesus, who is to be praised forever, knows that I am not lying. In Damascus the governor under King Aretas had the city of the Damascenes guarded in order to arrest me. But I was lowered in a basket from a window in the wall and slipped through his hands. (2 Cor 11:31–33)

He begins with a solemn oath and then presents the pathetic claim that he had to escape for his life as his most potent ministry credential. It is hard to imagine that a modern speaker or author would put something like this on the back cover of their new book rather than a list of academic degrees and impressive accomplishments. But this is Paul's logic: one's claim to authentic ministry is the extent to which their life looks like a rotting corpse hung on a tree.

Paul claims in 2 Corinthians 4:10 that he and his fellow ministers "always carry around in our body the death of Jesus, so that the life of Jesus may also be revealed in our body." And this mode of ministry magnifies God's glory: "We have this treasure in jars of clay to show that this all-surpassing power is from God and not from us" (v. 7). Those who seek prominence and praise demonstrate that they do not understand the way of Jesus, for "whoever wants to become great among you must be your servant, and whoever wants to be first must be slave of all" (Mark 10:43–44).

EXPLAIN the Story

This episode begins the final of three cycles in which Jesus predicts his betrayal and death, followed by the disciples failing to respond rightly. This third cycle ends in 10:52, with the healing of Bartimaeus the blind man, closing out the section that began in Mark 8:22 with a similar healing of a blind man. In this episode the disciples display a nearly comical—if it was not so tragic—failure to grasp what Jesus is saying, making a request that runs in exactly the opposite direction of "the way" of Jesus.

Jesus's Prediction (vv. 32–34)

Jesus continues "on the way" to Jerusalem, along with his disciples. Mark places Jesus ahead of them, "leading the way." The Greek expression for Jesus's position out in front of his disciples (*kai ēn proagōn autous*) may indicate his leading them to Jerusalem, but it can also indicate that Jesus "was going on ahead of them." That is, Mark is pointing to the gap between the agenda of Jesus and that of his disciples. Jesus is resolutely going on to Jerusalem to carry out the divine agenda, whereas the disciples are still captive to their selfish and worldly mindsets.[1]

The difference in their agendas is evident in the emotional state of the disciples. Mark notes that they were "astonished," which is the same Greek verb (*thambeō*) for their amazement at Jesus's words just previously about the difficulty of the rich to enter the kingdom (10:24), and a synonym of the verb used (*ekplēssō*) for their intensified reaction at Jesus's restatement (v. 26). Amazement in Mark is not always a positive reaction. The crowds can be amazed without any report of the result (1:27), and the disciples were previously overwhelmed with amazement (*existēmi*), which is an expression of their lack of faith and hardened hearts (6:51).

In addition to amazement, the disciples were afraid, a reaction that is the opposite of faith in Mark's Gospel and is often the condition that characterizes the disciples' failure.[2] While Mark does not comment on the reason the disciples are feeling this way, it may be their reaction to Jesus's steady persistence about going to Jerusalem and his insistence about what awaits him there. The tension is heightened, and their anxiety is growing as they near the city. The disciples may well have never been to Jerusalem, so their arriving there would be an intimidating prospect, and they have been unable to deter him or alter his agenda. They are indeed "following" (*akolouthountes*) Jesus, which is good. But they are still beholden to a different agenda, and this gulf between them is cranking up the anxiety.

For the third time, Jesus tells his disciples what is going to happen to him (10:33–34; cf. 8:31–32; 9:31). This is Jesus's most explicit and detailed prediction, functioning like a playbill for what is coming in the remainder of Mark's Gospel.[3] He begins with an interjection that the NIV leaves untranslated (*idou*): "Look!" "Behold!" Sensory perception in Mark's Gospel is crucial, indicating a genuine grasp of the kingdom's realities and Jesus's identity. Jesus is here calling on his disciples to open their eyes to discern what is happening. This is all the more important as the healing of blind Bartimaeus follows this episode (10:46–52).

1. Moloney, *Gospel of Mark*, 204.
2. Moloney, *Gospel of Mark*, 204.
3. Black, *Mark*, 229–30.

The Disciples' Request (vv. 35–41)

Immediately after each of Jesus's previous two predictions of his suffering and death, the disciples followed with serious failures. After the first, Peter took Jesus aside and rebuked him (8:32). Following the second prediction, the disciples argued about who was the greatest (9:34). Here, James and John ran out ahead of the other disciples to Jesus, who was walking on ahead of them, approaching him with a bold request: "Teacher, we want you to do for us whatever we ask" (v. 35). This is precisely the sort of blank-check request that raises serious suspicions. Jesus, however, invites them to lay their agenda openly before him, asking them the same question he will ask of Bartimaeus just after this (10:51). Bartimaeus requests that he be given sight, which is the desperate need of the disciples. They, however, demonstrate their blindness by completely ignoring what Jesus has just said about what awaits him in Jerusalem.

James and John ask that they be given seats on either side of Jesus when he comes into his glorious kingdom in the future (v. 37).[4] They perceive rightly that there will be a glorious kingdom to come, but they still do not recognize that they only arrive at this through suffering in the present. Jesus understands this, of course, so he asks if they are prepared to participate in the suffering that comes on the way to future glory (v. 38).

By answering "we can," the disciples reveal their arrogance and presumption (v. 39). They are confident in themselves, even though they have little basis for such self-regard. They had previously failed to look to God in prayer and were unable to cast out a demon (9:18, 29). They, along with others, will make boasts of loyalty that will ultimately prove baseless (14:27–31). They will flee, along with all the others, yet they are confident in themselves that they have what it takes to play these prominent roles. Jesus has in mind his suffering and their participation in it, which is the only way to exaltation. There is no crown without a cross.

It is interesting to consider the effect of this episode on Mark's audiences, many of whom already know how the story ends. Audiences will be aware that James and John do not know what they are talking about or what they are so confidently asserting. They do not know what it takes to go the way of the cross. They do not know that they will be overcome with fear and will flee in the face of Jesus's arrest, trial, suffering, and death. They do not know,

---

4. According to Greco-Roman honor codes, the placement of persons signals their status and social standing. Kings are seated higher than others, while conquered enemies are thrown at the feet of rulers. In the same way, "seating order at feasts and synagogues is an important signal of the relative status of the guests or worshipers." James and John ask Jesus for the best seats in order to be elevated above others and to be seen as having prestige, honor, and exalted social status (David A. deSilva, *Honor, Patronage, Kinship and Purity: Unlocking New Testament Culture* [Downers Grove, IL: InterVarsity Press, 2000], 31).

as Jesus indicates, that they, too, will be swallowed up in violence and death because of their loyalty to Jesus.

Audiences are in on this irony, but Mark intends for them to be self-reflective enough that they will see themselves in these disciples. We, too, want prominence and glory. We, too, did not know when we were baptized to identify with Jesus and the way of the cross that it would cost us. We, too, have not taken full account of the perils that attend "the way." And perhaps this is all by grace.

Jesus assures them that despite their current lack of awareness, they will indeed suffer as Jesus will (v. 39). Yet the prerogative to appoint people to positions of prominence in the kingdom lies with God alone (v. 40).[5] Jesus is being faithful to God and accepts the role God has appointed for him. And this is "the way" that he calls his disciples to follow. They also must join him in accepting what God will grant. There will indeed be positions of honor when the Son of Man comes in power, but all of this is up to God.[6]

When the other disciples heard about the request of James and John, they "became indignant" (*aganakteō*) with them. Their reaction is the same as that of Jesus when the disciples were preventing the children from coming to him (10:14). The motivation for their indignation, however, is quite different. They were outplayed by James and John in requesting positions of prominence and were not as quick thinking in seeking out privileges.

Jesus's Teaching on Servanthood (vv. 42–45)

Jesus does not directly rebuke the disciples as he did Peter in 8:33. Rather, as he so often does, he calls them all together and teaches them about true greatness in the kingdom. He speaks first of "those who are regarded as rulers of the Gentiles" (v. 42). The expression *hoi dokountes archein tōn ethnōn* ("those who seem to be rulers of the gentiles") captures well the character of earthly rule. It is delegated by God, as Nebuchadnezzar learned well in Daniel 4:28–37. Further, earthly rule is characterized by status seeking and is often reinforced through image-maintenance, intimidation, deception, and violence. Moloney states it well: "In the design of God, their all-powerful and self-sufficient rule is only apparent" and temporary.[7]

---

5. Black, *Mark*, 232.

6. Chrysostom writes: "In the fervor of their spirit they promise immediately, not knowing what they said, but looking to obtain that which they were asking. . . . He foretold great things for them; that is, you shall be held worthy of martyrdom, you shall suffer the things I have suffered, you shall end your life with a death from violence, and in this also you shall be sharers with me" (Oden and Hall, *Mark*, 142).

7. Moloney, *Gospel of Mark*, 206.

Worldly figures misuse and abuse their rule to exalt themselves and keep their people in subjection. While the disciples are craving the glory that comes with such positions, Jesus warns them they are not to behave this way. "Instead, whoever wants to become great among you must be your servant, and whoever wants to be first must be slave of all" (vv. 43–44). The mode of prominence and exaltation in the kingdom of God is radically different from the way of this world. Greatness for followers of Jesus is for those who become servants, for those who are slaves. A servant looks to the needs of others, and a slave gives up all rights and personal claims. The expressions about servants and slaves are set in synonymous parallelism and are meant to provoke the imagination about the sorts of attitudes toward others that characterize true greatness in the kingdom.[8]

Jesus gives the reason for the counterintuitive nature of true greatness in his climactic statement in v. 45: "For even the Son of Man did not come to be served, but to serve, and to give his life as a ransom for many." The Son of Man is the figure who will come in splendor and glory to rule (Dan 7:14, 27):

He was given authority, glory and sovereign power; all nations and peoples of every language worshiped him. His dominion is an everlasting dominion that will not pass away, and his kingdom is one that will never be destroyed. (Dan 7:14)

Jesus is this figure who will receive the kingdom and rule over it. Yet, he leads the way to the kingdom through suffering and death. Therefore, this is the way that all must go who will participate in his coming reign. If the Lord of the realm is a servant of others, giving himself up for their life, then those who desire prominence must follow him in servanthood and slavery on behalf of others. This is the paradox of the cross. Jesus's death is vindicated by his resurrection, so those will be likewise vindicated who join Jesus on crosses, "on the way" to his cross.

Jesus giving his life is the means whereby God redeems his people.[9] In the Old Testament, a "ransom" (LXX: *lytron*) refers to the payment to redeem an animal, property, a prisoner of war, or a person out of slavery (Exod 13:13, 15; 21:8, 30; Lev 25:47–52; Num 3:45–51). The verb (LXX: *lytroō*) was used of God's saving acts and of his redeeming Israel out of exile (Ps 34:22; 44:26;

---

8. Strauss, *Mark*, 457.

9. "Many" is a Semitic expression that means "all," and this points to the means of God's redemption of his people. Note the appearance of "many" in Isaiah 53:11–12 (Boring, *Mark*, 303).

78:42; Isa 35:9; 41:14; 43:14; 51:10–11; 52:3, 9; Jer 31:11).[10] Mark does not develop the ransom notion, so there is no indication to whom it is paid.[11] Jesus's point is that his suffering and death is the means whereby God saves his people.

LIVE the Story

Jesus-Shaped Leadership

Jesus contrasts the sort of leadership we find among worldly rulers with the kind of servant-oriented leadership that should exist among God's people. Much of the literature and advice on leadership in the church does not respect the dramatic contrast that Jesus sets up. Rather, because our culture is so dominated by economic ideologies and frames of reference, writers on church leadership often adapt principles and practices from business leadership to speak to ministry leaders, sprinkling in illustrations from Moses, David, Jesus, and Paul, along with some Bible verses.

If we reflect on the contrast that Jesus sets up, we might describe "worldly" leadership as follows: a desire to increase in prestige, status, and influence and a willingness to do whatever it takes to achieve these things, even if it means neglecting or hurting people who do not appear to be a means of one's own personal advancement. A person wrapped up in this pursuit is leader-oriented and leader-focused. This often results in churches becoming cults of personality. It is all about the leader's vision, his dream, and his plans. I once heard a pastor giving a talk about "how to get the most out of your people," which left me with the picture of him wringing every last ounce of energy and life out of those in his church. I wondered whether he was serving them, or if they were serving him.

The kind of leadership Jesus condemns is that which desires more and more influence, a greater platform from which to speak. This puts ministers in competition with others and generates great anxiety and anger when others appear to be growing or experiencing some kind of advancement. These kinds of leaders are also willing to identify people in sinful ways, valuing people in terms of whether they will advance the leader's agenda. These leaders are image conscious, manipulating situations in order to put the best spin on things. They

---

10. J. Dennis, "Death of Jesus," *DJG* 179; Black, *Mark*, 233; Boring, *Mark*, 302–3.

11. The "ransom" refers to the payment to some hostile power to liberate "the many" who are enslaved. According to McKnight, "the hostile powers are sin (1:5, 15), Satan and his destructive cohorts (e.g., 3:27), and the fearful self (8:34–9:1)" (Scot McKnight, *Jesus and His Death: Historiography, the Historical Jesus, and Atonement Theory* [Waco, TX: Baylor University Press, 2005], 357).

seek to control how they are seen and how people think of them. Again, this pursuit generates extreme anxiety, because they cannot let others see their failures. They end up cultivating inauthenticity, hiding from others who they truly are.

Jesus-shaped leadership is completely different, and we can describe it in these terms: it is an unrelenting commitment to the delivery of the love and grace of God into the lives of others and the taking of initiative to see to it that this happens. This mode of leadership follows God's agenda, which is to break into others' lives with love and grace to redeem, reclaim, restore, and save. God, who chose Israel to redeem the nations and who defends the cause of the poor, the orphan, and the widow is the one who determines the agenda for leaders as they consider how they might minister to God's people.

This makes leaders *others-directed* and *others-focused*. Jesus-shaped leaders are not focused on their own dreams and plans but rather on the people they are serving, in order to understand how the grace of God might arrive into their lives. The goal is community flourishing and not the pastor's prestige.

This sort of minister cultivates authenticity and rejects an image conscious orientation. I have an academic dean whose vision of leadership is servant oriented, so he spends his time thinking and strategizing in order to direct institutional resources toward faculty, so that we can thrive and serve our students well. That makes my life as a faculty person a serious delight! And while I am sure many pastors are like this, I know one who purposefully cultivates authenticity by building relationships with everyone in his congregation, enjoying long conversations that involve mutual sharing and openness. He purposefully rejects an approach that manages perception and builds an image of power and competence, knowing that such an inauthentic approach to ministry bears bad fruit in the long run.

Embracing authenticity in ministry frees ministers and churches from the grip of fear. We do not need to worry that others will see our weaknesses and our failures. We have no need to try to hide our true selves or manipulate the perception of others. When I speak frankly about my weaknesses, my shortcomings, and my slow progress in discipleship, I provide space for others to be equally authentic about their failures and struggles in the faith. Jesus-shaped leaders pursue authenticity in leadership and draw others in through their honesty.

Those who lead like Jesus are also very careful with how they use strength. Such leaders must be very careful to understand the nature of social capital, reflecting soberly on how socially magnetic they are, how others react to them, and how they draw others to themselves. Such social dynamics can be manipulated and exploited for one's own advancement and even used against others. Worldly leaders will not hesitate to do this and will even look for opportunities to use personal strengths, even if others are hurt. But Jesus-shaped leaders refuse to ever do such damage to people, using any social capital they have to draw in the marginalized and to radiate social significance to others.

Cross-oriented leaders are protective and shepherd-like, using resources and social connections on behalf of others and never against them. They are also very careful to avoid identifying people in ungodly ways, such as evaluating them based on whether they are on board with the pastor's vision. People must be known and loved on their own terms, since each person's story is of infinite value to God.

God's intentions for leaders among his people have always been the same. Deuteronomy 17 gives instructions for the sort of king God wanted for Israel. They were not to build up personal wealth (v. 17), and they were to learn the law, gaining an increasing sense of the heart of God for his people. And the king was not to "consider himself better than his fellow Israelites" (v. 20). Leaders after God's own heart behave toward God's people just as Jesus does, the one who gives his life for the blessing of others.

I know of a ministry leader who embodied this so well, a man I'll call "Kenneth." Kenneth was a lay leader who had run a successful business for many years and so engaged naturally with other executives and businesspeople in the church. At the same time, he took the initiative to develop relationships with a striking variety of people from different social classes and other ethnicities in the church. Kenneth told me once about a young man from another part of town who had been visiting the church, and this was someone with whom he had nothing in common. They had arranged to meet for an early morning breakfast each week to talk through the challenges and opportunities of life.

On one of those mornings, the young man didn't show up. So Kenneth called him a few times, but no one answered the phone. He drove to his apartment and knocked on the door. The young man was stunned to find Kenneth at his apartment, at which point Kenneth explained that their relationship meant a lot to him and that he cared deeply about their mutual growth in the Lord. They ended up having an abbreviated breakfast that morning and continuing their routine meetings after that day. Months later, this young man's girlfriend informed Kenneth that on the morning he didn't show up for breakfast, he was unusually discouraged and thought that Kenneth would just blow him off like others in his life had done. He was overwhelmed by Kenneth's commitment to him, which encouraged him to become increasingly open to Kenneth and to others in the church. I am grateful for his example of relational commitment and for this model of the sort of ministry leadership that is shaped by Jesus.

CHAPTER 44

Mark 10:46-52

📖 LISTEN to the Story

⁴⁶Then they came to Jericho. As Jesus and his disciples, together with a large crowd, were leaving the city, a blind man, Bartimaeus (which means "son of Timaeus"), was sitting by the roadside begging. ⁴⁷When he heard that it was Jesus of Nazareth, he began to shout, "Jesus, Son of David, have mercy on me!"

⁴⁸Many rebuked him and told him to be quiet, but he shouted all the more, "Son of David, have mercy on me!"

⁴⁹Jesus stopped and said, "Call him."

So they called to the blind man, "Cheer up! On your feet! He's calling you." ⁵⁰Throwing his cloak aside, he jumped to his feet and came to Jesus.

⁵¹"What do you want me to do for you?" Jesus asked him.

The blind man said, "Rabbi, I want to see."

⁵²"Go," said Jesus, "your faith has healed you." Immediately he received his sight and followed Jesus along the road.

Listening to the Text in the Story: 2 Samuel 7:4–16; 2 Kings 6:8–23; Psalm 89:3–4; Isaiah 35:1–7; Psalms of Solomon 17:21–25; John 9.

This episode brings to a close a section of Mark that began in 8:22 with the two-stage healing of a blind man. Together with that passage (8:22–26), this episode forms an *inclusio* (a literary device that brackets a section of text), within which is the threefold pattern of Jesus's prediction of his passion, the disciples' misunderstanding, and Jesus's teaching on discipleship.

Two-stage healing—8:22–26
　　Prediction of Son of Man's suffering and death (3x: 8:31; 9:31; 10:33–34)
　　Disciples' misunderstanding and selfishness (3x: 8:32–33; 9:32–34; 10:35–41)

Jesus teaches about discipleship (3x: 8:34–9:1; 9:35–37; 10:42–45)
Healing of Bartimaeus—10:46–52

This episode also concludes Jesus's journey "on the way" to Jerusalem, where he arrives in the following passage (11:1–11).

These two healings framing this section point to the desperate need of the disciples, which is *to see what Jesus's agenda is really all about*. They are failing to perceive it rightly at this point. They are still trying to figure out a way to accomplish God's purposes in some other way than submitting to suffering and death, which makes no sense to them. The disciples grasp Jesus's identity as Messiah, but they are confused about his mission, as is clear from Peter's testy conversation with Jesus just after the first healing (8:27–38). Here, Bartimaeus also rightly identifies Jesus, but he goes further to make a request that should be coming from the disciples: he wants to see.

EXPLAIN the Story

The traveling party consisting of Jesus and his disciples is nearing the end of its journey as it approaches Jerusalem. They now arrive at Jericho, which is about twenty miles northeast of Jerusalem, and they are only passing through on their way to Jerusalem. As they do, however, they are stopped by a blind man named Bartimaeus.

Mark gives the man's name and then explains that this means he is the "son of Timaeus" (v. 46). His name is ironic, since it means "son of honor," and Mark, no stranger to irony, intensifies it when he repeats his name by way of explanation. Bartimaeus is in a pathetic situation, reduced to begging because of his blindness. He has no social honor at all. Mark also notes that Bartimaeus is sitting "by the roadside" begging. This is the same expression (*para tēn hodon*, "along the path") that describes the seeds that are cast along the path that the birds came and ate up (4:4). Given the crucial role in Mark's Gospel of the parable of the soil and sower in 4:1–20, this detail is significant. The seed scattered along the path that the birds ate up represents a situation in which Satan "comes and takes away the word that was sown in them" (v. 15). This blind man, then, is in a vulnerable situation, with both his social shame and the hostility of the crowd working against the word bearing any fruit in him.

Bartimaeus is like other characters in Mark's Gospel who have true perception of Jesus, either seeing or hearing faithfully (5:6, 22, 27; 7:25). When he "heard" that Jesus was passing through town, he began to cry desperately,

"Jesus, Son of David, have mercy on me!"[1] The gathered crowd attempted to shut him up, rebuking him (10:48). This "rebuke" is a further link between the opening and closing passages that form the *inclusio* around this section of Mark. In 8:32–33, Peter rebuked Jesus who then turned around and rebuked Peter.

The crowd's attempts to shut him up only intensify Bartimaeus's desperate resolve: "Son of David, have mercy on me!" (v. 48). At this, Jesus stops and calls for Bartimaeus, an action that Mark stresses by repeating the word three times (*phōneō*; v. 49). Bartimaeus responds much like the disciples did when Jesus called them (1:16–19; 2:13–14). Immediately he threw off his cloak and jumped up and approached Jesus (v. 50). Like the disciples who responded immediately to Jesus and left everything behind, so, too, did Bartimeaus throw off what was likely his only possession and his only means of protection for his body. Boring notes that he likely had his cloak spread out before him to receive donations, so his throwing it off would have scattered his money as well.[2] His immediate response also stands in contrast with the rich young man, who could not bring himself to part with his riches to follow Jesus (10:22).

At this point, Jesus asks Bartimaeus the same question he put to James and John in 10:36 when they approached him by telling him that they wanted him to do for them whatever they asked. This sets Bartimaeus alongside not only Peter in 8:27–33 but James and John in 10:35–45. "What do you want me to do for you?" (v. 51; cf. with v. 36). The disciples throughout the Gospel, and certainly within 8:22–10:52, are in need of true perception and genuine understanding and insight, not only into Jesus's identity but into the suffering-and-exaltation dynamic of his ministry and mission. Bartimaeus's response, therefore, highlights what the disciples need and what they fail to ask for. "The blind man said, 'Rabbi, I want to see'" (v. 51).

Here, unlike most other healings in Mark, Jesus simply speaks a word to heal Bartimaeus rather than touching him: "'Go,' said Jesus, 'your faith has healed you'" (v. 52). The term for "healed" here is a form of the verb *sōzō*

---

1. This is the only episode in Mark that identifies Jesus as David's son. Boring states that Bartimaeus misidentifies Jesus when he calls him "Son of David," a title that Jesus does not seem eager to embrace, as is evident from the conversation in Mark 12:35–37 (Boring, *Mark*, 305). It may well be that the crowds, along with the disciples, have a deficient understanding of Jesus's identity as one who comes in David's line, but this does not mean that Jesus does not own this title. Certainly, the militaristic Davidic king spoken of in Psalms of Solomon 17:21–25 reflected a popular understanding of the sort of figure through whom God would triumph over his enemies. But Jesus is redefining what it means to be Son of David, just as he is redefining what it means to be the Son of Man, who enters into his triumph through suffering and death (cf. also Joel Marcus, *Mark 8–16*, AYBC [New Haven: Yale University Press, 2009], 759).

2. Boring, *Mark*, 306.

("to save"), indicating that his faith has drawn him into the power and presence of the kingdom, the space of spiritual and physical restoration. In commanding him to "go," Jesus is not driving him away but simply calling on him to go on from this point in whatever way he chooses.[3] As soon as Jesus spoke the words, Bartimaeus received his sight and began following Jesus "on the way" to Jerusalem (v. 52).

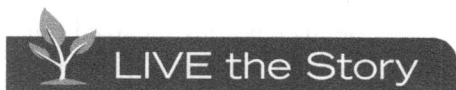

LIVE the Story

The Need for Clarified Vision

Mark identifies Bartimaeus as an honorable character, one that audiences of the Gospel should want to emulate. We had noted that Bartimaeus stands in contrast to Peter, in that Peter had rebuked Jesus when Jesus began to unfold his vision of the cross-oriented nature of the kingdom and his mission to go to Jerusalem to die (8:32). Peter, representing the disciples, resisted this vision. Moreover, Bartimaeus stands in contrast to James and John. When Jesus put the same question to them that he asked of the blind man, they answered that they wanted seats of prominence (10:36–37). Rather than seeking prestige and power, audiences of Mark are to be like Bartimaeus, pleading with God for a clarified vision of the sort of community they are to be.

I recently took part in a conference on the gospel and race relations among Christian communities. The conference focused on the ethnic and racial fractures among churches, especially among evangelicals. Several of the presenters pointed out how evangelicals have been shaped by the surrounding culture, so that cultural political divides between Republican and Democrat, conservative and liberal, have characterized how American Christians conceive of themselves and their church affiliations. Quests for political influence and power have consumed many evangelicals, with the result that they neglect the racial and ethnic divisions that hobble their Christian witness. Further, middle-class white evangelicals often fail to reckon fully with the history of American injustice and ongoing struggle of marginalized and oppressed communities.

Mark's Gospel is a wake-up call for Christians to identify how cultural divisions have shaped our communities and priorities. The seductions of political power and cultural prestige have distorted the vision of many churches and Christian leaders. These orientations that follow the promise of "influence" demonstrate a blindness that Mark's Gospel is designed to expose and heal.

---

3. Moloney, *Gospel of Mark*, 211.

Jesus calls the church to join him on the way to the cross and to cultivate community life oriented by the cross, which is embodied through service to the least and hospitality to the marginalized. Churches would do well to take on the posture of Bartimaeus and join him in praying not for greater power and prestige but for a clarified vision, in order to join Jesus "on the way" to the cross.

In addition to praying for insight, many resources are available for those who wish to develop new abilities to see how others in our communities have suffered injustice and marginalization, opening up possibilities for us to become people and churches that enact God's justice and embody his welcome and embrace. Heather Vacek has written a fascinating account of how mental illness was regarded among Christians over the last few centuries in America.[4] Her work is one of a number of excellent resources in a growing body of literature that reflects on disability from a Christian perspective and clears space for the church to consider how to support and welcome those who suffer with mental illness as well as those who care for them.[5] I have referred to works elsewhere in this commentary that reflect on race and gender relations in our current culture. Prayer for insight can be matched by taking steps to enlighten ourselves, so that God can empower us to embody his justice in the church.

---

4. Heather H. Vacek, *Madness: American Protestant Responses to Mental Illness* (Waco, TX: Baylor University Press, 2015).

5. See also Jean Vanier, *Becoming Human,* 2nd ed. (Mahwah, NJ: Paulist, 2008); Amy Simpson, *Troubled Minds: Mental Illness and the Church's Mission* (Downers Grove, IL: InterVarsity Press, 2013); Kathryn Greene-McCreight, *Darkness Is My Only Companion: A Christian Response to Mental Illness* (Grand Rapids: Brazos, 2015).

CHAPTER 45

Mark 11:1–11

📖 LISTEN to the Story

¹As they approached Jerusalem and came to Bethphage and Bethany at the Mount of Olives, Jesus sent two of his disciples, ²saying to them, "Go to the village ahead of you, and just as you enter it, you will find a colt tied there, which no one has ever ridden. Untie it and bring it here. ³If anyone asks you, 'Why are you doing this?' say, 'The Lord needs it and will send it back here shortly.'"

⁴They went and found a colt outside in the street, tied at a doorway. As they untied it, ⁵some people standing there asked, "What are you doing, untying that colt?" ⁶They answered as Jesus had told them to, and the people let them go. ⁷When they brought the colt to Jesus and threw their cloaks over it, he sat on it. ⁸Many people spread their cloaks on the road, while others spread branches they had cut in the fields. ⁹Those who went ahead and those who followed shouted,

"Hosanna!"

"Blessed is he who comes in the name of the Lord!"

¹⁰"Blessed is the coming kingdom of our father David!"

"Hosanna in the highest heaven!"

¹¹Jesus entered Jerusalem and went into the temple courts. He looked around at everything, but since it was already late, he went out to Bethany with the Twelve.

Listening to the Text in the Story: Psalm 118:26; Zechariah 9:9; Malachi 3:1; 1 Maccabees 13:51–52; Philippians 2:5–11; Revelation 5:11–14.

This episode initiates a new section of Mark's Gospel that runs from 11:1–12:44, with activity in and around the Jerusalem temple, which is much more than the setting for the confrontations between Jesus and the temple leadership throughout this section. This central Jewish institution becomes the object of

God's judgment because it has turned into a site of oppression and exploitation. From this point, Mark begins to portray Jesus more clearly as the new temple, the place on earth where God is encountered.

Jesus and his disciples have concluded their journey and are about to enter Jerusalem. While this episode is often regarded as "the triumphal entry," Mark hardly portrays it as triumphant. If anything, it is highly subversive and anticlimactic. After making preparations and then entering to joyful acclamation, Jesus merely enters, looks around, and leaves.

The force of this strikingly anticlimactic entry into Jerusalem can be seen when contrasted with Simon's entry into the city in 1 Maccabees 13:51–52. Simon was one of the heroes of the Hasmonean family that had defeated and driven out Antiochus Epiphanes and the Seleucids. In the early second-century BC, Judea was ruled by the Seleucids from Syria. Their rule became especially cruel with the rise to power of Antiochus and his effort to control Judea by imposing Hellenistic culture and seeking to eliminate the central features of Judaism. In 167 BC Mattathias, the local priest in Modein, a town northwest of Jerusalem, initiated a rebellion by killing Antiochus's representative. The rebellion was led by Mattathias's son, Judas "Maccabeus" ("the hammer"), and after Judas's death, by Simon, his brother. Judea gained political independence under Simon, who continued to lead military operations to liberate all of Judea and Jerusalem. He later purified the temple from its pollution by foreigners—the event commemorated in the Jewish celebration of Hanukkah—and subsequently led a celebratory entrance:

> Simon's men entered the citadel on the twenty-third day of the second month, in the year 171, with utterances of praise and palm branches and to the music of lyres and cymbals and lutes and hymns and songs, because a great enemy had been smashed and driven out of Israel. He decreed that the day be observed annually with rejoicing. (1 Macc 13:51–52)[1]

The heroic deeds of the Hasmoneans recorded in 1 Maccabees shaped the first-century Jewish imagination, as the people were once again under foreign domination, this time by the Romans. They longed for a heroic figure who had the charisma to lead a fighting force to drive out the Romans and liberate the nation, purifying the land from the pollution of foreigners, just as Judas and his brothers did two centuries prior. The disciples' hopes were also shaped

---

1. Jonathan A. Goldstein, *1 Maccabees: A New Translation with Introduction and Commentary*, AB (Garden City, NY: Doubleday, 1976), 480.

by these legendary figures, as they were anticipating that Jesus would somehow become this heroic figure who would be the agent of God's spectacular redemption of his people. But Mark's narrative subverts these hopes at every turn. Jesus knows that the crowds long for this sort of messiah, which is why he continually commands people to keep quiet about miracles he performs. He knows that Judea is filled with revolutionary fervor, but he is careful to avoid generating the sort of movement that will be shaped by Maccabean violence. He comes preaching a cross-shaped kingdom, calling on disciples to take up their crosses and join him on the way to Jerusalem, where he will not lead a military triumph but will be handed over, tortured, and killed.[2]

This entry into Jerusalem, then, is a subversion of cultural expectations shaped by Simon's triumphant entry. *It is an anti-triumphal entry!* In a culture that knew the stories of Maccabean heroism, Jesus intentionally plays against the type. He does not stir up the crowds at all but merely looks around and leaves. The disciples, however, are still trying to influence Jesus toward playing the role of a military hero. They continue in their role in Mark of being a group of people who have trouble with the way that God brings about his purposes. God works out his purposes in upside-down ways—through weakness, suffering, and death, and this is a pattern that is consistent throughout Scripture.

EXPLAIN the Story

Preparing to Enter Jerusalem (vv. 1–6)

After the long journey from Galilee, Jesus and his disciples arrive to the small towns of Bethphage and Bethany, just to the east of Jerusalem, on the eastern slope of the Mount of Olives. The traveling party stops first in Bethany, likely the easternmost of the two, and Jesus sends the disciples to Bethphage in order to secure a colt for Jesus's arrival into Jerusalem (v. 1).[3] Mark has already been portraying Jesus as an authoritative teacher throughout the Gospel, and he has seized the initiative in multiple encounters with his opponents and in conversations with his disciples. Mark intensifies this portrayal here as he depicts Jesus determining the action, fully in control of unfolding events.

---

2. For more on the relationship of this episode to 1 Maccabees, see Timothy Gombis, "1 Maccabees and Mark 11:1–11: A Subversive Entry into Jerusalem," in *Reading Mark in Context: Jesus and Second Temple Judaism*, ed. Ben C. Blackwell, John K. Goodrich, and Jason Maston (Grand Rapids: Zondervan, 2018).

3. Beavis, *Mark*, 167.

He predicts what will happen as he gives instructions to the two disciples whom he directs to secure for him a colt for his entry into the city.

Jesus has been walking everywhere he has gone throughout Mark, so his decision to ride a colt into the city is significant. He intends to enter the city in a manner that recalls the prophecy in Zechariah 9:9, speaking of a godly, royal figure:

> Rejoice greatly, O daughter of Zion!
> Shout in triumph, O daughter of Jerusalem!
> Behold, your king is coming to you;
> He is just and endowed with salvation,
> Humble, and mounted on a donkey,
> Even on a colt, the foal of a donkey. (NASB)

Jesus sends two of his disciples to Bethphage where they will find a colt that is tied up and which no one has ridden. This reference to no one having ridden the colt points to royalty, since no one else may ride a king's animal.[4] Jesus commands his disciples to untie it and bring it to him (v. 2). He then gives them strikingly specific instructions that are predictive of exactly what happens when they go to procure for him the colt. If anyone asks why they are untying it, they should report that "the Lord needs it and will send it back here shortly" (v. 3). The encounter proceeds just as Jesus predicted, and the people let them go (vv. 4–6). Jesus's predictive power here stresses his acceptance and embrace of the events that await him.[5] He is not an unwitting victim of the developing dynamics that will eventuate in his death. He is, rather, "the Lord," the sort of king whose royal coronation is his journey to the cross.[6]

This is yet another tantalizing note in Mark of people outside the scope of the disciples who are loyal to Jesus. In 4:36, Mark indicates that there were other boats with Jesus following him across the Sea of Galilee. In 9:38–41, John had pointed to other disciples who were casting out demons in Jesus's name. And throughout the narrative, there have constantly been crowds listening to Jesus, though much of Mark's focus has been on Jesus and the disciples. Here, Jesus indicates that in Bethany, there are disciples who know Jesus as "Lord" and who will gladly give up possessions in obedience to Jesus, "the Lord." Audiences who hear Mark's Gospel are here again challenged to see themselves as partners with other Christian communities, part of something

---

4. Garland, *Theology of Mark's Gospel*, 148; Boring, *Mark*, 314.
5. Moloney, *Gospel of Mark*, 218.
6. Boring, *Mark*, 315.

bigger than themselves—the worldwide kingdom of God made up of diverse communities of Jesus-followers.

The Approach to Jerusalem (vv. 7–10)

The disciples bring the colt to Jesus, who will ride it into the city and into the temple courts. Jesus is entering as a godly Davidic king, in fulfillment of Zechariah 9:9. Others, however, are acting according to the Maccabean script. The disciples threw their cloaks over the colt (v. 7), and as Jesus is being led to the city, the crowds lay their cloaks on the ground, symbolizing their offering of themselves to the hero they are acclaiming.[7] Others spread branches just as the crowds had done nearly two centuries earlier, welcoming Simon into the city as military conqueror (1 Macc 13:51).

Mark adds an intriguing note in v. 9 that indicates that the disciples and the crowds are not acting in accordance with Jesus's desires. He refers to "those who went ahead and those who followed" (v. 9). As Moloney states, indications of physical proximity to Jesus are important in Mark's Gospel. The disciples are called to be "with" Jesus (3:14), which means thinking and acting according to his agenda.[8] Here, however, they are acclaiming him a conquering king with the language of Psalm 118, a psalm that celebrates God's deliverance through military victory. This runs directly contrary to what Jesus has been explicitly teaching regarding his mission and purpose in coming to Jerusalem.

The crowd also celebrates "the coming kingdom of our father David" (v. 10), which they eagerly anticipate because they imagine that this kingdom will bring the triumph of God over the Romans and the liberation of God's people. They do not understand, however, that Jesus has already inaugurated God's kingdom in his arrival, demonstrating its reality by driving out demons and healing the sick. Kingdom inhabitants give their lives for others, just as their king does, rather than seeking violent revolution.

Jesus Enters Jerusalem (v. 11)

Jesus now arrives at the temple, and Mark's description narrows, zeroing in on only one actor. The crowds have fallen away, and Mark focuses on Jesus alone, who went into the temple courts, "looked around at everything," and left, returning to Bethany (v. 11). This is a stunningly abrupt visit! Mark notes that he left as he did "since it was already late," a detail that Garland finds pregnant with significance. This may be "a fateful nod to God's timetable

---

7. Boring, *Mark*, 315.
8. Moloney, *Gospel of Mark*, 219.

for the temple. It is already too late."[9] It is late in the day, and judgment is on its way. Given the cultural script of the triumphant Maccabean heroes, this entrance is shocking in its lack of drama. Mark builds the tension and completely deflates it with his terse and cryptic description of Jesus's entrance and exit in v. 11. But Jesus has his own agenda. He does not come to purify and rededicate the temple, as did Simon. Jesus comes in the manner of the God of Israel, who shows up to inspect the fruit of his people before rendering a verdict of judgment (cf. Isa 5:1-7). This judgment is coming, as Mark's Gospel will show in the episodes that follow.

LIVE the Story

Turning Jesus into a Conquering Hero

Mark portrays the disciples and the crowds as trying to turn Jesus into a Maccabean hero—a strongman who would fight for their cause. They longed for deliverance from the oppressive occupation of the Romans and were eager to follow someone who promised to bring in the kingdom of God. Jesus, of course, initiates the rule of God by going to the cross—through humble service and self-giving love. God triumphs in a manner that seems radically upside-down to humans, since God's wisdom is totally foreign to worldly wisdom. In the wisdom of the world, triumph comes through conquest, victory, and domination; God, however, triumphs through loss, defeat, and death.

Many Christians are familiar with the reality that God's thoughts and ways are different from the world's thoughts and ways, but they may be surprised about the thrust of the scriptural passages that unfold this reality. God's ways are not necessarily an affront to the world or people outside the Christian faith. They are an offense *to God's people who prefer worldly ways of doing things*. God's wisdom is foreign to Christians who look at worldly wisdom—conquest, domination, and power seeking—as the most reasonable way to accomplish God's purposes. One example of this is Paul's letter of sharp rebuke to the culture-accommodating Corinthian church (cf. 1 Cor 1:18–2:16). One of the ways that Christians adopt worldly wisdom is by preferring an image of Jesus as a triumphant strongman, a champion in terms of what our culture envisions as heroic, powerful, and impressive.

The problem of God's people transforming Jesus into a conquering hero made in our own image and who will fight for our cause did not end with

---

9. Garland, *Theology of Mark's Gospel*, 148–49.

the disciples. This is an impulse that continues to tempt the church today. When I taught at an evangelical Christian college, I wanted to help students discern how we are constantly affected by cultural hopes, fears, prejudices, presumptions, ambitions, and assumptions as we conceive of Jesus. We see him through our own cultural lenses, and it is a constant struggle to have a faithful vision of Jesus shaped by the Gospels and the rest of Scripture. I put together a slide show of various visual depictions of Jesus and asked them to reflect on the sort of values each revealed.

We discussed *Head of Christ* by Warner Sallman, a very common portrait of Jesus looking heavenward with a pious gaze. Students noted that Jesus did not look Jewish, but rather like an American man of northern European descent. It is perhaps this notion that Clifford Davis satirized in his portrait called *The Conformist*, which we also viewed. Jesus appears as a middle-class American man who is an earnestly striving businessman. He is patriotic, wearing an American flag pin on his suit-coat lapel.

Many artistic portrayals reveal the widely held assumption among American Christians that Jesus has a special relationship with the United States. And the confusion of Christian faith and American patriotism often goes hand in hand with a desire to turn Jesus into a conquering hero. When we hold tightly to our national identity, we inevitably make Jesus a champion of our nation's interests, goals, and ambitions. This is revealed in a painting called *Undefeated* by an artist named Stephen Sawyer. He portrays Jesus as a heavily muscled champion boxer standing in a ring. The color scheme is red, white, and blue. I showed this painting to the class, and we talked about the projection of power, triumphalism, and patriotism. We noted that it ran counter to the depiction of Jesus in Scripture, whose identity is revealed by the weakness and shame of the cross throughout the New Testament, and who reveals God by going to the cross.

Jesus calls disciples to follow him on the road to the cross, which is a rejection of triumphalism, questing for power, and the alliance of the king-dom of God with any earthly entity such as the United States of America. We inhabit God's kingdom by dying to this world and its national loyalties in order to enjoy God's kingdom in the future. Envisioning Christian exis-tence as compatible with seeking political power in order to control the larger culture leads to a triumphalist imagination that turns Jesus into a conquering hero. This is a dramatic departure from how Jesus speaks about himself in Mark's Gospel: he is the suffering Son of Man who has come to give his life as a ransom for many. He will indeed come in glory in the future, but that triumph only comes through suffering, rejection, and death (Mark 8:31;

9:31; 10:33–34). The disciples are fixated on glory, power, and prestige, which reveals that their imaginations are captive to a worldly mindset that Jesus describes as satanic (8:33).

Making Jesus in Our Image

Stephen Prothero examines a number of other ways that Christians have made Jesus in their own image in his book *American Jesus: How the Son of God Became a National Icon.*[10] In the mid to late nineteenth century in the United States, evangelical Christianity underwent a feminine revision. This stemmed from a range of cultural transformations during that era that resulted in the exaltation of feminine virtues. In this era, Jesus tended to be described as "pious and pure, loving and merciful, meek and humble."[11] Prothero points to the production of the Currier and Ives print *Christ Walking on the Sea,* a portrayal of Jesus in feminine pose and with female accents in his clothing and body, especially his hair, facial expression, and hips. Prothero goes on to discuss depictions of Jesus as African-American and female, as a cultural outlaw, as a Mormon, and many others.

It seems to me that Christians in any and every culture will struggle with the temptation to portray Jesus in terms of their cultural values, mostly aiming to put him in the most positive light. And this is precisely where we run into trouble. If, for example, we portray Jesus as a good-looking white man with the facial features that represent a northern European heritage, we may be wanting to cast him in the best possible light. Artists who do so may protest that they are simply depicting Jesus in terms of what they know. But what does this communicate to people of other ethnicities? Does this not send the message that somehow white people have a claim on Jesus, since he is white? If you do not think this is the case, how would you feel if Jesus were portrayed as a black person? Keep in mind that Jesus is not a white European but a Middle Eastern Jew.

We ran into precisely this problem at our seminary. Someone had donated a lovely piece of stained-glass art that depicts the crucifixion. I remember when it was originally given, and a handful of us commented that the portrayal was too beautiful and sanitary. The Gospel accounts indicate an awful scene in which Jesus was beaten brutally. But the stained-glass piece did not portray him as suffering all that much and left Jesus fairly well untouched. Yet because I observed it along with five other white men, none of us commented on

---

10. Stephen Prothero, *American Jesus: How the Son of God Became a National Icon* (New York: Farrar, Straus and Giroux, 2003).

11. Prothero, *American Jesus,* 59.

the features that indicated Jesus was a northern European white man, with sandy blond hair. But when nonwhite students saw it, this was the first thing they noted.

One way to avoid making Jesus in our own image is to cultivate conversations with Christians of other ethnicities and social classes. In this way, our speech about Jesus, our portrayals of him, and our inadvertent attachment of values to him will appear more obvious. This is not an insignificant issue. The New Testament teaches that the church must publicly display its international and multiethnic character so that God can be seen to be the Great King over all the earth (Rom 3:29–30). If we make Jesus in our own image, we run the risk of offending other Christians, but also of misrepresenting and offending God himself.

CHAPTER 46

Mark 11:12-25

📖 LISTEN to the Story

¹²The next day as they were leaving Bethany, Jesus was hungry. ¹³Seeing in the distance a fig tree in leaf, he went to find out if it had any fruit. When he reached it, he found nothing but leaves, because it was not the season for figs. ¹⁴Then he said to the tree, "May no one ever eat fruit from you again." And his disciples heard him say it.

¹⁵On reaching Jerusalem, Jesus entered the temple courts and began driving out those who were buying and selling there. He overturned the tables of the money changers and the benches of those selling doves, ¹⁶and would not allow anyone to carry merchandise through the temple courts. ¹⁷And as he taught them, he said, "Is it not written: 'My house will be called a house of prayer for all nations'? But you have made it 'a den of robbers.'"

¹⁸The chief priests and the teachers of the law heard this and began looking for a way to kill him, for they feared him, because the whole crowd was amazed at his teaching.

¹⁹When evening came, Jesus and his disciples went out of the city.

²⁰In the morning, as they went along, they saw the fig tree withered from the roots. ²¹Peter remembered and said to Jesus, "Rabbi, look! The fig tree you cursed has withered!"

²²"Have faith in God," Jesus answered. ²³"Truly I tell you, if anyone says to this mountain, 'Go, throw yourself into the sea,' and does not doubt in their heart but believes that what they say will happen, it will be done for them. ²⁴Therefore I tell you, whatever you ask for in prayer, believe that you have received it, and it will be yours. ²⁵And when you stand praying, if you hold anything against anyone, forgive them, so that your Father in heaven may forgive you your sins."

Listening to the Text in the Story: Isaiah 5:1–7; 56:7; Jeremiah 7:1–11; 19:1–13; Ezekiel 4:1–3; Micah 7:1; Acts 7:48–53; 1 Corinthians 3:16–17; Ephesians 2:19–22.

This passage is yet another Markan sandwich, a device common to this Gospel, in which Mark narrates Jesus cursing a fig tree (vv. 12–14, 20–25) with an account of his shutting down temple activity inserted into the middle (vv. 15–19). In the previous episode, Jesus had visited the temple, looked around briefly, and departed (v. 11). In the same way that the God of Israel visits his people to inspect their fruit before passing judgment (cf. Isa 5:2), Jesus examines the temple and discovers that it has become a place of corruption, and he renders his judgment on it.

Several Scripture passages use agricultural metaphors to speak of Israel, with the fruit they produce standing in for their character and conduct. Isaiah portrays God's relationship to Judah in terms of one who planted a vineyard and went to great lengths to provide for it the best conditions for fruitfulness (Isa 5:1–2). But because it yielded only bad fruit (v. 2), God would make the vineyard a wasteland (vv. 5–6).

> The vineyard of the LORD Almighty
> 　　is the nation of Israel,
> and the people of Judah
> 　　are the vines he delighted in.
> And he looked for justice, but saw bloodshed;
> 　　for righteousness, but heard cries of distress. (v. 7)

Micah uses a similar metaphor, this one directly relevant to that of the fig tree in Mark 11, which stands for the Jerusalem temple:

> What misery is mine!
> I am like one who gathers summer fruit
> 　　at the gleaning of the vineyard;
> there is no cluster of grapes to eat,
> 　　none of the early figs that I crave.
> The faithful have been swept from the land;
> 　　not one upright person remains.
> Everyone lies in wait to shed blood;
> 　　they hunt each other with nets. (Mic 7:1–2)

In Mark 11:17, Jesus indicts the Jerusalem authorities for turning the temple into a "den of robbers," a reference to Jeremiah 7:11. In that passage, God condemns the people of Judah for their complacent presumption that because they come to the temple they can freely treat others with injustice:

This is what the Lord Almighty, the God of Israel, says: Reform your ways and your actions, and I will let you live in this place. Do not trust in deceptive words and say, "This is the temple of the Lord, the temple of the Lord, the temple of the Lord!" If you really change your ways and your actions and deal with each other justly, if you do not oppress the foreigner, the fatherless or the widow and do not shed innocent blood in this place, and if you do not follow other gods to your own harm, then I will let you live in this place, in the land I gave your ancestors for ever and ever. But look, you are trusting in deceptive words that are worthless. (Jer 7:3–8)

The "deceptive words" Jeremiah twice warns about refer to their self-assurance that since they have the temple, where the God of Israel resides, they must be in good standing with God even though they mistreat the foreigner, the orphan, and the widow. Jeremiah continues with an ominous warning:

Will you steal and murder, commit adultery and perjury, burn incense to Baal and follow other gods you have not known, and then come and stand before me in this house, which bears my Name, and say, "We are safe"—safe to do all these detestable things? Has this house, which bears my Name, become a den of robbers to you? But I have been watching! declares the Lord. (Jer 7:9–11)

The judgment Jesus renders in Mark 11:17, then, is not aimed at the temple itself, as if it did not have a God-ordained function. Jesus passes judgment on the oppressive and exploitative practices of the temple authorities whereby they enrich themselves at the expense of the poor. In addition, like Jeremiah's audience, they are presumptuous and complacent, imagining that because of the temple's presence and their attendance at it, they may feel "safe," as if God turns a blind eye to their conduct. Like Jeremiah before him, Jesus is about to deliver God's verdict of judgment.

EXPLAIN the Story

Jesus Curses a Fig Tree (vv. 12–14)

In the previous episode, Jesus entered Jerusalem and went into the temple. That visit ended in a curiously anticlimactic fashion, with Jesus simply looking around and leaving for Bethany (v. 11). The next day, on returning to the city, Jesus and his disciples passed by a fig tree, and Jesus was hungry. Keeping in mind how significant verbs of perception (seeing, hearing) function in Mark's Gospel, it is crucial that Jesus *sees* the fig tree with leaves on it and "went to find out if it had any fruit" (v. 13). Just as the vineyard stands in for Israel in Scripture, the fig tree symbolizes the Jerusalem temple. Jesus's action of going over to the tree to discern whether it has any fruit on it is symbolic of what he has just done in the previous passage when he went into the temple. He was there to examine its fruit.[1]

Mark states that while the tree was full of leaves, "it was not the season for figs." This is a confounding statement. Why would Jesus expect to find fruit on the tree if it was not the season for it? Mark is most likely pointing to the temple's condition—it looks good on the outside, but there is no fruit.[2] Further, Mark's statements about time and seasons in this passage are significant. In v. 11, Jesus left the temple because "it was already late," pointing to the reality that God's judgment has already been rendered—it is now too late. Here, it is not the season for figs, but it does not matter because God can show up whenever he desires to determine the condition of his people.[3] The Lord has come to his temple, and it is not ready.[4]

In response to the fruitless condition of the fig tree, Jesus curses it: "May no one ever eat fruit from you again" (v. 14). Mark prefaces Jesus's statement dramatically in the Greek text: "And answering, he said to it" (*kai apokritheis eipen autē*). This is the typical formulation for how Jesus responds to someone with whom he is speaking in the Gospels, as if Jesus is responding to the tree's communication of its condition. And his judgment is just as remarkable; literally it reads: "No longer unto eternity may no one eat fruit from you" (*mēketi eis ton aiōna ek sou mēdeis karpon phagoi*). This is a final and settled judgment. Mark inserts the comment that his disciples heard what he said to the tree (v. 14).

Jesus Shuts Down Temple Activity (vv. 15–19)

Having arrived in the city, they went into the temple courts where Jesus proceeded to make a scene. It is important to note here that Jesus was not "cleansing" the temple, as this episode is commonly understood. Rather, *he was shutting it down*. He was bringing its operations to a close. He overturned tables and drove out those who were buying and selling (v. 15). These merchants were

---

1. Hooker, *Mark*, 267.
2. Black, *Mark*, 243.
3. "This is yet another case in which Jesus steps, at least functionally, into a role given exclusively to the Lord God in the Old Testament" (Hays, *Echoes of Scripture in the Gospels*, 76).
4. Garland, *Theology of Mark's Gospel*, 149.

not necessarily doing anything inappropriate. "Money changers" performed an important function for those exchanging coins in order to pay the temple tax. And those who came to offer sacrifices needed to purchase doves in order to offer the proper sacrifices.[5] Jesus also prevented those who were moving around the vessels and other items used in the temple's proper functioning (v. 16).[6]

Jesus is not "reforming" or "cleansing" the temple but rather halting its operation. This is a performed parable, symbolizing God's judgment on the temple. God had instructed the prophets to perform similar parabolic actions to explain his judgment on his people (Isa 20; Jer 13:1–11; 19; Ezek 4:1–3).[7] Jesus's disruptive action in the temple functions in the same way. The temple was no longer playing the role for which God had designed it, but had become corrupt. It was not the place on earth where people encountered God. Jesus is the new temple, and people know and encounter God through him and by belonging to communities of his followers.

Jesus proceeds to "teach," explaining what he is doing (v. 17). As he does elsewhere, Mark stresses Jesus's "teaching" through repetition ("taught," v. 17; "his teaching," v. 18). While at times Mark speaks of Jesus's teaching without mentioning the content of what he taught (cf. 1:21–28), here he cites Jesus's teaching in two sentences. Jesus refers to God's intended purpose for the temple, citing Isaiah 56:7. God intended it to be a house of prayer "for all nations," where Israel and the nations could encounter God.[8] Jesus enacts this reality throughout Mark by ministering to Jews and non-Jews (5:1–20; 7:24–37). Jesus condemns the temple authorities, however, for turning it into "a den of robbers," quoting Jeremiah 7:11 (v. 17). He is not here condemning the various systems of economic exchange at the temple. Those were all necessary for the temple to function properly. He is, rather, passing judgment on the Jerusalem leadership that had looked to the presence of the temple as God's endorsement of their complacency and toleration of their corruption. The temple had come to represent the tragedy that God's people had taken perverse comfort in their identity as God's people to excuse their disobedience.

The chief priests and the teachers of the law knew that Jesus was referring to them in his condemnation (v. 18). Like the Pharisees in 3:6, they began to plan for a way to kill him. Because the crowds in the temple were amazed at

---

5. Boring, *Mark*, 320.

6. The NIV translates *skeuos* as "merchandise," but this term likely refers to the various vessels used in the temple, such as containers used for transporting animal blood or other sacrificial elements (Marcus, *Mark 8–16*, 783).

7. Garland, *Theology of Mark's Gospel*, 149.

8. The Greek term translated here as "nations" (*ethnesin*) appears throughout the NT and is often translated "gentiles."

Jesus's teaching, however, they were unable to make their move at that point. They had to lay low for the time being. Just as the previous episode had ended in anticlimactic fashion, Jesus does not capitalize on the reaction of the crowds to further his own fame. When evening came, he and his disciples left the city and returned to Bethany (v. 19).

The Withered Fig Tree and Prayer (vv. 20–25)

They returned the next day, and on their way to Jerusalem they encountered the fig tree, which Mark notes was "withered from the roots," indicating complete and final judgment (v. 20). Like the temple, it was disconnected from its source of life and nourishment, being dead on the inside. Seeing the tree and remembering what Jesus had previously said, Peter remarked to Jesus, "Rabbi, look! The fig tree you cursed has withered!" (v. 21). This is yet another association between the fig tree and the temple. Later, when Jesus and the disciples leave the temple, one of them says to Jesus, "Teacher, look! What massive stones! What magnificent buildings!" (13:1). These twin exhortations for Jesus to "look," identifying him as "Rabbi" and "Teacher," lead audiences to link the temple and fig tree together. Just as the fig tree has been cursed and is now withered "from the roots," the temple, thoroughly corrupted, will be utterly destroyed (13:2).

The connection between the withered fig tree and the discussion of prayer in vv. 22–25 may not be immediately clear to readers of Mark. When we think of the temple's function, however, the relation comes into focus. The disciples may be wondering how they can pray if the temple is dead on the inside and under God's judgment. The temple was indeed supposed to be a place of prayer for all the nations, the place where heaven and earth came together, and where they could encounter God. If it is really no better than a lifeless pile of rubble, then what?[9]

For Jesus, God's judgment on the temple and its imminent destruction do not mean that God does not hear the prayers of his people. This looks ahead to the reality of the church as the new temple (1 Cor 3:16–17; Eph 2:19–22). Because the Jerusalem temple had become a corrupt institution, it was no longer the place where God would be encountered. Now, God is encountered among those who are in Jesus—the new temple—and who gather in the Spirit of Jesus. We encounter God in the church, the body made up of disciples from all nations.

And God hears and answers the prayers of his people who pray from

---

9. Cf. Garland, *Theology of Mark's Gospel*, 150.

genuine faith in him. It does not matter whether prayers are being offered from within the temple. The mountain in v. 23 refers to the temple mount, which has become a place of injustice and oppression of God's people. The prayer, then, for the mountain to be thrown into the sea is a prayer for justice. If God's people pray for the burden of injustice to be removed, they will be heard, and God will act on their behalf. The assurance that God will do "whatever you ask for in prayer" does not have to do with any and every prayer, however selfish (v. 24). This has to do with God's people crying out against injustice and the removal of impediments to humanity's enjoyment of God's presence on earth.

And God's people must be a people of ongoing reconciliation and renewal. This is the only way they can enjoy God's forgiveness. Therefore, if their praying has been accompanied by a lack of forgiveness of others, Jesus commands them to forgive. Only then will they enjoy truly being the people of God, the gathered community of those who are the temple—the presence of God on earth, and the forgiven people who are in right relation to God (v. 25).

LIVE the Story

Cultivating Justice among God's People

Jesus declares God's judgment against the temple because its leadership has tolerated and fostered injustice. Just as in Jeremiah's day, those entrusted as stewards of the temple have not served the needy, the vulnerable, and the marginalized but have rather exploited their positions to enrich themselves at the expense of the weak and disadvantaged. The imagery of the cursed fig tree also recalls other prophetic texts in which God declares his judgment against Israel because they have become a people tolerant of injustice (Isa 5:1–7; Mic 7:1–6).

God's vision for the temple as a place of care for the vulnerable and suffering, connecting people with God, especially the needy—the foreigner, the widow, and the orphan—ought to inform how we understand the ongoing life of God's new temple. In Mark's Gospel, Jesus is God's new temple, and in much of the rest of New Testament theology, the church is the temple of God, which is the community gathered in Christ by the Spirit. There is no contradiction between Mark's vision of *Jesus himself* as the temple and Paul, who envisions *the church* as God's new dwelling (1 Cor 3:16–17; Eph 2:19–22). Mark emphasizes Jesus as the temple in order to stress the absolute necessity of the church being a community of ongoing justice for the needy, hospitality for the marginalized, and service to the vulnerable. Mark's perspective reminds us that the church does not possess God or contain God, having the prerogative to dispense God to others as we see fit. On the contrary, it is only when the church welcomes the socially marginalized—those who "don't matter" in the world's estimation—that the church enjoys the presence of Jesus and of God (9:37).

Churches that are complacent about justice ought to be aware that they are subject to God's judgment in the same way that the Jerusalem temple was. Other New Testament writers capture God's vision for the church as a just community in different ways. James recalls prophetic critiques of Israel in his harsh rebukes to churches that tolerate economic injustice in their communities (2:1–13; 5:1–6). Paul excoriates the Corinthians for the same exploitative practices, telling them that it would be better for them not to gather as the church, because the mistreatment of their poorer members by the rich ones indicates that when they gather they are not participating in Christian practices (1 Cor 11:17–34). In fact, in a terrifying passage, Paul says that these behaviors are why God is causing some to be sick and others to die (v. 30).

This text in Mark—along with much of the rest of this Gospel—reminds us that throughout Scripture, God is a God of justice and that he has created a renewed people to carry out his justice in the world. The terms in Hebrew and Greek for "just" are the same as those for "righteous," and the terms in both testaments for "justice" are the same as those for "righteousness."[10] These terms describe who God is, and they constitute the vision of interpersonal and community life to which God calls his people. They are, after all, called to embody the life of God on earth. This was Israel's identity in the Old Testament, and this is the character and mode of life of the church in the New Testament.

It is important to have our imaginations shaped by a biblical vision of justice rather than one that comes from some other legal or ethical tradition. In Scripture, justice is not necessarily "each person getting what they deserve," and it is not always "punishment." Biblical justice has much to do with God's created order of flourishing—*shalom*. God calls his people to enjoy his gracious reign, living in community patterns that flow from and embody his just/righteous character. God's people look after one another and enjoy one another; they seek the best for each other and creatively plan in order to bring about community flourishing. When this order of *shalom* is violated or broken

---

10. It may be that translational issues have affected a loss of vision among English-speaking Christians of becoming a church that embodies the justice of the God of Christian Scripture in the wider world. It is easy to personalize and internalize "righteousness" as a status we have from God (i.e., we are declared righteous) and to imagine that if we are engaged in a certain kind of personal piety, we are practicing righteousness. We have lost the connection of God and his people to *justice*.

through interpersonal sin, with damage done by one person to another or one group violating the good order of the community by exploiting or oppressing others, *God's people must seek to enact biblical justice.*

Biblical justice does not necessarily involve seeking to lay blame and punish wrongdoers. The highest priority is to restore *shalom*, and this can take place in a variety of ways, as God's people seek God's wisdom to understand what has taken place and to reconcile offenders and the offended. God's justice, therefore, is active and community oriented; it is a positive pursuit carried out by God's people who seek to expand the reign of God's flourishing into the far reaches of their community life. And as a community, they seek to extend it beyond themselves in relationships with other communities.[11]

In Ephesians, Paul depicts the ongoing life of positive justice and the restoration of *shalom* to which Christian communities are called. He notes that when the recipients of this letter were taught about Christ and the vision of truth as it is in Jesus (Eph 4:20–21), this entailed an ongoing process of putting off their old humanity (v. 22), being transformed in their thinking (v. 23), and an ongoing process of putting on the new humanity (v. 24). The "old humanity" and "new humanity" are not internal, psychological dispositions of each individual Christian. The old humanity is how Paul envisions the corporate practices of humanity as they are mired in the enslavement of the present evil age through practices of exploitation and mistreatment of one another. And the new humanity consists of the corporate practices of humanity in Christ, those who are empowered by the Spirit to enjoy new ways of life that embody the presence of God among the church.

In Ephesians 4:25–32, Paul gives several examples of interpersonal practices to get rid of, along with positive practices to cultivate. When the church positively seeks to identify corrupted ways of life that exist among them and prayerfully seeks to cultivate new practices that embody God's justice, they are living into the fullness of their identity as the people of God of the new creation, "created to be like God in true *righteousness* [or, "justice"] and holiness" (v. 24).

After being a student of Scripture for a few decades and coming to see this vision of God's passion for his justice among his people, I have come to see that discerning injustices in our institutions, churches, and communities takes active listening and learning. I am so thankful for my colleagues and

---

11. For excellent and accessible introductions to biblical justice, with creative ways to embody God's justice in the modern world, see Bethany H. Hoang and Kristen Deede Johnson, *The Justice Calling: Where Passion Meets Perseverance* (Grand Rapids: Brazos, 2016) and Julie Clawson, *Everyday Justice: The Global Impact of Our Daily Choices* (Downers Grove, IL: InterVarsity Press, 2009).

administrators at the seminary where I currently teach. We have begun to engage vigorously with ways we have fallen short of inhabiting God's justice in the past and are seeking to rectify those by fostering conversations about gender and race. I have been enlightened by learning from female colleagues and students about their experiences in our school, especially the small slights they receive from male students and even insensitive faculty members. I recently finished reading *That's What She Said* by Joanne Lipman, which was a fascinating reflection on the pervasive injustices, both large and small, that characterize workplaces around the world.[12] She draws on extensive research and offers good and bad models for how men and women can work together. Further, she includes some wonderfully simple and practical advice for how men can advocate for their female counterparts.

My colleagues and I have also sought to educate ourselves on issues of race, and I have been astounded by the wealth of resources at our disposal. It is overwhelming to simply read the history about the persistent injustices suffered by black people in America. As a white, middle-class male, I grew up learning about the American Civil War and assumed that any and every injustice came to an end at the war's close in 1865. I have since learned about the constant efforts throughout the nation, above and below the Mason-Dixon line, to ensure that black people were degraded, mistreated, and denied good jobs and opportunities for education and advancement.[13] I have read about the practice of redlining in northern cities that denied black people access to home loans and intentionally segregated white and black neighborhoods.[14] And this is to say nothing of the terrorizing of black communities through lynching—barbaric murder that was routinely ignored by local law enforcement throughout the country—and mass incarceration of black men.[15]

I have learned over the last few years that I inhabit a place of privilege as a white male. I have also learned about "white fragility," the lack of stamina

---

12. Joanne Lipman, *That's What She Said: What Men Need to Know (and Women Need to Tell Them) about Working Together* (New York: William Morrow, 2018).

13. Beverly Daniel Tatum, *Why Are All the Black Kids Sitting Together in the Cafeteria?: And Other Conversations about Race*, 2nd ed. (New York: Basic Books, 2017); Ta-Nehisi Coates, *Between the World and Me* (New York: Spiegel & Grau, 2015); Carol Anderson, *White Rage: The Unspoken Truth of Our Racial Divide* (New York: Bloomsbury, 2017).

14. Linda Gartz, *Redlined: A Memoir of Race, Change, and Fractured Community in 1960s Chicago* (Berkeley, CA: She Writes Press, 2018); Richard Rothstein, *The Color of Law: A Forgotten History of How Our Government Segregated America* (New York: Liveright, 2018); Todd E. Robinson, *A City within a City: The Black Freedom Struggle in Grand Rapids, Michigan* (Philadelphia: Temple University Press, 2012).

15. D. L. Mayfield, "Facing Our Legacy of Lynching," *Christianity Today*, August 18, 2017; Michelle Alexander, *The New Jim Crow: Mass Incarceration in the Age of Colorblindness* (New York: The New Press, 2012).

in white people for handling discussions of race without reacting with anger, denial, shame, guilt, or simply shutting down.[16] There is doubtless also a corresponding "male fragility," the inability of men to reckon with discussions of cultural patterns and relational dynamics of gender.

My study of Mark has shaped me in such a way as to set me up perfectly for all of these discussions and this entire educational enterprise. If I have taken up my cross to follow Jesus on the road to the cross, then I have no place for defensiveness. My identifying fully with the death of Christ gives me no place to react with angry denials. I am situated perfectly to be ready to deny my self-defensive impulses and actively pursue justice on behalf of others, guaranteeing my participation in the glorious kingdom at the coming of the Son of Man. I am liberated from defensiveness as I have nothing to defend. I am set free to listen and to learn and to collaborate with others by thinking creatively about how to identify patterns of community injustice and cultivate dynamics of community justice. There are so many other obvious opportunities for a positive pursuit of justice as God's people, but I have decided to begin by having my eyes opened to ways the culture—and my own Christian tradition—has been shaped by injustice.

---

16. Robin DiAngelo, *White Fragility: Why It's So Hard for White People to Talk About Racism* (Boston: Beacon, 2018).

Mark 11:27–33

LISTEN to the Story

²⁷They arrived again in Jerusalem, and while Jesus was walking in the temple courts, the chief priests, the teachers of the law and the elders came to him. ²⁸"By what authority are you doing these things?" they asked. "And who gave you authority to do this?"

²⁹Jesus replied, "I will ask you one question. Answer me, and I will tell you by what authority I am doing these things. ³⁰John's baptism—was it from heaven, or of human origin? Tell me!"

³¹They discussed it among themselves and said, "If we say, 'From heaven,' he will ask, 'Then why didn't you believe him?' ³²But if we say, 'Of human origin' . . ." (They feared the people, for everyone held that John really was a prophet.)

³³So they answered Jesus, "We don't know."

Jesus said, "Neither will I tell you by what authority I am doing these things."

Listening to the Text in the Story: Genesis 1:1–2:3; 2:19–20; Daniel 7:13–14, 27; Matthew 28:16–20; Mark 2:1–12; Revelation 2:26–27; 12:10.

Jesus, as God's authorized agent, had come to Jerusalem, looked around, and assessed what was going on in the temple (11:1–11). He then rendered his judgment by shutting down the functions of the temple (11:12–25). As Mark develops, Jesus is the one through whom God may be encountered—he replaces the earthly temple, which no longer functions properly because of its corrupt leadership. Following Jesus's judgment on the temple, Mark narrates a series of conflicts between Jesus and the Sanhedrin. These engagements parallel Jesus's encounters with the Pharisees and teachers of the law in 2:1–3:6 that concluded with their plotting to kill him (3:6). The engagements in 11:27–12:34 involve questions put to Jesus. In response, Jesus sets before them his identity and invites them to recognize the divine logic at work whereby he is God's appointed agent of kingdom rule.

Jesus's authority has been a prominent issue in Mark. In the larger context of Scripture, God has ultimate authority as creator of all things, which he demonstrates in his creative acts. In Genesis 1:1–2:3, God speaks, and creation responds immediately. The functionaries in the heavens and everything on the earth and in the skies and seas derives its identity from him. And God delegates his authority in commissioning the human to name the animals. Just as God gives names to items within his creation (Gen 1:5), so too does the human for the animals (Gen 2:19), demonstrating the dominion God gave to humanity.

God also delegates authority to the king of Israel to rule on his behalf, as God's son (Ps 2:7–10; cf. also Ps 110). In Daniel 7, a passage that informs Jesus's designation as Son of Man in Mark, God delegates authority to "one like a son of man" and to the people loyal to him:

> In my vision at night I looked, and there before me was one like a son of man, coming with the clouds of heaven. He approached the Ancient of Days and was led into his presence. He was given authority, glory and sovereign power; all nations and peoples of every language worshiped him. His dominion is an everlasting dominion that will not pass away, and his kingdom is one that will never be destroyed. (vv. 13–14)

Later, Daniel points toward the eschatological reality in which God will gather together a people to embody the rule of the Son of Man over creation:

> Then the sovereignty, power and greatness of all the kingdoms under heaven will be handed over to the holy people of the Most High. His kingdom will be an everlasting kingdom, and all rulers will worship and obey him. (v. 27)

The book of Revelation depicts this same hope, holding out the promise of rule alongside God's Messiah for all those who are faithful to Jesus:

> To the one who is victorious and does my will to the end, I will give authority over the nations—that one "will rule them with an iron scepter and will dash them to pieces like pottery"—just as I have received authority from my Father. (2:26–27)

Then I heard a loud voice in heaven say:

"Now have come the salvation and the power
 and the kingdom of our God,
 and the authority of his Messiah.
For the accuser of our brothers and sisters,
 who accuses them before our God day and night,
 has been hurled down.
They triumphed over him
 by the blood of the Lamb
 and by the word of their testimony;
they did not love their lives so much
 as to shrink from death." (12:10–11)

Jesus is this figure to whom God has delegated authority to inaugurate the kingdom and declare God's judgments. The Jerusalem leadership objects to Jesus's claim that he plays this role in God's designs, and in this passage they call it into question.

EXPLAIN the Story

Jesus and his disciples arrive in Jerusalem after passing the withered fig tree that Jesus had previously cursed (11:14, 20–21). Three groups approach Jesus as he is walking in the temple courts: "the chief priests, the teachers of the law and the elders" (v. 27). Jesus has previously encountered "the teachers of the law" and often had contended with them (2:6, 16; 3:20; 7:15; 9:14). Just the day before, the chief priests and the teachers of the law heard Jesus condemn them for turning the temple into a den of thieves, after which they "began looking for a way to kill him" (11:17–18). These two groups are now joined by "the elders." Together, these represent the Sanhedrin, the Jewish "supreme court of justice," that exercised legal, political, and spiritual authority.[1]

They press Jesus with questions about the source of his authority to do "these things," referring to what he had just done the previous day in occupying the temple and shutting down its normal flow of operations (11:15–16). They may also have had in mind Jesus's entire ministry, since the teachers of the law had previously heard his teaching and seen him in action. They had

---

1. The authority of the Sanhedrin, a body comprised of 71 leaders, would be limited to some extent by the occupying Romans (G. H. Twelftree, "Sanhedrin," *DJG* 836–40; Edwards, *Mark*, 350–51).

already wondered about his authority to forgive sins (2:6–10).[2] In their view, they are the ones in charge of the temple and are God's appointed authorities over God's people. Their questions to Jesus are not sincere, however, and are more of a confrontational challenge. After all, they have long since cast their lot in opposition to Jesus, plotting to kill him (3:6; 11:18).

Mark has developed Jesus's authority at length to this point in the narrative. Audiences know Jesus's true identity as the Son of God, the divinely appointed and authoritative agent who ushers in the kingdom of God. Mark identifies him this way at the opening (1:1), and God declares Jesus's identity at his baptism (1:11) and the transfiguration, at which God pronounced, "This is my Son, whom I love. Listen to him!" (9:7). Jesus exhibited this authority by healing and casting out demons, who at points name Jesus as God's Son (1:24; 5:7). Further, the crowds recognized that Jesus taught with authority, unlike the teachers of the law, and that he had authority over demons (1:22–27). Even his disciples wondered at his power to command obedience from the wind and the waves (4:41). The Sanhedrin, however, refuses to recognize Jesus's authority, especially as he has now entered the very heart of Jewish life, the temple, and asserted his authority over it.[3]

Jesus responds to them by asking a question of his own, and he does so in commanding fashion. He frames his question with the repeated imperative verb, *apokrithēte*, that the NIV translates as "answer me" (v. 29) and "tell me!" (v. 30). He challenges them to identify the source of John's baptism, which stands in for John's ministry of calling for repentance: "Was it from heaven, or of human origin?"[4] Jesus is not evading their original question but rather forcing them to face up to the answer that is staring them in the face by setting the whole case before them. He is leading them to think through the divine logic that is unfolding according to Scripture, beginning with Elijah the forerunner—identified with John the Baptist in 9:12–13—who called God's people to repent and prepare themselves for the coming one. He puts the onus on them to reckon with events and discern what God is doing. Their opportunity to respond is open-ended at this point, though audiences already know that their hearts are hardened and that events will turn out as Jesus has predicted three times on the way to Jerusalem (8:31–32; 9:31; 10:33–34).

The Sanhedrin, along with other groups in Mark's Gospel, is caught in a bind because they are playing a political game in order to hold on to their

---

2. Boring, *Mark*, 326; Edwards, *Mark*, 351.
3. Timothy C. Gray, *The Temple in the Gospel of Mark: A Study in Its Narrative Role* (Grand Rapids: Baker Academic, 2010), 56.
4. Strauss, *Mark*, 505.

positions of power, prominence, and prestige. They must delicately navigate the tensions between keeping the population happy and maintaining good relations with their Roman overseers. If there is any disorder or disruption, the Romans could threaten them by noting that they can easily dispense with them and find other people to take their place. But they must keep their game out of view from the people and maintain peace in order to protect their authority and the appearance of integrity and authenticity. This precarious balancing act is made all the more difficult as the population of Jerusalem has swelled to bursting during this festival season.

The delegation from the Sanhedrin huddles to reason among themselves (vv. 31–32). If they admit that John was sent from God ("from heaven"), then they are acknowledging that he came with divine authority and that they should have listened to him, repented, and prepared their hearts to recognize Jesus as God's authorized agent. On the other hand, they want to avoid stating openly that John was not sent from God, confessing their belief that his ministry had a merely human origin, because "they feared the people," who regarded him as a genuine prophet (v. 32). Their reasoning reveals the true nature of their authority in contrast to what audiences already know about Jesus. They derive their authority "from below" because they fear the crowds rather than God. They are pretenders, merely playing political power games, occupying their places of authority illegitimately.

Afraid to commit themselves for fear of jeopardizing their self-appointed positions, they respond to Jesus that they do not know (v. 33). They are insincere because they have hardened their hearts. James Edwards writes, "When there is faith the size of a mustard seed, Jesus responds with 'truly I tell you,' but where there is hard-heartedness, he responds with 'neither will I tell you.'"[5]

LIVE the Story

Fearing God and Fearing People in Ministry

Jesus's question to the Sanhedrin strategically identified the precise nature of their power game. They do not operate out of fear of the God of Israel but rather want more than anything to hold on to their positions of power—that is their ultimate value. This is the reason they cannot give an honest answer. They cannot afford to be forthcoming, and their resistance to Jesus has led

---

5. Edwards, *Mark*, 353.

them to the place where they have hard hearts. They are utterly callous and completely resistant to God, unable to respond to him.

Contemporary ministry settings are filled with temptations to operate from a fundamental motivation of fearing people and wanting to make congregations happy rather than ministering from the fear of the Lord. This desire may drive us to put some distance between ourselves and the people to whom we minister, afraid that they may find out that we are somehow inadequate or not as personally impressive as we present ourselves to be in the pulpit. I knew one pastor who insulated himself from the people in his church, forging a high wall consisting of a pastoral staff that took care of everything but the preaching. Such a strategy bears bad fruit in many ways, both for the pastor who operates this way and the congregation that does not get to know their pastor.

Fear of people may drive us to avoid confronting a hard situation, especially if it might have a negative effect on the offering plate. Having spoken to a number of pastors who are bivocational, I've come to see how free a minister is when she or he does not earn their income from their ministry. They are able to give themselves fully to the church, loving people with abandon and pursuing authenticity. They can cultivate vulnerability and honesty with their churches, letting them in to see who they truly are, warts and all. Each minister must wrestle with their fundamental motivation for why they do what they do. Lifting up the hood on our ministries to tinker at the motivational level can be revelatory, and hopefully it will be salutary.

I have found it helpful to give frequent consideration to my fears, especially when it comes to my participation in ministry settings and even in my teaching. I am well aware of my desire to be seen by others as competent in what I do. When I teach the Bible in church settings, I don't like it when I don't have a ready answer to an unanticipated question. But I have learned to grow comfortable with admitting that I don't know, or to note someone's question and commit to searching out a good answer that I can pass on at some future point.

In my professional life as a seminary professor, I have faced this fear of others' opinions of me in the way that I posture myself in my classes. I note that I do what I do not because I imagine that I am the fount of all knowledge, but that I love being a student of Scripture. In fact, rather than "professor," I see myself as the "lead student" in my classes, the one responsible to direct our corporate learning. This grants dignity to everyone in the class, inviting them to fully participate in our shared project of discovery. It makes students responsible to me as I seek to grow in my understanding. I indicate that I would rather be called by my first name rather than "Dr. Gombis," as a crucial symbol of our shared status as those seeking to gain skills in interpretation for service to the church. This posture keeps me from feeling defensive or from giving in to the pressure to be seen as competent, having all the answers.

I think that all Christians, but especially pastors and ministry practitioners, would do well to consider the dynamics of power and fear that lurk in ministry settings. Doing so offers the promise of freedom from our fears of the opinions of others and invites others into full and joyful participation among the people of God.

CHAPTER 48

Mark 12:1-12

📖 LISTEN to the Story

¹Jesus then began to speak to them in parables: "A man planted a vineyard. He put a wall around it, dug a pit for the winepress and built a watchtower. Then he rented the vineyard to some farmers and moved to another place. ²At harvest time he sent a servant to the tenants to collect from them some of the fruit of the vineyard. ³But they seized him, beat him and sent him away empty-handed. ⁴Then he sent another servant to them; they struck this man on the head and treated him shamefully. ⁵He sent still another, and that one they killed. He sent many others; some of them they beat, others they killed.

⁶"He had one left to send, a son, whom he loved. He sent him last of all, saying, 'They will respect my son.'

⁷"But the tenants said to one another, 'This is the heir. Come, let's kill him, and the inheritance will be ours.' ⁸So they took him and killed him, and threw him out of the vineyard.

⁹"What then will the owner of the vineyard do? He will come and kill those tenants and give the vineyard to others. ¹⁰Haven't you read this passage of Scripture:

> "'The stone the builders rejected
>   has become the cornerstone;
> ¹¹the Lord has done this,
>   and it is marvelous in our eyes'?"

¹²Then the chief priests, the teachers of the law and the elders looked for a way to arrest him because they knew he had spoken the parable against them. But they were afraid of the crowd; so they left him and went away.

Listening to the Text in the Story: Genesis 37:18–20; Psalm 118; Isaiah 5:1–7; Jeremiah 7:25–26; Matthew 23:29–32; Luke 11:47–51.

In the previous episode, a group from the Sanhedrin had demanded that Jesus explain the source of his authority to act as he did in the temple, shutting down its operation. Jesus presented a question of his own, challenging them to commit themselves and name the source of John's baptism. Their refusal to do so closed that episode inconclusively. In this passage, however, Jesus speaks to them in parables that address the very issues of authority the Sanhedrin had just raised. These narratives draw on a range of biblical texts. The first parable is an adaptation of the song of the vineyard from Isaiah 5:1–7:

> I will sing for the one I love
>> a song about his vineyard:
> My loved one had a vineyard
>> on a fertile hillside.
> He dug it up and cleared it of stones
>> and planted it with the choicest vines.
> He built a watchtower in it
>> and cut out a winepress as well.
> Then he looked for a crop of good grapes,
>> but it yielded only bad fruit. (vv. 1–2)

Isaiah's tragic song is directed to the inhabitants of Jerusalem and the people of Judah (v. 3), declaring the basis for judgment because they have become a people of violence, exploitation, and oppression. Because of the vineyard's bad produce, the owner intends to take away its wall and hedge so that it is trampled and destroyed, making it a wasteland (vv. 5–6).

> The vineyard of the LORD Almighty
>> is the nation of Israel,
> and the people of Judah
>> are the vines he delighted in.
> And he looked for justice, but saw bloodshed;
>> for righteousness, but heard cries of distress. (v. 7)

Jesus adapts this song from Isaiah in Mark 12 and also alludes to another narrative from Scripture that involves evil plotting, betrayal, and vindication. In Mark 12:7, the tenants say to themselves, "Come, let's kill him," which is precisely what Joseph's jealous brothers say to each other:

"Here comes that dreamer!" they said to each other. "Come now, let's kill him and throw him into one of these cisterns and say that a ferocious animal devoured him. Then we'll see what comes of his dreams." (Gen 37:19–20)[1]

The Joseph story in Genesis 37–50 involves many of the same narrative dynamics as the parables that Jesus unfolds here in Mark 12. Joseph was the uniquely loved son of Jacob (Gen 37:3–4), was betrayed by his brothers, and was believed to be dead. However, God vindicated him by raising him to a high government position and through him provided for the salvation of many (cf. Gen 50:20).[2]

The Sanhedrin has pressed the issue of the authority by which Jesus is acting, and Jesus here responds to them by portraying in scriptural tones a larger scenario in which God has delegated authority to Jesus, his beloved Son. Jesus's parables also include characters that interpret and reveal the motivations and actions of the Sanhedrin. They are behaving unjustly and have placed themselves in danger of facing God's judgment.

EXPLAIN the Story

Jesus speaks to the Sanhedrin "in parables," addressing their question of authority but going well beyond it. Most commentators see one parable here, but Gray argues that there are two, claiming that the citation of Psalm 118:22–23 in vv. 10–11 is a distinct parable with its own plot, characters, conflict, and resolution.[3] *Parabolais* ("parables") can refer to a variety of stories, riddles, fables, or cryptic sayings.[4] Each parable has its own "story world" with

---

1. The wording of the speech of the tenants in Mark 12:7 in the Greek text is the same as that of Joseph's brothers in Gen 37:20 LXX: *deute apokteinōmen auton* ("come, let us kill him"; see Edwards, *Mark*, 359).

2. Boring, *Mark*, 330.

3. Gray, *Temple in the Gospel of Mark*, 70. It is possible to regard the expression *en parabolais* ("in parables") to mean that Jesus is speaking "parabolically." Yet, because the two earlier appearances of *en parabolais* in Mark indicate multiple parables, it is more likely that the expression has the same force here: Jesus speaks two parables rather than one (Rodney J. Decker, *Mark 9–16: A Handbook on the Greek Text*, Baylor Handbook on the Greek New Testament [Waco, TX: Baylor University Press, 2014], 107).

4. Jesus had taught in parables at length in Mark 3:23–4:34, but had not spoken in this way since that point. C. H. Dodd describes parables in this way: "At its simplest the parable is a metaphor or simile drawn from nature or common life, arresting the hearer by its vividness or strangeness, and leaving the mind in sufficient doubt about its precise application to tease it into active thought" (*Parables of the Kingdom*, 5).

its own integrity and employing its own imagery. Interpreters must therefore understand the two parables on their own terms before drawing points of comparison to the situation Jesus is addressing. One major feature of the two parables is that the main character in each one serves to answer the question posed to Jesus in the previous episode. In the first parable (vv. 1–9), the drama revolves around the owner of the vineyard. He is the subject of most of the verbs throughout the parable apart from the wicked actions of the tenants. In the second parable, it is "the Lord" who "has done this" (v. 11). The owner in the first parable and the Lord in the very brief second parable point to the God of Israel as the one who has sent Jesus as his Son. God is the source of authority for what Jesus is doing, and he will vindicate Jesus and construct the new temple with Jesus as its cornerstone.

The Parable of the Vineyard (vv. 1–9)

The first parable starts off just as the song in Isaiah does, with a man planting a vineyard, putting up a wall around it, digging a winepress, and building a watchtower (v. 1). Jesus, however, takes the original parable in a new direction. In Isaiah's song, the parable involved a vineyard that bore bad fruit, but Jesus tells of an owner who moved away and rented the vineyard to some tenant farmers. When "harvest time" came, the owner sent a servant to the tenant farmers to receive some of the fruit of the vineyard (v. 2). The Greek term translated "harvest time," is *kairos*, which had appeared earlier in an indication that the time of God's judgment has arrived. It was used to speak of the fig tree that Jesus cursed, which was not bearing fruit since "it was not the season [*kairos*] for figs" (11:13). And this had occurred the morning after Jesus had left the temple "since it was already late" (11:11). The appearance of *kairos* here is yet another indication in Mark's Gospel that the climactic moment of God's judgment has arrived.

The "servant" whom the owner had "sent," along with subsequent servants that are sent, recalls language used in Scripture to speak of the prophets that had been sent to Israel. In the same passage Jesus cited from Jeremiah to speak of the temple being turned into a "den of robbers" (Jer 7:11), the prophet says:

> From the time your ancestors left Egypt until now, day after day, again and again I sent you my *servants* the *prophets*. But they did not listen to me or pay attention. They were stiff-necked and did more evil than their ancestors. (Jer 7:25–26; cf. also Jer 25:4; Zech 1:6)[5]

---

5. Edwards, *Mark*, 357.

And like the servants that are assaulted and murdered by the tenants in Jesus's parable, Israel had likewise mistreated the prophets whom God sent to call them to repentance (1 Kgs 19:12–13; 2 Chr 24:20–22; 36:15–16).[6]

These servants are sent to collect some of the vineyard's fruit (Mark 12:2), which is a key departure from Isaiah's song, which condemns the vineyard itself for its production of rotten fruit. The antagonists in Jesus's parable, however, are the tenant farmers who insult the owner by mistreating the servants with increasing violence and refuse to share with the owner the portion of the fruit that rightly belongs to him.

The narrative takes an absurd turn in v. 6 as the owner has run out of available servants to send and is left with one possibility: his son, "whom he loved." It is outrageous that the owner would think to send his beloved son to the tenants that have proved themselves remorseless, murderous savages. Parables, however, do not have to work realistically, operating by conventions and rules of the real world, even though they reflect dimensions of life as we know it. It is crucial that Jesus portrays the owner of the vineyard in this way for what the parable has to say about Jesus's conflict with the Sanhedrin. The owner reasons that the tenants will surely respect his son, so he sends him last of all. The tenants, however, discern that the son is the heir to the vineyard, winepress, and tower, and they reason that if they kill him, they can lay claim to all of it. The tenants seize the son and kill him and throw him out of the vineyard (v. 8). Jesus now asks, "What then will the owner of the vineyard do? He will come and kill those tenants and give the vineyard to others" (v. 9).

The points of comparison between the parable and what is happening in Jerusalem are fairly straightforward. The owner of the vineyard is the God of Israel, the vineyard is Jerusalem and Judea, and the watchtower points to the temple.[7] The tenants are the Sanhedrin, who have oversight of the temple and the moral, political, and social life of the Jews. The parable makes clear, however, that they inhabit these positions on behalf of God and are responsible to him and thus subject to his judgment. Jesus's parable also situates them as characters that have mistreated and rejected God's prophets. Indeed, they are currently plotting evil against God's Son in order to seize the temple for themselves, inciting the wrath and judgment of the God of Israel who sent him. And this is the crucial point in the present context, since it answers

---

6. Black, *Mark*, 252.

7. Gray argues that the tower is a symbol for the Jerusalem temple, a common association in Jewish texts in the first century. He cites a Qumran fragment (4Q500) that regards Isaiah 5 as referring to Jerusalem and the temple and claims that 1 Enoch also makes this association (Gray, *Temple in the Gospel of Mark*, 63; cf. also Marcus, *Mark 8–16*, 812).

the question the Sanhedrin brought in 11:28: Jesus's authority to shut down temple operations comes from none other than the God of Israel, and the Sanhedrin is responding to God's authoritative agent by standing against God's purposes, inviting judgment on themselves.

Audiences of Mark's Gospel know that the Pharisees (3:6) and the Sanhedrin (11:18) have already committed themselves to killing Jesus. Moreover, they have heard Jesus predict his betrayal, suffering, and death three times on the road to Jerusalem (8:31; 9:31; 10:33). Here Jesus sets before them in narrative form a powerful presentation of the divine drama unfolding that climaxes in the destruction of the Jewish leaders who oppose Jesus. This will surely cause them to repent of their march toward judgment, will it not? Readers and hearers of the Gospel know otherwise.

The Parable of the Cornerstone (vv. 10–11)

The quotation of Psalm 118:22–23 is a distinct parable—it is a narrative in itself with its own story world.[8] While the first parable uses agricultural imagery, this one employs architectural imagery.[9] Though brief, the quotation suggests a drama with conflict, rejection, and ultimate vindication. The builders of the temple had considered and then rejected a stone for inclusion in the construction. But God had overturned and subverted their decision by choosing the rejected stone to become the temple's cornerstone. Indeed, "the Lord has done this," and it has become the cause of great celebration on the part of the people.

This parable informs the situation between Jesus and the Sanhedrin by affirming that the God of Israel is the one who grants authority to Jesus. Despite the Sanhedrin's rejection of him, God will vindicate Jesus by making him the cornerstone of his eschatological temple. Other New Testament texts cite Psalm 118:22 to speak of Jesus and the church as the new temple (e.g., Eph 2:20; 1 Pet 2:7), but this is the only place where v. 23 is included ("the Lord has done this, and it is marvelous in our eyes"). This is likely to emphasize that Jesus's authority comes from God.

Taken together, these two parables portray the Jerusalem leadership as guilty of rejecting Jesus, the authoritative agent sent from the God of Israel. But this will in no way override the plans of God, who will vindicate Jesus and judge the temple overseers.

---

8. This psalm is one of the most quoted in the New Testament (Matt 21:9; Luke 19:38; 20:17; Acts 4:11; Eph 2:20; 1 Pet 2:7).

9. Gray, *Temple in the Gospel of Mark*, 69.

The Sanhedrin Responds (v. 12)

These representatives of the chief priests, the teachers of the law, and the elders know that Jesus has spoken against them by portraying them as the tenants who have rejected God's messengers and are plotting to kill God's beloved Son. And they are the ones who have rejected the stone that God has chosen to make the cornerstone of the temple that he is building. Tragically, rather than responding to Jesus's striking parables with repentance, they look for a way to arrest Jesus. Because the crowd presents an obstacle to their scheming, however, they depart to wait for another opportunity.

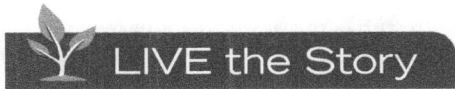

LIVE the Story

Rejection by Worldly Authorities

The rejection of Jesus by the temple authorities stems from their opposing agendas and modes of operating. The leaders of the Sanhedrin are grasping after power and control while also pursuing prestige and social honor, and all of this comes at the expense of faithfully overseeing the temple so that God's people are served. They are driven by selfishness, self-advancement, and self-preservation. Jesus, on the other hand, is utterly selfless, and because he knows that he is going to Jerusalem to die, he has already rejected the fundamental human impulse of self-preservation. He operates according to God's agenda, which includes here the task of confronting the temple leadership with their failure and unfaithfulness to the God of Israel. Because of his selflessness and rejection of self-preservation, Jesus is free to speak truth to power. He has no interest in accumulating power for himself.

This contrast between Jesus and the temple authorities reminds us that the church cannot seek to gain the approval of those in power but must remain free in order to speak prophetically to the powerful when they carry out injustice against anyone, especially the vulnerable and marginalized. This episode recalls the constant temptation of the church throughout the ages to cozy up to power in an effort to accomplish God's purposes. Cal Thomas and Ed Dobson were key figures in the rise of the religious right in America through the 1970s and 1980s. They were architects in the founding and building of the Moral Majority, a Christian political organization started by Jerry Falwell Sr. In their book *Blinded by Might*, they reflect on the compromises and corruptions that drew that movement away from the way of Jesus:

> The aphrodisiac of political power descended on Lynchburg, Virginia, with the impact of an asteroid. Politics was a better means to noble ends than

the hard and often invisible efforts mandated by Scripture. Who wanted to ride into the capital on the back of an ass when one could go first class in a private jet and be picked up and driven around in a chauffeured limousine? Who wanted the role of a servant when one could have the accolades given to leaders? Who wanted the pain of Good Friday when one could have the acclaim of the masses on Palm Sunday?

It is important to understand that the greatest temptation is not to do evil. Most of us could resist the big stuff. That's why fundamentalist preachers concentrated largely on the "sins" most of their members (though not all) had a pretty easy time avoiding—liquor, movies, dancing, promiscuity. They mostly avoided the positive tough stuff—the business about feeding the hungry, clothing the naked, and visiting those in prison, along with matters of justice (see Matthew 25:31–46).[10]

I write this in early 2020, with a presidential election later this year and during a time when American evangelicals are once again struggling with this very same temptation of imagining that God's purposes can be accomplished through grabbing hold of the levers of political power. The seductive attention from powerful leaders is overwhelming, but it is crucial to recognize that the fundamental character and the agenda of the church are at odds with institutions of power. Inevitably, such an alliance will diminish our faithfulness to our cross-shaped identity. This will be a constant challenge for Christians, and it is worth reflecting on the dynamics that are at work, especially from people who have experience, like Thomas and Dobson, of having surrendered to the seduction and can name it for what it is.

James Davison Hunter, in his book *To Change the World*, contends that the efforts of Christian leaders to initiate movements to "transform the culture" or "impact the world" are destined to fail, and he offers a different approach.[11] Rather than seeking to advance an agenda through the cultivation of political power, he commends "faithful presence" within the cultures in which the church is set as a way for Christians to imagine engaging with the world. What he means by this is multifaceted, but his vision includes a clear-eyed understanding of the temptations of worldly political power and its threats to Christian faithfulness. His vision is not a retreat from politics but is a radically different sort of politics altogether. What he writes resonates with

---

10. Cal Thomas and Ed Dobson, *Blinded by Might: Can the Religious Right Save America?* (Grand Rapids: Zondervan, 1999), 26 (emphasis added).

11. James Davison Hunter, *To Change the World: The Irony, Tragedy, and Possibility of Christianity in the Late Modern World* (New York: Oxford University Press, 2010).

the political vision of Mark's Gospel, which portrays Jesus as the ruler of the kingdom of God, gathering groups of people who embody kingdom life and who serve others in their local settings. It also involves speaking truth to power, prophetically reminding political figures that they are not ultimate but must answer to God.

Ministry and Accountability to God

The reality of Christian ministry is that those who serve the church of Jesus Christ are accountable for their conduct to God, who alone will examine the integrity of their ministries at the day of Christ. The basis for this will be whether ministers sought the flourishing of their communities, loving and serving the marginalized among them in the name of the crucified and risen Christ, or whether they were self-seeking, pursuing prestige and power over others. On the one hand, this is a fearsome reality, one that should make us hesitant to pursue ministry leadership or to be teachers of God's people, as James indicates (Jas 3:1). On the other, this dimension of Christian ministry can be the starting point for some fruitful reflections that are life giving and liberating, if we are creative and use our sanctified imaginations.

Ministers can draw on this reality to turn critics into friends. Pastors and ministry leaders know how draining criticism can be. It seems that some people in our churches have decided to note every fault with the church and every shortcoming in the service. Rather than let these critics drain us, we can reflect on the dynamics involved in critical interchanges, turning them into aids in our roles as stewards on behalf of God. I can use the occasion of a critical remark to ask myself whether the comment upsets me because I am trying to please people rather than pleasing God. Critics are also gifts from God because they help us to avoid falling into complacency. Since we will face judgment for how we carried out our ministries, critical people help us by arresting our attention and returning it to the tasks of ministry. And they are a slightly ironic gift from God, too, in the sense that they help us take ourselves less seriously. We need to remember that while we are *agents* of God's work among his people, we are also *objects* of his sanctifying work. God is forming ministers, too, into the image of his Son, and this involves developing mindsets of humility. Rather than reacting defensively, we might consider a humorous and self-deprecating remark, one that does not diminish a person who has brought a concern to us: "You know, Steve, I am so grateful for you. I think you are God's special agent, appointed to remind me that I have not fully arrived. I thank God for you!" If we are truly focused on this aspect of God's work in our lives, we can envision critics as partners rather than adversaries.

Ministers who are out for praise, adulation, admiration, and an easygoing ministry career path are bound to become complacent and long for seasons of relief from difficult people. Yet those who are aware of their accountability to God and the eschatological reality of the evaluation of their ministries will make space to allow critics to identify true blind spots in their ministry approach. Not only do we do damage to people from our lack of awareness, but we run the risk of provoking the wrath of a God who calls leaders to minister faithfully to those he loves and for whom he sent his Son.

CHAPTER 49

Mark 12:13-17

¹³Later they sent some of the Pharisees and Herodians to Jesus to catch him in his words. ¹⁴They came to him and said, "Teacher, we know that you are a man of integrity. You aren't swayed by others, because you pay no attention to who they are; but you teach the way of God in accordance with the truth. Is it right to pay the imperial tax to Caesar or not? ¹⁵Should we pay or shouldn't we?"

But Jesus knew their hypocrisy. "Why are you trying to trap me?" he asked. "Bring me a denarius and let me look at it." ¹⁶They brought the coin, and he asked them, "Whose image is this? And whose inscription?"

"Caesar's," they replied.

¹⁷Then Jesus said to them, "Give back to Caesar what is Caesar's and to God what is God's." And they were amazed at him.

Listening to the Text in the Story: Genesis 1:26–27; 1 Samuel 16:7; Isaiah 11:3; Romans 2:11; 1 Peter 1:17.

Jesus is in the midst of a series of contentious confrontations with the Jerusalem leadership—the Sanhedrin—stemming from his authoritative action in the temple the day before. He had shut down the temple's normal operations (11:15–16), delivering God's judgment on it and its custodians (11:17). The Sanhedrin had demanded to know by what authority Jesus had done this, and Jesus answered with two parables that indicated his authorization from God (12:1–12). These conversations took place in a threatening atmosphere, for Mark notes at several points that the Sanhedrin was looking for an opportune moment to seize Jesus in order that they might kill him (11:18; 12:12).

The Pharisees and Herodians in this episode approach Jesus with insincere praise in order to trap him, yet one of the qualities they ironically attribute to

Jesus is one that characterizes God throughout Scripture: impartiality. God reminded Samuel of his searching judgment as the prophet was evaluating which of Jesse's sons would be Israel's next king. Samuel had been impressed with some of the physical features of David's older brothers:

> But the LORD said to Samuel, "Do not consider his appearance or his height, for I have rejected him. The LORD does not look at the things people look at. People look at the outward appearance, but the LORD looks at the heart." (1 Sam 16:7)

When Isaiah prophesies about the "branch" from the "root of Jesse"—one of David's descendants—who will rule over Israel, he speaks of his impartial judgment:

> He will not judge by what he sees with his eyes,
>   or decide by what he hears with his ears;
> but with righteousness he will judge the needy,
>   with justice he will give decisions for the poor of the earth.
>   (Isa 11:3–4)

In his letter to the Romans, Paul argues that God's judgment on human behavior does not favor Jews or gentiles because "God does not show favoritism" (Rom 2:11). And Peter exhorts his audiences based on this same reality: "Since you call on a Father who judges each person's work impartially, live out your time as foreigners here in reverent fear" (1 Pet 1:17). People that have wealth or social standing in this world can often get away with mistreatment of others. God's searching judgment, however, means that no human can so impress God that he will overlook their injustice and abuse of others. While God's impartiality is good news for the downtrodden and oppressed, it is a warning for those who imagine that their status among God's people gives them license to treat others as they please.

EXPLAIN the Story

Having departed at the end of the previous episode (v. 12), after feeling the heat of Jesus's confrontational parables, the Sanhedrin sends some men from two groups to "catch him in his words" (v. 13). Mark gives the sense of constant waves of attackers peppering Jesus with rhetorical assaults in an effort to bring him down. The Pharisees and Herodians are two groups that have already been plotting for some time to kill Jesus (cf. 3:6), and they likely represent two alternative Jewish attitudes toward the occupying Romans. The Pharisees regarded the Romans as an idolatrous people whose presence was polluting God's holy land. The Herodians represented Jews that had accommodated to Roman rule, perhaps even finding ways to benefit from it.[1] These alternative postures are in play in this episode that revolves around the imperial tax imposed on Judea by Rome.

These groups approach Jesus with flattery that is obviously insincere though ironically true. They state that "we know that you are true" (*oidamen hoti alēthēs ei*), which the NIV translates as "we know that you are a man of integrity" (v. 14). Further, as noted above, they describe him in the same way that Scripture speaks of God: "You aren't swayed by others, because you pay no attention to who they are."[2] Finally, they confess that Jesus teaches "the way of God in accordance with the truth," a comment that would provoke Mark's audiences to wonder why they are not listening to his teaching!

After all this flattery, the Pharisees and Herodians put the question to Jesus: "Is it right to pay the imperial tax to Caesar or not? Should we pay or shouldn't we?" The imperial tax (*kēnsos*) was imposed by Rome in AD 6 when Judea became a Roman province. This move provoked great resentment and gave rise to a revolt led by Judas the Galilean (Acts 5:37).[3] Their question is designed to trap Jesus in a dilemma: if he answers that the Jews ought to pay the tax, he will turn nearly everyone against him, since most Jews objected to paying tribute to Rome. It was a constant reminder that they were dominated by a foreign power. Not only was the tax a hardship, but it drove home the tragic reality that they were not enjoying the kingdom of God the way they should have been. On the other hand, if Jesus said that Jews should not pay the tax, then he would be seen as an insurrectionist and invite the swift retaliation of the Roman authorities. Depending on his answer, either the Pharisees or Herodians hoped to report his words and have the Romans take him off their hands at once.

Jesus, however, saw through their pretensions and discerned their hypocrisy, asking, "Why are you trying to trap me?" (v. 15). He told them to bring

---

1. Larry W. Hurtado, *Mark*, NIBC (Peabody, MA: Hendrickson, 1989), 191–92.

2. The expression of the Pharisees and Herodians in the Greek text is very similar to the language Paul attributes to God in Rom 2:11. They say of Jesus, *ou gar blepeis eis prosōpon anthrōpōn* ("for you do not look to the face of men"). According to Paul, *ou gar estin prosōpolēmpsia para tō theō* ("for there is no receiving the face with God").

3. Moloney, *Gospel of Mark*, 236.

him a denarius *hina idō* ("in order that I might see it"). When they produced one, he asked them, "Whose image is this? And whose inscription?" (v. 16). On one side of a denarius was stamped the image of Tiberius, the reigning Caesar, with a Latin inscription that read, "Tiberius Caesar, son of the divine Augustus." The opposite side bore a Latin inscription for "High Priest."[4]

While the Pharisees and Herodians had acted deceitfully in setting their trap, Jesus responds to them in a very simple and straightforward fashion by examining the coin as if it is a lost item that may have the owner's name on it. "Let me see that piece of metal. I'll tell you whose it is!" His question about "whose image" is on the coin associates his reasoning with Genesis 1:26–27, in which humanity is made in God's image:

> Then God said, "Let us make mankind in our *image*, in our likeness, so that they may rule over the fish in the sea and the birds in the sky, over the livestock and all the wild animals, and over all the creatures that move along the ground."

> So God created mankind in his own *image*,
>   in the *image* of God he created them;
>   male and female he created them.

The Pharisees and Herodians respond that the image and inscription are those of Caesar (v. 16), to which Jesus replies in words that keep him from impaling himself on the horns of their dilemma. His response, however, is also powerfully resonant with meaning: "Give back to Caesar what is Caesar's and to God what is God's (v. 17).[5]

Without committing himself to either party's agenda, he has avoided aggravating both. He pushes his own agenda without being controlled or manipulated by anyone else's. Because Caesar's image is on the coin, give it to him. It appears to be his. But God wants far more than pieces of metal that can be carried in a leather pouch.

Jesus's statement raises the question of what belongs to God. In the immediate context and based on Jesus's mention of the word "image," he is referring

---

4. Beavis, *Mark*, 176–77; Garland, *Theology of Mark's Gospel*, 153.

5. Augustine writes, "We are God's money. But we are like coins that have wandered away from the treasury. What was once stamped upon us has been worn down by our wandering. The One who restamps his image upon us is the One who first formed us. He himself seeks his own coin, as Caesar sought his coin. It is in this sense that he says, 'Render to Caesar the things that are Caesar's, and to God the things that are God's,' to Caesar his coins, to God your very selves" (Oden and Hall, *Mark*, 160).

to all people. Every person is stamped with God's image, so they must give themselves to God. Further, Israel is God's own possession (Exod 19:5–6; Deut 32:8–9), so they must do the same. And, considering the parable of the vineyard (Mark 12:1–9), the leaders of the Sanhedrin have not cared for Israel as responsible tenants. They, too, must regard the vineyard and its watchtower—that is, Jerusalem and its temple—as belonging to God. Give Caesar his pennies. But give your whole self, and all of yourselves as a nation to the God of Israel. This would entail a radical repentance, transforming their posture toward God, their fellow Jews, and toward Jesus.

LIVE the Story

The Politics of Caesar and the Politics of Jesus

Jesus is here putting an absolute division between the identity of disciples as kingdom citizens and their loyalty to any other earthly cause. His audience was made up of subjects to Roman rule, and he was telling them to take care of what they needed to in order to live peaceably: "If there's a tax, pay the tax. Don't be insurrectionists or revolutionaries." He was warning them against a form of pagan idolatry that would involve them in allegiance to an earthly cause, whether that was pro- or anti-Roman. He was calling them to give their entire lives and their whole selves to God. This loyalty to God is primary and fundamental, and it cannot be mixed with any other commitments. And the daily form that this devotion to God takes is commitment to his people through the cultivation of practices of hospitality and service.

Jesus is the initiator of the kingdom of God, a realm and reign involving a new people that calls for our singular loyalty. We are baptized into a new political entity when we embrace Christian discipleship. That is, the kingdom of God is a social unit with its own ruler and a unique way of life. The body politic of Jesus—the church—can be considered like a nation, so that Christians have a new nationality when they become disciples of Christ. The odd thing about being part of the church, however, is that it is made up of people from every earthly nation and belongs to no one singular nation, even as it is situated within all nations.

This reality presents some special challenges, since we often confuse our earthly identities (city, state, nation, political party, or ethnicity) with our Christian identity. For example, if I am an American, I might assume that God has a special relationship to America and that he has uniquely blessed it. I might also be a regular supporter of either the Democratic or Republican party, voting for candidates from my preferred party each election cycle. What often happens over time is that I come to associate my earthly preferences with my Christian identity, and I begin to look on others (of other nations or political parties) as less than Christian.

When I associate God or the Christian faith with any earthly identity or cause, however, I am involved in the very same pagan idolatry Jesus warns against. This is a difficult temptation to resist, however, especially today when many of us live within conflicted and highly fraught culture wars. Cable news channels whip us up into a frenzy of hysteria and suspicion so that we come to view people with whom we disagree as mortal enemies. Families and friendships are torn asunder by partisan bickering. How can we see to it that we are not drawn into practicing the politics of Caesar and instead cultivate habits of life whereby we participate in the politics of Jesus?

I would suggest paying close attention to the forms of media that you consume, since these powerfully shape our mindsets, speech, and relationships. Do you see the world through the lens of this or that cable news channel, be it on the "left" or "right"? Do you assume the rightness of one political party and envision those that disagree as having evil motives? Do you find yourself speaking angrily and dismissively about people that disagree with your preferred political vision? We can be assured that we have become captive to the politics of Caesar if we are not prepared to view others with whom we may disagree with love, kindness, and respect.

The politics of Jesus involve a radically different reality and the cultivation of a different mindset. We must identify the sources that stir us up with anger and resentment of other people and learn to ignore them. And we must learn to see our political loyalty to King Jesus and to the political entity that he created in his death and resurrection—the church. And the church is indeed a *political entity*. It is a group of people constituted by God and called to a set of practices under his rule. Our political behaviors involve learning how to reconcile with one another, celebrating God's rule and his coming kingdom, and doing good to those in need among us and beyond the walls of our church communities.

Much more must be said to help Christian people disentangle their loyalties—the ways we confuse our commitment to Jesus with other earthly commitments. But in this passage, Jesus urges his followers to have a singular loyalty to God and to be wise in navigating this present age. That way, we can be liberated to give our whole selves to participate in the kingdom of God.

Mark 12:18-27

📖 LISTEN to the Story

¹⁸Then the Sadducees, who say there is no resurrection, came to him with a question. ¹⁹"Teacher," they said, "Moses wrote for us that if a man's brother dies and leaves a wife but no children, the man must marry the widow and raise up offspring for his brother. ²⁰Now there were seven brothers. The first one married and died without leaving any children. ²¹The second one married the widow, but he also died, leaving no child. It was the same with the third. ²²In fact, none of the seven left any children. Last of all, the woman died too. ²³At the resurrection whose wife will she be, since the seven were married to her?"

²⁴Jesus replied, "Are you not in error because you do not know the Scriptures or the power of God? ²⁵When the dead rise, they will neither marry nor be given in marriage; they will be like the angels in heaven. ²⁶Now about the dead rising—have you not read in the Book of Moses, in the account of the burning bush, how God said to him, 'I am the God of Abraham, the God of Isaac, and the God of Jacob'? ²⁷He is not the God of the dead, but of the living. You are badly mistaken!"

Listening to the Text in the Story: Exodus 3; Deuteronomy 25:5–10; Ruth 3–4; Daniel 12:1–3; Tobit 3:7–15; 1 Corinthians 15.

This encounter with the Sadducees is the third challenge in a row for Jesus. The day after he had shut down the functions of the temple, the Sanhedrin had questioned his authority for doing so (11:28). After they departed, the Pharisees and Herodians shrewdly came to him, drawing him into a rhetorical trap (12:13–17). The Sadducees now approach Jesus with similar intentions. In each of these challenges from groups that make up the Jerusalem leadership, Mark presents Jesus as the authoritative teacher. They all address him as "teacher" (12:13–17; 18–27; 28–34), and Mark notes regularly throughout the larger context that Jesus is teaching, even when he is merely responding in conversation (11:17, 18; 12:35, 38).

The Sadducees raise the issue of the resurrection, which is not a highly developed concept in the Old Testament. While there are scattered hints of the dead being raised to life (e.g., Job 19:26; Ps 16:9–11), Daniel 12 contains the clearest expression, a text from later in Israel's history:

> At that time Michael, the great prince who protects your people, will arise. There will be a time of distress such as has not happened from the beginning of nations until then. But at that time your people—everyone whose name is found written in the book—will be delivered. Multitudes who sleep in the dust of the earth will awake: some to everlasting life, others to shame and everlasting contempt. Those who are wise will shine like the brightness of the heavens, and those who lead many to righteousness, like the stars for ever and ever. (vv. 1–3)

> As for you, go your way till the end. You will rest, and then at the end of the days you will rise to receive your allotted inheritance. (v. 13)[1]

The Sadducees question Jesus about one of the marriage regulations from the Mosaic law (Deut 25:5–10). According to this arrangement, called levirate marriage, if a married man dies and has a brother, that brother will marry the widow in hopes that she might bear children and thus carry on the family name of the dead man. This was a merciful and compassionate social arrangement that provided protection for a widow. She could keep her first husband's land in the family, and bearing children would guarantee security and provision, since they could help to cultivate the land. This arrangement lies behind the drama between Judah and his daughter-in-law Tamar in Genesis 38:6–26 as well as that between Ruth and Boaz in Ruth 3–4.

Jesus responds to the Sadducees by citing the name of the God of Israel as he identifies himself to Moses in the episode of the burning bush (Exod 3). In that dramatic encounter, God states three times that he is "the God of Abraham, the God of Isaac, and the God of Jacob" (vv. 6, 15, 16). This narrative is strategic for the manner in which it informs God's identity in relation to Israel, which at the time was enslaved and horribly oppressed by Egypt. God is now returning to redeem Israel out of slavery because they are "my people" (cf. v. 7), and they are his people because he had bound himself

---

1. K. L. Anderson, "Resurrection," *DJG* 775–76; Strauss, *Mark*, 531; Edwards, *Mark*, 365.

in a covenant of promise to Abraham, Isaac, and Jacob, Israel's forefathers. The great saving event of the exodus is a display of God's faithfulness to his people and to the promises he had made to Israel's patriarchs.

EXPLAIN the Story

Mark presents these encounters between Jesus and various groups in the Jerusalem leadership in quick succession. The Sanhedrin sends wave after wave of contenders to Jesus to either trap him or reduce his teaching to absurdity, as the Sadducees attempt to do here. They do not believe Jesus has the authority to do what he did in bringing temple operations to a halt (11:15–17), and they have already planned to arrest and put him to death (11:18; 12:12).

The Sadducees' Challenge (vv. 18–23)

Little is known about the Sadducees from the first century. In addition to this text, Luke indicates in Acts 23 that they did not believe in the resurrection, a point that divided them especially from the Pharisees and that Paul exploits when he stands before the Sanhedrin (Acts 23:6–8). Josephus also notes that the Sadducees neither believed in the immortality of the soul nor punishments and rewards after death (*J. W.* 2.8.14).[2] The Sadducees were related to the priestly class and were tied in to the power structure of the temple, which is why they only appear when Jesus is in Jerusalem and in the temple area. The Pharisees, on the other hand, along with the scribes (*grammateis*, which the NIV regularly translates as "teachers of the law"), were more popular among the common people and so appear throughout Mark in different geographical locations. The Sadducees protected their positions of influence, privilege, and power by keeping peace in Jerusalem on Rome's behalf. This is likely why Josephus notes that the Sadducees were tougher on offenders than the Pharisees (*Ant.* 20.9.1).[3] They were less popular with the common people than were the Pharisees and were connected with the wealthy (*Ant.* 13.10.6).[4]

---

2. The rationale for their rejection of the resurrection is unclear. Boring points to their conservative posture toward tradition to explain it. Since hope in the resurrection was the result of developing tradition, and only hinted at in the Torah, the Sadducees maintained a skeptical attitude, seeing the resurrection as an unwarranted innovation (Boring, *Mark*, 338–39).

3. Michelle Lee-Barnewall, "Pharisees, Sadducees, and Essenes," in *The World of the New Testament: Cultural, Social, and Historical Contexts*, ed. Joel B. Green and Lee Martin McDonald (Grand Rapids: Baker Academic, 2013), 223.

4. Lee-Barnewall, "Pharisees, Sadducees, and Essenes," 222. While some commentators claim that the Sadducees only accepted the Mosaic law as Scripture, this may go beyond the evidence (Marcus, *Mark 8–16*, 1122; Lee-Barnewall, "Pharisees, Sadducees, and Essenes," 223).

The question that the Sadducees set before Jesus may have come from their stock of arguments against the resurrection.[5] It reflects a scenario in Tobit 3:7–15, a Jewish text written a couple hundred years before the first century, in which a woman named Sarah had been married seven times without having children. Her grief-stricken prayer is answered when she is given in marriage to Tobias, son of Tobit. Drawing on the Mosaic law's instruction regarding levirate marriage in Deuteronomy 25:5–10, the Sadducees construct a scenario in which a woman has been married to seven brothers in hopes of having children. Each husband dies without the woman conceiving, however, leaving her a widow to seven brothers. The Sadducees then ask Jesus whose wife she will be at the resurrection (Mark 12:23).

Jesus's Response (vv. 24–27)

Jesus responds authoritatively, asserting that the Sadducees are in error. He opens and closes his response with the repeated verb *planasthe* ("mistaken," "deceived"), which the NIV translates as "in error" in v. 24 and "badly mistaken" in v. 27. He had spoken in a similar way previously to the Sanhedrin, opening and closing his response with the imperative verb *apokrithēte* (11:29–30), challenging his questioners to "answer me!" With this strong assertion, Jesus seizes the initiative, just as he has done in each of these encounters. He is, after all, the authoritative teacher whose authority comes from God.

They are in error for two reasons: they do not know the Scriptures, and they do not understand the power of God (v. 24). These are strikingly confrontational claims to make to these temple authorities, who have reputations to protect as devoted students of Israel's Scriptures. Jesus first explains what he means by their deficient grasp of God's power in v. 25. The scenario constructed by the Sadducees assumed a direct continuity between this present age and the age of the resurrection. They imagined that the frameworks and structures of life would remain the same, along with cultural practices and everything else that oriented community life among God's people. Marriage, including the levirate marriage law, was for the protection of families and their property and inheritance rights, and the Sadducees assumed that these same needs and institutions would continue into the future age.

At the resurrection, however, God will powerfully transform all of creation. The needs of the present age and the structures that frame our existence—our cultural practices, social arrangements, and mechanisms in place for securing

---

5. Moloney, *Gospel of Mark*, 238.

justice and for the protection of the vulnerable, together with property and inheritance rights—will be obliterated as God radically renews, renovates, and overhauls the entire cosmos. This transformation includes the obsolescence of marriage, since resurrection realities make it unnecessary. God will transform human bodies so that "they will be like the angels in heaven" (v. 25). Resurrection bodies will not be "spiritual" bodies in a nonphysical sense, but rather bodies "from heaven," resurrected and transformed bodies that are not subject to death and that are fit for joyful participation in the life of the age to come (cf. 2 Cor 5:1–2).

This is not a thorough treatment of Jesus's view of resurrection in the age to come, nor an extensive discussion of what that new world will be like. Jesus is pointing to what life will *not* be like at the resurrection rather than providing a detailed description of what it *will* be like. Whereas the Sadducees had assumed that the resurrection age would be a simple continuation of life as we now know it in this age, Jesus is emphasizing the radical break between life now and that in the world to come. God will transform all things by his power, so that while we will still maintain our identities, our experience of that world will be profoundly different. Just what that will be like is difficult to imagine. Edwards captures this discontinuity well: "Present earthly experience is entirely insufficient to forecast divine heavenly realities: we can no more imagine heavenly existence than an infant *in utero* can imagine a Beethoven piano concerto or the Grand Canyon at sunset."[6]

Jesus continues his forceful response by explaining his first assertion—that the Sadducees do not know the Scriptures (vv. 26–27). He cites God's statement of his name to Moses during the encounter at the burning bush (Exod 3). Jesus is not appealing to Scripture as an authority in order to prove his point. Jesus is himself the authoritative teacher, and his assertions stand on their own. This is not an apologetic encounter in which Jesus must present arguments for the reliability or reality of the resurrection. His appeal to Scripture is a rebuke to the Sadducees since their position is a strike at the character of the God who has made promises to his people. They are not reading Scripture with the intention of getting to know God. If they humbly listened to the word of God, they would know that God's commitment to Abraham, Isaac, and Jacob means that they have not been captured by death and are in some way alive. Their current existence and future life are both powered by and guaranteed by God's faithfulness to them—a commitment that even death cannot break.

---

6. Edwards, *Mark*, 368.

LIVE the Story

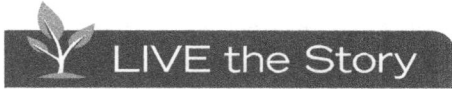

Reasoning about the Resurrection

Because I am a seminary professor, I receive some interesting emails, along with the occasional item through the regular post. More than once I have received a message from someone who has written a book or series of articles in which I can discover an airtight case for proving the resurrection to skeptical unbelievers. I appreciate the zeal that such people have for this crucial and central aspect of the Christian faith, but such pursuits are ultimately misguided.

The resurrection is a reality that Christians *confess* based on our belief in the testimony of God's authorized agents of revelation. It is not something that we can *prove* to skeptics. That is, Christians believe that God spoke through prophets and apostles to proclaim the reality of the resurrection and that some of these early figures later wrote documents that we regard as Scripture. These texts testify to the reality of the resurrection of Jesus Christ from the dead, and we believe their witness and confess it by faith. And our confidence that God dwells among the church currently by his Spirit, bringing us resurrection presence during this present age, is the basis for much of our Christian living.

Christians, therefore, confess faith in the resurrection, affirming that early prophets and apostles proclaimed the truth. Rather than *arguing to the resurrection*, we *live and speak from it*, basing our participation in community on it and ordering our lives by it. Our transformed communities, rather than rational arguments, are the most powerful earthly evidence for the resurrection.

Just as God brought forth a child of promise through Abraham and Sarah's "good as dead" reproductive capacities (Rom 4:19), God pours out resurrection life—an order of superabundance and *shalom*—on earth through the death and resurrection of Jesus. Where communities order themselves by the cross, they enjoy God's presence by the Spirit, bringing a superabundance of megaplenty and God's restored order of flourishing. This entails an entire array of community practices that runs directly against the ideology of scarcity that shapes our experience in this world. The present evil age orients our imaginations to pursue selfish and self-protective modes of life because we naturally see life as a zero-sum game. The kingdom of God, however, invites us into habits of life characterized by self-giving love in order to enjoy God's reign of plenty. And this reality has endless practical implications.

If I am involved in a relational conflict in community life, I am tempted to envision the situation from a zero-sum perspective—only one of us can "win," and I have to do whatever it takes to make sure I come out on top.

This conception of things drives all sorts of destructive relational strategies, such as gossip and slander, the cultivation of anger and resentment, and viewing the other party as having evil and corrupt motives. If I try to confront the situation, I will seek to prove my case, shutting down their arguments and demonstrating the righteousness of my cause, defending my behavior even to the point of employing irrational justifications.

But a resurrection mindset changes everything. It starts with the confidence that in the kingdom of God there is no zero-sum logic at work. It is not at all the case that one person must win while the other must lose. If God can bring life from the dead and feed many thousands from apparently meager resources, then there is more than enough to go around. And I have the assurance that God pours out resurrection life and power wherever there are people and communities shaped by the cross of Christ, so I know that if I adopt a cross-oriented posture, God will flood the conflicted situation with his restoring and renewing power.

I should approach conflicts, therefore, with the cruciform posture of a readiness to confess my sin and an eagerness to forgive others. I should have no interest in defending what I have said or done. Because I inhabit God's reign of plenty, I can be at rest and be ready to listen to the concerns of others, inviting them to share how they have been hurt. Kingdom space and resurrection presence enable "win-win" possibilities that radically reorient such situations, providing scenarios for redemption and reconciliation.

A resurrection approach also opens me up to the practice of rejoicing with those who rejoice (Rom 12:15). I remember speaking with a pastor friend who remarked that it is much easier to mourn with those who mourn than to rejoice with those who rejoice. This is especially true in an age of lifestyle and career competitiveness. Because we are all encouraged to strive for advancement and upward social mobility, we're all trying to "keep up with the Joneses," and we are tempted to see the success of others as somehow negatively affecting us. This is another symptom of the spirit of the age that shapes our mindsets according to a "win-lose" logic and forces us into relational practices of one-upmanship.

Again, a resurrection-shaped imagination radically transforms such situations, so that we can joyfully enter into the practice of rejoicing with the good things that arrive into the lives of others. If I see that I inhabit God's order of flourishing along with the rest of God's people, I will see that God has given me many good gifts and will expect that an outrageously generous and loving God will do the same for other kingdom inhabitants. Knowing that the good that others experience does not at all diminish me, I can celebrate others' successes with the assurance that as I do so, my heart and soul are expanded with resurrection life and joy.

In the same way that God brings life from the dead, churches can cultivate practices that stem from the confidence that God can transform hopeless situations into opportunities for bounty and plenty. And they will find that they can grow toward ever greater places of enjoyment, as their relationships grow richer and deeper than they previously imagined. Communities that reconcile and rejoice together display to the world God's resurrection power by embodying the life of the future resurrection age in the present. This is a far more compelling display of evidence for the resurrection than logical arguments that can never really do the job.

LISTEN to the Story

²⁸One of the teachers of the law came and heard them debating. Noticing that Jesus had given them a good answer, he asked him, "Of all the commandments, which is the most important?"

²⁹"The most important one," answered Jesus, "is this: 'Hear, O Israel: The Lord our God, the Lord is one. ³⁰Love the Lord your God with all your heart and with all your soul and with all your mind and with all your strength.' ³¹The second is this: 'Love your neighbor as yourself.' There is no commandment greater than these."

³²"Well said, teacher," the man replied. "You are right in saying that God is one and there is no other but him. ³³To love him with all your heart, with all your understanding and with all your strength, and to love your neighbor as yourself is more important than all burnt offerings and sacrifices."

³⁴When Jesus saw that he had answered wisely, he said to him, "You are not far from the kingdom of God." And from then on no one dared ask him any more questions.

Listening to the Text in the Story: Deuteronomy 6:4–5; 11:13; Leviticus 19:18; 1 Samuel 15:22; Hosea 6:6; Romans 13:9–10; 1 Corinthians 8:6; Galatians 5:14; James 2:8.

This episode delivers a small surprise. After several waves of Jerusalem leadership challenged Jesus after he shut down the temple (11:27–12:27), along comes another. He is a scribe (NIV: "one of the teachers of the law"), which leads audiences to expect another contentious conversation. But this is not what happens. The scribe grasps what Jesus teaches regarding Scripture and affirms it. The episode closes with the surprising verdict from Jesus that this teacher of the law is "not far from the kingdom of God" (v. 34).

This passage brings together a number of themes that appear throughout the story of Scripture. Jesus cites here Deuteronomy 6:4–5: "Hear, O Israel: The LORD our God, the LORD is one. Love the LORD your God with all your heart and with all your soul and with all your strength." This confession of the heart of Israel's faith was called the Shema, after the first Hebrew word, which means "to hear." It was recited daily by pious Jews in Jesus's day. When the nation confessed that "the LORD is one," they were claiming that the God of Israel was alone the creator God and that there was no one else like him. He is the Most High God over all the earth, far exalted above all gods, and the gods of the nations are as nothing (Pss 95:3; 97:9). Because the Lord alone is the one true God who created all things, he was to be worshiped exclusively. Israel was called to love God with all that they were, every part of themselves.

Jesus combines the Shema with the command in Leviticus 19:18 to "love your neighbor as yourself." This flows directly from God's identity as the one who adopted Israel as his own possession. When Jesus joins these two passages together, he is making the same point as many other biblical texts. The apostle John connects love of God and love of neighbor at several points:

> This is how we know what love is: Jesus Christ laid down his life for us. And we ought to lay down our lives for our brothers and sisters. If anyone has material possessions and sees a brother or sister in need but has no pity on them, how can the love of God be in that person? Dear children, let us not love with words or speech but with actions and in truth. (1 John 3:16–18)

> Whoever does not love does not know God, because God is love. This is how God showed his love among us: He sent his one and only Son into the world that we might live through him. This is love: not that we loved God, but that he loved us and sent his Son as an atoning sacrifice for our sins. Dear friends, since God so loved us, we also ought to love one another. No one has ever seen God; but if we love one another, God lives in us and his love is made complete in us. (1 John 4:8–12)

Paul and James agree in regarding love of neighbor as the fulfillment of the law. According to Paul, biblical commands "are summed up in this one command: 'Love your neighbor as yourself.' Love does no harm to a neighbor. Therefore love is the fulfillment of the law" (Rom 13:9–10). James likewise cites Leviticus 19:18 in rebuking his audiences for showing favoritism to the rich over the poor. He warns them not to take comfort in being otherwise faithful law-keepers if they are at the same time giving preference to the rich, for they are violating the law's command to love:

> If you really keep the royal law found in Scripture, "Love your neighbor as yourself," you are doing right. But if you show favoritism, you sin and are convicted by the law as lawbreakers. For whoever keeps the whole law and yet stumbles at just one point is guilty of breaking all of it. For he who said, "You shall not commit adultery," also said, "You shall not murder." If you do not commit adultery but do commit murder, you have become a lawbreaker.
>
> Speak and act as those who are going to be judged by the law that gives freedom, because judgment without mercy will be shown to anyone who has not been merciful. Mercy triumphs over judgment. (Jas 2:8–13)

When the scribe responds to Jesus here in Mark 12, he further emphasizes the biblical theme of loving one's neighbor and supplements it with a notion found in many places—"To love your neighbor as yourself is more important than all burnt offerings and sacrifices" (v. 33). This resonates with Samuel's words to Saul, when he rebuked him and informed him that he would no longer be king:

> Does the Lord delight in burnt offerings and sacrifices
>   as much as in obeying the Lord?
> To obey is better than sacrifice,
>   and to heed is better than the fat of rams. (1 Sam 15:22)

Other passages from the Psalms and the Prophets make the same point:

> Sacrifice and offering you did not desire—
>   but my ears you have opened—
>   burnt offerings and sin offerings you did not require. (Ps 40:6)

> You do not delight in sacrifice, or I would bring it;
>   you do not take pleasure in burnt offerings.
> My sacrifice, O God, is a broken spirit;
>   a broken and contrite heart
>   you, God, will not despise. (Ps 51:16–17)

> For I desire mercy, not sacrifice,
>   and acknowledgment of God rather than burnt offerings. (Hos 6:6)

This conversation between Jesus and the teacher of the law takes place after Jesus has shut down temple operations (Mark 11:15–17) and silenced the Jerusalem leadership (11:27–12:27). The teacher of the law understood what Jesus had done and what it means that God desires mercy and love of neighbor rather than participation in the sacrificial system. If that system is shut down because of corrupt temple authorities, God can still be worshiped by his people. As the writer of Hebrews puts it: "And do not forget to do good and to share with others, for with such sacrifices God is pleased" (Heb 13:16).

EXPLAIN the Story

This episode opens like the previous ones that began at 11:27, with groups that make up the Sanhedrin aggressively approaching Jesus in waves to engage in antagonistic debate. This teacher of the law, however, appears to have a different motivation. While he addresses Jesus as "teacher" (12:32) like the other opponents (vv. 14, 19), he does not appear to have dark or devious aims. Mark hints at his genuineness by differentiating his approach to Jesus from those of the scribe's colleagues. Keeping in mind the significance of verbs of perception in Mark's Gospel, the narrator adds "hearing" and "seeing" to the man's approach. He "*heard* them debating," and his question followed his "*seeing* that [Jesus] answered them well" (v. 28 NRSV).[1] The scribe inquired about the most important of all the commandments.[2]

Jesus responds by citing the Shema, the call to Israel to recognize God's absolute uniqueness and his singular worthiness of Israel's loyalty and love. He slightly expands the second half of it, supplementing an element among the commands.[3] He adds the exhortation to love God "from your whole mind" (*ex holēs tēs dianoias sou*). The four elements Jesus mentions are love from the whole "heart" (*kardia*), the whole "soul" (*psychē*), the whole "mind" (*dianoia*) and the whole of one's "strength" (*ischys*). These distinct aspects of the human person are not easily isolated, and Scripture does not indicate that humans are made up of three or four parts. These relative synonyms are meant to indicate

---

1. The NIV translates the participle *idōn* as "noticing."

2. The NIV captures well the sense of the scribe's question in Greek (*poia estin entolē prōtē pantōn*, "Which is the first command above everything?"). The term *prōtē* does not indicate "first" in an order of commands but focuses on the singular thing that is of primary importance.

3. Jesus cites the LXX version of Deuteronomy 6:4–5 with slight variation. He adds *ex holēs tēs dianoias sou* ("from your whole mind") and replaces *dynameōs* ("strength, power") with the synonym *ischyos* ("strength").

the entire self.[4] The original passage in Deuteronomy calls each Israelite and all Israel to give their entire selves to God and to love the God of Israel with everything that they are.

Jesus adds to this command a second, citing Leviticus 19:18: "Love your neighbor as yourself" (v. 31). He claims that these two commandments are greater than all the others. He has more or less blended the two into one singular thrust: to wholly love God and to love one's neighbor as oneself is the entirety of what the God of Israel wants from his people. These commands stand at the head, coming "first" and "second," not because they marginalize or eliminate the rest of the Mosaic law but because they sum it all up. Just as the Ten Commandments sum up the law's requirements of love of God and others, Jesus's concise citation of these two commands sums up the Ten Commandments and all of Torah.[5]

Surprisingly, the teacher of the law affirms Jesus's answer, implicitly recognizing him as God's authorized teacher who had the right to shut down the temple's regular functions the day before. He repeats the thrust of the Shema that "God is one," and adds to it a portion of Isaiah 45:21 that captures God's utter uniqueness: "There is no other but him" (Mark 12:32). The scribe also repeats the exhortations in the Shema but follows them with a provocative comment: loving God and loving neighbor "is more important than all burnt offerings and sacrifices" (v. 33). As noted above, Scripture repeatedly stresses the relative importance of love, mercy, and justice over sacrifices and offerings. However, the fact is remarkable that the scribe makes this claim in the temple and on the day when Jesus has been challenged for shutting down its operations. We might expect a scribe to rebuke Jesus for disrupting the proper order of temple activities as commanded by God in the Torah. But the scribe recognizes that Jesus is faithfully capturing the heart of Torah in acting as he has, and his identification of Jesus as "teacher" (v. 32) lacks the sarcasm and irony of his colleagues. He sees Jesus for who he is, the one who acts and teaches with God's own authority.

Jesus acknowledges that the man has responded wisely and notes that he,

---

4. One's "heart" (*kardia*) is who one truly is on the inside. It points to a person's entire inner life, without distinguishing between mental, spiritual, or emotional capacities. The term *psychē* ("soul") is a close synonym, pointing to the whole of a person or one's very life. The term *dianoia* ("mind") refers to one's reasoning capacity, what Black calls "discerning intelligence" (Black, *Mark*, 257). The term *ischys* ("strength") is straightforward, referring to one's ability "to function effectively" (BDAG 484).

5. The first four commands in the ten commandments relate to loving God, worshiping him alone for his uniqueness, while the final six commands have to do with loving others (Exod 20:1–17). It was common among rabbis to summarize the teaching of Torah. In response to a gentile who inquired whether the rabbi Hillel could teach him the entire Torah while he stood on one foot, Hillel said, "What is hateful to you, do not do to your neighbor; that is the whole Torah; the rest is commentary; go study it" (b. Shabbat 31a).

unlike his fellow members of the Sanhedrin, is "not far from the kingdom of God" (v. 34). This episode shows that not all members of the Jewish leadership were opposed to Jesus. After Jesus's death, another member of the Sanhedrin, Joseph of Arimathea, asked Pilate for Jesus's body and gave it a proper burial (15:42–47). Here, the scribe understood Jesus's mission and teaching and is not far from the kingdom, but his current condition is much like that of the rich young man who had approached Jesus earlier (10:17–22). It is one thing to recognize Jesus and assent to his teaching, but another to become a disciple and join him on the way to the cross (cf. Jas 2:14–26).

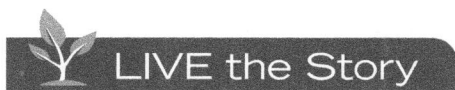

LIVE the Story

Loving God and Loving Others

When I was in college, I began to take my Christian faith seriously. My parents had given me a new Bible, and I read it voraciously. I had a small group of friends with whom I discussed various aspects of Scripture, theology, and Christian living. We would routinely ask each other how each of us was doing with regard to routine Bible reading and prayer by inquiring, "How are you doing with God today?" We usually took the measure of "how we were doing with God" by whether we were carving out time in our busy schedules for a quiet time in the morning and to what extent we were involved in Christian activities. Every once in a while one of us would report that while things were going fine "with God," there was this one person that was just driving us crazy. I can recall at times that discussions devolved into passing judgment on another person, and in certain instances we just flat out griped about certain people.

I remember being struck as I read through Deuteronomy repeatedly that God's heart for his people was that they intentionally and creatively love one another. And this was a theme I encountered repeatedly throughout the Old and New Testaments. One day I remarked to a friend that the questions we were asking each other probably needed to change, and that we should take the measure of "how we were doing with God" by how we were navigating relationships with other people. Loving God and loving others are inextricably linked, as can be seen from this text in Mark and in the other passages cited. As Scot McKnight writes, the way Jesus restates the Shema, "it is a Love-God-and-Others Shema. . . . Making the love of others part of his own version of the Shema shows that he sees love of others as central to spiritual formation."[6]

---

6. Scot McKnight, *The Jesus Creed: Loving God, Loving Others* (Brewster, MA: Paraclete, 2004), 9.

One aspect of loving God by loving others is putting ourselves in service to those in need. Our church in Springfield, Ohio, was a multiethnic community that brought together people from a variety of social classes and created loads of opportunities for service. A man named Ray was part of our church for several years. He had spent time in prison over the years and was struggling to get back on his feet, to keep a job, and to find a place to live. A handful of us established a rotation to drive Ray to his meetings with his parole officer and to job interviews. We encountered other situations with several people who were behind in paying bills and had difficulty keeping basic utilities running in their homes. While we were hesitant to create situations of dependence, we sometimes paid their bills but focused our efforts on being available to help people negotiate with utility companies to secure payment plans in order to keep the heat on during the winter months.

Another important aspect of loving God by loving others is forgiveness. McKnight notes that our relationship with God is rooted in and founded on forgiveness. God "preemptively strikes the human condition with an offer of grace. That strike of God's forgiving love to us produces in us a cascading flow of forgiveness to others."[7] While forgiveness is a fundamental component of being a disciple (Matt 6:15), it is also a complicated business. Nearly every situation of conflict in which harm has been done raises complex questions. Not everything can be sorted out neatly. I once had a conversation with a woman who asked how she could forgive her deceased grandfather who had abused her as a child. Situations like this one, and there are many like it, provide a challenge to those who long to respond faithfully to God and to enjoy the freedom that comes with forgiveness.

McKnight provides great help here by distinguishing two dimensions of forgiveness. He refers first to "objective forgiveness," by which he means "the elimination of the offense in the relationship." This is when two parties have an opportunity to reconcile. On the other hand, he identifies "subjective forgiveness," which "includes both a *disposition* to forgive and an *experience* of forgiving: release of anger, hatred, and resentment—ending the internal recycling of the offense."[8] This distinction between objective and subjective forgiveness is helpful because there will inevitably be situations where reconciliation is not possible, for a variety of reasons. In such cases, disciples can experience the liberating power of forgiveness by developing "a disposition to forgive that is ready to release the negative emotions caused by offenses."[9]

---

7. McKnight, *Jesus Creed*, 221.
8. McKnight, *Jesus Creed*, 224–25.
9. McKnight, *Jesus Creed*, 225.

McKnight goes on to enumerate a series of steps in pursuing forgiveness. First, "the victim of an offense *really confronts the offense and the offender's responsibility.*"[10] While this is difficult and may take some time, it is far better than ignoring what has been done and hoping that the pain will eventually subside. Such a destructive course only allows wounds to fester and bitterness to grow. Discussing how to do this with a counselor or trusted friend would be very wise at this point. Second, "the victim *recognizes the impact*" of what has been done, noting how it has damaged the relationship and unleashed "real emotions that have emerged because of the offense."[11]

Third, "the victim *chooses to pursue (objective) forgiveness.*" This difficult step involves creating dialogue with the offender, naming what has been done, offering to absorb the injustice and choosing to "accept the offender as a human who has sinned."[12] This is done with the hope that the offender will have a softened heart to own his or her offense. Fourth, "the victim *strives for justifiable reconciliation* (or, objective forgiveness)."[13] This may take time, and there may be a need for multiple conversations to meet this goal. And the complications may begin to pile up at this point, since reconciliation entails more than one party, and the offender may be unwilling.

Finally, "*forgiveness creates an alternative reality: those who forgive unleash a flow of love for others.*"[14] The wonder of life within the kingdom of God is that forgiveness creates a new situation in which God reconfigures the relationship by grace so that it is no longer ensnared within the corrosive dynamics of the present evil age. God's love and life-giving joy are now unleashed to alter the relationship between the parties, so that they can experience each other as liberated siblings in God's one new family and enjoy the rich gifts they have to give each other. Forgiveness is not sentimental. It is hard work. But the rich rewards we can enjoy are infinitely worth the effort.

---

10. McKnight, *Jesus Creed*, 225.
11. McKnight, *Jesus Creed*, 226.
12. McKnight, *Jesus Creed*, 226.
13. McKnight, *Jesus Creed*, 226.
14. McKnight, *Jesus Creed*, 226.

📖 LISTEN to the Story

³⁵While Jesus was teaching in the temple courts, he asked, "Why do the teachers of the law say that the Messiah is the son of David? ³⁶David himself, speaking by the Holy Spirit, declared:

> "'The Lord said to my Lord:
>> "Sit at my right hand
> until I put your enemies
>> under your feet."'

³⁷David himself calls him 'Lord.' How then can he be his son?"

The large crowd listened to him with delight.

³⁸As he taught, Jesus said, "Watch out for the teachers of the law. They like to walk around in flowing robes and be greeted with respect in the marketplaces, ³⁹and have the most important seats in the synagogues and the places of honor at banquets. ⁴⁰They devour widows' houses and for a show make lengthy prayers. These men will be punished most severely."

⁴¹Jesus sat down opposite the place where the offerings were put and watched the crowd putting their money into the temple treasury. Many rich people threw in large amounts. ⁴²But a poor widow came and put in two very small copper coins, worth only a few cents.

⁴³Calling his disciples to him, Jesus said, "Truly I tell you, this poor widow has put more into the treasury than all the others. ⁴⁴They all gave out of their wealth; but she, out of her poverty, put in everything—all she had to live on."

Listening to the Text in the Story: Exodus 22:22–24; Deuteronomy 24:17; Psalm 110; Isaiah 10:1–2; Ezekiel 34; Zechariah 7:10.

After a series of challenges by the Sanhedrin, and a conversation with an apparently sympathetic scribe (12:28–34), Jesus silenced the Jerusalem leadership: "No one dared ask him any more questions" (12:34). In this passage Jesus teaches in the temple courts.[1] He raises the question of his identity as David's son, warns about the teachers of the law, and laments the inequality of wealth at the temple treasury. He had entered the temple courts in 11:11, and after this teaching he will depart for the final time (13:1).

In 12:36 Jesus cites Psalm 110:1, which is one of the most significant biblical passages for the apostles in their proclamation of Jesus's resurrection and ascension to the right hand of power in his position as cosmic lord (Acts 2:34–35; 1 Cor 15:25–27; Eph 1:22; Heb 1:13; 1 Pet 3:22).[2] The psalm was originally a royal ascension psalm, conveying God's word to Israel's incoming king at the time of his coronation. The king is God's son, which refers to his authority to rule on God's behalf. For his part, God promises to subdue the king's enemies, though both God and the king participate in extending God's rule and subduing the enemies of both God and Israel (Ps 110:2–3, 5–7).

For the apostles and the New Testament writers, Psalm 110 became a crucial text to speak of how God had accomplished his powerful act of salvation in the death and resurrection of Jesus. God had raised him from the dead and installed him on his heavenly throne as cosmic lord over all creation, including his spiritual and cosmic enemies. Even though this victory had been won, however, God was still in the process of subduing all of his cosmic foes, including sin and death. Psalm 110, therefore, was crucial for the apostles in articulating the "already-not yet" character of God's work of salvation in Christ. While a victory had been won in God's climactic action in Jesus Christ, the final triumph over God's enemies awaited a future day when God and his appointed king—Jesus Christ—would fully defeat their enemies for good.

These notes of the surprising and progressive character of God's triumph are in view in this passage in Mark. Here, Jesus raises the question of the son of David's identity in order to provoke his hearers to question their own understanding of how Davidic sonship would look.

---

1. Throughout his Gospel, Mark portrays Jesus as the ultimate authoritative teacher. One of the striking features of this characterization is that Mark speaks of Jesus's teaching even in contexts where he is doing something other than teaching. Mark loads up terms for teaching in 1:21–27, where Jesus drives out an unclean spirit. In 11:17 he describes Jesus as having "taught" while shutting down the temple and condemning its unfaithful stewards. In this passage, Jesus continues to teach (vv. 35, 38), but the content of his teaching comes at his own initiative rather than being determined by his opponents.

2. It was common in apostolic proclamation to combine Psalm 110 with Psalm 8, replacing "make your enemies a footstool for your feet" (Ps 110:1) with some variation of "put everything under his feet" (Ps 8:6); see, e.g., 1 Cor 15:25–27; Eph 1:20–22. This modification of the wording of Psalm 110 with that of Psalm 8 also occurs in Mark 12:36.

EXPLAIN the Story

The Messiah and David's Son (vv. 35–37)

In this first portion of "teaching in the temple courts," Jesus asks some provocative questions regarding his identity, especially in relation to the identity of the Messiah as "son of David." Citing Psalm 110, with a modification from Psalm 8:6, Jesus notes that when David, being inspired by the Holy Spirit, declared that "the Lord" (indicating God) spoke to "my Lord" (i.e., David's lord), the "Lord" to whom God speaks must be someone greater than David. The question Jesus asks in v. 37, then, is this: How can this person whom David calls "my Lord" be David's son? The implication here is that while the teachers of the law speak of the Messiah as David's son (v. 35), there may be some sort of problem with that, since David does not address this figure as one who is merely one of his descendants but as one who is greater than David.

Clifton Black suggests that in this episode Mark objects to identifying Jesus as "son of David."[3] Davidic hopes had become thoroughly militaristic and triumphalistic, and Jesus as the Son of Man in Mark's Gospel comes as one who serves, suffers on behalf of others, and offers himself as a ransom for many. It is worth noting that while Bartimaeus addresses Jesus as "Son of David," Jesus does not positively affirm or clearly accept this identity (cf. 10:46–52).

There is too little in the passage to indicate that Mark (or Jesus) is rejecting Jesus's identity as David's son. If we consider this episode from the perspective of Mark's audiences, we can point to three important features. First, through the question Jesus raises here, Mark is provoking audiences to reflect on their own understanding of Jesus. Jewish texts like Psalms of Solomon 17:21–45 reveal that when Jesus speaks of what the scribes would have taught, they likely would have pointed to a messianic figure that generated hopes of conquest and triumphant liberation. Attaching such hopes to Jesus needs to be rethought. Jesus has been setting an entirely different pattern throughout Mark's Gospel. He is the Son of Man who is on his way to being put to death but who will be ultimately vindicated by God. And the movement that grows up around him—God's kingdom—is not one of triumphalism but service to the least and hospitality for the marginalized and outcast. Jesus is indeed David's son, but the popular conceptions of Davidic sonship need to be recast in light of Mark's narrative of Jesus.[4]

---

3. Black, *Mark*, 260–61.

4. Perhaps another way of saying this is to state that "the Messiah is the Son of David plus a whole lot more" (Michael F. Bird, *Jesus Is the Christ: The Messianic Testimony of the Gospels* [Downers Grove, IL: IVP Academic, 2012], 53).

Second, this is yet another instance of God speaking to Jesus. Audiences of Mark have already heard God's speech to and about Jesus at his baptism (1:11) and the transfiguration (9:7). In this episode, the audience is let in on an unfolding drama within the Trinity—Father, Son, and Spirit are each involved. The Holy Spirit inspired David's speech, and the audience knows that God is speaking to Jesus, the one who is greater than David. Just as God has spoken to God's Son throughout Mark, God speaks to him again. This is not a denial of Davidic sonship but rather another instance in which God plainly speaks about his authorization of Jesus—in the face of questions about Jesus's authority—to shut down the temple and pass judgment on it and its unfaithful stewards.

Third, and closely related to the previous point, the speech of God to Jesus indicates that Jesus—in his earthly ministry, in conversation with opponents, and now teaching in the temple courts—is already exalted as the authoritative Son of Man. The events unfolding in the temple courts and even what is to come in his betrayal, trials, suffering, and crucifixion *are the process of God subjecting his enemies to him*. What looks like defeat for Jesus is actually the paradoxical manner in which God accomplishes his triumph. Mark notes that the large crowd gathered in the temple courts "listened to him with delight" (v. 37).

Jesus Criticizes the Scribes (vv. 38–40)

Jesus had previously warned the disciples to "watch out" (*blepete*) for the yeast of the Pharisees and of Herod (8:15), and he now warns them to "watch out" (*blepete*) for the teachers of the law (12:38). We have just met a scribe who is not far from the kingdom (v. 34), so clearly not every individual scribe is like this. Jesus, however, is pointing out tendencies and typical behaviors of this group of leaders among the Jews who are enriching themselves and serving their own egos at the expense of the poor and vulnerable. He critiques them for their desire to be honored as especially pious and devoted, walking around in public in their garments (*stolais*) usually reserved for special festive occasions. The greetings in public would have strengthened their desired image as those who had exalted social status, as people of higher standing would expect to be greeted first, indicating their superior rank.[5] Jesus is both passing judgment on the scribes and warning his followers to avoid becoming like them, just as he warned them about cultivating the attitudes and behaviors of the Pharisees and of Herod.

Jesus seems to reserve harsh judgment for their exploitative practices toward

---

5. Boring, *Mark*, 350.

the vulnerable and needy. Sadducees were largely from wealthy families and were tied in to the temple apparatus with all its political connections. Scribes, on the other hand, were not wealthy and relied on gifts and donations.[6] We can imagine the development of manipulative and exploitative practices, especially preying on the vulnerable and poor, offering promises of divine blessing for donations from those who could not really afford to part with their money. Rather than teaching and serving, enabling others to walk in blessing, the scribes play their roles for their own benefit and to the harm of others, especially those who are vulnerable. One thinks of the many preachers today who are merely hucksters and who promise that those in dire situations will receive God's blessing if they send in money.

Scripture is filled with harsh warnings against mistreating the vulnerable. This is the heart of the God of Israel: "Do not take advantage of the widow or the fatherless. If you do and they cry out to me, I will certainly hear their cry. My anger will be aroused, and I will kill you with the sword; your wives will become widows and your children fatherless" (Exod 22:22–24; cf. Deut 24:17). God will judge Israel for their systemic injustice, passing laws that mistreat the vulnerable:

> Woe to those who make unjust laws,
>   to those who issue oppressive decrees,
> to deprive the poor of their rights
>   and withhold justice from the oppressed of my people,
> making widows their prey
>   and robbing the fatherless. (Isa 10:1–2)

Among a number of other prophetic texts that excoriate Israel and the nation's leaders for mistreating the needy, Boring notes that Malachi 3:5 is especially pertinent because of the role Malachi 3:1 plays in Mark's vision of the God of Israel showing up to the temple:

> So I will come to put you on trial. I will be quick to testify against sorcerers, adulterers and perjurers, against those who defraud laborers of their wages, who oppress the widows and the fatherless, and deprive the foreigners among you of justice, but do not fear me," says the LORD Almighty. (Mal 3:5)[7]

---

6. Edwards, *Mark*, 379.
7. Boring, *Mark*, 351.

Jesus's conclusion is both terrifying and perfectly consistent with the heart of God revealed in Scripture: "These men will be punished most severely" (Mark 12:40).

Judgment on the Temple Treasury (vv. 41–44)

In this final section of Jesus's actions in the temple, Mark does not repeat that Jesus is "teaching." This may be because Jesus is not so much teaching as he is passing judgment on the injustice of the temple and its treasury. Jesus "sat down," indicating a posture of judgment (cf. Dan 7:10), and did so "opposite" (*katenanti*) the treasury, about to pass judgment against this entity that has become a source of injustice and oppression of God's people. When Jesus entered Jerusalem and went into the temple in 11:11, he "looked around at everything," making his assessment before returning the next day to render his judgment (11:12–17). In the same way, Jesus here "watched the crowd putting their money into the temple treasury," discerning what was happening before delivering his prophetic judgment.[8] Just after this, Jesus will leave the city and sit on the Mount of Olives "opposite" (*katenanti*) the temple to prophesy its destruction (13:3).

Observing the many rich people putting their money into the temple and then the poor widow who put in "two very small copper coins" (12:42), Jesus notes that this woman has actually given more than the others, since she has "put in everything"—literally, "her whole life" (*holon ton bion autēs*; v. 44). Coming just after Jesus's condemnation of the scribes and their exploitative practices, and while Jesus is sitting "opposite," or "opposed to" the temple treasury, it is obvious that Jesus is lamenting this terribly unjust situation. The temple and its treasury represent a system of corruption and exploitation that grieves the heart of God and invites his judgment.

There is, however, another dimension to the widow's temple contribution. She is not merely a hapless loser. Without denying the larger unjust dynamics, Jesus commends her, since she embodies faithful discipleship. Like the disciples who "have left everything to follow" Jesus (10:28), this woman gives up everything, her whole life. It is unnecessary to choose a singular interpretation between these two—judgment of the corrupt system or commendation of a faithful widow. Both dynamics are present in the passage. This woman joins Jesus, who gives up his life before unjust and unfaithful rulers, and the vineyard owner, who gives up his son to scheming and murderous stewards (12:1–11).[9]

---

8. Marcus, *Mark 8–16*, 860.
9. Cf. Black, *Mark*, 263–64.

LIVE the Story

Pastoral Ministry and Economic Justice

I remember clearly hearing a Sunday school lesson as a child that held up the widow in this passage as a model for giving to the church. Whereas the rich people in this passage gave only a small portion of their wealth, the poor widow gave everything she had. We likewise were to give sacrificially so that we would also receive commendation from Jesus. Such lessons are common from preachers and teachers, but they neglect the wider dynamics in this text. Jesus does indeed commend this poor widow, but he also passes judgment on the temple treasury and its custodians for their exploitation of the poor and especially condemns the teachers of the law for cheating widows of their possessions: "These men will be punished most severely" (v. 40).

Rather than looking to this text in order to preach about the need for congregants to be faithful givers, pastors should consider that they themselves are the target of Jesus's rebuke insofar as they seek to exploit their status as teachers of Scripture as a means of financial gain. While the high-profile scandals of television preachers are obvious, such exploitation exists at local-church levels, too. I know of several pastors who regularly harangue their churches with the need to give increased sums and to contribute more regularly. In one instance, a pastor was a member of a local country club and was feeling the pinch when his membership dues increased!

Of course, many pastors and preachers are faithful to God, considerate of their churches, and carry out their ministries at great sacrifice. Further, some pastors go beyond this to live out the entire thrust of this passage in Mark to advocate against the exploitation of the poor. One great example of such a faithful minister is a person I am honored to call a good friend. Carl Ruby, who pastors Central Christian Church in Springfield, Ohio, had noticed the rapid growth of payday loan centers in his city, a city racked by poverty over the last half century, since the desertion of the city by several major industries.

> I was afraid immigrants were being taken advantage of. So I did some research and when I saw what the interest rates were, I was shocked. At one point, there were more payday lending stores than McDonald's in Ohio. I felt I had to do something.[10]

---

10. Renee Fox, "Short-Term Loan Reform Expected," *Tribune Chronicle*, July 29, 2018, www .tribtoday.com/news/local-news/2018/07/short-term-loan-reform-expected/.

Payday lending stores prey upon the poor and others who are in desperate need of cash. They offer short-term loans at predatory rates, as high as 591 percent.[11] Those who are trying to keep their lights on or feed their families after losing a job or falling into financial hardship for one reason or another find themselves in a cycle of debt that is nearly impossible to escape.

One Ohio elected official, Rep. Sean O'Brien, was stunned at his experiment in trying to secure one such loan:

I went in wearing jeans, a Cleveland Cavaliers T-shirt and a baseball hat and asked for a $5,000 loan with no collateral or co-signer. In 15 minutes, they quoted me a loan where I would pay back $1,000 a month for four months, and then owe $11,000 in the fifth month. They said I could finance the $11,000 with them, too," O'Brien said.

The lender wouldn't let O'Brien take home the paperwork to "mull it over."

"It was shocking," Rep. O'Brien said. "But I can't get this woman's face out of my mind. She was sitting there, a young lady in her 20s with a frown on her face and a baby on her lap, signing loan papers."

Pastor Carl got involved by holding a forum at his church to educate people about the exploitative dynamics involved in the payday loan industry. He organized a group of faith-based leaders to lobby the Ohio state government and worked with elected officials to craft a bill that severely limited the amount of interest lenders could charge. The bill was introduced by Rep. J. Kyle Koehler, a Springfield Republican, and was passed through Ohio's House and Senate.[12] In July 2018, it was signed into law by Ohio's governor, John Kasich.

This is a wonderful example of a pastor taking seriously the dynamics of this entire passage: Jesus is installed as God's appointed ruler, and he is attentive to the poor and vulnerable and will judge severely those who exploit their positions of power for their own gain. Those who minister to God's people on behalf of the Lord Jesus will be attentive to the social and economic environment of their local settings and advocate on behalf of those in need.

---

11. Fox, "Short-Term Loan Reform Expected."
12. Fox, "Short-Term Loan Reform Expected."

LISTEN to the Story

¹As Jesus was leaving the temple, one of his disciples said to him, "Look, Teacher! What massive stones! What magnificent buildings!"

²"Do you see all these great buildings?" replied Jesus. "Not one stone here will be left on another; every one will be thrown down."

³As Jesus was sitting on the Mount of Olives opposite the temple, Peter, James, John and Andrew asked him privately, ⁴"Tell us, when will these things happen? And what will be the sign that they are all about to be fulfilled?"

⁵Jesus said to them: "Watch out that no one deceives you. ⁶Many will come in my name, claiming, 'I am he,' and will deceive many. ⁷When you hear of wars and rumors of wars, do not be alarmed. Such things must happen, but the end is still to come. ⁸Nation will rise against nation, and kingdom against kingdom. There will be earthquakes in various places, and famines. These are the beginning of birth pains.

⁹"You must be on your guard. You will be handed over to the local councils and flogged in the synagogues. On account of me you will stand before governors and kings as witnesses to them. ¹⁰And the gospel must first be preached to all nations. ¹¹Whenever you are arrested and brought to trial, do not worry beforehand about what to say. Just say whatever is given you at the time, for it is not you speaking, but the Holy Spirit.

¹²"Brother will betray brother to death, and a father his child. Children will rebel against their parents and have them put to death. ¹³Everyone will hate you because of me, but the one who stands firm to the end will be saved.

¹⁴"When you see 'the abomination that causes desolation' standing where it does not belong—let the reader understand—then let those who are in Judea flee to the mountains. ¹⁵Let no one on the housetop go down or enter the house to take anything out. ¹⁶Let no one in the field go back to get their cloak. ¹⁷How dreadful it will be in those days for pregnant women and nursing mothers! ¹⁸Pray that this will not take place in winter,

¹⁹because those will be days of distress unequaled from the beginning, when God created the world, until now—and never to be equaled again.

²⁰"If the Lord had not cut short those days, no one would survive. But for the sake of the elect, whom he has chosen, he has shortened them. ²¹At that time if anyone says to you, 'Look, here is the Messiah!' or, 'Look, there he is!' do not believe it. ²²For false messiahs and false prophets will appear and perform signs and wonders to deceive, if possible, even the elect. ²³So be on your guard; I have told you everything ahead of time.

²⁴"But in those days, following that distress,

> "'the sun will be darkened,
>   and the moon will not give its light;
> ²⁵the stars will fall from the sky,
>   and the heavenly bodies will be shaken.'

²⁶"At that time people will see the Son of Man coming in clouds with great power and glory. ²⁷And he will send his angels and gather his elect from the four winds, from the ends of the earth to the ends of the heavens.

²⁸"Now learn this lesson from the fig tree: As soon as its twigs get tender and its leaves come out, you know that summer is near. ²⁹Even so, when you see these things happening, you know that it is near, right at the door. ³⁰Truly I tell you, this generation will certainly not pass away until all these things have happened. ³¹Heaven and earth will pass away, but my words will never pass away.

³²"But about that day or hour no one knows, not even the angels in heaven, nor the Son, but only the Father. ³³Be on guard! Be alert! You do not know when that time will come. ³⁴It's like a man going away: He leaves his house and puts his servants in charge, each with their assigned task, and tells the one at the door to keep watch.

³⁵"Therefore keep watch because you do not know when the owner of the house will come back—whether in the evening, or at midnight, or when the rooster crows, or at dawn. ³⁶If he comes suddenly, do not let him find you sleeping. ³⁷What I say to you, I say to everyone: 'Watch!'"

Listening to the Text in the Story: Deuteronomy 31:1–33:29; Jeremiah 7:1–8; Ezekiel 10:18–19; 11:22–23; Micah 3:11–12; Daniel 9:27; 11:31; 12:11; 1 Maccabees 1:54.

This passage contains Jesus's longest uninterrupted teaching in Mark's Gospel. In response to the disciples marveling at the magnificence of the Jerusalem temple, Jesus predicts its utter destruction, after which the disciples ask about when that will happen and what will be the sign that it is about to take place. Jesus then describes the sorts of tribulations that precede the temple's destruction and distinguishes this event from the coming of the Son of Man. The passage is dominated by exhortations to be alert and to discern what is happening in order to escape the coming destruction and avoid being taken in by deceitful interpretations of events. While the imagery of cosmic upheaval and the predictions of judgment grab our attention, Jesus's teaching is filled with practical wisdom for living as disciples amid a world that is coming apart.

Mark 13 functions as a bridge between chapters 11–12 and 14–15. In these earlier two chapters, Jesus had reached Jerusalem and examined the temple before passing judgment on it. He then shut down its operations and silenced the temple leadership in anticipation of its destruction. In the latter two chapters, Mark narrates Jesus's suffering and death. Mark 13 bridges these two sections that describe these two endings: the end of the temple and the end of Jesus. While the temple will be completely destroyed, God will vindicate Jesus by raising him from the dead, and he will return as the triumphant Son of Man in the future. Mark 13:5–37 is about how disciples are to live in this present age as they await the return of the Son of Man.

This passage is framed by the two women Mark describes in 12:41–44 and 14:1–11.[1] These two episodes have a number of similarities.[2] The widow gives everything she had to the lost cause of the temple, and the woman who anoints Jesus gives an expensive gift to Jesus on his way to death. These two temples—Jesus and the Jerusalem temple—are both headed for destruction, but Jesus will be raised from the dead as God's true temple.

Regarding the internal structure of Mark 13, vv. 1–4 set the stage for Jesus's teaching in the rest of the chapter. On their way from the temple, one of the disciples marvels at the impressive temple stones and buildings, after which Jesus forecasts the temple's complete destruction. The disciples then ask, "When will these things happen? And what will be the sign that they are

---

1. Beavis, *Mark*, 209.

2. First, Jesus praises the two women, the only times in Mark that Jesus does this, each time beginning with *amēn* ("truly") (12:43; 14:9). Second, Mark identifies the value of the gifts in both episodes: two small copper coins (12:42), and more than three hundred denarii (14:5; NIV, "more than a year's wages"). Third, both gifts are given sacrificially and at great personal cost. Fourth, the term "poor" (*ptōchos*) is repeated in each episode (12:42–43; 14:5, 7). Fifth, the two women are contrasted with wicked men. The widow stands in contrast to the financially rapacious scribes (12:40), and the woman who anoints Jesus contrasts sharply with Judas, who betrays Jesus for money (14:10; see Gray, *Temple in the Gospel of Mark*, 100–101; Marcus, *Mark 8–16*, 864).

all about to be fulfilled?" (v. 4). In vv. 5–23, Jesus addresses these questions by noting the signs that will precede the temple's destruction, and he also repeatedly urges them to cultivate discernment and watchfulness so that they will see these signs and take action. Not only is the destruction of the temple *not the end of the world*, but the coming age will be filled with tribulations for communities of disciples, none of which are the end of the world either.

Jesus goes on to address the end of the world in vv. 24–27, describing the upheaval of creation at the coming of the Son of Man. It is important to note that this latter event is distinct and separate from the destruction of the temple and the present age of ongoing tribulation. He then speaks two parables about readiness in vv. 28–37. The first one (vv. 28–31) has to do with the coming destruction of the Jerusalem temple. This event will be preceded by signs of which disciples should be aware. The second parable (vv. 32–37) concerns the behavior of disciples before the Son of Man arrives. They should be on guard and cultivate lives of faithfulness, for the Son of Man will come without warning. We can depict vv. 5–37 in this manner:

(A) Signs of the temple's destruction and of ongoing tribulation (vv. 5–23)
(B) The return of the Son of Man, for which there will be no sign (vv. 24–27)
   (A1) Parable of watchfulness for signs of the temple's destruction (vv. 28–31)
   (B1) Parable of faithfulness in light of the Son of Man coming with no sign (vv. 32–37)

Several commentators have described Jesus's teaching here as a "farewell discourse," much like those of Jacob (Gen 49:1–33), Moses (Deut 31:1–33:29), Joshua (Josh 23:1–24:30), and Samuel (1 Sam 12:1–25).[3] This may not seem like an appropriate comparison at first glance, since Jesus seems to be focused on end-times predictions and apocalyptic imagery. On closer reading, however, the predictions of the temple's destruction come amid instruction on how disciples should approach the troubles of this age. Knowing that he is about to leave his disciples, here he presents them with sober-minded and practical wisdom for living between the destruction of the temple and the return of the Son of Man.

In his farewell address to Israel, Moses recounted their journey and warned them about future disobedience. He exhorted them to faithfulness as they were entering the land of promise:

---

3. Others are of David (1 Kgs 2:1–9; 1 Chr 28:1–29:5), Tobit (Tobit 14:1–11), Mattathias (1 Macc 2:49–70), and Paul (Acts 20:17–35); see Moloney, *Gospel of Mark*, 250–51; Black, *Mark*, 264–65.

Take to heart all the words I have solemnly declared to you this day, so that you may command your children to obey carefully all the words of this law. They are not just idle words for you—they are your life. By them you will live long in the land you are crossing the Jordan to possess. (Deut 32:46–47)

In the same way, Jesus's concerns here are pastoral, as he warns his disciples—and subsequent audiences—about what they will face in the future. In the midst of an age that will be filled with horrific events that will feel like the world is ending and in which disciples will be persecuted, they are to remain faithful and watchful so that they are not shaken.

Ironically, Christian communities throughout the ages have encountered texts like Mark 13 with the result that they have grown fascinated about what will happen in the future and about the time of Christ's return. Jesus's aim in this discourse runs in exactly the opposite direction: *he is discouraging eschatological speculation*.[4] That is, disciples are not to be wrapped up with predicting end-time events, nor are they to listen to people interpreting horrifically traumatic events, such as the destruction of the Jerusalem temple, in terms of what God must be doing to bring an end to history. Jesus repeatedly warns throughout the passage that "these things must happen," as the present age continues to undergo convulsions in which apparently otherwise stable institutions are destroyed. None of these events is the end of history itself. God's people must be sober-minded and even flee from cities when they are facing destruction. The Son of Man will return, but no one knows when that will be, not even Jesus himself (v. 32). In the meantime, disciples are to cultivate faithfulness in the form of doing what Jesus has told them to do throughout Mark—to practice hospitality to the marginalized and to those with no social capital, and to serve the poor and needy.

EXPLAIN the Story

Jesus Predicts the Temple's Destruction (vv. 1–4)

This episode opens with Jesus and his disciples leaving the temple. He had been there since 11:27, just after cursing the fig tree (11:14), symbolizing God's judgment on the temple. After shutting it down and silencing the

---

4. The term *eschatological* points to discussions about what will happen in the future or at the end of time. *Eschatology* is the study of last things, or how God is going to wrap up history in the end.

Jerusalem temple leadership, Jesus departs and makes his way with his disciples to the Mount of Olives (13:1–3). The location for this passage sets an ominous tone. Jesus's movement from the temple to the Mount of Olives recalls Ezekiel's vision of the departing glory of the Lord as it left the temple, moving out toward the Mount of Olives and stopping there briefly before entirely departing (Ezek 10:18–19; 11:22–23).[5] Further, the Mount of Olives, just to the east of the Jerusalem temple, is the setting of oracles of judgment against Jerusalem (Zech 14:4; cf. Josephus, *Ant.* 20.169; *J. W.* 2.262).[6] Finally, just as he sat in a posture of judgment against the temple treasury, sitting "opposite" (*katenanti*) it in 12:41, Jesus sits on the Mount of Olives "opposite [*katenanti*] the temple" (13:3).

On their way out of the temple, an unnamed disciple marvels at the magnificent buildings of the temple complex and its massive stones.[7] Attentive audiences of Mark will remember when another disciple alerted Jesus to take notice of something. Such audience members will associate the two objects that the disciples highlight. In 11:21, the morning after Jesus had cursed the fig tree, Peter called to Jesus, "Rabbi, look!" (*rabbi, ide*), urging him to notice that the fig tree had been withered from the roots, thoroughly dead. Here, a disciple calls on Jesus, saying, "Teacher, look!" (*didaskale, ide*). While the disciple is marveling at the overwhelmingly impressive structure of the temple and its great beauty, Mark associates the two objects that the disciples notice. The fig tree and the temple are one and the same. The fig tree has been cursed and is withered from its roots, just as the temple stands cursed and is thoroughly dead on the inside. This same association is made by Jesus at the end of this discourse when he calls on his disciples to "learn this lesson from the fig tree" (13:28). Just as the budding fig tree signals the beginning of summer, so the signs of which Jesus speaks foretell the coming destruction of the temple.

---

5. Boring, *Mark*, 353.

6. Moloney, *Gospel of Mark*, 253.

7. Visitors to Jerusalem today can behold the massive foundation stones of the temple platform. Josephus speaks also of the glory of the temple by noting that it was covered in gold plates, so that at sunrise it "reflected back a very fiery splendor, and made those who forced themselves to look upon it to turn their eyes away, just as they would have done at the sun's own rays" (*J. W.* 5.222). Where it was not covered with gold, it was exceedingly white and appeared to travelers in the distance "like a mountain covered with snow" (*J. W.* 5.223; William Whiston, *The Works of Josephus: Complete and Unabridged* [Peabody, MA: Hendrickson, 1987], 707–8). Some of Josephus's estimates of the foundation stones are inaccurate, but "stones north of Wilson's Arch measure forty-two feet long, eleven feet high, fourteen feet deep, and weigh over a million pounds. The magnitude of the temple mount and the stones used to construct it exceed in size any other temple in the ancient world" (Edwards, *Mark*, 387).

Jesus responds in v. 2 by forecasting the complete destruction of the temple: "Do you see all these great buildings?" replied Jesus. "Not one stone here will be left on another; every one will be thrown down." The impressive grandeur of the buildings and the glory of the temple stand in stark contrast to the coming destruction. The apparent solidity of the temple might have engendered a sense of assurance and safety from judgment among inhabitants of Jerusalem, including the disciples, but this was the same self-deceived presumption against which the prophets cried out when they predicted the destruction of the first temple. Jeremiah warned that the inhabitants of Jerusalem were trusting in deceitful words, thinking that because the temple was standing they were assured of God's protection against enemies and that God's judgment against his own house was unthinkable (Jer 7:1–8). Micah used language similar to Jesus's when he prophesied Jerusalem's complete destruction:

> Her leaders judge for a bribe,
>> her priests teach for a price,
>> and her prophets tell fortunes for money.
> Yet they look for the LORD's support and say,
>> "Is not the LORD among us?
>> No disaster will come upon us."
> Therefore because of you,
>> Zion will be plowed like a field,
> Jerusalem will become a heap of rubble,
>> the temple hill a mound overgrown with thickets. (Mic 3:11–12)

The disciples who are with Jesus—Peter, James, John, and Andrew—ask him two questions that shape Jesus's discourse in the remainder of chapter 13: "When will these things happen? And what will be the sign that they are all about to be fulfilled?"[8]

Cultivating Discernment in This Age of Tribulation (vv. 5–23)

Jesus answers the disciples' question about the signs that will point to the destruction of the temple (and of Jerusalem) in vv. 5–23, but he also stresses that these tumultuous events are not signs of "the end" (v. 7; cf. also vv. 8c, 10). That is, they are not indications of the end of history or the return of

---

8. The disciples' questions recall language from Dan 12:4–7, which has a similar question and answer format. The "man clothed in linen" speaks of "the end" (v. 4), "all these things" (v. 7), and when these things "will be completed" (v. 7). In referring to what is "completed," he uses the verb *synteleō*, which also appears in Mark 13:4 where the NIV translates it as "fulfilled" (Boring, *Mark*, 355).

the Son of Man to save his people and judge the wicked. Throughout this section, Jesus repeatedly exhorts his hearers to "watch out" so that they will not be "deceived" into thinking that the upheavals of the present age, including the temple's destruction, are signs of the end. Disciples are not to give in to apocalyptic fervor but "must remain level-headed and not be perplexed by the persecutions they will endure in carrying out their mission."[9]

Just as throughout his Gospel, Mark includes terminology that has to do with discernment.[10] According to Jesus, this entire age will be filled with upheavals and destabilizing events that will shake believers. They, however, must not be unsettled. It may be that everything they hold dear is destroyed, even the institutions they associate with God and his people, such as the temple in Jerusalem. Despite such catastrophes, disciples must remain steadfast. They need to "see through" times of unrest and tumult in order to properly understand what is really going on.

Jesus tells his disciples that this age will be marked by faithful disciples being mistreated, suffering, and being killed, just like Jesus. As they cultivate communities of hospitality and service and as they resist cultivating political power and cultural influence because they are a cross-shaped people, the whole world will feel like it is coming apart. They must be discerning so that they are not deceived by messages of false hope—either that the end has come or that God will save their institutions and prevent them from suffering. The *inclusio* that holds vv. 5–23 together highlights this need for discernment. This framing device consists of the repetition of *blepete* ("watch out," v. 5; "be on your guard," v. 23) and *planaō* ("deceive," vv. 5, 6, 22 [*apoplanaō*]).

Jesus exhorts his disciples to "watch out so that no one deceives" them (v. 5). During the tumultuous times that precede the destruction of the temple, "many" will claim to speak on behalf of Jesus, even claiming to be him (v. 6). Such supposed spokespeople for Jesus will claim that these cataclysmic events are the end of history. They may also claim that though these tumultuous events seem to foreshadow the destruction of Jerusalem, certainly that would never happen, since Jerusalem contains the temple of the God of Israel. Surely, he will protect it! Jesus also predicts that some will claim to be the Son of Man himself, and though many will be deceived Jesus warns his disciples against being alarmed; this is not yet the end (v. 7). Further, they should not

---

9. Garland, *Theology of Mark's Gospel*, 158.

10. Jesus's parable of the sower and the seeds is crucial for Mark, as is his emphasis on "seeing," "hearing," and "understanding" (4:12). Throughout Mark 4–10, various characters see and hear Jesus, while the disciples repeatedly do not, failing to rightly perceive what Jesus and his teaching are all about.

be deceived by any messages of reassurance that God will dramatically rescue the Jerusalem temple from destruction.

Several features of the destabilizing events that Jesus mentions in vv. 6–8 appear in prophetic texts that speak of the coming destruction of Jerusalem.[11] After prophesying that God was going to judge the city, Jeremiah warned against people claiming to speak on God's behalf that God was actually going to preserve the temple:

> Then the LORD said to me, "The prophets are prophesying lies *in my name.* I have not sent them or appointed them or spoken to them. They are prophesying to you false visions, divinations, idolatries and the delusions of their own minds. Therefore this is what the LORD says about the prophets who are prophesying *in my name*: I did not send them, yet they are saying, 'No sword or famine will touch this land.' Those same prophets will perish by sword and famine. (Jer 14:14–15)

Prophetic texts also mention earthquakes in association with God coming to judge Jerusalem: "The LORD Almighty will come with thunder and earthquake and great noise, with windstorm and tempest and flames of a devouring fire" (Isa 29:6; cf. Jer 4:24; Mic 1:3–4). In several places, Ezekiel mentions God bringing famine upon Jerusalem in judgment (Ezek 6:11–12; 7:15; 12:16; 14:13, 21).[12] Finally, the prophets refer to "birth pains" that precede the destruction of a city, often Jerusalem (Isa 26:16–19; Jer 4:31; 6:22–26; 22:23–27; 30:4–8; Mic 4:10–14).[13]

Jesus's use of this range of prophetic imagery that referred to a previous, imminent judgment of Jerusalem indicates that similar traumatic social dynamics will precede the destruction of Jerusalem and point to the certainty that it will take place. He warns his disciples to avoid any deceptive talk that somehow the temple and the city will escape destruction. Even if well-meaning or pious people issue assurances based on God's faithfulness to his people and his protection of Zion throughout the generations, disciples must "watch out" to avoid false hope. God has already rendered his verdict on the temple, and its destruction will come soon.

Jesus's words have just as much relevance for Mark's audiences living *after* the temple was destroyed as for the original audience consisting of Peter, James, John, and Andrew. His warnings remind audiences that vaunted religious

---

11. Gray, *Temple in the Gospel of Mark*, 111–20; Moloney, *Gospel of Mark*, 255.
12. Gray, *Temple in the Gospel of Mark*, 116–17.
13. Gray, *Temple in the Gospel of Mark*, 118–19.

institutions and powerful Christian organizations are not guaranteed perpetual divine protection. If the very house where the God of Israel resided on earth could be abandoned and judged by God, then God's people throughout the ages must avoid putting their faith in the perceived strength of institutions and imagining that they are forever solid and reliable. The prophets warned Israel against trusting in false promises of protection. Jesus likewise warns his disciples to reject similar claims in his day. And Jesus's word resonates across the ages to sound the same note of caution and to urge the cultivation of discernment. Such times of upheaval are indeed destabilizing and provoke believers to imagine that the end is near, but none of these are signs of the coming of the Son of Man. Jesus calls God's people to cultivate discernment and learn to see these events for what they are—indications that in the present evil age creation continues to come apart, and the powers of evil continue to wreak havoc. These dynamics in the present age do not signal the end.

Again, Jesus exhorts his disciples to exercise discernment, with another appearance of *blepete*, which the NIV translates "be on your guard" (v. 9). Jesus tells his disciples that this age will be a time of suffering and persecution as they carry out the mission of preaching the gospel to all the nations. His statement that the gospel must be preached to all the nations (v. 10) indicates that the present age will continue beyond the destruction of the temple. Not only is the temple's destruction not the end of history, but the present age will be a time of persistent persecution, in which faithful disciples will be arrested and brought to trial. When this happens, they are not to worry, but just to say what comes to their minds. When they do this, "it is not you speaking, but the Holy Spirit" (v. 11). Faithful disciples of Jesus will be treated just as he will be. He will soon be betrayed by one of his disciples, and Christians throughout the ages will face similar circumstances. They will be hated and put to death (vv. 12–13), but those who endure faithfully will be saved in the end (v. 13). God will vindicate them just as he vindicated Jesus by raising him from the dead.

Amid these prophecies of upheaval that will characterize the present age, Jesus makes this mystifying reference to the future prospect of his disciples seeing "the abomination that causes desolation" (v. 14). When they see this "standing where it does not belong," those in Judea are to flee to the mountains. Making this verse even more difficult to understand, Mark inserts an editorial comment into the middle: "Let the reader understand." Just what does Jesus mean by this future event, and what does Mark mean by this inserted editorial comment?

The expression "abomination that causes desolation" comes from several

places in Daniel (9:27; 11:31; 12:11) that looked ahead to Antiochus IV
Epiphanes desecrating the temple by erecting a pagan altar within it in 167 BC
(1 Macc 1:54; 2 Macc 6:5). This was an abomination that caused "desolation"
in that it defiled the temple, preventing Jews from worshiping there.[14] It is
unclear to what event or events Jesus refers in this passage, but he indicates
that when they see it, they are assured that the destruction of the city and the
temple is right around the corner, and they must flee the city.[15]

Considering Jesus's words from an audience-oriented approach, it seems
that Mark's first audiences, perhaps even those outside Judea, would have
understood the event to which Jesus refers. Yet the larger point remains for
subsequent audiences that have no connection to the destruction of Jerusalem:
Jesus is exhorting his disciples to adopt a posture of readiness. They must not
assume that earthly institutions have God's endorsement, and when calamitous
events point to devastating destruction, they should pay no attention to words
of reassurance, but rather flee.

This is what Mark means by his editorial insertion "let the reader understand." It is an extraordinary moment in the narrative when the narrator himself turns to audiences hearing the Gospel and urges them, "You need to grasp
the significance of this!" He is adding stress to Jesus's warnings to be watchful
and to understand what is happening. Institutions are going to fall—Christian
organizations, large churches, even nations and empires—*so do not trust in
them.* God is not going to come and rescue any earthly entity. This present age
is one that ends in destruction, and for the people of God this age will be one
of persecution and hardship, even death. The only hope that disciples of Jesus
have is that they will be raised from the dead to inhabit the kingdom when it
comes fully in glory. In the meantime, however, Jesus's disciples must discern
the signs that the temple is about to be destroyed and flee. Audiences that hear
the Gospel after AD 70 must develop the same discernment to understand
what is happening and develop the wisdom to act accordingly.

The exhortation for the reader to understand builds on Mark's use of sensory language for discernment.[16] Jesus had spoken of "seeing," "hearing," and
"understanding" in the parable of the sower and the soils (4:12). Outsiders of

---

14. Boring, *Mark*, 367; Moloney, *Gospel of Mark*, 259.

15. This could refer to the emperor Gaius Caligula seeking to erect a statue of himself and placing
it in the temple in AD 40. It may also refer to the entrance of the Romans into the temple to set
up their military standards there in AD 70. Their presence certainly would have defiled the temple.
There are other events leading up to the siege of Jerusalem and the destruction of the temple that
could be in view here. Yet, as frustrating as it is for modern interpreters, there is no way to be certain
as to what Jesus refers here.

16. Gray, *Temple in the Gospel of Mark*, 132–33.

the kingdom are those who might "see" and "hear," but will fail to "perceive" and "understand." After demonstrating their progressively darkening vision of Jesus and his teaching, Jesus questions his disciples: "Do you still not see or understand? Are your hearts hardened? Do you have eyes but fail to see, and ears but fail to hear?" (8:17–18). "Do you still not understand?" (v. 21). When Jesus cursed the fig tree, the disciples "heard" it (11:14), and later the disciples "saw" it in its withered condition (v. 20). There is no mention, however, of "understanding" because they did not grasp its meaning. When they leave the temple and point to its impressive grandeur and stunning beauty (13:1), they indicate that while seeing and hearing *they have not understood what Jesus has been teaching them.*[17]

This lack of understanding on the part of the disciples and Mark's audiences will be devastatingly costly. If they listen to persuasive voices that provide assurances of God's continuing protection of Jerusalem and the temple, they will not take seriously Jesus's words to flee the city. And if subsequent generations of Mark's audiences do not pay close attention to what Jesus has said, they likewise will suffer disasters that would otherwise have been avoidable.

The gospel of the kingdom in Mark specifically has its cross-orientation in view, a call for disciples to join the cross-directed Messiah on the way to the cross. This present age is headed for destruction, and all institutions that partake of it are also headed for destruction. Yet the innate impulse toward self-preservation and self-protection, which leads people to seek safety in supposedly secure institutions, will constantly drive resistance to identifying with the cross.

Jesus exhorts his audiences to avoid any delay, but to flee immediately when they see signs of temporal destruction: "Let those who are in Judea flee to the mountains" (v. 14). The imagery of vv. 15–17 recalls the flight of Lot and his family from the city of Sodom at its destruction (Gen 19:17).[18] The terror of flight and the awfulness of the destruction of the city were to be beyond imagination.[19] If the devastation on Jerusalem was not limited by God, then no one would survive, not even those who belong to him. But for the sake of "the elect"—the disciples of Jesus—the destruction is limited (v. 20).

Again, Jesus returns to his warnings to avoid listening to anyone who claims to be speaking in Jesus's name, or even claiming to be Jesus himself

---

17. Gray, *Temple in the Gospel of Mark*, 132.

18. Boring, *Mark*, 368.

19. In books 4–6 of his work *The Jewish War*, Josephus gives an account of the arrival of the Romans into Galilee and their march through Judea to Jerusalem. His description of the siege of Jerusalem and the destruction of the temple is harrowing.

(vv. 21–22). The destruction of Jerusalem is not the sign of the coming of the Son of Man. Moreover, upheavals during the present age are not signs of Jesus's return. These are the ways that the present age *must* work out. It is going to be a time of distress that will see the rise and fall of nations and the growth and destruction of earthly institutions. While wars, famines, and economic hardships all cause great anxiety during this age, faithful disciples are not to read these as signs of the end of history. Such false messengers may be so convincing that they could even have led astray God's elect, if that were possible (v. 22). The church will need to exercise great caution and extreme discernment in order to remain faithful to its mission in the present age amid the great upheaval that will characterize it.

Jesus concludes his sobering talk about this age in v. 23 with a repetition of *blepete* ("be on your guard"). He has told them everything in advance. These upheavals are bound to come—indeed, they "must happen" (v. 7). But Jesus has told his disciples and subsequent audiences in advance, so that they might be discerning—*so that they might understand.*

The Coming of the Son of Man (vv. 24–27)

After addressing the tribulation and distress that precede the destruction of the Jerusalem temple and that will characterize the present age, Jesus now speaks about the coming of the Son of Man. This event that brings an end to the present age is therefore distinct from the ongoing destruction throughout this age. Jesus makes a transition at the beginning of v. 24: "But in *those days*, following *that distress.*" The expression "in those days" often indicates eschatological judgment or salvation (Jer 3:16, 18; 31:29; 33:15–16; Joel 3:1; Zech 8:23).[20]

The "distress" refers to the horror of Jerusalem's destruction and the terrorized flight out of the city (vv. 14–23). Jesus has given signs for when this would happen. Now, however, he describes the coming of the Son of Man, which is distinct from the temple's destruction, *an event for which there are no signs whatsoever*. In fact, as Boring notes, when "the signs can be seen, it will be too late to get ready."[21]

The sun being darkened and the stars falling from the sky are not "signs" that the Son of Man is on his way but rather descriptions of the entire cosmos convulsing at God's appearance. A number of biblical passages speak of creation being violently shaken when God shows up in power. For example:

---

20. Strauss, *Mark*, 590.
21. Boring, *Mark*, 372–73.

See, the day of the LORD is coming
    —a cruel day, with wrath and fierce anger—
to make the land desolate
    and destroy the sinners within it.
The stars of heaven and their constellations
    will not show their light.
The rising sun will be darkened
    and the moon will not give its light.
I will punish the world for its evil,
    the wicked for their sins.
I will put an end to the arrogance of the haughty
    and will humble the pride of the ruthless. (Isa 13:9–11)

I will show wonders in the heavens
    and on the earth,
        blood and fire and billows of smoke.
The sun will be turned to darkness
    and the moon to blood
        before the coming of the great and dreadful day of the LORD.
        (Joel 2:30–31)[22]

Another indication that vv. 24–27 speak of an event that is distinct from the age of destruction is that v. 26 mentions that "*people* will see the Son of Man." In vv. 5–23, Jesus has been addressing "you." Here, however, he refers to "people," referring to a different group and not his immediate audience, indicating an event that lies beyond the temple's destruction. Jesus does not indicate how much time separates the destruction of the temple from the appearance of the Son of Man. The point Jesus is making is that the appearance of the Son of Man has no signs to identify it. He will show up suddenly, and creation will violently react to his arrival. It will indeed be a great and dreadful day (cf. Joel 2:31).

At that event that culminates the present evil age, the Son of Man will gather the elect as the kingdom of God is fully realized. In this age, the temple will be destroyed, as will Jesus. But God will vindicate him by raising him from the dead, so that he becomes God's new eschatological temple. And at his return he will gather his people to himself. God had intended the Jerusalem temple to be a house of prayer for all nations, though this tragically did not

---

22. Cf. also Isa 34:4; Joel 2:10; Zech 2:6.

happen (11:17). Jesus, however, will be just this sort of temple, gathering his people from the farthest ends of the earth (13:27).

The Parable of the Fig Tree (vv. 28–31)

After speaking about the eschatological appearance of the Son of Man in vv. 24–27, Jesus returns to speaking about the coming destruction of Jerusalem. He mentions the fig tree, which he has already associated with the temple (11:13–20), and he refers to seeing "these things" in anticipation of something being near: "When you see these things happening, you know that it is near, right at the door" (v. 29). "These things" (*tauta*) goes back to the same expression in v. 4, where the disciples inquire about the destruction of Jerusalem: "Tell us, when will these things happen? And what will be the sign that they are all about to be fulfilled?" Moreover, in v. 30 Jesus states that "this generation will certainly not pass away until *all these things* have happened," indicating that the temple's destruction is going to happen during the lifetime of those who were the first of Jesus's disciples.

Just like fig trees give signs that summer is near by bearing leaves, so the disciples need to pay attention to the signs of growing chaos and violence that are going to lead up to the destruction of Jerusalem. Jesus's association of the fig tree's development with the coming destruction of the Jerusalem temple recalls his cursing of the fig tree for failing to bear fruit. Jesus has already seen that the temple is dead from the inside, just like the cursed fig tree. And he announced God's judgment on it by shutting down its operations. When they "see" the signs that the temple is about to be destroyed, they need to recognize that its destruction is at hand.[23]

Jesus assures his audience in v. 31 of the certainty of these events in language that recalls the power and absolute reliability of God's word in Isaiah 40:8: "The grass withers and the flowers fall, but the word of our God endures forever." This is yet another instance in which Mark depicts Jesus participating in the divine identity of the God of Israel. His word is as sure as that of God's.

---

23. The NIV rightly translates the Greek expression *ginōskete hoti engys estin* as "you know that it is near," referring to the destruction of the temple (cf. Robert H. Stein, *Jesus, the Temple and the Coming Son of Man: A Commentary on Mark 13* [Downers Grove, IL: IVP Academic, 2014], 124; Strauss, *Mark*, 594). Because there is no explicitly stated subject of the third-person singular verb *estin*, it could be either a person or thing. It might be taken to refer to the Son of Man rather than the temple's destruction ("you know that *he* is near"). Among the major translations that have the Son of Man in view here are the CEB, NASB, ESV, CSB, NRSV, and NET. For reasons stated above, however, it makes better sense to read vv. 28–31 as a parable referring to the temple's destruction rather than to the appearance of the Son of Man.

The Parable of the Watchman (vv. 32–37)

Whereas the parable of the fig tree has to do with the destruction of the temple, this parable concerns the distinct eschatological event of the coming of the Son of Man (vv. 32–37). Jesus had been speaking about "these things" that are the signs of the coming destruction of the temple (v. 29). He now turns to speak of "that day or hour," referring to his future return. That day will come suddenly, and no one knows when it will occur. In fact, no one knows anything at all about that day, not even the Son of Man (v. 32). Only God the Father knows when this will take place.

In the meantime, before the Son of Man returns, Jesus exhorts his disciples once again with the imperative verb *blepete*: "Be on guard!" He supplements that with another imperative—*agrupneite*: "Be alert!" (v. 33). These are not exhortations to be engaged in eschatological speculation, predicting when the end of history will come. Disciples, rather, are like the servants and the watchman that have been appointed tasks by the master of the house (v. 34). No one in the house knows when the master will return, but the one thing they cannot be doing when he comes back is sleeping (v. 36). They must be about their tasks! Jesus, therefore, exhorts his disciples again to "keep watch" (v. 35). Then Mark again makes an arresting move: he pauses his narrative of Jesus's address and has Jesus turn from addressing his four disciples to speak to all of Mark's subsequent audiences. Just as in a movie when a character turns to the camera to speak directly to the audience, Jesus speaks directly to the church. This is so important that Jesus wants to tell everyone himself: "What I say to you [the disciples], I say to everyone [Mark's audiences]: 'Watch!'" (v. 37).

This parable has to do with being watchful in the present age in anticipation of the coming of the Son of Man. Jesus commends "being watchful" and warns against "sleeping." What does he mean? Being watchful and diligent involves paying attention to what Jesus has said to do throughout Mark's Gospel. Disciples are to cultivate communities that embody the cross-shaped Messiah by offering hospitality to the marginalized and serving the poor and needy. To be "sleeping" means to become complacent about cultivating these sorts of communities. Communities that are "asleep" are those that are formed by the habits and social patterns of their surrounding cultures. The tragedy is that such churches and Christian communities will continue to exist, but they will be communities formed by the word of a kingdom with no cross. Satan will have snatched away the word. Or worries about other things will have crept in ever so subtly, so that other sorts of concerns smother the word and make it lifeless (4:15–19).

LIVE the Story

Eschatological Speculation

Throughout history, many Christian groups have been consumed with events surrounding the end of history. Study of "the last days" or "eschatological speculation" has only grown in strength over the last century or so. Reading the Bible, especially its prophetic passages, to gain an exact picture of what precisely will unfold at the end of the world is a pursuit that fascinates millions of Christians.

William Miller was one such person. A farmer from New York, he was a Baptist layperson who was fascinated by the study of prophecy. From his study of Daniel, he calculated that Christ would return in 1843, though he later settled on the exact date of October 22, 1844.

> Utilizing tracts, prophecy conferences, and tent services; periodicals with titles such as *The Midnight Cry* and *Signs of the Times*; and colorful illustrated charts with menageries of lions, bears, and dragons from the Book of Daniel, the movement won followers across New England, upstate New York, the upper Midwest, and as far away as England.[24]

The hopes of "Millerites," numbering in the tens of thousands, were tragically dashed when that day passed without event.

In his study of evangelicalism in the twentieth century titled *American Apocalypse*, Matthew Avery Sutton chronicles the central place that speculation about the future occupies for evangelicals in modern America.[25] Since the decades before the First World War, prominent preachers have been seeking to identify in contemporary events of their day who was playing the roles of the Antichrist and various other biblical characters in end-times conflicts. Because evangelicalism developed with a strong patriotic impulse, nations in conflict with America were often seen to be playing these sinister roles, including presidential candidates with whom a given evangelical leader might disagree.

The movement known as premillennial dispensationalism spawned countless books, conferences, and magazine publications, focused on identifying contemporary events with prophetic passages from the Old Testament and the

---

24. Paul Boyer, *When Time Shall Be No More: Prophecy Belief in Modern American Culture* (Cambridge, MA: Belknap, 1992), 81.

25. Matthew Avery Sutton, *American Apocalypse: A History of Modern Evangelicalism* (Cambridge, MA: Belknap, 2014).

book of Revelation. The most famous of these is Hal Lindsey's *The Late Great Planet Earth*, which is purported to be the best-selling book of the 1970s.[26] The most recent instance of this prophetic fascination is the series of novels in the *Left Behind* series.[27]

Because of its future orientation and its use of imagery from the biblical prophets, Mark 13 has become a source for speculation about future events. What can Jesus's speech to his disciples teach us about all of this? First, Jesus says that all the upheavals and various destructions of history have nothing to do with the end of the world. That is, World Wars, the rise and fall of nations, and various economic collapses *are not signs of the end-times. These are not eschatological events.* These are the sorts of things that happen as this present evil age unfolds. And Jesus tells his followers emphatically that they must cultivate wisdom to discern how these events will affect their communities—especially the vulnerable among them—and take steps to look out for each other.

I have heard Bible teachers state that they feel that the Lord's return is near. When I asked one of them why he felt that way—I was genuinely curious—he gave a variety of reasons that had to do with the flow of history, economic instability, international relations, and various intergenerational dynamics. Even though such dynamics in our culture are upsetting and feel enormously significant to us, *these are precisely the sorts of unsettling dynamics and destabilizing events that have nothing at all to do with the return of the Son of Man to judge the living and the dead.* Jesus teaches his disciples plainly that they should not interpret contemporary events, no matter how momentous, with relation to the end of history.

Second, not only are contemporary, troublesome developments in our world not signs of the end of history, but Jesus indicates that *no signs at all will point to his appearance at the last day.* Moreover, no one can possibly know when this will happen, since Jesus himself is unaware of when his return will take place. Only God the Father knows the timing of this consummating event. Therefore, even though studying biblical prophecy and related Bible passages to discern the timeline leading up to the end may feel productive or leave one feeling awakened to a significant reality, it is actually highly unproductive. In terms of Mark 13, such a pursuit is actually *a failure* to be alert, to be on guard, and to be watchful (vv. 33–37). It is actually a strategy that puts one at risk of being found "asleep."

Being "alert" and "on guard" involves paying close attention to the directives

---

26. Hal Lindsey, *The Late Great Planet Earth* (Grand Rapids: Zondervan, 1970).

27. The original novel, cowritten by Tim LaHaye and Jerry B. Jenkins, appeared in 1995 and was followed by more than ten sequel volumes, several of which were made into films.

that the Lord has given to his church, which involve cultivating communities of service to the poor and hospitality to the marginalized despite all the conflicts and cultural upheavals going on in our world. "Being awake," therefore, points to a community effort of becoming the sort of church that discerns within our wider communities who is suffering and who is being marginalized. Such an effort will put us in touch with strangers who will make us uncomfortable, certainly, but such practices are precisely the means whereby we enjoy the presence of the Lord Jesus and of God who sent Jesus (Mark 9:37). "Being watchful" entails doing the sort of things that we may perceive through the eyes of the flesh as unsettling, such as welcoming immigrants into our communities and looking after refugees and others who live in fear and in need.

Third, and closely related to the previous point, as Michael Gorman indicates in his critical analysis of the *Left Behind* series, a fascination with end-times eschatology typically creates internal dispositions of fear and a posture of suspicion toward others that runs directly counter to the sort of character that the Spirit of Jesus is working to produce in the church.[28] Because the series of novels prioritizes *escapism*—longing for the day when Christians leave this world and go to heaven—it has no ethical vision for life on this earth and becomes fascinated with violence and fearmongering. Sutton's work details how reading contemporary events in terms of prophetic speculation typically went hand in hand with hostility toward foreigners, immigrants, and especially African-Americans throughout the twentieth century.[29]

The fears and suspicions fostered by prophetic speculation, however, are precisely what biblical faith is meant to overcome; *this is exactly what Jesus warned his disciples about.* Throughout the Gospel of Mark, such fear is equivalent to unbelief. Suspicion of others who are unlike us causes us to cultivate church community life that excludes others and closes ourselves off from others. While we may feel safe, secure, and certain, this is actually a community mode of life that embodies unbelief, according to Mark. Such churches are actually seeing but not perceiving what the kingdom is all about. They are hearing but not understanding what God wants for them and from them. Tragically, while they imagine that they are kingdom insiders, they run the risk of being revealed as outsiders (Mark 4:11–12).

Like Bartimaeus, the church must cry out to Jesus, "Rabbi, we want to see!" (cf. Mark 10:51). Calling out to God for an expanded kingdom vision will help us to see the plenty around us so that we can be charitable, open-hearted,

---

28. Michael J. Gorman, *Reading Revelation Responsibly: Uncivil Worship and Witness: Following the Lamb into the New Creation* (Eugene, OR: Cascade, 2011), 70–73.

29. Sutton, *American Apocalypse*, 114–47.

welcoming communities of rest for outsiders, foreigners, immigrants, and others whom our culture presses us to fear and regard with suspicion. In Mark 13, Jesus teaches the church to live with wisdom and discernment in this present age, to hope in no earthly institution, and to be wrapped up thoroughly in the joy of becoming communities of hospitality and service.

And what do Jesus's disciples have to fear? Nothing, so long as we are looking forward to receiving the eternal kingdom when the Son of Man comes in power. But we do have reason to fear if we become wrapped up in anything that presses us into becoming communities of paranoia and suspicion or misled by any speculation that moves us away from loving others with abandon.

Interpreting God's Purposes in Historical Events

The vision of this present age that Jesus unfolds has much to teach us about Christian reticence when it comes to interpreting events in history. By Christian reticence, I mean that Christians ought to be extremely cautious about interpreting cataclysmic events as if they can somehow discern the mind of God. The twentieth century was an age of mass media—newspapers, television, and radio, along with mass mailing, and we now live in an era dominated by social media because of the internet. These tools of mass communication allow Christian figures with large followings to weigh in on events and give their opinions about how such things fit into a scheme of God's work in the world.

After the unspeakably awful events of September 11, 2001, Jerry Falwell Sr., in a conversation with Pat Robertson on the television program *The 700 Club*, claimed that the attacks were divine judgment against America. Falwell stated:

> I really believe that the pagans, and the abortionists, and the feminists, and the gays and the lesbians who are actively trying to make that an alternative lifestyle, the ACLU, People For the American Way, all of them who have tried to secularize America. I point the finger in their face and say "you helped this happen."[30]

Robertson agreed with him:

> "We have sinned against Almighty God, at the highest level of our government, we've stuck our finger in your eye," said Robertson. "The Supreme Court has insulted you over and over again, Lord. They've taken your

---

30. "Falwell Apologizes to Gays, Feminists, Lesbians," CNN, September 14, 2001, www.cnn.com/2001/US/09/14/Falwell.apology/.

Bible away from the schools. They've forbidden little children to pray. They've taken the knowledge of God as best they can, and organizations have come into court to take the knowledge of God out of the public square of America."[31]

Falwell later apologized:

Namely, I do not believe that any mortal knows when God is judging or not judging someone or a nation. In my listing of groups and persons who might have assisted in the secularization of America, I unforgivably left off the list a sleeping church, Jerry Falwell, etc. . . . It was a pure misstatement, unintentional, and I apologize for it uncategorically.[32]

Unfortunately, this was not the last time that popular Christian figures claimed to discern the hand of God in large-scale catastrophes and other significant events. In 2005, Robertson explained the divine logic behind Hurricane Katrina and attributed the devastating earthquake in Haiti to that small nation's "pact with the devil."[33] After the election of Donald Trump in 2016, Franklin Graham claimed that "God showed up."[34]

The proclivity of evangelical public figures to interpret epoch-making events such as natural disasters or national elections in terms of what God is doing in the world runs counter to the teaching of Scripture in general and of Mark 13 in particular. From the perspective of the entire narrative of Scripture, we must keep in mind where we are located in the story. We are currently situated *after* human rebellion (Gen 3), which took the specific form of humanity's preference for chaos and disorder rather than participation in manifesting the rule of God in creation as the divine image.[35] And we are

---

31. "Falwell Apologizes."

32. Peter Carlson, "Jerry Falwell's Awkward Apology," *Washington Post*, November 18, 2001, www.washingtonpost.com/archive/lifestyle/2001/11/18/jerry-falwells-awkward-apology/c4b30199-ce51-4b35-bf38-29a60476cd03/. See also Peter Carlson, "Bearing Witness to the Gospel according to Falwell," *Washington Post*, May 16, 2007, www.washingtonpost.com/wp-dyn/content/article/2007/05/15/AR2007051502368.html.

33. Megan Friedman, "Top 10 Pat Robertson Gaffes," *Time*, September 16, 2011, http://content.time.com/time/specials/packages/article/0,28804,1953778_1953776_1953771,00.html; John Hudson, "Pat Robertson Blames Natural Disaster Victims," *The Atlantic*, January 14, 2010, www.theatlantic.com/technology/archive/2010/01/pat-robertson-blames-natural-disaster-victims/341489/.

34. Mark Price, "Franklin Graham: It Wasn't Russians Who Intervened in Election, 'It Was God,'" *Charlotte Observer*, December 19, 2016, www.charlotteobserver.com/news/local/article121721213.html.

35. John H. Walton explains the significance of the serpent and related imagery in Genesis 2–3 against the backdrop of the ancient world in his excellent *The Lost World of Adam and Eve: Genesis 2–3 and the Human Origins Debate* (Downers Grove, IL: IVP Academic, 2015).

situated *before* God has fully redeemed creation. So we still await God's coming salvation and the transformation of the children of God and creation. Because of this, we are in an era when creation and all humanity groan under the burden of a condition where nothing is experiencing God's rule of shalom as it should (Rom 8:19–27).

Not only has humanity rebelled against God's purposes, but the entire cosmos has been hijacked by cosmic forces that are working to ruin creation and ensure that the character of all life on earth is marked by oppression and degradation. Satan, the "god of this age" (2 Cor 4:4) and the "ruler of the kingdom of the air" (Eph 2:2), along with the powers and authorities and the rulers of this present evil age (Eph 6:10–12), have perverted and corrupted creation, and they hold it in their enslaving grip. Even though they are defeated entities and will be destroyed at the day of Christ (1 Cor 15:25–28), they still work to corrupt, distort, pervert, and ruin human experience in God's good but not yet fully liberated world. Because of their corrupting work, God's creation is not yet fully experiencing his rule of shalom. And since this is the case, we simply cannot discern with any accuracy the extent to which large-scale events take place by God's design. To claim to have a God-authorized interpretation of an event like an earthquake or a political election is self-deception that dishonors God.

When it comes to Mark 13, Jesus relays to his disciples a vision of this age as one of ongoing, relentless, and regularly occurring destruction. And because there is no logic to the ongoing destruction, Jesus says that Christians are not exempt, and they will at times be captured by the chaotic character of this age's destructive dynamics. They may be like John the Baptist, who was caught up in the pursuit of revenge and the power dynamics of the Herodian royal family (Mark 6:14–29). The capricious Herod's foolish and drunken boast opened him up to manipulation and exploitation by his wife and her daughter, and all these power games led to John's death. To attempt to discern the mind of God in these events is pointless and fruitless. Such a course leads one to endlessly speculate with no clear answer ever coming. It is far better to reckon with the broken character of God's world and grieve over the destructive folly of humanity.

In the same way that John the Baptist was mistreated, the disciples of Jesus would be turned over to authorities and would be mistreated and put to death. But none of these events in history should be read as God's specific judgments on these individuals for their misbehavior. They can be attributed to the chaotic and destructive character of this age, in which disciples must be aware that the world does not reflect the rule of the creator God as it will one day when the Son of Man comes in power to finally bring all creation under God's sovereign authority. Until that day, we cannot attempt to discern a straightforward logic to things.

Such interpretations are inevitably myopic. They miss larger dynamics in the world, and they flow from one's own resentments and fears and from one's cultural setting. For example, Pat Robertson and Jerry Falwell have both stirred up and participated in the divisive culture wars in America over the last half century, so they almost inevitably see the political groups they oppose as God's enemies. Because their resentments and anger at such groups are well cultivated, they understand terrible events as God's judgments on those very people. When they are forced to reconsider their rashly spoken words, however, they often, though not always, return to their senses and remember that as mere mortals they do not have access to God's secret councils.

The church of Jesus must remember that it is unwise to seek to discern the mind of God in cataclysmic events such as natural disasters and epoch-changing cultural dynamics. In Mark 13 Jesus tells his disciples that this present age will be filled with catastrophes and cultural upheavals. We should not be shocked when they occur, and we ought to be ready to respond in order to protect the vulnerable and continue to do what Jesus has said to do: serve the needy and provide hospitality to the marginalized.

Confidence in Earthly Institutions

Jesus's words to the disciples were no doubt very unsettling and highly disturbing. The Jerusalem temple was one of the most impressive structures in the ancient world, projecting stability, reliability, and strength. And since Jerusalem and the temple had many promises of God attached to them from Israel's Scriptures, there was an even stronger sense that the temple would be a lasting reality. Though they were living in an occupied land, faithful Jews were confident that at some point God would return and save them and drive out the Romans. For the disciples, this was all in the process of happening in the person whom they were following—Jesus, the one to whom they had committed their lives. It must have been very exciting! The rescue of the God of Israel was on its way!

The only bummer was that their teacher kept bringing up how he was going to die! But even though they couldn't quite figure out what he was getting at, what they were certain of was that the liberation of Israel was right around the corner. To this point in Mark's Gospel, the disciples have not been paying close enough attention to catch the reality that Jesus is not the Messiah they think he is, and none of this is going to work out like they imagine it is.

All this optimism drives their overawed observation of the wonder and grandeur of the temple at the beginning of Mark 13: "Look, Teacher! What massive stones! What magnificent buildings!" Jesus's message is clear, however, even though it was equally devastating to hear: this beautiful structure and these magnificent buildings that they imagine have God's promises attached to them are all going to be destroyed. The temple was intended for the blessing of God's people and for the refreshment of the nations, but it has become a place of exploitation and oppression. It is dead on the inside, all the way down to the roots. It will not survive. It is going to be destroyed in devastating fashion.

This is a hard lesson to learn. Humans inevitably look to impressive earthly institutions and regularly attribute God's blessing to them, inspiring confidence and a sense of peace and order. The "Christian" empires of late nineteenth and early twentieth-century Europe celebrated their power and were confident in God's promised blessings on them as they went to war for their glorious kingdoms in what we call the First World War. This mind-boggling miscalculation and tragic folly upon which these empires embarked issued in more than a century of violence and chaos involving the reordering of Europe and ongoing destruction and devastation in the Middle East.[36]

A similar ideology affects the context in which I was raised and in which I currently live. White evangelical Christian culture in America is shaped by an ideology that resides in our collective consciousness. It is very subtle, but it was taught to us over the last four centuries in our churches and in our schools; it comes to us in our language, in our imagery, in the blending of the cross and the American flag, in our hymns, and in our celebration of Christian freedom and American liberty.

This particular narrative that we have inherited is one that *associates the kingdom of God with America*. To be a good Christian is to be a patriotic American. Our culture looks back to a glorious past—one that never really existed as we think it did—as a heritage that has been lost, for various reasons.[37] It's been taken away by others who mean to do us harm. And we imagine that it is our mission to reclaim it or to fight to regain it.

This identification of America as a nation that is especially blessed by God and that enjoys a special relationship with God is an idolatry that has

---

36. David Fromkin, *A Peace to End All Peace: The Fall of the Ottoman Empire and the Creation of the Modern Middle East* (New York: Holt, 2009). See also Scott Sanderson, *Lawrence in Arabia: War, Deceit, Imperial Folly and the Making of the Modern Middle East* (New York: Doubleday, 2013).

37. Cf. Stephanie Coontz, *The Way We Never Were: American Families and the Nostalgia Trap* (New York: Basic Books, 2016).

produced a variety of corrupted fruits. I say that it is an idolatry because in the Bible, idolatry is the inappropriate association of anything created by humans (an object, a city, a nation) with the one true God. We will see later that Mark suggests that the temple had become an idolatrous reality, since people associated it with God, while God had rejected it (Mark 14:58).

Moses took a similar misstep, aligning himself too closely with God and suffering the consequences of being barred from entering the promised land (Num 20:10–13; Deut 4:21–24). He castigated Israel in the wilderness: "Listen, you rebels, must *we* bring you water out of this rock?" (Num 20:10). God regarded Moses's aligning of himself with God as a disregard for his holiness: "Because you did not trust in me enough to honor me as holy in the sight of the Israelites, you will not bring this community into the land I give them" (v. 12).

Throughout his long speech recounting the past for the generation that was to enter the land of promise, Moses repeatedly warned Israel not to make any images when they entered there (Deuteronomy 1–4). It was regular practice for people in the ancient world to make images for their deities, so it would have been the easy and natural thing to do to make images of the God of Israel. But since God is the living God, *humanity* is his image, and anything that humanity makes—anything "made with hands"—must never be seen as representing the creator God. The danger of idolatry is the temptation to revere anything that humanity creates as if it represented the God who rules creation and is only imaged through humanity.

This reality lies behind the exhortations of the writer of Hebrews when he writes to his Jewish Christian audience and warns them against aligning the current work of God in Christ with the earthly city of Jerusalem and the temple. He notes that they are receiving a heavenly kingdom, a coming reality, which allows them to let go of these current earthly realities:

See to it that you do not refuse him who speaks. If they did not escape when they refused him who warned them on earth, how much less will we, if we turn away from him who warns us from heaven? At that time his voice shook the earth, but now he has promised, "Once more I will shake not only the earth but also the heavens." The words "once more" indicate the removing of what can be shaken—that is, created things—so that what cannot be shaken may remain.

Therefore, since we are receiving a kingdom that cannot be shaken, let us be thankful, and so worship God acceptably with reverence and awe, for our "God is a consuming fire." (Heb 12:25–29)

The citation of the statement that "God is a consuming fire" comes from the concluding line of Moses's speech to Israel in Deuteronomy 4:24. God had judged Moses for the inappropriate move he made, and God will judge Israel if they view the God of Israel as imaged through any created thing: "For the LORD your God is a consuming fire, a jealous God" (Deut 4:24). God will not tolerate such an inappropriate association.

White American Christians have an especially difficult time disentangling their American identity from their Christian identity, since the assumption that these two identities are one and the same is deeply embedded in our national narrative. It is a seduction that calls to us repeatedly and relentlessly, and it hearkens our imaginations back to a time in the distant past when things were as they ought to have been. And I am referring to an assumption that *white* American Christians make, because for nonwhite Americans the distant past is an era when they experienced unspeakable oppression and exclusion. One of the awful realities of this particular idolatry, therefore, is the way it divides Christians in America. White Christians hear slogans that recall a previous era of American greatness, and they resonate with it. But Christians of color hear such slogans, and they imagine a terrible era when they were pushed out or kept down—treated as property to be owned or as noncitizens or second-class citizens. This is intensely problematic, for it divides the body of Christ, grieving and angering the heart of God.

Many white Christians have some work to do to sort through their identities as white Americans and as Christians. Reading evangelical history in America is a step in a fruitful direction.[38] This will allow us to see how we have been affected by a particular narrative that associates being Christian with being American. We might consider the regrets of Billy Graham, who said that one of his chief regrets is that for many years he had associated the kingdom of God with the American way of life. Another one of his regrets is that he did not discern how he had been manipulated by American presidents for their own political purposes.[39] He saw all of this later in his life, but did not understand the dynamics involved while they were going on.

Unfortunately, we do not have fruitful ways of talking about this in our current hotly contested political climate. We imagine that one must be either intensely patriotic or anti-American. But there are other options we might

---

38. An excellent place to start is Jemar Tisby, *The Color of Compromise: The Truth about the American Church's Complicity in Racism* (Grand Rapids: Zondervan, 2018).

39. Collin Hansen, "What I Would Have Done Differently: Billy Graham's Regrets, in His Own Words," *Christianity Today*, February 21 2018, www.christianitytoday.com/ct/2018/billy-graham/what-i-would-have-done-differently.html.

explore, including how to be *faithfully Christian in America*, as opposed to being *Christians that are entitled to control American destiny*. We can love this land and *all* the people in it, without associating the nation with God's purposes. Returning to the Gospel of Mark, this present age involved the destruction of Jerusalem, the city that many of the psalms celebrate, including the building that was at one time considered the dwelling place of the God of Israel. If that building and that city did not survive, then we can be assured that the earthly construct called "the United States of America" will also be a passing reality. If we attach our ultimate identity to this earthly reality, we put ourselves in a place of judgment, potentially sharing the destruction of this present age. Yet if we "lose" our lives in this present age, holding our national identity with an open hand while living fully into our identification as Jesus-followers, then we will receive the kingdom that is coming when the Son of Man returns in power to set up his eternal reign.

CHAPTER 54

Mark 14:1–11

📖 LISTEN to the Story

¹Now the Passover and the Festival of Unleavened Bread were only two days away, and the chief priests and the teachers of the law were scheming to arrest Jesus secretly and kill him. ²"But not during the festival," they said, "or the people may riot."

³While he was in Bethany, reclining at the table in the home of Simon the Leper, a woman came with an alabaster jar of very expensive perfume, made of pure nard. She broke the jar and poured the perfume on his head.

⁴Some of those present were saying indignantly to one another, "Why this waste of perfume? ⁵It could have been sold for more than a year's wages and the money given to the poor." And they rebuked her harshly.

⁶"Leave her alone," said Jesus. "Why are you bothering her? She has done a beautiful thing to me. ⁷The poor you will always have with you, and you can help them any time you want. But you will not always have me. ⁸She did what she could. She poured perfume on my body beforehand to prepare for my burial. ⁹Truly I tell you, wherever the gospel is preached throughout the world, what she has done will also be told, in memory of her."

¹⁰Then Judas Iscariot, one of the Twelve, went to the chief priests to betray Jesus to them. ¹¹They were delighted to hear this and promised to give him money. So he watched for an opportunity to hand him over.

Listening to the Text in the Story: Exodus 12; Deuteronomy 15:11; 2 Samuel 24; Amos 2:6–7; James 2:1–13; 5:1–6.

Mark 14–15 narrates Jesus's betrayal, suffering, and death (or, his *passion*, a term that relates to Greek and Latin words for "suffering"). This episode in Bethany, at Simon the Leper's house, initiates a larger section in which Jesus is betrayed by Judas, denied by Peter, and increasingly abandoned by the rest of his disciples until he is finally alone. Throughout the passion account, Jesus is largely a passive figure, which is a dramatic shift from the rest of Mark. To this point in the Gospel, Jesus has been driving the action and setting the agenda, but in Mark 14–15 he gives himself willingly and becomes subject to the evil scheming of other characters. Despite their plotting and apparent control of the narrative, however, everything that unfolds has been predicted by Jesus. The divine plan is being worked out, for these things "must" take place (8:31; 9:12; 14:49).

This episode plays a pivotal structural role in Mark's Gospel. We have already noted in introducing Mark 13 that the present episode forms an *inclusio* with 12:41–44. The poor widow who gives "all she had to live on" to the temple that was about to be destroyed stands in contrast to the scribes who are getting rich from their exploitation of such widows (12:38–40). In the same way, the unnamed woman here who anoints Jesus gives an overwhelmingly sacrificial gift to Jesus who is about to die, contrasting sharply with the Sanhedrin who are plotting Jesus's death and Judas who is seeking to betray him for money. In addition to framing Mark 13, this episode also relates to 16:1–8, forming an *inclusio* with the end of Mark's Gospel. Just as this woman anoints Jesus for burial, the women come to Jesus's grave to anoint Jesus's body (16:1). Both episodes also refer to Jesus's absence: "You will not always have me" (14:7); "He is not here" (16:6).[1]

This episode is another Markan sandwich, with the account of the woman anointing Jesus (vv. 3–8) framed by the Sanhedrin scheming to kill Jesus (vv. 1–2) and Judas planning to betray him for money (vv. 10–11). The woman performs a "beautiful" (*kalos*) act for Jesus, preparing him for burial. The Sanhedrin and Judas, however, plot and scheme to betray and kill Jesus. Mark provides verbal links between the outer portions of this episode that demonstrate that Judas has allied himself with the murderous agenda of the Sanhedrin:

Mark 14:1	Mark 14:11
And the chief priests and the scribes	And Judas
were seeking (*ezētoun*, from *zēteō*)	was seeking (*ezētei*, from *zēteō*)
how him (*pōs auton*)	how him (*pōs auton*)
by stealth (*en dolō*)	opportunely (*eukairōs*)
having arrested, might kill (*kratēsantes apokteinōsin*)	might deliver up (*paradoi*)[1]

[1] Marcus, *Mark 8–16*, 943.

---

1. Placher, *Mark*, 196.

The costly gift that elicits Jesus's effusive commendation recalls David's statement about his desire to give a costly gift in 2 Samuel 24:24. David had sinned by taking a census of the people (vv. 1–2). He had been warned by Joab that he should not do this, but he stubbornly went ahead, disregarding Joab and the other commanders' admonitions (vv. 3–4). This incited the Lord's anger, and he brought about a devastating slaughter among the Israelites, stopping only when the angel of the Lord reached Jerusalem (vv. 15–16). When David went to build an altar at Araunah's threshing floor, which was the place the angel of the Lord had ceased from judgment, Araunah offered to give the property to David (vv. 22–23). The king, however, refused: "No, I insist on paying you for it. I will not sacrifice to the LORD my God burnt offerings that cost me nothing" (v. 24). Though her situation is quite different from David's, the unnamed woman who anoints Jesus offers her gift from the same spirit.

EXPLAIN the Story

The Scheming of the Sanhedrin (vv. 1–2)

Mark opens the scene by noting that Passover and the Feast of Unleavened Bread, which was a seven-day festival that followed Passover, was two days away (v. 1). This was, of course, the holiday during which Jews celebrated God's liberation of Israel from slavery in Egypt (Exod 12). During such festivals, Jewish pilgrims from around the Mediterranean world filled Jerusalem so that the city swelled to many times its normal population. This put the Sanhedrin on edge as they sought to maintain the peace in order to protect their positions with the occupying Romans. The Romans were also on high alert during such times, being well aware of the resentment on the part of the Jewish people and the revolutionary fervor pulsing through the visiting crowds.

All of this informs Mark's comment that the chief priests and the scribes wanted to be rid of Jesus but needed to plot their moves cautiously so as not to provoke a riot among the people (v. 2). These two groups have been trying to figure out a way to kill Jesus since he arrived in Jerusalem, shut down the temple (11:18), and told the parable of the absent vineyard owner and wicked tenants, which was directed at them (12:12).[2]

---

2. Garland, *Theology of Mark's Gospel*, 160.

The Woman's Gift (vv. 3–8)

After introducing the evil scheming of the Sanhedrin, Mark narrates the inner portion of the literary sandwich. The setting is Simon the Leper's house in Bethany, just a few miles from Jerusalem on the eastern slope of the Mount of Olives. Jesus and his disciples have been staying there since they arrived in 11:1. Mark does not state whether Simon was healed of his condition, but this is another indication of Jesus's preference for outsiders.[3]

During a meal, an unnamed woman entered with an alabaster jar that contained very expensive perfume.[4] Rather than opening the jar and preserving the possibility of holding some back, she broke it, giving her gift with absolute abandon. Having done so, she poured the perfume on Jesus's head, grabbing everyone's attention (14:3).[5] As Jesus will explain, the woman is preparing Jesus's body for burial. She identifies completely with Jesus in his death. She has held nothing back but has fully given "what she could" to Jesus as he goes to his death. Mark sets her up as an ideal disciple, starkly contrasting her with Peter in 8:29–38. Peter had identified Jesus as the Christ, but rejected Jesus's prediction that he was going to suffer and be killed. Mark's audiences need to move from Peter's mindset toward that of this woman, abandoning any reservations and identifying themselves fully with Jesus's death.

Some of those gathered around the table complained indignantly to one another about the woman's wasteful act and "rebuked her harshly" for "wasting" the expensive perfume (v. 4). That the cost of the perfume added up to

---

3. Leprosy can refer to a range of skin conditions in the ancient world. Simon may still have retained his identity as a leper after being healed. After Jesus drives the "legion" of demons from the man in Mark 5:1–20, he is called "the man who had been demon-possessed" three times (vv. 15, 16, 18; the NIV translates each of these slightly differently). While Mark expresses this in the past tense, it still shapes his identity for the sake of the narrative. In the same way, Simon's current health condition is irrelevant, but Mark uses this identity effectively for his narrative purposes in that it identifies him as an outsider, which contrasts sharply with Judas, an insider, "one of the Twelve" (14:10).

4. This episode is often conflated or associated with other Gospel accounts in order to supply details that Mark does not include (Matt 26:6–13; Luke 7:36–50; John 12:1–8). Mark does not indicate her name, however, nor does he identify her as a sinner or a prostitute. The woman in Luke 7:36–50 is a sinner, and Mary is named in John 12:1–8, though there is no indication there that she is a prostitute, a tradition that derives from a mistaken association with another Mary (cf. Boring, *Mark*, 381). It is important to consider this episode within Mark's Gospel to understand how Mark characterizes her for his own narrative purposes.

5. Some commentators have suggested that this is a royal anointing, so that the woman recognizes Jesus as king, with his death as the means whereby Jesus assumes his rule (Black, *Mark*, 284; Moloney, *Gospel of Mark*, 281). Mark uses the term for "perfume" (*myron*), however, and not that for olive oil (*elaia*). The verb for royal anointing (*chriō*) also does not appear here. The objectors focus on the waste of something extremely valuable rather than a mistaken royal anointing. And among beautifully elaborate commendations of her, Jesus does not mention anything about royal anointing, but focuses on her preparation for burial (cf. Boring, *Mark*, 383).

a year's wages is truly staggering (v. 5).[6] Mark does not comment on whether those who criticized the woman were Jesus's disciples, but if they were, their concern for the poor here is somewhat hypocritical. They had previously suggested that the hungry crowds fend for themselves (6:36), and they have been selfishly consumed with pursuing positions of prominence in the kingdom (9:34). And Judas, who was present at the meal, is about to betray Jesus for money (14:10–11). Given these larger narrative dynamics, it may be that the concern for the poor is little more than pretense.

Jesus shuts down the objectors in v. 6: "Leave her alone. Why are you bothering her?" His strong commendation of the woman sets her alongside several other characters in Mark's Gospel who, unlike the Twelve, are exemplary disciples. Whereas the Twelve have been consistently obtuse, others have rightly perceived the reality of what Jesus is talking about and have responded accordingly. Like the characters who after *seeing* (5:6) or *hearing* (5:22, 27, 33) Jesus run to him and fall down before him, the woman boldly intruded on a meal and performed an act of stunning devotion, sacrificing something indescribably valuable. And just as he did with the Syrian-Phoenician woman, Jesus commends her (7:29).

Jesus elaborately describes what the woman had done and offers a strikingly meaningful commendation. First, he says that she had done a "beautiful thing" to Jesus. He then addresses his meal companions' objection about feeding the poor. Citing Deuteronomy 15:11, he notes that it is always appropriate to provide for and serve the poor, but there is something unique about this specific situation (Mark 14:7). While he is present with them at that moment, he will soon depart. Her gift, then, is strategic and wholly appropriate.

Jesus also states in v. 8 that "she did what she could." Like the widow in 12:42–44 who gave "all she had," this woman gave a gift that was personal and overwhelmingly meaningful to her.[7] Jesus notes that she is preparing him for burial, indicating that she fully identifies herself and all she has with the death of Jesus. By doing so, she not only takes her place with other commendable characters in Mark's Gospel but stands as *the supreme example of an ideal disciple*: she publicly identifies with Jesus and his death at great personal cost and without reservation, in the hope of resurrection. Unlike Peter, she is unashamed of Jesus and his words about being a cross-shaped Messiah who calls disciples to take up their crosses (Mark 8:34–38). In contrast to the disciples, she discerns that this is the manner in which God is accomplishing his purposes, and she commits herself fully to it.

---

6. The NIV translates *dēnariōn triakosiōn* (lit. "three hundred denarii") as "a year's wages" in v. 5, and this translation is based on the calculation that one denarius is the pay for one day's labor; cf. Matt 20:2 (Marcus, *Mark 8–16*, 935).

7. Edwards suggests that the perfume may have been a family heirloom (*Mark*, 413–14).

Her actions are a proclamation of the gospel, therefore, just as Paul says that eating the Lord's Supper is itself a proclamation of Jesus's death until he returns (1 Cor 11:26).[8] And, just as they have been resistant to Jesus's talk about going to the cross throughout Mark, Jesus's disciples object to the unnamed woman's performed proclamation. Jesus gives her a supreme commendation, however, by stating that wherever and whenever the gospel is preached throughout the world, this ideal disciple will be remembered for what she has done (v. 9).

The Betrayal of Judas (vv. 10–11)

Mark now returns to narrate the outer portion and second half of the sandwich. He notes that Judas was "one of the Twelve," an insider. Consistent with Mark's subversion of presumed identity throughout his Gospel, Jesus dined with *an outsider*—Simon the Leper—while Judas, *an insider*, threw in his lot with those scheming to arrest Jesus secretly and to kill him. Mark does not indicate explicitly what Judas's betrayal might mean, but it is likely that it consists in his serving the Sanhedrin's aim of secretly arresting Jesus. That is, they want an opportunity to do away with Jesus in a way that does not incite the crowds gathered in Jerusalem.

Judas was not seduced into doing what he did by the chief priests and scribes. Rather, he went to them on his own initiative. Mark's portrayal of their reaction is chilling: *hoi de akousantes echarēsan* (lit. "when they heard, they rejoiced"). From then on, Judas began looking for a chance to inform the Sanhedrin of a good opportunity to deliver him up.

The characters of the chief priests and scribes, along with Judas, appear to have the initiative as they are plotting and scheming to do their evil work in a way that will surprise the unsuspecting. But Jesus has already predicted three times the very thing that Judas is plotting and what the Sanhedrin will carry out (8:31; 9:31; 10:33–34). God is working out his great program of salvation, and he triumphs over the present evil age by using the evil scheming of the wicked to do so.

LIVE the Story

Serving the Poor

I studied political science as an undergraduate student in an evangelical university, and I well remember hearing and also citing Mark 14:7 in policy

---

8. I owe this insight to Elizabeth Davidhizar, with whom I enjoyed extensive discussion about Mark's Gospel in general and this episode in particular.

discussions about poverty. I was taught an economic theory that emphasized individual responsibility and placed the burden for getting out of poverty on individuals. We would cite this text as a reason not to get too worked up about the poor, because even after all the efforts expended on relieving poverty, there would always be a group of people living in relative poverty. No matter how prosperous a culture, there is always going to be a "bottom 20 percent."

But Jesus's statement in v. 7 that "the poor you will always have with you" is not meant to endorse complacency about the poor. The statement comes from a passage in Deuteronomy 15:1–11 that casts an economic vision that includes purposeful care for the poor. The God of Israel calls his people to live with open hands and to avoid being tightfisted or cold-hearted toward the needs of the poor.

Israel did not have a capitalist economy oriented around individual responsibility. God instead instituted a *Jubilee economy*. Every seven years they were to forgive the debts of their fellow Israelites. Further, God held out the possibility of completely eliminating poverty among the people, if they would have been whole heartedly obedient:

> However, there need be no poor people among you, for in the land the LORD your God is giving you to possess as your inheritance, he will richly bless you, if only you fully obey the LORD your God and are careful to follow all these commands I am giving you today. For the LORD your God will bless you as he has promised, and you will lend to many nations but will borrow from none. You will rule over many nations but none will rule over you. (Deut 15:4–6)

At the same time, the passage is realistic about the possibility of the ongoing existence of people in need in Israel. And it is in this context that God warns his people about becoming complacent or contemptuous toward the poor:

> If anyone is poor among your fellow Israelites in any of the towns of the land the LORD your God is giving you, do not be hardhearted or tightfisted toward them. Rather, be openhanded and freely lend them whatever they need. Be careful not to harbor this wicked thought: "The seventh year, the year for canceling debts, is near," so that you do not show ill will toward the needy among your fellow Israelites and give them nothing. They may then appeal to the LORD against you, and you will be found guilty of sin. Give generously to them and do so without a grudging heart; then because

of this the LORD your God will bless you in all your work and in everything you put your hand to. *There will always be poor people in the land.* Therefore I command you to be openhanded toward your fellow Israelites who are poor and needy in your land. (Deut 15:7–11)

The reality of poverty in our world, therefore, is not something that Christians ought to take for granted. Yes, there will always be the poorest 20 percent among the regions in which we live, but this reality is not one about which we should be complacent. The church of Jesus Christ is to be a people shaped and oriented by the economic vision found in Deuteronomy 15:1–11. We are to be a people of generosity, a gathered community that is not "hardhearted" toward the needy or "tightfisted" with our resources, but who live with open hands. The church should not have an economic vision that is worldly—that derives its economic theories primarily from its culture. Every worldly economic theory begins with the conviction that we live in a world of limited goods. But twice in Mark's Gospel Jesus brings forth outrageous abundance from extremely limited resources, feeding both Jews and gentiles (6:30–44; 8:1–10).

We should be unsurprised at this, since Jesus Christ represents the very same God who holds out the promise of eliminating poverty among his people in Deuteronomy 15. The only obstacle is our vision and our glad obedience to the way of life to which God calls us.

Beyond merely being hardhearted toward the poor, I have encountered a theological problem among Christian people that keeps us from serving the poor. That is, there is a conceptual or ideological obstacle that some churches struggle to overcome. I have heard several times from Christians that it is one thing to meet the *physical needs* of people, but we should also seek to meet their *spiritual needs*. Sometimes this is stated as an imperative: *we should not meet physical needs without also meeting spiritual needs.* According to this way of thinking, our service to the poor has little or no value unless it is also connected with an evangelistic thrust or some teaching of the Bible. This conviction has the immediate ring of truth and seems to come directly from a sound biblical frame of reference.

Yet this thought does not represent sound biblical teaching and runs against the grain of Mark's Gospel. Jesus teaches the church that when they care for the poor and the marginalized, *they are looking after their own spiritual needs.* That is, when the church welcomes the marginalized, they are welcoming Jesus and the God who sent him, and this is how God meets their needs. Jesus speaks of this reality in Mark 9:36–37:

He took a little child whom he placed among them. Taking the child in his arms, he said to them, "Whoever welcomes one of these little children in my name welcomes me; and whoever welcomes me does not welcome me but the one who sent me."

The author of Hebrews represents the same logic when he exhorts his audience to practice hospitality to strangers. He makes a clever reference to the episode in Genesis 18 when Abraham welcomed three strangers into his tent for a meal and inadvertently welcomed God to join him for dinner! "Do not forget to show hospitality to strangers, for by so doing some people have shown hospitality to angels without knowing it" (Heb 13:2; cf. Gen 18:1–15).

We see this same logic at work in Jesus's conversation with the Samaritan woman in John 4. The disciples encounter Jesus speaking with this woman, and they exhort him to eat something (v. 31). Jesus responds that he has "food to eat that you know nothing about" (v. 32). As the conversation proceeds, Jesus indicates that his food is to do God's will, which is carried out as he enjoys conversations like the one he is having with the woman at the well (v. 34). That is, *Jesus's own mission is what sustains him.* Jesus has his own spiritual and physical needs met as he engages his mission.

This is the underlying gospel logic that drives the Christian church's mode of community life as it cares for the poor and serves the marginalized. God floods our communities with sustaining power and life-giving joy as we meet the needs of the poor. We should reject any notions that prevent us from gladly pursuing the mission to which Jesus calls us, even if they sound high-minded and spiritual. The deeply felt sense that we should care for the *physical and spiritual* needs of others is one such idea that appears at first glance to be faithful to Scripture, but it is not. And it ends up keeping us from doing what Jesus says to do.

CHAPTER 55

Mark 14:12-31

📖 LISTEN to the Story

¹²On the first day of the Festival of Unleavened Bread, when it was customary to sacrifice the Passover lamb, Jesus's disciples asked him, "Where do you want us to go and make preparations for you to eat the Passover?"

¹³So he sent two of his disciples, telling them, "Go into the city, and a man carrying a jar of water will meet you. Follow him. ¹⁴Say to the owner of the house he enters, 'The Teacher asks: Where is my guest room, where I may eat the Passover with my disciples?' ¹⁵He will show you a large room upstairs, furnished and ready. Make preparations for us there."

¹⁶The disciples left, went into the city and found things just as Jesus had told them. So they prepared the Passover.

¹⁷When evening came, Jesus arrived with the Twelve. ¹⁸While they were reclining at the table eating, he said, "Truly I tell you, one of you will betray me—one who is eating with me."

¹⁹They were saddened, and one by one they said to him, "Surely you don't mean me?"

²⁰"It is one of the Twelve," he replied, "one who dips bread into the bowl with me. ²¹The Son of Man will go just as it is written about him. But woe to that man who betrays the Son of Man! It would be better for him if he had not been born."

²²While they were eating, Jesus took bread, and when he had given thanks, he broke it and gave it to his disciples, saying, "Take it; this is my body."

²³Then he took a cup, and when he had given thanks, he gave it to them, and they all drank from it.

²⁴"This is my blood of the covenant, which is poured out for many," he said to them. ²⁵"Truly I tell you, I will not drink again from the fruit of the vine until that day when I drink it new in the kingdom of God."

²⁶When they had sung a hymn, they went out to the Mount of Olives.

²⁷"You will all fall away," Jesus told them, "for it is written:

"'I will strike the shepherd,
    and the sheep will be scattered.'

²⁸But after I have risen, I will go ahead of you into Galilee."
²⁹Peter declared, "Even if all fall away, I will not."
³⁰"Truly I tell you," Jesus answered, "today—yes, tonight—before the rooster crows twice you yourself will disown me three times."
³¹But Peter insisted emphatically, "Even if I have to die with you, I will never disown you." And all the others said the same.

Listening to the Text in the Story: Exodus 24:8; Leviticus 17:10–14; Psalm 41:9; Isaiah 53:11–12; Zechariah 9:11; 13:7; 1 Corinthians 11:17–37.

This episode, in which Jesus celebrates Passover with his disciples, takes place on Passover Friday, which begins at sundown on Thursday. Jesus shares his final meal with his disciples, often called the Last Supper. In the opening scene, preparations are made for the meal, while in the middle scene Jesus eats with his disciples in Jerusalem. Afterward, they leave and make their way to the Mount of Olives. There are four sections to this passage:

1. Preparation for Jesus's Passover meal (vv. 12–16)
2. Jesus predicts a disciple's betrayal (vv. 17–21)
3. Jesus shares his body and blood (vv. 22–26)
4. Jesus predicts the disciples' desertion (vv. 27–31)

Jesus's instructions to his disciples to make preparations for Passover in Jerusalem parallel his instructions to two of his disciples in 11:1–6 whom he directs to prepare for him a donkey to ride into the city. The parallels are striking, especially the expressions in the Greek text. Mark clearly wants audiences to notice the similarities between these two sets of instructions and to inquire as to what his narrative intentions are. Literal translations are provided here in an attempt to bring out these parallels:

Similarities	Mark 11:1–6	Mark 14:12–16
In the village, awaiting entrance into Jerusalem	In Bethany and Bethphage, on their way to Jerusalem (v. 1)	In Bethany, the disciples ask where in Jerusalem they should prepare the Passover
Jesus sends two disciples	"he sent two of his disciples" (*apostellei dyo tōn mathētōn autou*; v. 1)	"he sent two of his disciples" (*apostellei dyo tōn mathētōn autou*; v. 13)
Prediction of encounter and second-person aorist imperative command	"And he said to them, 'Go into the village . . . ; untie it'" (*kai legei autois hypagete eis tēn kōmēn . . . lysate*; v. 2)	"And he said to them, 'Go into the city . . . ; follow him'" (*kai legei autois hypagete eis tēn polin . . . akolouthē-sate*; v. 13)
Jesus instructs them what to say, using a conditional conjunction with subjunctive verb and aorist imperative form of *legō* ("to say")	"And if anyone should say to you . . . say, 'The Lord . . .'" (*kai ean . . . eipē . . . eipate ho kyrios*; v. 3)	"And if he should enter a place . . . say . . . 'The teacher says . . .'" (*kai . . . ean eiselthē eipate . . . ho didaskalos legei*; v. 14)
They do as Jesus instructs, and events unfold just as Jesus predicted	"They answered just as Jesus had told them" (*hoi de eipan autois kathōs eipen ho Iēsous*; v. 6)	"And they found things just as Jesus had told them" (*kai heuron kathōs eipen autois*; v. 16)

The links between these two passages indicate that a number of dynamics are at work. First, Mark begins these two larger sections (11:1–12:44 and 14:12–15:47) with Jesus's predictions in order to demonstrate that the subsequent events unfolding in both instances are doing so according to God's intentions to bring about God's saving purposes. As Jesus has mentioned several times already, and will say again, all these things "must" take place (8:31; 9:12; 14:49). The conflicts in Jerusalem that followed Jesus's judging (11:12–13) and then shutting down the temple (vv. 15–17) and confronting its leadership (12:1–12) are not signs that Jesus is not God's authorized agent or that God's purposes are being thwarted. In the same way, Jesus's betrayal, suffering, and death that Mark narrates in 14:32–15:47, during which Jesus is mistreated at the hands of others, have been predicted and are the manner in which God works out his saving ends. While it appears at first glance that other characters are in control and are doing with Jesus "everything they wished" (cf. 9:13), *God is at work to accomplish his purposes.*

Second, by beginning these two major sections in such similar fashion, Mark invites his audiences to associate what happens after each set of predictions. Subsequent to the first (11:1–6), Jesus passes judgment on the temple and shuts it down. After the second (14:12–16), Jesus celebrates the Passover meal with his disciples and invites them to share in his body and blood. Mark's association of these two episodes indicates that the temple in Jerusalem is no longer the place where Israel (and humanity) encounters God, and it is no longer the site of sacrifice and the forgiveness of sins. *Jesus* is the new temple, and those who eat the meal in his name share in him and enjoy reconciliation with God through forgiveness of sins. This device is one further way that Mark portrays Jesus as the new temple that replaces the physical one in Jerusalem, which is about to be destroyed.[1]

EXPLAIN the Story

Preparation for Jesus's Passover Meal (vv. 12–16)

Jesus and his disciples were in Bethany, where they had been staying, when the first day of the Feast of Unleavened Bread arrived. This opening scene takes place just before sundown on Thursday that would be the start of Passover Friday. This was the time when Passover lambs would begin to be sacrificed, as Mark indicates (v. 12).[2] The narrator signals the importance of the Passover by repeating it four times (vv. 12, 14, 16). This is not just any Passover; it is to be *Jesus's Passover.* The disciples ask him where they should prepare things "for you to eat the Passover" (v. 12). When they arrive in Jerusalem, Jesus directs them to ask his host where he will be staying "where I may eat the Passover with my disciples" (v. 14).[3]

It was customary for Jews to eat the Passover meal in Jerusalem, according to Deuteronomy 16:2: "Sacrifice as the Passover to the LORD your God an animal from your flock or herd at the place the LORD will choose as a dwelling for his Name." The associations of Jesus's impending sacrifice during the Passover celebration invite the comparisons: Jesus is in Jerusalem as the sacrificial lamb.

1. Gray, *Temple in the Gospel of Mark*, 158.
2. Edwards, *Mark*, 419.
3. Garland, *Theology of Mark's Gospel*, 162.

And just as the Passover celebrates God's salvation of his people, the meal he will eat with his disciples will be a celebration of God's salvation accomplished in Jesus and that looks ahead to ultimate redemption.

Jesus sends two of his disciples to Jerusalem and tells them that they will see a man carrying a water jar (v. 13). This would have been unusual, since it was customary for women to carry water in jars.[4] Jesus instructs the disciples to follow this man and ask the owner of the house that he enters where Jesus will stay and celebrate "with my disciples" (v. 14). Jesus does not elsewhere refer to his disciples in this way in Mark's Gospel, and here it stands as a powerful note of grace. One of his disciples is about to betray him, and the rest are going to abandon him, and Jesus is about to predict this. Yet he calls them "my disciples." In fact, there is a subtle and sweet irony here. Jesus had called the disciples to be "with him" (3:14), though they have routinely failed to be attentive to him and do what he says. Jesus, however, plans to be *with them* and claims them as his own.

The Passover meal would have been eaten with family members, including those who had come from outside Jerusalem. This gathering, then, is an instance of Jesus being with his reconfigured family, recalling Mark 3:33–35:

> "Who are my mother and my brothers?" he asked. Then he looked at those seated in a circle around him and said, "Here are my mother and my brothers! Whoever does God's will is my brother and sister and mother."

While the disciples are about to fail Jesus in dramatic fashion, Jesus treats them as his family members. Though they will abandon him, he proves faithful to them.

Jesus Predicts a Disciple's Betrayal (vv. 17–21)

Jesus arrived at the house where his Passover meal had been prepared for him and his disciples. In the evening, during the meal, Jesus made a dramatic prediction that stunned his hearers: "Truly I tell you, one of you will betray me" (v. 18). His emphasis on the fact that it will be "one who is eating with me" is a bitter irony. Meals were intimate settings that embodied social solidarity and reinforced the bonds that tied people together. The fact that someone whom Jesus had called "my disciple" and who was part of his reconfigured family would betray him is staggering. Jesus's statement recalls the sense of betrayal articulated in Psalm 41:9:

---

4. Edwards, *Mark*, 420.

Even my close friend,
>
> someone I trusted,
>
> one who shared my bread,
>
> has turned against me.

Jesus's prediction drops like a bombshell in the midst of the meal. The disciples were deeply grieved (*lypeō*; NIV, "saddened") at Jesus's words, and each one of them began asking whether it was them. The form of their persistent question indicates a mixture of panic, self-doubt, and insistence that surely none of them would be the one to betray him. Inflaming the sense of frantic self-doubt is the reminder that Jesus had just predicted in detailed fashion how two of his disciples would find the location of their shared meal. His prophecies in Mark's Gospel do not fail. *This is going to happen, and it will be one of them.*

Jesus responds that, indeed, one of his intimate companions—an insider—will be the one who does this. It will be, in another irony, "one of the Twelve" (v. 20). Jesus had previously noted that the disciples were insiders, those to whom the mystery of the kingdom had been revealed, while it had been hidden from outsiders (4:11–12). Mark's narrative unfolds in tragically ironic fashion, however, as the disciples grow increasingly confused about Jesus and the kingdom, while supposed outsiders regularly recognize Jesus and perceive the realities of the kingdom. This is yet another instance of this dynamic. "One of the Twelve" stands in contrast to Simon the Leper and the woman who anoints Jesus with perfume. Simon provides hospitality for Jesus in his home, and the woman identifies with his death, while an insider will be ashamed of Jesus and his words, seeking to save his own life and thereby losing it (8:35–38).

The events of Jesus's betrayal, suffering, and death are unfolding according to the divine plan, as Jesus repeats in v. 21: "The Son of Man will go just as it is written about him." This does not mean, however, that those who carry out the awful injustice will escape judgment. And the disciple who betrays Jesus to the Sanhedrin will likewise be culpable for what he does. Jesus's words are chilling: "But woe to that man who betrays the Son of Man! It would be better for him if he had not been born."

Mark has not left his audiences in suspense as to the identity of the betrayer, having identified Judas already in 3:19 as the one "who betrayed him." And he has indicated in two of his three predictions of his suffering and death that he would be "delivered" to the chief priests (9:31; 10:33).[5] Here, however, Jesus does not identify his betrayer. One can imagine Mark's early audiences,

---

5. Boring, *Mark*, 389.

to whom the Gospel would be read aloud, hearing the solemn words, "one of you will betray me," and being unsettled at Jesus's searching statement.

Jesus Shares His Body and Blood (vv. 22–26)

Mark places the account of Jesus sharing his body and blood with the disciples between the predictions of a disciple's betrayal and of all the disciples deserting him. This is another overwhelmingly gracious note. Jesus shares himself with his disciples and stresses that they belong to him. He does not return their unfaithfulness with harsh rebuke, nor does he retaliate in some other way.

It may be impossible to read this text apart from the later development of what has come to be known as "the Lord's Supper" and the various ways it is celebrated by church traditions, but we must first reckon with this account within Mark's narrative. Mark does not give any details of the meal, and he does not associate the bread and the cup with any specific parts of the traditional Passover meal. For centuries, Jews had eaten the Passover to recall, celebrate, and embody their participation in the deliverance of the God of Israel. When they ate, they looked back to the exodus, God's liberation of the nation from slavery in Egypt. In the same way, the meal that the disciples share with Jesus is the celebration and embodiment of their participation in Jesus and his death, which liberates God's new people from enslavement to the present age and delivers them into God's kingdom.

During the meal, Jesus took bread that was an unspecified part of the Passover meal and did what he had done before other meals in Mark: he "took," "and when he had given thanks, he broke it and gave it to his disciples" (cf. 6:41; 8:6). He told his disciples that the bread "is my body," indicating *himself*—his person or his identity. Their eating the meal with Jesus is their participation in Jesus himself, identifying themselves with him and especially with his death. Again, Mark's note that he gave it "to his disciples" is significant. They are *his*—those who will abandon him, one of whom will betray him.

Jesus then did the same with the cup (v. 23). He gave thanks and passed it around so that each one drank from it. He said that the cup "is my blood of the covenant, which is poured out for many" (v. 24). The "blood of the covenant" recalls Moses's words in Exodus 24:8: "Moses then took the blood, sprinkled it on the people and said, 'This is the blood of the covenant that the LORD has made with you in accordance with all these words.'" The covenant between God and Israel was ratified by the blood of a sacrificed animal, which stood in for the lives of the people who enjoyed the blessings of the covenant. In the same way, Jesus establishes a new covenant in his death, and the disciples enjoy the blessings of that covenant by their identification with him, signaled by their drinking from the cup. Jesus's death is for others—"for many," an echo of Isaiah 53:11–12 that points to Jesus's disciples and all who identify with Jesus and his death.[6]

Jesus concludes by looking ahead to the kingdom of God coming in its fullness, when he will again drink wine while feasting with his people (v. 25). This recalls the paradox of Jesus's presence and absence that he described earlier (2:18–20). When pressed about his disciples not fasting, Jesus had said that fasting was appropriate during his absence and not during his presence. When he would depart, they would fast again in anticipation of his return. Here, Jesus invites his disciples to envision this meal—*his* Passover—as a celebration of their identification with him that looks ahead to the feast they will enjoy at his return.

Mark's audiences would certainly hear this episode in terms of their participation in what came to be called "the Lord's Supper" (1 Cor 11:17–37). While this has come to be celebrated in a variety of ways among different Christian traditions, in the first century it was a meal that the church enjoyed together. In whatever way it is celebrated today, those who eat it indicate that they belong to Jesus Christ. Further, it is a participation in his death.[7] Disciples who take up their crosses to follow Jesus eat this meal, not only looking back and giving thanks for his death but fully identifying with it so that the cross determines the shape of their lives. And it is eaten in anticipation of the return of the Son of Man when he comes to judge and bring in the fullness of God's kingdom. The meal, therefore, has *a cruciform character* and *an eschatological focus*. The eating proclaims the death of Christ and anticipates his return (cf. 1 Cor 11:26).

Jesus and his disciples conclude the meal by singing a hymn (v. 26). The Passover meal typically concluded with the singing of Psalms 110–118, and so the hymn with which they concluded their meal very well may have been one of these.[8] Mark, however, does not give any indication. Afterward, they make their way out of the city and go to the Mount of Olives (v. 26).

Jesus Predicts the Disciples' Desertion (vv. 27–31)

After narrating the supper, Mark stuns his audience by quoting, without warning, Jesus's stark prediction that his disciples will abandon him: "You

---

6. As Moloney states, "the many" does not stand in contrast to "all" but stands rather in contrast to the singular person who dies on behalf of others (*Gospel of Mark*, 286).

7. I am using the language of participation to capture how it is that disciples of Jesus fully identify with the cross-oriented and cross-directed life of Jesus in order to share in his resurrection, vindication, and exaltation. Paul expresses this dynamic with his language of co-suffering, co-crucifixion, co-resurrection, and co-ascension (cf. Gal 2:20; Rom 8:17; Eph 2:5–6).

8. Hurtado, *Mark*, 240.

will all fall away" (v. 27). The Greek verb for "fall away" (*skandalizō*) is passive in form, indicating that events will transpire that will cause the disciples to abandon Jesus.[9] This verb appeared in the parable of the sower and the soils in 4:17 when Jesus described the seed that found rocky ground:

> Others, like seed sown on rocky places, hear the word and at once receive it with joy. But since they have no root, they last only a short time. When trouble or persecution comes because of the word, they quickly fall away [*skandalizontai*]. (4:16–17)

The disciples, then, are not rooted and are going to face trouble and persecution because of the word—the reality of a cross-directed Messiah. Mark elsewhere indicates that the disciples need to cultivate their perception so that they can *see* and *hear* Jesus rightly, leading to *understanding*. Here, Mark indicates that they stand in need of becoming cultivated soil.

In another indication that events are unfolding according to God's plan, Jesus cites Zechariah 13:7: "I will strike the shepherd, and the sheep will be scattered" (v. 27). Even though the disciples will be scattered like sheep as a result of their shepherd's death, he will not abandon them. After his resurrection, Jesus will gather his sheep and lead them back to Galilee (v. 28). The NIV translates the expression *proaxō hymas*, "I will go ahead of you." The verb *proagō*, however, can mean "to lead," and the plural pronoun *hymas* ("you all") is accusative in form, so that it receives the action of the verb. Further, with the shepherding imagery in such close context, Jesus is more likely predicting that he will lead them like a shepherd to Galilee.[10] The disciples will fail utterly, but Jesus will not abandon them. He will gather them as a faithful and loving shepherd and lead them home.

In the same way that Peter objected to Jesus's initial prediction of his suffering and death (8:32), he now defiantly rejects Jesus's prophecy. "Even if all fall away, I will not" (v. 29). For the third time in this passage, Jesus precedes a statement with *amēn* ("truly"; v. 30; cf. vv. 18, 25). On that very evening, Jesus tells him, Peter is going to disown Jesus three times before the rooster crows twice (v. 30). Peter protests, however, that he will prove to be the ideal disciple—one who is faithful to Jesus to the point of death (v. 31; cf. 8:34–38). Peter had previously objected to Jesus identifying himself and his mission in cruciform terms (8:32). Now he pronounces that he is willing to abandon his

---

9. Edwards, *Mark*, 428.
10. Moloney, *Gospel of Mark*, 288.

impulse for self-preservation and to die with Jesus. "Even if I have to die with you, I will never disown you." Peter was not the only one protesting. All the disciples were proclaiming their loyalty to Jesus in the same way.

LIVE the Story

Jesus's Scandalous Meal

The notes of grace and the faithfulness of Jesus to his disciples in this passage are overwhelmingly beautiful. Throughout Mark the disciples have been failing repeatedly and have grown increasingly obtuse. And now, as Jesus is about to enter into his suffering through betrayal, false accusation, physical abuse, and death by crucifixion, his disciples will prove utterly faithless and will abandon him. Jesus, however, continues to claim them as "my disciples," repeatedly giving himself to them and inviting them to participate in his body and his blood.

The grace of God demonstrated by Jesus's behavior with his disciples is scandalous to our sensibilities that are shaped by *worthiness*. We want to think that there are standards for eating at Jesus's table, expectations that must be met. "We must be responsible! Surely, we can't just let any old sinner eat at Jesus's table—what kind of message would we be sending?"

Mark goes right after this sensibility by setting Jesus's words about his table (vv. 22–26) between Jesus's prediction of Judas's betrayal (vv. 17–21) and his indication that all the disciples will desert him (vv. 27–31). The disciples are utterly unworthy to be eating with Jesus, for they are acting and behaving as perfect examples of non-disciples. Rather than being "with him," they will abandon him. Rather than being faithful to him and listening to him, one of them is plotting to betray him, and another will deny that very night that he even knows him.

The scandalous realities of the Lord's table came home to me during a season of reflection about how the church is to engage this practice. Our church in Springfield, Ohio, was in a very poor section of town filled with all the problems of a mid-size Midwestern city that had been abandoned by a few key industries half a century earlier: poverty, drug addiction, alcoholism, domestic abuse, and homelessness. Our church met on Saturday nights and held our service at 5:00pm, after which we ate a meal together and invited everyone from the neighborhood to join us. Over a period of months and years, people from the neighborhood would join us for our service and then also stay for the meal, though we never required them to come to the service in order to enjoy a free meal.

Each week during our service we celebrated communion, and we did this in different ways to keep its meaning always fresh in our minds. Most of the time we had a freshly baked loaf of bread on the front table along with a bowl of grape juice, and people could come forward, tear off a piece of the bread, dip it in the juice, and eat it. We then had opportunities to do something tactile in order to confess sin or celebrate forgiveness, such as tables with paper and crayons for kids to draw scenes or write notes. We also had tables for people to write reflections on the meaning of the death and resurrection of Jesus and what that meant for life as a community of Jesus-followers.

Yet one aspect of our gatherings raised some significant questions for us. Our invitation to the community to join us for our service along with our practice of communion led to people walking in off the street and fully participating in all that we were doing. Some church members inquired as to whether we ought to make it clearer that *communion was specifically for Christians*, since only those who are saved and members of Christ's body can celebrate this. Were we running the risk of putting some of these people in a place where they were eating and drinking judgment on themselves since they were eating the Lord's Supper in an unworthy manner (1 Cor 11:29)?

These questions provoked rich reflections and fruitful discussions. First, we reminded ourselves about the character of the "Lord's Supper" in the first-century church, which was a common meal that churches ate together. Meals in the ancient world were occasions that depicted and reinforced social solidarity, so people ate common meals with others who shared their socioeconomic status or who were of the same household. And meals would display social hierarchies, with people of importance occupying honored places and those of less importance sitting on the margins or perhaps eating in a different room.

The "Lord's Supper," however, was supposed to be a radically different meal, and it depicted and reinforced the radical new reality that God had brought about in the death and resurrection of Jesus Christ. Christians gathered for a meal, sat together, and served one another in a way that depicted publicly that they were each honored guests of the Lord Jesus Christ. Each of them had the same status, being siblings in the one new family that God had created in Christ and by the Spirit. This certainly would have raised questions in the wider culture, for such a meal challenged all the assumptions that anyone and everyone would have had across all cultures in the first-century Mediterranean world. This meal would need some explanation, providing a great opportunity to talk about what was happening. And the physical act of eating and sharing together with others would drive home to each participant the reality of new siblingship in Jesus. Each person had dignity, each was worthy of honor, and all of them belonged to one another without respect to the social ranking that a person had in the eyes of the wider culture. Eating the meal was the proclamation of the death of Jesus Christ, displaying publicly what God had created through the cross.

Paul's rebuke of the Corinthians in 1 Corinthians 11:17–34 reflects their violation of the character of the Lord's meal. The rich Corinthians were eating together and consuming all the good wine, bread, and cheese, getting drunk and eating until they were full, and only then inviting the poorer Corinthian Christians to eat the leftovers. By doing this, Paul said they were despising the church of God and humiliating the poor (v. 22). This is why some of the Corinthian Christians were dying and some were getting sick (v. 30). This is an astounding statement! God was judging the church in a severe manner because of their failure to have proper Christian table manners!

The character of the Lord's Supper in the early church, therefore, led our church to conclude that it was actually the common meal we ate together after our service that was the Lord's Supper rather than the simple practice in which we participated at the end of each week's service. This, after all, was more organically related to Paul's instruction in 1 Corinthians 11. Each week, those with greater means purchased food or made it at home and brought it to the church. And each week, those with little or no money were required to bring nothing but their appetites. We all ate together, and everyone was free to eat as much as they wanted. And most weeks we had some leftovers to bring to local people we knew had trouble getting out and about.

Yet we still kept practicing the traditional communion ritual at the end of each service, though we changed the language a bit. We noted that our common meal was actually "the Lord's Supper," but we were going to continue this practice, as it was an opportunity to say "yes" and "thank you" to God for what he had done in sending Jesus to die, for bringing us to himself and uniting us to one another, and for the promise of participating in his kingdom at Christ's return. And we also noted that this practice is for all who want to say "yes" and "thank you" to the God and Father of the Lord Jesus Christ. We felt that by doing this we were making clear what these practices were for, while also keeping us from playing the inappropriate role of "the God Squad," checking out each person's salvific status.

Further, we had some good conversations about the scandalous nature of Jesus's meals throughout the Gospels. The sort of people whom Jesus invites to his table and to whom he gives himself are those like Judas, who was planning to betray him, those like Peter, who was about to deny that he knew him, and those like Thomas who doubted him. In fact, Jesus gives himself to all his disciples at the meal in this passage in Mark, even though they all abandon him.

Moreover, throughout the Gospels Jesus's meals raise serious questions among those who are intensely committed to Scripture—the Pharisees. In Mark 2:15–16, the Pharisees and scribes are offended that Jesus is eating with tax collectors and sinners. Tax collectors were traitors to the Jewish people and nation, and sinners were those the Pharisees were shunning in attempts to get them to repent. Jesus, on the other hand, was eating with them, demonstrating social solidarity with them! This was utterly confusing and scandalous.

Jesus's most well-known parable was provoked by his scandalous table manners. In Luke 15:11–32, Jesus tells the parable of the prodigal son and the angry older brother, which was sparked by Luke's note in vv. 1–2 that the Pharisees were muttering to themselves that Jesus was welcoming sinners and eating with them. Again, his table fellowship indicated that he was perhaps "soft on sin" and blurring lines in an inappropriate way.

Luke also narrates the story of the beginnings of the outreach to the gentiles in terms of Jesus's offensively inclusive table. In Acts 10–11, God had spoken to Peter in a dream about no longer regarding certain foods as unclean. The subsequent narrative involved Peter welcoming gentiles into his house, going to Caesarea, and entering into the house and enjoying table fellowship with non-Jews (10:21–48). While this may not seem like a big deal today, this was scandalous to the first-century Jewish church. When Peter returned to Jerusalem, he was called on the carpet for what he had done:

> The apostles and the believers throughout Judea heard that the Gentiles also had received the word of God. So when Peter went up to Jerusalem, the circumcised believers criticized him and said, "You went into the house of uncircumcised men and ate with them." (Acts 11:1–3)

Peter subsequently explained the sequence of events that led to his journey to Caesarea and how God was driving this mission of including the gentiles into the one new, international, multiethnic people of God in Christ.

Coming to grips with all of this led our church to conclude that our practice needed to reflect the character of Jesus's table fellowship. Rather than reinforcing an exclusive regard toward outsiders, Jesus's table regularly scandalized precisely those people who wanted to draw sharp distinctions between "the righteous" and "sinners." Jesus's table manners raised all sorts of questions precisely for those who felt they were upholding a concern for the holiness of the God of Israel. To all these people in the pages of the Gospels,

Jesus's behavior was reckless, scandalous, irresponsible, unholy, and soft on sin. Jesus, however, made it clear that he was not endorsing practices of sin but rather calling all people to repentance (Luke 5:32).

We concluded, then, that our table would be inclusive and welcoming. We would be clear that the practices of our communion time during the service and the common meal afterward were for anyone and everyone, since God in Christ is a magnanimous lover, whose love and grace scandalize the self-righteous. And we would state that these are for anyone who wants to say "yes" to what God has done for us in Jesus as well as for those who want to say "thank you." And we noted that God continues to call to all of us to turn from our sinful ways and cultivate social practices of kingdom life whereby we can enjoy the life and blessing of God on earth.

We did all this in the confidence that we would enjoy the life and blessing of God by welcoming others into our fellowship and that this was a set of practices whereby we could also reinforce that we are sinners who are welcomed by God in Christ (Rom 15:7). We were not the righteous who *merely tolerated* the presence of sinners or who *condescendingly permitted* them to have the privilege of our company. And we were confident that in doing all this we were faithfully capturing the scandalously inclusive table of Jesus while also making clear to everyone that Jesus calls sinners to repentance.

Mark 14:32-52

📖 LISTEN to the Story

³²They went to a place called Gethsemane, and Jesus said to his disciples, "Sit here while I pray." ³³He took Peter, James and John along with him, and he began to be deeply distressed and troubled. ³⁴"My soul is overwhelmed with sorrow to the point of death," he said to them. "Stay here and keep watch."

³⁵Going a little farther, he fell to the ground and prayed that if possible the hour might pass from him. ³⁶"*Abba*, Father," he said, "everything is possible for you. Take this cup from me. Yet not what I will, but what you will."

³⁷Then he returned to his disciples and found them sleeping. "Simon," he said to Peter, "are you asleep? Couldn't you keep watch for one hour? ³⁸Watch and pray so that you will not fall into temptation. The spirit is willing, but the flesh is weak."

³⁹Once more he went away and prayed the same thing. ⁴⁰When he came back, he again found them sleeping, because their eyes were heavy. They did not know what to say to him.

⁴¹Returning the third time, he said to them, "Are you still sleeping and resting? Enough! The hour has come. Look, the Son of Man is delivered into the hands of sinners. ⁴²Rise! Let us go! Here comes my betrayer!"

⁴³Just as he was speaking, Judas, one of the Twelve, appeared. With him was a crowd armed with swords and clubs, sent from the chief priests, the teachers of the law, and the elders.

⁴⁴Now the betrayer had arranged a signal with them: "The one I kiss is the man; arrest him and lead him away under guard." ⁴⁵Going at once to Jesus, Judas said, "Rabbi!" and kissed him. ⁴⁶The men seized Jesus and arrested him. ⁴⁷Then one of those standing near drew his sword and struck the servant of the high priest, cutting off his ear.

⁴⁸"Am I leading a rebellion," said Jesus, "that you have come out with swords and clubs to capture me? ⁴⁹Every day I was with you, teaching in the temple courts, and you did not arrest me. But the Scriptures must be fulfilled." ⁵⁰Then everyone deserted him and fled.

⁵¹A young man, wearing nothing but a linen garment, was following Jesus. When they seized him, ⁵²he fled naked, leaving his garment behind.

Listening to the Text in the Story: Psalms 6; 42; 43; 55:4–5; Amos 2:6, 16; 1 Corinthians 11:23–26.

After eating the Passover meal with his disciples and predicting both Peter's denial and the rest of the disciples' abandonment, Jesus and his disciples went to Gethsemane. This episode is filled with passion and deeply felt emotion, as the critical moment has arrived. Jesus had predicted that he would be "delivered into the hands of men" (9:31; 10:33), and that one of his close companions would betray him (14:18–21), events that would initiate the sequence of his suffering and death. All of this is now about to take place, and here we see the overwhelming emotional burden that all this places on Jesus.

Knowing the awful physical suffering that was about to take place, along with the horrors of enduring God's judgment, Jesus retreats to pray, urging his disciples to "keep watch" (*grēgoreō*). Jesus repeats this verb three times in this passage, emphasizing that this is precisely the time when the disciples need to be alert. Yet three times he finds them sleeping rather than being alert and staying awake.

In his long discourse about the tribulations that disciples will encounter in the coming age of destruction (13:5–37), Jesus had repeatedly stressed the necessity of being alert, discerning, watchful, and not falling asleep. The verb *blepō* ("watch," "be on guard") appears four times in Mark 13 (vv. 5, 9, 23, 33), *agrypneō* ("be alert") appears once (v. 33), and *grēgoreō* appears three times, including the climactic command at the close of that chapter: "What I say to you, I say to everyone: 'Watch!' [*grēgoreō*]" (v. 37; see also vv. 34, 35). Jesus had also just warned his disciples, "If he comes suddenly, do not let him find you sleeping" (v. 36). In doing so, Jesus exhorts the disciples to be faithful during this present age of destruction and tribulation. In this episode, such diligence is precisely the need of the moment, since the destructive dynamics about which Jesus spoke in Mark 13 are about to overwhelm and overcome him.

The dramatic tone of Mark has already been steadily intensifying. After the discussion of the tribulations that will dominate the present age in chapter 13, Mark narrates the powerful gift of the woman who anointed Jesus for burial (14:3–9). This was followed by the Passover meal, at which Jesus both gave himself fully to his disciples and predicted their betrayal and abandonment of him (14:12–31). The tension in the narrative heightens, as audiences know what is coming. This passage is the climax of emotional intensity as Jesus nearly breaks down, becoming "deeply distressed and troubled" (v. 33). He laments that his "soul is overwhelmed with sorrow to the point of death" (v. 34). He calls out passionately to God to somehow allow this moment to be averted and pleads with his companions to join him in prayer rather than falling prey to temptation (vv. 35–38).

His prayers recall the language of the Psalms, which express the emotional trauma of suffering. Psalms 42–43 repeat the mournful question, "Why, my soul, are you downcast?" (42:5, 11; 43:5). Other psalms also express this sort of traumatic struggle:

> My soul is in deep anguish.
>   How long, LORD, how long? (Ps 6:3)

> Listen to my prayer, O God,
>   do not ignore my plea;
>   hear me and answer me.
> My thoughts trouble me and I am distraught
>   because of what my enemy is saying,
>   because of the threats of the wicked;
> for they bring down suffering on me
>   and assail me in their anger.
> My heart is in anguish within me;
>   the terrors of death have fallen on me.
> Fear and trembling have beset me;
>   horror has overwhelmed me. (Ps 55:1–5)

Jesus does not endure suffering in stoic fashion, as if he is unaffected and untroubled by impending suffering and death. Nor does he grow defiant like the main character in a heroic narrative. He faces suffering in biblical terms, lamenting and crying out to God, knowing the awfulness of the traumatic suffering that awaits him.

EXPLAIN the Story

Jesus in Gethsemane with His Disciples (vv. 32–34)

Jesus and his disciples had just eaten the Passover meal together and had departed for the Mount of Olives. Here, they are in "a place called Gethsemane" (v. 32), which is now a lush garden of olive trees at the base of the Mount of Olives just east of the Jerusalem temple mount. Jesus directed his disciples to sit in one place while he went to pray. As he had done on other occasions, he then took Peter, James, and John with him to go further (v. 33). At this point, Jesus begins to break down and reveals how traumatized he has become. The two terms that Mark uses, *ekthambeisthai* (NIV, "deeply distressed") and *adēmonein* (NIV, "troubled") indicate a crushing terror that brings Jesus to the brink of complete breakdown. Boring translates these two terms as "overwhelmed with horror and anguish," and he states that Mark portrays Jesus as

> barely in control, on the verge of panic, reflecting not only the depth of suffering of a human being who shudders on the threshold of torture and death, but also the numinous terror of the eschatological, transcendent nature of what is about to transpire, a sorrow and anguish so intense it already threatens his life.[1]

Jesus shares his traumatized state with his disciples: "My soul is overwhelmed with sorrow to the point of death" (v. 34). He has responded to situations throughout Mark with intense reactions, but here his emotional trauma brings him to the verge of being completely undone: *he feels like he is dying*. He knows the horrors he will suffer at the hands of the chief priests and the terrors of crucifixion. But he is also aware that his death is the eschatological moment of God's judgment, indicated by his references to "the hour" (v. 35) and "this cup" (v. 36).[2] He had just noted at the Passover meal that his death would initiate a "covenant," indicating that his impending death would accomplish God's judgment on human sinfulness (14:24). With all this before him, Jesus is overwhelmed.

He urges Peter, James, and John to "stay here" and "keep watch" (*grēgoreō*; v. 34). This is not for his sake, as if he wants them to protect him from what

---

1. Boring, *Mark*, 397.

2. In prophetic passages, the word "cup" often refers to divine judgment against human sinfulness (e.g., Isa 51:17, 22; Jer 25:15, 17, 28; 49:12; Rev 14:10), and references to "the hour" also indicate notes of judgment (Rev 14:7; 18; see Marcus, *Mark 8–16*, 978; Moloney, *Gospel of Mark*, 293).

is about to take place or perhaps even to signal a warning so he can somehow escape. He knows that he is God's appointed agent to bring about the new creation in his death. What awaits him is ordered according to what "must" take place (8:31; 9:31; 10:33–34, 45; 14:49). He wants them to "keep watch" for their own sake. He knows what is about to happen and wants them to be prepared in order to endure this moment of tribulation with faithfulness.

Jesus's Passionate Praying and the Disciples' Failure (vv. 35–42)

Jesus now leaves behind his three closest disciples and goes a little further to be alone. Dramatically, he falls to the ground, being utterly overcome by the stress of the moment, and implores God that "if possible the hour might pass from him" (v. 35). Jesus had formerly been the one to whom others were pleading for healing, such as the leper, who "came to him and begged him on his knees, 'If you are willing, you can make me clean'" (1:40). A man with a demon-possessed son had appealed to Jesus, "But if you can do anything, take pity on us and help us" (9:22). Now Jesus is pleading with God, using similar language.

Jesus asks that "the hour" might pass from him (14:35), and he will also refer to "this cup" in v. 36. He had just mentioned "the hour" in 13:22 to refer to the return of the Son of Man to judge and to save. And "cup" is often used in biblical contexts having to do with God's pouring out of judgment on human sinfulness (e.g., Isa 51:17, 22; Jer 25:15, 17, 28; 49:12; Rev 14:10). The crucial moment is upon him, in which Jesus is about to endure God's eschatological judgment, and he cries out to God in desperation, asking that this unspeakably terrifying experience might, if possible, be averted.

Mark cites Jesus's own words in v. 36. Addressing God directly as "Abba, Father," Jesus prays with words that audiences of Mark have previously heard.[3] "Everything is possible for you" (*panta dynata soi*), which is similar to what Jesus said to the father of the demon-possessed boy (*panta dynata tō pisteuonti*, "everything is possible for the one who believes," 9:23) and to his disciples regarding the salvation of the rich (*panta gar dynata para tō theō*, "all things are possible with God," 10:27). Mark states Jesus's request in starkly simple terms: "Take this cup from me."

Jesus knows how things "must" go, however. He is God's appointed agent to initiate God's kingdom and to accomplish the salvation of God's people.

---

3. Mark is the only Gospel to include the Aramaic word *Abba* along with the Greek word for "Father" (*patēr*). There is no evidence that this is an unusually personal address or something like "daddy." Rather, it is the normal word for father used by both children and adults (M. M. Thompson, "God," *DJG* 317).

He strongly recoils from the terrors that await him, but he ultimately yields his will to God's: "Yet not what I will, but what you will" (v. 36). Moloney notes that this is precisely the opposite of the disciples' request to Jesus, coming just after he had predicted his suffering and death for a third time: "We want you to do for us whatever we ask" (10:35).[4] It might be tempting to say here that this is Jesus's humanity wrestling with what is God's will for him, but Mark, like the other Gospel writers, does not psychologize Jesus and attempt to distinguish between his humanity and deity. Mark simply portrays Jesus as the one who faces down the horrible prospect of what awaits him. As he does so, he recoils but ultimately embraces that which *must* take place.[5]

Jesus returns to Peter, James, and John and finds them doing what he had warned against in 13:36: they are sleeping and failing to keep watch! Jesus singles out Peter, calling him "Simon," and questions him: "Are you asleep? Couldn't you keep watch for one hour?" (14:37). Jesus is undergoing indescribable stress, and he knows that his disciples will soon face their own climactic moment of temptation. He orders them all to watch and pray so that they might prove faithful and avoid failure in the face of what is about to unfold. After all, the "spirit is willing, but the flesh is weak" (v. 38). By "spirit," Jesus has in mind here the internal disposition and determination for goodness in the form of desiring to be faithful to God. Peter had just protested that he would remain faithful to Jesus even if it led to his death and that he would be faithful no matter who else deserted (vv. 29, 31). The "flesh," however, is weak. That is, humanity is prone to wither, wilt, and shrink back, driven by self-preservation and motivated by self-protection.[6] This latter impulse inevitably overwhelms us and will soon drive the disciples to abandon Jesus. Jesus in effect says, "You may have great resolve, Peter, but if you are not being watchful and looking to God in prayer, you will fall easily in the crucial moment."

Jesus left the disciples a second time and went away by himself and uttered the same prayer to God that somehow there might be another way (v. 39). And a second time he returned to find his three companions asleep, "because

---

4. Moloney, *Gospel of Mark*, 294.

5. This passage, especially its depiction of Jesus as emotionally overcome and struggling to embrace God's will, may present a challenge to common assumptions among Christians about the character of God. We have a window into the emotional torment within one who is the definitive revelation of the one true God. Christians ought to embrace the challenge, however, to develop a more dynamic and biblically faithful conception of God and to confront their own assumptions about the God revealed in Jesus. Assumptions about God drawn from other sources inevitably creep in and distort our thinking about God. This passage may reveal that one of the notions that must be jettisoned is the assumption that God does not have emotions or that God does not respond emotionally to suffering.

6. Black, *Mark*, 294.

their eyes were heavy" (v. 40). Their flesh was indeed being overpowered. When he again questioned them, "they did not know what to say to him" (*ouk ēdeisan ti apokrithōsin autō*). Mark makes a similar comment to explain Peter's ill-considered words in response to seeing Jesus transfigured. He spoke because "he did not know what to say" (*ou gar ēdei ti apokrithē*, 9:6). Whereas Peter previously should have kept quiet, in this instance the disciples can only respond in ashamed and bewildered silence.

Jesus went away a third time to pray, and upon returning he again finds Peter, James, and John sleeping (vv. 39–40). Jesus's clipped and rapidly fired short statements capture the intensified drama of this moment. "Enough!" he exclaims (v. 41). It is now too late. The moment is here, initiating the awful events that will unfold. Jesus warned the disciples to watch and pray to avoid falling into temptation, but they are unprepared for this moment. It is too late. "The hour" is upon them. As Jesus had predicted, "the Son of Man is delivered into the hands of sinners" (v. 41). "Rise! Let us go! Here comes my betrayer!" (v. 42).

Judas Betrays Jesus (vv. 43–49)

At that very moment, Judas arrived, along with a "crowd armed with swords and clubs" (v. 43).[7] Mark calls Judas "one of the Twelve," hitting again the note of tragic irony. He has already referred to Judas as "one of the Twelve" in 14:10, stressing his status as an insider. This stands in contrast with the woman, an obvious outsider, who had just anointed Jesus's body for burial (14:3–9). Earlier in the Gospel, when Jesus had originally called and appointed his disciples, Judas was the one "who betrayed him" (3:19). The earlier description of Judas serves Mark's purposes of portraying Jesus's entire ministry under the cloud of threat. And these latter descriptions partake of Mark's dynamic whereby he turns the status of presumed insiders and outsiders upside-down.

Mark also intensifies another important narrative feature. Judas arrives with a "crowd," which further contributes to Mark's construction of them as an ambivalent and unstable character in the narrative. The NIV rightly translates *ochlos* as "crowd," referring to the group led by Judas, rather than something like "a mob." While modern readers might imagine the regular large crowds that gather anytime Jesus preaches as a positive phenomenon, Mark does not portray them this way. The large crowds drawn to Jesus indicate a desperate populace longing for liberation from oppression and freedom from satanic

---

7. The appearance of *euthys* ("immediately") in v. 43 captures the drama in which the moment overtakes them. The NIV portrays this with its translation, "Just as he was speaking . . ."

enslavement. They often, however, prove to be an obstacle to his ministry (e.g., 1:45; 2:2–4). Further, Mark hints that the overwhelming response to Jesus may also be an indication that people are not hearing the true character of the gospel that Jesus preaches. When the cross-oriented nature of the kingdom is rightly proclaimed, it provokes a reaction of rejection or rebuke, like that of Peter (8:32). The fact that so many have responded to Jesus indicates that they have not rightly heard "the secret of the kingdom" (4:11). Crowds had cheered Jesus's arrival into Jerusalem just a few days before (11:8–10). Yet soon the crowd will demand Jesus's execution (15:6–15). Here, a crowd arrives with Judas to do the work of "my betrayer," initiating a sequence of sinister injustice. This "crowd" has come as an armed delegation to accompany Judas from the Sanhedrin, which includes the chief priests, the scribes (NIV, "teachers of the law"), and the elders.

A striking transition takes place at this point. Throughout Mark, Jesus has had the initiative in nearly every episode. He is the character who drives and determines the action, causing other characters to respond to him. A decisive shift takes place between vv. 42 and 50. Jesus sternly orders his disciples to get up in v. 42, because his betrayer has arrived. From this point, however, Jesus will become a passive figure for the remainder of Mark's Gospel. After he is "delivered [*paradidōmi*] into the hands of men" (14:41), he becomes like John the Baptist, who was first "delivered" (*paradidōmi*, 1:14) and then mistreated by those who did to him "everything they wished" (9:13). Aside from his question to the representatives of the Sanhedrin in vv. 48–49, Jesus seldom speaks for the rest of Mark.

At this point in the narrative, Judas seizes the initiative, driving the action in vv. 44–46. Judas "had arranged a signal with" the group carrying swords and clubs who were charged with arresting Jesus on the authority of the Sanhedrin (v. 44). The signal adds another layer of tragic irony to the betrayal—a kiss, a greeting that expresses intimate familiarity. And Judas issues commands to the men regarding the one he will kiss: "Arrest him and lead him away under guard" (v. 44). Judas then approached Jesus, addressing him as "Rabbi," and kissed him, after which the men seized Jesus and arrested him (v. 46).

At this, "one of those standing near drew his sword and struck the servant of the high priest, cutting off his ear" (v. 47). Mark makes no comment about this act, neither identifying who did it nor why.[8] Moloney notes that Mark does not identify this person as one of Jesus's disciples, since this act of violence is not an act befitting a disciple of Jesus. This one is not a "disciple," but a

---

8. John's Gospel identifies Simon Peter as the one who did this (18:10).

bystander.[9] Not only does this detail portray the chaos of the situation, but it once again indicates that the disciples are behaving like non-disciples who are opposed to Jesus's agenda—they are still trying to prevent him from going to the cross. They still have not grasped that violent rebellion is not the way of the kingdom. God's reign comes through the Son of Man giving himself up to death on the cross, and God's kingdom is inhabited by people who go the way of the cross. Disciples do not retaliate, recognizing that doing so is the way of self-destruction and death, behavior that signals Satan's reign. Jesus is not looking for his disciples to be alert so that they can defend him, preventing his arrest. Disciples are called to be "with" Jesus, identifying with him as he is betrayed and goes to the cross. *Watching* and *praying* would prevent them from abandoning Jesus. It may even have led to their being delivered over and being seized along with Jesus. But watchfulness would not have driven them to violently defend him.

The question Jesus asks in v. 48 distinguishes the kingdom of God from a revolutionary movement. He is not interested in violent overthrow or armed rebellion. The kingdom of God, and Jesus as the one who initiates it, does indeed challenge every established power and any and all political interests, but violent overthrow and insurrection are the manifestation of satanic enslavement. The members of the Sanhedrin reasoned that they needed to execute their injustice surreptitiously because they feared the people (11:18; 12:12). Jesus exposes their machinations with his question in vv. 48–49. In effect he states, "I conducted my ministry and confronted your hypocrisies in the plain light of day. I did not hide myself, but taught in the temple courts and was vulnerable to whatever plan you wanted to carry out. But I am not leading a rebel band, so why do you come to arrest me with arms?" The representatives of the Sanhedrin ought not to imagine that they have gained the upper hand and are carrying out their own will. *All of these things must happen*, for "the Scriptures must be fulfilled" (v. 49).

The Disciples Desert Jesus (vv. 50–52)

At this, Jesus's prediction that all his disciples would fall away is tragically realized. Mark states this bluntly: "Then everyone deserted him and fled" (v. 50). The cross-shaped kingdom cannot be inhabited by those dominated by their impulse for self-preservation. Jesus had already said that disciples must take up their crosses and follow him on the road to his cross. The journey toward salvation takes place on the pathway of losing one's life:

---

9. Moloney, *Gospel of Mark*, 297.

Whoever wants to be my disciple must deny themselves and take up their cross and follow me. For whoever wants to save their life will lose it, but whoever loses their life for me and for the gospel will save it. (8:34–35)

The disciples have not been watchful in prayer and so are overcome by their impulse to self-preserve. Though they all protested that they would remain faithful to their teacher even until death (14:31), each one of them fled, abandoning Jesus.

The detail about the young man who flees naked is provocative and raises all sorts of questions, which is just as Mark would want it. As Black indicates, Mark is far more interested in provoking his audiences' imaginations and teasing their minds into active reflection than in resolving all mysteries.[10] The young man's anonymity prevents audiences from assigning blame and responsibility to someone else. They are left questioning themselves: Would we likewise abandon Jesus?[11] This young man represents the disciples in their frantic flight from Jesus. Their drive for self-preservation keeps them from sharing in Jesus's suffering and death, which is his entrance into his glory as the Son of Man.[12] They had previously left everything to *follow* Jesus (10:28), but here they are embodied in the young man's leaving everything behind to *abandon* Jesus. He becomes a symbol of an "anti-disciple."[13]

The young man also points ahead to Peter. Just as the young man "was following Jesus" (v. 51), apparently lurking just out of view, Peter also follows Jesus to the chief priest's house (vv. 53–54). But in the same way that the young man flees naked, a mark of shame, Peter will mourn in shame over his denials (v. 72). In speaking of God's judgment on Israel, Amos 2 captures the tragic dynamics we find in this passage:

> For three sins of Israel,
>   even for four, I will not relent.
> *They sell the innocent for silver,*
>   and the needy for a pair of sandals. (v. 6)

> *Even the bravest warriors*
>   *will flee naked on that day,*
>   declares the Lord. (v. 16)

---

10. Black, *Mark*, 300.
11. Edwards, *Mark*, 441.
12. Moloney, *Gospel of Mark*, 299–300.
13. Marcus, *Mark 8–16*, 1000.

LIVE the Story

Praying for God's Will, Not Our Will

In v. 36 of this passage, Jesus passionately prays: "Abba, Father, everything is possible for you. Take this cup from me. Yet not what I will, but what you will." He knows the awful torment that awaits him, the terrible torture and the unspeakable horrors of bearing eschatological wrath on behalf of God's people. He is about to become the ultimate God-forsaken one (Mark 15:34). In the face of this, Jesus is not dispassionate or stoic but is profoundly shaken. He prays that if there was some other way to accomplish God's saving purposes, he would much prefer that, but defers to what he knows "must" take place. As he has stated repeatedly throughout Mark's Gospel, this is how all things "must" unfold (8:31; 9:34; 14:49). Going the way of suffering and death on the cross is how God has determined to accomplish his purposes.

This fundamental contrast—"not my will, but what you will"—has specific reference to Jesus's desire that God's purposes be worked out by some other path than his suffering an awful death on the cross, even though he knows that this is "God's will." Unfortunately, this prayer is often adopted by Christians when they pray passionately for what they desire, and for what are ultimately God's purposes, yet feel that they are being demanding to God in prayer. *We use Jesus's words inappropriately when we find ourselves deferring to what will happen anyway.* Underlying this misappropriation is a misunderstanding that whatever happens is God's will.

For example, say a young person in my church is suffering a terrible sickness and appears to be near to losing her life. I might gather with others to pray that God would heal this person, out of a shared sense that it is a tragedy that a young woman would not live to a ripe old age. We might pray passionately that God would heal her, raise her up from her sickness, and restore her to health. And out of a sense that we cannot demand anything from God, we might add to our prayers, "yet not what we will, but what you will."

The underlying assumption here is that whatever ends up happening in this situation is God's will: good or bad, triumph or tragedy, all events that take place are the result of God's control over the world and are unfolding according to his will. This is such a common way of thinking that it is seldom questioned. But this is a *misappropriation* of Jesus's words in his Gethsemane prayer. I say this because *God's world is currently in a condition where God's will is not being done.* God did not intend his world to be a place where people get sick and die. Rather, God created his world to be a hospitable place where humanity enjoyed God's order of flourishing. Because of human rebellion and the enslavement of creation to sin and death, the world is currently a place where people suffer pain and loss and where we will all face death unless God comes soon to transform his world.

In the restored creation, when the Son of Man returns to transform the world and fully restore God's order of flourishing, the will of God will be done in every place and at all times. Until then, Jesus has taught his disciples to pray, "*May your will be done* on earth as it is in heaven" (Matt 6:10). The reality Jesus reveals here is that this world is not a place where God's will is being done. Only in the heavenly world is God's will being done. Yet Jesus is preparing a world that is our future inheritance and ultimate destination. God's people will dwell there, and it will be free from the terrible and oppressive reign of sin and death. Jesus teaches his disciples to pray that God would bring that world soon, so that God would be glorified by his people inhabiting creation according to God's original design.

Until that world comes, we cannot say that the terrible things that happen to us and to those that we love are "God's will." Unfortunately, many Christians feel the need to explain the pain and suffering that we experience as somehow within God's design. We name these experiences as "God's will" and seek to justify how they are part of our lives as somehow within God's good intentions, as if they are part of an ultimate plan. It seems to me that we often do so in order to get God "off the hook," to somehow answer the question of how a good God could intend for the brokenness of the world to be a normal state of affairs.

We do not realize, however, that we are justifying the presence of evil in this world as what God intended. But this is not the condition that the world was meant to be in. God has acted in Jesus to begin to set things right, and in the end when Jesus returns to restore creation, God will banish pain and suffering, along with sin and death, forever. Only in that future reality will things ultimately make sense.

It is always "God's will" that people would be restored and healed. It is never God's will that we would suffer sickness, heartache, relational betrayal, and the deep wounds of loss and death. But that is the current condition of this world. Because the world is currently in this condition, God's people lament the suffering we face, and the pain that we feel should fuel our praying that God would return soon to his world and heal it. It is a profound misunderstanding of God's intentions for creation to justify the presence of suffering in this world. When we say things like, "Well, God has a purpose in your loss, you just need to trust him," we misrepresent God and do further damage to already wounded hearts.

Now, it is certainly the case that God is very near to those who are suffering and works amid tragedy and pain to further his purposes and to provide his people fuel for perseverance (Rom 5:3–5; Jas 1:2–4). This is a crucial way that God triumphs over the tragedies of how his creation has been marred by the suffering caused by sin and death. Moreover, it is indeed the case that because of the world's currently broken condition, God's people are called to bear suffering (Phil 1:29; 1 Pet 2:21). It is not the case, however, that whatever happens in this world is what God intends.

Scripture portrays God as the sovereign king over his world, and his kingship was supposed to be embodied by humanity ruling over creation on God's behalf. Because humanity rebelled and decided not to oversee the spread of God's order of flourishing in the world, we do not currently see God's sovereign kingship being enacted within the whole of creation (Heb 2:8). We can see God's kingship enacted within Christian communities that acknowledge the truth about the world, namely, that it is God's good world and that he has installed his ruler, Jesus Christ, as cosmic Lord. And Christians seek to spread God's order of shalom to the extent that we can, though this will always be accompanied by the suffering that inevitably comes our way. This process involves churches praying that God would return to his world to heal and transform it, so that we can finally see God's will being done on this earth (Rev 22:20). Until that day, we ought to exercise care when we pray "not our will, but yours be done."

Returning to the example of praying for a young person who is sick and near death, we can pray with confidence that it is God's will that the person will be raised up and restored to health. Of course, we do not know whether the person will be healed or not. But it is not God's will that anyone endure sickness and die. God's will ultimately will be done when all those who have died in Christ will be raised from the dead, never to die again. We will indeed ultimately all be healed! But we do not have any guarantees in this life other than that we will participate in the resurrection if we are truly disciples of Christ. Yet because God's will is not being done in this world, we ought not to assume that if God does not heal a person, that somehow means it is God's will that a person suffer and die.

Bifurcating Jesus

It is common to read passages that display Jesus's intense emotional reactions as a revelation of his humanity over against his divinity. When Jesus suffers from the overwhelming pressure of facing his impending torture and death, he recoils and prays to God that somehow this moment would pass from him. Because we imagine that God is unmoved in the face of tragedy and awful suffering, we are tempted to somehow attribute this response to Jesus's humanity. Certainly God would not respond this way, would he?

Christian tradition has rightly spoken of Jesus being fully human and fully divine, but this should not be a hermeneutical lens through which we view episodes in the Gospels, thinking that we can attribute certain actions or reactions as "Jesus in his divinity" or "Jesus in his humanity." The Gospels simply present us with Jesus—the revelation of the one true God as he truly is. And in the Gospel of Mark, Jesus is *Jesus*, the Christ, the Son of God, who is also the Son of Man and the chosen agent of the kingdom of God. He speaks for God and acts within creation as God himself, who has returned to his people to establish the kingdom and to accomplish salvation.

Therefore, when we come to this episode and find Jesus responding with intense emotion, we ought not to lose nerve and see Jesus as behaving in some other way than how God would behave when faced with such suffering. After all, in Scripture, when God faces the horrors of judgment and wrath, he recoils, just as Jesus does.

First Chronicles 21 and 2 Samuel 24 both narrate a riveting episode in which God judged Israel because of David's foolishness. David had ordered a numbering of the fighting men, which in some way was inappropriate. He was warned against this by Joab, but he went ahead with his plan anyway (2 Sam 24:3–4). In response, the prophet Gad confronted David and said that David had incited God's wrath against Israel (1 Chr 21:9–12). He was presented with three punishments from which to choose, though David refused and instead threw himself on God's mercy (2 Sam 24:14; 1 Chr 21:13).

God then sent a plague among Israel, and this is where we see God's response to the judgment he had declared:

> So the LORD sent a plague on Israel, and seventy thousand men of Israel fell dead. And God sent an angel to destroy Jerusalem. But as the angel was doing so, the LORD saw it and relented concerning the disaster and said to the angel who was destroying the people, "Enough! Withdraw your hand." The angel of the LORD was then standing at the threshing floor of Araunah the Jebusite. (1 Chr 21:14–15; cf. 2 Sam 24:15–16)

The angel of the Lord is God himself, sent by God to enact this judgment.[14] This is a fascinating window into the drama within God. As God watches God

---

14. In Scripture the angel of the Lord is both identified as Yahweh, the God of Israel (Gen 16:13; 22:15–18; Judg 6:13–14; 13:21–23), and is distinct from him (Exod 23:20–23; 32:34–35).

carrying out his own judgment, he sees the horror of it and relents, stopping the disaster that he himself was carrying out.

To fill in the picture of God's own emotional responses to the suffering of this world, we ought also to consider Romans 8:18–27. In response to the suffering and pain of the current condition of the world, Paul says that creation itself groans under the weight of the frustration of being in bondage to decay (vv. 20–21). Christians, too, groan, as we long for the completion of our salvation, the renewal of our bodies and the complete restoration of creation. Yet we are not alone in this intense groaning and longing for ultimate redemption:

> In the same way, the Spirit helps us in our weakness. We do not know what we ought to pray for, but the Spirit himself intercedes for us through wordless groans. And he who searches our hearts knows the mind of the Spirit, because the Spirit intercedes for God's people in accordance with the will of God. (vv. 26–27)

God's Spirit, too, feels intensely the pain, frustration, and longing of creation and of God's creatures, as we all await liberation from this current bondage. And in v. 27 Paul indicates that Jesus Christ himself—the one who "searches our hearts" and "knows the mind of the Spirit"—also appeals to God to restore creation. Paul depicts Jesus and the Spirit, feeling deeply the pain of creation and praying along with the saints for ultimate restoration and renewal.

These passages indicate that God is not dispassionate when he sees the groaning of creation as it bears the frustration of its current broken condition. In fact, we should say that *God feels more deeply than anyone else* the pain of creation and the suffering of his creatures. God knows fully that the world is not experiencing his order of flourishing as it should, and it grieves him deeply. So when we see Jesus recoil from leaning into the horrors of judgment, we should not imagine that this is merely Jesus's humanity. *This is our God.* Jesus is the fullest and most complete revelation of God, and when we see Jesus's torment at facing suffering, we ought to imagine that this is precisely how God reacts at facing the cost of healing the brokenness of creation.

CHAPTER 57

Mark 14:53–72

📖 LISTEN to the Story

[53]They took Jesus to the high priest, and all the chief priests, the elders and the teachers of the law came together. [54]Peter followed him at a distance, right into the courtyard of the high priest. There he sat with the guards and warmed himself at the fire.

[55]The chief priests and the whole Sanhedrin were looking for evidence against Jesus so that they could put him to death, but they did not find any. [56]Many testified falsely against him, but their statements did not agree.

[57]Then some stood up and gave this false testimony against him: [58]"We heard him say, 'I will destroy this temple made with human hands and in three days will build another, not made with hands.'" [59]Yet even then their testimony did not agree.

[60]Then the high priest stood up before them and asked Jesus, "Are you not going to answer? What is this testimony that these men are bringing against you?" [61]But Jesus remained silent and gave no answer.

Again the high priest asked him, "Are you the Messiah, the Son of the Blessed One?"

[62]"I am," said Jesus. "And you will see the Son of Man sitting at the right hand of the Mighty One and coming on the clouds of heaven."

[63]The high priest tore his clothes. "Why do we need any more witnesses?" he asked. [64]"You have heard the blasphemy. What do you think?"

They all condemned him as worthy of death. [65]Then some began to spit at him; they blindfolded him, struck him with their fists, and said, "Prophesy!" And the guards took him and beat him.

[66]While Peter was below in the courtyard, one of the servant girls of the high priest came by. [67]When she saw Peter warming himself, she looked closely at him.

"You also were with that Nazarene, Jesus," she said.

⁶⁸But he denied it. "I don't know or understand what you're talking about," he said, and went out into the entryway.

⁶⁹When the servant girl saw him there, she said again to those standing around, "This fellow is one of them." ⁷⁰Again he denied it.

After a little while, those standing near said to Peter, "Surely you are one of them, for you are a Galilean."

⁷¹He began to call down curses, and he swore to them, "I don't know this man you're talking about."

⁷²Immediately the rooster crowed the second time. Then Peter remembered the word Jesus had spoken to him: "Before the rooster crows twice you will disown me three times." And he broke down and wept.

> *Listening to the Text in the Story*: Exodus 20:16; Numbers 35:30;
> Deuteronomy 5:20; 17:6; 19:15; 1 Kings 18:1–15; Isaiah 53:7;
> Jeremiah 19:14–20:6.

Jesus's thrice-repeated predictions are being realized. He had said that he would be "delivered into the hands of men" (9:31), would "suffer many things" (8:31), and that he would be "delivered over to the chief priests and the teachers of the law" who would "condemn him to death" (10:33). The transition from Jesus driving the action, which he has done throughout Mark, to his being a passive character in the hands of others, is now complete. That transition took place in the previous episode, where Judas led a crowd to arrest Jesus (14:43–49). In this episode, Jesus is taken to the high priest and is put on trial before him and the Sanhedrin. At the same time, Peter has followed along at a distance and ends up in the courtyard of the high priest's house. He is questioned there by a servant girl and later by others, and he tragically fulfills another one of Jesus's predictions—that Peter would deny him three times before the rooster crowed twice (14:30).

Events have overtaken Jesus so that, like John the Baptist before him, others are doing to Jesus "everything they wished" (9:13). From this point to the end of the Gospel, Jesus is a passive figure, known only from a distance, and other characters—their reasoning and their actions—become the focus of the narrative. Whereas throughout the Gospel, Mark revealed Jesus's motives and emotional reactions, he now portrays him as an opaque character. He is in the hands of others, and other characters are carrying out their will, doing to Jesus as they please.

Attentive audiences of Mark notice, however, that everything is unfolding according to Jesus's repeated predictions. As Jesus had just remarked at his arrest, things are happening as they are because "the Scriptures must be fulfilled" (14:49). While Jesus is controlled by others who mistreat him in this episode, everything is taking place precisely as he had predicted. He is rejected by the chief priests, elders, and teachers of the law, which he predicted in 8:31. And this group condemns him to death, and soldiers mock him, spit on him, and flog him, which he foretold in 10:33–34. Everything is unfolding according to the divine plan.

This episode is another of Mark's many intercalations—the blending of two accounts. Mark often does this by "sandwiching" one episode within another, but here he introduces them both in vv. 53–54 and then narrates one after the other. This indicates that Jesus's trial and the confrontation of Peter in the courtyard are happening simultaneously. This is the final scene in which any of the disciples appear. It is the lowest point of a developing dynamic in Mark whereby the disciples began well, but gradually grew in their confusion until they manifested that they were the ones with hardened hearts (8:17–21). A series of outsiders, however, have manifested the sort of behavior that the disciples should have been embodying. By blending the trial of Jesus with the denials of Peter, Mark is portraying the sort of behavior that is *unbecoming of a disciple*. That is, *Peter is behaving dramatically unlike Jesus*.

Jesus had previously told his disciples what they should do when arrested and put on trial: "Whenever you are arrested and brought to trial, do not worry beforehand about what to say. Just say whatever is given you at the time, for it is not you speaking, but the Holy Spirit" (13:11). In this episode, Jesus behaves in a way that is consistent with his exhortation. His behavior is cross-shaped: he does not argue, fight, retaliate, or try to escape. He simply opens his mouth and speaks his identity plainly. Black notes a series of contrasts between Jesus and Peter:

- Jesus submits himself fully to unfolding events, knowing that these things *must* happen, while Peter is driven by self-preservation and self-protection.
- Jesus is being acted upon by others and is passive, while Peter is active, unconstrained in choosing how he will respond to the questions put to him.
- Jesus is the center of attention in the chief priest's house, while Peter lurks on the fringes outside.

- Jesus is questioned by authorities with the power to bring about his death, while a servant girl and then an anonymous person question Peter, who is never under threat.
- Jesus is subject to false accusations, while the questions asked of Peter have to do with the truth.
- Jesus faithfully answers, revealing his identity; Peter lies about his knowledge of Jesus and denies his own identity.
- Jesus is accused of blasphemy, and Peter calls down curses.
- Jesus is beaten after being sentenced, while Peter humiliates himself.[1]

The manner in which Jesus is mistreated at the hands of the Sanhedrin follows the very similar mistreatment of John the Baptist at the hands of Herod (6:14–29). And Jesus has already foretold that the disciples would be treated in the same way during the present age of tribulation (13:9–13). This is how God's faithful servants have always been treated. In 1 Kings 18:1–15, God calls Elijah to confront Ahab, after which he engages in a contest with the prophets of Baal (18:16–40). On his way to speak to Ahab, however, Elijah runs into Obadiah, who had hidden one hundred of God's prophets in caves to protect them from Jezebel's program of purging faithful prophets from her husband Ahab's royal court through murder (v. 4).

Jeremiah was one of God's prophets who was mistreated by others, which is significant in this context since Jesus echoes many of Jeremiah's prophesies against the temple when he announces God's judgment on this institution in Mark 11–13. Jeremiah had declared God's judgment against the temple throughout Jeremiah 19. In response, Pashhur the priest "had Jeremiah the prophet beaten and put in the stocks" (Jer 20:2). Jeremiah, not to be silenced, then prophesied God's terrifying judgment against the wicked priest (vv. 3–6):

The LORD's name for you is not Pashhur, but Terror on Every Side. For this is what the LORD says: "I will make you a terror to yourself and to all your friends; with your own eyes you will see them fall by the sword of their enemies. I will give all Judah into the hands of the king of Babylon, who will carry them away to Babylon or put them to the sword. I will deliver all the wealth of this city into the hands of their enemies—all its products, all its valuables and all the treasures of the kings of Judah. They will take

---

1. Black, *Mark*, 313.

it away as plunder and carry it off to Babylon. And you, Pashhur, and all who live in your house will go into exile to Babylon. There you will die and be buried, you and all your friends to whom you have prophesied lies." (vv. 3–6)

God's promise to vindicate faithful disciples in the end brings comfort, but it does nothing to prevent the faithful from enduring the mistreatment of those who deceive themselves and others that what they are doing is the will of God.

EXPLAIN the Story

Introduction of the Blended Episode (vv. 53–54)

Mark narrates the action inside and outside the chief priest's house together, for just as Jesus is being questioned by the Sanhedrin, Peter is subject to an interrogation in the courtyard. The "crowd" of representatives of the Sanhedrin that had accompanied Judas to arrest Jesus now "took" him to the high priests. Jesus is under their control. The rest of the Sanhedrin, the ruling body over political, religious, social, and economic affairs in Jerusalem and Judea, now come together.

At the same time, Peter, having just fled from Jesus out of self-preservation, follows "at a distance" (v. 54). Mark portrays Peter moving farther and farther away from Jesus. While he was supposed to be "following Jesus," he now follows from afar. And whereas Jesus had called Peter to be "with him" (3:14), Peter is now "with the guards," warming himself by the fire. Mark repeats this detail in v. 67, indicating that Peter is looking out for his own needs and desires.

Jesus, the Chief Priests, and the Sanhedrin (vv. 55–65)

The chief priests and the Sanhedrin gather to obtain some evidence so that they could credibly accuse Jesus and sentence him to death. They are not weighing evidence and seeking to determine what is the best course of action. Their minds have been made up for some time. The Pharisees had long since committed themselves to killing Jesus (3:6), though they have been off the scene since 12:13. The temple leadership—the Sanhedrin and the chief priests—have been after Jesus ever since he shut down the operations of the temple and passed judgment on it in 11:15–17. Just after this had happened, Mark states that "the chief priests and the teachers of the law heard this and began looking for a way to kill him, for they feared him, because the whole crowd was amazed at his teaching" (11:18).

Mark further depicts their motives through his use of *zēteō* ("to seek"), which he employs in several places to describe characters who behave badly—often faithlessly or with malicious intent. Jesus's family *seeks* him, thinking that he is out of his mind (3:32). The Pharisees *seek* a sign, and Jesus laments the faithless generation that *seeks* a sign (8:11–12). The Sanhedrin *seeks* to kill Jesus (11:18), they *seek* to arrest him (12:12), and they *seek* to arrest him secretly and kill him (14:1).[2] Here, they *seek* evidence to condemn Jesus, though they fail to find any (v. 55).

So they take an alternative path and solicit false testimony. Mark notes that many people gave false testimony against Jesus, but since they couldn't find any that agreed, they were frustrated.[3] At this point, someone falsely testifies that Jesus had spoken about the temple's destruction: "We heard him say, 'I will destroy this temple made with human hands and in three days will build another, not made with hands'" (v. 58). From among the many accusations that Mark could have cited, it is strategically significant that he chooses this bit of false testimony. This detail contributes to Mark's theme of Jesus replacing the Jerusalem temple.

The term *cheiropoiētos* ("made with hands") is used fourteen times in the Greek translation of the Old Testament, and each time it refers to idols.[4] According to Gray, this description of the temple "is not simply saying that the temple is of this world—man-made—but that it has become an idol."[5] This idolatrous temple is going to be destroyed, and Jesus is building a new one "not made with hands" (*acheiropoiēton*). Christian audiences discern that what is in view here is the establishment of a new place of worship, a new means of relating to God, one established and authorized by God. Jesus is the new temple, and all those gathered in his name enjoy his presence by his Spirit. This is another instance of Mark putting something true—or, at least close to the truth—in the mouth of a character opposed to Jesus (cf. 12:14).

---

2. Black, *Mark*, 306; Moloney, *Gospel of Mark*, 301. Early audiences of Mark would likely have heard the Gospel read aloud repeatedly, and after noting the regular negative use of *zēteō* throughout the narrative, would have given renewed consideration to the first use of the verb on subsequent hearings. While Jesus goes off alone to pray in 1:35, "Simon and his companions went to look for him, and when they found him, they exclaimed: 'Everyone is looking [*zēteō*] for you!'" (1:36–37). Considering how Mark portrays crowds with some ambivalence and the disciples as growing in confusion and increasingly failing, this early appearance of *zēteō* would alert audiences to the beginning of these dynamics quite a bit earlier in the Gospel than they had previously noted.

3. Jesus cannot be condemned with false testimony (Deut 17:6; 19:15), so it may be that they are frustrated that they cannot obtain the kind of testimony that would seal their case.

4. Gray, *Temple in the Gospel of Mark*, 175.

5. Gray, *Temple in the Gospel of Mark*, 175.

It is intriguing that Mark calls this testimony "false" because it is so close to the truth of what Jesus has said, and it certainly adds another dimension to Mark's critique of the Jerusalem temple. The specific reason it is false is because Jesus did not explicitly say that he was going to do this himself, but rather that the temple would be destroyed, without indicating an agent (cf. 13:2). But Mark's larger purposes involve provoking audiences to lean forward and figure out just what the difference is between this "false" accusation and what Jesus had said. In doing so, they will likely look more closely at the meanings of "made with hands" and "made without hands," adding layers to their understanding of the Jerusalem temple and the reality of Jesus replacing it.

When the high priest presses Jesus to answer the charge, Jesus remains silent (vv. 60–61), recalling Isaiah 53:7:

> He was oppressed and afflicted,
>   yet he did not open his mouth;
> he was led like a lamb to the slaughter,
>   and as a sheep before its shearers is silent,
>   so he did not open his mouth.

The high priest then asked Jesus directly about his identity: "Are you the Messiah, the Son of the Blessed One?" This last description ("the Blessed One") is a typical Jewish circumlocution for God, a way of referring to the God of Israel without saying his name. Jesus answers in a straightforward way: "I am" (v. 62). He then describes the vindication he will enjoy at the hand of God, which the Sanhedrin will witness: "And you will see the Son of Man sitting at the right hand of the Mighty One and coming on the clouds of heaven" (v. 62).

Jesus's profession of his identity is dramatic enough, considering the tense drama unfolding in the high priest's house. But several dimensions of Mark's narrative make Jesus's confession of his identity climactic. First, this is the singular revelatory moment that brings to a close all of the calls for silence and secrecy about Jesus's identity. At the opening of the Gospel, God had clearly identified Jesus as his beloved Son, but this acclamation was heard only by Jesus (1:11). Throughout the proceeding narrative, Jesus continually ordered people to be quiet about him (1:34, 44–45; 3:11–12; 7:35–37). God later proclaimed Jesus's identity as his beloved Son at the transfiguration in 9:7, though again Jesus ordered his disciples to keep silent about what they saw until after the resurrection (9:9).

Now, however, is the time for Jesus to speak plainly about his identity.

This is the culminating moment of revelation, when Jesus is vulnerable and at his weakest, having already been delivered into the hands of others and abandoned by his followers. *It is in being betrayed, being rejected, and while on the way to his cross that Jesus's identity is fully disclosed.*

Second, and closely related to this, Jesus again affirms that he is the Messiah—the Christ—in terms of suffering, rejection, death, and vindication. He is not the power-grabbing, sensational, and socially prominent military leader that Peter and the disciples wanted. Jesus is the Son of Man who is a faithful prophet and God's appointed agent of salvation and kingdom rule.

He associates his identity as the Son of Man with his being the Christ, so that on repeated readings and hearings of Mark, audiences would learn to interpret what it means to be Messiah in terms of Jesus being the *now-suffering* and *later-exalted* Son of Man. This dynamic transforms culturally constructed notions of a messiah figure developed out of the resentment of the Romans and shaped by Maccabean hopes and dreams. Jesus, specifically as the suffering Son of Man, is the Christ—he is a cruciform Christ. Jesus is a cross-directed Messiah who calls disciples to take up their crosses and follow him on the way to the cross. The cross determines the nature of the kingdom, and only communities shaped by the cross will be vindicated by the returning Son of Man.

Yet another irony here is that Jesus stands before his judges who are administering anything but justice. They are executing a grave *injustice* in order to protect their positions of authority over the people and are doing so in a surreptitious way so as not to provoke an insurrection and to protect their positions with the Romans. Yet Jesus, who stands before them, will be vindicated by God and will return as the Son of Man, *the one appointed by God to judge these very people headed for God's judgment.*

After hearing Jesus confirm his identity, the high priest tears his clothes (v. 63), a dramatic act signaling extreme distress.[6] He declares that Jesus has blasphemed and indicates that there is no need for further witnesses. The rest of the Sanhedrin confirms this judgment and agrees that he must be put to death (v. 64). Mark's audiences will detect another dark irony. It is the high priest who is blaspheming, as he is denying the reality about the one who stands before him. After all, at Jesus's baptism and transfiguration, God himself had declared his verdict about who Jesus is. The high priest is committing a sin that cannot be forgiven (3:28–29).

After the Sanhedrin reached their verdict, they began to abuse Jesus (v. 65). Some of them spit at him, a sign of rejection and humiliation (Num 12:14;

---

6. Moloney, *Gospel of Mark*, 305; Edwards, *Mark*, 448.

Deut 25:9; Isa 50:6–7).[7] They also strike and punch him, having blindfolded him, and mock him by demanding that he prophesy (v. 65). The guards also manhandle Jesus and beat him. The awful ironies at this point are piling up. While the Sanhedrin and the guards appear to be the ones in control, demanding that he prophesy, Jesus has already prophesied that all of this would happen, *including these very details*: he would be rejected (8:31), mocked, spit upon, and beaten (10:34).

Peter Disowns Jesus (vv. 66–72)

At the same time as the chief priests and the Sanhedrin were interrogating Jesus and finally condemning and abusing him, Peter was "below in the courtyard," and Mark repeats the detail that he was warming himself by the fire (vv. 54, 67). He had followed along "at a distance," after fleeing when Judas had arrived with a crowd to arrest Jesus. Peter and Jesus are both interrogated, but there is a stark contrast between their questioners: Jesus is before the chief priests and Sanhedrin, while Peter is confronted by a mere servant girl.

Considering the importance of verbs of perception (seeing and hearing) throughout Mark's Gospel, the details of this encounter are highly significant: "When she *saw* Peter warming himself, she *looked closely* at him" (v. 67). Mark uses verbs of perception when Jesus sees and calls his disciples (1:16, 19; 2:14). Jesus later stresses how crucial it is that the disciples *listen* and *see* what he is talking about when he speaks in parables so that they may move toward understanding (4:1–24). Further, Mark inverts insiders and outsiders throughout the Gospel by indicating that outsider characters *see* and *hear* Jesus (e.g., the demon-possessed man, Jairus, the unclean woman, Bartimaeus), while the disciples rarely have verbs of perception attributed to them and do not move toward understanding. *Seeing* and *hearing* in Mark indicate *a true and penetrating perception of reality*, especially the discernment by other characters of Jesus's identity.

This description of the servant girl, therefore, is yet another device that intensifies the tragic irony. She truly perceives who Peter is and knows the truth about him: "You also were with that Nazarene, Jesus" (v. 67). She articulates Peter's identity in terms of being a disciple. Jesus had called the Twelve to be "*with* him" (3:14), the very thing she attributes to Peter. She does not question him, and this is not necessarily a threatening accusation. She merely identifies him and does so in terms of the truth.

Peter, however, denies the truth, being ashamed of the Son of Man and of

---

7. Boring, *Mark*, 415; Garland, *Theology of Mark's Gospel*, 168.

his words (cf. 8:38). "I don't know or understand what you're talking about" (v. 68). His admission is ironically loaded with truth! He does not understand what it means to be a disciple of Jesus, having had his understanding diminished over the course of the Gospel's narrative because of his resistance to Jesus's message of the cross. He was supposed to be seeing and hearing, moving toward understanding, but since this has not happened, his statement is pathetically accurate. At the same time, Peter intends this as a denial of his connection to Jesus. He was supposed to be "with Jesus," but he is now here in the courtyard, "with the guards" (v. 54). He has situated himself with those who are abusing Jesus. Ironically, as the supposedly consummate insider character in Mark, he fully claims the status of an outsider—one who does not know himself or understand his connection to Jesus.

Peter left the courtyard to escape the discomfort of the girl's searching gaze and went into the entryway of the high priest's house (v. 68). The girl followed him there and again "saw him," once more truly perceiving who Peter is and what he is all about (v. 69). Speaking to everyone who had assembled there, she identifies him once more, this time associating him with the Twelve: "This fellow is one of them" (v. 69). Again, Peter denies his connection to Jesus and to Jesus's other disciples (v. 70).

Other people who were standing around in the courtyard and the entryway and who have heard the girl's identification of Peter, along with his denials, now press the issue. They indicate to Peter that his accent gives him away: "Surely you are one of them, for you are a Galilean" (v. 70). At this, Peter vehemently denies that he has any connection whatsoever to Jesus, and does so in pathetically ironic terms: "I don't know this man you're talking about" (v. 71). Truly, Peter seems to not know him. He is at the lowest point in the narrative. He had begun so well in immediately dropping everything to follow Jesus when he was called, along with his brother Andrew (1:16–18). And he had witnessed and experienced the power of the kingdom, seeing Jesus's miracles and ministering with kingdom power while on mission (6:8–14). But after growing increasingly confused at Jesus's identity and teaching, he has devolved as a disciple, demonstrating that even the little bit of kingdom reality he possessed is now being taken away from him (4:25). He calls down curses on himself by swearing that he wants awful things to befall him if he is lying about knowing Jesus.

Immediately, another of Jesus's predictions is painfully realized. Peter hears the rooster crow a second time and instantly remembers Jesus's prediction (v. 72). While Peter had protested that he would never abandon Jesus but would go to his death out of loyalty, Jesus solemnly predicted that "before the rooster crows twice you yourself will disown me three times" (v. 30). Peter recalls "the word Jesus had spoken," and "he broke down and wept" (v. 72).

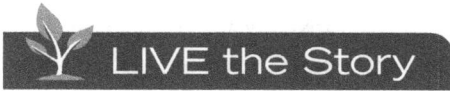

LIVE the Story

Perseverance as Disciples

When I teach about the New Testament depiction of the necessity for disciples to persevere in the faith, I find that people often get nervous. Many of them have received assurances that because of an initial profession of faith in Christ, their final salvation is secure. Because of the promises of Jesus to lose none of his disciples, it seems that there is no need to expend any effort to persevere in the faith. It sounds as if these twin realities of God's holding on to us and our need to continue in the faith are somehow mutually exclusive. And it strikes many that if Scripture teaches that disciples need to persevere, then salvation "by grace" is somehow threatened. And these questions inevitably arise: How much obedience is enough? What if I stumble and fall? What happens if I sin, or find myself in a season of wandering?

I think that the contrast between Peter and Jesus in this passage is instructive for this discussion. In this episode, Peter denies his identity and his attachment to Jesus and the other disciples. He is an example of failing to persevere, whereas Jesus is a model of perseverance in that *he owns his identity when he is questioned.* I think we have some significant misconceptions when we think about living as Christians that prohibit us from thinking rightly about perseverance. We imagine that living as Christians is drudgery. We tend to see life as non-Christians as somehow the more desirable path, with Christian discipleship as a hard slog. We forget that Scripture portrays discipleship to Jesus as inhabiting the reality of freedom and the realm of liberation. It is a life in community that is empowered by God's Spirit. Yet we tend to imagine that living as Christians is in some way a life of achievement, and that it is hard. When we think about perseverance, therefore, we wonder, "Do I have to keep doing this forever? What if I get worn out and can't continue?"

But in this episode, Jesus perseveres in faithfulness to God simply by owning his identity. He knows who he is and what his mission is, and he does not deny those. Yes, it is the difficult path of the cross, but when pressed he does not need to do anything other than speak the truth about who he is and what it is that God has called him to do.

While there is much else to say about perseverance, from this passage we can say that it involves the simple task of knowing who we are in Christ and then faithfully embodying that reality by continuing to claim it. We don't have to achieve anything impressive or accomplish great things for God. We simply must know who we are and remain in a posture of thanksgiving to God by receiving his grace alongside our sisters and brothers in the faith.

When I think of examples of perseverance in the faith, I think of one of my heroes, a woman named Lynne. She recently passed into the presence of the Lord, and to many she may have seemed like a pretty unremarkable person. She wasn't famous, didn't wield personal power, and was not a great leader. To me, however, she epitomizes what it means to persevere in faithfulness to God and to his people. Lynne was baptized as a child in the church of which she was a part for most of her long life. That is remarkable in a city filled with churches and many thousands of Christians that move from this megachurch to that one based on what is exciting and who is generating buzz. She, however, remained in the same church and was supportive of the various ministers who had served over the decades. She was a faithful mainstay through good times and bad. For her, commitment to God was embodied through commitment to her community.

I spoke to her one time about our minister, mentioning that we were so blessed to be led so well. I said that I hoped he didn't leave so that the character of the church wouldn't change and that people wouldn't look for someplace else. She gave me a puzzled look and said that this was her community and that she would be part of it no matter who was the pastor.

I've thought about that conversation quite a bit in the years since, and especially in light of some recent unpleasantness we have experienced in our community. Some people have left, and I must admit that I have had moments of uncertainty about my future there. But I have found myself asking, "What would Lynne do?" I am jealous of her longevity in one community over many decades, and I am struck by that sort of faithfulness. Like Jesus speaking frankly about his identity, Lynne knew who she was, knew the God to whom she belonged, and was in no doubt that her faithfulness to God entailed nothing other than her identity as part of her church.

When we think about perseverance as disciples, then, we do not have any need to be anxious. In an age dominated by consumerism, in which we are pressed to own identities as "shoppers" who follow our desires for what is attractive, interesting, and impressive, it just might be that perseverance entails knowing *who we are* and *who we are not*. We are people baptized into Christ and into a local expression of Christ's social body—the church. We persevere by remaining faithful to that identity and by resisting our culture's push to do whatever immediately pleases us.

CHAPTER 58

Mark 15:1-20

📖 LISTEN to the Story

¹Very early in the morning, the chief priests, with the elders, the teachers of the law and the whole Sanhedrin, made their plans. So they bound Jesus, led him away and handed him over to Pilate.

²"Are you the king of the Jews?" asked Pilate.

"You have said so," Jesus replied.

³The chief priests accused him of many things. ⁴So again Pilate asked him, "Aren't you going to answer? See how many things they are accusing you of."

⁵But Jesus still made no reply, and Pilate was amazed.

⁶Now it was the custom at the festival to release a prisoner whom the people requested. ⁷A man called Barabbas was in prison with the insurrectionists who had committed murder in the uprising. ⁸The crowd came up and asked Pilate to do for them what he usually did.

⁹"Do you want me to release to you the king of the Jews?" asked Pilate, ¹⁰knowing it was out of self-interest that the chief priests had handed Jesus over to him. ¹¹But the chief priests stirred up the crowd to have Pilate release Barabbas instead.

¹²"What shall I do, then, with the one you call the king of the Jews?" Pilate asked them.

¹³"Crucify him!" they shouted.

¹⁴"Why? What crime has he committed?" asked Pilate.

But they shouted all the louder, "Crucify him!"

¹⁵Wanting to satisfy the crowd, Pilate released Barabbas to them. He had Jesus flogged, and handed him over to be crucified.

¹⁶The soldiers led Jesus away into the palace (that is, the Praetorium) and called together the whole company of soldiers. ¹⁷They put a purple robe on him, then twisted together a crown of thorns and set it on him. ¹⁸And they began to call out to him, "Hail, king of the Jews!" ¹⁹Again and

again they struck him on the head with a staff and spit on him. Falling on their knees, they paid homage to him. [20]And when they had mocked him, they took off the purple robe and put his own clothes on him. Then they led him out to crucify him.

Listening to the Text in the Story: Psalm 110; Isaiah 50:6; 52:13–53:12; John 6:15; 1 Corinthians 2:7–8; 1 Peter 2:18–25.

Just after the Sanhedrin finds that Jesus is worthy of death, they bring him to Pilate in order to convince him to condemn Jesus to be crucified.[1] Mark portrays the trial before Pilate with some similarities to Jesus's trial before the Sanhedrin in 14:53–65:

- In both instances, Jesus is in the hands of others: "They took Jesus to the high priest" (14:53); they "led him away and handed him over to Pilate" (15:1).
- Both trials indicate that the Sanhedrin is responsible for crucifying Jesus, as Mark lists the various groups within the Jerusalem leadership (14:53; 15:1) and includes in both passages the expression "the whole Sanhedrin" (*holon to synedrion*; 14:55; 15:1).
- The Sanhedrin is scheming in both episodes. In the first, they are not *weighing* evidence but *looking for* evidence that will give them grounds to put Jesus to death (14:55). In the second, they "made their plans," strategizing to convince Pilate that Jesus is worthy of death (15:1).
- Jesus is asked a question about his identity by both rulers: "Are you the Messiah, the Son of the Blessed One?" (14:61). "Are you the king of the Jews?" (15:2).
- Jesus affirms his identity before the Sanhedrin (14:62) and Pilate (15:2).
- Jesus is silent when pressed to answer accusations (14:61; 15:5).
- Jesus suffers mockery and physical abuse at the close of each episode (14:65; 15:15–20).
- The abuse of Jesus in both passages is tragically ironic. The Sanhedrin strikes him and calls on him to prophesy, just as they are fulfilling Jesus's prophecies (14:65; cf. 8:31; 9:31; 10:33–34). The Roman soldiers

---

1. The Sanhedrin did not have the power to execute a person, something only the Roman authorities could carry out (Marcus, *Mark 8–16*, 1026).

mockingly hail Jesus as king, not realizing that going to the cross is God's appointed means of Jesus assuming his kingship.

In both passages, Mark portrays Jesus in terms taken from Isaiah's depiction of the suffering servant. Jesus is passive before both the Sanhedrin and Pilate, and twice he suffers abusive mockery and spitting.

> I offered my back to those who beat me,
>> my cheeks to those who pulled out my beard;
> I did not hide my face
>> from mocking and spitting. (Isa 50:6)

As was just indicated above, in both trials Jesus acknowledges his identity but does not answer the false accusations brought against him, also recalling Isaiah:

> He was oppressed and afflicted,
>> yet he did not open his mouth;
> he was led like a lamb to the slaughter,
>> and as a sheep before its shearers is silent,
>> so he did not open his mouth. (Isa 53:7)

This passage is loaded with intensely tragic irony. The soldiers mock Jesus and hail him as "king of the Jews" (Mark 15:18). Of course, they do this, imagining that they are putting an end to the political dreams of a pathetic figure over whom they are in total control. Yet the way of suffering and death is precisely the manner in which Jesus inaugurates the kingdom of God and enters into his reign as God's appointed king. Jesus had already spoken of this while he was in the temple courts in Mark 12:35–37. Citing Psalm 110:1, Jesus had indicated that God had spoken by the Holy Spirit to one whom David had called "Lord," indicating that God was addressing Jesus himself:

> The LORD says to my Lord:
> "Sit at my right hand
>> until I make your enemies
>> a footstool for your feet."

Therefore, the opposition that Jesus was facing from the temple leadership and the entirety of Jesus's suffering and death is the long process of Jesus's coronation as God's appointed king.

While Jesus's passion is tragic from one perspective, it is also consistent with everything Jesus has taught throughout Mark regarding the kind of Messiah he is. Jesus is a cross-directed Messiah, initiating God's cross-shaped kingdom made up of disciples who take up their crosses and follow Jesus on the way to the cross. He is the suffering Son of Man, who enters into his glory through death and calls his followers to inhabit his kingdom through self-giving love. This entails losing their lives so that they may gain them in that future kingdom when the Son of Man comes in power. While it appears, from one perspective, that Jesus is in the hands of others and that he is being subdued by them, this is ultimately the process by which God is putting his enemies "under his feet."

This is a radically counterintuitive way for any king to enter into his glory. Yet this is the way that the God of Israel carries out his work. A suffering and crucified Messiah is the most explicit expression of the wisdom of God. It is lunacy to a worldly way of doing things and makes no sense to those who pursue worldly forms of power. Paul and his fellow apostles

> declare God's wisdom, a mystery that has been hidden and that God destined for our glory before time began. None of the rulers of this age understood it, for if they had, they would not have crucified the Lord of glory. (1 Cor 2:7–8)

The injustice, suffering, cruel mockery, and abuse that Jesus endures is difficult to consider. But we must keep in mind that Mark is displaying not merely *what happened. He is portraying the mode of life for kingdom inhabitants.* If Jesus takes up his reign in this countercultural fashion, then the kingdom of God cannot be embodied by a community that quests after power. Kingdom communities must be oriented by their counterintuitive ruler.

Structurally, this passage in Mark consists of three sections:

1. Jesus before Pilate (vv. 1–5)
2. Jesus and Barabbas (vv. 6–15)
3. The soldiers ironically hail Jesus as king (vv. 16–20)

An *inclusio* marks off the first two sections, one that fulfills Jesus's prophecies in 9:31 and 10:33. He predicted that he would be "handed over" (*paradidōmi*) to the chief priests and then to the gentiles, before being put to death. The same verb is used here in 15:1 to speak of the Sanhedrin handing Jesus over to Pilate, and then Pilate handing him over to be crucified in v. 15.

The middle section (vv. 6–15) is the longest, in which Pilate goes back and forth with "the crowd" over whether to release Jesus or Barabbas. This invites audiences to compare the two figures. Jesus is a cross-identified king who calls disciples to go the way of the cross, while Barabbas is a revolutionary figure who has pursued an agenda with which the disciples and the crowds identify. They long for independence from Rome and seek the kingdom of God through a violent military engagement with the Roman occupiers. This comparison serves Mark's narrative purposes in identifying Jesus with the rejection of violent overthrow as the manner in which the kingdom of God is established. Resenting enemies and resorting to violence make sense according to a worldly way of thinking. But this is a manifestation of satanic enslavement and demonstrates that the crowds, along with the Sanhedrin "do not have in mind the concerns of God, but merely human concerns" (Mark 8:33).

EXPLAIN the Story

Jesus Before Pilate (vv. 1–5)

Mark sets the trial before Pilate "very early in the morning," a typical time for such events (v. 1).[2] The Sanhedrin has been up throughout the night in an attempt to carry out their plans, and they now arrive before Pilate to make their case. Mark emphasizes that the entire Sanhedrin has gathered together, and they are all in on the plot. He ponderously lists each party that makes up the ruling council ("the chief priests, with the elders, the teachers of the law") and then adds a summary comment: "And the whole Sanhedrin." Mark thus puts the responsibility for the death of Jesus on the temple leadership. They are the ones against whom Jesus declared God's judgment for corrupting the temple of God. It was meant to be "a house of prayer for all nations," but they had "made it a den of robbers" (11:17).

The council had gathered and "made their plans," scheming in order to present to Pilate a case that would force him to carry out their murderous intentions. They "bound Jesus, led him away and handed him over to Pilate,"

---

2. Pilate appears as an unfavorable figure in extrabiblical sources. Both Philo and Josephus paint him in a very negative light as heavy-handed, cruel, and inflexible, provoking the Jews in Judea when he could have governed in such a way as to keep the peace more effectively. See Helen K. Bond, "Political Authorities: The Herods, Caiaphas, and Pontius Pilate," in *Jesus among Friends and Enemies: A Historical and Literary Introduction to Jesus in the Gospels* (Grand Rapids: Baker Academic, 2011), 229–33.

in fulfillment of Jesus's predictions (9:31; 10:33). The verb for "handed over" (*paradidōmi*) is important in Mark's Gospel, indicating the sort of treatment disciples of Jesus can expect in this present evil age. Jesus's ministry began under the shadow of threat, just after John was "handed over" (*paradidōmi*; NIV, "put in prison," 1:14). Jesus uses this term twice in speaking of the persecution his disciples would face in this age of ongoing distress and destruction:

> You must be on your guard. You will be handed over [*paradidōmi*] to the local councils and flogged in the synagogues. On account of me you will stand before governors and kings as witnesses to them. And the gospel must first be preached to all nations. Whenever you are arrested [*paradidōmi*] and brought to trial, do not worry beforehand about what to say. Just say whatever is given you at the time, for it is not you speaking, but the Holy Spirit. (13:9–11)

Jesus is treated just as John was, and his disciples will be treated just as Jesus was.

The Sanhedrin bound Jesus, even though he never presented himself as a threat. He preached and taught openly and did not defend himself when they came for him in the garden of Gethsemene (14:48–49). But the ruling council needed to present Jesus to Pilate as a dangerous figure—a revolutionary—the very sort of person that a Roman governor would see as a threat to order and stability.

Pilate's question to Jesus indicates the Jewish council's strategy: "Are you the king of the Jews?" (v. 2). When they "made their plans," the Sanhedrin plotted to present Jesus as a figure who would foment instability and social unrest. If they had presented Jesus as a Jewish prophetic figure that had called out the hypocrisy and corruption of the temple leadership, Pilate would not have cared. Nor would he have paid any mind to the particulars of a dispute among Jewish groups over messianic titles (cf. Acts 25:19–20). But this specific charge represents a danger to Rome's rule over Judea, as if Jesus were a Maccabean figure leading a movement to establish independence. They knew that Pilate, as governor of that region on behalf of Rome, would need to be on the lookout for people stoking revolutionary fervor in a quest for liberation. Jesus, of course, has not presented himself in this way and has explicitly condemned such a course of action as satanic (cf. 8:33).

Jesus's answer to Pilate's question is cryptic and mystifying: "You have said so" (v. 2). Is it an affirmation, so that Jesus accepts the title? Or is he resisting Pilate's characterization of him? It appears that Jesus affirms that he is indeed "the king of the Jews," based on the parallel with the high priest's question in 14:61. The questions of Jesus's identity from the high priest and Pilate are asked in the same form, and because Jesus affirms his identity to the high priest, it is likely that Jesus also affirms his identity as king to Pilate.[3] In a Roman context, Jesus's identity as the Son of Man who is coming in power would not make much sense. But the title "the king of the Jews" resonates in a non-Jewish setting, and this serves Mark's purpose of portraying Jesus as the ruler of God's kingdom as the Gospel is read throughout the world in non-Jewish contexts.

Jesus is not, then, resisting Pilate's characterization of him as "the king of the Jews." Rather, he embraces it. And if we consider the setting of this conversation within the narrative of Mark's Gospel, we can understand Jesus's subsequent silence. There is no need for him to elaborate, for he has already spoken at length about the sort of ruler he is. He is the king who serves others and does not seek to be served (10:45). He is a ruler who goes the way of the cross and resists being pressed into the shape of one who seeks after power (8:31–38; 11:1–11). His kingship will not be vindicated in this age, but only when he returns in power, which follows his going to the cross. And while Jesus does not seek to ignite a revolution, he also shows no deference to Pilate and his authority. He merely notes that Pilate has spoken rightly of his identity: "You have said it."[4]

The chief priests now step in and accuse Jesus of "many things" (v. 3), which Mark repeats in Pilate's question to Jesus: "Aren't you going to answer? See *how many things* they are accusing you of" (v. 4). The narrative makes no mention of the content of these accusations, but they would have reflected the Sanhedrin's strategy of portraying Jesus as a political threat to Rome, and thus as a personal danger to Pilate.

Jesus, however, remains silent, refusing to justify himself to Pilate. The Roman ruler "was amazed" by this (v. 5), a response of wonder that is largely negative throughout Mark's Gospel. While crowds are often amazed at what Jesus says and does (1:22, 27; 2:12), they are also obstacles to his ministry and will eventually call for his death. The townspeople who encounter the formerly demon-possessed man are amazed at what Jesus did, but they plead with Jesus to leave their region out of fear (5:17–20). The people in Jesus's hometown are amazed at Jesus, yet they do not believe in him, which causes Jesus to be amazed (6:2–6). And his disciples are amazed at what is happening in Jesus's ministry at the same time that their confusion grows (6:51).

---

3. Moloney, *Gospel of Mark*, 310.
4. Marcus, *Mark 8–16*, 1034.

Amazement, therefore, is not a positive response in Mark, and it usually goes together with unbelief. As audiences heard the Gospel over and over, they would consider the earlier incidences of amazement in Mark in light of Pilate's amazement, leading to a growing realization that they should have a healthy skepticism about an enthusiastic initial response to Jesus. What matters is not an immediately positive reaction to Jesus but a *seeing* and *hearing* that leads to understanding, repentance, and persevering discipleship.

Jesus and Barabbas (vv. 6–15)

In the middle of narrating the trial before Pilate, Mark notes that the Roman ruler had a "custom at the festival to release a prisoner whom the people requested" (v. 6).[5] A man named Barabbas was in prison for participating in a violent insurrection against Roman rule, during which he had committed murder (v. 7). It is important to understand the narrative significance of Barabbas and how he is set in contrast to Jesus, for he represents precisely the sort of revolutionary figure that Jesus is not. When Jesus spoke with his disciples about his mission as Messiah to go to Jerusalem to die, Peter "took him aside and began to rebuke him" (8:32). The disciples wanted to follow a figure who would accomplish salvation *as they understood it*—liberation from Roman oppression and the restoration of God's people as an independent nation. When they entered Jerusalem, the disciples were still committed to pressing Jesus into the role of triumphant hero, as they whipped up crowds to celebrate his arrival (11:8–10). Barabbas represents, therefore, the hopes of the disciples and the crowds for a worldly sort of figure—a revolutionary committed to liberating God's people by violence.[6] According to Mark's Gospel, however, this conception of God's salvation is satanic (cf. 8:33).

The character of Barabbas as just this sort of figure is the reason why he is appealing to "the crowd" (*ochlos*). He is a revolutionary hero in a way that Jesus is not. And the chief priests are there to manipulate the crowd toward their end of being rid of Jesus. "The crowd" has been an ambivalent character throughout Mark's Gospel, and here we see why Jesus has never played to

---

5. There is no record of Pilate's practice of releasing a prisoner outside the Gospels (cf. Matt 27:15; John 18:39). This, however, does not mean that such a practice did not exist.

6. "Barabbas" in Aramaic means "son of the father," but Mark leaves his name untranslated. This is unusual since Mark elsewhere interprets Aramaic expressions and names, especially the term "Abba," which means "father," in 14:36 and "Bartimaeus," which means "son of Timaeus" in 10:46 (cf. also 7:34; 15:34). Marcus suggests that audiences encountering the name "Barabbas" after hearing "Abba" and "Bartimaeus" translated for them, would be provoked to inquire as to its meaning, causing them to make the connections and comparisons between Jesus, the Son of the Father, and Barabbas, the "son of the father" who is utterly unlike Jesus (cf. Marcus, *Mark 8–16*, 1028).

them. Upon repeated hearings of the narrative, audiences will have in mind the crowd's behavior in preferring Barabbas over Jesus, as they hear of their apparently positive response to Jesus at the beginning of his ministry. The crowd has been an obstacle to Jesus in his ministry (2:1–12; 3:7, 20; 5:24), and "a crowd" accompanied Judas at Jesus's arrest (14:43).

"The crowd" now approaches Pilate and asks him to once again "do for them what he usually did" in releasing a prisoner (v. 8). Because Jesus is right there with him, Pilate asks them if they want him to release "the king of the Jews" (v. 9). Mark notes that Pilate discerns the motivations of the chief priests, that it was "out of self-interest" that they had "handed over" (*paradidōmi*) Jesus to him (v. 10). The Greek term that the NIV renders "self-interest" can also be translated as "envy" (*phthonos*). The chief priests are certainly acting out of self-interest, but Pilate perceives that they are envious of Jesus. Jesus is not wrapped up in the plays for power that captivate the Sanhedrin, who must hold on to their positions by manipulating both the Roman authorities and the Jewish people. Jesus, because he is headed for death on the cross, is utterly free to prophesy against the temple authorities and to announce the arrival of God's liberating reign. His freedom to speak and his identifying the corruptions of the temple leadership make him a mortal threat to the Sanhedrin, and Pilate knows that.

Because of this, the chief priests manipulate the crowd to pressure Pilate to release Barabbas instead of Jesus (v. 11). When Pilate asks what the crowd wants him to do with Jesus, they reply passionately, "Crucify him!" (vv. 12–13). Pilate protests, however, with words that would resonate with any audience hearing the Gospel: "Why? What crime has he committed?" (v. 14). But the crowd at this point is whipped up into a frenzy and is beyond reason: "They shouted all the louder, 'Crucify him!'"

Though he is baffled by their choice of a revolutionary murderer rather than the innocent Jesus, the crowd, moved by the chief priests, has confirmed their choice. They do not want Jesus as their king, and they are rejecting the reign of God as it truly is—oriented toward the cross and ruled by a cruciform Lord. Ironically, their choice to see Jesus crucified is the means whereby God establishes his kingdom in fulfillment of Jesus's predictions.

Because he wanted to satisfy the crowd, Pilate released Barabbas and fulfilled Jesus's prophecies by ordering Jesus to be flogged. He then "handed him over to be crucified" (v. 15; cf. 9:31; 10:33–34). Mark portrays Pilate in much the same way he had characterized Herod, who knew that John the Baptist was "a righteous and holy man" (6:20). Herod's wife wanted John dead because John had confronted the couple for their shameful marriage

(6:18–19). But Herod protected John by keeping him in prison. Later, however, he was manipulated by Herodias after his drunken boast, which led to his reluctantly putting John to death (6:26–28). Jesus's condemnation comes about in the same way, through a corrupted leader who knows better but is manipulated by the crowd, controlled by the chief priests.

The Jewish leaders had seized an opportune moment to accomplish their murderous desires. The Pharisees had plotted with the Herodians to destroy (*apollymi*) Jesus (3:6). And the temple leadership, along with the scribes, had long sought how they might arrest Jesus and have him killed (11:18; 14:1). Their chance had arrived, and they jumped at the opportunity. Mark notes repeatedly, however, that they are not ultimately in control of anything. Events are unfolding according to God's design to accomplish his saving purposes (8:31; 9:12; 14:49).

The Soldiers Ironically Hail Jesus as King (vv. 16–20)

After Pilate handed Jesus over to be crucified (v. 15), the soldiers led him away into the palace, and just as "the whole Sanhedrin" had previously gathered to Pilate (v. 1), "the whole company of soldiers" gathered together around Jesus (v. 16). What follows is an awful account of their mocking abuse of Jesus that is also powerfully ironic, for this process of Jesus suffering terrible mistreatment on his way to the cross is actually the route of his coronation as God's appointed king. The soldiers, of course, intend to demean and utterly humiliate Jesus, not knowing that God triumphs through defeat.

Mark emphasizes Jesus's identity as "king of the Jews" throughout this passage, mentioning the title three times to this point (vv. 2, 9, 12), and he notes it again when the soldiers mockingly call out to him, "Hail, king of the Jews!" (v. 18). Marcus indicates that in a Roman triumph—the celebratory military parade of a victor returning to Rome—a victorious Caesar was saluted by his soldiers, "Hail, Caesar!"[7] In the same way, then, it is fitting that Jesus is acclaimed by soldiers who do not know that they are participating in the counterintuitive celebration of the triumph of God. Because they do not know the wisdom of God, they are unaware that they are greeting the truly triumphant one, who accomplishes a victory in completely upside-down ways.

The soldiers proceed to carry out a mockery of the Roman triumph, clothing Jesus in a purple robe, an expensive color and a symbol of Roman authority.[8] They put on him a crown made of thorns and repeatedly strike him on

---

7. Marcus, *Mark 8–16*, 1046; Moloney, *Gospel of Mark*, 316.
8. Boring, *Mark*, 425.

the head while spitting on him (v. 19), fulfilling once again Jesus's predictions (10:34). They fall before their victim and pay homage to him, and after putting Jesus's own clothes back on him "they led him out to crucify him" (v. 20). In doing so, they continue to participate unwittingly in the accomplishment of God's purposes in bringing Jesus to his position of universal rule.

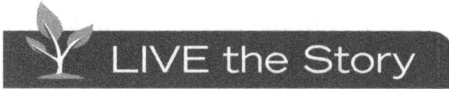

LIVE the Story

Jesus's Silence and the Holy Spirit's Enablement

It is interesting that Jesus does not say much in his trials before the Sanhedrin and before Pilate. When he stands before the high priest and is asked about his identity, Jesus affirms that he is indeed the Messiah—the Christ—and that the high priest "will see the Son of Man sitting at the right hand of the Mighty One and coming on the clouds of heaven" (14:62). And when Pilate asks him if he is the king of the Jews, he merely responds: "You have said so" (15:2). He does not answer the many false accusations brought to the high priest, nor those that the Sanhedrin bring to Pilate. He simply remains silent.

This raises questions in light of what Jesus says to his disciples in his long discourse about the destruction of the coming age, a time when they will be turned over to authorities and put on trial. Jesus had said, "Whenever you are arrested and brought to trial, do not worry beforehand about what to say. Just say whatever is given you at the time, for it is not you speaking, but the Holy Spirit" (13:11). In light of Jesus's silence before his accusers, what sort of divine enablement can believers expect? How is Jesus a model for how we ought to bear witness to the gospel in our day?

This came home to me in a very direct way many years ago when I was a young Christian. I was on a flight from Los Angeles to Chicago and had brought along a magazine. The person seated next to me initiated a conversation, which I regarded at first as a distraction from my reading. I eventually engaged the discussion, and we talked about a number of topics before he asked me what I did. When I told him I was in seminary, he asked me some questions about what that involved, and I sensed that this was the sort of gospel opportunity that I had heard preachers talk about, one that I should not pass up. I thought that perhaps then and there the Holy Spirit would give me words to say, and it would not be me speaking, but God himself. I launched into an explanation of the gospel, the big story of what God is up to in the world, explaining all the particulars as I understood them. At the end of my long discourse that I thought was unusually power-packed, the man sat back, thought for a moment, and said, "Okay." He took out a book he brought with him, and we didn't say another word to each other the entire flight.

I must say that I felt pretty let down after that experience. I pondered the passage in Mark 13 about the Holy Spirit giving us the words to say in moments just like this and wondered why it had no effect. Wasn't something supposed to happen? Did I not just unfold for this man, and for others who heard me, a compelling explanation of the plans of God for humanity? Why then was there no response? Did the Holy Spirit speak through me or not?

I wonder if other Christians have had similar experiences. I wonder whether some have encountered challenges to their faith in a conversation and have felt overwhelmed. Perhaps they have had opportunities to speak a word about the gospel, but failed to come up with the right words at strategic moments, making them feel guilty that they have somehow let God down when it really mattered. How can Jesus before the high priest and Pilate be a model for how Christians should speak in strategic moments?

It is important to note that what Jesus does before the Sanhedrin and Pilate is to claim his true identity. When he is asked who he is, he speaks plainly about himself—nothing more and certainly nothing less. And this is consistent with what disciples are called to do throughout Mark. Jesus calls disciples to be "with him" and do the things he does. And Mark portrays faithfulness to Jesus in terms of owning our identities as Jesus's disciples, *especially our identification with the cross of Christ*. Unfaithfulness, on the other hand, is depicted as being ashamed of Jesus as a Messiah who goes to the cross. This happened to Peter when he rebuked Jesus for speaking about his mission to go to Jerusalem and be killed (8:32–33). Just after this, Jesus said, "If anyone is ashamed of me and my words in this adulterous and sinful generation, the Son of Man will be ashamed of them when he comes in his Father's glory with the holy angels" (v. 38).

We are unfaithful to Jesus, then, when we are overcome, like Peter, by an impulse of self-preservation, with the result that we deny Christ, failing to identify with him in his death, refusing to participate in his cruciform kingdom through service and hospitality to the marginalized. This is the mode of life to which Jesus calls disciples, and it is the manner of life he models. When Jesus plainly owns his identity at his two trials, he is setting the template for how disciples ought to speak.

Further, Jesus says nothing about the Holy Spirit enabling us to provide compelling presentations of the gospel that will unleash divine power and move people to repent of their sins and embrace the kingdom. *He says nothing at all about the effect of our words.* I wonder if our expectations reveal our corrupted imaginations. Why is it that we imagine the Holy Spirit's empowerment to look like a spectacular sermon or an impressive display? We need to learn the strategically important lesson of the ambivalent portrayal of the crowds in Mark. *Mark never portrays huge crowds and overwhelming responses in a positive light.* We ought to be skeptical, therefore, about compelling presentations or when a gospel articulation makes a big splash. Dramatic moments work well in movies, but have no value when it comes to God's kingdom. Jesus says nothing about the effect of our words. He only says that we should not worry about what we will say. We should speak plainly of our identity and of our association with Jesus and the cross. When we do so, it is the Holy Spirit enabling us to do that.

The same dynamic runs through Peter's exhortations in his first letter. I have heard 1 Peter 3:15 used to endorse apologetics enterprises, which is a complete misunderstanding of what Peter is instructing his audiences to do. Some teachers note that Peter uses the Greek term *apologia* for "answer," when he gives the following exhortation:

> But in your hearts revere Christ as Lord. Always be prepared to give an answer [*apologia*] to everyone who asks you to give the reason for the hope that you have. But do this with gentleness and respect, keeping a clear conscience, so that those who speak maliciously against your good behavior in Christ may be ashamed of their slander. (1 Pet 3:15–16)

Such teachers claim that this is an endorsement of the need for Christians to undergo training in providing a rational defense of the Christian faith in the face of various attacks. Such pressure is often compelling to Christian people who simply want to be faithful to God. They may feel that becoming equipped to answer objections to the faith is something to which God calls us.

Peter, however, is speaking largely to slaves and to others who are on the margins of society. His audiences are almost entirely illiterate, and he does not intend for them to undergo training in providing compelling defenses of the Christian faith. The context of this exhortation clearly indicates that he is speaking of situations where Christians are treated badly by others. When they are mistreated while doing good and asked why they are not retaliating, they ought to be prepared to say that they are followers of a Lord who did not retaliate. And because God vindicated Jesus Christ by raising him from the dead, they too will be raised from the dead if they persevere in doing good and resist the temptation to retaliate. *This is the reason for the hope that they have,* and it is the reason that they do not retaliate against those that abuse them.

Peter therefore simply exhorts his audiences to do the same thing that Jesus did: claim their identity as followers of Jesus and do this "with gentleness and respect." Nothing more is required of us.

Christians are not responsible to defend Christianity or the public behavior of other Christians. Unfortunately, the public reputation of many Christians is not all that great. Many high-profile Christian leaders have participated in fomenting the hotly contested cultural climate in the West, creating political and cultural enemies by attacking groups with which they disagree. In addition, some Christian figures have behaved in hypocritical and scandalous ways. When people point these out to us, we might consider the course of plainly acknowledging that this is so and commenting that it is a grievous reality that brings shame to the name of Christ.

When good people who are not Christians are repulsed by such public episodes, they are responding rightly. In fact, in my experience, agreeing with people that such incidents are repugnant opens up rich conversations and often creates good friendships. In the previous chapter of his letter, Peter urges his audiences, "Live such good lives among the pagans that, though they accuse you of doing wrong, they may see your good deeds and glorify God on the day he visits us" (1 Pet 2:12). Like Jesus, we do not have to answer every accusation that comes our way. Doing good in the larger culture and considering how to say less rather than more just might be the evidence of the Holy Spirit's powerful work among us.

The Proverbs are filled with wisdom for how to think about our speech with others. There are times to be silent (Prov 10:19; 12:23; 13:3; 21:23), and times to give consideration about how to answer patiently and graciously (Prov 17:28; 25:15). We do not need to feel the pressure to offer strong defenses or compelling presentations. In the Gospel of Mark, faithful speech before others involves simply owning our identities as people claimed by the cross, remaining loyal to a cruciform Lord who gave his life for the life of his people.

CHAPTER 59

Mark 15:21–47

²¹A certain man from Cyrene, Simon, the father of Alexander and Rufus, was passing by on his way in from the country, and they forced him to carry the cross. ²²They brought Jesus to the place called Golgotha (which means "the place of the skull"). ²³Then they offered him wine mixed with myrrh, but he did not take it. ²⁴And they crucified him. Dividing up his clothes, they cast lots to see what each would get.

²⁵It was nine in the morning when they crucified him. ²⁶The written notice of the charge against him read: THE KING OF THE JEWS.

²⁷They crucified two rebels with him, one on his right and one on his left. ²⁹Those who passed by hurled insults at him, shaking their heads and saying, "So! You who are going to destroy the temple and build it in three days, ³⁰come down from the cross and save yourself!" ³¹In the same way the chief priests and the teachers of the law mocked him among themselves. "He saved others," they said, "but he can't save himself! ³²Let this Messiah, this king of Israel, come down now from the cross, that we may see and believe." Those crucified with him also heaped insults on him.

³³At noon, darkness came over the whole land until three in the afternoon. ³⁴And at three in the afternoon Jesus cried out in a loud voice, "*Eloi, Eloi, lema sabachthani?*" (which means "My God, my God, why have you forsaken me?").

³⁵When some of those standing near heard this, they said, "Listen, he's calling Elijah."

³⁶Someone ran, filled a sponge with wine vinegar, put it on a staff, and offered it to Jesus to drink. "Now leave him alone. Let's see if Elijah comes to take him down," he said.

³⁷With a loud cry, Jesus breathed his last.

³⁸The curtain of the temple was torn in two from top to bottom. ³⁹And

when the centurion, who stood there in front of Jesus, saw how he died, he said, "Surely this man was the Son of God!"

⁴⁰Some women were watching from a distance. Among them were Mary Magdalene, Mary the mother of James the younger and of Joseph, and Salome. ⁴¹In Galilee these women had followed him and cared for his needs. Many other women who had come up with him to Jerusalem were also there.

⁴²It was Preparation Day (that is, the day before the Sabbath). So as evening approached, ⁴³Joseph of Arimathea, a prominent member of the Council, who was himself waiting for the kingdom of God, went boldly to Pilate and asked for Jesus' body. ⁴⁴Pilate was surprised to hear that he was already dead. Summoning the centurion, he asked him if Jesus had already died. ⁴⁵When he learned from the centurion that it was so, he gave the body to Joseph. ⁴⁶So Joseph bought some linen cloth, took down the body, wrapped it in the linen, and placed it in a tomb cut out of rock. Then he rolled a stone against the entrance of the tomb. ⁴⁷Mary Magdalene and Mary the mother of Joseph saw where he was laid.

Listening to the Text in the Story: Exodus 10:21–22; Psalms 22; 38:11; 69:19–21; 109:21–25; Isaiah 53:12; Amos 8:9–10; Wisdom of Solomon 2:17–18.

As Mark narrates the crucifixion of Jesus, he intensifies some of the narrative dynamics on display throughout his Gospel. While the disciples have already fled from Jesus, and he dies alone and completely abandoned, several characters behave like true disciples. Simon from Cyrene is pressed by the Roman soldiers into carrying Jesus's cross. Mark uses the same expression from Jesus's instruction in 8:34: "Whoever wants to be my disciple must deny themselves and take up their cross [*ton stauron autou*] and follow me." Here, Simon was forced "to carry the cross [*ton stauron autou*]" (15:21).

At the close of the passage, Joseph from Arimathea courageously asks Pilate for Jesus's body in order to give it a proper burial (v. 43). Joseph, much like the woman who anointed Jesus's body for burial (14:3–9), carefully took down the body from the cross, wrapped it in linen, and placed it in a tomb (15:46). The woman in Mark 14 is portrayed as the ideal disciple because she fully identified with Jesus in his death, and Joseph courageously does the same here in Mark 15. Throughout the Gospel, Mark has depicted Jesus's twelve disciples as failing to be true disciples, while "outsider" characters repeatedly do the things that the disciples should be doing. This pattern is on display at the open and close of this episode.

This dynamic regarding insiders and outsiders finds its ultimate expression in the confession of the Roman centurion, who "saw how [Jesus] died" and said, "Surely this man was the Son of God!" (v. 39). The disciples repeatedly failed to *see* and *hear* and come to full understanding, and they had abandoned Jesus at his arrest, trial, and death. They had resisted Jesus's teaching about his going to Jerusalem to die (8:32), but the centurion *saw how Jesus died* and confessed the reality of Jesus's identity as the Son of God. He takes his place alongside the many other "outsider" characters who rightly perceive and understand Jesus's identity: the demon-possessed man (5:1–20), Jairus and the woman with the continuous bleeding (5:21–43), the Syrian-Phoenician woman (7:24–30), and the woman who anointed Jesus for burial (14:3–9). The centurion is the climax of this pattern of "outsiders" realizing the truth in that he is the only human character in Mark who identifies Jesus as the Son of God.

Mark also replays here the dynamic of the drift of the disciples away from Jesus. They began well by leaving everything to follow him, yet they abandoned him at his arrest. As Jesus was taken to the Sanhedrin, Peter "followed him at a distance" before eventually denying him in the courtyard of the high priest's house (14:66–72). In the same way, Mark introduces a group of women that had accompanied Jesus to Jerusalem from Galilee. Mark notes that they "had followed him and cared for his needs" throughout his ministry, acting as ideal disciples by following and serving (15:41). Now, however, they "were watching from a distance" (v. 40). This repeated pattern of moving from following Jesus to now watching "from a distance" raises the question of whether they, too, will abandon Jesus, just as everyone else has done.

A final dynamic that Mark recapitulates here is the contrast of perception that leads to confusion and perception that leads to insight and understanding. The mockers *hear* and *see* in vv. 35–36, but they do not understand. The centurion, however, *sees* and comes to a true understanding of Jesus's identity as the Son of God (v. 39). All of this recalls Jesus's words in Mark 4:11–12:

He told them, "The secret of the kingdom of God has been given to you. But to those on the outside everything is said in parables so that,

'they may be ever seeing but never perceiving,
    and ever hearing but never understanding;
otherwise they might turn and be forgiven!'"

Throughout the Gospel, Mark depicts the disciples as in need of a more faithful understanding of Jesus and the character of the kingdom. Jesus's teaching about the cross on the way to Jerusalem opens and closes with the healing of two blind men (8:22–26; 10:46–52). Mark does this, of course, to highlight the disciples' blindness. They are in danger of "ever seeing but never perceiving" and of "ever hearing but never understanding." They, along with Mark's audiences, would do well to call out to Jesus in the words of Bartimaeus, "Rabbi, I want to see" (10:52).

While this episode is filled with drama, Mark narrates the events with simple prose, unadorned and spare. He does not play up the horror of crucifixion by adding grisly details. His narration strikes with rhythmically blunt clarity: "And they crucified him" (v. 24); "it was nine in the morning when they crucified him" (v. 25); "they crucified two rebels with him" (v. 27); "those crucified with him also heaped insults on him" (v. 32).

Crucifixion was an especially gruesome form of death, meant to prolong the agony and torture of those being executed. "Sometimes victims would remain alive for days, with death coming by either loss of blood (due to previous tortures) or asphyxiation."[1] This torturous method of execution was practiced throughout the ancient world, but the Romans used it extensively, especially as a deterrent to those tempted to resist their rule. "This is why the ancients placed crosses along well-traveled highways, on hilltops, and at city gates."[2] Public crucifixions served as billboards advertising the fate of anyone who threatened Rome's rule.[3]

Mark portrays Jesus as the righteous sufferer with images drawn from the Psalms, Isaiah, and the Wisdom of Solomon:

> My God, my God, why have you forsaken me?
>> Why are you so far from saving me,
>> so far from my cries of anguish? (Ps 22:1)

> All who see me mock me;
>> they hurl insults, shaking their heads.
> "He trusts in the LORD," they say,
>> "let the LORD rescue him.
> Let him deliver him,
>> since he delights in him." (vv. 7–8)

---

1. J. Dennis, "Death of Jesus," *DJG* 174.

2. Dennis, "Death of Jesus," 173.

3. Martin Hengel, *Crucifixion in the Ancient World and the Folly of the Message of the Cross* (Philadelphia: Fortress, 1977), 49–50.

All my bones are on display;
　　people stare and gloat over me.
They divide my clothes among them
　　and cast lots for my garment. (vv. 17–18)

You know how I am scorned, disgraced and shamed;
　　all my enemies are before you.
Scorn has broken my heart
　　and has left me helpless;
I looked for sympathy, but there was none,
　　for comforters, but I found none.
They put gall in my food
　　and gave me vinegar for my thirst. (Ps 69:19–21)

Therefore I will give him a portion among the great,
　　and he will divide the spoils with the strong,
because he poured out his life unto death,
　　and was numbered with the transgressors.
For he bore the sin of many,
　　and made intercession for the transgressors. (Isa 53:12)

Let us see if his words are true,
and let us test what will happen at the end of his life;
for if the righteous man is God's child, he will help him,
and will deliver him from the hand of his adversaries.
　　　　(Wis 2:17–18 NRSV)

EXPLAIN the Story

The Roman Soldiers Crucify Jesus (vv. 21–27)

The Roman soldiers drive the action throughout vv. 21–27, as Mark states routinely what "they" do.[4] They force Simon, a man from Cyrene in North Africa, to carry Jesus's cross (v. 21). Mark mentions that Simon is the father of Alexander and Rufus, presumably because either Simon or his sons would be known to some of the early audiences of Mark.[5] Simon had likely traveled

---

4. Moloney, *Gospel of Mark*, 319.
5. Beavis, *Mark*, 227.

to Jerusalem for the festival. As noted above, Mark portrays him as an ideal disciple, one who literally had taken up "his cross." While the cross that Simon carries is not his own, Mark uses the same expression that Jesus does in 8:34 when he states that anyone who wants to be a disciple of his must "take up his cross" (*ton stauron autou*). Here, Simon is forced to "carry his cross" (*ton stauron autou*).

Readers of Mark should not be distracted by the fact that Simon was forced, perhaps against his will, to do this. The awful reality of Roman occupation is that the occupying army could grab anyone and force them to do whatever they wanted. While modern readers might trip over questions about inner motivation, this is not on Mark's radar. His narrative purpose is to portray Simon doing what the disciples should be doing—identifying with Jesus in his death by taking up his cross as their own. Mark portrays this striking episode in order to provoke audiences to reflect on these dynamics.

The soldiers bring Jesus to Golgotha, an Aramaic term that Mark translates as "the place of the skull" (v. 22). This is yet another reminder that Mark did not provide a translation for the name "Barabbas," provoking audiences to again inquire into the meaning and significance of his place in the Gospel (see on 15:6–15).

The soldiers then offer Jesus "wine mixed with myrrh," which is most likely a narcotic meant to prolong suffering. They intend to keep their victim alive for as long as possible to revel in his misery. Jesus is the righteous sufferer, portrayed in terms of Psalm 69:21: "They put gall in my food and gave me vinegar for my thirst." Jesus, however, refuses it (Mark 15:23).

Mark then states, without flourish, what the soldiers did next: "And they crucified him" (v. 24). Because the Romans usually crucified people naked, the soldiers would divide among themselves the victim's belongings.[6] This is yet another detail that alludes to the Psalms: "They divide my clothes among them and cast lots for my garment" (Ps 22:18).

Mark mentions the Romans' crucifixion of Jesus a second time, in similarly stark terms: "It was nine in the morning when they crucified him" (v. 25). Crucifixion was gruesome advertising of what happened to revolutionaries, and the reason for the victim's death was noted by a placard hung around the neck or placed somewhere else on the cross.[7] Mark does not indicate where the sign was placed, but he notes the charge for which Jesus was crucified. It read: "THE KING OF THE JEWS" (v. 26). This partakes of the irony that has been

---

6. Dennis, "Death of Jesus," 174.
7. Dennis, "Death of Jesus," 174.

developing since 12:35–37, in that the way of opposition, betrayal, unjust suffering, and cruel treatment is Jesus's path of coronation. All of this is how Jesus assumes his royal throne as ruler of God's kingdom. And now, put on the inhumane cross by the Roman soldiers, Jesus assumes his kingship in his death. In the completely upside-down, counterintuitive logic of the cross, Jesus portrays publicly how God exercises his ultimate sovereignty.

The Romans crucified "two rebels with him, one on his right and one on his left" (v. 27), which recalls the request that James and John had made to Jesus in 10:35–40. The two disciples had asked to be given prominent places when Jesus came in his glory, with one sitting "at your right and the other at your left" (10:37). Jesus responded by saying that they did not know what they were asking: "Can you drink the cup I drink or be baptized with the baptism I am baptized with?" (v. 38). Jesus will only enter into his glory through suffering and death—enduring the awful torture of the cross, as is now clear. James and John at that point were boastful: "'We can,' they answered" (v. 39). They similarly trumpeted their loyalty to Jesus, along with Peter, in 14:31, insisting that they would never abandon him, even if it meant their death. Of course, at this point in the narrative, they have fled with all the others. Upon repeated hearings of the Gospel, audiences would consider the request of James and John and recall the crucifixion of the two rebels on Jesus's right and left. For these disciples to have a place in the kingdom of God, they must forsake their pursuit of glory and take up the cross, suffering along with Jesus in order to enter his glory with him.

It is ironic that Jesus is crucified along with these two "rebels." The Greek term *lēstēs* does not indicate petty thieves or "robbers," as some translations indicate. As Boring notes, the Romans did not punish thieves with crucifixion, a fate reserved for rebels against their rule. Josephus uses this term to refer to revolutionary figures who attempted to throw off Roman rule through violence.[8] The NIV captures this sense by rendering this term as "rebels." Jesus had taught throughout Mark that he was not this sort of character, but the Romans crucify him as a political threat. Pilate knew that he had done nothing wrong (15:14), but the crowd had rejected him. And now he is crucified among this band of rebels, recalling Isaiah 53:12:

> He poured out his life unto death,
>   and was numbered with the transgressors.
> For he bore the sin of many,
>   and made intercession for the transgressors.

---

8. Boring, *Mark*, 428–29.

The irony, of course, is that Jesus *is* a political figure. He truly is the "King of the Jews," Israel's rightful ruler. His political domain is the kingdom of God, and his crucifixion is his coronation. Jesus's mode of politics is radically unlike anything generated by this world, which tempts people and groups to quest after power in order to dominate others, so that they might determine the course of life for tribes, states, and nations. The politics of Jesus, however, is determined by the cross, and it is embodied by service to the poor and hospitality to the marginalized.

Various Parties Blaspheme and Mock Jesus (vv. 29–32)

The mockery and abuse of Jesus continues in this section, as three groups of people blaspheme and hurl insults at him. First, random passersby "blaspheme" Jesus. The NIV translates the Greek term *blasphēmeō* as "hurled insults," as it can indeed refer to abusive speech aimed at humans or at God.[9] The high priest had accused Jesus of blasphemy (*blasphēmia*) upon hearing Jesus claim to be the Son of Man who would come in power (14:63–64). Early audiences hearing the Gospel read aloud to them in Greek would associate the blasphemy aimed at Jesus with the high priest's claim that Jesus had blasphemed and would understand that it was actually the high priest who was blaspheming. The scene recalls Psalm 22:

> All who see me mock me;
> > they hurl insults, shaking their heads.
> "He trusts in the LORD," they say,
> > "let the LORD rescue him.
> Let him deliver him,
> > since he delights in him." (Ps 22:7–8)

The mockery of the passersby is ironic. They identify Jesus as "you who are going to destroy the temple and build it in three days" (v. 29), referring back to the charge leveled at him before the Sanhedrin (14:57–58). Jesus had indeed rendered God's judgment on the temple in 11:12–12:44. His cursing of the fig tree symbolized his condemnation of that institution, which he then demonstrated by shutting down temple operations (11:12–16). He articulated God's verdict, citing prophetic judgments on the temple: "Is it not written, 'My house will be called a house of prayer for all nations'? But you have made it 'a den of robbers'" (11:17; cf. Isa 56:7; Jer 7:11). Mark had further intimated

---

9. BDAG 178.

that the temple had become an idolatrous institution in 14:58 when he cited the false accusation made against Jesus, calling it "this temple made with human hands."[10]

Ironically, Jesus's death will signal the temple's destruction, bringing God's final judgment on it, though it is not Jesus who is responsible. The guilty parties are those that make up the temple leadership. They have turned it into a site of exploitation and oppression rather than the place where humanity encounters the God of Israel.

The passersby taunt Jesus to "come down from the cross and save" himself (v. 30), which furthers Mark's theme of outsiders completely misunderstanding the sort of Messiah that Jesus is. Audiences of Mark's Gospel will recognize that the passersby's suggested course of action flies in the face of Jesus's mission. Jesus accomplishes God's salvation by dying, so saving himself is out of the question. He did not come to be served but to serve and to give his life as a ransom for many (10:45). And he had called disciples to lose their lives so that they might save them, for anyone seeking to save themselves would only lose their lives in the end (8:35). If Jesus were to come down from the cross and save himself, he would betray his identity as the suffering and dying Son of Man and would also forfeit his ultimate vindication from God, along with entrance into the kingdom in power.

In addition to the passersby, the chief priests and the teachers of the law mock Jesus "among themselves" as they gather to speak abusively about him (v. 31). Their taunts reflect the same spiritual blindness as that of the onlookers. They ironically speak the truth about what Jesus was doing during his ministry when they note that he had "saved others." As the agent of God's reign, Jesus was spreading salvation throughout his ministry as he healed many and exorcised demons. Mark uses the verb *sōzō* ("to save") in several places, which the NIV often translates as "healed" (e.g., 5:23, 28; 6:56; 10:52).[11]

They mock Jesus because while he saved others, "he can't save himself!" (v. 31). Again, they misunderstand Jesus's identity as the suffering Son of Man and his mission of establishing God's reign through his death. His crucifixion is the means whereby he will fully and finally save others, giving his life as "a ransom for many" (10:45). Because of his faithfulness, God will vindicate him by raising him from the dead.

In their dismissive mockery, they ironically acknowledge Jesus for who he is, the "Messiah," the "king of Israel." They call for him to "come down

---

10. In Old Testament contexts, the expression "made with hands" is used to speak of idols. See comments on 14:58.

11. Moloney, *Gospel of Mark*, 323.

now from the cross, that we may see and believe" (v. 32). In their blindness, they do not realize that his death on the cross is precisely how Jesus enters into his reign as the "king of Israel," initiating God's kingdom. Their demand represents the same error as that of the Pharisees in 8:10–12, when they "asked him for a sign from heaven" (v. 11). Jesus had refused to provide them with a sign in that conversation, since in Mark's Gospel genuine faith is "the *condition* of restoration, not its outcome."[12] Their demand signals hardened rejection rather than an openness to considering Jesus's identity.

The rebels crucified alongside Jesus "also heaped insults on him," which is extraordinary (v. 32). This detail indicates once again that Jesus is not one of them. He is not a revolutionary seeking liberation from Rome through violence, even though he is crucified as a political threat. This is yet one further note that Jesus dies utterly alone, completely abandoned and rejected by everyone, even those suffering the same torturous death.

The Death of Jesus and God's Eschatological Judgment (vv. 33–39)

The account of the death of Jesus is bracketed by two signs of God's eschatological judgment "over the whole land" (v. 33) and on the temple (v. 38). These two signs form an *inclusio*, within which Mark brings to the fore once again his theme of perception accompanied by misunderstanding.[13] In the previous section, Mark had noted the misunderstanding of the passersby and the members of the Sanhedrin who had blasphemed and mocked Jesus. Mark foregrounds this dynamic once again, including verbs for perception accompanied by misunderstanding.

> Sign of eschatological judgment (darkness) (v. 33)
> > Jesus's loud cry (v. 34)
> > > Hearing and misunderstanding (v. 35)
> > > Seeing and misunderstanding (v. 36)
> > Jesus's loud cry (v. 37)
> Sign of eschatological judgment (temple curtain torn) (v. 38)

Mark notes that at noon, "darkness came over the whole land until three in the afternoon," at which point Jesus died (vv. 33, 37). The darkness, then, signals a crescendo of judgment, since it lasts for the three hours leading up to Jesus's death, at which point the temple curtain is torn in two. This is the

---

12. Black, *Mark*, 326.
13. Gray, *Temple in the Gospel of Mark*, 184–85.

climax of judgment, which gathers and stands over the whole of Israel, but lands with a crash on the temple and the temple leadership.

The darkness covering the whole land for three hours recalls the plague of darkness that had covered Egypt for three days in Exodus 10:21–22:

> Then the LORD said to Moses, "Stretch out your hand toward the sky so that darkness spreads over Egypt—darkness that can be felt." So Moses stretched out his hand toward the sky, and total darkness covered all Egypt for three days.

This sign of judgment also alludes to God's declaration of destruction against the temple in Amos 8:9, when darkness would again cover the land during the noon hour:

> "In that day," declares the Sovereign LORD,
>
> > "I will make the sun go down at noon
> > and darken the earth in broad daylight."

The darkness does not occur at Jesus's death but rather concludes when he dies, and that is when the temple curtain is torn.[14] The death of Jesus, then, is God's accomplishment of salvation for his people, but it is also God's judgment on Israel—specifically the temple and its leadership.

At three in the afternoon, "Jesus cried out in a loud voice, '*Eloi, Eloi, lema sabachthani?*'" (v. 34). Mark translates this anguished cry from Aramaic: "My God, my God, why have you forsaken me?" Jesus has been abandoned by his disciples and dies utterly alone. On the cross, he is the focal point of the turning of the ages, bearing eschatological judgment and accomplishing salvation for God's people. He utters the awful cry of the psalmist from the opening lines of Psalm 22:

> My God, my God, why have you forsaken me?
> > Why are you so far from saving me,
> > so far from my cries of anguish?
> My God, I cry out by day, but you do not answer,
> > by night, but I find no rest. (vv. 1–2)

---

14. Boring, *Mark*, 429.

Jesus's words dignify for all time the agonized laments uttered by God's people who feel forsaken by God, *as he becomes the God-forsaken one.* But God is not absent from the scene, as he will demonstrate in the tearing of the temple curtain (v. 38).

Mark now focuses on the misunderstanding of those who hear Jesus's anguished cry. Some bystanders thought he was crying for Elijah, mishearing Jesus's "*Eloi*" and thinking he was calling for Elijah, which sounds similar in Aramaic. Mark repeats two terms for auditory perception: when they "heard" his cry, "they said, 'Listen, he's calling Elijah.'" As had happened earlier with the offer to Jesus of wine mixed with myrrh (v. 32), someone ran to get a sponge filled with wine vinegar to again offer it to him (v. 36). This is likely for narcotic purposes, and it is not done out of mercy. Because of the wider context of mockery and mistreatment, it is best to understand this as an attempt on the part of the soldiers to prolong Jesus's suffering.

Mark notes again the misunderstanding on the part of those witnessing Jesus on the cross: "Let's *see* if Elijah comes to take him down." The cross, however, has been Jesus's destination throughout Mark, and he is accomplishing God's work of salvation and judgment by dying. The *hearing* and *seeing* that takes place while Jesus is on the cross partakes of Mark's larger narrative purposes. Jesus's identity, teaching, and ministry are utterly countercultural, demonstrating the counterintuitive nature of the kingdom. He had said that for those who possessed the "secret of the kingdom," they would *see* and *hear* and increase in their understanding (4:11, 24–25). But those outside the kingdom would *see* and *hear* and only increase in misperception:

> They may be ever seeing but never perceiving,
> and ever hearing but never understanding;
> otherwise they might turn and be forgiven! (4:12)

This has happened throughout the Gospel to the disciples, as they have had front-row seats to all that Jesus said and did, yet their hearts were hardened. On the other hand, Mark portrays "outsider" characters as routinely demonstrating kingdom-oriented hearts by their ability to see and hear of Jesus and respond rightly to him. Here, this dynamic comes to full expression, with people witnessing God's climactic revelation of Jesus as the exalted cruciform king, but failing to understand what they hear and see.

Mark expresses the death of Jesus, again, without flourish: "With a loud cry, Jesus breathed his last" (v. 37). At just that moment, "the curtain of the temple was torn in two from top to bottom" (v. 38). The passive verb points to God as the actor. This tearing provides an *inclusio* to Mark's Gospel. At the very beginning of the Gospel of Mark, God had "torn open" (*schizō*) heaven to declare his delight in Jesus at his baptism: "You are my Son, whom I love; with you I am well pleased" (1:10–11). Here, God once again dramatically enters the drama with another tearing (*schizō*), but this time in judgment on the temple. Jesus felt utterly abandoned, but God was not absent. His Son, God's authorized agent of kingdom rule, has been rejected by his people, and God in turn passes judgment.

According to Gray, the curtain to which Mark refers is the one that protects the Holy of Holies, into which only the high priest could enter. The curtain was embroidered with stars and constellations, representing the heavens and reflecting the reality that in Scripture and Jewish tradition, the temple was a microcosm of the cosmos.[15] The tearing of the temple curtain, then, is God's judgment not only on the temple and its leadership but on a corrupted cosmos that is enslaved under the bondage of Satan and the powers of this present evil age. The death of Jesus signals the destruction of this age and the inauguration of the new creation. The cross of Christ is "the turning point of the ages."[16]

In a Gospel full of surprises and subversions, Mark has yet another one up his sleeve, and this is the culmination of the dynamic of "outsider" characters perceiving Jesus and responding rightly to him. The centurion who had "stood there in front of Jesus, *saw* how he died," and makes the ultimate confession of faith: "Surely this man was the Son of God!" (v. 39). Mark sets forth this consummate outsider character as the most strategic insider, even though he was part of the group that had tortured and mocked Jesus and had put him to death. He *saw how Jesus died*—abandoned and alone, having suffered at the hands of others, rejected by his followers and his own people, shamed and stripped bare, utterly humiliated. Seeing all of this, the centurion makes the ultimate confession of faith, identifying Jesus as the Son of God, the only human character in Mark's Gospel to do so.[17]

---

15. Gray, *Temple in the Gospel of Mark*, 189–91.

16. Moloney, *Gospel of Mark*, 328. It is inappropriate to understand the tearing of the curtain as somehow symbolizing the way being open to God now that Jesus has died. That is an imposition on this text of a theological construct that does not belong. Throughout Mark, the temple, meant to be the place where humanity encountered God, had become corrupt and stood in need of being destroyed and replaced by God's authorized agent of God's rule. Jesus is the new temple, and being gathered to Jesus is how humanity encounters God.

17. Mark introduces Jesus as the Son of God at the beginning of the Gospel (1:1), and God identifies Jesus as his own Son in 1:11 and 9:7. Demons recognize Jesus as the Son of God in 3:11 and 5:7, and the chief priest, in order to set Jesus up, asks him, "Are you the Messiah, the Son of the Blessed One?" (14:61). Jesus then affirms his identity in v. 62. The centurion, then, is the only character besides God, Jesus, and the demons to recognize and confess the reality of Jesus's identity as God's Son.

For Mark, this is true faith: to see Jesus entering his reign through his death and to identify him as the Son of God. Peter had rebuked Jesus when he spoke about the cross. The disciples had argued about prominence when Jesus spoke about the cross. And everyone abandoned him when he was on his way to the cross. Now the centurion stands before him and takes in all that has transpired, and he says about Jesus what God had said about him at his baptism and transfiguration: he is the Son of God.

Mark situates this confession of faith immediately after God's ultimate judgment on the temple in Jerusalem. That institution had become idolatrous, and the temple authorities had corrupted it, so that rather than being "a house of prayer for all nations" it had become a "den of robbers" (11:17). The transition is now complete. The temple in Jerusalem no longer houses the God of Israel. Jesus is God's new temple, gathering a family of worshipers from all nations, symbolized here by the Roman centurion.[18]

Women Followers of Jesus (vv. 40–41)

For the first time in his Gospel, Mark identifies the other followers of Jesus. He had intimated earlier that there were more followers than just the Twelve. When they had taken a boat to the other side of the Sea of Galilee, "there were also other boats with him" (4:36). And John had remarked to Jesus that the disciples had seen "someone driving out demons in your name and we told him to stop, because he was not one of us" (9:38). Jesus urged the disciples to leave them be, "for whoever is not against us is for us" (9:40). Now we discover that some women had accompanied Jesus ever since his time in Galilee (15:41). And they had been acting as true disciples, *following him* and *serving him* by caring for his needs. And there were "many other women" who also were disciples, since they had been "with him" on the way to Jerusalem. These are in addition to the women Mark names: "Mary Magdelene, Mary the mother of James the younger and of Joseph, and Salome (v. 40).

But there is an ominous dynamic here. The women "were watching from a distance" (v. 40). Mark hints that their "watching" may not be the kind of perception that is commendable. Edwards notes that Mark uses a term for their watching in vv. 40 and 47 (*theōreō*) that he uses elsewhere of mere observation and not of true perception that leads to understanding (3:11; 5:15, 38; 12:41).[19] It is indeed remarkable that the women are there, for they are more faithful than the Twelve, who have long since abandoned Jesus out

---

18. Garland, *Theology of Mark's Gospel*, 176; Gray, *Temple in the Gospel of Mark*, 194–96.
19. Edwards, *Mark*, 485.

of self-preservation. At the same time, Mark indicates a threatening scenario in which the "dynamics of drift" away from Jesus that overtook the disciples may be at work here among the women. Jesus appointed the disciples to be "with him" (3:14), and they did indeed follow him to Jerusalem. But after they fled, Peter followed "at a distance" (*apo makrothen*, 14:54), before ultimately denying Jesus. Now the women watch "from a distance" (*apo makrothen*, 15:40). Will they also ultimately abandon him? Mark doesn't say, but rather leaves his audiences to inquire into what is happening. This will be important to keep in mind at the close of Mark's Gospel, when the women fail to say anything to anyone out of fear (16:8).

Joseph of Arimathea Buries Jesus (vv. 42–47)

Mark notes that it was "Preparation Day," the day before the Sabbath (v. 42). The Sabbath was a day when no work was to be done. If Jesus's body was left on the cross at sundown, the start of the Jewish Sabbath, it would have to remain there throughout the following day, fully exposed to being picked apart by scavenger birds. To prevent this from happening, a man named Joseph of Arimathea gives Jesus a proper burial.

Mark portrays Joseph as an ideal disciple who, like the woman who anointed Jesus for burial, performs a beautiful service to Jesus. He was "a prominent member of the Council," which can only mean that he was part of the Sanhedrin (v. 42).[20] Joseph takes his place alongside other characters who do not behave like the group to which they belong. Jesus warns against the scribes in 12:38–40, for they exploit widows for economic gain. But there is one scribe who engages in honest conversation with Jesus (12:28–34), and Jesus says that he is "not far from the kingdom of God" (v. 34). And while the whole company of Roman soldiers mocks and abuses Jesus (15:16–20), one Roman centurion confesses that Jesus truly was the Son of God (15:39).

In the same way, Joseph is a member of the Sanhedrin, and even though "the whole Sanhedrin" (15:1) had schemed to manipulate Pilate and the crowd to have Jesus put to death, here is one character who behaves against the grain of the evil orientation of the larger group. Mark notes that Joseph "was himself waiting for the kingdom of God" (v. 43). What Joseph does next manifests his recognition that in the crucified Jesus, God has initiated his reign. He "went boldly to Pilate and asked for Jesus' body," recalling both the meal at which the woman anointed Jesus and the meal that Jesus ate afterward with his disciples. When the woman

---

20. Mark does not explicitly indicate that this "Council" is the Sanhedrin, but Moloney points out that in 15:1 the term for the Sanhedrin's holding council is *symboulion*, which shares the same root for the term used here for "Council" (*bouleutēs*; Moloney, *Gospel of Mark*, 333).

interrupted the meal at Simon the Leper's house and performed her "beautiful" act (14:6), Jesus noted that she was preparing his "body" (*sōma*) for burial (v. 8). And at the supper with his disciples, Jesus offered to them bread and told them, "Take it; this is my body [*sōma*]" (v. 22). When Joseph courageously went to Pilate, therefore, and "asked for Jesus' body [*sōma*]," it is as if he is requesting to partake of Jesus's meal so that he might fully identify with him. Joseph associates himself with Jesus in his death so that he might have life. Unlike the Twelve who fled out of self-preservation, Joseph risks his life and reputation to identify with Jesus's body. Like a true disciple, he "loses" his life, letting go of self-preservation, so that he might inhabit the kingdom of God (8:35).

Pilate is surprised that Jesus has already died, for victims of crucifixion could often survive for much longer, even days. He learns from the centurion, however, that Jesus has in fact died (15:44–45). In a stunning irony, Pilate grants Joseph his request, doing to Joseph what Jesus had done to the Twelve at his final meal with them. Just as Jesus broke bread and "gave it to his disciples," saying, "This is my body" (14:22), Pilate, ironically standing in for Jesus, "gave the body to Joseph" (15:45).

Like the woman who anointed Jesus at great personal cost, Joseph purchased some linen cloth in order to prepare Jesus's body for burial. Mark then expresses what Joseph did in the same cadence as when Jesus distributed the bread and cup to his disciples.

> While they were eating, Jesus took bread, and when he had given thanks, he broke it and gave it to his disciples, saying, "Take it; this is my body."
>
> Then he took a cup, and when he had given thanks, he gave it to them, and they all drank from it. (14:22–23)

Similarly, Joseph "took down the body, wrapped it in the linen, and placed it in a tomb cut out of rock. Then he rolled a stone against the entrance of the tomb" (15:46). Like Simon from Cyrene at the opening of this episode who carried Jesus's cross, Joseph is an ideal disciple. Simon had identified with Jesus in his death, and Joseph does the same.

LIVE the Story

The God-Forsaken God and Lament

I have found that many Christians in the West have a difficult time with lament. American Christianity, the culture with which I am most familiar, is oriented by positivity. We like encouragement and uplifting messages and pep talks. We typically regard lament and complaint as things to avoid, perhaps a sign that someone is not as thankful as they ought to be. Closely tied to this is the desire to make God look good. Because we are God's people and believe that God is king over his creation, we feel that we ought to cultivate a positive outlook and a grateful disposition. After all, the things that happen to us are all orchestrated by God, aren't they? And if we are ungrateful or if we complain or question God, then we run the risk of indicating that God has somehow made a mistake or that we feel that he has gotten something terribly wrong.

This avoidance of the biblical tradition of lament springs from a lack of deep engagement with the rich narrative of Scripture. I say this because it fails to account for the true condition of the world. As I have indicated in a previous reflection on Mark 14:32–52, we do indeed inhabit God's good world, but his world is in a terribly tragic condition. God's cosmic enemies have hijacked God's good creation, so that currently it is cosmically enslaved space. In the death and resurrection of Jesus Christ, God has powerfully broken the enslaving grip of sin and death, along with Satan and the powers of evil. But this creation is not yet fully redeemed and restored. Our experience of life in this world is "both/and" and not "either/or." While this is God's good world, we still experience tragedy, suffering, and pain, even feeling at times like God is absent. We will all endure times of feeling, like Jesus, abandoned by God.

Jesus's cry from the cross, citing Psalm 22:1 ("My God, my God, why have you forsaken me?"), is powerful for precisely this reason. Jesus was experiencing God's world in a manner that was not at all consistent with God's original intentions. According to God's creational purposes, when the creator shows up to his creation he is supposed to be received warmly and welcomed with celebration. But Jesus is abandoned by his followers, betrayed by one of his friends, beaten and mocked, and put to death. The profound reality of Jesus's cry from the cross is that God does not merely have a silver lining for those who feel abandoned by God. Rather, Jesus himself knows precisely what it is like to be abandoned by God. And because Jesus is God himself, the wonder of the Christian faith is that *God himself becomes the God-abandoned one*. God fully leans into the awful reality of experiencing creation as "God-less."

Jesus demonstrates that the appropriate response to such an experience is lament. Lament in Scripture is complaining to God skillfully about the awful current condition of God's world. Lament is driven by the conviction that the God of Christian Scripture is actually the creator of all things and that he will indeed come to save and renew his creation. Lament is the manifestation of impatience that God's world is in pain, that God's creation suffers, and that God has not yet acted to relieve this suffering and fully heal his world. Lament is speaking truthfully about the broken and messed-up condition of the world, calling out to God to vindicate himself as creator and to manifest his rule over creation by ridding it of evil.

There is a rich tradition of lament in Scripture. Along with Psalm 22, there are numerous psalms of lament in which the righteous cry out and complain to God (e.g., Pss 43, 44, 55, 88). In places, these laments strike modern readers as extremely rude and nearly blasphemous:

> Awake, Lord! Why do you sleep?
>   Rouse yourself! Do not reject us forever.
> Why do you hide your face
>   and forget our misery and oppression?
> We are brought down to the dust;
>   our bodies cling to the ground.
> Rise up and help us;
>   rescue us because of your unfailing love. (Ps 44:23–26)

Many Christians would resist ever accusing God of sleeping and hiding his face, or that he has forgotten our "misery and oppression." At the same time, many psalms of lament contain strong confessions of faith in God's unfailing love, that he is the only source of hope.

At least one psalm, however, is an unrelenting complaint that ends without any hint of hope:

> But I cry to you for help, LORD;
>   in the morning my prayer comes before you.
> Why, LORD, do you reject me
>   and hide your face from me?
> From my youth I have suffered and been close to death;
>   I have borne your terrors and am in despair.
> Your wrath has swept over me;
>   your terrors have destroyed me.
> All day long they surround me like a flood;
>   they have completely engulfed me.
> You have taken from me friend and neighbor—
>   darkness is my closest friend. (Ps 88:13–18)

Just imagine attending a prayer gathering and listening to a person who is going through an intense time of suffering, lamenting and crying out with these words, ending with "darkness is my closest friend." Would such a person be rebuked for questioning God? Or for being such a downer?

Beyond the Psalms, there is an entire book of the Bible devoted to the expression of grief: Lamentations. And this is not just an Old Testament thing. John 11 narrates the emotionally intense experience of two of Jesus's closest friends, Mary and Martha, whose sick brother, Lazarus, had died. They had sent word to Jesus: "Lord, the one you love is sick" (v. 3). Jesus had delayed his journey to Bethany, and in the meantime Lazarus had died. When he finally arrived, both Mary and Martha greeted him with the same words of lament and complaint: ""Lord, if you had been here, my brother would not have died" (vv. 21, 32). Jesus did not reprove them for doing this but rather entered into their shared grief:

> When Jesus saw her weeping, and the Jews who had come along with her also weeping, he was deeply moved in spirit and troubled. "Where have you laid him?" he asked.
>
> "Come and see, Lord," they replied.
>
> Jesus wept. (vv. 33–35)

In the reflection on Mark 14:32–52, we considered the groanings of the Spirit and of Jesus himself, as they share in the longings of creation for restoration as it bears the weight of brokenness. Moreover, lament will not end with death. The vision of the souls of the martyrs under the heavenly throne indicate that even after death, when God's people are "with the Lord" awaiting resurrection, we will yearn with eager anticipation for God to set all things right:

> When he opened the fifth seal, I saw under the altar the souls of those who had been slain because of the word of God and the testimony they had maintained. They called out in a loud voice, "How long, Sovereign Lord, holy and true, until you judge the inhabitants of the earth and avenge our blood?" Then each of them was given a white robe, and they were told to wait a little longer, until the full number of their fellow servants, their brothers and sisters, were killed just as they had been. (Rev 6:9–11)

When we consider Jesus's words of lament and complaint on the cross, crying out to God and expressing his sense of God-forsakenness, we can see that this is not an anomaly. Jesus is dignifying for all time the cry of God's people who sojourn through this world of pain and suffering and at times feel abandoned by God.

Being Christian involves living in God's world truly and authentically according to its actual condition. Currently it is broken and hijacked by evil forces, and though God has won the victory in Christ, creation is not fully redeemed. Our present experience of this world is not what we were made for. God knows it. So when we lament, we are joining with God, speaking with God, speaking according to God, and joining with God's faithful throughout the ages who have spoken truthfully about the condition of the cosmos. Indeed, Christians do celebrate that we enjoy the blessings of living in God's good world. But we also grieve that it is broken, and this fires our hopes and prayers for the day when the Son of Man returns to make all things new.

When we were part of a church set within a neighborhood ravaged by poverty, we would often devote our weekly gathering to prayer. During certain seasons, we would offer praise and thanksgiving, but we also devoted times to lament. Below is an excerpt that includes a psalm of lament and a prayer that expressed the grief of our experiences:

Psalm 13

How long, LORD? Will you forget me forever?
How long will you hide your face from me?
How long must I wrestle with my thoughts
and day after day have sorrow in my heart?
How long will my enemy triumph over me?
Look on me and answer, LORD my God.
Give light to my eyes, or I will sleep in death,
and my enemy will say, "I have overcome him,"
and my foes will rejoice when I fall.
But I trust in your unfailing love;
my heart rejoices in your salvation.
I will sing the LORD's praise,
for he has been good to me.

A Prayer

Father, we hate that your world is broken,
and we confess that we are broken, too.
Our hearts break at the brokenness of this neighborhood,
and at our own inadequacy to fix any of it.
How long, O Lord, will you let your people suffer,
and let those created in your image bear long with poverty,
fear, rejection, abuse, imprisonment, addiction, relentless sorrow?
Come and save; come and restore;
heal our hearts; without you we are completely lost.

CHAPTER 60

Mark 16:1-8

📖 LISTEN to the Story

¹When the Sabbath was over, Mary Magdalene, Mary the mother of James, and Salome bought spices so that they might go to anoint Jesus' body. ²Very early on the first day of the week, just after sunrise, they were on their way to the tomb ³and they asked each other, "Who will roll the stone away from the entrance of the tomb?"

⁴But when they looked up, they saw that the stone, which was very large, had been rolled away. ⁵As they entered the tomb, they saw a young man dressed in a white robe sitting on the right side, and they were alarmed.

⁶"Don't be alarmed," he said. "You are looking for Jesus the Nazarene, who was crucified. He has risen! He is not here. See the place where they laid him. ⁷But go, tell his disciples and Peter, 'He is going ahead of you into Galilee. There you will see him, just as he told you.'"

⁸Trembling and bewildered, the women went out and fled from the tomb. They said nothing to anyone, because they were afraid.

Listening to the Text in the Story: Exodus 34:2; Psalm 30:5; Daniel 6:17–20; Hosea 6:2; Malachi 4:2; Romans 1:4; 1 Corinthians 15; Revelation 21–22.

Mark's Gospel concludes with a focus on the recently introduced women (15:40–41). They had been "following" Jesus and "serving" him since his ministry in Galilee and had been "with him" also in Jerusalem. All of these are descriptions of what disciples do, according to Mark. While the appointed Twelve had drifted away and finally fled, these women are still attending to Jesus. But Mark had already inserted an ominous sign in 15:40, noting that the women were "watching from a distance." A dynamic of drift and desertion had overtaken the Twelve: they had originally been "with" Jesus

559

(3:14) and had left everything to follow him (10:28). But they had all fled, with Peter following "at a distance" (14:54) before he ultimately denied that he knew Jesus (14:66–72). With his portrayal of the women as "watching from a distance," Mark hints that this same dynamic of drift and desertion is at work among them, too, prompting audiences to wonder whether it ultimately will overtake them.

For church audiences that are familiar with versions of the gospel story, Mark's ending is highly subversive. Until v. 8, everything unfolds according to expectation: early in the morning the women show up to the tomb in which Joseph had laid Jesus and are stunned to find it empty. A young man exhorts the women not to be afraid, for Jesus has been raised and is no longer in his grave! He is alive and has gone ahead to meet the disciples in Galilee, just as he had promised! To this point, everything is going according to the wonderful and glorious plan, and triumphant choruses seem to be swelling in the background.

But all of this comes to a screeching halt with v. 8, which could be translated as follows: "And going out of it they fled from the tomb, for trembling and amazement had seized them; and they said nothing to no one; because they were afraid."

The end.

That's it? What kind of an ending is that? That's no way to end a Gospel at all! Mark's ending is a real head-scratcher, leaving audiences feeling completely unsettled, and this is likely his intent.[1]

What response does Mark want to elicit from his audiences? Rather than providing a conclusion that relieves tension and brings resolution, Mark is far more interested in provoking readers and hearers to continued reflection on his Gospel narrative. Just as he has done throughout his Gospel, he challenges audiences to probe more intensely into the character of Jesus and the nature of the kingdom he inaugurates, in order to make sure they truly understand.

EXPLAIN the Story

The Women Go to Anoint Jesus's Body (vv. 1–3)

As the sun was coming up on the third day after Jesus had been crucified, Mary Magdalene, Mary the mother of James, and Salome set out for Jesus's tomb (v. 1). Mark creates a growing sense of expectation by narrating the details of

---

1. See the appendix for a discussion of Mark's ending and various longer, alternative endings.

the dawning of a new day: "When the Sabbath was over" points to sunrise, which from a Jewish perspective is the end of the previous day (v. 1). Mark makes this explicit in v. 2: "Very early on the first day of the week, just after sunrise."[2] The women take off in the dark, and the action takes place as the sun is coming up. And just as it is rising, the light is breaking on what God has brought about with the raising of his Son.

The women, however, are not there with any sense of wonder-filled expectation. They have brought spices to anoint Jesus's body, which means they fully expect him to still be dead when they arrive. Their spices are not for the purposes of preservation through embalming but rather to cover the smell as the body decayed, after which the bones would be gathered and kept in a box.[3]

The women ask themselves, "Who will roll the stone away from the entrance of the tomb?" (v. 3). They were there when Joseph had buried Jesus and had seen that he had rolled a stone against the entrance (15:46–47). Their question indicates that they are still expecting Jesus to be in the tomb, still buried and dead. They are acting out of devotion to and love for Jesus, aiming to care for him even in his death. Yet while they are well-motivated, *their imaginations are limited by the horizons of this present age.* They have been with Jesus all this time in Galilee and Jerusalem, listening to the same predictions of his death and resurrection that the disciples had heard (8:31; 9:31; 10:34; cf. 14:58; 15:29). Why, then, do they expect him to be in the tomb?

This impresses upon audiences of Mark the sobering reality that it is possible to follow Jesus for an extended period, to hear his teaching and his predictions and even to be well-motivated, *but still to be mired in misunderstanding.* Their question also creates an expectation of the need for someone to act. They are not merely asking a factual question regarding a stone but expressing despair and helplessness regarding the massive obstacle they face: "Who will be there to help us with this impossible task?"[4]

The Women Encounter a Young Man (vv. 4–7)

Mark continues to focus on the women, narrating their perception of the events. They had come to the tomb well-motivated to do something loving and respectful for Jesus, but they did not have any expectation of God having acted. They were concerned, understandably, with the obstacle they would face—the stone, "which was very large" (v. 4). But they are about to encounter

---

2. Moloney, *Gospel of Mark*, 343.
3. Edwards, *Mark*, 491.
4. Marcus, *Mark 8–16*, 1079–80.

the action of God: they are about to *see* that what Jesus had predicted has already happened.

The first thing they see is that God has taken care of the biggest obstacle that they had imagined. "When they looked up, they saw that the stone, which was very large, had been rolled away" (v. 4). The appearance of the Greek verb for "when they looked up" (*anablepō*) recalls the two times that Jesus raised his eyes to heaven just before performing miracles in 6:41 and 7:34. Mark's description here fuels the expectation of something miraculous.[5] Having raised their eyes, they "saw" the result of God having already miraculously acted. And they are about to behold even more of God's cosmically transformative work.

When the women entered the tomb, they "saw a young man dressed in a white robe sitting on the right side" of the tomb (v. 5). This is clearly an angelic figure, since a heavenly messenger could appear as a "young man" (cf. 2 Macc 3:26, 33). Further, the encounter unfolds according to the pattern of biblical angelophanies (angelic appearances), with human fright followed by an exhortation not to be afraid, along with further revelation (e.g., Gen 21:17).[6] Why, then, does Mark refer to this figure as a "young man" rather than an angel? Mark uses this device to give the episode some background strokes of redemptive reversal, emphasizing the depiction of God's dramatic act of vindicating the crucified Jesus by raising him from the dead. This becomes evident when we consider the young man in contrast to the earlier appearance of the young man who fled when Jesus was arrested (14:51–52). Mark uses the same term for "young man" (*neaniskos*) in both texts, and in each episode Mark indicates what the young men are "clothed with" (*periballō*). The terms for their clothing are different, however. In 14:51, the young man has on a "linen garment" (*sindōn*), while here the young man wears a "white robe" (*stolē leukē*). But the similarities certainly grab an audience's attention, and this is just the effect Mark intends: one young man had fled, while another announces Jesus's resurrection. While the two figures are not the same, Mark subtly introduces a dynamic of redemptive reversal that is at work now that God has acted powerfully in Jesus.[7]

Upon encountering all of this, the women are terrified (v. 5). One of several words for amazement Mark uses throughout his Gospel is the verb *thambeō* (1:27; 10:24, 32). Here, Mark adds the prefix *ek-* as if to indicate that the women are "amazed out of themselves."[8] Using the same verb, the young man

---

5. Marcus, *Mark 8–16*, 1084.
6. Edwards, *Mark*, 493; Boring, *Mark*, 445.
7. Moloney, *Gospel of Mark*, 345.
8. Moloney, *Gospel of Mark*, 344.

exhorts the women to get hold of themselves: "Don't be alarmed" (*ekthambeō*, v. 6). Such an exhortation is typical in angelophanies, but here it has special force, since throughout Mark's Gospel reactions of amazement are often the opposite of faith, indicating that characters are moving toward unbelief and hard-heartedness (e.g., 6:51–52). The women need to keep their senses and take careful note of what God has accomplished in raising Jesus from the dead. It is understandable that they are blown away, but this is a crucial moment to focus on what has happened and on the realities of the kingdom of God.

When the young man identifies what the women are doing, he reveals yet another ominous sign: they are seeking (*zēteō*, NIV, "looking for") Jesus the Nazarene. In one sense, their "seeking" is well-motivated, for they want to care for Jesus's body and honor him in his death. But *zēteō* is only used negatively in Mark. It appears when the disciples seek after Jesus, but turn out to be obstacles to him praying (1:37). It is used when his family wants to take him home because they think he is out of his mind (3:32). And it appears when Jesus's opponents are seeking to arrest and kill him (11:18; 12:12).[9] What the women are doing, then, is driven by "merely human concerns" rather than "the concerns of God" (cf. 8:33). They have heard Jesus predict his death and also his resurrection, but their intention to anoint his body indicates that they do not expect the miraculous power of the kingdom to break forth and for God to raise Jesus from the dead. Just as others who sought Jesus were dealing with him as a "this-worldly" figure, the women cannot see beyond the limited horizons of human imagination.

The women ought not to be alarmed, according to the young man, because God has raised the crucified one from the dead. Mark uses the expression "[the one] who was crucified" as something of a title for Jesus. The Greek expression *ton estaurōmenon* (lit. "the one who was crucified") is set next to *ēgerthē* ("he has been raised"), so that we encounter a tightly formulated Christian confession here at the close of Mark. As Marcus notes, because of the tense of this Greek verb, it can indicate an action that has only just occurred: "The crucified one has just been raised!"[10]

With two more expressions, the young man attempts to impress upon the women the reality of what has happened, and he does this in terms of visual perception. He states bluntly that "he is not here," and then with an imperative verb (*ide*) he exhorts them: "See the place where they laid him."[11] It is as if he

9. Edwards, *Mark*, 494.
10. Marcus, *Mark 8–16*, 1080.
11. The young man's exhortation should be punctuated as follows: "Look! The place where they laid him." The term "place" (*ho topos*) is nominative in Greek, which means it is not receiving the

is saying, "Open your eyes! Take in and process what is going on here! You saw Joseph bury Jesus in this very place. Do you see him here? No, because God has raised him!" His exhortations draw on the dynamic that Mark has developed throughout his Gospel regarding the necessity of *hearing* and *seeing* and moving toward understanding and sustained discipleship. The women behold the evidence of the reality-transforming work of God, and the young man calls on them to process it faithfully—*to see it for what it really is.*[12]

The young man gives the women two more commands, exhorting them to "go" and to "tell his disciples and Peter" (v. 7). Jesus claims the disciples as his own and never rejects them, even though they routinely misunderstood him and had finally abandoned him. They remain "his disciples." The expression "and Peter" (*kai tō Petrō*) may also be translated "*even* Peter," as if to emphasize that Peter's thrice-repeated denial has not canceled Jesus's claim on him. They continue to belong to him, even Peter. This is a powerful note of grace.

The young man tells the women to relay a specific message: "He is going ahead of you into Galilee. There you will see him, just as he told you" (v. 7). When he shared the final supper with them, Jesus had predicted that they would all fall away, but that "after I have risen, I will go ahead of you into Galilee" (14:28). There will be a reunion with Jesus in the place where he had originally called them to himself. This is the promise of a new start, an opportunity to refresh and renew their discipleship to Jesus. It will be a new chance to *listen, look,* and move toward understanding, so that they might carry out their discipleship with special attention to the cross-shaped character of Jesus and the kingdom.

Yet they will not merely *meet* or *encounter* Jesus in Galilee: they will "see him" there (16:7). This is the promise of perception. They will have their eyes opened to see and perceive, and their ears will be unstopped so that they will listen and understand. Their hard hearts will be softened, and they will do as God commands them in 9:7: "This is my Son, whom I love. *Listen to him!*"

There is so much hope at this point in the narrative. The women arrive to the tomb to discover that God has already been active. He has invaded the tragic situation of Jesus's death and powerfully reversed it, raising the crucified one to life and inaugurating the kingdom in power. Moreover, Jesus is on the

---

action of the verb, nor is it an indirect object; rather, it is the subject of a statement that has the sense, "The place where they laid him is empty."

12. Edwards points out that this is a fulfillment of Jesus's prediction in 9:1: "Truly I tell you, some who are standing here will not taste death before they see that the kingdom of God has come with power." The women had been following Jesus and serving him throughout his ministry in Galilee and in Jerusalem and would have been standing there when Jesus made this prediction. They are now the ones who see that the kingdom of God has come with power (Edwards, *Mark*, 494).

move, heading to Galilee to launch a new start. Mark's audiences are primed to enjoy the continued dawning of hope as the sun continues to rise and the promise continues to grow, reversing the failures from previous moments in the Gospel narrative.

The Women Flee in Fear (v. 8)

Yet what happens next is stunning. Mark's ending subverts all expectations and dashes the hope that the young man's words have generated. The Greek text is dramatic, depicting the women backing out in shock before fleeing in terror: "And going out they fled from the tomb" (NIV, "[they] went out and fled from the tomb; *kai exelthousai ephygon apo tou mnēmeiou*). Their panicked flight is depicted with the same verb (*pheugō*) as when the disciples and the young man bolted from Jesus at his arrest (14:50, 52). The women fled because trembling and amazement had seized them (*eichen gar autas tromos kai ekstasis*). Throughout Mark, amazement is often a negative response to Jesus, associated with fear and unbelief (6:51; 15:5). They were overcome by what they saw and were shaken to their core.

The same dynamic of drift and desertion that affected the disciples now appears to have overtaken the women. They were "with him" at the start of his ministry, a description of faithful discipleship, but at Jesus's crucifixion they were watching "from a distance" (15:40). Now, just as they fully perceive the power of the kingdom, they behave like the disciples did when they were overcome by fear (4:41; 6:50; 9:32; 10:32), and they respond in precisely the wrong way.[13] It is all too much for them, and they flee. Mark's conclusion comes as a total shock: "They said nothing to anyone, because they were afraid."

This abrupt ending of Mark raises all sorts of questions. When Christian audiences hear this ending, they will inevitably ask why Mark does not conclude his Gospel the way the other Gospel writers do. Why are there no resurrection appearances to eyewitnesses? Why is there no account of a reunion of Jesus with his disciples, and no commission for them to preach the gospel to the ends of the earth? How can Mark close with this note of failure on the part of the women to tell anyone, especially when others *did* eventually hear about Jesus's resurrection and churches *were* established? If no one said anything, how did we get here? Christians are hearing and reading this Gospel, so the news did spread. Why does Mark do this?

Unfortunately, we don't have Mark around to answer these questions, and

---

13. Moloney, *Gospel of Mark*, 348.

we are left to reflect on how to respond faithfully to Mark's narrative and its conclusion. Certainly the ending would provoke discussion among audiences, forcing them to ask themselves these very questions. And this may be just what Mark intended. This is the brilliance of an unsatisfying narrative ending. It leaves audiences without any resolution, forcing them to grapple with all the tensions and unsettling issues that the narrative raises. Audiences and readers will need to revisit the story repeatedly to inquire into the dynamics that led to this point. And with the promise of a new beginning in Galilee, they might ask themselves what various characters might do differently that would lead to an alternative ending. In what follows, I will note some aspects of Mark's narrative that audiences may consider.

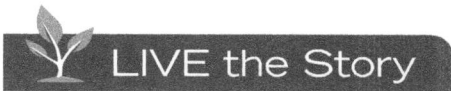

LIVE the Story

Responding to the End of Mark

I remember well the first time I watched the film *No Country for Old Men* with some friends. Several of them had already read the novel on which the film was based, but I was unfamiliar with the story. When it ended abruptly, I was stunned and upset. "What was that?!" I exclaimed. I'll never forget my friend Bob turning to me and saying, "Think about it." I certainly did. I couldn't get it out of my head for several weeks. I read reviews of it online in order to discern its meaning. I read the novel and watched the film a few more times, continuing to converse with friends about various characters and turns in the plot. I have come to see the brilliance of the ending and how it drives readers and viewers back into the narrative itself to search out its meaning. If a writer wants to agitate an audience, provoking them to reflect on what they've heard and what it means for them, then a satisfying resolution may hinder his aims. What, then, are some ways we can respond faithfully to the surprising ending of Mark?

First, even though the final statement lingers in our minds, we ought to remember the wonder that God has already acted to bring about a cosmic victory and a new creation. Yes, the women are overwhelmed, but we must note that God has shattered the present evil age and raised Jesus from the dead. Jesus is on the move to Galilee to begin anew and enact his kingdom reign. Everything in the Gospel has unfolded just as Jesus has foretold. He was handed over to be abused and crucified, and God raised him up on the third day. He had predicted that he would go ahead of them to Galilee, and that is just what he has done. Throughout Mark, God has been active and faithful. God entered the stage early in the narrative when he ripped open the heavens to declare his delight in Jesus (1:10–11), and he was faithful to Jesus in vindicating his faithful Son. In a Gospel so filled with human failure, God's faithfulness and saving activity stands out as a constant and the bedrock of Christian hope.

Second, it is instructive to consider the specific failure of the disciples throughout the narrative. Mark's portrayal of the disciples is strongly negative. Jesus calls them and appoints them, and they have privileged access to Jesus. But they do not listen to Jesus like they should. They prove themselves to be the first three soils at various points rather than the fruitful fourth (4:1–20). Throughout the Gospel, they prove themselves to be the ones who see but do not perceive and who hear but do not understand. They are the ones who hear Jesus's word, but receive it as confusing parables. Outsider characters, however, see and hear Jesus and move toward understanding and enjoy the blessings of God's kingdom as a result. When the disciples hear about Jesus's suffering and death, they don't pay close attention and reflect or even ask questions for clarification. They rebuke Jesus (8:31–33), fight with each other for prominence (9:30–34), and quest after power and prestige (10:35–40).

As we give renewed and repeated consideration to the disciples, we subject ourselves to the searching question of whether we are people who consider ourselves to be kingdom "insiders" but do not really understand what Jesus is all about. Do we really know him? Are we faithful Bible readers and consistent participants in the church without diligently attending to what Jesus has actually said? In what ways are we drawn to Jesus because of what we imagine we will gain? And in what ways are we trying to fit Jesus into our conceptions of what we want him to be? Are we like Peter, following Jesus in some sense, but rejecting the reality that he is a cross-shaped Messiah who calls disciples to embrace the cross in a cross-oriented kingdom? Do we long for power and prestige and reject Jesus's call to serve the needy and offer hospitality to the marginalized?

The human tendency to be presumptuous, to give ourselves the benefit of the doubt, is a constant danger. We commend ourselves and presume that surely we are the ones who are uniquely attentive to Jesus. We assume that we are an objective audience as we read or listen to Mark's Gospel, standing safely at a distance and judging the disciples for their flaws. Mark, however, has his crosshairs trained on us. We are the target of his portrayal of the disciples. We are the ones who have not listened to Jesus as we should. This is why Jesus continually—and uncomfortably—tells nearly everyone in the Gospel to keep quiet about him.

This feature of Mark is especially shocking for Christian audiences that have heard repeatedly that they ought to tell as many people as possible about Jesus. Certainly any public speech about Jesus is an unmistakably good thing, right? Then why all the talk about remaining silent? As we have said throughout the commentary, Mark seems to assume that many Christian audiences have paid insufficiently close attention to the cross-orientation of Jesus's identity and the cruciform character of the kingdom of God. It would be easy to assume that the role of Christians is to tell others about Jesus and that it is for outsiders—non-Christians—to listen. But when God invades Mark's narrative, it is the disciples that he commands, "Listen to him!" (9:7). Christian audiences would do well to reflect on the ways in which they consider themselves loyal followers of Jesus but ignore what he says.

A third feature of Mark ripe for reflection is Jesus's commitment to his disciples despite their abandoning him. Here, the young man commands the women to relay the message to "*his* disciples and Peter" (16:7). Just before he eats his Passover meal with the disciples—a meal at which he will predict that one of them will betray him and all will abandon him—he makes preparations to eat the Passover "with my disciples" (14:14). And sandwiched between his predictions of Judas's betrayal and Peter's denial, he gives to his disciples his body and blood, giving himself fully to them (14:18–27). In a Gospel of unrelenting human failure, Jesus remains utterly faithful and fully committed to those whom he has called. The profound notes of grace that ring through Mark's Gospel are powerfully struck.

A fourth aspect of Mark has great relevance for audiences in so-called "Christian" cultures. These exist beyond the West, but I am most familiar with my cultural location in the United States. These are contexts in which the church is easily seduced by triumphalism. When believers surrender to the temptation to associate the faith with a political party, so that a subtle but rock-solid alliance is formed between the church and an entity that belongs to this present age, the dynamics of triumphalism easily take over. Christians begin to quest after cultural domination, seeking political power and cultural approval.

Such a move is directly contrary to Jesus's kingdom proclamation in Mark. Rather than going to the capital city to take power or triumph, Jesus is going to die. Peter represents a triumphalist vision, the longing for a victorious messianic figure who will defeat enemies and win the culture war. When he hears about Jesus going to die, he rebukes him! But Jesus calls him "Satan" and says that his imagination is captive to human concerns rather than those of God (8:33). Christian audiences ought to consider carefully the clash between these visions.

As noted above, Jesus's kingdom proclamation involves disciples cultivating the practices of serving the needy and offering hospitality to society's marginalized. When the disciples try to exclude children—those with no social value—from encountering Jesus, he reproves them. And Jesus sets these marginalized figures at the very center of his community, identifying himself with them. He then told his disciples that when they welcome the marginalized, they welcome Jesus himself and God who sent him (9:36–37). Reading this text while a national debate rages about immigration has been quite unsettling. Many Christians in America resonate with a vision that seeks to keep out people who have been traumatized and are fleeing for their lives. While the Gospel of Mark does not provide us with specifics about public policy, the stark contrast between Jesus's call to welcome the marginalized and a policy stance of exclusion of those who are suffering ought to compel Christians to reflect on whether they belong to this present evil age or to the kingdom of God's beloved Son.

While we could list features of Mark's narrative endlessly, one final aspect of the Gospel should be considered. Jesus has foretold that he will meet his disciples in Galilee, where there will be a new start, a new beginning. Thus far they have failed to see and hear and move toward perception and understanding. If they were to start again, what would they do differently? A good exercise after hearing the Gospel a few times is to consider each episode in which the disciples appear to fail or Jesus reproves them. What alternatives can audiences imagine for the disciples? For example, what should the disciples have done when Jesus was arrested rather than fleeing? Should they have tried to feed the 5,000 when Jesus told them to (6:37)? What would that have looked like? Answering questions like these activates our imaginations, so that we begin to think through faithful responses to Jesus in our day—how we might watch, be alert, and be on guard rather than falling asleep (13:32–37).

Alternative Endings to Mark's Gospel

A lmost without exception, New Testament scholars maintain that the Gospel of Mark concludes with 16:8 and that all other material is not part of the original composition. Because of Mark's abrupt ending, however, the first few centuries of the church bear witness to several attempts to provide an ending that brings resolution. The King James Version, the dominant English translation until relatively recently, included one of these endings, giving readers the sense that it was the natural and intended conclusion of this Gospel (vv. 9–20). Most English translations produced in the last several decades set vv. 9–20 apart in brackets and include a note that other endings apart from vv. 1–8 are not found in the earliest manuscripts (e.g., CEB, ESV, CSB, NASB, NIV, NRSV). They do so because text-critical scholars who study the history of copying biblical texts throughout the centuries are in agreement that such alternative endings are not original and come from the second century or later. What follows is a brief survey of alternative endings and other opinions about the close of Mark.

Alternative 1. A minority opinion is that Mark 16:8 is *not* the original ending of Mark's Gospel, but neither are any of the extant "endings" of Mark. The original may have been lost, possibly through the mutilation of part of a manuscript that contained the original conclusion.[1] Or it may be that Mark intended to supply a suitable conclusion to his Gospel, but like Mozart's *Requiem*, he somehow never finished it.

Alternative 2. A "longer ending," reproduced below, is found in vv. 9–20, printed in the KJV without any indication of its distinct character from the rest of Mark. This ending is not found in the earliest and most reliable manuscripts, and while some church figures in the first four centuries knew of its existence, they did not regard it as original.[2] This portion of text contains a series of appearances that are clearly constructed from accounts in the other Gospels and Acts in order to provide an ending that brought resolution and

---

1. This view remains speculative and has very few adherents. Clayton Croy has mounted a recent defense (N. Clayton Croy, *The Mutilation of Mark's Gospel* [Nashville: Abingdon, 2003]).

2. Hurtado, *Mark*, 288; Garland, *Theology of Mark's Gospel*, 538.

reversed the failure of the women and the Twelve. Not only are vv. 9–20 not in the earliest manuscripts, but the language is strikingly different from the rest of Mark. On the one hand, we might say that vv. 9–20 are an important portion of text that reveals how the early church responded to Mark's Gospel. On the other, we might assert that this is one of the first instances of *resistance* to Mark's actual ending. Certainly Mark's Gospel is challenging, mystifying, unsettling, and confrontational, but if the church believes that this Gospel is inspired by God, then it will be received as a gift from a gracious God who wants to lead his people into greener pastures of kingdom flourishing. The abrupt and uncomfortable ending at 16:8 has a crucial role to play in that purpose, especially the destabilized and unsettled condition in which it leaves audiences. The following is from the NIV, which sets the text in italics in most print editions to indicate its questionable status.

> 9When Jesus rose early on the first day of the week, he appeared first to Mary Magdalene, out of whom he had driven seven demons. 10She went and told those who had been with him and who were mourning and weeping. 11When they heard that Jesus was alive and that she had seen him, they did not believe it.
>
> 12Afterward Jesus appeared in a different form to two of them while they were walking in the country. 13These returned and reported it to the rest; but they did not believe them either.
>
> 14Later Jesus appeared to the Eleven as they were eating; he rebuked them for their lack of faith and their stubborn refusal to believe those who had seen him after he had risen.
>
> 15He said to them, "Go into all the world and preach the gospel to all creation. 16Whoever believes and is baptized will be saved, but whoever does not believe will be condemned. 17And these signs will accompany those who believe: In my name they will drive out demons; they will speak in new tongues; 18they will pick up snakes with their hands; and when they drink deadly poison, it will not hurt them at all; they will place their hands on sick people, and they will get well."
>
> 19After the Lord Jesus had spoken to them, he was taken up into heaven and he sat at the right hand of God. 20Then the disciples went out and preached everywhere, and the Lord worked with them and confirmed his word by the signs that accompanied it.

Alternative 3. A shorter ending, which the NIV prints in a footnote. In some manuscripts, this ending follows 16:8 so that it concludes the Gospel.

In others, it comes between vv. 8 and 9 and is followed by the "longer ending" (alternative 2, above). Its manuscript support is very weak.

> Then they quickly reported all these instructions to those around Peter. After this, Jesus himself also sent out through them from east to west the sacred and imperishable proclamation of eternal salvation. Amen.

Alternative 4. The "longer ending" with an addition. The NRSV reproduces a portion of text that is found in at least one manuscript between vv. 14 and 15 of the "longer ending" (alternative 2, above).

> And they excused themselves, saying, "This age of lawlessness and unbelief is under Satan, who does not allow the truth and power of God to prevail over the unclean things of the spirits. Therefore reveal your righteousness now"—thus they spoke to Christ. And Christ replied to them, "The term of years of Satan's power has been fulfilled, but other terrible things draw near. And for those who have sinned I was handed over to death, that they may return to the truth and sin no more, that they may inherit the spiritual and imperishable glory of righteousness that is in heaven."

Nearly without exception, biblical scholars agree that the Gospel of Mark ends at 16:8 and that these other "endings" are from a later period. The vast majority also maintains that 16:8 is Mark's intended conclusion. While this leaves us with all the questions that an abrupt ending inevitably raises, this is likely the author's intention. After all, his Gospel begins abruptly and continues at a breathless pace. It confronts its Christian audiences through the device of the disciples' routine failures and Jesus's tough talk to them. Mark portrays Jesus as a confrontational prophet, often being confused with Elijah and John the Baptist.

All these devices—and more, besides—are ways that Mark works on audiences to provoke them to reflect on how their communities fall short of being faithful to the ways of Jesus revealed in his journey toward the cross, his identity shaped by the cross, and a kingdom oriented by the cross. That the narrative would leave us unsettled, disturbed, and asking questions, especially of ourselves, makes perfect sense. It is also understandable that a later scribe would want to blend Mark's account with the other Gospels, perhaps out of concern that the original, satisfying ending was lost. The manuscript evidence is as conclusive as can be that 16:8 is the original ending of the text of Mark. And from the narrative itself, it seems that this was Mark's intention.

Scripture Index

Genesis

1.	47, 50, 97
1–2.	36
1:1	21, 24
1:1–2:3.	400, 401
1:5	401
1:26–27	417, 420
1:27	339, 340, 343
1:28	162
1:31	260, 261
2–3.	467
2:2–3	96
2:19	401
2:19–20	400
2:24	339, 340, 342, 343
3.	190, 467
3:14–21	31
4.	2
4:2–8	51
4:5	53
4:7	2
6:1–4	2
7:1	277
12:1–3	2
12:3	201
14:18–20	168
15:4–6	153
16:1–2	153
16:1–3	292
16:13	510
17:3–8	112, 113
18.	482
18:1–5	322, 327
18:1–15	482
18:9–15	153
19:8	205
19:17	458
21:17	562
22:1–2	23
22:2	21
22:15–18	510
25:23	258
35:9–10	112, 113
35:10	42
37–50.	409
37:3–4	409
37:18–20	407
37:19–20	409
38:6–26	324
39:20	36, 409
49:1–33	450
49:10	26
50:20	193, 409

Exodus

3.	42, 112, 423, 424, 427
3:1	112
3:1–14	42
3:6	424
3:7	424
3:14	226
3:15, 16	424
4.	261
4:8–9	276
4:10–12	260, 261
4:17	276
4:22–23	26
4:28	276
7–14.	102
7:17	79
8:10	79
8:22	79
9:14	79
9:33–35	223, 227
10:1–2	276
10:2	79
10:21–22	539, 548
12.	474, 476
13:13, 15	371
15.	172
15:1	172
15:4	172

15:5 172
15:10 172
16. . . . . .97, 200, 201, 212, 266
17:1–7 275
18:1–25 217
18:21 217
19. 112
19:1–25 113
19:3–25 . . . . .304, 305
19:5–6 421
19:6 . . . . .2, 201, 313
19:22 236
20:1–17 325
20:8–11 . . . . .96, 97
20:12 240
20:12–17 358
20:16 513
21:8 371
21:10–11 . . . . .339, 340, 341
21:17 240
21:30 371
22:21 . . . . .2, 348
22:21–24 352
22:22–24 .439, 443
23:20 . . . . .21, 22
23:20–23 510
23:21 28
24:8 . . . . .484, 489
24:9–16 304
24:15–16 306
24:15–18 305
30:18–21 239
32:9–14 62
32:34–35 510
33. 80
33–34. 62
33:12–13 81
33:17–34:7. . . . . .223, 224
33:18 62
33:19 224
33:19–34:8. 62
33:20 224
34. . . . . .304, 305
34:2 . . . . .225, 559
34:4–7 . . . . .74, 81
34:6 . . . . .224, 225
34:6–7 . . . . .75, 78
40:23 98
40:31 239

40:34–38 307

Leviticus

4. . . . . .74, 78
7:26–27 242
10:1–3 236
11. . . . . .242, 243
11:1–8 167
11:7–8 172
12:1–8 236
13–14. . . . . .67, 68
13:1–46 236
15. . . . . .58, 185
15:19 236
15:19–23 184
15:19–27 .181, 184
17:10–14 484
18:13 200
18:16 . . . . .200, 205
18:24 236
19:18 . . . . .71, 431, 432, 435
19:26 242
19:33–34 2
20:9 240
20:21 . . . . .200, 205
21:11 187
24:5–9 98
25:37–42 371
26:3–12 236
26:14–33 236

Numbers

3:45–51 371
5:2; 6:6; 9:6 169
11:1–25 212
12:1–16 68
12:14 519
14:11 313
15:38–39 230
18:8–13 . . . . .235, 239
19:11 187
20. 332
20:1–5 330
20:1–13 . . . . .212, 213, 329
20:6–8 330
20:8 213
20:10 . . . . .213, 471
20:10–11 330
20:10–13 471

20:12 . . . . .213, 330, 471
20:13 331
24:16 168
24:17 26
27. 213
27:12–14 213
27:15–23 212
27:16–17 214
27:17 213
35:30 513

Deuteronomy

1–4. 471
1:19–46 298
1:20 299
1:21 299
1:27 299
1:35 277
1:35–36 299
1:44 299
4:8 251
4:20 236
4:21–24 471
4:24 472
4:34 276
5:1–27 112
5:16 240
5:16–21 358
5:20 513
6:4–5 . . . . .431, 432, 434
6:4–9 131
6:20–23 42
7:6 236
8:4 . . . . .200, 201
8:10 217
8:10–18 355
10. 352
10:12–22 . . . . .348, 352
10:16–20 349
10:18 345
11:13 431
12:21–25 242
14. 243
14:8 . . . . .167, 171
14:10 243
14:28–29 67
15. 481
15:1–11 . . . . .480, 481
15:4–6 480

15:7–11 481
15:11 . . . . .474, 478
16:2 486
17. 374
17:6 . . . . .513, 517
17:14–20 . . . . .322, 365
17:15 323
17:16–20 323
17:17 374
17:20 374
18:15 . . . . .304, 306
19:15 . . . . .513, 517
22:12 230
23:25 96
24. 343
24:1 . . . . .340, 342
24:1–3 342
24:1–4 . . . . .339, 342
24:4 342
24:17 . . . . .439, 443
25:5–10 . . . . .423, 424, 426
25:9 520
28. 355
28:1–14 355
28:49 270
29:5 200
29:5–6 201
29:12 28
29:22 270
30:19 28
31:1–33:29 .448, 450
32:5 277
32:8 168
32:8–9 421
32:20 . . . . .277, 313
32:46–47 451
33:26 . . . . .230, 231
34:5–8 305

Joshua

7. 329
9:6, 9 266
15:8; 18:16. 334
23:1–24:30. 450

Judges

5:4–5 47
6. . . . . .275, 276
6:11–24 226

6:13–14 510
11:12 . . . . .49, 170
13:21–23 510
14:1, 3, 7 205

Ruth

1:20–21 113
3–4 . . . . .423, 424

1 Samuel

1:1–2:11 55
1:6 55
2:1–10 55
2:1 56
2:7–8 56
5 . . . . .108, 167
5:1–4 108
5:1–5 107
5:2 167
5:3 168
5:4 168
5:6 . . . . .108, 168
5:7–12 168
6:6 223
12:1–25 450
15:22 . . . . .431, 433
16:7 . . . . .78, 258, 417, 418
18 52
18:6–9 53
20:30–33 53
21:1–6 . . . . .96, 98
25:25 113

2 Samuel

7:14–16 375
7:13–14 27
24 . . . . .474, 510
24:1–2 476
24:3–4 . . . . .476, 510
24:14 510
24:15–16 . . . . .476, 510
24:22–23 476
24:24 476

1 Kings

2:1–9 450
8:10–11 307
14:11 . . . . .253, 255
16:29–19:3 .200, 205

17:7–16 212
17:17–24 . . . . .181, 182
17:18 . . . . .49, 170
18 . . . . .37, 47, 167, 169, 170
18:1–15 . . . . .513, 525
18:4 515
18:15–18 . . . . .36, 37
18:16–40 515
18:16–46 201
18:26 169
18:28–29 169
19 305
19:1–18 . . . . .113, 304
19:2 201
19:8 224
19:8–18 112
19:9 224
19:11 . . . . .224, 225
19:11–12 223
19:12–13 411
19:13 224
19:19–21 . . . . .42, 43
21 . . . . .200, 201, 205
21:19–24 . . . . .253, 255
22:1–40 36
22:17 215

2 Kings

1:8 . . . . .21, 30
2:9–12 305
2:11–12 27
4 182
4:1–37 55
4:14 182
4:16 182
4:18–21 182
4:18–37 . . . . .181, 182
4:27–28 182
4:42–44 212
5:1–14 . . . . .67, 68
5:19–27 68
6:8–23 . . . . .286, 375
16:3 334

1 Chronicles

21 510
21:9–12 510
21:13 510
21:14–15 510

28:1–29:5 450

2 Chronicles

7 29
7:12–14 29
18:16 215
24:20–22 411
26:19–21 68
28:3; 33:6 334
36:13 227
36:15–16 411

Ezra

7:1–11 49

Esther

1 200
2:9 206
5:1–8 200
5:6 205

Job

1–2 143
9:8–11 . . . . .223, 224
19:26 424
31:10 205
38:1 307
38:11 . . . . .159, 162
42:7 355

Psalms

2 . . . . .23, 37
2:7 . . . . .23, 27
2:7–10 401
6 498
6:3 499
8 440
8:6 . . . . .440, 441
13 557
15 . . . . .235, 244, 358
16:9–11 424
18 231
18:8–16 47
22 . . . . .539, 545, 548, 555
22:1 . . . . .541, 554
22:1–2 548
22:6 308
22:7–8 . . . . .541, 545
22:17–18 542

22:18 543
23:1 217
29:1–11 47
29 . . . . .131, 133, 134
29:3 133
29:3–10 . . . . .159, 161
29:3–11 226
29:10 133
30:5 559
32:5 81
34 231
34:17 162
34:22 371
38:11 539
40:6 433
41:9 . . . . .484, 487
42 498
42–43 499
42:5, 11 499
43 . . . . .498, 555
43:5 499
44 555
44:23–24 161
44:23–26 . . . . .320, 555
44:26 371
47:1–9 36
49 355
50:10 274
51:16–17 433
55 555
55:1–5 499
55:4–5 498
68:18–20 119
69:19–21 . . . . .539, 542
69:21 543
77:16–20 . . . . .223, 224, 226
78 298
78:8 299
78:42 372
82 170
82:3 345
82:6; 83:18 168
86:11 313
88 555
88:13–18 555
89:3–4 375
95:3 . . . . .36, 108, 432
95:6–8 227
95:7 215

95:10–11 277
96:4 108
96:4–5 171
97:9 . . . . .168, 432
100:3 . . . . .42, 45, 87
103:3 190
103:19 36
107. .230, 231, 268
107:1–9 266
107:4–9 268
107:23–29 161
107:23–32 159
109:21–25 539
110. . . . . .21, 401, 439, 440, 441, 525
110–18. 490
110:1 . . . . .440, 526
110:2–3, 5–7 440
111:10 . . . . .131, 150
113. 67
113:4–9 68
113:5–9 181
113:7–9 183
118. . . . . .291, 384, 407
118:22 . . . . .304, 308, 412
118:22–23 .409, 412
118:23 412
118:26 380
138:6 . . . . .55, 56
139:23 . . . . .74, 78
142. 62
145:11–13 36
147:2 56
147:6 . . . . .55, 56
147:10–11 56
148:14 270

Proverbs

1:5–7 148
1:20–33 147
1:32–33 148
2:1–11 262
2:1–22 147
6:16–19 329
8:18–21 355
10:19 537
10:22 355
11:4, 25, 28 355
12:23; 13:3. 537
17:28 537

19:17 355
21:23 537
22:16 355
23:5 355
24:12 78
25:6–7 365
25:15 537

Ecclesiastes

3:11 . . . . .260, 261

Isaiah

3:14–15 67
5. 411
5:1–2 .132, 390, 408
5:1–7 . . . . .135, 385, 389, 395, 407, 408
5:2 390
5:3 408
5:5–6 . . . . .390, 408
5:7 . . . . .390, 408
5:8–9 248
6. 231
6:8–10 132
6:9–10 . . . . .131, 239, 280, 281
10:1–2 . . . . .439, 443
11:1–2 30
11:1–6 16
11:3 417
11:3–4 418
11:6–9 31
13:9–11 460
14:14 168
20. 393
23. . . . . .253, 255
26:16–19 455
29:6 455
29:13 . . . . .235, 240
31:9 334
34:4 460
35:1–7 375
35:5–6 . . . . .260, 261
35:9 372
40–55. . . . . .22, 28
40:3 . . . . .21, 22
40:8 461
40:9 . . . . .21, 24
41:14 372
42:1 23
42:1–4 23

42:6 313
43:14 372
43:16–17 . . . . .223, 224, 226
43:25; 44:21–22. .74
45:1 26
45:1–7 26
45:21 435
45:23 36
49:6 . . . . .105, 107, 160, 313
49:24–25 119
50:6 . . . . .525, 526
50:6–7 520
51:10–11 372
51:17, 22 . . . . .500, 501
52:3 372
52:7 24
52:7–10 21
52:9 372
52:13–53:12. . . . . .291, 292, 525
53. 324
53:1–12 365
53:3 304
53:3–12 308
53:7 . . . . .513, 518, 526
53:10–12 324
53:11–12 . . . . .371, 484, 490
53:12 .539, 542, 544
54:4–7 89
54:4–8 88
55. 74
55–56. 83
55:1–56:8. 83
55:6–7 . . . . .76, 128
55:6–9 81
55:8–9 76
56:7 . . . . .389, 393, 545
56:9–12 286
66:24 334

Jeremiah

1:19 193
2:2 28
2:9–19 192
2:10–11 193
3:16 459
3:18 459
4:5–6 89
4:24 455
4:31 455

5. 281
5:2 281
5:13 281
5:21 .131, 280, 281
6:22–26 455
7:1–8 . . . . .448, 453
7:1–11 389
7:3–8 391
7:9–11 391
7:11 . . . . .390, 393, 410, 545
7:25–26 . . . . .407, 410
7:30–33 334
9:23–24 . . . . .355, 356
13:1–11 393
14:14–15 455
16:16–17 . . . . .42, 44
19. . . . . .393, 515
19:1–13 . . . . .334, 389
19:14–20:6. .512–13
20:1–6 . . . . .192, 193
20:2 515
20:3–6 . . . . .515, 516
20:7–8 318
22:23–27 455
25:4 410
25:15, 17, 28 . . . . .500, 501
30:4–8 455
31:11 372
31:29 459
32:34–35 334
33:5–9 29
33:15–16 459
37–39. 36
38:1–6 193
38:4 193
49:12 . . . . .500, 501

Ezekiel

2:1 8
2:1–10 192
3:27 131
4:1–3 . . . . .389, 393
6:11–12 455
7:15 455
10. 196
10:18–19 . . . . .448, 452
11:22–23 . . . . .448, 452
12:1–3 . . . . .131, 132
12:2 . . . . .280, 281

12:16 455
14:13, 21 455
16:49 67
17. 155
19:4–5 44
26:1–28:19. . . . . .253, 255
31:1–14 155
31:6 152
31:23–40 89
33:27–29 121
33:30–32 121
33:30–33 . . . . .65, 119
34. . . . . .102, 215, 439
34:1–5 102
36:24–28 132

Daniel
2:21 147
3:26 168
4:10–12, 14 155
4:17 168
4:28–37 . . . . .322, 370
4:30 323
4:34–37 26
6. 62
6:17–20 559
7. . . . . .8, 291, 401
7:9 . . . . .304, 306
7:10 444
7:13–14 . . . . .8, 292, 294, 400, 401
7:14 371
7:21–22 . . . . .36, 292, 294
7:26–27 8
7:27 . . . . .292, 294, 371, 400, 401
9:27; 11:31. . . . . .448, 457
12. 424
12:1–3 . . . . .423, 424
12:4 453
12:4–7 453
12:7 453
12:11 . . . . .448, 457
12:13 424

Hosea
1:9 . . . . .119, 120
2:14 28
6:2 559
6:6 . . . . .431, 433
9:10 28

11:1 26

Joel
2:10 460
2:28–32 30
2:30–31 460
2:31 460
3:1 459
3:13 152

Amos
2. 506
2:6 . . . . .498, 506
2:6–7 474
2:16 . . . . .498, 506
4:2 44
8:9 548
8:9–10 539

Jonah
1–4. 159
1:1 160
1:1–16 159
1:6 159
1:11–12 159
1:14 159
1:16 159
4:1–11 3
4:2 160
4:3 160

Micah
1:3–4 455
3:11–12 . . . . .448, 453
4:10–14 455
6:8 358
7:1 389
7:1–2 390
7:1–6 395

Habakkuk
1:13 319

Zechariah
1:6 410
2:6 460
3:1–2 143
7:10 439
8:20–23 . . . . .107, 108

8:23 459
9:9 . . . . .380, 383, 384
9:11 484
13:1–2 . . . . .47, 50
13:7 . . . . .484, 491
14:4 452
14:9 36

Malachi

2:13–17 . . . . .339, 340, 344
3:1 . . . . .21, 21, 27, 390, 433
3:5 . . . . .28, 433
4. 304
4:2 559
4:5 . . . . .27, 28
4:5–6 21

Matthew

3:7–10 121
4:1–11 295
4:10 170
4:17 35
5:1 113
5:1–7:29. 112
5:17–18 251
5:27–30 333
5:43–47 71
6:10 508
6:15 437
6:17 203
9:9–13 84
10:1 51
11:28–30 83
12:32 127
13:33 282
16:18 153
20:2 478
21:9 412
23:29–32 407
25. 228
25:6 229
25:31–46 .219, 414
25:43 229
26:6–13 477
27:15 531
28:16–20 400

Mark

1:1 . . . . 8, 23, 24, 26, 293, 403 550

1:1–13 . . . . .21, 36
1:1–45 18
1:2–3 22
1:3 22
1:4 . . . . .28, 30, 63, 215
1:5 . . . . .30, 372
1:6 30
1:8 30
1:10 . . . . .30, 124
1:10–11 . . . . .550, 567
1:11 . .12, 23, 31, 305, 357, 403, 442, 518, 550
1:12 . . . . .31, 63, 215
1:12–13 .9, 139, 295
1:13 . . . . .31, 58, 276, 295, 341
1:14 . . . . .37, 115, 200, 324, 504, 529
1:14–15 . . . . .36, 42
1:14–3:6. 112
1:15 . . . . .1, 37, 38, 64, 372
1:16 . . . . .43, 226, 358, 520
1:16–18 521
1:16–19 377
1:16–20 . . . . .42, 45, 112, 113, 125, 173
1:17 44
1:17–20 361
1:18 . . . . .44, 145
1:19 . . . . .43, 226, 358, 520
1:19–20 44
1:20–28 202
1:21–22 48
1:21–27 . . . . .77, 84, 440
1:21–28 . . . . .7, 47, 104, 215, 393
1:21–31 16
1:22 . . . . .49, 50, 530
1:22–27 403
1:24 . . . . .64, 168, 170, 403
1:25–26 57
1:26 70
1:27 . . . . .48, 49, 50, 314, 368, 530, 562
1:28 50
1:29 57
1:29–31 56
1:29–34 55
1:30 57
1:31 57
1:32–34 . . . . .56, 58, 230
1:32a 230
1:32b 230
133. 230
1:34 . . . . .17, 58, 187, 189, 230, 518

1:35 . . . . 215, 517
1:35–37 . . . . 214, 225
1:35–39 62
1:36 63
1:36–37 517
1:37 . . . . 63, 125, 563
1:38 64
1:39 64
1:40 . . . . 69, 501
1:40–45 . . . . 67, 189
1:41 . . . . 69, 110, 350
1:42 70
1:43–44 17
1:44 50
1:44–45 518
1:45 . . . . 50, 70, 214, 504
2. 80
2:1 . . . . 64, 84
2:1–5 76
2:1–12 . . . . 74, 75, 83, 102, 104, 231,
                                   262, 400, 532
2:1–3:6. . 19, 74, 84, 85, 88, 96, 102, 120, 400
2:2 77
2:2–5 504
2:3 288
2:3–4 316
2:3–5 77
2:4 77
2:5 . . . . 77, 226
2:6 . . . . 96, 402
2:6–10 . . . . 76, 78, 403
2:6–12 48
2:8 78
2:10 . . . . 78, 79
2:11 79
2:11–12 79
2:12 . . . . 75, 79, 530
2:13 84
2:13–14 . . . . 113, 173, 377
2:13–15 84
2:13–17 . . . . 75, 83, 85, 87, 124, 125
2:14 . . . . 43, 84, 226, 358, 361, 520
2:15 . . . . 43, 85
2:15–16 495
2:15–17 . . . . 59, 350
2:16 . . . . 84, 85, 96, 146, 402
2:17 . . . . 64, 85
2:18 . . . . 84, 89, 96
2:18–20 490

2:18–22 . . . . 75, 88
2:19 90
2:19–20 89
2:20 90
2:21–22 91
2:23 . . . . 84, 97
2:23–24 97
2:23–28 . . . . 75, 96
2:24 . . . . 96, 97
2:25–26 98
2:26 98
2:27 98
2:27–28 99
3. . . . . 127, 128
3:1 84
3:1–6 . . . . 75, 83, 102, 232, 239, 288
3:2 104
3:4 104
3:5 . . . . 69, 105, 227, 359
3:6 . . . . . 9, 75, 88, 108, 115, 276, 341, 393,
                      400, 403, 412, 419, 516, 533
3:7 . . . . 109, 532
3:7–12 . . . . 107, 230, 232
3:7–35 19
3:7a 230
3:7b–8 230
3:8 . . . . 107, 109
3:8–10 109
3:9 . . . . 109, 231
3:10 . . . . 109, 110, 232
3:10a 230
3:10b 230
3:11 . . . . 108, 550, 551
3:11–12 . . . . 109, 518
3:12 50
3:13 . . . . 113, 123
3:13–15 203
3:13–19 . . . . 112, 120, 125, 173
3:13–8:21. 112
3:14 . . . . . 163, 173, 270, 315, 332, 384, 487,
                            516, 520, 552, 560
3:14–15 114
3:15 . . . . 187, 332
3:16–19 . . . . 84, 115
3:18 84
3:19 . . . . 488, 503
3:20 . . . . 231, 402, 532
3:20–21 . . . . 120, 122
3:20–35 . . . . 119, 195

3:21 . . . . .122, 124, 125
3:22 . . . . .122, 276
3:22–29 120
3:22–30 122
3:23 . . . . .123, 125, 187
3:23–29 48
3:23–4:34. 409
3:23b–26 123
3:27 . . . . .4, 37, 123, 189, 372
3:28 129
3:28–29 . . . . .124, 127, 519
3:28–30 123
3:29 124
3:30–35 120
3:31 124
3:31–35 . . . . .120, 122, 124, 361
3:32 . . . . .63, 125, 517, 563
3:33–35 . . . . .186, 487
3:34 . . . . .125, 226, 359
3:34–35 145
3:35 . . . . .65, 120, 125
4. . . . . .132, 152
4–8. .15, 16, 131, 133
4–10. 454
4:1 . . . . .133, 155, 214, 262
4:1–2 . . . . .131, 133, 134
4:1–20 . . 12, 15, 19, 120, 130, 131, 132, 147,
155, 182, 242, 254, 256, 280,
294, 301, 376, 567
4:1–24 520
4:1–34 . . . . .19, 155
4:1–8:17. 256
4:1–8:21. . . . . .136, 137, 256, 281, 287
4:3 . . . . .134, 149, 241
4:3–8 154
4:3–9 . . . . .131, 134
4:4 . . . . .135, 138, 376
4:5 . . . . .135, 140
4:6 135
4:7 . . . . .132, 135, 140
4:8 . . . . .135, 141
4:9 . . . . .134, 135, 148, 231, 241
4:10 173
4:10–11 125
4:10–12 . . . . .131, 134, 136, 137, 283
4:11 . . . . .163, 227, 504, 549
4:11–12 . . . . .15, 19, 112, 137, 153, 254,
280, 281, 465, 488, 540

4:12 . . . . .18, 131, 136, 149, 173, 239,
454, 457, 549
4:12–13 163
4:13 138
4:13–20 . . . . .131, 138
4:13a 132
4:15 . . . . .17, 138, 139, 295, 376
4:15–19 462
4:15–20 205
4:16–17 . . . . .140, 491
4:16–19 51
4:17 . . . . .140, 491
4:17–19 65
4:18–19 140
4:20 . . . . .141, 254
4:21–25 . . . . .147, 227
4:23 . . . . .148, 241
4:24–25 549
4:24a 149
4:24b–25 149
4:25 . . . . .207, 521
4:26–29 . . . . .152, 154
4:26–34 152
4:27 154
4:28 154
4:30–32 . . . . .153, 154
4:33 . . . . .153, 155
4:33–34 155
4:34 155
4:35 . . . . .161, 230
4:35–39 160
4:35–41 . . . . . . .133, 159, 172, 223, 226, 231
4:36 . . . . .160, 383, 551
4:38 . . . . .159, 161
4:39 . . . . .48, 50, 159, 162
4:40 . . . . .149, 161, 163, 307, 325
4:40–41 . . . . .162, 173
4:41 . . . . .159, 163, 181, 227, 403, 650
5. . . . . .15, 18, 145, 163, 168, 170, 175,
178, 192, 231, 358
5:1 . . . . .169, 174
5:1–5 169
5:1–6 357
5:1–20 . . . .114, 159, 160, 165, 393, 477, 540
5:1–8:21. 19
5:2 . . . . .169, 170
5:2–9 170
5:3 169
5:3–4 169

5:5 169
5:6 . . . . 69, 145, 167, 170, 181, 231,
255, 376, 478
5:6–10 170
5:7 . . . . .167, 168, 171, 403, 550
5:8 . . . . .170, 171
5:9 170
5:10 . . . . .167, 170, 171
5:11 171
5:11–13 171
5:12 . . . . .167, 170, 171
5:13 170
5:14 173
5:14–17 . . . . .173, 177
5:15 . . . . .173, 307, 325, 477, 551
5:16 . . . . .173, 477
5:17 . . . . .167, 173
5:17–20 530
5:18 .167, 173, 477
5:18–20 173
5:19 174
5:21 184
5:21–24a 181, 183
5:21–34 159
5:21–43 . . . . .16, 50, 58, 180, 540
5:22 . . . . 69, 145, 170, 181, 184, 231,
239, 255, 357, 376, 478
5:22–23 316
5:23 .181, 184, 546
5:24 .184, 231, 532
5:24a 184
5:24b–34 . . . . .181, 184
5:25 . . . . .181, 184
5:25–34 . . . . .110, 232
5:26 . . . . .184, 185
5:27 . . . . .170, 181, 185, 231, 376, 478
5:27–31 110
5:28 . . . . .181, 185, 546
5:28–31 185
5:29 185
5:30 . . . . .185, 232
5:33 . . . . 69, 145, 170, 173, 181, 185,
231, 239, 255, 257, 478
5:34 . . . . .181, 182, 185, 186, 188
5:35 186
5:35–43 . . . . .159, 181, 186
5:36 . . . . .186, 307, 325
5:37 . . . . .113, 187
5:38 551

5:39 187
5:39–40 187
5:40 187
5:41 . . . . .57, 317
5:41–42 187
5:42 181
5:42–43a 187
5:43 . . . . .17, 50
5:43b 187
6. 224
6:1 43
6:1–6a 192
6:2 . . . . .192, 194, 196
6:2–6 530
6:3 . . . . .195, 333
6:5 . . . . .189, 195, 196
6:5–6 232
6:6 196
6:6–13 227
6:6b–13 . . . . .200, 202, 216
6:6b–30 199
6:7 . . . . .51, 202
6:7–13 213
6:8–9 202
6:8–11 . . . . .201, 202
6:8–14 521
6:9–10 136
6:10 203
6:12–13 . . . . .14, 202
6:12–14 . . . . .215, 315
6:14 204
6:14–15 . . . . .201, 293
6:14–16 204
6:14–29 . . . . .30, 468, 515
6:15 253
6:16 204
6:17 122
6:17–20 205
6:17–29 205
6:18 . . . . .30, 341
6:18–19 433
6:19 205
6:20 . . . . .205, 307, 325, 532
6:21–29 205
6:22 205
6:24 206
6:26–28a 533
6:29 206
6:30 . . . . . . .14, 200, 206, 213, 215, 216, 227

6:30–44 481
6:31 . . . . .214, 267
6:31–34 214
6:31–44 . . . . .206, 212, 213, 214, 266
6:31–45 . . . . .267, 271
6:32 . . . . .214, 215, 267
6:32–33 215
6:33 215
6:34 . . . . .213, 215, 267, 268, 269
6:34–36 267
6:35 214
6:35–36 267
6:35–37 . . . . .215, 231, 267
6:36 . . . . .216, 225, 478
6:37 . . . . 163, 207, 216, 227, 231,
 242, 256, 270, 569
6:38 . . . . .217, 267
6:38–44 217
6:39 217
6:41 . . . . .267, 270, 489, 562
6:42 . . . . .217, 267
6:43 267
6:44 267
6:45 . . . . .225, 267
6:45–45 225
6:45–52 223
6:45–56 133
6:46–50 63
6:47–50 225
6:48 . . . . .223, 226
6:49 239
6:49–50 226
6:49–51 307
6:50 . . . . .307, 325, 565
6:51 . . . . .368, 530, 565
6:51–52 . . . . .226, 314, 563
6:52 . . . . . .149, 226, 231, 239, 252, 268, 270
6:53 230
6:53–56 . . . . .230, 238, 239
6:54–55 230
6:55–56 231
6:55b–56a 230
6:56 . . . . .110, 232, 350, 546
6:56b 230
7. 237
7:1–5 238
7:1–23 . . . . .234, 238, 254
7:2 239
7:3 239

7:3–4 239
7:6 22
7:6–8 240
7:6–13 240
7:8 240
7:8–13 342
7:9 240
7:10 240
7:13 240
7:14–15 241
7:14–23 241
7:15 .235, 241, 402
7:16 241
7:17 343
7:18 242
7:18–19 242
7:18–23 242
7:19 . . . . .242, 252
7:20–23 243
7:21–22 243
7:24–30 . . . . .114, 238, 253, 540
7:24–36 160
7:24–37 393
7:25 . . . . .18, 239, 255, 357, 376
7:25–26 316
7:26–27 255
7:27 . . . . .13, 255
7:28 256
7:29 478
7:31 . . . . .262, 269
7:31–35 314
7:31–37 . . . . .38, 260, 281
7:32 . . . . .262, 288
7:33 . . . . .110, 350
7:34 . . . . .263, 277, 531, 562
7:35 263
7:35–37 518
7:36 . . . . .50, 263
8. 269
8:1 269
8:1–3 267
8:1–9 160
8:1–10 . . . . .266, 267, 271, 481
8:2 . . . . .267, 269
8:2–3 . . . . .267, 270
8:3 . . . . .267, 268
8:4 . . . . .269, 270
8:5 . . . . .267, 271
8:6 . . . . .267, 270, 271, 489

8:7 267
8:8 . . . . .267, 270, 271
8:9 . . . . .267, 271
8:9–10 271
8:10 267
8:10–12 547
8:11 .276, 341, 547
8:11–12 . . . . .63, 517
8:11–13 . . . . .275, 283
8:12 . . . . .277, 315
8:13 277
8:14–18 137
8:14–21 280
8:15 . . . . .282, 288, 313, 315, 332, 442
8:16 283
8:17 262
8:17–18 . . . . .18, 19, 149, 163, 458
8:17–21 . . . . .288, 514
8:18 . . . . .131, 281
8:19–20 283
8:21 . . . . .107, 112, 131, 458
8:22 . . . . .110, 288, 367, 375
8:22–26 . . . .18, 281, 286, 287, 291, 375, 541
8:22–10:52. . . . . 19, 287, 291, 292,
293, 357, 377
8:23 288
8:25 288
8:26 288
8:27 . . . . .291, 293
8:27–30 . . . . .262, 287
8:27–33 . . . . .9, 291, 377
8:27–38 376
8:28 . . . . .30, 37, 253, 293
8:29 .26, 27, 293
8:29–38 477
8:30 293
8:31 . . . . 187, 287, 292, 294, 301, 375,
386, 412, 475, 479, 485, 501, 507,
513, 514, 520, 525, 533, 561
8:31–32 . . . . .9, 27, 307, 368, 403
8:31–33 . . . .90, 164, 232, 262, 287, 330, 567
8:31–35 31
8:31–38 530
8:31–9:29. 322
8:32 . 293, 294, 301, 369, 378, 491, 504, 531,
540
8:32–33 . . . . .287, 299, 375, 377, 535
8:33 . . 17, 139, 226, 295, 298, 300, 307, 359,
370, 387, 528, 529, 531, 563, 568

8:34 . . . . . . .43, 146, 299, 300, 345, 539, 543
8:34–35 506
8:34–38 . . . . .332, 478, 491
8:34–9:1. . . . . .287, 298, 372, 376
8:35 . . . . .300, 301, 546, 553
8:35–38 . . . . .300, 488
8:36 301
8:37 301
8:38 . . . . .299, 301, 315, 521, 535
9. . . . . .305, 328
9:1 . . . . .301, 302, 306, 564
9:2 . . . . .113, 187, 301, 306
9:2–3 8
9:2–13 .37, 301, 304
9:4–5 293
9:5 307
9:6 . . . . .306, 503
9:7 . . . . . 5, 12, 145, 300, 305, 307, 357, 403,
442, 518, 550, 564, 568
9:8 307
9:9 . . . . .307, 518
9:11 308
9:11–13 293
9:12 . . . . .308, 475, 485, 533
9:12–13 403
9:13 .486, 504, 513
9:14 . . . . .314, 402
9:14–29 . . . . .64, 312
9:15 314
9:16 314
9:17 314
9:18 . . . . .315, 369
9:19 . . . . .313, 315
9:20 315
9:22 . . . . .315, 501
9:23 501
9:24 .146, 316, 320
9:27 . . . . .57, 317
9:28 343
9:29 .315, 317, 369
9:30–31 90
9:30–32 313
9:30–34 567
9:30–35 232
9:30–37 322
9:30–50 338
9:31 . . . 9, 187, 287, 324, 336, 368, 375, 387,
403, 412, 479, 488, 498, 501, 513,
525, 527, 529, 532, 561

9:31–32 292
9:32 565
9:32–34 . . . . .287, 375
9:33 .324, 325, 343
9:33–34 .324, 325, 343
9:34 . .293, 314, 324, 325, 331, 369, 478, 507
9:35 . . . . .58, 322, 325, 332
9:35–37 . . . . .15, 287, 348, 372
9:36 325
9:36–37 . . . . .333, 350, 481, 569
9:36–50 348
9:37 . . . . .6, 323, 326, 396, 465
9:38 . . . . .47, 330, 331, 332, 551
9:38–41 383
9:38–50 . . . . .329, 336, 350
9:39–40 332
9:39–48 332
9:40 551
9:41 . . . . .26, 332
9:42 333
9:42–48 333
9:43–48 333
9:44 333
9:45 334
9:46 333
9:47 334
9:49 335
9:49–50 335
9:50 335
10. 352
10:1 341
10:1–12 339
10:2 341
10:3 341
10:5 343
10:6 343
10:7–8 340
10:8 343
10:9 343
10:10 343
10:10–16 356
10:11 343
10:12 343
10:13 350
10:13–14 69
10:13–16 . . . . .273, 348
10:14 .226, 350, 370
10:15 . . . . .355, 358
10:16 . . . . .350, 352

10:17 . . . . .356, 357
10:17–22 . . . . .146, 357, 436
10:17–23 7
10:17–31 164
10:18 . . . . .357, 403
10:20 358
10:21 . . . . .43, 358
10:22 . . . . .359, 377
10:23 359
10:23–27 359
10:24 . . . . .359, 360, 368, 562
10:25 360
10:26 . . . . .360, 368
10:27 . . . . .360, 501
10:28 . . . . .43, 361, 444, 506, 560
10:28–31 361
10:30 361
10:31 .146, 322, 361
10:32 . . . . .43, 307, 325, 562, 565
10:32–34 . . . . .239, 292, 355, 368
10:32–45 . . . . .232, 365
10:33 . . . . .412, 488, 498, 513, 527, 529
10:33–34 . . . . 9, 90, 287, 368, 375, 387, 403,
479, 501, 514, 525, 532
10:34 . . . . .187, 520, 534, 561
10:35 . . . . .369, 502
10:35–37 293
10:35–40 . . . . .544, 567
10:35–41 . . . . .287, 369, 375
10:35–45 377
10:36 . . . . .188, 377
10:36–37 378
10:37 .146, 369, 544
10:38 369
10:39 . . . . .369, 370
10:40 370
10:42 370
10:42–45 . . . . .283, 287, 370, 376
10:43 58
10:43–44 . . . . .6, 10, 367, 371
10:43–45 15
10:45 . .9, 10, 58, 64, 310, 371, 501, 530, 546
10:46 .291, 376, 531
10:46–52 . . . . 18, 286, 287, 355, 368,
375, 376, 441, 541
10:47 18
10:48 377
10:49 377
10:50 377

10:51 . . . . 188, 369, 377, 465
10:52 . . 43, 188, 291, 367, 377, 378, 541, 546
11. 390
11–12. 449
11–13. 515
11:1 .382, 477, 485
11:1–6 . . . . .382, 484, 485, 486
11:1–11 . . . . .376, 380, 400, 530
11:1–12:44. . . . . .19, 380, 485
11:2 . . . . .383, 485
11:3 . . . . .383, 485
11:4–6 383
11:6 485
11:7 384
11:7–10 384
11:8–10 . . . . .504, 531
11:9 384
11:9–10 50
11:10 384
11:11 . . . . 384, 385, 390, 391, 392,
410, 440, 444
11:12–13 485
11:12–14 .390, 391
11:12–16 545
11:12–17 444
11:12–25 .389, 400
11:12–12:44. 545
11:13 . . . . .392, 410
11:13–20 461
11:14 . . . . .392, 402, 451, 458
11:15 392
11:15–16 .402, 417
11:15–17 . . . . .425, 434, 485, 516
11:15–19 .390, 392
11:16 393
11:17 . . . . . 37, 390, 391, 393, 417, 424, 440,
461, 528, 545, 551
11:17–18 402
11:18 . . . . . 63, 125, 307, 325, 393, 412, 417,
424, 425, 476, 505, 517, 533, 563
11:19 394
11:20 . . . . .394. 458
11:20–21 402
11:20–25 .390, 394
11:21 . . . . .394, 452
11:22–25 394
11:23 395
11:24 395
11:25 395

11:27 .402, 434, 451
11:27–28 48
11:27–33 400
11:27–12:27. . . . . .431, 434
11:27–12:34. 400
11:28 . . . . .412, 423
11:29 403
11:30 403
11:31–32 404
11:32 . . . . .307, 325, 404
11:33 404
12. .408, 409, 433
12:1 410
12:1–9 . . . . .410, 421
12:1–11 444
12:1–12 . . . . .407, 417, 485
12:2 .410, 411, 425
12:6 411
12:7 . . . . .37, 408, 409
12:8 411
12:9 411
12:10–11 .409, 412
12:11 410
12:12 . . . . . 63, 122, 125, 307, 325, 413, 417,
418, 476, 505, 517, 563
12:13 . . . . .418, 516
12:13–17 .417, 423
12:14 .419, 434, 517
12:15 419
12:16 420
12:17 420
12:18–23 425
12:18–27 423
12:19 434
12:26–27 427
12:28 434
12:28–34 . . .78, 279, 314, 331, 423, 440, 552
12:32 434
12:33 433
12:34 . . . . .431, 436, 440, 442, 552
12:35 . . . . .26, 424, 440, 441
12:35–37 . . . . .377, 441, 526, 544
12:36 440
12:37 . . . . .441, 442
12:38 .424, 440, 442
12:38–40 . . . . .37, 442, 475, 552
12:40 . . . . .444, 449
12:41 . . . . .452, 551
12:41–44 . . . . .444, 449, 475

12:42 . . . . .444, 449
12:42–43 449
12:42–44 478
12:43 449
12:44 444
13. . . . . . . 12, 449, 451, 464, 466, 467, 468,
469, 470, 475, 498, 499, 535
13:1 .394, 440, 458
13:1–3 452
13:1–4 . . . . .449, 451
13:1–37 . . . . .12, 20, 447
13:2 .394, 453, 518
13:3 . . . . .113, 444, 452
13:4 .450, 453, 461
13:5 . . . . .454, 498
13:5–23 . . . . .450, 453, 454, 460
13:5–37 . . . . .449, 450, 498
13:6 454
13:6–8 455
13:7 . . . . .453, 459
13:8c 453
13:9 . . . . .456, 498
13:9–11 529
13:9–12 324
13:9–13 515
13:10 . . . . .453, 456
13:11 . . . . .456, 514, 534
13:12–13 456
13:13 456
13:14 .12, 456, 458
13:14–23 459
13:15–17 458
13:20 458
13:21 26
13:21–22 459
13:22 . . . . .454, 459, 501
13:23 . . . . .454, 459, 498
13:24 459
13:24–27 . . . . .450, 459, 460, 461
13:26 460
13:27 461
13:28 452
13:28–31 . . . . .450, 461
13:28–37 450
13:29 . . . . .461, 462
13:30 461
13:31 461
13:32 . . . . .451, 462
13:32–37 . . . . .450, 462, 569

13:33 . . . . .462, 498
13:33–37 464
13:34 . . . . .462, 498
13:35 . . . . .462, 498
13:36 . . . . .462, 498, 502
13:37 .12, 462, 498
14. 539
14–15 . . . . .449, 474, 475
14:1 533
14:1–15:47 20
14:1 . . . . .63, 125, 475, 476, 517
14:1–2 . . . . .475, 476
14:1–11 . . . . .449, 474
14:2 476
14:3 477
14:3–8 . . . . .475, 477
14:3–9 . . . . .146, 499, 503, 539, 540
14:4 477
14:5 . . . . .449, 478
14:6 . . . . .478, 553
14:7 . . . . .449, 475, 478, 479, 480
14:8 . . . . .478, 553
14:9 . . . . .449, 479
14:10 . . . . .449, 477, 503
14:10–11 . . . . .475, 478, 479
14:11 .63, 125, 475
14:12 486
14:12–16 . . . . .484, 485, 486
14:12–31 . . . . .483, 499
14:12–15:47 485
14:13 . . . . .485, 487
14:14 . . . . .485, 486, 487, 568
14:16 . . . . .485, 486
14:17–21 . . . . .484, 487, 492
14:18 . . . . .487, 491
14:18–21 498
14:18–27 568
14:20 488
14:21 488
14:22 553
14:22–23 553
14:22–26 . . . . .484, 489, 492
14:23 489
14:24 . . . . .489, 500
14:25 . . . . .490, 491
14:26 490
14:27 491
14:27–31 . . . . .369, 484, 490, 492
14:28 .57, 491, 564

14:29 . . . . .491, 502
14:30 . . . . .491, 513, 522
14:31 . . . . .491, 502, 506, 544
14:32 500
14:32–34 500
14:32–42 64
14:32–52 . . . . .497, 554, 556
14:32–15:47 .485
14:33 . . . . .113, 187, 499, 500
14:34 . . . . .499, 500
14:35 . . . . .500, 501
14:35–38 499
14:35–42 501
14:36 . . . . .500, 501, 502, 507, 531
14:37 502
14:38 502
14:39 502
14:39–40 503
14:40 503
14:41 . . . . .503, 504
14:42 . . . . .503, 504
14:43 . . . . .503, 532
14:43–49 . . . . .503, 513
14:44 504
14:44–46 504
14:46 . . . . .122, 504
14:47 504
14:48 505
14:48–49 . . . . .504, 505, 529
14:49 . . . . .475, 485, 501, 505, 507, 514, 533
14:50 . . . . .114, 504, 505, 565
14:50–52 505
14:51 . . . . .506, 562
14:51–52 562
14:52 565
14:53 525
14:53–54 . . . . .506, 514, 516
14:53–65 525
14:53–72 512
14:54 . . . . .516, 520, 521, 552, 560
14:55 . . . . .63, 517, 525
14:55–65 516
14:57–58 545
14:58 . . . . .471, 517, 546, 561
14:60–61 518
14:61 . . . . .26, 525, 530, 550
14:62 . . . . .518, 525, 534, 550
14:63 519
14:63–64 545

14:64 519
14:65 . . . . .519, 520, 525
14:66–72 . . . . .520, 540, 560
14:67 . . . . .114, 516, 520
14:68 521
14:69 521
14:70 521
14:71 521
14:72 . . . . .506, 521, 522
15. 539
15:1 . . . . .525, 527, 528, 533, 552
15:1–5 . . . . .527, 528
15:1–20 524
15:2 . . . . .525, 529, 533, 534
15:3 530
15:4 530
15:5 . . . . .525, 530, 565
15:6 531
15:6–15 . . . . .504, 527, 528, 531, 543
15:7 531
15:8 532
15:9 . . . . .532, 533
15:10 . . . . .104, 532
15:11 . . . . .231, 532
15:11–15 50
15:12 533
15:12–13 532
15:14 . . . . .532, 544
15:15 . . . . .527, 532, 533
15:15–20 525
15:16 533
15:16–20 . . . . .527, 533, 552
15:18 . . . . .526, 533
15:19 534
15:21 . . . . .539, 542
15:21–27 542
15:21–47 538
15:22 543
15:23 543
15:24 . . . . .541, 543
15:25 . . . . .541, 543
15:26 543
15:27 . . . . .541, 544
15:29 . . . . .545, 561
15:29–32 545
15:30 546
15:31 546
15:32 . . . . .26, 541, 547, 549
15:33 547

15:33–39 547
15:34 . . . . .319, 507, 531, 547, 548
15:35 547
15:35–36 . . . . .293, 540
15:36 . . . . .547, 549
15:37 . . . . .547, 549
15:38 . . . . .30, 544, 547, 549
15:39 . . . . 8, 10, 16, 27, 137, 171, 540,
544, 550, 552
15:40 . . . . .540, 551, 552, 559, 565
15:40–41 . . . . .551, 559
15:41 . . . . .43, 302, 540, 551
15:42 552
15:42–47 . . . . .436, 552
15:43 . . . . .539, 552
15:44–45 553
15:45 553
15:46 . . . . .539, 553
15:46–47 561
15:47 551
16:1 . . . . .475, 561
16:1–3 560
16:1–5 302
16:1–8 . . . . .20, 475, 559
16:2 561
16:3 561
16:4 . . . . .561, 562
16:4–7 561
16:5 562
16:6 . . . . .57, 187, 302, 475, 563
16:7 . . . . .14, 564, 568
16:8 . . . . 12, 18, 307, 325, 552, 560,
565, 571, 572, 573
16:9 573
16:9–20 . . . . .571, 572
16:14 573
16:15 573

Luke

1. 276
1:5–25 275
1:18 275
1:26–38 275
1:34 275
1:39–45 275
1:46–55 56
1:46–56 55
4:1–13 295
4:8 170

4:14–30 192
5:32 496
7:36–50 477
9:1–2 51
11:29–30 426
11:43 365
11:46 251
11:47–51 407
12:10 127
12:23 426
12:24 426
12:24–27 426
12:25 . . . . .426, 427
12:26–27 427
12:27 426
12:31 435
12:32 435
12:33 435
13:33–34 . . . . .192, 193
12:35–44 439
14:7–11 365
15. 74
15:1–2 495
15:11–32 495
16:19–31 355
19:38 412
20:17 412
20:45–47 365
24:13–35 212
24:28–29 327

John

1:1 327
1:1–18 22
1:18 80
2:24–25 51
3:1–21 348
3:14 197
4. 482
4:21 170
4:31 482
4:32 482
4:34 482
6:15 525
6:35 . . . . .197, 282
6:54–57 197
6:60 197
6:61–62 197
7:17 150

8:28 197
8:31–32 150
8:37–44 54
8:42–44 121
9. . . . . .67, 74, 286, 375
9:1–2 68
10:17–31 354
11. 556
11:3 . . . . .186, 556
11:21 . . . . .186, 556
11:32 . . . . .186, 556
11:33–35 556
12:1–8 477
12:23–26 112
12:25–26 228
13:35 71
16:7 . . . . .88, 91
17:20–23 327
18:10 504
18:39 531
20:30–31 11

Acts

2:34–35 440
2:38 34
2:39 266
4:11 412
5:3 144
5:12 252
5:15–16 230
5:17–42 36
5:36 28
5:37 419
7. . . . . .192, 200
7:9–16 193
7:17–29 193
7:48–53 389
7:52 193
10. . . . . .243, 255
10–11. 495
10:1–11:18. . . . . .235, 348
10:8–17 237
10:21–48 495
10:23 255
10:25 255
10:28 . . . . .237, 238, 269
10:34–36 349
11:1–3 495
11:2–3 238

11:3 255
11:12 255
12:12 10
13:13 10
14:15 171
15. . . . . .83, 207, 252
15:4 207
15:5 105
15:37 10
15:39 10
16:16–24 170
18:5–6 203
19. 117
19:5 29
19:13–16 117
19:13–17 54
19:13–19 47
19:21; 20:16. .252
20. 284
20:17–35 450
20:28 284
21. 207
21:17–20 207
21:18 125
21:24–26 252
21:38 . . . . .28, 63
22:21 . . . . .266, 270
23. 425
23:6 . . . . .105, 252
23:6–8 425
25:19–20 529
26:5–7 252

Romans

1. 170
1:1–5 291
1:1–7 21
1:4 559
1:18–3:31. 330
1:21–25 167
1:23 170
1:24 170
2:11 . . . .55, 56, 258, 329, 330, 417, 418, 419
2:24 124
3:21–24 348
3:29–30 388
4:18–21 153
4:18–24 313
4:19 428

5:1–2 335
5:3–5 509
5:6–8 . . . . .83, 84
7:12, 16 251
8:1 335
8:5–17 280
8:9 91
8:12–30 260
8:15 336
8:18–23 264
8:18–27 . . . . .191, 511
8:19–27 468
8:20–21 511
8:22 263
8:23 263
8:26 263
8:26–27 511
8:27 . . . . .263, 511
8:28 191
9:6–33 119
9:12 258
12:1–2 . . . . .145, 198, 289
12:15 429
13:9–10 . . . . .431, 432
13:11 92
14:5 . . . . .99, 101
14:5–9 96
14:14 243
14:14–17 235
14:17 . . . . .39, 310
15:7 496
16:25 137

1 Corinthians

1:12 366
1:18 283
1:18–25 275
1:18–2:16. . . . . .137, 280, 385
1:20–25 197
1:23 333
2:1–5 . . . . .66, 366
2:1–8 . . . . .291, 292
2:7 137
2:7–8 . . . . .525, 527
2:10–11 327
3:5–9 .135, 365, 366
3:5–15 . . . . .152, 156
3:16 327
3:16–17 . . . . . . .249, 329, 337, 389, 394, 395

5:6 282
6:1–11 362
6:16 339
6:20; 7:23. 100
8:6 431
11. . . . . .220, 494
11:17 . . . . .220, 221
11:17–34 . . . . .266, 396
11:17–37 490
11:18 221
11:17–34 . . . . .212, 356, 362, 494
11:17–37 484
11:20 221
11:21–22 221
11:22 . . . . .362, 494
11:23–24 220
11:23–26 498
11:26 .222, 479, 490
11:27 . . . . .220, 221
11:28–30 337
11:29 493
11:30 .221, 396, 494
11:32 . . . . .220, 221, 337, 362
11:33–34 222
11:34 220
12:12–31 334
15. . . . . .523, 559
15:1–8 21
15:25–27 440
15:25–28 . . . . .92, 116, 468
15:35–55 111

2 Corinthians

4. 31
4:3–6 147
4:4 . . . . .119, 123, 143, 189, 468
4:7 367
4:7–18 365
4:10 . . . . .345, 367
5:1–2 427
8:9 365
11:1–12:10. . . . . .365, 367
11:18 367
11:23–30 367
11:31–33 367
12:7–8 111
12:8 190
12:9 111

Galatians

1:4 143
1:6–10 298
1:8–9 250
2. 249
2:12 . . . . .266, 269
2:14 . . . . .249, 269
2:15–16 84
2:15–21 . . . . .83, 348
2:20 . . . . .309, 490
2:21 222
3:28 253
5:9 282
5:14 431
6:10 102
6:14 . . . . .42, 309

Ephesians

1. 290
1:3–4 45
1:13 145
1:15–23 286
1:17–19 289
1:20–22 440
1:22 440
2:1–3 . . . . .119, 143
2:2 . . . . .123, 143, 468
2:5–6 490
2:8 92
2:8–9 87
2:11–14 249
2:11–22 235
2:12 266
2:13 270
2:17 . . . . .266, 270
2:19–22 . . . . .389, 394, 395
2:20 412
2:21–22 327
3:2–13 137
3:4–5 137
3:7–8 365
3:9 171
3:10 116
4:3 145
4:7–13 88
4:11 246
4:20–21 397
4:22 397

4:22–24 290
4:23 397
4:24 397
4:25–32 397
4:26 144
4:26–27 .52, 53, 116
4:27 144
4:31–32 144
5–6. 117
5:21–6:9. . . . . .54, 116
5:22–33 . . . . .339, 340
6:10–12 468
6:10–18 . . . . .54, 116

Philippians

1:19 263
1:29 509
2:1–18 298
2:5–11 . . . . .322, 323, 380
2:6–8 323
2:9 323
2:9–11 . . . . .107, 108, 109
3. 298
3:2 . . . . .253, 255
3:5 105
3:20 92

Colossians

1:13 . . . . .39, 310
1:13–14 36
1:26–27 137
2:8 248
2:16 96
2:16–17 . . . . .99, 101
3:19 340
4:10 10

1 Thessalonians

4:13 . . . . .94, 265

1 Timothy

3:1–7 245
3:2 327
3:16 291
6:4 124
6:4–5 364
6:6–10 . . . . .355, 364
6:11–12 313
6:17–19 355

2 Timothy

3:10–12 36
4:11 10

Titus

1:5–9 245

Philemon

1–25 67
24 10

Hebrews

1:1–3 80
1:6 170
1:13 440
2:1–4 128
2:8 509
3:12–14; 4:1–11 .128
4:12 47
6 128
6:1–12 119
6:4–8 . . . . .127, 128
6:7–8 135
6:9–12 129
10:19–39 128
10:24–25 129
12:7 336
12:7–11 191
12:25–29 471
13:2 . . . . .322, 327, 482
13:16 434

James

1:2 336
1:2–4 .93, 191, 336, 509
1:5 76
1:9–11 181
1:12 93
1:13 190
1:19–25 131
1:25 251
2:1–4 363
2:1–13 . . . . .348, 355, 356, 396, 474
2:4 . . . . .349, 363
2:5 349
2:8 431
2:8–11 349
2:8–13 433
2:9 363

2:14–17 219
2:14–26 436
3:1 415
3:13–18 198
3:14–17 . . . . .47, 54
4:1–10 . . . . .117, 144
4:3 144
4:7 144
4:11–12 144
5:1–6 . . . . .355, 363, 396, 474
5:14 203
5:17–18 62

1 Peter

1:17 . . . . .55, 56, 347, 417, 418
2:7 412
2:9–10 45
2:12 537
2:18–25 525
2:19 42
2:21 509
3:7 . . . . .339, 340
3:15 536
3:15–16 536
3:21 34
3:22 440
4:17 336
5:6–11 117
5:13 10

2 Peter

1:10 283
2:10–12 . . . . .117, 124

1 John

2:19 336
3:2 336
3:16–18 . . . . .219, 432
4:8–12 432
4:16–21 71
5:3 100
5:16 128
5:16–17 . . . . .119, 126, 128
5:18 . . . . .118, 145
5:18–19 . . . . .47, 54

Jude

1 145
8–10 . . . . .54, 117

21. . . . . .336, 337
24–25. 336

Revelation

1:12–14 306
1:13–14 304
2:5 196
2:26–27 .400, 401
3:17 363
3:17–18 363
3:20 . . . . .322, 327
4:10 170
5:11–14 380
6:9–11 556

6:10 319
7:9 348
12:10 400
12:10–11 . . . . .298, 402
14:7 500
14:10 . . . . .500, 501
14:14–20 152
14:18 500
21–22. 559
22:7 92
22:15 255
22:17 264
22:20 509

Subject Index

Aaron, 236, 330
Abel, 51–52, 53
Abiathar, 96, 98n. 4
Abigail, 113
Abihu, 236
Abraham, 2, 23, 113, 153, 292, 327, 340n. 1, 428, 482
abstraction, 157
accountability to God, 415–16
Adam, 1
adultery, 339, 342–43n. 7, 343–44
Advent, 32
Ahab, 7, 37, 201, 205, 515
Ahasuerus, 205, 206
Ahimelech, 98n. 4
Andrew, 42, 44, 112, 447, 453, 455, 521
Angel of the Lord, the, 510, 510n. 14
anointing woman, the, 449, 449n.2, 474, 475, 477–79, 499, 503, 540, 552–53
Antiochus Epiphanes, 3, 381
Apollos, 366
apostasy, 129, 129n. 9
Araunah, 476
authority, of Jesus
    God as source of, 48, 400–402, 403, 404, 409, 410, 412, 417, 442
    over the Sabbath, 99
    to cast out demons, 48, 49–50, 167–68, 171, 403
    to control the wind and the see, 50, 133, 172, 403
    to forgive sins, 48, 74, 78, 79n. 6, 80, 403
    to shut down the temple, 48, 402, 403, 408, 409, 412, 417, 423, 425, 442

baptism
    of Jesus, 21, 30, 124, 403, 442, 519, 550, 567
    identification of Jesus as God's son at, 12, 21, 23, 31, 403, 442, 518, 519, 550n. 16, 551, 567
    as initiation into corporate movement of repentance, 28–30
    significance of, 33–34
    what it is, 33
Barnabas, 10, 202, 207
Barabbas, 525, 528, 531–32, 543
Bartholomew, calling of, 112
Bartimaeus,
    desire of to see, 18, 188, 369, 375, 376, 377, 465, 541
    healing of, 375, 377–78
    identification of Jesus as son of David, 188, 377, 441, 520
    perception as contrasted with disciples' blindness, 18, 188–89, 286–87, 369, 376, 377–78, 520, 541
    place of his healing in the broader story arc of Mark, 286, 287, 355, 367, 368, 375–76
Basil, 44
blasphemy, 124
bleeding woman
    faith of, 181, 185–86, 192, 196, 232, 540
    healing of, 180, 184–86, 232
    worship of, 185, 192, 231, 239
Boaz, 424

Cain, 2, 51–52, 52
Caleb, 299
casting out demons. See exorcisms
church, the
    accountability to God of, 415–16
    and care for the marginalized, 54, 395–96, 481
    and casting out demons, 115–18
    creating inclusive cultures in, 85–86, 257–59
    cultivating an attitude of abundance in, 271–74
    consumerism in, 219
    division within, 52, 53, 143–45
    everyone welcome in, 59–61, 65, 71, 83–84, 86, 137

individualism in, 218–19
and justice, 395–97
and mental illness, 176–77
need for watchfulness among leadership of, 284–85
as the new temple, 394, 395–96
opposition of to Satan and the powers and authorities, 116
and white flight, 177–79
clean vs. unclean, 235–37, 241
commands for silence, Jesus
after exorcisms, 17, 55, 58, 107, 109
after healings, 17, 67, 70, 189–90, 260, 263
after a resurrection, 181, 187
after the transfiguration, 304, 307–8, 518
reason for, 9, 12, 17, 50, 55, 58, 65, 70, 139, 225, 263, 293, 296, 382, 567
to the disciples, 291, 293, 304, 307–8, 518
confession, 39, 40, 82, 146
consumerism, 219
creation
chaos as threatening to undo, 134n. 1, 161, 468
God as King of all, 36, 274, 349, 440, 554
as God's dwelling place, 1, 96
groaning of, 191, 263, 264, 468, 511
healing as work of new, 260–61, 262
humanity's relation to, 1, 31, 36, 162, 260, 343, 509
Jesus's resurrection as ushering in new, 226, 308n. 5, 324, 426, 469, 501, 508, 550
new, longing for, 263, 264–65, 511, 556
cross-shaped kingdom, the
crowds as hindrance to message of, 50, 65, 70, 263, 277, 382, 504
disciples called to, 9, 143, 294, 301, 505, 527
need for revelation of, 147–48, 153, 242, 568
Peter's rejection of, 295, 378
radical character of, 17, 138, 140, 141, 282, 297, 573
crowds
delighting in Jesus, 439, 442, 532
demanding Jesus's execution, 504, 524, 532, 544
as evidence of desire for restoration, 70, 107, 110, 231, 503

as evidence that the true nature of the gospel is obscured, 17, 50, 70, 139, 504
as hindrance to basic needs of, 119, 122, 125, 212, 214–15, 225
as hindrance to work of Jesus, 17, 50, 67, 109, 110, 130, 133, 134, 137, 139, 183–84, 231, 504, 532
at Jesus's arrest, 503–4, 532
Cyrus, 26

Daniel, 62
darkness, as sign of God's judgment, 538, 547–48
David, 52–53, 62, 96, 98, 441, 450n. 3, 476, 510
Decapolis, the, 160, 167, 174, 260, 262, 269
demons, casting out. See exorcisms
disciples, the
abandonment of Jesus, 20, 474, 498, 505–6, 551–52, 560
being with Jesus and aligned to his mission, 163, 170, 173n. 11, 214, 384, 505, 516, 520, 535, 552, 559
being with Jesus while being sent out, 114,120, 203, 206, 213, 216, 315
calling of, 42, 43–44, 45, 46, 112–15, 120, 145, 173, 203, 520
casting out demons, 43, 51, 112, 114, 115, 116, 163, 199, 202, 203, 210, 213, 216
desire of for military victory by the messiah, 9, 385, 531
desire for place of prominence, 287, 293, 294, 322, 365, 366, 369, 370, 371, 378, 478, 551, 567
failure of to perceive, 170–71, 181, 207, 226–28, 231, 239, 242, 254–55, 262, 270–71, 280–81, 283, 286–87, 293, 324, 375–76
faithful devotion of Jesus to, 14, 487, 489, 491, 492
faithlessness of, 313, 314, 316–17, 369
and fasting, lack of, 88, 89, 490
and the feeding of the five thousand, 163, 207, 212, 215–17
fishing for people, 44
hardened hearts of, 18, 155, 223, 226–27, 242, 280, 283, 314, 360, 368, 403, 458, 514, 549

healings by, 43, 163, 199, 202, 203, 210, 213, 216

Jesus's rebuke of, 162–63, 235, 242, 348, 350, 355

necessity of perseverance as, 522–23

as outsiders, 136, 207, 227, 283, 287, 520, 521, 539–40, 567

persecution of, 200, 447, 451, 454, 456, 468, 515, 529

preaching of, 112, 114, 447, 456

presentation of in Mark, 14

profession of loyalty to Jesus of, 484, 492, 506, 544

as reconstituted Israel, 114

renaming of, 113, 115

requirement for watchfulness among, 447–48, 449, 451, 454, 456, 457, 459, 462, 464, 497, 498, 500–501, 502, 505

return of, 206–7, 210

sarcasm of, 14, 207, 216, 242, 256

selfishness of, 286, 287, 292, 322, 375

sending of to proclaim the gospel, 19, 112, 114, 120, 199, 201, 202–3, 210, 213

discipleship
    as hospitality to the marginalized and service to the needy, 14, 15, 88, 150, 288, 297, 300, 340, 348, 451, 462, 465, 469, 569

    Jesus teaching about, 19, 286–87, 294, 298–99, 300–302, 304–5, 339–41, 375–76

    in Mark, 14–15

    wealth as obstacle to, 361–64

divorce, 339–44. 342–43n. 7, 344–45, 347

Eleazar, 47

Elijah
    and Ahab and Jezebel, 7, 37, 201, 205, 515

    and call of Elisha, 43

    encounter with God at Horeb, 113, 224, 225, 305

    healing by, 182, 190, 202

    and Jesus, 7, 37, 44, 201, 202, 204–5, 253, 291, 293, 316, 357, 573

    and John the Baptist, 30, 37, 44, 403

    prayer of, 62

    as sent to prepare the way, 27, 304, 308, 403

    and transfiguration of Jesus, 304, 305

    vindication of, 305

Elisha, 43, 182–83, 190

Elizabeth, 275

Esau, 83

Esther, 206

Eve, 1

exclusivity, 331–332, 333, 334, 335, 348

exodus, the,
    from Egypt, 2

    new, 4n. 3, 201

    second, 3

exorcisms
    in the ancient world, 47

    in Capernaum, 47, 49–50, 51, 55, 58, 104

    in the modern church, 115–18

    of the deaf and mute boy, 312, 315–17

    done by the disciples, 19, 43, 51, 112, 114, 115, 116, 163, 199, 202, 203, 210, 213, 216

    done by others, 47–48, 329, 331, 332

    Holy Spirit and, 48

    of the leper, 69–70

    of the man in the tombs, 166–67, 171–73

    as manifestation of advance of God's kingdom, 4, 43, 48, 64, 105, 115, 123–24, 160, 163, 166–67, 181–82n. 1, 189, 260, 332, 384, 403

    in the New Testament, 47–48

    as resurrections, 57

Ezekiel, 8, 65, 120–21, 196, 294

faith
    as condition of restoration, 547

    definition of, 40

    dimensions of, 317–20

    and healing, 188–91, 232

    and the power of God, 195–96

    versus fear, 163–64, 173, 181, 307, 325, 368

false messiahs and prophets, 447–48, 454

Falwell, Jerry, Sr., 413, 466, 467, 469

fear
    and departure, 177

    versus faith, 163–64, 173, 181, 307, 325, 368

Feast of Unleavened Bread, the, 474, 476

forgiveness
    of God, 75–76, 80–82, 83, 126, 127, 129, 437

    of Jesus, 48, 74, 75, 76, 77, 80

objective, 437
as root of relationship with God, 437
steps to pursuing, 438
subjective, 437

Gabriel, 275
Gad, 510
Gideon, 276
God
as above all other gods, 108, 161, 167–68,
170, 170–71n. 6, 432
calling of, 42, 45–46, 83
command of the sea, 162
compassion of, 75, 81, 90, 160
creation as dwelling place of, 1, 96
and forgiveness, 75–76, 80–82, 83, 126,
127, 129
generosity of, 71–73
grace of, 33, 42, 46, 56, 71, 75, 87, 99,
111, 126, 129, 160, 176, 218, 268,
492
and growth of kingdom of God, 152–53
humans in image of, 1, 259, 420–21, 471
impartiality of, 347, 349, 418, 419
as king of all creation, 36, 274, 349, 440,
554
and marriage, 340. 341, 343
over all nations, 259, 269
promises of restoration of, 3, 5, 107–8
provision of for his people, 201, 202, 215,
216, 217, 271
self-revelation of, 223–25, 226, 323
special attention of to the vulnerable, 56,
67–68, 273, 340–41, 345–47, 352,
373, 395, 443, 480–81
subjecting his enemies, 442
treading upon the sea, 224, 226
and treatment of foreigners, 348–49,
351–52
and triumph through defeat, 20, 292–93,
294, 442, 479, 505, 527, 533, 544
gospel, the, 39–40
Graham, Billy, 472
Graham, Franklin, 467

Hagar, 292
Hannah, 55
Hanukkah, 4, 381
healing, praying for, 111

healings
of Bartimaeus, 18, 355, 367, 368, 375,
376-77
of the bleeding woman, 184–86
crowds of people seeking, 230–31
of the deaf and mute man, 260, 262–63
done by the disciples, 163, 199, 202, 203,
210, 213, 216
done by Elijah, 182, 190, 202
and exorcism, 70
faith and, 188–91
to highlight disciples' blindness, 18, 541
of Jairus's daughter, 180–81, 183–84,
186–87
in Jesus's hometown, 189, 192, 195
of the leper, 67, 68–70, 189–90
of the man with the shriveled hand, 102, 104
as manifestation of advance of God's
kingdom, 43, 115, 123, 160, 163,
189, 384, 403, 546
of the paralyzed man, 74, 75, 79, 104–5
and the resurrection of Jesus, 57
and salvation, 181–82n. 1, 546
of Simon's mother-in-law, 55, 56, 57–58
of the Syrian Phoenician woman's daughter,
253
two-stage, 286, 287, 375
as work of new creation, 260–61, 262
hell, 334n. 6
Herod Antipas, 199–200, 204, 204n. 9,
205–6, 208, 282, 341, 468, 532–33
Herodians, 19, 102, 105, 341, 419–20, 423,
533
Herodias, 199, 204, 205, 206, 533
holiness, 244–47
Holy Spirit, the
baptism with, 21
blasphemy against, 119, 124
and David, 439, 441, 442, 526
and exorcisms, 48
as presence of Jesus among the church,
91, 92
and speaking at trial, 447, 456, 514, 529
holy vs. common, 235, 236
humanity
commission of, 162, 401
diversity among, 1
dominion of over creation, 1, 31, 36, 162,
260, 343, 509

in image of God, 1, 259, 420–21, 471
rebellion of, 2, 190
suffering of as training, 191
traditions of, 247–50

identity markers, 86–87
idolatry, 116, 123, 170, 271, 346, 421,
    470–72
impartiality, of God, 347, 349, 418, 419
inclusio, 30–31n. 15, 131, 286, 291n. 1,
    375–76, 377, 454, 475, 527, 547, 550
individualism, 218–19
intercalation. *See* Mark: literary sandwiches in
intercommunity relations, 332–34
investment, 71–73
Isaac, 23
Isaiah, 22
Israel
    agricultural metaphors in relation to, 390
    calling of, 42, 45, 83, 268–69, 313
    as disobedient to God, 299, 313
    drawing nations to, 107, 160, 160n. 2
    exile of, 3, 5
    as God's chosen people, 2, 45, 160
    as God's son, 26
    as holy, 235, 236, 247
    as kingdom of priests, 2, 45, 313
    as a light to the nations, 107, 114, 160n. 2,
        268–69, 313
    longing of for reestablishment of God's
        rule, 4, 5, 24–27, 30, 36, 63, 64–65,
        70, 110, 139, 381–82, 528
    as "not my people," 120
    as people of justice, 114, 160
    rejection of God's messengers, 192–93
    as spiritually captive, 4
    treatment of foreigners, 348–49, 351–52
    treatment of the oppressed, 2–3, 88, 443

Jacob, 83, 113, 193, 340n. 1, 450
Jairus
    faith of, 196
    healing of daughter of, 180–81, 186–87
    perception of, 18, 180, 183, 192, 231,
        520, 540
    worship of, 145, 170, 180, 184, 231, 239
James (son of Alphaeus), calling of, 112
James (son of Zebedee)
    calling of, 42, 45, 112

and destruction of the temple, 447, 453, 455
at Gethsemane, 497, 500–503
and healing of Jairus's daughter, 180, 187
and healing of Simon's mother-in-law, 55
profession of loyalty to Jesus of, 544
renaming of, 112, 115
request of for place of prominence, 14, 188,
    365, 369, 378, 544
and transfiguration of Jesus, 304, 305, 306
jealousy, 51–53
Jeremiah, 88–89, 193, 318, 515
Jesus
    abandonment of, 20, 474, 498, 505–6,
        539–40, 544, 547, 548, 551, 560
    abuse of, 512, 519–20, 524–25, 526,
        533–34, 545–47
    and the anointing woman, 449, 449n. 2,
        474, 475, 477–79, 499, 503, 540,
        552–53
    arrest of, 122, 497–98, 504, 513, 529
    ascension of, 197
    authority of. *See* authority, of Jesus
    baptism of, 21, 30, 124, 403, 442, 519, 550
    betrayal of, 474, 497, 503–5
    and the bleeding woman, 180, 181, 184–
        86, 192, 196, 231, 232, 239, 540
    as bread of life, 197, 282
    burial of, 436, 552–53
    call of to repent, 35–38, 64, 86, 115, 141,
        163, 167, 196, 202, 327, 496
    and calling of the disciples, 42–46, 83,
        84–85, 112–15, 120, 125, 145, 163,
        173, 203, 520
    casting out demons. *See* exorcisms
    as challenge to status quo, 28, 37, 88, 125
    and children, 348, 350–51, 355, 482, 569
    command of to pay attention, 147–49,
        231, 241, 282
    commands of for silence. *See* commands for
        silence, Jesus
    and community judgment, 335
    compassion of, 69, 212, 213, 215, 218,
        226, 231, 266, 267, 268, 269–70
    as confrontational, 5, 7, 202, 205, 253,
        293, 316, 573
    contrasted with Peter, 514–15
    controlling the weather and the waves, 48,
        50, 133, 159, 160–62, 172, 223,
        226, 403

conversation with the rich man, 354–55, 357–59

as cross-oriented, 9–10, 20, 65, 143, 242, 277, 294–97, 301, 366, 478, 514, 519, 527–28, 568, 573

and crowds. *See* crowds

crucifixion of, 538, 541, 543, 546

death of, 538, 547, 548, 549

denial of, 114, 474, 491, 492, 494, 506, 513, 520–22, 542

direct address of readers by, 12, 457, 462

and discipleship, 19, 286–87, 294, 298–99, 300–302, 304–5, 339–41, 357, 375–76

and divorce, 339–44

eating with sinners and tax collectors, 83, 84, 85, 89, 495

and Elijah, 7, 37, 44, 201, 202, 204–5, 253, 291, 293, 316, 573

entrance of to Jerusalem, 384–85

and establishment of God's kingdom, 7, 25, 36–38, 63, 64, 74, 112, 114, 160, 162, 310, 421

faithful devotion of to the disciples, 14, 487, 489, 491, 492, 564, 568

and false messiahs and prophets, 447–48, 454

family of, 119, 120, 122, 124–26, 145, 186, 192, 487

and the feeding of the five thousand, 163, 206, 212, 217–18, 266–68

and the feeding of the four thousand, 266–68, 270

and the fig tree, 389, 390, 391–92, 394, 402, 451, 461, 545

and forgiveness of sins, 48, 74, 75, 76, 77, 78, 79n. 6, 80

at Gethsemane, 187n. 7, 497, 498–503

as God's appointed agent of kingdom rule, 6, 109–10, 123–24, 183, 295, 403, 510, 519

and the greatest commandment, 431, 435

healings by. *See* healings

and hospitality to the marginalized, 6, 14–15, 288, 297, 300, 322, 325–26, 329, 331, 332, 333, 348, 351, 441

identification of as David's son, 439, 440, 441

identification of as God's Son. *See* Son of God, identification of Jesus as

and insiders and outsiders, 120, 124, 172, 163, 254, 280, 294, 488, 539–40

and intercommunity relations, 332–34

and Jerusalem, 193

and John the Baptist, 7, 37, 291, 293, 573

judgment of on the temple treasury, 439, 440, 444, 445

as king of the Jews, 524, 529–30, 533–34, 538, 543, 545

and the Last Supper, 483, 489–90

as the Messiah, 8, 26, 127, 137–38, 167, 293, 376, 512, 518, 519, 534, 546

mission of, 6, 63, 64, 85, 112, 141, 293, 298, 332, 378, 531, 546

and the Mosaic law, 98–99, 105, 242–43, 250–52

and Moses, 201

as the new temple, 28, 393, 395, 400, 410, 412, 449, 460, 486, 517, 550n. 16

"on the way," 291, 291n. 1, 324, 326, 331, 332, 356, 368, 376, 378, 382

in our image, 387–88

as passive, 475, 486, 504, 513, 514, 526

and the Pharisees. *See* Pharisees, the

and the poor widow, 439, 444, 449, 449n. 2

prayer of, 62, 63–64, 223, 225, 497, 498, 501–3, 507, 509

prediction of abandonment of, 484, 489, 490–92, 498, 499

prediction of betrayal of, 483, 484, 487–89, 492, 498, 499, 527

prediction of destruction of Jerusalem temple, 20, 444, 447, 451–53, 470

predictions of suffering and death of, 9, 19, 90n. 1, 286–87, 291–92, 294, 296, 322, 324, 331, 365–68, 375, 412, 479, 513

presence and absence of, 89–90, 91–92, 475, 490

as prophetic, 7, 8, 37, 195, 294, 357, 519

reaching out to the gentiles, 114, 137, 138

rebuke of by Peter, 9, 27, 291, 292, 294–95, 299, 369, 377, 378, 531, 535, 551

rebuke of his disciples, 162–63, 291, 348, 350, 355

rebuke of Peter, 287, 295, 298, 377

rejection of by his hometown, 192–96

resurrection of, 187, 324, 356, 440, 559, 563–64, 566

and the return of the Son of Man, 20, 449,
    447–48, 449, 451, 459–61, 462
and the Sabbath, 47, 48–49, 96, 99, 102,
    104
as sacrificial lamb, 486
and salvation, 8, 9, 26, 58, 90, 226, 324,
    440, 487, 501, 510, 519, 546
and the Samaritan woman, 482
and the Sanhedrin, 400, 402-4, 408,
    417–21, 423, 425, 426
and the scribes. See scribes, the
second coming of, 90
self-revelation of, 225, 226, 227
as servant-oriented, 10, 14–15, 58, 322–23,
    325, 332, 370–72, 441, 530, 545, 546
and service to the needy, 6, 14, 15, 219,
    220, 297, 300, 322, 329, 331, 332,
    333, 348, 441
as shepherd, 212, 213, 215, 217, 218
and the shutting down of the temple, 19,
    389–94, 400, 402, 408, 417, 423,
    425, 434, 449, 461, 476, 485, 516,
    545
as the Son of Man, 8, 294, 306, 442, 519,
    527, 534, 546
sovereignty of over impure spirits, 108, 109
and the Spirit's groaning, 263, 264
as (authoritative) teacher. See teaching,
    Jesus
and the teachers of the law, 122–24, 439, 440
teaching of. See teaching, Jesus
temptation of, 9, 21, 31, 138–39, 276–77,
    291, 295, 341
touching people, 57, 58–59, 60, 67,
    69–70, 110, 181, 182, 187, 257,
    262–63, 287–88, 312, 350
transfiguration of, 8, 12, 145, 187n. 7, 301,
    304, 305, 306, 403, 442, 518, 519
trial before Pilate of, 524–25, 528–31
trial before the Sanhedrin of, 512, 513,
    514, 516, 525
vindication of, 8, 441, 449, 460, 518, 519,
    530, 536, 546, 562, 567
walking on water, 133, 223, 226
women followers of, 551–52, 559–66
as Yahweh, 323
Jethro, 217n. 6
Jezebel, 7, 37, 201, 205, 515
Joab, 476, 510

John
    calling of, 42, 45, 112
    and destruction of the temple, 447, 453, 455
    at Gethsemane, 497, 500–503
    and healing of Jairus's daughter, 180, 187
    and healing of Simon's mother-in-law, 55
    ministry partnership of, 202
    and mistake of exclusivity, 330–32
    profession of loyalty to Jesus of, 544
    purpose of in writing his Gospel, 11–12
    renaming of, 112, 115
    request of for place of prominence, 14, 188,
        365, 369, 378, 544
    and transfiguration of Jesus, 304, 305, 306
John the Baptist
    arrest of, 122, 205, 341
    baptism of Jesus, 21, 30
    and baptism as initiation into corporate
        movement of repentance, 28–30, 37
    burial of, 200, 206
    and Elijah, 30, 37, 44, 403
    and Herod, 199–200, 201, 205–6532–33
    imprisonment of, 37, 115, 199, 529, 533
    introduction of, 18
    Jesus as similar to, 7, 37, 291, 293, 573
    and judgment, 37
    killing of, 200, 204, 205–6, 341, 468, 533
    and membership in God's family, 121
    mistreatment of after arrest, 504, 513, 515
    and the Pharisees, 121
    popularity of, 30
    preparing the way for Jesus, 21, 22, 27–30,
        31, 37, 308–9
    as prophet, 37, 205, 400, 404
    and repentance, 21, 28, 34, 35, 37, 89, 121,
        308, 403
    source of baptism of, 400, 403, 408
    vindication of, 208
Jonah, 3, 160
Jonathan, 53
Joseph, 193, 409
Joseph of Arimathea, 436, 539, 552–53, 561,
    564
Joshua, 213–14, 450
Judas the Galilean, 419
Judas Iscariot
    and betrayal of Jesus, 324, 449n. 2, 474, 485,
        478, 479, 488, 494, 497, 503–4, 513
    calling of, 112, 115

as an insider, 477n. 3, 479, 503
    judgment of, 488
Judas Maccabeus, 3, 381
judgment, 335–37
justice, 395–97

Kasich, John, 446
kingdom of God, the
    abundance of, 271–72
    "already-not yet" character of, 190, 440
    arrival of, 37–38, 90
    astounding growth of, 153, 154–55, 160
    cross-shaped. See cross-shaped kingdom, the
    and destruction of the kingdom of
        darkness, 50, 51–54, 57, 109–10,
        115, 123, 162, 189, 190
    growth of, 132–33, 152, 153, 154
    inclusion of gentiles in, 160, 201, 207,
        235, 252, 268–69, 393, 495
    as invasion of purity, 58–61, 69–70, 105,
        110, 162, 182, 185, 187, 238, 260,
        263, 288
    longing of Israel for reestablishment of, 4,
        5, 24–27, 30, 36, 63, 64–65, 70, 110,
        139, 381–82, 528
    as over and against all other entities, 26
    secret of, 130, 137–38, 141–43
    those welcome within, 234–35, 238, 241–
        44, 252, 254, 256, 257–59, 349–51
    wealthy, the, and, 359–61
    as worldwide empire, 155, 155n. 3, 160,
        201, 252, 259, 384
Koehler, J. Kyle, 446

lament, 553–58
law, the
    Jesus's view of, 98–99, 100, 105
    Pharisees' view of, 99
leadership, worldly vs. Jesus-shaped, 372–74
Lent, 35
Levi, 83, 84, 84n. 1, 85, 124. See also Matthew
levirate marriage, 424, 426
Levites, the, 247
Lord's Supper, the, 220–22, 362, 479, 493–94
Lot, 458
love of neighbor, 431, 432–35
Luther, Martin, 86

Magnificat, the, 56, 56n. 1

Mara, 113
Mark, book of
    alternative endings to, 571–73
    as anti-imperial, 25–26, 25n. 6
    author of, 10–11
    as climax of story of God, 1, 5
    as continuation of the unfinished story
        of God, 24
    direct address of readers in, 12, 457, 462
    inclusio in, 30–31n. 15, 131, 286, 291n. 1,
        375–76, 377, 454, 475, 527, 547, 550
    insiders and outsiders in, 15–16, 19, 109,
        112, 120, 124, 130–32, 136–37,
        152–53, 155, 182, 207, 503, 539–40,
        546, 549
    intended audience of, 11–13, 17
    literary and theological features of, 14–18
    literary sandwiches in, 16–17, 120, 122,
        181, 200, 390, 475, 514
    map of, 18–20
    pace of, 16, 44, 57, 63, 84, 133, 217, 325
    parables in. See parables
    purpose of, 12
    setting of, 4
    as subversive, 5–6, 18, 131
    term "immediately" in, 16, 44, 57, 503n. 7
    verbs of perception in, 15, 17–18, 134,
        170, 182–83, 239, 255, 281–82,
        314, 368, 392, 434, 520, 540, 547,
        549, 564
    women in, 55–56, 57
Martha, 186n. 5, 556
Mary (mother of James), 539, 551, 559–66
Mary (mother of Jesus), 125, 275, 276
Mary (sister of Lazarus), 186n. 5, 556
Mary Magdalene, 539, 551, 559–66
Mattathias, 381, 450n. 3
Matthew, 45, 112. See also Levi
mental illness, church response to 176–77
Messiah
    Jesus as, 8, 26, 127, 137–38, 167, 293,
        376, 512, 518, 519, 534, 546
    meaning of, 26, 293
messianic secret, the. See commands for silence,
        Jesus
Miller, William, 463
Miriam, 172
money changers, 393
Moral Majority, the, 413

Mosaic Law, the, 230–52
Moses
    and the blood of the covenant, 489
    and the burning bush, 112, 424
    calling of, 42
    confronting Pharaoh, 79, 102
    and divorce, 339, 341–42
    encounter with God at Mount Sinai, 305
    farewell discourse of, 450–51
    God revealing glory to, 75, 80–81, 224, 225
    at Horeb, 112–13
    identifying himself with God, 213, 215,
        330, 332, 471
    and idolatry, 471
    lack of eloquence of, 261
    and the Mosaic Law, 251
    and polygamy, 240n. 1
    prayer of, 62
    rejection of, 193, 195
    and revelation of divine identity, 79
    song of, 172
    as teacher and lawgiver, 201
    and transfiguration of Jesus, 304, 305
    and transition of leadership to Joshua,
        213–14
    vindication of, 305
Mount of Olives, the, 380, 382, 444, 447,
    452, 483, 484, 490, 500

Naaman, 68
Nabal, 113
Nadab, 236
Naomi, 113
Nebuchadnezzar, 323, 370

Obadiah, 515
obedience, as creative and proactive, 105–6
O'Brien, Sean, 445–46

Papias, 10
parables
    binding of the strong man, 119, 123
    of the bread and the dogs, 253, 255–56
    of the cornerstone, 407, 412
    definition of, 134
    of the fig tree, 448, 450, 461, 462
    of the lamp, 147
    of the mustard seed, 152, 154–55
    of newness, 91
    of the prodigal son, 495

purpose of, 130, 131, 134, 136
    of the sower and the seed (first parable), 15,
        17–18, 19, 51, 130–32, 134–36, 138,
        140–41, 256, 280, 376, 454n. 10,
        457, 491, 567
    of the sower and the seed (second parable),
        152, 154
    of the vineyard, 135, 407, 410–12, 421, 476
    of the watchman, 448, 450, 462
Pashhur, 515
Passover, 474, 476
Paul
    calling of, 45, 246, 252
    as crucified with Christ, 309
    farewell discourse of, 450n. 3
    humble ministry of, 65–66, 137, 207, 211,
        309–10, 366–67
    as a Jew, 252
    and Mark, 10
    ministry partnerships of, 202
    and non-Jews as members of God's people,
        84, 207
    as Pharisee, 105n. 6, 252
    shaking the dust off, 203
perichoresis, 326–27
perseverance, necessity of, 522–23
Peter
    calling of, 112, 521
    confession of Jesus as Messiah, 8, 9, 27, 139,
        287, 291, 293, 477
    contrasted with Jesus, 514–15
    and Cornelius, 237
    denial of Jesus, 114, 474, 491, 492, 494,
        506, 513, 520–22, 542, 560
    and destruction of the temple, 447, 453, 455
    and the fig tree, 389, 452
    following Jesus, 506, 512, 516, 520, 542,
        552, 560
    and gentiles, 255, 269, 349, 495
    at Gethsemane, 497, 500–503
    and healing of Jairus's daughter, 180, 187
    and Mark, 10–11
    ministry partnership of, 202
    profession of loyalty to Jesus by, 484, 491–92,
        502, 521, 544
    rebuke of by Jesus, 287, 295, 298, 377
    rebuke of Jesus, 9, 27, 291, 292, 294–95,
        299, 369, 377, 378, 477, 504, 531,
        535, 551

renaming of, 112, 115
and transfiguration of Jesus, 304, 305,
    306–7, 309, 503
as triumphalist, 568
See also Simon
Pharisees, the
and divorce, 339, 341–43
fasting of, 75, 88, 89
and hand washing, 234, 235, 237–38, 239
hardened hearts of, 69, 102–3, 104, 234,
    277, 339, 343
holiness standards of, 85, 237–38, 239,
    245, 246, 254, 255, 288
and human traditions, 234, 240–41, 247
and Jesus eating with tax collectors and
    sinners, 75, 83–85, 89, 495
and Jesus's activities on the Sabbath, 49, 75,
    96–99, 102–5
and the law, 98, 99
as outside the family of God, 121
lack of perception of, 255
plot to kill Jesus, 19, 75, 102–5, 115, 232,
    238–39, 276, 282, 400, 412, 419,
    474, 516, 533
questioning of Jesus's authority, 75, 400
request for a sign, 275, 276
and restoration of Israel, 98, 99, 105
and the resurrection, 425
and the Romans, 105, 419
testing of Jesus, 275, 276–77, 339, 341–43,
    417, 419–20, 423
as unfaithful shepherds, 103, 104–5
Philip, calling of, 112
Pilate
awareness of Jesus's innocence, 524, 532,
    544
and release of Barabbas, 524, 528, 531–32
releasing of Jesus's body, 539, 553
and trial of Jesus, 524, 525, 528, 529–31
as unfavorable figure, 528n. 2
polygamy, 340n. 1
Pompey the Great, 4
prayer
of Jesus. 62, 63–64, 223, 225, 497, 498,
    501–3, 507, 509
of Moses, 62
and the temple, 394–95
premillennial dispensationalism, 463–64
preparation, theme of, 31–33

purity
codes, 57, 58
as contagious, 58–61, 69–70, 105, 110,
    162, 182, 185, 187, 238
rituals, 234, 237–38

ransom, 371–72, 372n. 11
repentance
gospel as a call for, 40
Jesus calls for, 35–38, 64, 86, 115, 141,
    163, 167, 196, 202, 327, 496
John the Baptist calls for, 21, 28, 34, 35,
    37, 89, 121, 308, 403
resurrection
bodies in, 427
of Jesus, 187, 324, 356, 440, 559, 563–64,
    566
Jewish notions of, 308, 308n. 5
marriage in, 423–24, 426–27
in the Old Testament, 424
Robertson, Pat, 466–67, 469
Ruby, Carl, 445–46
Ruth, 424

Sabbath, the
contemporary observance of, 99–101
creation of, 96–97
Jesus and, 47, 48–49, 96, 99, 102, 104
Pharisees' objection to Jesus about, 96–98,
    104, 105
purpose of, 97
timing of, 58
Sadducees, the, 423–24, 425–26, 425n. 2,
    443
Salome (daughter of Herodias), 204, 205,
    205n. 12, 206
Salome (follower of Jesus), 539, 551, 559–66
Samuel, 418, 450
Sanhedrin, the
conflicts with Jesus, 400, 402–4, 408,
    417–21, 423, 425, 440
desire of for secret arrest of Jesus, 479, 517
hardened hearts of, 404–5
limiting of authority of, 402n. 1, 403–4
plot to kill Jesus, 412, 413, 417, 474, 475,
    476, 516–17, 525, 528, 529, 533,
    552
Sarah (wife of Abraham), 153, 292, 428
Sarah (wife of Tobias), 426

Satan
    chief agent of evil, 116, 122–23, 143, 189
    and division within the church, 143–45
    as god of this age, 468
    opposition of, to Jesus's crucifixion, 9, 138,
        277, 295, 296
    subject to God, 116
    temptation of Jesus, 9, 138–39
Saul, 52–53
Scribes
    accusation of Jesus as working by the power
        of Satan, 276
    and authority of Jesus to forgive sins, 19,
        49, 76, 77–79, 78n. 4, 80
    believer among, 431, 434–36, 440, 442
    and disciples' eating with unclean hands,
        238–41
    and disciples' lack of fasting, 89
    exploitative practices of toward the needy
        and vulnerable, 439, 442–45, 475, 552
    geographical locations of, 425
    and the greatest commandment, 431
    and Jesus eating with sinners and tax
        collectors, 83, 84, 85–86, 89
    plot to kill Jesus, 474, 476, 533
    as skeptical of Jesus, 85
    who they were, 49, 78n. 4, 194–95,
        238–39n. 6, 314n. 2, 443
Sea of Galilee, size of, 134n. 1, 161n. 4
self-harm, 166, 169–70
Sermon on the Mount, the, 113
Shema, the, 432, 434, 435, 436
shepherds, unfaithful, judgment against, 102,
    104–5
Silas, 202, 203
Simon (the Cyrene), 538, 539, 542–43, 553
Simon (the disciple)
    calling of, 42, 44, 112
    renaming of, 112, 115
    See also Peter
Simon the Leper, 477, 479, 488
Simon the Zealot, calling of, 112
sin, 2, 52, 282
Solomon, 29
Son of God, identification of Jesus as
    at his baptism, 12, 21, 23, 31, 403, 442,
        518, 519, 550n. 16, 551, 567
    by the centurion, 10, 137n. 5, 539, 540,
        550, 550n. 17, 551, 552

by demons, 17, 107, 109, 1166–68, 170
by God, 12, 21, 23, 31, 145, 300, 304,
    305, 307, 357, 403, 442, 518, 519,
    550n. 17, 551, 567
by Mark, 23–25, 26–27, 174n. 12, 403
self-identification as, 512, 518, 519, 550n. 17
through performance of miracles, 16, 18,
    57, 79
at the transfiguration, 145, 300, 304, 305,
    307, 403, 442, 518, 519, 551
spiritual warfare, 54, 116, 144
Stephen, 192–93

Tamar, 424
tax collectors, 83, 84
teachers of the law. See scribes
teaching, Jesus
    as authoritative, 7–8, 47–48, 49, 77,
        133–34, 202, 215, 3314, 341, 382,
        423–24, 426, 440n. 1
    about discipleship, 339–40, 344–47
    by parables, 130, 131, 134, 155
    casting out spirits and, 7, 47–49, 440n. 1
    in his hometown, 192, 193–94
    on the destruction of the temple, 447–48,
        449
    lack of details of content of, 5, 7–8, 48, 77,
        84, 202, 212, 215, 341
    on marriage and divorce, 339–40, 341–47,
        423
    about the resurrection, 393, 426–27
    in shutting down the temple, 440n. 1
    in the temple courts, 393, 439, 440, 441
temple, Jerusalem
    church, the, as the new, 394, 395
    corruption of, 380–81, 390–91, 393, 394,
        395, 400, 410, 470, 528, 545–46,
        550n. 16, 551
    curtain torn, 538, 547, 548, 549–50
    fig tree as symbolizing, 392, 394, 452, 461,
        545
    God's intended purpose for, 393, 551
    Jesus as the new, 28, 393, 394, 395, 400,
        410, 412, 449, 460, 486, 517, 550n.
        16, 551
    John's presence in the wilderness as critique
        of, 28
    judgment of God on, 547–51
    judgment on treasury of, 439, 440, 444, 445

as idol, 471
    as place of care for the needy and suffering,
       395
    prediction of destruction of, 20, 444,
       447–48, 449, 451–53, 470
    shutting down of by Jesus, 19, 48, 389,
       390–91, 392–94, 400, 402, 408, 412,
       417, 423, 425, 449, 476
Thaddaeus, calling of, 112
Thomas, 112, 493
Timothy, 10, 203
Tobias, 426
Tobit, 450n. 3
Torah, the, 98, 98n. 3
transfiguration, the
    disciples with Jesus at, 187n. 7
    and Jesus's glory, 8, 304, 305, 306, 307
    identification of Jesus as God's Son at, 12,
       145, 304, 305, 306, 307, 403, 442,
       518, 519

triumphalism, 568

vindication
    of God's servants, 208, 456, 490n. 7, 516
    of Jesus, 8, 441, 449, 460, 518, 519, 530,
       536, 546, 562, 567
    of John the Baptist, 208
    longing of Israel for, 142

wealth, 355–56, 361–64
white flight, 177–79, 178n. 16
wilderness, the, 28, 63, 215
worship, importance of 145–46

Yahweh, 323
yeast, 282

Zebedee, 42
Zechariah, 275, 276

Author Index

Alexander, Michelle, 398
Anderson, Carol, 398
Anderson, K. L, 308, 424
Augustine, 110, 127, 420

Bates, Matthew W., 40, 317–18
Bauckham, Richard, 11, 27, 169
Beale, G. K., 1
Beavis, Mary Ann, 217, 255, 382, 420, 449, 542
Beilby, James K., 54
Bendroth, Margaret Lamberts, 258
Berry, Wendell, 157
Bird, Michael F., 27, 238, 293, 441
Black, C. Clifton, 26–27, 43–44, 57–58, 63,
    75, 84, 109, 112, 115, 125, 135, 154,
    161, 168, 183, 202, 215, 217, 227, 230,
    255, 267, 276–77, 282, 287, 291, 301,
    325, 334, 358, 368, 370, 372, 392, 411,
    435, 441, 444, 477, 502, 506, 514–15,
    517, 547
Blomberg, Craig L., 59–60, 364
Bond, Helen K., 105, 204–5, 528
Boring, Eugene M., 23, 28, 104, 155, 195,
    203, 226–27, 239, 242, 256, 261–62,
    277, 282, 287–88, 291, 295, 299–300,
    314, 324–25, 334, 341, 344, 371–72,
    377, 383–84, 393, 403, 409, 425,
    442–43, 452–53, 457–59, 477, 488,
    500, 520, 533, 544, 548, 562
Boyer, Paul, 463

Carlson, Peter, 467
Chilton, Bruce, 109
Chrysostom, John, 69, 79, 208, 278, 370
Clawson, Julie, 397
Coates, Ta-Nehisi, 398
Collins, Adela Yarbro, 288
Coontz, Stephanie, 470
Croy, N. Clayton, 571

Dahl, Nils A., 12

Davidhizar, Elizabeth, 279
DeBerg, Betty A., 258
Decker, Rodney J., 409
Dennis, J., 372, 541, 543
deSilva, David A., 236, 369
DiAngelo, Robin, 399
Dickens, Charles, 22
Dobson, Ed, 413–14
Dodd, C. H., 134, 409

Eddy, Paul Rhodes, 54
Edwards, James R., 49, 98, 109, 402–4, 409–
    10, 424, 427, 443, 452, 478, 486–87,
    491, 506, 519, 551, 561–64
Emerson, Michael O., 258
Eusebius, 10
Evans, Craig, 26

Fea, John, 351
FitzGerald, Frances, 302
Fox, Renee, 445–46
France, R. T., 37
Friedman, Megan, 467
Fromkin, David, 470

Galli, Mark, 316
Garland, David E., 49, 98, 383–85, 392–94,
    420, 454, 476, 486, 520, 551, 571
Gartz, Linda, 398
Goldstein, Jonathan A., 381
Gombis, Timothy G., 116, 382
Gorman, Michael J., 324, 465
Gray, Timothy C., 403, 409, 411–12, 449,
    455, 457–58, 486, 517, 547, 550–51
Green, J. G., 334
Greene-McCreight, Kathryn, 379
Gundry, Robert H., 197

Hall, Christopher A., 24, 31, 45, 50, 70, 79,
    105, 110, 127, 151, 171, 208, 278, 326,
    370, 420

Hansen, Collin, 472
Hardin, Michael, 117
Hays, Richard B., 25, 44, 162, 198, 225, 294, 346, 392
Hengel, Martin, 541
Hoang, Bethany H., 397
Hooker, Morna D., 63, 91, 124, 195, 203, 255, 294, 342, 360, 392
Hudson, John, 467
Huizenga, Leroy A., 163
Hunter, James Davison, 303, 414
Hurtado, Larry W., 419, 490, 571

Instone-Brewer, David, 340, 346

James, Carolyn Custis, 258
Jenkins, Jerry B., 464
Jipp, Joshua W., 351
Johnson, Kristen Deede, 397
Jones, R. N., 68
Josephus, 31, 47, 63, 458, 528, 544
Joyce, Kathryn, 258

Kinnaman, David, 303
Kruse, Colin G., 128

LaHaye, Tim, 464
Lee-Barnewall, Michelle, 425
Lindsey, Hal, 464
Lipman, Joanne, 398
Luther, Martin, 35
Lyons, Gabe, 303

Marcus, Joel, 23, 30, 38, 43, 50, 57, 64, 76, 78–79, 91, 109, 113–15, 134, 155, 168, 183, 186–87, 201–4, 206, 215–16, 226, 239, 256, 270–71, 282, 377, 393, 411, 425, 444, 449, 475, 478, 500, 506, 525, 530–31, 533, 561–63
Mathews, Mary Beth Swetnam, 258
Mayfield, D. L., 398
McCormick, Neil, 320
McKnight, Scot, 26, 41, 125, 129, 372, 436–38
McNeil, Brenda Salter, 258
Melville, Herman, 22
Miller, Chris A., 243
Modica, Joseph B., 26
Moloney, Francis J., 31, 44, 57, 64, 75, 96, 102, 109, 112, 115, 171–72, 183,

202–3, 207, 217, 225–26, 239, 270, 301, 305, 314, 324, 342, 360, 368, 370, 378, 383–84, 419, 426, 452, 455, 457, 477, 490–91, 500, 502, 504–6, 517, 519, 530, 533, 542, 546, 550, 552, 561–62, 565
Mulder, Mark T., 178–79

Nelson, Arthur A. R., 32–33
Nock, A. D., 25

Oden, Thomas C., 24, 31, 45, 50. 70, 79, 105, 110, 127, 151, 171, 208, 278, 326, 370, 420
Omiya, T., 68

Pankaj, Mishra, 218
Perkins, John, 258
Perrin, Nicholas, 28
Peterson, Dwight H., 11
Peterson, Eugene H., 156–58, 320
Placher, William C., 195, 204, 217, 239, 262, 271, 305, 307, 359, 475
Plantinga, Cornelius Jr., 326
Price, Mark, 467
Prothero, Stephen, 387

Rediger, G. Lloyd, 209
Robinson, Todd E., 398
Rothstein, Richard, 398

Sanderson, Scott, 470
Shuman, Joel, 111
Simpson, Amy, 379
Smith, Christian, 258
Snodgrass, Klyne, 137
Stein, Robert H., 98, 461
Storkey, Alan, 4
Strauss, Mark L., 104, 123, 155, 183, 187, 230, 239, 255, 276–77, 282, 301, 308, 333, 341, 371, 403, 424, 459, 461
Sutton, Matthew Avery, 248–49, 302, 463, 465

Tatum, Beverly Daniel, 398
Thellman, G., 49, 78, 239, 314
Thomas, Cal, 413–14
Thompson, M. M., 501
Tisby, Jemar, 472
Twelftree, Graham H., 48, 402

U2, 320
Ulansey, David, 31

Vacek, Heather H., 176–77, 379
Vanier, Jean, 379
Volck, Brian, 111

Waetjen, Herman C., 4
Waltke, Bruce K., 279

Walton, John H., 1, 97, 467
Watts, Rikki E., 4
Whalen, C., 203
Whiston, William, 452
Willitts, Joel, 3
Wink, Walter, 117
Winn, Adam, 25
Wright, D. P., 68

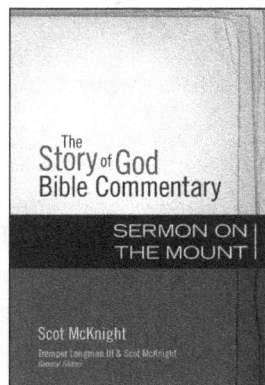

Acts

Dean Pinter

A new commentary for today's world, The Story of God Bible Commentary explains and illuminates each passage of Scripture in light of the Bible's grand story. Its story-centric approach is ideal for pastors, students, Sunday school teachers, and laypeople alike.

Three easy-to-use sections designed to help readers live out God's story:

- LISTEN to the Story: Includes complete NIV text with references to other texts at work in each passage, encouraging the reader to hear it within the Bible's grand story
- EXPLAIN the Story: Explores and illuminates each text as embedded in its canonical and historical setting
- LIVE the Story: Reflects on how each text can be lived today and includes contemporary stories and illustrations to aid preachers, teachers, and students

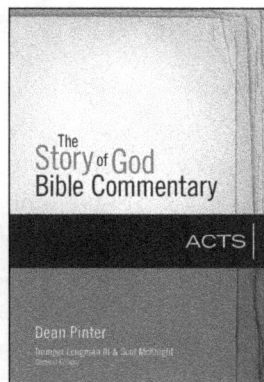

Available in stores and online!

ZONDERVAN®
.com

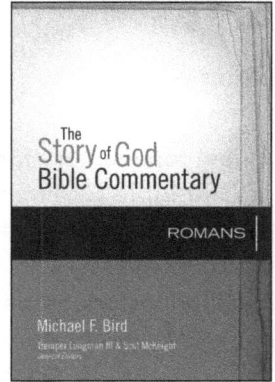

2 Corinthians

Judith A. Diehl

A new commentary for today's world, The Story of God Bible Commentary explains and illuminates each passage of Scripture in light of the Bible's grand story. Its story-centric approach is ideal for pastors, students, Sunday school teachers, and laypeople alike.

The
Story of God
Bible Commentary

2 CORINTHIANS

Judith A. Diehl
Tremper Longman III & Scot McKnight

Three easy-to-use sections designed to help readers live out God's story:

- LISTEN to the Story: Includes complete NIV text with references to other texts at work in each passage, encouraging the reader to hear it within the Bible's grand story
- EXPLAIN the Story: Explores and illuminates each text as embedded in its canonical and historical setting
- LIVE the Story: Reflects on how each text can be lived today and includes contemporary stories and illustrations to aid preachers, teachers, and students

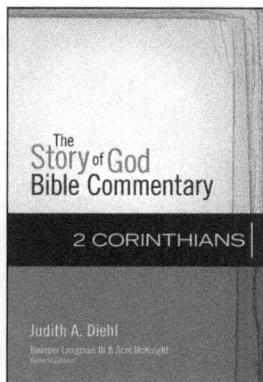

Available in stores and online!

ZONDERVAN®
.com

www.ingramcontent.com/pod-product-compliance
Lightning Source LLC
Chambersburg PA
CBHW070406100426
42812CB00005B/1652